TIBERIUS
with a
TELEPHONE

TIBERIUS
with a
TELEPHONE
the life and stories of
William McMahon

Patrick Mullins

SCRIBE
Melbourne • London

Scribe Publications
18–20 Edward St, Brunswick, Victoria 3056, Australia
2 John St, Clerkenwell, London, WC1N 2ES, United Kingdom
3754 Pleasant Ave, Suite 100, Minneapolis, Minnesota 55409, USA

First published by Scribe 2018

Typeset in 11.5/15 pt Adobe Caslon by the publishers
Index compiled by Mei Yen Chua

Printed and bound in Australia by Griffin Press

Scribe Publications is committed to the sustainable use of natural resources and the use of paper products made responsibly from those resources.

9781925713602 (Australian edition)
9781911617860 (UK edition)
9781947534759 (US edition)
9781925693324 (e-book)

A CiP entry for this title is available from the National Library of Australia and the British Library.

scribepublications.com.au
scribepublications.co.uk
scribepublications.com

To my parents

Contents

CHAPTER ONE

End to End

1982–1983

When he finally started it, the book was late. By 1982, Sir William McMahon was nine years gone from power. He was jaded, frustrated. The ambition and energy that had sustained him through thirty-three years in the House of Representatives—twenty-one of them as a minister, almost two as Australia's prime minister—had not gone away but, since the 1972 election, they had been without use. His influence had faded. His relevance seemed gone. His time, people said, had passed. For years now, he had languished on the backbenches, ignored by his leader, discounted by colleagues, pitied by opponents, derided by the press, mocked by the public.

But by 1982 he decided that it was enough. McMahon was angry, frustrated with politics, done with Canberra's bureaucrats, finished with his prime minister. The last of the famous 'forty-niners'—those elected in the wave that brought Robert Menzies to power in 1949 and kept the Liberals on the government benches for over two decades—he resigned his seat. McMahon did not mind that he was causing inconvenience and discomfort. Nor did he mind that his once-safe, blue ribbon Liberal Party electorate was likely to elect a Labor successor.[1]

He had decided he would write his book. Long threatened but never started, it was going to be an autobiography, and it was going to be history. It was going to be serious and also sensational. Above all, it was going to be a revelation. 'When I publish my autobiography and tell of the things I had to put up with,' he said, 'none of you will believe it.'[2]

McMahon would follow Churchill's line and write history himself.[3] He would bridge the gap between participant and historian, would intertwine his own experiences with the story of the past. Not for him the scattershot 'reminiscences' of George Reid, the 'patchwork blanket' of Menzies, or the 'stories' of Billy Hughes.[4] His would be a 'multi-volumed masterpiece', a magisterial history that illuminated the 'substantial issues': the Menzies era, the Vietnam War, the troubled days of Harold Holt and John Gorton, the Dismissal—and, of course, his own prime ministership.[5] He would not be discreet.[6] McMahon would be frank; in fact, he promised 'bombshells'.[7] He would supply freewheeling character assessments of Robert Menzies, Harold Holt, John Gorton, Gough Whitlam, Richard Casey, Billy Snedden, and his longtime foe, John McEwen. The present political elite would not be left unscathed: McMahon promised hard words for Malcolm Fraser and John Howard, too.

McMahon was not unaware of his reputation; indeed, the supposed falsity of that reputation was one of his hooks. His book would be the real story. It would peel back the veneer. 'When I write about it one day, people will wonder how we did as well as we did,' McMahon said. The book would be a rebuke to his critics in the press and in his party. It would be rehabilitation for his derided prime ministership. 'What we achieved in those twenty months was unbelievable,' he said, 'because we left the economy in the healthiest state I have known it to be in the thirty-three years I was in Parliament.'[8]

McMahon had been preparing for the book for a long time. For thirty-three years, he had followed the old lawyer's habit of safeguarding papers, filing away briefings, retaining correspondence, making and remaking aide-mémoires of conversations of significance. Nine years before, he had donated the bulk of his papers to the National Library, in Canberra; now, he requested their return. Using his entitlements as a former prime minister, McMahon retreated to his longstanding office on the nineteenth floor of Westfield Towers, on Sydney's William Street, close by the offices of his old foe Gough Whitlam. He employed a secretary and an assistant, and, with those papers around him, he began to write.

Soon, he had an agent. The author and journalist Michael Morton-Evans offered representation after hearing from McMahon that a manuscript was almost complete. Morton-Evans spread word among Sydney publishers. Thomas Nelson, which a decade before had published a satirical compilation of McMahon's utterances, *The Wit and Wisdom of William McMahon*, was the first to bite.[9] But when they caught sight of the manuscript that McMahon had been working on, they were aghast. Why? According to Morton-Evans, they were daunted by the manuscript's size. 'It was huge,' he said. 'It would have run to four volumes.'[10]

As ever, intransigence was McMahon's first response. He waved off concerns about the size of the book. He would not countenance cutting, and he would not allow another hand to intervene. He had ploughed through the files, and this was what he had produced. 'The whole concept of someone fiddling with his words was anathema to him,' said Morton-Evans. The book had to be done his way: 'It was all or nothing.'[11] Believing the book unpublishable and McMahon unpersuadable, Thomas Nelson backed away.

In August 1983, the publisher at William Collins, Richard Smart, expressed a guarded interest. Invited to Westfield Towers to discuss the possibility of a deal, Smart arrived accompanied by his two-year-old-daughter. With her, McMahon was gentle and polite. He offered her biscuits while he and Smart talked. They discussed the scope of the book, the style of its telling, the title. *End to End: Menzies to McMahon* caught the budding author's ear.

Eventually, McMahon asked Smart if he would like to see the autobiography. To Smart's nod, McMahon guided him out of the office and through a labyrinth, 'a dark Russian gulag' of a corridor, into a room whose walls were lined with twenty-seven cheap metal filing cabinets, each stuffed full of the papers that had been returned by the National Library. 'There it is!' McMahon said.

Smart did not understand. Where was the book?

'It's in the files,' McMahon told him.

Smart had had concerns before the meeting. McMahon was no Menzies, no Whitlam. Publishers were not queuing at his door the way they had for those giants. McMahon was not renowned for his way with words, and he was not remembered in terms that suggested a wide, waiting readership. If this book was to work, Smart knew, it would have to be good. It had to be about the story.

McMahon had an interesting one to tell, didn't he? His life, conceivably, was a thread that weaved through the twentieth century, running from Chifley and post-war reconstruction to Menzies and the communist scares; it was entwined with Holt and Vietnam, and the feuds with McEwen and Gorton; it knotted around the clash with Whitlam, and it twisted through the Dismissal and Fraser, and the emerging order of the 1980s. McMahon's life was coloured with dramatic oppositions—of tragedy, farce, triumph, failure, tenacity, and disregard. And he had been prime minister!

With a proper writer to help him, Smart thought, McMahon *could* produce something worth reading. He *could* produce something of value. A whole chronicle of Australian politics and history *could* hang on the thread of McMahon's experiences. But, as matters stood, there was nothing to publish.

The publisher decided to be polite. 'Let me know when you've got something,' he told the former prime minister, and left.[12]

CHAPTER TWO

Building Character

1908–1926

The McMahons were well known when William was born. By 1908, wagons emblazoned J. McMahon & Co. had been trundling through Sydney's streets for nearly forty years. Whether loaded with guns, livestock, clothes, or heavy sacks of greasy wool, those wagons had ensured that the McMahon name was recognisable to all.

For Sydneysiders awake early, the most famous owner of that name was a familiar sight.[1] James McMahon would drive his Abbott buggy to his yards in Redfern at four o'clock each morning, ready to supervise the first departures for Darling Harbour and Circular Quay. His dark beard was always neatly groomed, and, though his customary trilby suggested otherwise, the burly Irish carrier never had an air of frivolity or gentility about him. Mornings were for work, and he tolerated no slacking off. 'I am uneasy if I think there may be stores or goods exposed to the weather lying on the wharves or elsewhere,' he said.

James was the source of the McMahon family's considerable wealth and power. As a child of nine, he had fled County Clare and the misery of Ireland's Potato Famine to come to Australia with his parents. He had been working almost since his feet had touched the shore. He had earned seven shillings and sixpence a week as a baker's boy on George Street before moving on to work for a wine merchant, a railway contractor, and then a carrier named Patrick Murphy. While working for Murphy in Parramatta, he saw a team of carriers' wagons, five of them, all laden with wool and pulled by teams of sixteen or eighteen bullocks. He was deeply impressed: 'The great wool teams were a very fine sight.'

It kindled his ambition. Beginning his own carrier's business with one horse and a rented, dilapidated dray, he expanded it to 250 workers and some 500 horses. Contracts grew from the ordinary—ferrying guns and railway sleepers—to the larger, more notable. His big break was the awarding, in 1871, of a monopoly contract for shifting wool between the railway station where it had been delivered and the warehouses from which it could be exported. In the absence of a rail connection to the wharves, this was a lucrative victory.

He had been aggressive throughout. Scornful of unionists and unionising employees, James crossed swords with Billy Hughes and railed against the forty-eight-hour workweek. 'It makes a man feel that the moment his eight hours are up his responsibility is done,' he said, in 1906. He had no time for the Labour Party, which he regarded as a den of demagogues living 'at ease while workers toil'.

Violence was second nature to James. Nicknamed 'Butty' for his tendency to head-butt antagonists, he had nonetheless made an exception for the picketers and strikers who had blocked his yards during the maritime strikes in 1890. Picking up a stave from a cask, he rushed at one and beat him around the head with it.[2] In another notorious incident, he 'prepared'—as he termed it—three men for the hospital, and cheerfully declared that it was 'just a little bit of the spirit of the Donnybrook Fair' that had made him to do it. When the court summonses came, he bought off his victims with £25 and a bottle of whiskey.

James had augmented his ambition and aggression with a sharp eye for a deal. 'I foresaw the rapid progress that Sydney was certain to make, and began to invest in city property,' he boasted. He snapped up land in the city and the country, raised sheep in Amaroo, agisted horses in Cowra and Mount Druitt. He improved his land by building on it, and lined his pockets by insisting that his workers rent lodgings from him or work elsewhere. He bought hotels near his yards and stables to recoup his drivers' wages when they went for drinks. He was poorly educated, but he was not poor and he was not stupid.

James was gruff and proud, fixed in his ways and unwilling to change. 'He would carve the roast on a silver salver, and no one ever got to ask for the first helping,' a grandson later said.[3] Everything James had done was for his family. 'I have come through a life of hard toil, but I have succeeded,' he said. 'I do not want my children to have the struggle without the same prospect of reward.'

James had looked after his six of his children by involving them.[4] He trusted his eldest son and namesake to manage the extensive and unwieldy business. He expanded into farming to allow sons Thomas and John to engage in 'pastoral pursuits'.[5] He employed the twins, Ernest and Joseph, as foremen. His sole daughter, Agnes, had been put to work collecting rents for the McMahon properties. With an armed guard at her side, the work would take her five days—a testament to the size of the empire James was building.

But James's fourth son, William Daniel, was different. Educated at the Jesuit-run St Aloysius' College on Milsons Point, he wanted no part of the family business.[6] He seemed intent on making his own way. A 'rationalist' in a family of devout Irish Catholics, he crossed religious lines when he married in 1903.[7] His wife, Mary Ellen Walder, was from a respectable family that manufactured sailcloth, tents, and canvas in a steam-powered factory a little way from the McMahon stables in Redfern. Her family was English in faith and English in outlook, with a proud adherence to the British Empire and a belief in the virtues of making good through hard work.[8]

It was an unusual match. The Walders were thrifty teetotallers who were well aware of the way chance governed life: Mary Ellen's father had died young and left them adrift until the eldest son, sixteen-year-old Samuel, rescued the family business. The McMahons, in turn, were rough, ambitious, and physical. All James's sons played rugby union. They were built for it: bulky and heavy, thick-necked and big-shouldered. William Daniel did not have the skill of his eldest brother—whose exploits playing full-back for Randwick saw him represent New South Wales for twelve years, and subsequently manage the 1908–09 Wallabies tour of England, Wales, and North America—but he refereed club matches on weekends to stay involved.[9]

However mismatched William Daniel and Mary Ellen might have seemed, their marriage was working. They were making their way. Their family was burgeoning. Though their first child had died shortly after birth in 1905, William Daniel and Mary Ellen had welcomed another, James, the following year.[10] By 1908, Mary Ellen was pregnant again, due late in February. William Daniel's years as an articled clerk were soon to finish. He would take the exams for a certificate of Supreme

Court practice in November. Assuming he passed, he would open a legal practice in Sydney's inner north, and handle civil suits and minor criminal matters. Work there would earn William Daniel his own name, one that could provide for his family and compete with the fame of his father's wagons and his elder brother's football prowess.[11]

And so, on 23 February 1908, as summer rains washed out the weekend and Mary Ellen gave birth to another boy, they gave this child his father's name: William Daniel McMahon.[12]

THREE years later, there were four children. James and William had been joined by Sam and Agnes.[13] The law practice was doing well: William Daniel McMahon's name was becoming well known in and of its own right.

But there was a problem: Mary Ellen was sick. 'She was never very well,' Sam later said. 'They said she had tuberculosis.' Cures of all variety were tried. The Walder family put up a tent in their garden in Kensington. 'She used to sit out there, and they would lift up the sides to let the air in,' Sam recalled.[14] The ineffectiveness of these treatments worried the family. Eventually, the fear of contagion spurred the decision to keep the children away from their mother. William Daniel, still working away at making his name, did not take charge of them. Though he employed a guardian to care for his children, he had them sent to live elsewhere.

James, William, Sam, and Agnes were split up and juggled between their aunts and uncles, grandparents, and cousins. They would change home as their relatives needed, always subject to the whims and desires of their elders. On occasion, siblings would end up in the same house—but it was never permanent. It was always ad hoc.

The children drifted across Sydney, moving from the Catholic homes of the McMahons to the Church of England homes of the Walders. They lived in Kensington, Killara, Redfern, Centennial Park, Beecroft, and Point Piper. There were so many homes that William later said he would need a full half-hour to list them all. It was an errant life, insecure, always in flux. The children were conscious they were never in a home of their own. They were aware that they were always guests, wherever they went. Knowledge of these circumstances makes it possible to see why the siblings, in later life, were not particularly close; moreover, it becomes possible to sense that this constant movement would have inhibited the feeling—at least for William—of belonging among his immediate family. What is likely to have grown from this is the anxiety, insecurity, and isolation that William's colleagues would observe in his adult behaviour, and the urgent, needful ambition that would compel him to dangerous prominence.[15]

Yet William would also observe that there was one place where feelings of belonging did exist: at his maternal aunt and uncle's. Samuel and Elsie Walder's home offered as much material comfort as other relatives' did, but available in that home was much more than bed and bread. The Walders were the emotional ballasts that William's parents could not be. William knew that whenever he went to see Elsie, it was with the constant assurance that she loved him. In the absence of his mother's presence and comfort, Elsie was everything. Samuel Walder, meanwhile, was support and strength, generosity and care. Walder guided William to do better, to make something of himself.

Yet the nature of William's life, of moving from home to home, often without a consistent authority to restrain him, led the boy to manifest a headstrong and often carefree attitude. He was adaptable, yes: 'I think by nature I was probably a child who learned to adjust himself pretty quickly to changing circumstances,' he said later.[16] But he was also undisciplined and reckless. It came from wanting attention—most particularly, from his father.

Caught up in his work and trying to make a name for himself, his father was a gadfly. William once went to see him in Penrith, and had to wait four hours for him to make the time. When he finally did appear, it was with another man in tow, and they took William for a beer.

The relationship between father and son was amicable, but it was never close. William's father was happy to provide help but never presence in his children's lives. He was preoccupied with his own concerns.

In 1913, William's father decided to turn his standing as a solicitor into a political career. He stood under the banner of the Liberal Party for the New South Wales state seat of Camperdown: solidly Labor and, despite suggestions to the contrary, unlikely to change. He was beaten soundly. He could muster barely 30 per cent of the vote. His poor showing was compounded by the knowledge that the defeat was at the hands of the brother of his own articled clerk. He hardly felt comfortable standing for office, though. On the stump, he told his audience that he felt like a cat on a hot tin roof. Hearing the speech, the five-year-old William was arrested by this image: he simply could not imagine his enormous father tiptoeing on *anyone's* roof.[17]

A year later, in November 1914, as the storm of the Great War started to rage, the patriarch of the McMahon family died unexpectedly. James left a monumental business.[18] His teams were transporting 750,000 bales of wool annually. His employees numbered in the hundreds. Drafted in to settle the estate, William's father became enmeshed in a drawn-out and taxing process. The extent of the McMahon holdings—all the pockets of land that had been snapped up, the assets, and the contracts—was huge and complex. The final valuation, of £236,325, was controversial. Some thought it was unearned: by the *Bulletin's* reckoning, the McMahon family's wealth had come about only 'by the grace of the Congestion policy of N.S. Wales'.[19]

Two years later, after returning to the law, the desire for a political career compelled William's father to make a futile stand as an independent in the 1917 New South Wales election. The humiliations of electoral politics were even more visceral this time. In the 24 March ballot, there were more informal votes than there were for his candidacy. With only 1.46 per cent of the vote—just sixty-five ballots—he was soundly defeated once again.[20]

Worse followed. Little more than two weeks later, on 9 April, Mary Ellen died.[21] Tuberculosis had kept her from her husband and her children for years; finally, it took her from them completely. But she had always been a ghost to her son. Much later, William professed not to have any memory of his mother. He could not recall seeing her at all, he would say.[22] When prompted for more, he could only state the most mawkish and romanticised things: that she was beautiful, that she was lovely, that she was extraordinary.

For William, her death was never fixed to a particular date or year. He told some interviewers that he was three-and-a-half when she died; he told others that he was four, or six.[23] He was, in fact, nine—old enough, it would seem, to remember. The indecision and inconsistency is a suggestion both of the regular disruptions of William's childhood and how little that childhood altered after Mary Ellen passed away.

William's father wanted little to do with his four grieving children. Mourning the loss of his wife, aware of his tendency to work to the exclusion of everything else, he decided to formalise the arrangements already in place. Agnes would live permanently with her aunt and namesake in Redfern. Samuel would live with the Blunts—Elsie Walder's family—in Lucknow. William would live with Samuel and Elsie Walder. Where James went is unknown.

To ensure their security, their father organised to have his portion of James's estate held in trust. His children would inherit it when they were old enough to look after it.

It was a neat arrangement that would not last. In 1919, when William was eleven, his elder brother died. James was thirteen. According to his death certificate, 'exhaustion' and 'a cerebral disease' were the causes of death.[24] Whether it was caused by the influenza pandemic that spread across the globe after the Great War is unknown. Certainly, the effect of the pandemic was pronounced: in Sydney, more than 4,000 people died, and the disease affected 40 per cent of the city's population.[25]

James's existence consists of two brief flashes: one for his birth and one for his death. William never mentioned James. He was always treated as the eldest child. The grief of the McMahon families, so far as it appears on the public record, was restrained. But for a notice of his funeral and burial in the family vault in the Catholic section at Rookwood Cemetery, there is nothing. On the same day, *The Daily Telegraph* editorialised:

> After a war involving practically all civilised mankind, carried on for nearly five years with unexampled carnage, and stopped at last only by the exhaustion of one of the belligerents, the world could not be expected to regain its normal condition merely by the signing of some names to a Peace Treaty.[26]

William's father could easily have made the same lament. Within the space of five years, the world had plunged into war; his father had died; his wife had died; and now his eldest son had died, too. The normal condition of the world, to him, would surely have felt to have passed.

He returned to his practice. A political career was not for him. But, as his son would later say, William Daniel knew the law. And that was where he would find his keep. He was intelligent enough to get by. He was good enough to win more often than he lost. But his ambition softened. He became louche: he drank heavily, and he gambled heavily. He was loose with his attention and his work, so much so that he was sued by one of his own clerks for unpaid wages.[27] His reputation suffered. He became a source of family embarrassment.

AS an adult, William spoke of his father with some wariness. There were occasions when he claimed to have inherited his interest in the law from him: 'Naturally I went into law because my father had been a lawyer, and I just accepted that I would be one too.'[28] At other times, he dismissed the idea of having absorbed anything from his father at all. Shame seemed to tinge his statements about the man. He did not even see physical similarities, he said. They had bypassed him completely, going to his own son instead.

He was not entirely wrong. From youth to old age, William did not look much like a McMahon. Thin where his father was immense, short where his father was tall, the blue-eyed boy had missed out on the family's rugby-appropriate build, and was always thought, because of his slender frame, to be susceptible to the disease that had claimed his mother's life. He was a small kid with a thin neck, a messy mound of dark hair, and ears that jutted from his head like round flowers.

Possibly to develop his physical resilience, William was dispatched to board at Abbotsholme College when he was thirteen.[29] Located in Killara and well regarded in Sydney's society, the school considered development of the body as important as that of the mind. *Virtute non verbis* ran the school's motto: By deeds, not by words. Students were made to do military drills and play rugby, cricket, and tennis each afternoon for two hours. They slept in dormitories that were open to the night, ate produce grown on the school grounds, and studied in open-air classrooms, all to build their health. The school had a military ethos that was thought suitable for ill-disciplined and unhealthy boys. Frank Packer was sent there; Harold Holt attended, and knew William.[30] Abbotsholme boasted that it aimed 'at the highest development of body, mind and character. Send us the boy,' the school said, 'and we will return you the man.'[31]

Yet William only attended Abbotsholme for two years before transferring to Sydney Grammar School in 1923. The change is beguiling. Despite producing a prime minister in Edmund Barton and counting many of the New South Wales elite as alumni, the Darlinghurst school was not an attractive proposition at the time.[32] An exodus of staff during the war had damaged Sydney Grammar's standing, and results from its students had not yet returned to their earlier lofty levels. Enrolments had dropped, prompted by high fees and run-down facilities that even the school magazine admitted were not 'worthy'.[33] Its ageing headmaster had just resigned and been replaced by Herbert Dettman, a gentle professor of classics who believed that a 'schoolmaster's business is to sympathise with his boys'.[34] Stern when the occasion warranted, this bespectacled, unruly-haired fellow rarely used the cane.[35] Dettman encouraged study of the classics and extra-curricula activities; he increased hours for tuition, and reduced free periods. He believed that the glory of education lay in 'character building'.

In this respect, William's character was a work in progress. He studied the classics—Latin, Greek, French, English, and History—and deliberately eschewed study of mathematics and the sciences, subjects that would demand a total commitment. Aside from a prize for French when he was in third form, his academic record was undistinguished. He was a rowdy student, and he enjoyed himself. His peers regarded him as an extrovert, always talkative, always up for some fun. As a member of the school debating team, his contributions were limited to the comic. On a trip to the Hawkesbury Agricultural Institution, his peers recorded, William gave an insistent rendition of 'Thanks for the Buggy Ride', and came stomping around his slumbering schoolmates at four o'clock in the morning wearing a pair of military boots. Apparently intent on milking some cows and 'banishing the spirit of sleep from his neighbours', William then 'betook himself to the arms of Morpheus'.[36] Areas where discipline might have seemed certain, such as the senior cadets, were lacking. Uniforms were scarce; rifles with which to practise were non-existent; the schoolmasters who led the training were themselves untrained. As the school itself admitted later, its cadet training was ineffective, an irksome obligation observed only by perfunctory routine.[37]

'I couldn't say it was an unhappy childhood,' William said later. 'That would be wrong.'[38] But it was a lonely childhood. Isolated from his siblings, kept from his father, moving from school to school, he learned to rely on himself, to follow his own desires, to do what he wanted. It led to a very firm belief in the virtue of going in his own direction, always on his own: 'I received very little guidance as to what I should or should not do. You had to make your own way.'

His uncle may not have agreed. Samuel Walder's hand is evident in many of William's later choices, and it is difficult to ignore the work, habits, and loves that his nephew shared with him: politics, art, and devotion to physical exercise. A believer in the virtues of sport, Walder pushed William to play tennis, to box, and to golf. He made him swim regularly at Sydney's beaches. Notably, he pushed William in rowing: when William was seventeen, Walder told him he had to get out of Fours rowing, that it was now time for the Eights.

The obstacles to success here were many. Rowing Eights demanded a physical strength that William simply did not possess. He was only sixty kilos, lean as a length of wire.[39] He was not a natural-born athlete. But when convinced of a course of action, he was doggedly determined. The knowledge that he had to do things for himself met with a deep hunger to prove himself, to demand attention. Walder hurt his back helping William train, but the result was worth it: the handicap of William's slender build was overcome by the disciplined and resolute work.

William came home one night while in his final year of school, and was offered a glass of wine and congratulations. He had made the Sydney Grammar School Eight, Walder said. Though the team was unsuccessful in competition that year, the training had paid off in more ways than Walder knew. William had developed a good technique: 'He had a free movement, with a good length of body swing,' the team's coach wrote. 'The hands were smart and the blade work clean. Although on the small side he rowed a powerful blade.'[40]

Walder's efforts had also unearthed a strength that William's political rivals would grudgingly acknowledge: his persistence. 'He was tenacious alright,' recalled John Courlay, the number-two oar in the

Eight. 'He had to battle mighty hard ... What he lacked in weight,' Courlay said, tapping his chest, 'he made up for in what it took *here*.'[41]

Walder also influenced William's decision to convert to the Church of England. Though he had been baptised into the Catholic Church at St Vincent de Paul, in Redfern, on 20 March 1908, William's association with Catholicism was only slight.[42] He did not attend Sunday school, and he later doubted that he had even read a Bible before he was seventeen.[43] He certainly had not studied religion at school: religious teaching was not introduced to Sydney Grammar until the year after William left.[44] When he was asked about it later in life, he claimed that he had not converted from Catholicism so much as not having had a connection with it in the first place. 'There had been a vacuum there before,' he said, 'a pretty big vacuum.' He attributed it to the 'strong divisions' between the two families from which he had sprung.[45]

According to William, this changed when he was sixteen or seventeen. He met the son of a rector named Rook, and, through Rook, became interested in the Church of England.[46] With a seriousness of intent that belied his other actions, William investigated, read, thought, and decided. It was an unusual process for one so young, and the fervour of William's faith was surprising. Taking the words of the theologian John A.T. Robinson, he later described himself as 'twice-born'.[47] He believed. 'I sort of proved to myself that there was a God,' he said, 'and that I was ... able to make up my mind about it.'[48]

When William discussed his faith some forty years later, he named the Archbishop of Canterbury, William Temple, as among the most influential figures.[49] The vigorous, action-based Christianity that Temple recommended in *Christus Veritas* and *Christ's Revelation of God* appealed to him greatly. 'The Christian who, on whatever grounds, has accepted the Gospel ... is engaged in working out what is involved in that assumption,' Temple wrote. Debate was not the way to test and strengthen one's faith. That could only come about 'by the life of active and practical discipleship, in prayer and service,' Temple argued.[50] It was a message that William absorbed, and years later he would return to it in politics.

Walder's influence was similarly evident in William's developing political and philosophical beliefs. After consolidating his family's business, Walder had made its name supplying tents to the army during

World War I. His business acumen and values—which had a clear affinity with those of James McMahon, and were the common values of Sydney's commercial world—were extended to politics. These included fewer and less cumbersome restrictions on the exchange of goods and services, a dislike for the power of trade unions, and a conservative approach to financial matters.

Achieving financial security by 1924, Walder switched his attention to politics, declaring his desire to serve 'the interests of the city'.[51] His initial foray was local. He stood for the Sydney Municipal Council, running for the Citizens' Reform Association in a by-election, and served as an alderman on the council until 1927, and the party's secretary from 1925.

Living in Walder's home, witness to the prominent identities who came through the door, already aware of the lure of public life through his father's defeated ambitions, William gained a close familiarity with Sydney politics. In old age, he could recall the teetotaller Sir Bertram Stevens and the reserved Sir Thomas Bavin, future New South Wales premiers, visiting Walder's home; through Walder, he became friends with Billy Hughes and a host of other notables.[52]

Just as he had absorbed Walder's religious beliefs, so did William absorb Walder's political values. The social circumstances of his upbringing were exerting themselves. They must have had a 'good effect', William once said.[53] And, as he neared the end of his final year at school, Walder's influence was felt again when William decided to study at the University of Sydney.

But the end of William's school years also marked the end of his childhood. On 18 October 1926, his father died.[54] Aged eighteen, poised on the boundary of adulthood, William McMahon was now well and truly alone.

CHAPTER THREE

The Ghostwriter

1984

Eventually, McMahon agreed that he would have to make changes to his draft. He went to the public service and to the universities, sought advice about form and style, made enquiries about people, asked for recommendations and help.

Some were forthcoming; others less so. Sir Halford Cook, who had worked with McMahon in the Department of Labour and National Service, was willing to help, but Harry Bland, McMahon's former permanent head at the same department, gave the request short shrift: 'No way.'[1] McMahon passed a chapter to Cameron Hazlehurst, a biographer of Menzies and research fellow at the Australian National University. 'My advice is that you should try to tell of what you know that no one else knows,' Hazlehurst told him after reading it. He suggested that McMahon be more personal: 'I believe your readers would prefer to read more of your experiences.'[2] But wary of McMahon and the book, Hazlehurst begged off assisting further. Another scholar, Mark Hayne, an historian from the University of Sydney, agreed to help but resigned after two months, pleading ill-health.[3] Then McMahon approached Ian Wilson, head of the ANU's political science department, and asked him to find a graduate student who would be willing to help. 'Someone like Clem Lloyd,' McMahon said.[4]

When he did not hear back from Wilson, McMahon looked around again. Early in January 1984, he eschewed academics and plumped for a journalist—someone who could work quickly and write clearly for all readerships. On a recommendation from the chief of staff at the *Sydney Morning Herald*, McMahon approached David Bowman.

Bowman was a seasoned South Australian–born journalist who, in his youth, had been a champion chess player. Since joining the Adelaide-based *News* in 1949, he had worked his way from a cadetship to the top of the newsroom. Smart and observant, Bowman was as notable for his mop of grey hair as he was for his nose for a story. As managing editor of the *Canberra Times* and editor-in-chief of the *Herald,* among other publications, Bowman had been energetic and meticulous, and had shown that he was as skilful with sentences as with managing egos. Finding himself a 'sort of Kerensky figure' after a reorganisation of Fairfax management, he had left the company in 1980 and begun building a career as a media critic.[5] When McMahon called, Bowman was cautious. He agreed to a six-month contract only, with his task explicitly stated: to edit McMahon's manuscript to a publishable length and quality.

Bowman arrived at Westfield Towers on 16 January 1984 to find an elderly man clearing out a desk. Breaking off from his task, George Campbell introduced himself. An historian and former Coldstream Guards officer, he was one of two staffers employed in the McMahon office. In a posh accent, Campbell told Bowman that he would be around for a fortnight or so to help him understand the voluminous files, and then be gone. Campbell was decent and helpful, Bowman thought, with the manner of a retired public servant or schoolmaster. Moreover, he had a thorough knowledge of the files and obvious literary experience. Why was he leaving?

McMahon arrived in the office at half-past nine. Spritely, friendly, impeccably dressed in a suit and tie, the former prime minister stopped in to see how Bowman was getting on. Their conversation began as work, but turned towards contemporary politics. McMahon chatted about the prospect of an amalgamation between the Liberal Party and the National Party, mooted in that morning's papers. He was sceptical. 'Doesn't believe it ever will or should come off,' Bowman wrote in his diary that night. 'The primary producers and the miners both need a National Party, he says.'

Once McMahon was gone Bowman began reading the manuscript. As he had been told, it was huge. He counted words and pages, and took notes. He made considerable progress, but by mid-afternoon he was sleepy. Though it had a good opening sentence, the book was oddly structured and seemed full of irrelevancies. A prologue on political ideology and the dangers of socialism was followed by an abbreviated account of McMahon's childhood that diverged into a long section on Billy Hughes. Given his grandfather's history, a discussion of Hughes might have been appropriate in passing, thought Bowman; but at such length and so early on, it was simply confusing. This was followed by a chapter on the family background of McMahon's wife, Sonia. 'Not appropriate for here. Later, with marriage?' Bowman wondered. The manuscript then jumped several decades, to McMahon's political career. It was not an improvement. 'No good,' Bowman jotted in his notes, of a discussion of McMahon's period as minister for labour and national service. 'Various aspects might be transferred somewhere else. Tells us nothing we don't already know.' It was not all bad. There were bright spots. A chapter on Menzies had 'some excellent stuff', and a thumbnail sketch of Evatt was 'good', but then a long section on foreign affairs was 'dull', 'hollow', and 'incomprehensible'. On the Vietnam War, Bowman was scathing: 'No insight. Not worth using!' Overall, the editor was disheartened by what he had read: 'It is very badly done.'[6]

Late in the day, McMahon called past to give Bowman a copy of the *Age*, and the two men got to chatting again. Bowman told McMahon that there had been no problems so far. 'Oh, I don't think there will be,' McMahon replied, and Bowman suddenly realised that the former prime minister thought he was talking about the autobiography.

'Oh,' he said, pointing at the manuscript to correct McMahon, 'there's problems in this.'

McMahon said nothing but, Bowman noticed, his eyes narrowed to 'small blue spots'.[7]

It was a warning sign, but the former prime minister seemed intent on being friendly. Three days later, he invited Bowman to dinner. He had the logistics all worked out: 'The car can drop you back and you can catch your bus.'[8] Though he cancelled the next day, McMahon kept up the invitations. He asked what Bowman liked to drink in case they got to talking on Friday afternoons. He invited him to his country property, boasting that it was a picture.

McMahon was opening up to Bowman, looking back over his life and allowing him to see it, to help him understand it. Over a scotch in the first week of February, McMahon talked about his childhood.

While riding a big draught horse when he was twelve, McMahon said, an official of some kind had stopped him. How long, asked the official pointedly, had the horse been away from her foal?

'This morning,' McMahon said.

'Well, she's in pain, you'd better help her,' the official told him.

McMahon hopped down and 'sucked and sucked' until the official was satisfied. 'Surely you've got the lot now,' said the official.

When he went home and told his aunt about it, McMahon said to Bowman, 'She laughed and laughed and laughed.'[9]

On days like this, Bowman could have been forgiven for thinking that his job would be simple. McMahon seemed forthcoming, trusting, energetic, and on task. But if Bowman ever thought this, he was quickly disabused. In repeated conversations, Campbell enlightened Bowman about McMahon's oddities. On one occasion, Bowman was told, Campbell had been ordered to find a file that he just *knew* was sitting on McMahon's desk, but which McMahon refused to recognise. After McMahon left for the day, Campbell retrieved it, copied it, put the original back, and the next day handed the copy over as though he had found it. McMahon took it without question, without comment.[10]

Joyce Cawthorn, the other staff member, was likewise full of stories. A thickset and formidable woman in her late fifties who managed the accounts and calendar, she told Bowman of the man who telephoned to say that he had lent McMahon a slide-viewer a few months before. Could he have it back, please? McMahon refused without explanation. The slide-viewer would have to stay in the office over the weekend, he told Cawthorn, despite having decided to go that evening to the Isle of Capri, on the Gold Coast. She made no attempt to conceal her embarrassment when she relayed the decision. The caller was indignant, declaring that he would think twice before lending anything to McMahon ever again.[11]

Bowman tried not to be distracted. His concern had to be the book. By his reckoning, the voluminous work that had dissuaded publishers was nowhere close to the oft-stated 400,000 words. A proper reading revealed duplication and extraneous material such as letters and unabridged speeches: 'By the time it's cut into shape we shall probably have no more than 50,000–60,000 words,' he wrote. But even cutting this away would be insufficient. A simple edit would not do, he decided.

To address the problems he saw, the manuscript needed to be almost entirely rewritten.[12]

In coming to this view, Bowman apprehended that the terms of his employment would have to change. No longer would he be merely editing. Now, he would become a ghostwriter, writing a book that McMahon, it seemed, could not write for himself.

Bowman had a long talk with Campbell about how to approach McMahon and handle him. The elderly historian was supportive. He had already confided that he thought little of the manuscript. The plan that Bowman laid out would require big changes, but they were necessary, both men agreed, if there was to be any prospect of publication.

CHAPTER FOUR

Shelter and the Law

1927–1939

'As I read I noticed that a particular factor cropped up over and over again,' wrote Lucille Iremonger.[1] While studying the lives of British prime ministers, Iremonger, an historian and novelist, observed a characteristic shared by almost two-thirds of her subjects: the loss of a parent in childhood or early adolescence.[2]

Theorising that the deprivation of a parent's love in childhood manifests in later life as the desire to find it in the embrace of voters and political power, Iremonger decided upon a name for her observation: the Phaeton Complex. It was named for the illegitimate son of Apollo, whose unyielding demands for love and recognition led to his being struck from the sky. Disaster, as with all Greek myths, was the fate for Iremonger's Phaetons.

The deaths of McMahon's mother and father mark him for inclusion in Iremonger's pantheon. The isolation of his childhood; the influence of Samuel Walder; the unconditional love that McMahon found in his aunt Elsie Walder; the heated religious beliefs that led to McMahon's description of himself as 'twice-born'; the fervent declarations of love for his wife, Sonia: all of these, too, align with Iremonger's catalogue.

There are differences, however. There is little to suggest that McMahon grieved 'extravagantly' for the dead, but his silence on the existence of his elder brother, James, is conspicuous. No demonstration of reserve is on the record, though McMahon's feelings of injustice always coloured his statements and conduct. Nor does it seem that McMahon sought the love of the public in quite the same fashion that Iremonger suggests. McMahon was vain and needy, certainly—but more for the recognition of his peers and the trappings of power than crowds.

From any reading of his life, William McMahon did not allow his father's death to affect him. There is no notable change recorded in his behaviour after his father's death. He seems to have carried on just as he had for the decade before.

He skied. He rowed. He boxed. He swam in the surf at Bondi. He attended the ballet and the theatre. He became involved in horseracing to the point of owning a few horses. McMahon was happy to bet, and profligate about it. His religiosity did not restrain him. He was not particularly lucky. By his own admission, he lost often and he lost big. But he hardly worried about it. For McMahon, the thrill of watching loss and success contend around a grass track could outweigh the prospect of financial loss or gain. It could make him careless. On one occasion, police raided a party that he was attending. A friend who had been gambling at the tables and who was about to be arrested passed McMahon £1,000 and told him to use the money to bail him out in the morning. McMahon decided on a different course of action. He took the money out to the racetrack and bet it all on a sure thing. Luck, this time, smiled on him.[3]

He had gained admission to St Paul's College, a residential hall for male Church of England students of the University of Sydney. The austere sandstone buildings in Newtown, designed in the 1850s by the architect Edmund Blacket, were the home of many establishment figures before McMahon. Clergymen, solicitors, politicians, and doctors had passed through its doors and established traditions to accompany a cultural philosophy that emphasised involvement in Australian society. The college's motto, *Deo Patriae Tibi* (For God, Country, and Thyself), foregrounded this involvement and the influence of the Church of England.

McMahon's attendance at the college caused some dismay within his father's family, who were not aware that he had been received into the Church of England.[4] Yet the decision to attend St Paul's was as much attributable to his religiosity as it was for his choice of study.

McMahon later said that Law was an automatic choice for him. According to him, he never considered any other study. It is not quite true. His ambitions almost went another way:

I was a balletomane. I adored the ballet and music. But I realised I had
to be totally committed. I did a fair bit of ballet dancing and then after
that I had high falutin' ideas of being a good 'ordinary' dancer.[5]

At university, he was a lax student, a libertine, content to party and
live leisurely. What regimentation college life tried to impose did not
bind him. 'He would sally forth about nine o'clock,' wrote his peers,
'returning in the small hours to clatter about the corridors … Morning
revealed him lying in a tumbled bed in improper relation to his
pillow.'[6] Richard Kirby, president of the Conciliation and Arbitration
Commission when McMahon was minister for labour and national
service, knew him in these 'party days': he was 'quite the man about
town', Kirby recalled, often seen at nightclubs and parties.[7]

Years of taking in the sons of the wealthy and well-off had developed
an unofficial culture in St Paul's that was heavy on sport, excess, and
chummy, boyish humour. St Paul's, one student suggested, developed in
its fellows 'a sense of the value of things':

> Here there is freedom of conscience and freedom of speech: here is
> legislation healthily ignored: here one may grow a beard seven days
> together and lunch, sockless, in a torn blazer; work silently, drink
> noisily, laugh hilariously, moan lugubriously—and always will be found
> company to fit the mood, and none to say one nay. Surely this is Utopia!
> I can conceive of no greater freedom nor of any better soil in which to
> sow the seeds of individuality.[8]

McMahon would have enjoyed his Fresher year, but it is unlikely
that he would have found much that was new in it. The 'delights of its
newly discovered liberty, the novelty of its experiences and the absence
of responsibilities' that ensured college men regarded their first year as
the happiest in their college life would have been, to McMahon, passé,
everyday. He would have already been well accustomed to this kind of
living, for he walked on the same path as his father. He dated, partied,
was wild and disordered. 'You could do what you liked,' he said later. 'If
you wanted to work you did; if you didn't, you didn't. If you wanted to
go out at night, you went out at night. I think I was a pretty wild sort of
bloke when I was there.'[9]

He was the same gregarious, charming young man that his school friends had observed—if a little louder and prouder. 'He would talk volubly and hyperbolically on most subjects, with or without knowledge of them, and his remarks were the more vivid on account of complete, if temporary, self-conviction,' wrote his peers in the *Pauline*.[10] McMahon was fun and merriment. He rowed cox for the Eight in 1928, swam in 1930, and was on the college sub-committee for dance between 1929 and 1931.[11] He won a round of golf at Killara Golf Club; had a 'paternal look' when a guinea pig was presented at a Seniors supper in 1929; and fell into a yawning trench between the main building and garage when some copper piping was being installed. 'As Fortune had it, Bill McMahon was the only person to fall down, and he did not kill himself,' his peers snickered.[12] The wealth his uncle had begun to entrust to him allowed McMahon to dress fashionably. He bought and wore clothes with free abandon, not minding to take care of them or keep them in order. The 'sundry pots' he kept by the mirror of his dressing table showed the attention he paid to his appearance.

He was healthy and happy. Playing his gramophone incessantly, grinning from ear to ear, talking with a 'spluttering utterance' and walking with a 'swaggering gait' around the university, clad in his blue-flannel college coat with brass buttons that tinkled on the sleeve, McMahon was carefree.[13] St Paul's was a shelter from the outside world, 'an asylum for the sane,' one old boy wrote,[14] and it inured McMahon to the economic calamity that, by the middle of his first year of Law, began to engulf the world.

INITIALLY, the Depression did not affect McMahon. He said later that it had not worried him. He possessed all the money he needed. Ensconced in the libertine sphere of St Paul's, his life seemed hardly to change as the Depression deepened. The only effect it had, it seemed, was in conversation: his aunt and uncle might occasionally bring it up. To McMahon, the Depression was simply something that happened to other people.

For many other people, the Depression *was* change—of a dramatic, absolute, and unequivocal kind. In Australia, it fuelled the ascendancy of the non-Labor parties and the predominance of their orthodoxies in economic and financial policy. Under Joseph Lyons, who deserted Labor to lead the United Australia Party to victory at the 1931 federal election, a fiscal straitjacket—of honouring overseas debts, of cutting government spending, of reducing constraints on business ventures—would be coupled with devaluation and cuts to wages and the entitlements of lenders, and would eventually lead to Australia's economic recovery and stability in the subsequent decade.

For Samuel Walder, the economic and political upheaval wreaked by the Depression was an ingredient in his rise and an opportunity. Becoming Sydney's lord mayor in 1932, still a member of the Citizens' Reform Association, he led efforts to cope through measures such as the Citizens' Employment Committee, which helped some 3,000 people obtain work within two months. He oversaw the construction of Martin Place and Macquarie Street in order to put more people to work; with his wife, he took an active interest in finding employment opportunities for women.

He also exercised a wider influence by persuading the various non-Labor parties to band together under the United Australia Party banner. As vice-president of the National Association of New South Wales, Walder was party to the negotiations that led to its merger with the populist, right-wing All for Australia League in 1932. This in turn led to his becoming vice-president of the UAP. Then, in September, still serving as lord mayor of Sydney, Walder was nominated for a seat in the New South Wales Legislative Council by premier Bertram Stevens. From there, Walder had an immediate and close experience of all the frenzied efforts to alleviate the problems wrought by the Depression.

As McMahon drove between Walder's home at Point Piper and his room at St Paul's, as he accompanied Walder around Sydney, as he sat through meetings of the UAP, he made connections between the speeches he was hearing and the news he was reading—and the law that his teachers had begun to drum into him.

The Law School in his day had none of the roseate glow of a university. Located off-campus, in the veins of Sydney's legal precinct, the school was staffed by working solicitors and barristers who taught around sessions in the morning and evening. The school was designed not for the butterflies of abstraction but for the teaching of a 'systematic body of legal knowledge'. Students were expected to attend lectures in the morning, work as articled clerks during the day, and return for further classes in the late afternoon and early evening.[15] In keeping with the orthodoxy of the legal profession, the facilities in which this took place were shabby: old and uncomfortable, cramped and small, with a cloakroom that was a 'black hole of Calcutta'.[16]

What it lacked in material comforts the school made up for in the quality of its staff. McMahon came under the tutelage of the leaders of Sydney's bar: Charteris, Treatt, Windeyer. But it was the famed professor of law, Sir John Peden, who was the most memorable.

McMahon encountered Peden in 1929.[17] The dean of the Law School taught constitutional law, and was famous for enmeshing it with contemporary circumstances in order to ensure students understood its practical working.[18] President of the Legislative Council of New South Wales, of the Law Council, and chair of the Royal Commission on the Constitution (1927–30), Peden combined the perspectives of an academic, silk, and legislator, and was a fierce defender of high standards. 'You've got to *work* here. You've got to know your law,' he would rasp. 'You can't expect us to turn loose a man who'll be a menace to his profession':

> He [Peden] hammered into them [his students] the importance of exact knowledge. With all the grim fervour of his Covenanting ancestors he would turn, in the middle of explaining some case, to denounce the ignorance and indolence of the solicitor who had made a false step and 'slaughtered his client!'[19]

Exacting and conservative, Peden was an advocate of the theories of A.V. Dicey, the English jurist who had promoted monarchical powers as a bulwark against the Home Rule movement in Ireland in the 1880s.[20] He regarded Dicey as 'almost sacred', said one student.[21] Setting Dicey's *Introduction to the Study of the Law of the Constitution* as a class text, Peden would expound on the unwritten powers that could regulate governments.[22] 'The discretionary power of the Crown occasionally may be, and according to constitutional precedents sometimes ought to be, used to strip an existing House of Commons of its authority,' Dicey had written. When might such an action be necessary? 'A dissolution is allowable, or necessary, whenever the wishes of the legislature are, or may fairly be presumed to be, different from the wishes of the nation.'[23]

Peden was able to inculcate these views among three generations of lawyers in New South Wales. The future attorney-general and chief justice of the High Court, Garfield Barwick, thought 'Jacko' treated his students like kindergarten children, but found much to agree with in his lectures.[24] The power to withdraw the commission, he would later say, is 'always available as a last resort'.[25] Herbert Vere 'Doc' Evatt, leader of the federal parliamentary Labor Party (1951–60) and Peden's most brilliant student, agreed that the reserve powers existed, but found their unwritten status a cause for despair.[26] His doctoral thesis, published as *The King and His Dominion Governors*, was an extended plea that these powers be set down and codified.[27] For John Kerr, studying at Sydney University shortly after McMahon, the influence of Peden, Barwick, and Evatt was undeniable. The question of reserve powers was a 'reality' for him from his 'early student days'.[28]

Debate over those powers became a reality for many people in May 1932.[29] Since his election two years before, Labor premier Jack Lang had aroused the ire of Sydney's elite with his policies to shorten the working week, and to provide endowments for children and relief for the Depression-hit mortgagors, tenants, and unemployed.[30] 'Man before money,' he called it, but his opponents called him 'six feet of uncouth, untrained political pugnacity'.[31] Bad enough, they thought, were Lang's insistent attempts to abolish the Legislative Council. Worse still were his slights on royalty, most evident in his decision to open the Sydney Harbour Bridge in the place of the governor. But these paled next to Lang's vow to withhold payment of New South Wales's share of the interest on debts that had been raised in Britain. By 1932, the unrelenting criticism from his opponents had caused Lang's support to dissipate. Unemployment had hit 31 per cent. The press was openly hostile. The Scullin Labor government had cracked apart at Lang's defiance, and been replaced by the Lyons-led UAP, which was determined to use Commonwealth law to check the rogue premier.

In March, with his state £7m in debt to the Commonwealth, Lang let New South Wales default on its interest repayments to British bondholders. The prime minister responded by passing the *Financial Agreement Enforcement Act 1932*, which allowed the Commonwealth government to appropriate New South Wales' revenue from the banking system. Lang ordered all state funds to be withdrawn from the private banks, and mandated the use of cash for state transactions. The New South Wales Treasury vaults were filled with cash, and public servants with bulging leather satchels walked the city making payments under the watchful eye of police. Then Lang introduced a Bill that would impose a 10 per cent levy on banks and lenders. The financial institutions began to panic. Seven King's Counsel wrote to the New South Wales governor, Sir Philip Game, calling on him to act. Game could not accept their advice, but he 'generally' agreed with it.[32] He believed Lang was breaking the law. Unwilling to allow the Crown and his representative to be a party to it, Game asked Lang to withdraw the orders.

Lang refused. On 13 May, after a long night and a flurry of letters, Game dismissed Lang from office and commissioned the leader of the opposition, Bertram Stevens, a former head of the New South Wales Treasury, to form a government. Stevens advised an immediate election. Amid the Lyons government's subsequent suspension of the *Financial Agreement Enforcement Act* and sudden provision of some £600,000 relief for the unemployed, the stock market soared. At the election, Lang's Labor Party was trounced; its fifty-five seats were cut to twenty-four.

McMahon did not agree with Peden's views on the reserve powers, and he did not agree with Game's dismissal of Lang.[33] An admirer of the former premier's tenacity and ability, McMahon thought the context from which the reserve powers had sprung was too different, too removed, from Australia, where the political systems were coming of age.

Yet he thought highly of Peden. 'He seemed to me to stress the duty of the lawyer to protect the individual *against* the State,' McMahon said. 'This has been one of my fundamental political beliefs.'[34]

It is unlikely that Peden would have thought much of him. Peden was severe, hardworking, and 'puritanical in his outlook', said Margaret Hay, the faculty clerk.[35] The dominating scholar would have found much that was wanting in McMahon, a mediocre student who was in need of a tutor at each exam period. 'I only got through by the skin of my teeth without failing,' McMahon said later.[36] Yet the relationship was possibly tinged with some care: Peden once told McMahon not to bother sitting an exam because he would fail it. McMahon took no small measure of pride in noting that he sat the exam anyway and passed. The story was possibly an exaggeration, a bit of self-flattery to counter the declaiming professor. Yet late in his studies, McMahon *did* begin to take on the work ethic that would make the story believable.

An apprenticeship in a solicitor's office was a necessary step in McMahon's career. The demands of articles were mostly time-based: five years' experience in a master solicitor's office. The expectation that articles would begin during a student's study was implicit.

Enter Norman Cowper. A tall, confident, and elegant solicitor, Cowper had an expertise in commercial law that was as sharp as his mischievous wit. He was an alumnus of Sydney Grammar School, and deeply involved in non-Labor politics. He had been a branch president of the Nationalist Party, and had unsuccessfully stood as its' joint candidate, with the United Australia Party, against Billy Hughes in the 1931 federal election, when Hughes was a candidate of his own Australia Party. Transferring his allegiance to the UAP thereafter, Cowper helped to draft the party's constitution, and served on its policy committee from 1932 onwards. Rarely seen out of a suit, a habitual pipe smoker, and, in his leisure, a gardener with a murderous eye for shrubs and bushes, Cowper was also a partner at the law firm Allen Allen & Hemsley.[37]

Cowper knew Samuel Walder and, by dint of McMahon's association with Walder and Sydney Grammar, he knew McMahon. He took the young man on as his articled clerk in 1932.[38]

ALLEN Allen & Hemsley was old and reputable, and took pride in both.[39] It had been around for more than a century when McMahon stepped through its doors. Stationed on the corner of Castlereagh Street and Hosking Place in the old Athenaeum Club building, signs of the firm's history were everywhere. Its strongroom held books of letters that dated from 1840, and the familial link to George Allen—its founder and the first solicitor to have been educated in Australia—was evident in the penthouse offices afforded to his descendants Reginald, Herbert, and Arthur. None of the three was particularly interested in the law, though. Reginald played cricket for Australia and bred bloodstock;

Herbert liked to travel; Arthur preferred to manage his real estate interests and record the minutiae of his life in a diary that he dictated to his secretaries. As those diaries attest, the Allen men were partners in the firm, but largely uninvolved in it. The real work went on in the lower floors.

Alfred Hemsley and Norman Cowper were the leaders of the firm. Hemsley, an Englishman married as much to the law as he was to his spouse, looked after big clients J.C. Williamson Ltd and Australian Gas Light while serving as a UAP-aligned member of the New South Wales Legislative Council. When not searching for a way into politics, Cowper managed the work emanating from the Bank of New South Wales, for whom Allen Allen & Hemsley had acted for almost ninety years.

Both men were Protestant, intellectual, and influential. Their work ethic was considerable. Their skill was notable. But, McMahon said later, it was their 'sort of generous liberalism' that he admired, a kind on display when Cowper represented Mabel Freer, an Indian-born British woman who had been refused admission to Australia after failing a dictation test in Italian; the real grounds for her refused entry was her intention to marry a still-married Australian army officer.[40]

Though McMahon also came under Hemsley's eye, Cowper was a good master for him. Believing that 'in the *majority* of offices an articled clerk can, if he has initiative and curiosity as well as ability and application, obtain a great deal of very useful experience',[41] Cowper nurtured his clerks and jostled them along, even gingering them up. The gentleman solicitor would later surprise one of his clerks by encouraging him to attend an anti-Vietnam War moratorium march: 'He made you wonder what you were doing with your life.'[42] McMahon had much the same experience with Cowper in the 1930s: 'He tried to give you every opportunity he could to let you study and understand.' Cowper was cognisant of the practical problems of studying law, and he was willing to trust his clerks' initiative and application. 'I can't remember in all the time I was with him,' McMahon said, 'that he ever sought to try and steer you in any direction.'[43]

The guidance may not have been overt, but it was there. The nature of the clientele, Cowper's involvement with the UAP, and Hemsley's position in the Legislative Council, ensured that a conservative political orthodoxy pervaded the office. This was increased by the presence of non-Labor politicians. Thomas Bavin, who had served as premier before Lang, was a frequent visitor to Arthur Allen. S.M. Bruce, the former prime minister, was a correspondent of Allen's and a dinner companion of Cowper's. Thus, when Lang was dismissed, Arthur Allen could write with confident jubilation that 'everybody [is] terribly thrilled at the political news to-day … Certainly one can look at the future with more hope than we could this morning.'[44]

Cowper's expertise in commercial law meant that McMahon became intimately involved with the business side of the practice. And, as his university studies moved from constitutional law to the more mundane and practical, McMahon was increasingly assigned to the commercial work at Allens.[45] The involvement allowed him to become familiar with commerce and industry in Sydney, and to make his own forays into it. One of these early moves became increasingly important in the years that followed.

In October 1932, the journalist George Warnecke conceived a plan to scratch at the protective instincts of Hugh Denison, chairman of the Sydney-based Associated Newspapers. Warnecke's plan was simple: form a syndicate to take on the loss-making Australian Workers' Union newspaper, *The World*, and then, by announcing plans to set up *The World* as a direct rival to Denison's evening paper, *The Sun*, provoke a panicked takeover bid from Denison, a tidy proportion of which would be profit.[46]

Unable to raise the capital for the idea, Warnecke approached his old boss, Clyde Packer. Packer was intrigued, but could not take part. He told Warnecke to talk with his son, Frank, who was smarting from his recent ejection from Associated Newspapers. The young Packer seized on Warnecke's plan with glee. He brought James Scullin's former treasurer, E.G. 'Ted' Theodore, into the loop, and together they purchased a nine-day option on *The World* and its premises for £100. Via a front-page report on *The Newspaper News* on 1 November 1932, Packer announced that he and Theodore would remodel *The World* along the lines of the London evening dailies and undercut the price of *The Sun* by a ha'penny. 'We are busily organising so that the new production will make its first appearance on November 9,' he said.[47]

To ensure the scratch could not be ignored, Packer had his solicitors register a new company to publish the paper: Sydney Newspapers Ltd. According to the announcements it made, the company had a formidable authorised capital of £150,000. But only £30,000 was actually paid at the time. Packer and Theodore, respectively managing director and chairman, invested £5,000 apiece; Warnecke scraped together £1,000; the remainder came from 'friends and business associates'.

Where did McMahon fit into this? As he described it forty years later, McMahon's involvement with Sydney Newspapers Ltd was simple:

> On 8th November 1932 or somewhere about that time I did sign the memorandum and articles of association of his [Packer's] company. I was then an articled clerk in Allen Allen and Hemsley. I had never met Frank Packer; I had never met his associates. I did not know who he was. The men to whom I was clerking, Sir Norman Cowper and Mr Arthur Hemsley [sic], asked me to sign the document. Of course I signed it. Any person with a knowledge of law and a knowledge of the way companies are formed would have done exactly as I did.[48]

McMahon may certainly have signed the papers, but to leave it there is to understate his role. McMahon was an original subscriber to the infant company, one of those who stumped up part of the remaining capital. Cowper and Hemsley were not among those others; indeed, the articles of association were not even drawn up by Allen Allen & Hemsley.[49] How Cowper and Hemsley would have been involved, if they were at all, is unclear. It is likely, however, that McMahon was alerted to the opportunity by a relative, Maisie McMahon, a stenographer for the lawyers who drew up the papers.[50]

However it happened, it was among the best investments that McMahon ever made—for the scratching worked. Denison and the board at Associated Newspapers panicked. They paid Packer and Theodore £86,500 in exchange for their promise not to publish an afternoon daily or Sunday newspaper in Sydney for three years. The only modesty that Denison managed to insist upon was keeping the figure private: 'It was inadvisable to make this public,' Denison said.[51] The discretion did not last. It was common knowledge within a few months.

The money, and the company that had been formed in the ploy to obtain it, was the seed of the Packer family's wealth and power. From that money sprang the *Australian Women's Weekly*; from that came Australian Consolidated Press; from that grew the clout that Packer would wield unabashedly in the service of McMahon's political ambitions. However new it was in 1932, the connection between McMahon and Packer would strengthen in the years that followed: Packer would bring his business almost permanently to Allen Allen & Hemsley in 1936, and McMahon would count the press tycoon as a close friend.

As the year concluded so, too, did McMahon's law studies. He finished the last of his exams in February 1933 and awaited his results. In March, there was news. 'I notice the University Law examinations results are in the paper this morning,' Arthur Allen recorded on 14 March. 'McMahon, in our office, got through in all his subjects.'[52]

McMahon was promoted to managing clerk soon afterwards.[53] He talked in later life of acting for the Bank of New South Wales and the Commonwealth Bank, but his exact role is unclear. It is the familiar puzzle of legal biography: lawyers are shadows, mouthing words that are not theirs, acting for interests that are not their own. On the basis of McMahon's presence at Allen Allen & Hemsley, it is reasonable to assume that he was good at the work. He would not have been kept around for long had he been anything else.

Meanwhile, Norman Cowper began to shake at the foundations of Allen Allen & Hemsley. The gentleman solicitor's concerns were initially personal. In 1933, he murmured discontentedly about his future.[54] His efforts to break into politics had proved fruitless. He had considered going to the bar. He was agitated. Arthur Allen tried to assuage him, initially with success. 'I had a very nice letter from Norman Cowper appreciating the suggestions made by us to him for the future,' Allen wrote afterward.[55] But two years later, Cowper's concerns had resurfaced. He was a partner of the firm and the driver of much of its work. He had a good salary, more than £1,000 per annum. Yet he was souring and restless. Another firm had offered him a position; he had nothing to lose. Cowper demanded that his salary be doubled. When Allen demurred, Cowper asked why he received only a salary and not a share of the profits. Allen told Cowper that there were no profits. 'No profits!'

Cowper did not believe the misanthropic heritor, so he called his bluff. 'If there are no profits, let's share the losses.'[56]

Cowper's concerns were not entirely self-serving. He could foresee that the genteel and nepotistic inclinations rife among law firms would soon be replaced by a hard-nosed sense of business. For Allen Allen & Hemsley to survive, he believed, it needed to change. Training and retaining talent with the prospect of promotion and reward was the only way to ensure the firm did not ossify.

His efforts to drive change were aided by upheaval within the firm. Taken ill in January 1936, Alfred Hemsley died in July the following year. In between, Allen Allen & Hemsley vacated its offices on Castlereagh Street and moved to the APA building in Martin Place.

All this left Cowper the dominant figure. He used that dominance to pull Allen Allen & Hemsley into the future. He led efforts to recruit partners and poach people irrespective of the autobiography of a school tie. In doing so, he brought energy to Allen Allen & Hemsley, expanded the list of partners, and ensured opportunity was present.

The effect was not lost on Arthur Allen. Early in 1939, as McMahon neared completion of his articles, Allen spoke with him about his future. It was a time for decisions.[57]

Whether to confirm himself as a solicitor or go to the bar was a decision made at the end of a clerkship. McMahon had hoped to become a barrister for years. It may have stemmed from a desire to one-up his father, or to place himself in the most conspicuous place possible, at the centre of attention. He had the talents for it: he was able to speak to and charm different audiences, modulating his approach as needed; he was thorough in preparation and able to prosecute arguments.

But it was not to be. McMahon had begun to go deaf. He found himself missing snatches of conversation, and unable to hear arguments. The realisation that this precluded him from becoming a barrister was stark. 'I would have gone to the bar without any doubt had it not been for that difficulty,' he lamented later.[58]

He chose the only course open to him. On 10 March 1939, he was admitted as a solicitor.[59] There was some consolation. Arthur Allen made the necessary arrangements for the newly admitted lawyer. A few weeks later, all was done. 'I wrote a letter this morning to Bill McMahon confirming my promise to take him in as a partner now that he is a Solicitor,' Allen wrote on 3 April, 'the partnership to begin as from 1st instant.'[60]

In accepting the offer, McMahon became only the eighteenth partner at Allen Allen & Hemsley.[61] The offer would not have been made without Cowper's efforts to shake up the firm and to modernise it. Nor would it have even been in prospect without the model of discipline and hard work that Cowper provided to his young clerk.

Yet it is possible, for only the second time, to discern in the offer of the partnership some recognition of McMahon's work and discipline. He had evidently worked well enough to earn the advancement. And he reaped its rewards for years.

CHAPTER FIVE

The Central Figure

1984

Bowman put his criticisms to McMahon at the end of January 1984. The autobiography's structure was unsatisfactory, he said. There was no start, no end. The book jumped from point to point, and was written in a needlessly official manner, he said. It had a gaping hole at the centre. It needed to develop and unfold more naturally and more smoothly. It had to be coherent. It had to be a narrative, to tell a story.

'The unifying factor,' Bowman argued later, putting his concerns into writing, 'is the central figure—what he does, what he knows, what he thinks—and only rarely should he step aside for some other character to dominate the stage.'[1]

What was required was a nearly complete overhaul of the work. By Bowman's reckoning, it was possible to get the whole thing done in six months. But for that to happen, Bowman's role would have to change. He would now be a ghost: he would have to haunt McMahon's past, investigate and document it, in order to write the book.[2]

Bowman knew it was a change, and he knew it was a big job, especially with the urgency McMahon attached to finishing the book. He was undaunted. He was willing to take it on. But there was a condition, he told McMahon: George Campbell would have to be retained as a full-time researcher.

This was a problem. McMahon's entitlements as a former prime minister did not cover the employment of a third set of hands, and he did not want to pay for Campbell out of his own pocket.

Bowman did not care for these concerns. 'I said that the first priority was to get the book out quickly and to make it a first-class job,' he wrote in his diary that night. 'The profits were secondary.'[3]

McMahon seemed to agree with that. Bowman left the meeting believing he had convinced McMahon. But that afternoon McMahon wanted to speak about it again. It remained important to him, McMahon said, to make some money out of the book. He wanted to discuss it with Richard Smart.

One week later, Smart came to the office. Meeting the publisher for the first time, Bowman was reminded of a bird: 'Smart looks like an emu, dresses like one too.'[4] The encounter was short. What to do about Campbell was not Smart's problem. The publisher averred from doing anything more than advancing money against royalties for a researcher.

It took another week and a half to sort out Campbell's fate. McMahon asked him to go part-time, but Bowman would have none of it. It would not be acceptable, he told McMahon. He needed Campbell's research skills. McMahon received the ultimatum coolly. The atmosphere in the office was 'a bit thick' for a few days, thought Bowman, a bit tense, but then McMahon announced he would pay Campbell to stay on.[5]

And then, suddenly, McMahon was back to his old self, 'cheerful and forthcoming', happy to recount stories and to gossip about personalities old and new. He chatted with Bowman about the turmoil at Fairfax and how he had just advised young Warwick Fairfax, working at Chase Manhattan, to defy his father's wishes that he return home.

But the good moods did not last. Joyce Cawthorn stormed into Bowman's office one afternoon to complain about a booking she had arranged that McMahon had upset. 'I *told* you,' McMahon had said, to her protests. 'I may hesitate and stammer at times, but I don't get things like that wrong.'[6]

'These people are impossible,' McMahon told Bowman the next morning on the phone,[7] but Bowman was not convinced that Cawthorn and Campbell were at fault. In the short time he had worked for McMahon, Bowman had seen repeated lapses of memory, from the trivial and transient to the significant and problematic. 'He confuses periods as well as forgetting names and places,' Bowman observed. Aware of the effect it could have on the book, Bowman lamented that McMahon had left the job so late. 'He should have written the book ten years ago.'[8]

In mid-February, having trawled through *Hansard* and rewriting thoroughly, Bowman handed McMahon new drafts of the first two chapters. They were an early test of the relationship. Would McMahon like them? Would he find them satisfactory? They were returned three days later with substantial annotations and commentary. Friends had told him that his early life *had* to be in the book, McMahon wrote to his ghostwriter. Bowman was happy that these friends had echoed his recommendations, but disgruntled when he read McMahon's edits. 'I don't mind having to work harder at his style,' Bowman groused, 'but [I] won't accept this much alteration as a normal thing. His "style" is as dry and unimaginative as it could possibly be.'[9]

More worryingly, the agreement they had made about the structure and the nature of the work seemed to be slipping. In a meeting, McMahon expressed second thoughts about the old draft. Daunted by the amount of work involved in producing a new draft, touchy about Bowman's involvement, he talked of returning to the huge manuscript that had sent Bowman to sleep. He liked its limited scope, its fixation on the great and powerful he had known. Bowman tried to stop it. 'I told him he should be the centre of it, not other political figures such as Menzies.'[10] But the disagreement was more fundamental, and stemmed from a misunderstanding on the part of both men.

Bowman's understanding had always been that McMahon was producing an autobiography. Implicit in the drafts, it was the word McMahon had always used to describe the book in conversation and in the press. He had always spoken of the comprehensive, documented story of his life and the times he had lived through, of moving sequentially from youth to old age—from Menzies to McMahon, even. Was this not autobiography? Certainly he did not ever seem to mean a memoir, marked more by selection and whimsy than a sturdy, credible autobiographical tome.

Bowman sought to clarify this. He asked McMahon whether he wanted to produce a political autobiography or political memoirs. The reply staggered him.

'Memoirs,' McMahon said.[11]

CHAPTER SIX

A Time of Transformation

1939–1948

In the same week that McMahon made partner at Allen Allen & Hemsley, the prime minister died. Joseph Lyons had been under immense strain for months. The ramshackle government that he had led for seven years was coming apart. The United Australia Party's purpose had faded. The Depression had eased. Economic recovery was well underway. Yet war was looming, and the horrified Lyons seemed unwilling to confront its likelihood. His party began to whisper of casting him aside. Exhausted, isolated, bereft of direction, Lyons wondered if he should quit.[1]

In January, as newspaper baron Keith Murdoch dismissed Lyons as 'a born rail-sitter' who had 'lost his usefulness', the prime minister tried to persuade S.M. Bruce, now high commissioner in London, to return to Australian politics.[2] 'Look here, you've got to come back,' Lyons pleaded. 'I can't carry on, in view of the obviously difficult and threatening times ahead.'[3]

Times were difficult: Labor was regrouping; Europe was rearming; and Japan was expanding. But Lyons was wavering. The next day, he returned to Bruce and told him he had changed his mind. By March he was contemplating retirement again. The UAP organisation pressed him to stay until the next election was won; they saw him as a winner, still popular in the country. But his parliamentary colleagues were less enamoured, more exasperated: Lyons' longtime ally Henry Gullett had deserted him; Billy Hughes was white-anting him; and the lordly and immense Robert Menzies, the glittering star of Victorian politics and a senior minister since September 1934, had resigned from Lyons' cabinet in a swirl of controversy barely three weeks earlier.

Lyons was on the rack, pressed and harried. Over a drink on Wednesday 5 April, he told the clerk of the House of Representatives, Frank Green, that he should never have left his home state of Tasmania. 'I had good mates there, and was happy,' Lyons said to Green, 'but this situation is killing me.'[4]

He boarded a car bound for Sydney. He was to open the Royal Easter Show in a few days' time. But somewhere along the road through the pale-khaki paddocks beyond Goulburn, the prime minister had a heart attack. He clung to life for two days, enough time for his wife to race to Sydney's St Vincent's Hospital to take his hand. She held it in the unfamiliar room until Good Friday came and he passed away.

'It all seems so sudden,' Arthur Allen commented, when news broke.[5] He was not wrong. Many things were sudden. German troops were finalising their annexure of Czechoslovakia. Italy had invaded Albania. Europe's shadows were growing darker and casting further, reaching to Australia.

Sir Earle Page, the deputy prime minister and Country Party leader, crafty and temperamental, with a high-pitched voice and frequent chortle, was commissioned as prime minister until the UAP chose Lyons' successor. He announced that neither he nor his party would serve under Menzies should he be chosen. It was an attempted reprise of tactics that Page had used to dislodge Billy Hughes from the prime ministership in the aftermath of the 1922 elections. Back then, Page's motive had been to force a coalition between the Country Party and the Nationalists; this time, personal motivations outweighed any political ends.[6]

He would not desist from his opposition to Menzies, even after Menzies was elected leader of the UAP. Speaking in an adjournment debate before Menzies was to be commissioned as prime minister, Page told the House of Representatives that the government needed a leader possessing 'qualities of courage, loyalty, and judgment'. Finding the new UAP leader wanting on all fronts, Page accused Menzies of disloyalty to Lyons and cowardice for his resignation from the military during World War I:

All I say is that if the right honourable gentleman cannot satisfactorily and publicly explain to a very great body of people in Australia who did participate in the war his failure to do so, he will not be able to get that maximum effort out of the people in the event of war.[7]

Hoping that this had poisoned Menzies' merits, Page announced that, like Lyons, he had entreated Bruce to return to Australia as the head of a government which he would happily serve in or make way for. For his part, Bruce would only agree to do so if it were a 'nonparty' government. Page's high-minded, self-sacrificial proposal did not divert attention from the main content of his carefully prepared jeremiad.

Inside the House, outraged interjections punctured the speech. 'This is very cheap,' muttered UAP member John Lawson.[8] 'That is dirt!' shouted Rowland James, a Labor parliamentarian.[9] Another Labor man, Gerald Mahony, was disgusted: 'Nobody wants you. You have let your mates down, whatever else you have done.'[10] The feeling was so vehement that four of Page's colleagues in the Country Party, Arthur Fadden among them, moved to the crossbenches to protest their leader's action.

The speech was an act of inadvertent yet spectacular self-immolation. Menzies immediately denied Page's claims; aware of Menzies' flaws yet confident of his capacities, the UAP would not revisit his election as leader. Menzies went to the governor-general that afternoon. 'If I commission you to form a government,' the governor-general, Lord Gowrie, said to him, 'how long do you think you will last?'

'Six weeks, Your Excellency.'

The governor-general smiled. 'Well, that will do for a start.'[11]

After accepting his commission, aware of the public support that he enjoyed in the wake of Page's attack, Menzies drew up a ministry composed only of members of the UAP. He laid the responsibility for this squarely at Page's feet:

You remind me in your letter that my party has not a majority in either House … I am not prepared to purchase that security by inviting into my Cabinet, which is composed of men who have confidence in and loyalty to me, one who has repeatedly and bitterly (and I assume sincerely) charged me with a want of courage, loyalty and judgment.[12]

Come September, Page had resigned as leader of the Country Party amid turmoil from his speech and the party's ejection from government. In the ensuing contest for the leadership, the irascible wowser and croweater Archie Cameron managed to forestall, by seven votes to five, the ambitions of a craggy-faced, self-educated, and aloof backbencher from Victoria. The failure to win at this time meant that John McEwen had to wait almost twenty years to take the Country Party leadership. When he finally did take the leadership, however, he would exercise power with far greater shrewdness and determination than Page—and a very senior Liberal with whom he would deal would be William McMahon.

BEING a partner at Allen Allen & Hemsley gave McMahon much to be concerned about. He was not an apprentice anymore: he had a direct stake in the work being produced. Many were surprised by the promotion. A student who had lived with McMahon at St Paul's College was astonished that his 'earlier diversions' had not hampered his career.[13] Richard Kirby was similarly amazed: 'We never regarded him [McMahon] as having much brains at all,' he said later. '... We laughed at the idea of him being a solicitor, and suddenly found him not only a solicitor but a partner in Allen Allen & Hemsley—a very big firm.'[14]

What did hamper McMahon's career was a sense of restlessness, a growing disenchantment with his life. As 1939 progressed, the young solicitor grew bored. The work at Allen Allen & Hemsley was repetitive: setting up companies, issuing claims, writing correspondence, dealing with matters small, litigious, commercial, and everyday. None of this was unexpected. It was an office job. Yet the devotion that his new role demanded left little time for socialising. McMahon began to feel isolated by the corridors of the office, by not being able to mix with others. Nor did his work offer much in the way of recognition. The satisfaction that he drew from his work ebbed. Then he lost interest entirely. 'By the time the war came I really felt I'd had enough,' he said later. 'I think if the war hadn't come I would soon have branched out into some other area of activity, the stock exchange or something.'[15]

When it came, World War II found Australia largely unprepared.

In the aftermath of the Depression, the Lyons government had been parsimonious with defence spending. In 1932–33, defence spending represented only 0.61 per cent of national income; in 1936–37 it was 1.09 per cent. Though it would continue to rise further over the next three years, this 'tiny proportion' of the national income was enough to fund little more than the maintenance of existing defence equipment.[16] When he looked back, the treasurer at the time, Richard Casey, privately admitted that he could not summon 'any arguments to support the belief that the Lyons government went out, horse, foot, and artillery to improve and increase Australia's defensive equipment'.[17]

Menzies surveyed the emasculated defence forces with apprehension. Australia's navy was small; the air force had few modern planes and limited capability; the army was only a few thousand strong. Although the militia had been swelled by a frenetic recruitment campaign to some 75,000 men, it was poorly regarded.[18] The militia was a social club for 'Toy Soldiers', claimed veterans of the AIF. They sneered that it was 'fit only for half-wits'.[19]

Despite this parlous state, nothing would prevent Australia's entry into the war. When Britain declared hostilities on Germany for its violation of Poland's sovereignty, Australia duly followed. The 'melancholy duty' that was Menzies' to announce on 3 September 1939 was spurred by the 'coldblooded breach' of the 'solemn obligations' that Hitler had undertaken.[20]

The government hastened to place the country on a war footing. Three days after declaring war, Menzies introduced the National Security Bill to the House of Representatives. The Bill gave the Commonwealth sweeping power to regulate every aspect of daily life, and it provoked outrage from the Labor opposition, which held it up in stormy sessions that lasted until the early hours of the morning of 9 September. Six days later, Menzies announced that the government would raise a volunteer military force of 20,000 men serving in Australia and abroad; this 'special' force would become the 6th Division of the AIF, succeeding the five that had been sent overseas during World War I.

McMahon did not enlist immediately. He later claimed to have served briefly with the navy and the army before war broke out, but the documentary record does not contain evidence of this.[21] McMahon could have been confusing his service with the militia, or simply exaggerating. Like many other Australians at the time, McMahon is likely to have been sanguine about the war.

Between September 1939 and April 1940, it was possible to be so. Frustrated by the European winter, Germany made no move to attack the French on land; Australia's relationship with Japan, while strained because of the latter's aggression in the Pacific, still remained intact. There were no shortages of food or fuel, and the effects of the National Security Act were not yet understood beyond the lawyers who saw opportunities to prosper because of the poorly drafted regulations that were promulgated under it. Menzies had stressed the need for 'calmness, resoluteness, confidence and hard work', and the public had paid attention, to the point that plans for rationing petrol were resisted by the motor trade on grounds that it was unnecessary.[22] These were the quiet months, later called the 'phoney war', when a new peace was still in prospect.

This changed in the European spring of 1940. On 9 April, the Germans came with speed and force. They took Denmark in a night, and seized vital land in neutral Norway. During the next few weeks, as the British infantry in France was repeatedly routed, the muddle of English military preparedness and the failings of its political leadership were brutally exposed. Neville Chamberlain resigned. Winston Churchill became prime minister.

In Australia, complacency fell away. Any notion that peace would be quickly restored was quashed and quashed again as news came of the German advance through undefended Holland and Belgium. By early June, the Germans were storming through the Ardennes and encircling the French troops on the Maginot Line while pressing the British back towards the beaches of Dunkirk. It was a shock to all. 'The news struck cabinet like a bomb,' recalled Percy Spender, the then-treasurer in the Menzies government. Henry Gullett, a distinguished veteran of World War I and the vice-president of the Executive Council, was staggered. 'I just can't believe it,' Gullett kept saying. 'I just can't believe it.'[23]

McMahon enlisted in the Citizen Military Force—the equivalent of the modern-day Army Reserves—on 26 April 1940. He was given the provisional rank of lieutenant for the year's experience that he claimed as a former member of the university militia, and was assigned to the

1st Battalion of the 9th Army Brigade. But the enlistment did not last. Within a few weeks, he was back at work at Allen Allen & Hemsley.[24]

Six months later, McMahon was posted for duty, this time with the Australian Military Forces, and assigned to the Machine Gun Training Battalion. He was thirty-two years old, single, and, when asked for his address, wrote that of Allen Allen & Hemsley's. The address was no small point. 'Arrangements' had been made with Arthur Allen to allow Cowper, McMahon, and the other partners to enlist, serve, and return when the war was over.[25] McMahon named his brother, Sam, as his next of kin, and wrote 'Nil' on the line available for statement of his religious denomination. It was not necessarily an indication that he had abandoned his faith. He did not record it on any of the remaining records.[26]

The medical officer who examined McMahon deemed him Class II: fit for duties for which a disability was no bar. That disability was a 'limited flexion' of McMahon's left knee, the reason for which was an 'old injury'.[27] The injury, along with his hearing problems, had the effect of keeping McMahon in Australia. He never served abroad.

His war years, thus, were modest. 'I can't be pretentious about them,' he later said.[28] Kept on staff duties, McMahon was seconded to train in field marks and topography at Glenfield before rejoining his unit for further training in Dubbo. Late in February 1941, he was transferred to make use of his legal training in the Courts of Enquiry. Promoted to temporary captain in October, McMahon was an aide-de-camp before his appointment the following January as a staff captain with the deputy assistant quartermaster general (movements) at the headquarters of II Corps.

In July 1942, his medical fitness was re-assessed, and he was classified as Class I—fit for active service. But the assessor noted McMahon's hearing trouble: 'Very slight disability hearing. Possibly from boxing.' McMahon volunteered for the AIF, hoping to be sent overseas. It was not to be. Participating in night exercises, he failed to hear some danger signals. As a result, his fitness was re-assessed and downgraded to Class IIb: fit for any duty other than with field formations. The medical examiner's diagnosis, of chronic bilateral middle-ear inflammation, was wrong, but the assessment of McMahon's hearing capacities was correct. His hearing difficulties were hampering him again, restricting his choices and his opportunities.[29]

He would later wonder about what might have happened had his hearing problems been accurately diagnosed and properly handled. That he had not been able to join the II Australian army's move to Papua New Guinea in 1943 frustrated him. The fight against the Japanese on the Kokoda Track was hard, wearing, and cruel, but he wished he had gone. 'I suffered from a slight deafness then … and that made it difficult for me to command troops in a battle line,' he said.[30] Would he have commanded troops if his hearing had not been a problem? It is unlikely. McMahon was older than most recruits, and better educated. He knew how to handle paperwork. He knew how to administer. He would have been most useful in positions that utilised these talents. Serving in the field would have been a waste.[31]

His promotion to major—temporary, at first, but then confirmed—was some solace, proof that he was making a contribution. He was happy. He had wanted out of an office, and in the army he got that. Moreover, he was close to Sydney: close enough to his friends and family, should he wish to see them; close enough to keep an eye on political developments, should he wish to as well.

THE government that Menzies took over in the wake of Lyons' death had been teetering by the time an election was called in 1940. The deaths of three cabinet ministers in an aeroplane crash in August that year had severely weakened the government's capacities and its morale. Despite the restoration of a coalition between the UAP and Country Party, the government was too riven by conflict, and the Labor Party, under John Curtin, was resurgent. At the election, Menzies lost his slender majority. A year later, in August, his party's restlessness and division forced his resignation from the prime ministership. 'I have been done,' Menzies told his private secretary afterward.[32] The big man had tears in his eyes, yet was wry enough to quote an old children's song: 'Ile lay mee downe and bleed a while, and then Ile rise and fight againe.'[33]

The stout and gregarious Arthur Fadden, who had returned to the Country Party fold and taken over the leadership from Archie Cameron, was thrust into the prime ministership by a combined vote of his party and the UAP. Treasurer after the election, Fadden was not enthusiastic. He was nervous. Percy Spender, sitting next to Fadden at the meeting, recalled the perspiration 'running in little rivulets down his face'.[34] Fadden knew his time as prime minister would be short. So did his colleagues. 'Artie,' Cameron said to him, 'you'll scarcely have enough time to wear a track from the back door to the shithouse before you'll be out.'[35]

And so it was. Forty days later, with the vote on the budget imminent, aware that the 'rotten reeds' of the mercurial independents Arthur Coles and Alex Wilson were likely to bring his government down, Fadden went without lunch. 'My table was piled with files,' he recalled, 'and I worked on these to give my prospective successor a reasonable start.'[36]

A reasonable start seemed hardly in prospect for his successor, John Curtin. Like Fadden and Menzies before him, the security of his government rested on the whims of the two independents. Like Menzies, Curtin came to the prime ministership with a divided, rancorous, and fractious party in tow. That 'tangle of impulse[s]',[37] Dr Herbert Vere Evatt, had stepped down from the High Court to take a place in the House of Representatives in 1940. Ambitious and restless, he thought Curtin was 'woefully timid', and criticised his caution and tendency towards moderation.[38] The puppeteer of the factions in New South Wales, Jack Beasley, had designs on the leadership himself; both men, wrote the British high commissioner to Australia, Sir Ronald Cross, were 'determined to stab the other on the steps of the throne'.[39] Moreover, a history of stress-related illnesses, bouts of depression, and drinking problems did not auger well for Curtin's resilience in the face of the demands of the office. No one wanted a prime minister with the flagging energies that had mired Scullin and Lyons.

Yet Curtin, for all his apparent unsuitability, was a quick study and a sure hand. Within a few weeks, one journalist judged, Curtin 'had the job completely at his fingertips. He felt he was master of it and he *was* master of it.'[40] Notwithstanding that his body would eventually give out, Curtin was able to overcome the difficulties that had plagued his predecessors. Unlike Menzies, he was able to quell the criticism and infighting of his colleagues. Unlike Menzies and Fadden, he was able to place his government's parliamentary foundations on stable ground. And, by harnessing all of the restless energies around him, Curtin managed to bind his party, his government, and the Parliament towards one goal: defending Australia.

He was aided by the onset of war with Japan. For two years, Japanese aggression in China and over the Pacific had been checked by a policy of economic isolation. Finally, on 7 December 1941, Japan lashed out against its enemies. Woken with the news of Japan's attack on Pearl Harbor, Curtin was calm: 'Well, it has come.'

Aware that war would now be fought on Australia's doorstep, Curtin demanded from Churchill and US president Franklin Roosevelt a strong Allied presence in the Pacific. These demands grew more urgent as the rapid Japanese advance through Malaya continued towards Singapore, destroying the illusion of British-enforced security in the region. Alarmed, aware of Australia's vulnerability, Curtin appealed publicly to the United States for help: 'Without any inhibitions of any kind, I make it quite clear that Australia looks to America, free of any pangs as to our traditional links or kinship with the United Kingdom.'[41] The loss of Singapore was the shock Curtin needed in order to capture America's attention. Late in March 1942, the American general Douglas MacArthur was appointed supreme commander of the south-west Pacific area, and took responsibility for strategic military decision-making. Though the threat of a Japanese invasion was effectively removed by the presence of American troops and naval vessels, and the victories of the Coral Sea and Midway Island, the Japanese landing in New Guinea and its thrusts over the Kokoda Track kept an edge and an urgency to the Australian war effort. In Sydney, barbed wire was uncoiled along the beaches; shopkeepers replaced glass frontages with boards; and the red double-decker buses that heaved through the streets were repainted in dull khaki.[42]

The unity Curtin had wrought, and the effectiveness with which he prosecuted the war, saw him rise in the estimation of many. It was a complete contrast to the UAP and the Country Party, whose division and disunity had continued in opposition.

After Fadden's resignation from the prime ministership, Menzies had stepped down from the leadership of the UAP in order to leave his party 'free to decide, without regard to individuals, whether it should become the official opposition or combine with the Country Party'.[43] His colleagues in the UAP decided on joint party action, and allowed

Fadden to stay as leader of the opposition. Menzies, adamant that the UAP, as the senior partner of the coalition, should hold the position, went to the backbench in despair, while remaining a member of the Advisory War Council. 'Well, a party of our numbers which is not prepared to lead is not worth leading,' he told colleagues.[44]

Billy Hughes took over as leader of the UAP and deputy leader of the opposition. Wizened and deaf, but still full of fire and thunder, the Little Digger set himself two goals: to help win the war, and to keep hold of the UAP leadership for as long as he was able to.

By 1943, Menzies had had enough. Labor was doing too well. The UAP was not prosecuting its case effectively. Divisions over conscription had afflicted it more than the government—a staggering fact, given the splits that had crippled Labor when the issue was confronted during World War I. On 1 April, Menzies and seventeen colleagues wrote to Hughes to inform him of their decision to not attend party-room meetings. 'We consider it essential to reorganise the UAP under new and vigorous leadership,' they wrote. Releasing the letter to the press, they formed what they called 'a national service group' that would operate within the UAP and help sharpen its attacks on the Curtin government.[45]

Hughes was no fan of Menzies. 'He couldn't lead a flock of homing pigeons!' he once said.[46] Now a mesh of wrinkles, just skin, bone, and indomitable energy, the former prime minister had no reticence about lashing out. Calling the group 'wreckers', Hughes declared that they would be 'as helpless in the House of Representatives as a beetle on its back'.[47]

This was, however, a better description of the UAP and Country Party's position after the Labor Party's bomb-thrower, Eddie Ward, got involved. Sharp-tongued, often provocative, and never deferential, Ward suggested in October 1942 that the UAP and Country Party had planned to abandon northern Australia to a Japanese invasion. The so-called Brisbane Line was evidence of its rank defeatism, he argued. The attack was untrue and unacceptable, as Curtin himself acknowledged in an off-the-record briefing he gave to the press. Ward was a 'bloody ratbag', Curtin said,[48] yet he did not quash the rumour until late in June 1943. Moreover, after the dissolution of the House of Representatives for the August election, Curtin would allude to the rumour by his comparison of the handling of the war under the Coalition and the Labor Party.

It was in the lead-up to that election that McMahon made his first moves towards a political career. At the urging of Samuel Walder, he scouted Sydney for a seat that he could win. There were few options. The Labor Party held sway over much of the city. Seats inclined towards the UAP were held by the big men of the party: Percy Spender, Eric Harrison, Billy Hughes, and Frederick Stewart, who were firmly in control. McMahon would have no hope of toppling any of them in a preselection battle. 'I came down to Sydney, but the notice was too short,' McMahon reasoned later, 'and I didn't relish standing for preselection against the sitting Liberal Member [sic].'[49]

It was for the best that he did not try. The 1943 election was a debacle for the non-Labor parties. The UAP was left with only fourteen members in the House of Representatives. Contesting only thirty-seven of the seventy-four seats in the parliament, the UAP attracted only 16 per cent of the primary vote. The popular support that buoyed the Curtin government almost swept away the big men that McMahon had shied away from challenging. 'This is the first election in which my return has not been a foregone conclusion,' wrote a shocked Billy Hughes, still leading the UAP. 'We've been struck by a cyclone.'[50] That cyclone stripped the party bare. On show were its institutional failings, its bereft leadership, and its lack of a policy direction beyond opposition to Labor.

After this debacle, Menzies returned to the UAP leadership with *carte blanche* authority to rescue the non-Labor side of politics, excluding the Country Party, from complete annihilation. The problem, Menzies told his colleagues, was not that they were without popular support. There were, he said, 'many thousands of people all desperately anxious to travel in the same political direction'. But those many thousands were 'divided into various sects and bodies with no federal structure, with no central executive … and, above all, with no clearly accepted political doctrine or faith to serve as a banner under which all may fight'.[51] In Menzies' view, the cyclone that had struck the UAP was an opportunity to bring these parties together, to unite them under a single banner. Yet in spite of a general recognition of the problem, initial attempts to address it failed. A proposal for unity in New South Wales foundered when the Country and Liberal Democratic parties walked, leaving only the Commonwealth Party and the UAP to merge. It would take the authority of a federal leader, in Menzies, and a concerted, sustained effort by many within the state-based parties to bring about the unity required to take on Labor.

Efforts were helped by Labor's decision to hold a referendum on the so-called 'Fourteen powers' in 1944. Evatt, serving as attorney-general and desirous of maintaining the wartime powers for use after the war's end, pushed Curtin to have a question to that effect put to the people. The referendum, cloaked in an innocuously framed question, would consolidate Commonwealth control over employment, corporations, health care, and trade for five years following the end of hostilities. Menzies recognised the political danger. As he argued later, 'if things were allowed to settle down into a continuance of this political pattern, Labor's future would be bright and that of its opponents shadowy indeed'.[52] He also recognised the opportunity to portray the referendum's passage as a necessary step in the establishment of a centralised, socialist government in Canberra.

Between his campaign against the referendum, Menzies worked at promoting the formation of a single non-Labor party, one that could emerge from the ashes of the 1943 defeat as a cohesive political force. Dining with press barons Keith Murdoch, Frank Packer, and Rupert Henderson, Menzies put forth his arguments for the new party and the defeat of the referendum, gaining crucial support that could be exercised down the line. Meanwhile, lieutenants at the state level, such as William Spooner, in New South Wales, and Elizabeth 'May' Couchman, of the Australian Women's National League, in Victoria, set about recruiting the splintered non-Labor parties to the Menzies-led cause.[53]

When Labor's referendum was defeated in August, Menzies sensed the moment had come. 'The fields were ready for sowing and we could hope for a great harvest.'[54] He wrote to the leaders of the non-Labor organisations, inviting them to Canberra for a springtime conference: 'The time seems opportune for an effort to secure unity of action and organisation.'[55]

Eighty delegates came to the Masonic Temple in Canberra, and among trestle tables and hard seats they set about debating and discussing the formation of the new party. On 16 October, they unanimously agreed on the need for a new party that would, stemming from state branches, support a federal organisation, council, and executive. At a subsequent conference in Albury in December, the delegates wrote a party constitution. It was enough to constitute a triumph. In the eyes of the press, Menzies' efforts had wrought a whole new party, one that he would be acclaimed as birthing nearly single-handedly.[56]

The success enabled Menzies to make an announcement when Parliament resumed in February the following year. 'Those who sit with me in this House,' he said, 'desire to be known in future as members of the Liberal Party.'[57]

SIX months later, the war was over. Germany had surrendered amid fire and ruin in May. Japan had held out longer, but the destruction of Hiroshima and Nagasaki brought its capitulation in August.

'At this moment, let us give thanks to God,' the new prime minister said, announcing the news. Ben Chifley had taken over from Frank Forde following John Curtin's death on 5 July. Though he had a voice like 'old rusty chains knocking together',[58] the former train driver could blend gravity with hope: 'Let us remember those whose lives were given that we may enjoy this glorious moment and may look forward to a peace which they have won for us.' Then came the words that so many wished to hear: 'And now our men and women will come home.'[59]

Requests for transfer and demobilisation poured into the offices of the navy, army, and air force. McMahon's was one of them.[60] He had moved on from the military, in mind if not in body. He had been studying economics for the previous year and a half. His interest in commerce had survived the monotony of Allen Allen & Hemsley, and his aborted tilt for preselection had provoked an interest in political thought. The programme at the University of Sydney seemed to marry both of those interests. McMahon had enrolled as an External Service Student for 1944. He had taken the exams in December, and passed.[61]

It took a month to process McMahon's demobilisation paperwork. By 11 October, he was out. He was tanned and healthy, body blessed with some vaccination marks, uniform studded with a War Medal,

Australian Service Medal, and General Service Badge. He returned to an apartment he had taken in Kings Cross, and, by December, had passed his next set of exams.[62]

Another two years of study beckoned, but McMahon decided to delay them. Although he had been abroad before, McMahon later claimed that he was conscious of not having served abroad during the war and not having seen much of the world.[63] Like many a young person before him, he decided to travel. There was another reason for the trip. Medical advances in post-war America offered McMahon the chance to make his hearing troubles a thing of the past. Deafness had prevented him from becoming a barrister and from serving outside Australia; who knew what it could do in the future? It was already isolating him, making communication difficult, affecting his voice. His pitch could slide extravagantly up and down, or hold in a slumberous monotone. In social settings, he could speak in a volume that was harsh and grating. Why not try to have his hearing fixed?

McMahon made his way to New York to see Dr Julius Lempert, a pioneer of effective but controversial advances in the treatment of hearing loss, most notably through a one-phase fenestration to treat otosclerosis.[64] On his arrival, however, McMahon confronted the problem that Australia's new diplomatic mission to the United Nations had also faced: prices. Unable to afford more than three nights' stay in a Manhattan hotel, McMahon went to Alan Renouf, then third secretary at Australia's mission to the UN, and begged for a spare bed. Renouf, who had attended the University of Sydney Law School a few years after McMahon, and who would in due course become secretary of the Department of Foreign Affairs, had been forced by the same problem to live in an apartment in Westchester County, an hour's drive from Manhattan.

It might have been better had McMahon found the money for a hotel. On the night before McMahon underwent his operation, Renouf held a party for a friend. McMahon begged off attending, and went to bed early. He did not sleep long. A combination of unsuccessful romantic advances and unintentionally strong martinis led to Renouf's friend becoming 'resolved on satisfaction'. As a prize-winning boxer, 'satisfaction' for the inebriated fellow meant a pile of victims, Renouf among them.

Having been dispatched to the floor, Renouf dazedly noticed the door to McMahon's room open. Suitcase in hand, McMahon tiptoed out, heading for the front door of the apartment. He was halfway to safety when his escape was detected. 'I'll have you too, McMahon,' the drunk yelled. McMahon was out the door and down the steps 'like a bullet', Renouf saw from the floor. The drunk gave chase, but McMahon was fleet of foot.[65]

The operation the next day was not wholly successful. It restored some of McMahon's hearing, but it took three more operations, dotted over the next twenty years, to fix his deafness fully. For now, consolation would have to be found in his surroundings.

The United States was full of vitality. 'They really felt they could do anything they wanted to do,' Renouf said. He thought it made for an inescapable, infectious atmosphere: 'It's like a madhouse at any time. It's an extremely invigorating place for a young person to live, certainly.'[66] McMahon would undoubtedly have experienced something of this atmosphere, which was just as well—for it would have underlined the dramatic contrast between the United States and Europe.

After he had recuperated, McMahon went to Canada, Ireland, England, France, and West Germany. The destruction caused by the war was still apparent throughout Europe. So, too, was the threat posed by communism. Germany had been cleaved in two. The Soviet Union had subsumed half of Eastern Europe as a buffer against any future conflict. For all the energy and optimism McMahon would have encountered in the United States, the communist presence had a greater effect on him. The political truths instilled in his upbringing were reinforced by what he saw. What was supposed to be an adventure became a study tour.

In later years, McMahon spoke of the trip almost wholly in this vein. His tour was spent studying the 'political trends' of Europe, he said. 'On this trip I was particularly interested in the future of democracy and the threat of communism.'

In his efforts to emphasise the importance of what he saw, McMahon would sometimes deny entirely the original, innocent curiosity that had prompted the trip, and completely elide the attempt to address his hearing issues. That he did so speaks to how important the trip was to his conception of himself and his politics. It was an integral part of the story that he would later tell about himself, whereby he was a self-declared authority on Marxism and communism by virtue of having studied and seen the latter in operation at first hand.[67]

BY the time McMahon returned to Australia in March 1947, he had missed two important events. The first was the re-election of the Labor government under Chifley in September 1946. Though the ALP lost six seats, it obtained 49.7 per cent of the vote to the Liberal Party and Country Party's combined 43.7 per cent—a rebuff, it seemed, to the hopes of the new Liberal Party.[68] The second was the death of his uncle four months before.

Samuel Walder's death was not unexpected. By all accounts, Walder had been ill for some time. Aged sixty-seven, he had cancer of the bowel and liver that an operation in 1945 had failed to stem.[69] McMahon would have known of his uncle's ill-health before he departed Australia. The possibility that Walder would pass away could not have been remote.

Nonetheless, McMahon had returned just in time for the resumption of the university year; within no time at all, he had resumed the life of a student.

Economics offered McMahon a university experience much more typical than Law. The teaching was academic in style, and progressive in purpose. Liberal European scholarship was well-represented on the syllabus, and the faculty, under the much reserved and dry-humoured dean, Syd Butlin, nurtured 'an emphasis on academic understanding rather than vocational training', also unlike Law.[70]

The faculty was in the middle of a change when McMahon re-enrolled in 1947.[71] Four years before, Syd Butlin had pressed his colleagues to revise the undergraduate economics degree. He wanted to address the over-use of courses from other faculties, the reliance on part-time staff whose availability was never guaranteed, and he wanted a greater emphasis on economic history.[72] Butlin secured his changes, but there were dangling threads and exceptions that were still working themselves out years later.

McMahon took advantage of the exemptions on offer to returned servicemen. When he met with Butlin in April, he was given a

programme that exempted him from four of the fifteen courses that
constituted his degree, and allowed him to claim credit for courses
in English and Philosophy he had taken almost twenty years before,
during his Law degree. With Butlin's blessing, McMahon enrolled in
two courses.[73]

The first of these focused on the economy, and was broken into
three key streams.[74] 'My task,' recalled Heinz Arndt, the lecturer, 'was
to teach ... basic income theory in the first term, money and banking
and fiscal policy in second term and international monetary economics
in third term.' Oxford-educated and a recent émigré to Australia,
Arndt set liberal amounts of Keynes for the income theory; drew on
topical work to cover the third term's study; and, after a bout of fruitless
searching, resolved to write a 'suitable textbook' for the study of banks
and financial institutions. Believing that economic theory should guide
policy, Arndt said that his chief concern was 'to pass on to students
some of my own excitement about Economics as an exercise of the
mind and as a guide to better policies in the post-war world'.[75]

Arndt's enthusiasm would rub off on McMahon, who would
forever take pride in his familiarity with economics and its centrality
to government. But Arndt's political beliefs, which he never bothered
to conceal, would raise McMahon's hackles. He and Gordon Barton,
an ambitious and mischievous man studying for three degrees at once,
who later caused much political trouble for McMahon, were 'articulate
critics' of their then left-leaning lecturer.[76] The conservatively oriented
McMahon found much to argue about with Arndt, most notably on
the nationalisation of the banking system.

This 'holy ikon of Socialism', as one Labor parliamentarian
described it,[77] was among the ALP's most deeply held policy objectives,
regarded by the party's rank and file as an article of faith. For Chifley,
nationalisation had been spurred by the callousness of the banking
system and the intransigence of the High Court, which, in striking
down section 48 of the Banking Act in August 1948, had all but dared
him to enact the policy. 'If there be a monopoly in banking lawfully
established by the Commonwealth,' Justice Owen Dixon had written,
'the State must put up with it.'[78]

So, a week later, after declaring to his cabinet that he was committed
to the policy 'to the last ditch', Chifley had his press secretary read

a forty-word statement that prompted one startled journalist to bite through the stem of his pipe:

> Cabinet today authorised the Attorney-General and myself to prepare legislation for submission to the federal Labor parliamentary party for the nationalisation of banking, other than State banks, with proper protection for the shareholders, depositors, borrowers and staffs of private banks.[79]

Opposition materialised immediately. Menzies said that it was a 'tremendous step towards the servile State', and called the government 'aspiring dictators'. He quoted Milton's *Second Defence of the People of England*. He told the House of Representatives that the debate was 'a second battle for Australia'.[80] The banks, too, geared up for a fight. They called in the lawyers they kept on retainer, including Norman Cowper, by now returned to Allen Allen & Hemsley. In the argument over who would lead the inevitable court challenge to the legislation, Cowper's voice was decisive. He picked Garfield Barwick, at that point best known for his part in a suit brought against the winner of the 1943 Archibald Prize, William Dobell.[81]

In Sydney, Heinz Arndt joined with colleagues to form the Fabian Society of New South Wales. With its imprimatur, he published a pamphlet supporting nationalisation. The Chifley government found it so much to its liking that it purchased 40,000 copies to distribute. Arndt wrote letters to *The Sydney Morning Herald* railing against the paper's opposition to nationalisation, and at public forums he added his voice to the debate.[82]

McMahon was unequivocally opposed to the idea. When Arndt gave a lunchtime talk to students for the Economics Society, McMahon ensured that he had a front-row seat from which he could heckle his lecturer and answer his arguments supporting nationalisation.[83]

Much more agreeable to McMahon was Professor Francis Armand Bland, his lecturer for Public Administration I. Bland had told *The Sydney Morning Herald* that if nationalisation were carried out 'we can say good-bye to popular government and, with it, our cherished rights and liberties'.[84] Shortly to retire from the university and seek Liberal Party preselection for the federal seat of Warringah, following Percy

Spender's appointment as ambassador to the United States in 1951, Bland was preoccupied by questions of government and management. A frequent advisor to New South Wales premier Bertram Stevens, Bland described himself as 'an uncompromising opponent of the extension of centralised authority'.[85] His course was designed to 'appraise the role of the official in the scheme of modern government' through the whole field of personnel management: from recruitment, to remuneration, management, arbitration, and political rights.[86] McMahon admired the man. Bland's teachings, McMahon said later, 'revived my interest in liberal philosophies ... I was particularly impressed by his views on free men and free institutions.'[87] These were the views that he took into politics and exercised as a minister.

McMahon passed his course with Bland, and the following year completed the next course in Public Administration.[88] He scooped several prizes: the Frank Albert Prize for Proficiency at the Annual Examinations and the John D'Arcy Memorial Prize for Public Administration were both his. He also did well with Arndt. In Economics III, Arndt acknowledged, McMahon 'wrote a good essay (with the policy conclusions of which I strongly disagreed) on company tax. Imperfectly familiar with the regulations, I gave him a Distinction in the end-year examinations.'[89]

Arndt's confusion was understandable. The dangling threads of Butlin's changes to the Economics degree were as confusing for staff as they were attractive for students looking for loopholes. McMahon was one of them. The dean had told McMahon in 1947 that he could do the Distinction work in Economics III and IV—but this was 'on the distinct understanding that you are not a candidate for Honours'.[90]

When McMahon was told this again, in 1948, he grew angry. 'He threatened to sue the University Senate, claiming that the regulations were ambiguous on the point', Arndt claimed.[91] Despite having documentary proof that he had known about this condition, the university gave in and let McMahon have his way. He finished his degree in 1948, breezing through his remaining courses.

The prizes he had received and the marks he had been given were the credentials that McMahon would refer to when demonstrating his expertise. He repeated the claim over and over again. 'Then back home I did the four-year Economics course in two years,' he told one journalist.[92] To another, he claimed, 'I wanted to go back to the university to attempt to get a degree in economics, which I did, graduating with distinction after a two-year course which normally takes four years.'[93]

The claim was false. McMahon had started the degree in 1944; had claimed credit for courses he had finished in 1928; and had used the exemptions afforded to students who had war service. It had not taken him two years. He did not receive honours.

But, veracity aside, the claim was important to McMahon for it was the culminating moment of his narrative of transformation. The story he told and came to believe split his life into two phases. The first contained the errant years of his childhood and his wild days at St Paul's, the boredom of the law, and the modesty of his time with the army. 'I didn't have any precise goals and I moved from one field to another because the mood caught me,' he said of it. 'As I was able to do it, I took advantage of what I thought would be the most entertaining and enjoyable thing to do.'[94] In his telling, this first phase of his life was without a mission: his abilities and education were lying idle, going to waste.

The second phase began after 1945. 'It was then, immediately after the war years, that I changed,' he said.[95] By his trip abroad, McMahon would say that he became awake to the threat of communism and the need for individual liberty. By his studies, he would say, he became convinced of the importance and enthused by the possibilities of economics in the post-war world. With all this—plus his familial background, his social circumstances, and his networks of supportive friends and family—he had become disciplined and dedicated, prepared for a new life.

It was a transformation. In his own eyes, by his own lights, McMahon was now ready. He would put to use the education he had gained, the abilities he had honed in law and in economics. He would live a life of service, one that William Temple might be proud of. He would do so in a noble profession, where it was possible to find recognition and status. He would live up to the idealised image he had of himself and his talents. Never acknowledged, but perhaps crucial, he would succeed in a field where his father had failed.

CHAPTER SEVEN

Rumours

1984

On 23 February 1984—his seventy-sixth birthday—McMahon surprised his staff by being in a good mood. Two days before, he had lunched with some oyster farmers, and the meal had left him ill and bad-tempered. He was in a 'shocking mood', Bowman wrote the next day. He, Campbell, and Cawthorn were not the only ones to bear the brunt of it.

'Don't Sir William me!' they had heard McMahon bellow from his office. Whoever was on the phone had the call and the relationship abruptly terminated: 'I never liked you anyway!'[1]

By his birthday, however, McMahon was better, and he was apologetic. The oysters had affected him badly, he told Bowman. He was glad when the day had ended. 'We all were,' his ghostwriter muttered, *sotto voce.*[2]

The good mood and the consequent energy lasted. Recovering from McMahon's earlier about-face, Bowman was rewriting the draft again, and the whole office was swinging in to help him. Campbell wrote to Sydney Grammar School for McMahon's school records.[3] McMahon sought information about the movements of the Second Australian Army after his fitness had been downgraded. If his hearing difficulties had been properly handled, he told the Central Army Records Office, he was sure that he would have gone to New Guinea.[4]

Abundant energy spurred McMahon to work on other things. On 27 February, he told Bowman he wanted to write about the constitutional aspects of the Hawke government's dispute with the AMA. The clash had been making headlines for weeks. Bowman was cautious about the diversion, but interested. He told McMahon he had not seen anyone mention a constitutional question. 'Ah,' McMahon replied, 'that's because they haven't got my memory.'[5]

The article he gave Bowman for editing was verbose and overlong, with extensive quotes from Menzies and Evatt and their debate in 1946 over section 51 of the constitution. It required a harsh edit. But it was better than he had expected, Bowman allowed. 'And he seems to be making a good point.'[6]

Bowman cleaned it up and sent it on to *The Sydney Morning Herald*, which published it with some indifference on the following Monday. McMahon did not mind. He liked being in the public eye again. When *The Age* published transcripts of conversations suggesting that an unidentified justice of the High Court had been involved in improper behaviour, McMahon did the media rounds to offer his opinions. 'He said the PM, the A-G, and Solicitor-General had all pronounced on the tapes and it was proper not to name names,' Bowman recorded, after McMahon arrived late into the office and happily recapitulated everything.[7]

His good mood allowed McMahon to relax. Between appointments and work, he continued to talk to Bowman about his youth, and about his life. He gabbed about old friends and enemies. He yakked about Clyde Packer, about the Lloyd family, about the woes of Fairfax. Peculiarly, for a man who had spoken of the hurt that rumours had caused him, McMahon seemed to have no compunction about trafficking in gossip and half-truths. He did it often, almost compulsively. Snippets were tantalising, but much of it was grubby. On other occasions, McMahon's talk seemed simply hare-brained. 'You'll have to excuse me if I say this,' he said to Bowman on 9 March, 'but Dame Pattie [Menzies] always thought I should marry her daughter.'[8]

CHAPTER EIGHT

Lowe

1948-1949

By 1948, the number of seats in the House of Representatives had not been increased since Federation in 1901. In that time, Australia's population had grown from 3.5 million to 7.5 million. The average number of voters in each electorate was more than 60,000. MPs complained that their local-member work had become too onerous, too difficult—particularly in rural areas, where electorates were large and sparsely populated. In response, and with some self-interest, the Chifley government passed legislation to enlarge the House from seventy-four seats to 121. At the same time, the Senate was expanded from thirty-six to sixty, in accordance with the constitution, and proportional voting was introduced.

No electorate was left unchanged once the country was carved up. Old electorates were broken up, and the pieces cobbled together to form new ones. The names of explorers and Labor heroes were given out, with the slightest of nods to Australia's Indigenous people in the naming of the Sydney electorate of Bennelong.

Lowe was one of the new electorates. Proclaimed on 11 May 1949, it was located in Sydney's inner west, and centred on Strathfield, Concord, and Burwood. Neighbouring the newly created Blaxland and Evans, its creation reflected Sydney's continued growth after World War II. Assembled from pieces of old Labor-leaning seats, it was unclear which way the electorate would go in an election.

McMahon would not have been ignorant of the seat. Since 1943, at least, he had been angling for a political career. His studies in economics had been a part of the plan to build his credentials and reputation. He would have been aware of the opportunity that the forty-seven extra

seats offered ever since the measure was mooted. And even before
Lowe was proclaimed, McMahon was politicking.

When Heinz Arndt wrote a critical appraisal of an article by
prominent Liberal William Spooner on production and taxation early
in 1949, McMahon picked up the pen to respond. Writing that his old
lecturer had the views of a 'doctrinaire armchair socialist', McMahon
said that Arndt's critique was deceitful and riddled with errors. 'We have
heard this before,' he wrote, 'but not in Australia. It is the technique of
the Communist.'[1]

Use of the term was deliberate. The non-Labor parties had been
invoking the spectre of communism everywhere they could, stoking
fear and raising alarm. International news reinforced the urgency and
gravity of their message. The Iron Curtain had been drawn. Democracy
in the Eastern European states was being stamped out. In western
Europe it was under threat. Communist-driven insurrections had flared
throughout Asia. As the Nationalist government of Chiang Kai-shek
fled across the Taiwan Strait to set up a government in exile, Mao Tse-
Tung was soon to declare the end of a costly civil war and proclaim the
creation of the communist-governed People's Republic of China. The
suggestion that communist revolutions would continue was virulent,
effective, and, for many, terrifying—so much so that Arthur Fadden
declared that the Country Party regarded the Australian communist as
'a venomous snake' that had 'to be killed before it kills'.[2]

The Liberal Party was less savage, but no less critical. It worked
to link the Chifley government to the communists. It paid for a series
of propaganda broadcasts that were thinly disguised as discussions of
current affairs, and used them to lacquer the ALP until it was dripping
in red. The fictional 'John Henry Austral' told listeners:

The Communist Party in Australia has fastened itself on the Labor
Party as a tick fastens itself to the skin of a dog. Its propaganda is to urge
the support of Labor. But remember this. Lenin himself said, 'Whoever
we support in this way is supported in the same way as the rope supports
one who is hanged.' *Whoever communism supports is supported in the same
way as the rope supports one who is hanged.* Therefore, whoever supports
communism plays the hangman; assists in the annihilation of freedom
[and] the destruction of liberty.[3]

Despite attempts to prove that it, too, was opposed to communism, most notably expressed in the establishment of the Australian Security Intelligence Organisation, the Chifley government's measures to smooth Australia's path through peacetime were too easily tarred. Its reintroduction of petrol rationing, and its proposals to nationalise the banking system, smacked of the state ownership and control that were the hallmarks of communist-governed countries.

The Liberal Party's message was harsh. Its members thought the country was in danger. And notwithstanding that the Chifley government broke a Communist Party–driven strike on the coalfields of New South Wales in August 1949, the Liberal Party feared that the ALP was susceptible to communist influences. It approached the imminent election with the zealous belief that it *had* to be won in order to protect Australia.[4]

To that end, preselection committees began work early. They looked for new blood and for candidates who were well prepared. Party nominees, wrote the general secretary of the New South Wales division, John Carrick, should have the ability to legislate 'with courage and conviction along the progressive lines of a Liberalism which is completely independent of either conservative or socialistic pressure groups'.[5] The party and its committees had a checklist of the perfect candidate: 'A Protestant male in his thirties or forties, who had a war record, professional qualifications, a commitment to the public good, and a loathing of socialism,' as Ian Hancock summarised it.[6] McMahon could not have been unaware that he ticked all these boxes; nor could he have been unaware of the markers of acceptability that he carried with him: his schooling, memberships of reputable clubs and societies, networks of friends and politicians, and connections in the business and law communities. All of these were valuable, and would become more so when he bumped into an old friend while walking along Phillip Street some time in 1947.

Jack Cassidy, a leading Sydney barrister, had taken silk ten years before, and had since been kept on retainer for *The Daily Telegraph*, *Truth*, and *Daily Mirror*. An energetic man with impeccable connections, Cassidy had taught at Abbotsholme College while working his way through degrees in Arts and Law at the University of Sydney. While his time at Abbotsholme had not overlapped with

McMahon's, the connection between the two was strong enough to make them friendly.[7]

According to McMahon, Cassidy begged a favour.[8] There was a function out in the west of Sydney for women and younger members of the Liberal Party. He was supposed to be speaking—part of his pitch to be the candidate for the seat that was likely to encompass the area. But suddenly, Cassidy said, he had been called to court. Could Bill do him a favour and speak in his stead? Could he speak on Cassidy's behalf?

With nothing to do and nowhere to be, McMahon readily agreed. Taking a cab to the hall in Strathfield, he spoke to an audience composed largely of women about his studies in the law and his time working for Allen Allen & Hemsley. He spoke about economics and politics, what he had observed of communism and democracy in North America and Europe, and what he was seeing in Australia.

Once his talk had finished and the audience broke for afternoon tea, McMahon was asked to stay for a few minutes. He sat outside. Shortly afterwards, the tall woman who had chaired the meeting, Mrs Beale, came out to speak with him.

She asked if he was a tyke. He had not heard the word before. He asked her what in the hell it meant.

She told him.

The question became clear. Was he, as his surname suggested, a Roman Catholic?

Redeemed at last was Samuel and Elsie Walder's guidance, and McMahon's allegiance to the Church of England. For, to his reply that he was not a tyke, Mrs Beale was pleased. 'Yes, well, we are very interested in you, and the women of Strathfield would like to promote you as candidate for Lowe.'

'But Mr Cassidy is the potential candidate,' McMahon said.

Beale was nonplussed. 'We've decided to ask you.'

McMAHON'S objections faded quickly, likely the result both of Cassidy's decision to let bygones be bygones and his own, innate sense that Beale's approach to him was correct—that he was the better candidate. Beale became his quasi-official campaign manager. She prompted him to come along to branch meetings. She pointed out potential rivals. She ensured that he joined the Liberal Party and became well known around the traps. He did not know the area. Strathfield, Burwood, and Concord were not home: he was living in a red-brick, art-deco apartment in Elizabeth Bay. Inner western Sydney was a whole new area for him.

He was lucky to have Beale and contacts within the party he could draw upon. Billy Hughes advised McMahon to make an impression on those who would form the electoral conference for Lowe. When he was told a reference from Hughes would be invaluable, McMahon wrote to ask for one. Hughes asked him to send a draft. A week later, McMahon sent him a short passage that emphasised his studies and his family's involvement in politics. After Hughes' amendments came through, McMahon was ready to float the nomination.[9]

McMahon's platform was straightforward, but tinged with ideas drawn from his studies and his background. According to drafts of his autobiography, he wished to break up the Commonwealth Bank; roll back changes made by the Chifley government and reserve the use of tariff protection for infant industries; ensure that the Commonwealth did not usurp the states in areas such as health care and education; spread a gospel of efficiency, innovation, and entrepeneurship; offer government support to private schools; and means-test pensions and welfare payments. Unusually, too, McMahon stated that he was in favour of abortion when recommended by medical advice, and that he believed in equal pay for equal work.[10]

His nomination succeeded. Despite the presence of sixteen other candidates, McMahon won preselection on the first ballot. But almost immediately there was an outcry. When the Liberal Party had been formed there had been considerable attention paid to ensuring it would attract and promote women. Elizabeth 'May' Couchman had exacted a commitment to equal representation within the Victorian division when she led the Australian Women's National League to merge with the Liberals in 1945. Committees had been set up in the four years since to address 'women's issues', most notably in equality of opportunity, equal pay, and ending discrimination for appointments to the public service.[11]

But by 1949 the party's commitment had not been turned into action. It was simply not choosing women for preselection. Roberta Galagher, who had worked and pushed fruitlessly, had considered resigning from the party because 'women are not allowed to work'.[12] The Liberal Party seemed happy to have women organise meetings, raise funds, staff polling places, canvass for votes, and cater for events—yet there was little evidence it was willing to preselect them. Parliament, it seemed, was a place for the men.

There were some gestures made to address the disparity. War hero Nancy Wake won preselection for a seat in the House of Representatives in the lead-up to the 1949 election—but it was for Barton, held by the deputy prime minister, Dr Evatt, on an insurmountably high margin. In Western Australia and Victoria, two women were preselected in winnable spots in the Senate, and Dame Enid Lyons was still serving in the House of Representatives. But in New South Wales, the efforts of three self-styled female 'pioneers' to force the issue were defeated when none was selected for a position on the party's Senate ticket at the end of March 1949. When the state council subsequently agreed to a motion that at least one woman should be selected for the Senate ticket in third place or higher, William Spooner—who headed the ticket—rubbished it, ruling that the 1949 preselections had already been conducted and that retrospective measures were inappropriate.

Edith Shortland, chair of the Women's Central Movement and a former vice-president of the New South Wales Liberals, was incensed by the party's continued indifference. A university graduate and school teacher who had become well known for her involvement in the Strathfield community while her husband served as mayor, Shortland was loud with her opinions and an outspoken critic of the Labor Party.[13] Its efforts to nationalise the banks were 'a flagrant injustice', she believed.[14] Its encroachment on civil liberties followed the 'example of Russia and its subservient states'.[15] Under the Chifley government, she argued, 'home life is crumbling'.[16]

'She is a grand lady,' wrote one newspaper, commending Shortland's candidacy for the Senate ballot.[17] When she and the other 'pioneers' were shut out of that ballot, she called it a 'tactical error' on the party's part.[18] But by early June, she declared it was enough. She resigned from the Liberal Party. Arguing that she wanted to 'justify the status of women as laid down in the [party] platform', Shortland announced that she intended to stand for Lowe as an 'Independent Liberal':

As an erstwhile leader of the women of the New South Wales Liberal Party, I feel that a stand has to be taken against the unofficial discrimination against women within the party. The New South Wales Liberal Party has never endorsed a woman for the Senate and only once has [it] endorsed a woman for the House of Representatives. In every democratic country in the world the prejudice against women has been entirely removed and the right of women representation has been considered as being coincident with that of the vote.[19]

McMahon was panicked by her decision. Already, he and the party were unsure about Lowe. Would it vote Labor? Would it go Liberal? The presence of another candidate, well known in the area and possessing the potential to split the non-Labor vote, could derail his candidacy. He tried to persuade Shortland to withdraw from the race. She refused, for what he thought were reasons all to do with her vanity.[20]

Within the Liberal Party, there was criticism of Shortland. Eileen Furley, a vice-president of the state and federal party, and one of the women who had put themselves forward for Senate preselection, subtly called into question Shortland's merits as a candidate. 'The reason why more women were not chosen,' Furley said later, 'was because women of high calibre did not stand for selection. The men were outstanding in their field and women would have found it very difficult to compete against the men's qualifications.'[21]

Shortland would not have a bar of it. She would not resile from criticisms of her party. Attention needed to be paid to women. Shortland told one journalist that the war had created a 'politically conscious type of Australian housewife' who found politicians uninterested in their concerns.[22] Her candidacy, she argued, was not just for her own benefit: 'If I win the seat, it will be easier for other women to follow; if I fail, the women of Australia will go back fifty years.'[23]

The Labor Party, meanwhile, preselected a forty-year-old schoolteacher named H.L. McDonald as its candidate. As the year progressed, the three campaigns swung into action.

McMahon boarded with a local family for a few weeks, living on Shaftesbury Road, Burwood, doorknocking and distributing a flyer advertising his policy positions.[24] They were straightforward, uncontroversial Liberal policies: the elimination of the socialist changes made by the Labor government, a ban on the Communist Party, a restriction of Commonwealth powers to those set out by the constitution, and the breaking up of the Commonwealth Bank.[25]

He was aided by press coverage that favourably garbled his resumé. McMahon was a 'business executive', wrote *The Sydney Morning Herald*, when he won preselection.[26] *The Sun* described him as a 'barrister and economist' who, after leaving the army, had 'lectured in law by day, [and] studied economics at night'.[27] The falsities piled up, and Heinz Arndt, observing the campaign with some amusement, now understood why McMahon had become so angry about being refused entry to the Honours subjects in his Economics degree. 'His motives became apparent the following year when, in his election literature as a candidate for Lowe, he listed among his qualifications, "B. Ec. with Honours in Economics III and IV",' Arndt noted.[28]

Campaigning allowed people to see McMahon's quirks and personality. Alan Wright, a member of the Liberal Party, found him busy to the point of hyperactivity. 'He was a like a fly in a bottle,' he said. 'He never stayed long. He'd go from here to there to there again.'[29] McMahon was small and lithe, his movements somewhere between a dancer's graceful step and a mouse's furtive scurry. His dark hair was rapidly thinning, revealing a high, tanned scalp and emphasising the size of his ears. In spite of his wealth, McMahon rarely carried money or used it freely. Lorna Wright—whose brother, Lerryn Mutton, a New South Wales MLA, had considered McMahon's nomination—observed McMahon nudging her brother during a church service, just before the collection plate came around, asking if he could borrow a pound. She noticed that McMahon would always kiss the older women of the electorate but, potentially wary of any romantic distractions, never the younger ones. He always looked 'smart', was always dressed in expensive clothes, and his hearing difficulties could become apparent in conversation. 'He always came close when talking to you,' she said.[30] Possibly because of this, he rarely indulged in small talk.

The Chifley government's lacklustre campaign aided McMahon's efforts. Despite an accomplished record in office, including presiding over the transition to peace, the maintenance of full employment, and a visionary programme in infrastructure, education, immigration, and social welfare encapsulated in the hopeful and oft-quoted objective of 'the light on the hill', the ALP was as complacent as it was exhausted. Calling a seventy-four day campaign that would culminate on 10 December, the worn-out prime minister offered 'no rosy promises' or 'economic bribes' to voters. He asked them to judge him and his party on its record.[31]

That was a place that the Menzies-led Coalition was happy to fight on, particularly once the Privy Council decision to strike down bank nationalisation laws was announced on 29 October. Free to raise the spectre of socialisation and nationalisation, the non-Labor parties and the daily presses ran amok, creating what Chifley later called 'a fear complex in the minds of a percentage of the middle-class vote'.[32]

Menzies, meanwhile, continued a yearlong effort to cultivate a more homely image. No longer the glittering, lordly prime minister of 1939–41, an advertising campaign by the same people who had composed the John Austral ads sought to portray Menzies as a man of the people. He was depicted in widely distributed photographs chatting to miners and drinking a beer, ironing a shirt, engaging with hecklers. While Menzies would never match Chifley's gruff ordinariness, these efforts were intended to develop another Menzies—a Bob to go with R.G. Menzies.[33]

'The best years of my life have been given to what I deeply believe is a struggle for freedom,' Menzies declared in his policy speech. 'That struggle has reached a climax. Victory is in front of us. We can fail to achieve it only by indolence, or indifference, or a failure to realise that on December 10 we will be deciding the future of our country. It is in your hands, Australia.'[34]

THE same kind of appeal was being made throughout Lowe. McMahon enlisted the son of his official campaign director, A.V.S. Walker, to spruik his candidature all over the electorate. All of nine years old, the boy had to stand on tiptoes to reach the microphone. Reading from a script, Adrian told people that:

December 10 is a very important day for us children too. In twelve years time I should have a vote and I want you to help me so that I can be sure of having that vote. To do that I ask you to vote for Mr William McMahon. My daddy says he is a very good man.[35]

It was kitsch, but it garnered attention. McMahon was intent on winning, and had no time for half-hearted efforts. He door-knocked until his knuckles were sore. He begged Billy Hughes to visit the seat and speak for his candidacy.[36] He persisted with the discipline that had characterised his attempts to get into the Eights in those days back at Sydney Grammar. 'From the time that I was selected to be the representative for the Liberal Party in the division of Lowe,' he later said, 'I devoted all my attention to it. I can't give you a reason for it, it just happened naturally.'[37]

The commitment was absolute. Bill Wakeling, a famed Liberal Party organiser with thick cloudy glasses, who boasted of papering the ceilings of Kings Cross brothels with posters for Billy Hughes, was changing a light in the roof of the builder's hut from which McMahon was running his campaign. It had been raining, and his shoes were slippery. 'I fell down and hit the chair on the way down and laid myself out,' Wakeling recalled. McMahon looked through the window, and thought the worst. 'You thought I was a corpse!' Wakeling said to McMahon later. But McMahon's immediate reaction was not grief. It was horror—for himself. He called Liberal Party headquarters: 'Send me another organiser. Wakeling's dead!'[38]

Lowe was a key seat, according to some, but, as the campaign neared its end, both parties believed it would go Liberal, just as the country was expected to. A Roy Morgan poll the weekend before had suggested that neither party would receive a substantial majority, but 10 December broke with much of the press predicting a change of government.

The press was correct. Labor lost government in a resounding fashion, but had the consolation of retaining control of the Senate, with thirty-four seats to the Coalition's twenty-six. Of the 121 seats in the newly enlarged House of Representatives, Menzies' Liberal Party took fifty-five, including many of the new seats. The Country Party snared nineteen. Labor held forty-seven.

Menzies was vindicated. Chifley was humbled. McMahon was elated.

He had no trouble in Lowe. With more than 20,000 votes—4,000 ahead of the ALP, and far above the 2,470 that Edith Shortland received—McMahon's time in Parliament and in government had begun.[39]

CHAPTER NINE

Gaps

1984

Working through the course of McMahon's life could prompt cynicism and dislike. Trawling through McMahon's twenty-seven filing cabinets, reading the innumerable speeches he had made and the countless articles he had appeared in, confronted with inevitable contradictions and gaps between words and actions, Bowman perceived a man difficult to understand.

'To whom did McMahon appeal as a politician?' he wondered privately. 'To the brainless, the scheming, the mean, the petty, the muddled, the get-rich-quick, the I'm-alright-Jack ...'[1]

He wondered how McMahon had succeeded in politics, how he had gotten so far ahead. He agonised over how to confront McMahon's pervasive reputation as an incompetent, schemer, and inveterate liar. With Whitlam's famous sobriquet in mind—Tiberius with a telephone—Bowman asked in his notes whether it should be met 'head-on' in the book.[2]

At other points, however, he was less adamant about McMahon and his reputation. 'In many ways W.M. seems to have been the victim of false rumours and false perceptions,' Bowman wrote. He had heard the former prime minister yap away about rumours of homosexuality and how he had triumphed over them, how he had been knocked down many times but always gotten back up. There was a lot of commentary around McMahon, and much of it seemed scurrilous.

'And yet,' Bowman was moved to write, 'when that is said, there remains something odd. He appears *undeserving*. What is it?'[3]

CHAPTER TEN

Red

1950–1951

The opening of the nineteenth Parliament was an occasion for pomp and circumstance. It was a clear, sunny February day. Well-dressed spectators and finely clad dignitaries attended Parliament House in droves. Menzies and his ministers turned up wearing formal black jackets, grey striped trousers; some MPs went further and arrived in full morning dress. Inside, the chief justice of the High Court, Sir John Latham, deputised for the governor-general and swore in new MPs while clusters of diplomats looked down from the crowded galleries. Likening himself to the bramble that ruled over the trees in the Book of Judges, Archie Cameron took the Speaker's chair wearing the full rig of British tradition: a horsehair wig, long black robes, lace cravat and cuffs, buckled shoes replacing his usual elastic-sided boots.[1] The governor-general, William McKell, arrived wearing a top hat amid the smoke and powder of a twenty-five-gun salute and a guard of honour from Duntroon.

In the Senate chamber, crowded with members of both newly enlarged houses and thronged with members of the public in the galleries, McKell opened the Parliament with a speech that was weighty in its emphasis on national security and the scale of change to come under the Menzies government. He foreshadowed measures to impede government intrusion into industry and to invest in infrastructure. The government would legislate to 'protect the community against the activities of subversive organisations and individuals' (that is, the Communist Party), to alter the governance of the Commonwealth Bank, and would bring in policies to improve welfare and child endowments.[2]

Surveying the faces of all the new members and senators assembled in the crowded chamber, one journalist noted that the 'predominant impression was that of youth'.[3] He was not wrong. The 1949 election had lowered the average age of MPs and senators, raised the average level of education, raised the number of Australian-born representatives, and raised the number of women from four to a still-paltry five. Predominantly ex-servicemen of World War II, those elected in December were 'ready to remake Australia', Edgar Holt wrote later.[4] They were young, driven, idealistic. Many of them, coming from the Liberal side of politics, were fervent opponents of anything that smacked of government control. Key members included West Australians Paul Hasluck and Gordon Freeth, the Victorian senator John Gorton, Queenslanders Reg Swartz and Alan Hulme, New South Welshmen David Fairbairn and William Wentworth, and the South Australian Alexander 'Alick' Downer. As a parliamentary class, 'the forty-niners' were notable for the generational shift they heralded.

With so many colleagues around him having similar backgrounds and outlooks, McMahon needed to distinguish himself if he were to have any prospect of advancement. His degrees in Law and Economics were to his credit, but he needed much more than this.

His initial efforts to gain notice were not promising. In his first speech, given on 2 March, McMahon recited the standard objections to Labor Party policies, and invoked the new gospels of the Liberal Party. Exaggerating the former and underlining the virtues of the latter, McMahon cited Keynes, Schumpeter, and academic monographs to support his argument that the Coalition would be better for the country than the ALP. He sprinkled statistics throughout. He professed to be nervous:

> I may say that some of my colleagues have told me that they experienced considerable nervousness when making their maiden speeches in this debate. They said their hearts were in their mouths. They fared better than I have done, because I am sure that my heart has been lost somewhere in the corridors. It is not marked, 'Please return to the owner' or 'Reward to finder', but if any honourable gentleman should find it I should be pleased if he would return it to me.

He boasted about his credentials. To underscore a point about socialism, he told the House that:

> I do so as a person who, during the last two or three years, has made a study of scientific socialism. When I say that I have studied socialism, I do not mean that I have merely read a couple of books on the subject. I have spent two years of hard effort and mental sweat in the university.

Concluding that the Menzies government was 'pro-worker, pro-woman, pro-family', he predicted prosperity within the decade should the Coalition remain in office. Then, despite the fact that it was just after 2.30pm, McMahon finished with a weak, prepared joke. 'As this is the first occasion on which I have made a speech before dinner, I trust that it has not proved too indigestible.'[5]

Listening to the speech on a bench on the government side of the House was John Cramer, member for the neighbouring seat of Bennelong. A real estate agent, former mayor of North Sydney, and a Catholic in the Protestant-dominated Menzies parliamentary forces, Cramer thought little of his colleague's introduction. McMahon's was an 'academic speech', Cramer sniffed derisively—'as one would expect from a lawyer'.[6]

At other times, McMahon gained attention for less desirable reasons. His tendency to be well dressed was soon noticed by other members, some of whom—particularly on the Labor side, such as Evatt—could be positively dishevelled. In May, in lieu of the grey or blue double-breasted suit that was the invariable attire of a Liberal Party member, McMahon entered the House wearing a rather less-formal navy-blue sports coat and grey trousers. The next day, he received a letter from the Speaker, Archie Cameron. Indignation was apparent in the query as to whether McMahon's attire was due to 'ignorance or arrogance'. McMahon replied immediately to assure the Speaker of his regret and to explain that he had somehow lost his regular coat during the journey between Sydney and Canberra.

The letter never reached Cameron. The government whip, Jo Gullett, who took from the incident great amusement, saw to it that his practical joke was leaked to the press but did not reach the ears of the short-tempered Speaker.[7]

McMAHON was a quick learner. After Arthur Fadden introduced the Commonwealth Bank Bill on 16 March—which would, among other things, repeal the Chifley government's Banking Act of 1947 and re-establish the board of the Commonwealth Bank—McMahon spoke seven times on the Bill, drawing upon his knowledge of economics in a manner that was far more direct and effective than his first speech. 'It is practically impossible for anyone outside to determine whether this organisation [the Commonwealth Bank] is being efficiently managed,' he said on 28 March. 'However, there is a strong suspicion that it is inefficient.' Defending the idea of a governing board, and arguing that the advantage enjoyed by the Commonwealth Bank—working as a central reserve bank and trading bank simultaneously—was unfair, McMahon argued for what he believed was the fundamental point: 'All we say is that there should be fair competition with the other trading banks … Ultimately, the Parliament itself must have the power to review or to control the financial affairs of Australia.'[8]

But, for the Labor Party, the scars of the Depression went deeper than those of the 1949 election. It was convinced neither by the government's arguments nor by political expediency. Blaming the banking system for the upheaval and turmoil of the 1930s, Labor used its majority in the Senate to neuter the Bill of its main provisions.[9] The government refused to countenance any changes. A second Bill, exactly the same as the first, was passed by the House and sent to the Senate with the same result. It was a deadlock.

Less deadlocked, but no less contentious, was the government's effort to ban the Communist Party. The proposal, which had originated with the Country Party, had caused much unease within the Liberals, who were ostensibly opposed to state attempts to restrict liberty and freedom. In an influential article in the *Australian Quarterly*, McMahon's old master, Norman Cowper, had criticised the proposed ban, arguing that it would 'constitute a grave threat to the right of association and all civil liberties, and make a lamentable precedent … The Communist Party will be outlawed, not because of what it or its members have been proved to have done but because of what the ruling party in Parliament thinks of it.'[10]

After expressing initial unease, Menzies had turned in favour of the proposal. He brushed aside objections such as Cowper's, and declared that Australia was 'not at peace today, except in a technical sense'. The state of 'cold war' between the Soviet Union and the West required action. The Bill that he commended would declare the Communist Party and its associated bodies illegal, and dissolve them. Members of the Communist Party would be disqualified from employment by the Commonwealth and from holding office in most trade unions. In this way, Menzies argued, the government would have the power to deal with 'the King's enemies in this country'.

But the Bill had its flaws, most particularly in sections 9 and 10, which dealt with the declaration and disqualification of people as communists. These sections placed the onus of proof *not* on the Commonwealth but on the declared person. As Menzies put it, 'If you want to demonstrate that you are not within this net, prove it, because, after all, you should be the one who knows the facts.'[11]

Controversial because it appeared to contravene the accepted principle in legal proceedings that the onus of proof was placed on the affirming party, the issue became especially glaring when Menzies, in the same speech, read into *Hansard* the names of fifty-three men whom he identified as members of the Communist Party.[12] Within days, finding that five were not members, he was obliged to make a correction.[13]

The ALP was divided. Some of its members wanted to offer unqualified support and do away with the issue. Others wanted to amend the Bill to address the problems regarding the onus of proof and the possibility of appeals to the Supreme Court and the High Court. Eventually, the latter approach won out. But the government was unwilling to give much ground: it accepted amendments on the right of appeals, but refused to countenance changes to the onus of proof. When the ALP-controlled Senate amended the legislation once more, the government refused the amended Bill, and deadlock resulted again.

A few days later, North Korean troops invaded South Korea. Australian troops were dispatched to fight under the banner of the United Nations. Amid a wave of renewed anti-communist sentiment, the government reintroduced the Communist Party Dissolution Bill in October, lining it up as a potential trigger for a double-dissolution election.

McMahon was an eager speaker. He had told the House in May

that the ALP's concerns about the onus of proof were ill-founded: 'There is not a single rule about the burden of proof, and so far as I am aware, there has never been such a rule,' he said, addressing his remarks to Evatt. Taking Evatt on in the domain where he had made his name was bold, yet McMahon had been forthcoming with his criticisms:

> How can it be argued that the burden of proof should be placed on any shoulders other than those of the conspirators and the criminals themselves? I wholeheartedly agree with the advocacy of the Prime Minister, who said that it would completely neutralise the principles of, and completely nullify, the Bill if we were to accept the contention of the Right Honourable Member for Barton [Evatt] that the onus of proof should be placed fairly and squarely on the Crown.[14]

The speech was punchy and incisive; according to McMahon, this was largely the result of advice from the deputy leader of the Liberal Party and senior New South Wales Liberal, Eric Harrison.[15]

A handsome, solidly built man whose penchant for rhetorical force was once checked by Menzies' advice to use the rapier in lieu of the bludgeon, Harrison came up to McMahon in the House and asked to see his notes. McMahon handed them over, only to see Harrison tear them up with painstaking care. 'This will be your moment of trial,' Harrison told him, still tearing, 'and one of decision. You are rotten when you read, but not too bad when you speak without notes.' According to McMahon, the speech he proceeded to give prompted Menzies to tell him he would soon be in the ministry. 'You are the next one in there,' Menzies allegedly said, pointing to the cabinet room.

A similar prediction was made in July 1950 when McMahon drew the eye of Alan Reid, a journalist for *The Sun* and close observer of the internal workings of the ALP. Slight of build, gimlet-eyed, sharp-chinned, and dabbed with thinning, auburn-coloured hair, Reid had assiduously cultivated the new generation of MPs, both in government and opposition. He perceived in McMahon skills and talents that had long been in abundance in Labor politicians but in short supply among the Coalition parties—principally, the awareness that politics was a 'tough, professional fight for existence,' as he would later term it.[16] In a glowing profile, Reid wrote that McMahon was the first of the new

Liberal members to 'find and exploit the secret inner life of politics that goes on behind the showy and posturing front of parliamentary histrionics'.

According to Reid's 'information', McMahon was the principal internal lobbyist for changes to the rights of appeal and compensation in the Communist Party Dissolution Bill. The changes, supposedly, had been achieved by McMahon's awareness that 'it is much easier to get agreement in privacy than in public, where dignity is a matter of honour and "face" is all important'. To Reid, this was in marked contrast to McMahon's colleagues: 'McMahon got no publicity, but inclusion of his ideas.' After favourably garbling McMahon's resumé, Reid cited Chifley's supposed judgement that McMahon was 'the most promising' of the crop of Liberal men, and, most importantly, alluded to McMahon's comfort and ease within the political arena—'of being at home there'.[17]

This was certainly true. Despite McMahon's shaky start and his later statements to the contrary, he was comfortable in politics. His years living with Samuel Walder and his work at Allen Allen & Hemsley ensured he was familiar with many of the people he met in the Parliament. He had the measure of his colleagues and the political world. He was no novice, nor was he an ingénue with pressmen like Reid. The relationship went both ways: they cultivated each other.

By October 1950, aware of the colour and attention that a full-throated, if exaggerated, political attack could bring, McMahon homed in on ALP divisions and told the House that:

> It is a well-known device to say, with tongue in cheek, 'We agree with your objectives,' and then systematically to attempt to prevent the achievement of those objectives. That is a Marxian tactic, and it is one freely used by honourable gentlemen opposite.[18]

Boasts of his legal training and contacts within the legal world were hardly subtle. He had not heard of *one* eminent constitutional lawyer with objections to the Bill, he said. 'Universally it has met with approval by all the barristers and solicitors with whom I have discussed it.'

But he could sometimes overreach; in particular, his willingness to ingratiate himself with the fervent anti-communist sentiments of his party led him into controversy. During Question Time on 11 October, McMahon asked Menzies:

> [...] whether the gentleman named H.W. Arndt, who was recently appointed as a professor of economics at the University College, Canberra, took a very prominent part, both in university circles and in public, in opposing the Communist Party Dissolution Bill? Is this gentleman a prominent and dogmatic member of the Fabian Society and did he support the Chifley Socialist Government in its attempt to nationalise the trading banks? ... Does the Prime Minister consider that people of known and biased views should be appointed to a faculty in which complete impartiality and freedom from political bias is absolutely essential? Will the Prime Minister ensure that the appointment is reviewed?[19]

Menzies evaded an immediate answer by having the question placed on the notice paper. In the meantime, however, McMahon's question about his former lecturer caused uproar and, along with his defence of the onus of proof in the Communist Party Dissolution Bill, blotted the classic liberalism in which he professed to believe. When he was asked, some twenty years later, how he could square his 'small "l" liberalism' with these positions, McMahon initially dismissed the question: 'I couldn't fiddle around with stupid little things like this.' Then he argued that it had to be considered within the context of a long career:

> I believed—and I believed more at that time—that Communism was a danger to Australia, that this was the method chosen by my party and once it was accepted by the party naturally I would accept it too ... So, you can't look at life as though you've fitted it into tiny little compartments and say I'm a small-L Liberal, and then say, 'Why did you back your party?' I wouldn't have been there but for the party![20]

When Menzies did provide an answer, it was careful and restrained. 'I am not concerned with the politics of men appointed, so long as they have the academic qualifications,' he told journalists. 'Even if it had been the National University to which the appointment was made I could not be called upon to examine the political position regarding it. However, if somebody raised the security aspect that would be a different matter.'[21]

BY the end of October 1950, Labor's infighting over the Communist Party Dissolution Bill prompted its federal executive to intervene. Its resolution, directing the parliamentary Labor Party to allow the Bill through, forced a reluctant Chifley to wrangle his senators to pass the Bill. Immediately upon its assent by the governor-general, the legislation became the subject of a High Court challenge. Evatt, acting in accordance with the barrister's rule of the 'first cab on the rank', with the fierce belief of his brilliant mind, and with the most disastrous of political instincts, led the challenge.[22]

The division within the Labor Party and its continued intransigence—exercised through its use of a Senate majority that had, in large part, been established at the 1946 election—frustrated the Menzies government. Its attempts to re-introduce compulsory military training were blocked. Its attempt to resolve what Chifley called the 'crossword puzzle business' of deadlocks in the Senate after double dissolutions, caused by the introduction of proportional representation, was refused passage.[23]

In the following year, when Parliament reassembled in March, an election was in the offing. Menzies had returned from the Commonwealth Prime Ministers' Conference warning of war and continued unrest. When the High Court struck down the Communist Party Dissolution Bill, with only chief justice Latham dissenting, Menzies saw an opportunity to exacerbate the Labor Party's troubles and entrench his government more securely. He told the House that it was time to 'let the machinery of the Constitution work':

> Let us go to our masters, the Australian people, and ask them to say where they stand on these crucial issues of the communist conspiracy, of law and order in industry, of the public safety, of the preparation of this country to meet as heavy a cloud of danger as free men have looked at for many long months. This is perfectly simple. The Government will welcome the verdict of the people.[24]

But the occasion for the election was not the Communist Party Dissolution Bill. It was, instead, the stalled Commonwealth Bank Bill, which, following its reintroduction in October, had been held up in the Senate before being referred to a Senate committee. Though some suggested this was a reasonable stage in legislative proceedings, Menzies obtained legal advice to support his contention that the Senate had failed to pass the legislation, and therefore requested that the governor-general dissolve both houses of Parliament to break the stalemate.

McMahon had little to fear in the election. With no chance that Edith Shortland would reprise her candidacy, the considerable margin he enjoyed was certain to increase. He was also aided by indecision in the Labor Party about its candidate.

John Kerr, then thirty-six years old and a barrister in sympathy with the right wing of the ALP, had been considering an entrance to politics for some time. Possessing a high self-regard, he surveyed House of Representatives seats in New South Wales as the election approached in 1951. After seeing that a winnable seat was 'not available', Kerr was told that he should stand nonetheless and earn 'an honest scar' in the service of the party. He was thus persuaded to stand against McMahon in Lowe.

But amid Kerr's abilities and ambitions was a crucial streak of vanity. Glumly conceding defeat before the contest even began, that vanity began to get the better of him. Kerr had no appetite for a loss. An honest scar held no appeal. When Dr John Burton, the young and iconoclastic high commissioner to Ceylon and former secretary of the Department of External Affairs, rang him to say that he was going to gamble on a political career, Kerr leaped at the chance to squirm out of his candidacy. 'I told Burton that I had the Labor endorsement for Lowe; that it was not in my opinion winnable, that I was not very keen to stand myself and would step aside in his favour,' Kerr wrote.[25]

Burton took him up on the offer. A few hours later, he was on a dawn plane from Ceylon to Darwin. He left without his passport, without the knowledge of his minister, without resigning from his position, and, thereafter, without any kind of a future in the public service. Landing in Australia on 27 March, he was endorsed the next day as the ALP's candidate in Kerr's place. Burton was not unaware of the difficulty of the task that awaited him, but he had his reasons. 'I walked out because

I objected to certain things I was ordered to do,' he told journalists. 'I cannot discuss what they were, but they were against my conscience.' He had sought preselection for the ACT seat in 1948, but without success. However slight it was, this, in 1951, was his chance.[26]

Ostensibly called to resolve the problem of the banking Bills, the election campaign was, in the event, all red. The ALP's internal divisions were mercilessly exploited by the Coalition, which hammered Labor on its use of the Senate to frustrate the government's programme of reform and its alleged softness on communism. The Coalition's anti-inflationary measures—principally, a temporary 20 per cent tax on woolgrowers, to combat the international wool boom—lost it some support, but it came through the polls relatively unscathed. It lost five seats in the House, but was returned to office with a 32–28 majority in the Senate.

In Lowe, McMahon had no trouble. The circumstances of Burton's departure prompted a lengthy outburst of criticism from the minister for external affairs, Percy Spender.[27] During the campaign, Eric Harrison travelled to Strathfield to attack Burton, calling him 'completely untrustworthy'.[28] Years later, McMahon would laugh about Burton's cack-handed candidacy, its ineptitude and silliness—and why would he not? With 22,000 votes, a sharp increase on his 1949 majority,[29] McMahon's majority was enough to assure him that promotion could now be a realistic prospect—and not one he was willing to give up lightly.

Three weeks after the poll, Menzies announced a reconstituted cabinet of nineteen ministers, with a twentieth to be added once an amendment to the Ministers of State Act had been passed by Parliament to allow it. Speculation abounded immediately about who it would be. Within days, word had leaked that Menzies intended to promote Fred Osborne, the member for the New South Wales seat of Evans.[30]

Dark-haired and sharp-nosed, Osborne was a decorated war hero, a well-regarded solicitor, and an ardent anti-communist who had also entered the House in 1949. He had a soft, gravelly voice and an incisive manner that had allowed him to make strong contributions in debates on the banking Bill and in foreign affairs. Like McMahon, Alan Reid had picked Osborne as someone worth watching.

Osborne heard enough about the rumour of Menzies' intent

to check its veracity. Through friends and intermediaries, the forthcoming promotion was confirmed. But the time between Menzies' announcement of the opening spot and his statement of who would fill it left a crucial gap, a window of opportunity.[31]

Three New South Wales Liberals went in secret to Eric Harrison, in his capacity as the senior minister in the state, to voice their objections to Osborne's promotion. Osborne did not enjoy their confidence, they told Harrison. They thought him too arrogant, they said.[32]

Surprised, Harrison dutifully reported the meeting to Menzies.

The prime minister was similarly surprised, but he noted the objections. And so, come July, when he announced the new minister, it was not Osborne. It was McMahon.

Surprised, disappointed, and humiliated that he had been led astray so publicly, Osborne was only then told about the deputation that had waited on Harrison. He went to see the deputy party leader, and demanded to know if it was true. Harrison confirmed it.

'I want to ask one thing only,' Osborne said to him, suspicions hardening. 'Was Bill McMahon a member of that deputation?'

Harrison looked down his nose. 'Yes.'

The experience profoundly affected him, Osborne said later. He had gone into politics full of self-confidence, ebullient about what he could do. This experience inflicted an irrevocable wound. It 'destroyed' his confidence and optimism.

Osborne blamed Menzies for allowing the situation to occur, Harrison for not telling him about the deputation, and McMahon for the blatant treachery. He was surprised by it. They had had some association, after all: fellow lawyers, both from Sydney, from adjoining Sydney seats. McMahon had given Osborne a lift in his car to Canberra before Parliament had opened, so they could work out where they would sit in the House. This seemed a betrayal of all that.

A journalist who spoke with Osborne told him that it was not uncommon to have your throat cut in politics. 'But what is unforgiveable,' the journalist went on, 'is to let you walk around for weeks without knowing that it's been cut.'

McMahon had no regrets about what he had done. According to him, he had been promised the spot. It was his, and friends and colleagues had joined with him to ensure he received what was rightfully his. 'I had to wait some weeks,' he said later, 'during which time I was informed on a couple of occasions that somebody else might be appointed in my stead.'

> Then I received advice from a Cabinet Minister. I went to Ezra Norton of the *Daily Mirror* and sought his support. Within a couple of days I became a member of the Cabinet ... I learned in those days that there always is someone able to give us guidance of a very helpful kind.[33]

McMahon's account of this episode was telling for his character and view of politics. The promotion was the due reward for his talents and abilities, he believed, and the methods to get it were simply those that were necessary. There was no shame in treachery; no embarrassment in self-promotion. Politics had to be played hard, ruthlessly, if he were to receive his reward. Loyalty, friendship, truth—all of these were secondary considerations, and dispensable, too, should circumstance demand they be dispensed with.

Plainly, McMahon had learned much in his first term in the Parliament. He knew how to work in the House. He knew how to work in the backrooms. He knew how to work the press. Now, on the first rung on the ministerial ladder, he had proved he knew how to get ahead.

CHAPTER ELEVEN

Disgust

1984

There were times when McMahon's conduct simply disgusted his ghostwriter, when the past and the present came together to prompt an instinctive, deep dislike of McMahon. In March, after a day spent working on the prologue, which had been re-designed as a summary of McMahon's political outlook and beliefs, Bowman simply could not hold himself back. When the time came to write in his diary, he was scathing.

'McMahon really is a third-rate politician and that he could be PM is a damning indictment of the country,' Bowman wrote. 'He is, really, a rather nasty bit of work. Half-truths, lies, Commo can, cheap attacks—what an unpleasant little turd.'[1]

CHAPTER TWELVE

The Colours of Ambition

1951–1956

On the morning of 17 July 1951, McMahon made the four-kilometre trip from his flat in Elizabeth Bay to Government House. There, he watched the governor of New South Wales and his old commanding officer, Lieutenant-General Sir John Northcott, stand in for the absent William McKell and sign legislation expanding the cabinet to twenty. Then it was McMahon's turn: the governor swore him in as minister for the navy and minister for air. The two men went outside and milled in the morning sunshine, shaking hands as the press took photographs. There was no further opportunity for McMahon to savour the moment. Within five minutes, it was all over. The new minister was off. Police escorted his car to Mascot, where he took a plane to Canberra for that afternoon's cabinet meeting.[1]

McMahon was the second-youngest man in the room and the lowest in seniority that day. Harold Holt was younger by a few months, but vastly senior to McMahon in experience and in ranking as minister for labour and national service and minister for immigration. With the exception of Paul Hasluck and Athol Townley, respectively ministers for territories and for social services, the other members of the Menzies ministry were an average of fifteen years older and comfortably ensconced around the large, polished table in the cabinet room at Parliament House. They had experience of government and of opposition. They were well versed in how everything was to work.

Top of the agenda that day was the sombre economic outlook. Difficult economic conditions were in their infancy. Fuelled by the war in Korea, wool prices had soared, and consumer demand was rising to unsustainable heights. 'We are grossly overstretched on investment—both public and private,' Menzies said. The meeting, which ran for two days, was wholly concerned with addressing these problems. Menzies and his ministers canvassed ways to reduce costs, whether by reducing Commonwealth employment, freezing wages, or raising the rate of interest. Undaunted by the fact that it was his first meeting, McMahon was not shy about contributing. In what would become a regular display of his familiarity with economics, he pointed out the dangers of inflation, and stated his belief that the Commonwealth Bank had not done enough. Arthur Fadden's response to this interloper's criticism was sharp: 'I think it has been well watched.'[2]

Less than three weeks before, the government had passed a Bill to hold a referendum on amending the constitution to ban the Communist Party. It was to be the fourth time that communism was debated in the Parliament within an eighteen-month period, and what was said in the debate was little more than an echo of the past. 'The whole danger to peace in the world today springs from the policies, plans, underground activities and promoted local wars of the Communists,' Menzies told the House. He pointed towards the war in Korea as an example of the dangers that awaited any kind of tolerance or delay. 'Having the clear instruction of the nation to deal with the Communist fifth column swiftly, vigorously and unrelentingly, we propose to perform that task if we are given power to perform it.'[3]

For Evatt, it was a matter of fierce belief that Menzies should never receive this power. Upon the death of an exhausted Chifley on 13 June, Evatt had taken over the Labor Party leadership, and set about opposing the government's case for a Yes vote. The political damage that the communist issue had inflicted on the ALP had not caused him to doubt the righteousness of his actions; nor had his unexpectedly narrow victory against a returning Nancy Wake at the election prompted any deviation from principle. 'If I had to make the same decision again,' Evatt said, when it seemed that he had been defeated, '… I would not hesitate for one moment.'[4]

As winter thawed into spring, Evatt barnstormed the country, campaigning for the No vote. He lashed the government in apocalyptic tones that reached an apogee in Perth, where he told people that the

Menzies government was 'following the old totalitarian road', and recalled Pastor Niemöller:

> It is the Hitler technique over again. First the Reds, then the Jews, then the trade unions, then the Social Democratic Parties, then the Roman Catholic Centre Party, then the Roman Catholic and Lutheran Churches.[5]

The leader of the opposition's high visibility in the campaign was in marked contrast to most members of the ALP, a fact that McMahon noted as he stumped for a Yes vote in the final weeks of the campaign. At a meeting at Strathfield Town Hall early in September, McMahon suggested that the ALP had deserted Evatt: 'They will let Bert accept full responsibility for a crushing and ignominious defeat of the advocates of a No vote.'[6]

Confidence in the result did not deter McMahon from trying to blunt Evatt's attacks. He told people that the 'legislation under this power could not, under any circumstances, be extended to include political parties, the trade unions, or social and religious organisations'. The Communist Party Dissolution Act could be repealed once the danger had been neutralised, he added, a point that Menzies used in the days that followed to try to stem Evatt's campaign.[7] McMahon also linked passage of the referendum with the prosecution of the war in Korea. 'As we are fighting the Communists in Korea, so must we fight them in Australia, because they are fighting us,' he said. 'The sooner we get to grips with them the better.'[8]

The public was not persuaded, and on 22 September voted the referendum down. For the government, the humiliating defeat caused bewilderment and carried an extra sting because of the knowledge that it had been returned to office only a few months before on the very same platform. What had gone wrong? At first, senior figures pointed the finger at treachery, misinformation, and low intelligence on the part of voters.[9] Soon, more reasonably, they blamed the difficulties of prosecuting any referendum without the support of the opposition, the complexity of the proposal, the conservatism of the Australian electorate, and the unfavourable reception to the budget that Fadden had handed down only a few days before the referendum.[10]

McMahon moved on quickly from the unsuccessful campaign. He had to become acquainted with an area he knew little about, yet whose presence in the public eye was conspicuous. HMAS *Anzac* was in Korean waters, part of a blockade of the North Korean port of Songjin; the light aircraft carrier HMAS *Sydney* was heading north to patrol the west coast of the Korean peninsula with the Americans; the No. 77 Squadron, flying Gloster Meteors that had been hastily supplied to counter-act the threat posed by the Soviet-made MiG-15, was in its eighth year of an overseas basing, and soon to battle the Soviet Union's 176th Guards Fighter Aviation Regiment in the skies above the North Korean city of Sunchon.[11] For McMahon, not involved in the details of combat operations, the weight of his responsibilities would have been keen, particularly when he had to announce the deaths of Australian military personnel.

His portfolios had become accepted training posts for junior ministers, and were rarely the subject of intense political debate.[12] But both were undergoing change. The navy was moving away from procedures and practices it had inherited from Britain, becoming receptive to new ideas in public administration and the changes wrought by technological advances, most notably in the increased utility of missiles and submarines over battleships.[13] The RAAF was increasing its intake, training pilots, and updating equipment and planes, notably in its critical decision to purchase American-designed F-86 Sabres in lieu of British-designed Hawker F3s.[14]

McMahon's first months attracted derision and disapproval. A report that he had been seen on a Sydney golf course with a naval officer in tow, apparently a caddy for his game, barely six days after his appointment, prompted criticism from Labor firebrand Eddie Ward.[15] McMahon's newfound liking for being driven by uniformed RAN personnel also provoked scorn from his colleagues.[16] His references to the RAN as 'my Navy' and senior naval officers as 'good boys' hardly prompted warmth from his department.[17] His driver, however, liked his new minister. 'He was very, very easy to speak to,' said Lawrie Anderson, 'and we often had conversations about things that were highly irrelevant to anything in the navy.' Once, when Anderson's mother was sick in Melbourne and the navy was refusing to allow him leave to see her, McMahon intervened and told him to go. Later, Anderson invited McMahon to his wedding, where he made an impromptu speech.[18]

Even from his earliest days in the portfolio, McMahon would display behaviours that would become standard in subsequent years. First, as already seen, was McMahon's use of the privileges of ministerial office; second was his willingness to reach beyond typical sources of advice. 'As Minister for the Navy and Air,' recalled Alan Wright, 'he went down to Rushcutters Bay and ate with the able-bodied seamen. Then he went up to the Officers Club. *Then* he went to the Naval Board. He knew what he was doing.'[19] Third was McMahon's zealous protection of his authority as minister.

This was most evident following the appointment of the British-born Air Marshal Donald Hardman to the position of chief of the air staff. A decorated veteran of both world wars, Hardman came with a reputation as 'an innovative manager'.[20] But there was criticism for the perceived slight of not appointing an Australian to the position. Though the decision had been made before McMahon took office, the brunt of that criticism came his way. He did not help himself when he explained that Hardman had been appointed because 'there was no one in Australia with the experience or the necessary qualifications for the position'—news to the RAAF officers who had been successfully fighting a war only six years earlier.[21] However inept the justification, Hardman's appointment was a response to the perceived failings of the RAAF's area-based system of command. Put in place in 1939, the flexibility offered by that decentralised command system had been highly prized during the war. In peacetime, however, this system was an organisational tangle, with overlaps of responsibility, divided commands, and glaring limitations of co-operation and resources. Under the previous chief of the air staff, Air Vice-Marshal George Jones, the system had been maintained on grounds that it suited Australia's divides of geography and small, sparsely located population. The government was unconvinced by this reasoning, and Jones received a summons to McMahon's office. 'Cabinet has decided that you are to be retired,' McMahon told him, once greetings were out of the way.[22] Hardman's appointment came with the expectation that he would draw upon his familiarity with functional commands, from his experience with the Royal Air Force, and re-organise the RAAF into a system of commands based around the service's main activities and functions—operations, maintenance, training, and administration.[23]

McMahon was careful to aid Hardman where he could and to ensure that the change was never in doubt. During 1952, as the chief of the air staff laid the groundwork with the help of the newly appointed secretary of the Department of the Air, Edwin (Ted) Hicks, McMahon signalled that the new system would be non-negotiable. Countering opposition from members of the Air Board, who questioned the logistics and effectiveness of the new system,[24] McMahon noted that an unofficial functional system had evolved from necessity in some places of Australia. He was blunt, intent on ensuring he had his way. 'We should make up our minds one way or the other which system we wish to adopt,' he wrote to the board.[25]

McMAHON'S work as a minister could be uneven and surreal. The structure of the air force and navy and their departments meant that McMahon regularly juggled the momentous with the small and niggling. Amid the shake-up of the RAAF and combat operations in Korea, he approved the introduction of 'wet' canteens on RAAF bases, negotiated a renewal of the lease on Cockatoo Island, signed off on the purchase of equipment, and persuaded the cabinet to approve the purchase of land near Glenbrook, New South Wales, in order to alleviate crowded conditions on an adjacent RAAF base.[26] McMahon summed up the proposal delicately, writing that the situation in the base:

> [...] seems to have been organised by P.G. Wodehouse. At present the women are accommodated in the Sergeants' Quarters, the Sergeants are living in the Airmen's Quarters and the Airmen are crowded into the huts. It is only going to need a Sergeant to come home late and go into his accustomed rooms by mistake and there will be a terrible scandal.[27]

In this light, the £16,000 asking price was a bargain. Cabinet approved the submission without debate, yet was less willing to approve more costly measures: it took McMahon two years to convince his colleagues that a radar air-defence system should be a priority, and longer still to convince them to fund it.[28]

In spite of the calm hand he usually wielded, McMahon's naivety could be evident. In April 1952, aware of the high financial costs of the Korean war effort and the mounting strain of casualties, McMahon suggested withdrawing the No. 77 Squadron. He thought the RAAF was over-committed and that withdrawal of the squadron, which had lost some 25 per cent of its pilots to death or capture, should be considered. The Americans, he argued, would not mind. Menzies gave this proposal short shrift. The Americans *would* object, Menzies told him, and, furthermore, the move had the potential to damage the relationship between their two countries.[29]

At other times, McMahon's connections could cause problems. In the course of 1952, there was controversy about the government's plan to shutter the oil-shale plant at Glen Davis, a small town in Capertree Valley, New South Wales. For McMahon's younger brother, Sam, this was an opportunity. Now an entrepreneur who owned limestone deposits at the site, Sam developed a proposal to turn the plant into a cement-making factory. But he and the group of Sydney businessmen he gathered wanted government support. So, ahead of Glen Davis's proposed closure in May, Sam lobbied the government. He found a favourable reception from New South Wales senator William Spooner, the minister for national development. 'I encouraged him to proceed with his proposition,' Spooner said.[30]

But the optics were poor. Using government funds to support a proven unsustainable venture? A venture led by the brother of a government minister? It was all too fraught, a point driven home when Eddie Ward seized on the issue and cast Glen Davis's closure and the pending disposal of its equipment as evidence that the Menzies government was looking after its own. 'For months past,' Ward said in the House, 'a brother of the Minister for the Navy has been lobbying in this building and in Sydney in an endeavour to secure advantages over other persons who are interested in the purchase of the plant.'[31]

A cabinet subcommittee that did not include McMahon examined Sam's proposal in May and knocked it on its head. The need for a tender, the disposal of equipment, the economics, and the vested interests of so many of those involved made the decision an easy one. They turned it down flat, said the minister for supply, Howard Beale, 'and that was the end of it'.[32]

But it was not. In August, a report that journalists at *The Sun* were directed not to mention the relationship between the minister and his brother forced McMahon to reply in the House: 'I have had no business associations or discussions with my brother for at least ten years.' He told the House that he had no knowledge of the offer, that he had not talked about the matter in cabinet or with colleagues, and that he had not asked any newspaper to suppress 'the alleged relationship' between him and Sam: 'I could not have done so because no relationship in fact existed.'[33]

For McMahon, such incidents were a distraction from the exercise of his authority as a minister. As the year went on, he worked to close the rifts between civilian and military personnel in the air and navy departments by clarifying questions of status and responsibilities. He resisted moves to alter the composition of the air and navy boards. Most notably, and again demonstrative of the way he would handle himself in later years and subsequent portfolios, McMahon involved himself in a long-running dispute about the consecration of colours, the heraldic flags of great ceremonial significance within the military services.[34]

Shortly after her accession to the throne, Queen Elizabeth II confirmed her late father's decision to grant a colour to the RAAF. The presentation of that colour was set for 17 September, with the governor-general, William McKell, to represent the Queen. News of the pending presentation attracted the ire of the archbishop of Melbourne and Catholic chaplain-general of the army, Dr Daniel Mannix. He had long been opposed to the Anglican 'consecration' that was embedded within these ceremonies. For Mannix, forcing Catholic personnel to attend these ceremonies smacked of an institutionalised sectarianism.

Moreover, it was unlawful constitutionally. Section 116 of the constitution was clear: 'The Commonwealth shall not make any law … for imposing any religious observance.'[35] By its maintenance of the Anglican elements of the ceremony, was the RAAF not contravening this? Was it not trying to impose a religious observance on some members, prohibiting the free observance of their own religion? Even if there were no constitutional questions, Catholic law was unequivocal: it forbade active participation 'in the worship of non-Catholics'.[36] How could Catholic military personnel, in all good conscience, be commanded to attend these ceremonies? Catholic clergy had asked this question as far back as 1905, but a series of ad hoc compromises and exploitation of unofficial loopholes had ensured it was addressed without ever being answered.

As the time for presentation of the Colour drew near, the military hierarchy sought to silence the opposition and protests raised by Catholic personnel who had been ordered to attend. Cadets at the RAAF College at Point Cook were told that they were risking their careers. Officers were threatened with courts martial. The Catholic chaplain was accused of violating his oath of allegiance.

Ineptitude and intransigence characterised the RAAF's handling of the matter, and McMahon backed them up. His conversion, his upbringing, and his party: all these now insulated him from the objections. He was uncompromising. In the name of tradition, he insisted that the presentation proceed without change.[37] Against this refusal to engage and the possibility of repercussions to Catholic military personnel, Mannix backed off. With great reluctance, the archbishop granted a dispensation to those personnel to attend, and the parade went ahead with only one disruption to tradition: when the governor-general's plane was delayed, McMahon was obliged to stand in for McKell and present the light blue, wattle-embroidered flag to an airman, who received it on bended knee.[38]

Two months later, McMahon left Australia for his first international trip as a minister. He inspected efforts to rebuild the naval base on Manus Island. He stayed overnight in Guam, somehow lost his wallet,[39] and flew on to Tokyo and then to Korea, where he spent four days meeting servicemen from all three branches of the defence force. He moved among generals and diplomats; had a 'wonderful flight' in a Meteor aircraft; and, in a gaberdine coat and dark homburg, visited the front lines to shake hands and meet troops.[40] From there, he travelled to the Philippines and then Hong Kong. On the border, he was confronted by Chinese guards who, from across the river, pointed guns at his party while taking surveillance photographs. 'It is rather a horrifying experience to be looking down the barrel of a Sten gun,' he said afterward. 'Naturally we backed away rather hastily.'[41] In Laos, he took part in an air strike on communist targets; then he returned to Australia via Singapore, arriving home on 14 December.

McMahon did not confine himself to his portfolio. In cabinet meetings, he was reputed to contribute regularly to discussions about economic matters, often to the chagrin of Arthur Fadden; in private, he could be sanctimonious, as when he wrote to John McEwen to tell him that the release of price estimates by the Bureau of Agricultural Economics had caused 'unnecessary harm' to the government because they were not adequately explained.[42] After explaining the real issue, McEwen offered a sardonic rebuke: 'How lucky you are to have only the Navy and the Air Force to worry about.'[43] In the House, McMahon's speeches were similarly directed towards economics and taxation.[44] They were notably heavy on statistics. McMahon loved numbers, and delighted in figures that he could lob across the chamber. He would reel off astronomical-sounding sums, one on top of the other, as though they could bludgeon his opponents. He fancied himself a performer, an attack dog, yet was often mocked as a lightweight.[45] 'Was not the Minister selected by a newspaper as one of the best-dressed men in the Commonwealth?' Eddie Ward sneered at him.[46]

The image was deceptive. McMahon was capable of deeper things. He could engage with ideas, as he demonstrated in a paper presented to the Australian Institute of Political Science in September 1953. In an address significant for its exposition of his political beliefs and notable for its peculiarity among Liberals of this period, McMahon spoke about the Liberal Party and the intersection of religion, politics, and philosophy. Beginning with the caveat that 'in the short run, political activity undoubtedly bows to expediency'—a key admission of the necessity of pragmatism in politics—McMahon said that four basic assumptions about nature influenced his views of political action.

The first was his explicitly Christian belief that the individual was the 'central feature of society'. From this followed his rejection of the views of Hegel and Marx, of Plato's ideas of the Republic, and any suggestion that the state had an inherent value that might trump the value of the individual. Second was his emphasis on the individual as the changing force in society, ahead of the 'forms or conditions of production' that McMahon argued communism and socialism emphasised. 'As the individual is the driving force in society and undoubtedly responds to external stimulae—to rewards of one kind or another,' McMahon said, 'he must have satisfactory incentives for effort and achievement.' Third, the Doctrine of Original Sin meant that Man was fallible and susceptible to sin. Power should therefore be distributed in order to prevent the abuse that arose from this inherent fallibility. Fourth, possession of a free will was the source of all good and evil: 'Without free will there can be no evil.'

From these four assumptions followed his argument that parliamentary democracy, as 'the source and custodian of our essential liberties', was the way by which the individual could develop and liberties be safeguarded; and from them also stemmed his regard for the government and Parliament as 'the responsible authority for keeping healthy the economic climate in which society works'. For McMahon, the political foundation of the liberal system was based upon the need to preserve the 'essential civil freedoms' of speech and worship, assembly and association, of choice of occupation, of management of income and property. These were the ultimate ends of liberalism, and 'the liberal view' held that constraints of the law and constitution were the bulwarks for the protection of these freedoms.

Liberalism was 'not a dogma', he said. 'It is more an opportunity than a way.' Comparing this favourably with the fixed theories of communism and socialism, McMahon argued that the flexibility offered by liberalism was more likely to lead to happiness. Yet he also noted that within his own party there were oddities and impracticalities: the lack of an 'apostolic succession' ensured that personality would predominate. 'What one Prime Minister would attempt might be quite beyond the wish or capacity of his successor.'[47]

If the paper did nothing else, it confirmed that McMahon had given serious thought to the principles that girded his politics, and that they were based, in no small part, on his religious beliefs, which he practised by his weekly attendance at services at St Mark's, Darling Point. For all the contradictions that his arguments raised—between freedom of association and assembly and the attempts to ban the Communist Party, between freedom of speech and his question of the appointment of Heinz Arndt—the address was notable for its acknowledgement of religious influence, the rarity of such discussions among Liberal Party politicians, and the concessions that McMahon made towards pragmatism and reality. One day, however, his caution about the capacities of a succeeding prime minister would seem prescient.

THE year 1954 opened with widely felt anticipation about the Queen's imminent visit to Australia. Amid a buoyant-seeming economy, the royal tour was widely acknowledged to precede the dissolution of the House of Representatives and the holding of an election. Behind the scenes, the parties were gearing up for the contest, but amid the preparation for the Queen's visit they allowed some issues to slide—among them, military colours.

In the two years since the events at Point Cook, Archbishop Mannix had become resolved to ensuring that his objections to the entrenched Anglican tradition in the consecration of colours were recognised and properly answered. In mid-1953, as plans were made for the Queen to present a new colour to the Royal Military College at Duntroon during her tour, Mannix contacted the government to make it known that he would not give dispensation to Catholic cadets to attend the parade. The fair warning resolved nothing. The government procrastinated, leading to a frenzied series of negotiations in the following January and February that saw Menzies himself travelling to Melbourne to attempt to meet with the archbishop. Menzies had certainly recognised Mannix's objections: when the archbishop cabled him on 12 February, he noted that Menzies had admitted the service at Point Cook was 'indefencable [sic]'.[48]

Evidence also suggests that Menzies' colleagues were less willing to recognise the grievance. Amid criticism in newspapers, Mannix released to the press the letters he had exchanged with the prime minister. 'The press comments, based on leakage of information from the Federal Cabinet,' Mannix explained to Menzies on 16 February, 'had given the impression that the whole difficulty arose solely from an attempt on my part to embarrass Her Majesty, the Queen, at Duntroon.'[49]

By now they were too close to the presentation, and Menzies believed that press publicity 'had greatly reduced the likelihood of a settlement'.[50] The prime minister told Mannix that the situation would be resolved afterward—but, on this occasion, Mannix had to yield. The archbishop reluctantly complied, lifting the ban on Catholic cadets and their involvement. The Duntroon ceremonies went ahead.

It was not over. On 18 February, at HMAS *Cerberus*, the naval base in Victoria, while observing a dress rehearsal for the presentation of another colour by the Duke of Edinburgh on 2 March, members of

THE COLOURS OF AMBITION 101

the press were startled to see some 400 white hats bobbing through the rigid ranks of navy personnel assembled. It was the Catholic personnel, falling out and running from the parade ground before the dedication and consecration. As the Anglican senior chaplain recited the prayers, the Catholic personnel formed up under the shade of some trees by the Catholic chaplain, Father Lake, who said a prayer for the Queen. Then, once the eight-minute ceremony had finished, the Catholic members ran back to the main parade.[51]

The press was aghast. It looked like chaos. At best, it was unseemly; at worst, it was disgraceful. For the Catholic personnel, however, this 'undignified action' was a rehearsal for a worst-case scenario. 'Catholics at the depot are not at all happy about having to leave the ground in the middle of the parade,' Father Lake was quoted saying. 'But if they turn it into an Anglican service, there is no alternative. No Catholic of conscience can participate in it.'[52]

These comments, and the imprimatur that the fallout apparently enjoyed from the Department of the Navy, prompted Menzies to call McMahon and demand an explanation. Cabinet had already noted that the issue was likely to linger, and had 'invited' Menzies to discuss it with McMahon.[53] The publicity and outrageous comments from Lake led the prime minister to view the fallout as an embarrassment. According to McMahon, Menzies threatened demotion for seeming to allow it.[54]

But it was all a miscommunication. Lake had said no such thing to the press, McMahon told Menzies. Moreover, he had already sorted things to the satisfaction of all parties, and could defend the arranged fallout on grounds that the ad hoc compromises used before had become standard practice. He had written to Mannix and to the Catholic Archbishop of Sydney, Cardinal Norman Gilroy, to say as much.[55]

The next day, McMahon told the press that an agreement had been reached between the Department of the Navy and the Catholic Church. 'Catholics will rejoin the ranks after the religious ceremony. This procedure complies with the age-long Royal Navy and Royal Australian Navy practice.' The resentment and grievance could be easily healed, said the man who not two years before had insisted tradition was more important. 'There is no good reason why there should not be a mutually satisfactory arrangement and I am sure a solution will be found in a more congenial atmosphere.'[56]

The ceremony went off as rehearsed. The Duke of Edinburgh presented the new colour. The Catholic personnel fell out in well-rehearsed order and rejoined the parade once the consecration had been made. Following the ceremony, the Duke met with dignitaries and shook hands. He met men he had served with during World War II: 'Well, well,' he said, 'this is a pleasure.' He had a beer with them before leaving. The pageantry, the medals, and the shows of bonhomie were enough to crowd out any embarrassment from the break with tradition.[57]

WHEN the Queen and the Duke left Australia on 31 March, attention turned to the election. The twenty-ninth of May was to be the day of reckoning.[58] Communism was hardly to be an issue: the government's loss of the 1951 referendum and the political scars borne by the ALP seemed to have deterred both parties from raising it.

But on 13 April, the day before Parliament was to be prorogued, Menzies stood in the House just after the dinner adjournment and announced the defection of Vladimir Petrov, the third secretary at the Soviet Embassy: 'Mr Petrov, who has been carrying out in Australia the functions of the Russian Ministry of State Security—the MVD—has disclosed a complete willingness and capacity to convey to our own security people a great number of documents and what may turn out to be much oral information and explanation.' Asylum for this stocky, big-jowled man had been granted on 3 April, and he had brought with him a trove of documents that Menzies declared showed 'there are matters affecting Australia's security which call for judicial investigation'. The matter was too important to wait until the election was over, Menzies said. A Bill would be introduced the next day to make some requisite amendments to the royal commission legislation.[59]

The Labor Party greeted the news with silence. Evatt was in Sydney with no knowledge of what was happening, and in his absence the party made no reply to Menzies' speech. As debate in the House moved to the Superannuation Bill, Evatt's press secretary hurried to phone his leader. A short statement was issued within the hour; the next morning in the House, Evatt declared his support for the establishment of the royal commission.

However fiercely he did so, Evatt must have been aware that Petrov's defection was a blow to his party and his chances of becoming prime minister—a blow that continued to reverberate throughout the subsequent election campaign. Evdokia Petrov, distraught in the firm grip of two hulking Soviet officials, was dragged through a roaring crowd to a plane to return to Russia, and then rescued in dramatic fashion at Darwin airport and reunited with her husband. The first formal hearings of the Royal Commission into Espionage, held in the Albert Hall, Canberra, were conducted against a backdrop of velvet curtains, with a cast of leading barristers and an audience of baying press. And while Menzies refrained from mentioning Petrov, others on the government side were not quite so decorous. In whose hands, Arthur Fadden asked voters, would you place the results of the royal commission—'R.G. Menzies with his splendid record, or H.V. Evatt with his?'[60]

Evatt tried to shift the terms of debate: in his policy speech on 6 May, he announced a programme of lower taxes, higher pensions, increased finance for housing, and the abolition of the means test on pensions within the next parliamentary term. He called it a 'fighting programme', but he was the one being fought.[61] The papers dismissed it as a 'gimme' gimmick; the Coalition sneered that it was uncosted and expensive; William Bourke, a hardliner in the Victorian ALP, publicly criticised it.[62]

With no serious threat in his own seat, McMahon was free to campaign in aid of other Coalition candidates.[63] He told audiences that Labor was set on gerrymandering electoral boundaries, that abolishing the means test so quickly was impracticable, that the ALP was changing its tune on arbitration, and that it had no credentials on housing.[64] Without mentioning Petrov directly, McMahon pointed his audiences that way: 'Communism is an issue in this election; make no mistake about that.'[65]

When the ballots were counted, it became evident that the Coalition's success in Queensland, where it won thirteen of the state's eighteen seats, would keep it in office. The ALP attracted 50.1 per cent of the vote, but it was not able to spread those votes throughout the country. The government lost five seats, but gained one, resulting in a seven-seat majority.[66]

Almost immediately after the election, the press began to speculate about whether there would be a reshuffle of the ministry.[67] The Liberal Party backbench, largely composed of idealistic and zealous 'forty-niners', had been grumbling at the government's direction and the apparently immovable layer of ageing, sick men in the ministry. Menzies was disinclined to promote younger men, Alexander Downer thought, with the result that the front bench 'was clouded by others of lesser magnitude who contrasted unfavourably with many of the men who sat behind them'.[68] Although he, too, was a forty-niner, McMahon was the most junior minister, and goodwill towards him was scant, given the manner in which he had been promoted and conducted himself since 1951. There were suggestions that he, Howard Beale, and Paul Hasluck were all in the frame for demotion. The press wrote of whispered rebellions and of proposals for the backbench to elect a portion of the ministry.[69] Journalist Harold Cox, who thought McMahon a hard worker and man of quick understanding, recalled that it was common wisdom that McMahon was to be dropped from the cabinet that year. Surprised, he raised it with John McEwen, who confirmed that the reports were true. Cox told McEwen that he thought it a shame: 'He's made blunders, but, after all, he's a new minister.' McEwen said that he agreed, and volunteered that he had often thought of who could take over his portfolio. 'Obviously the next best man, or another man who could do it and do it superbly well, would be Menzies himself.' Menzies, obviously, was not available to take the portfolio, McEwen went on, so it was a matter of the next best choice. 'Now, the third man on my list for the job would be McMahon. That's what I think of McMahon.'[70]

If true, it is likely that McEwen's favour saved McMahon. For, despite the press reports and rumours, he was not dropped. McMahon was given Athol Townley's former portfolio of social services. Was it a demotion? Potentially. The new role did not give him any extra seniority, but, as *The Sydney Morning Herald* noted, the portfolio itself was more fitted to McMahon's 'natural bent'.[71] Largely an administrative outpost that was heavily influenced by Treasury, the social services portfolio funnelled McMahon's predilection for economics into a useful outlet and gave him valuable experience.

His work was aided by a gradual convergence between the

Coalition and Labor Party on social-security measures. For although the government had roundly criticised Evatt's promise to abolish the means test within the next term, its objection was only to the speed of the idea. The Coalition itself had promised the abolition of the means test at the 1949 election; the difficulties and the delay in doing so had not dissuaded it from the goal. 'We will continue vigorously the work of modifying it, having in mind the majority of hard cases,' Menzies had said, in the May campaign.[72]

In September, now settled into the social services portfolio, McMahon introduced further modifications. The *Social Services Act 1954* provided for a 75 per cent increase in the permissible income allowed to pensioners, liberalised the property test to exclude income derived from property, and raised the limits on property tests by £500.[73] The first measure was not as generous as it sounded, considering the rise in price levels, but the changes to the tests on property were among the ways that the government would encourage home ownership, work, and thrift. 'It is an essential element of Liberal policy that people should be given incentives to work and save, and by this means to increase the amount of property owned by them,' McMahon said. 'Both work and savings are necessary if we are to ensure full employment and progress, with a reasonable level of stability for the purchasing power of money.'[74]

The ALP was keen to criticise the meagre increase to pensions, and McMahon's circumstances—his personal wealth and his bachelorhood—gave them the opening. Their criticisms were such that Percy Joske, a Liberal backbencher from Victoria, leaped to McMahon's defence with a curiously convoluted argument. McMahon, he said:

> [...] does not need to worry about his own domestic troubles—as he does not have any—and he does not have to engage in the battle for money, because he is sufficiently well furnished with it now. Therefore, he can devote his attention to the work of his department.[75]

McMahon was certainly hardworking, but he did have help. Bill Wakeling, a field officer of the Liberal Party who was not on McMahon's payroll, kept a close eye on the electorate, so much so that some jokingly called him the 'real member for Lowe'. McMahon's private secretary, the tall and elegant Val Kentish, took care of his diary and personal affairs, and was the first point of contact for those wanting him to do anything. 'If you wanted something done,' said Alan Wright, by now treasurer of the Liberal's Lowe federal electorate conference, 'you went to Val, not to McMahon.'[76] And although he had a reputation for being a social butterfly, McMahon was hardly much for parties. He ate most of his meals in restaurants, and rarely drank. Undistracted by the needs of a family or a volatile electorate, McMahon would work long hours in his flat in Elizabeth Bay, delving into his portfolio, telephoning officials all through the night, in his efforts to master it completely. In cabinet, he would be well prepared as a matter of routine, able and willing to speak on matters outside his portfolio, occasionally to the annoyance of his colleagues.

Proving his merit seemed to occupy his mind. McMahon was determined to succeed. Eddie Ward had declared him a 'hopeless failure' in the departments of navy and air, and greeted news of his new appointment with a moan: 'God help the pensioners of this country when they are placed at the mercy of this kind of Government and this type of Minister.'[77] Whether or not this stung more than his near dropping from cabinet, McMahon worked to establish himself in the portfolio and make his mark.

On 21 October, he introduced an amendment to the *War Service Homes Act*, which had been passed in the aftermath of World War I to help ex-servicemen and their dependents finance and build homes. McMahon's Bill extended its provisions to eligible ex-servicemen living in Papua New Guinea and Norfolk Island, and increased the size of the maximum loan available. The changes were again aimed at increasing home ownership and emphasising the primacy of the family. 'Family life is the foundation of a vigorous, contented and healthy community,' he said. 'Homes are essential if the family is to live a dignified and full life.'[78] Critical of the slow rate of the construction of homes, Labor was forthcoming with support; the colourful Les Haylen even commended McMahon for his 'great skill' in handling the Bill.[79] Labor was less enamoured, however, with McMahon's propensity for endless gabbering.

'Will the Honourable member come in and land?' deputy opposition leader Arthur Calwell interjected, as McMahon offered a nine-minute reply to the congratulations that were extended to him.

'What does that mean?' asked McMahon.

'Finish quickly,' Calwell barked.[80]

Two weeks later, McMahon introduced the *Aged Persons Homes Bill*, which allowed the Commonwealth to make grants, on a pound-for-pound basis, to churches, charitable bodies, and institutions that provided homes for the elderly. It was, to some extent, an overdue measure. For years, as McMahon noted, volunteer organisations had been the only ones working in the area, developing, building, and maintaining roughly 200 aged-care institutions throughout the country, almost entirely without aid.[81] Menzies had long resisted calls for the Commonwealth to step in, arguing that the federal government's authority to engage in home building was limited. But during the election, prompted by an offhand comment from his wife, he had announced a pledge to intervene.[82] An appropriation of £1.5m was made for 1954–55. 'A flea-bite, economically speaking,' Les Haylen commented, but nonetheless 'a happy beginning to a good scheme'.[83]

It was. The Act provided a model for future schemes within Aboriginal housing, aged persons hostels, women's refuges, and accommodation for the homeless. Within ten years, more than 1,000 grants had been approved through the Act, providing accommodation for more than 18,000 people.[84] For a minister attuned to opportunities for publicity and tirelessly able to exploit them, the measure was unalloyed gold. McMahon could—and did, repeatedly—visit a home with press in tow and show to the country, by the presentation of a cheque, that it had a government and a minister that cared. It was McMahon's biggest triumph as minister for social services, and Labor *hated* it.[85]

But McMahon was not always concerned about the press and public relations, according to Queensland senator Annabelle Rankin. He had a personal investment in the work that went with the social services portfolio, particularly where it related to children. She observed seeing tears in his eyes while they visited one establishment:

> On one occasion a little child was learning to walk again. His father had come for this special occasion and stayed at one end of the room offering words of encouragement. The little child, with all the confidence he could muster, and with hope in his bright little eyes, stepped out bravely

one or two steps to take his father's hands. I can remember as we left Bill McMahon saying, 'What courage! I must never forget it when the path for me is getting rough!'[86]

By this time, the path was getting rough for Labor. Evatt's failure to win the 1954 election and concern about his ability to lead the ALP, intensified by his decision to appear before the Petrov royal commission on behalf of members of his own staff, saw his authority challenged and his suspicions provoked. In August, the right-wing West Australian MP Tom Burke sought to unseat Evatt from the party's leadership. The attempt failed, but subsequent publication of Alan Reid's profile of Bartholomew Augustine Santamaria, the 'Svengali' of a shadowy group nicknamed The Movement, gave Evatt's seething paranoia and frustrations something real to latch onto. Early in October, he issued a statement condemning Santamaria, an act that enraged the hardline anti-communists within the federal caucus. On 20 October, the Tasmanian senator George Cole moved a spill of leadership positions. The motion was lost on the voices, but Evatt decided to flush out his enemies. He leaped onto a table, grasping a pencil and paper, red-faced and excited. 'Get their names, get their names!'[87] he demanded.

Over subsequent months, the ALP fractured and split, with seven MPs expelled from the party, only to reconstitute themselves as the 'Australian Labor Party (Anti-Communist)' when Parliament resumed in April the following year. And after the royal commission's final report into the Petrov matter was tabled in September, Evatt's conduct caused further alarm. The leader of the opposition announced that he had written to the Soviet foreign minister, Vyacheslav Molotov, to ascertain the veracity of the documents brought over by Petrov. To gales of laughter, Evatt argued that Petrov's defection had been used as a 'rabbit out of a hat' to revive the communist bogey-man, that the royal commission had been a stunt, and that facts had been kept from the public until the 1954 election was over. Evatt accused the prime minister of knowing all about Petrov since as far back as 1953. 'He did not!' McMahon yelled, but Evatt remained glued to his narrative of trickery and deceit, of dishonour and conspiracy.[88]

Menzies responded by calling an election. As he wrote, 'it would be flying in the face of Providence not to seize the opportunity'.[89]

Terminating Evatt's career would be a bonus to enlarging the government's majority, which was exactly what happened on 10 December. The Coalition's hold on government tightened. Its seven-seat majority became twenty-eight. McMahon's 6 per cent margin in Lowe became 10 per cent.[90]

'For many years I thought that when Sophocles made Oedipus Rex kill his father and marry his mother it illustrated the inscrutable workings of fate and unpredictability of life,' McMahon had written to Menzies in August. But this, he went on, was not really the truth. 'The story is intended to show that life follows certain immutable patterns and works out according to the designs of Apollo. This explanation is an enormous help to me,' McMahon declared, 'as I was becoming a little uneasy about destiny.'[91]

For the moment, it might have seemed, design was keeping McMahon and the Liberal Party in government.

CHAPTER THIRTEEN

The Undoctored Incident

1984

Early in March 1984, Campbell passed Bowman a 'thought for the week'. Addressed 'to the editor', it was a bit of verse of Campbell's own composition:

> Ah! What avails Sir William's sense,
> And what the cultured word,
> Against the undoctored incident
> That actually occurred.[1]

Lighthearted though it was, that slip of paper summed up one of the most difficult questions that Bowman and Campbell were confronting: the gulf between what McMahon believed had happened and what the documentary record could establish.

Sometimes the gap was insignificant, and stemmed from the way words were used. On an early draft that described the hardships of McMahon's service in the militia in the 1920s, for example, Bowman could be cutting: 'This must surely have been the school cadets.'[2] At other times, Bowman had to reason with McMahon. When they discussed the colours controversy, which McMahon wanted to cover in-depth, McMahon told Bowman that the Queen and Duke of Edinburgh had been present for the RAAF presentation at Point Cook. 'I explained as gently as possible that the ceremony was in September 1952 and they weren't in Australia,' Bowman wrote in his diary that night. 'He kept on and eventually trailed off into incoherencies.'[3]

At other times, McMahon could be as adamant and implacable as

Bowman had ever seen. While trying to straighten out the chronology of McMahon's 1952 visit to Korea and Japan, he came up against a wall. McMahon insisted that he had been in Korea at Christmas. Bowman checked McMahon's passport. It was stamped with a 14 December return to Australia. This did not convince McMahon that he was mistaken: 'He was *certain*.'[4] McMahon suggested Bowman call Sir Thomas Daly, who had been serving in Korea during McMahon's visit. Daly backed the ghostwriter. 'He says he has a distinct memory of that Christmas and you were not there,' Bowman wrote to McMahon. 'He recalls your carrying a message from the Army Minister, Jos Francis, for delivery to the troops. However, the men were widely scattered and only a few could be brought together.'[5]

When he received the note, McMahon came to Bowman's office. He denied carrying a message from Francis, and said he would call Daly himself. McMahon cited the *Parliamentary Handbook*, said he was in Japan and Korea from November to December, and 'that should be good enough'.

Angered, frustrated, Bowman threw McMahon's passport onto the desk. 'Then what do I do—burn this?'

McMahon's eyes widened, and he glared at his ghostwriter. He brandished the *Parliamentary Handbook* and asked the same question.

Bowman tried to point out that the *Handbook* was correct, that McMahon *had* been in Japan and Korea in November and December—but that it did *not* mean he was there at Christmas.

McMahon would not hear it. He left Bowman's office, arguing as he went, only to return a few minutes later: 'I don't want to pursue it further,' he announced.[6]

There were also claims that could not be backed up by documents. McMahon wrote that he had attempted to resign when the House of Representatives jailed the journalists Frank Browne and Raymond Fitzpatrick for offences under parliamentary privilege, in 1955. McMahon had objected to the whole affair on grounds that their criticism of the offended member, Charles Morgan, centred on actions taken before Morgan was elected. The Clerk of the House, McMahon said, had agreed with him, based on a common reading of Erskine May's *Parliamentary Practice*, the widely used authority on parliamentary procedure. When Menzies canvassed jailing the two journalists in a cabinet meeting, McMahon had stormed out, saying he would not go along with it. It was only when Eric Harrison confronted him in a lavatory and asked him to talk to Menzies that McMahon stayed his hand. At Menzies' request, McMahon withdrew the resignation. How could that be proven?[7]

At other points, McMahon seemed to wish to overblow minor matters, even if they had the potential to backfire. The Canberra bomber episode was one example that he intended to include in the book. In 1954, *The Sunday Telegraph* had quoted him suggesting that a new bomber would soon be a necessary addition to the RAAF fleet. Menzies had cabled him immediately: 'I can find no record of submission of any such proposals to Cabinet and would therefore be glad to have either your denial or your explanation.'[8] Touring the country, McMahon *had* said that the Canberra's limited capability meant Australia would need a new bomber: 'We need bigger and faster jet bombers like the Victor Vulcan and Valiant just going into production in England.'[9] Nonetheless, from Darwin, McMahon denied all. 'I have never criticised Canberra bomber in any form ... Statement alleged to have been made by me in one paper not made and I understand was subsequently withdrawn by paper,' he cabled Menzies.[10]

The prime minister was not to let him off the hook. 'That being so you should take steps to have denial issued in Sydney,' he cabled McMahon. 'Statement will have been received with glee by our opponents.'[11]

What could McMahon say, here? What new light could he shed on this?

Some points were tantalising. A story McMahon told of the origins of the Aged Persons Homes Bill struck Bowman as possessing some consequence. At McMahon's request, he called Billy Wentworth to hear more. What he heard surprised him. 'Wentworth seemed to confirm some of W.M.'s story about origins of Aged Persons Homes Act.'[12] Was it different from the explanation that Menzies had given? The prime minister had claimed the measure as his own—did McMahon's story conflict with that?[13] Or was it the same?

Exposed everyday in the process of writing the autobiography was an abyss: between what the documents could and could not establish; what the individual could recall, forget, and believe; between different ways of reading and understanding the past; between reality and perception; between truth and falsity. Bowman could hardly tell McMahon that his truthfulness, or lack of it, would harm the book: he needed to retain McMahon's trust and goodwill to get the job done. But, repeatedly, Bowman was asking himself the same question. What actually occurred?

CHAPTER FOURTEEN

Control

1956–1958

John McEwen was facing a dilemma. By the mid-1950s he could foresee that he would soon become leader of the Country Party. Arthur Fadden was ageing and unlikely to continue for much longer; when he retired, McEwen was sure to take over. But McEwen was aware that the realisation of this ambition would be accompanied by problems. With Fadden gone, the Liberal Party was sure to demand that one of its own become treasurer. Unless he was prepared to take the portfolio himself, and thereby surrender control of the areas that were his party's chief concern, McEwen had to find a way to counter the influence of a Treasury not controlled by the Country Party.

A possible solution came after the 1955 elections. Conscious of Australia's serious balance-of-trade problems, Menzies reshaped the landscape of government departments and established the Department of Trade, headed by McEwen, with a remit to get control of trade.[1] Consolidating all trade-related responsibilities, hiving off powers from the Department of Customs and Excise, McEwen's became the 'central policy department of a triumvirate' of departments 'that covered nearly all aspects of Australia's trade and her primary export industry'. Managed properly, McEwen saw, his new department could conceivably become a counter to Treasury.[2]

The responsibilities left over from the abolished Department of Commerce and Agriculture became those of the new Department of Primary Industry. They were a motley lot: stabilisation schemes for wheat, fruit, dairy, and sugar; administration of Commonwealth policy on wheat, dairy, fisheries, and whaling; administration of industry boards, research grants, and marketing efforts. 'All the chickens west of the Namoi,' went one popular sneer. It was a portfolio perfect for a Country Party MP—but this was not in the offing, as the government's success at the election had not extended to the Country Party. Numerically, it had emerged in a weaker position relative to the Liberal Party. The Country Party could not claim the Primary Industry portfolio for one of its own; therefore McEwen settled on the next best option. He urged McMahon's appointment.

It is likely that this peculiar choice stemmed, as Harold Cox argued later, from McEwen's regard for McMahon's work ethic and discipline.[3] But even if Cox's assertion was not true, McEwen's choice of McMahon is oddly understandable. McMahon was a city slicker, a 'Sydney tycoon,' Arthur Calwell had said.[4] His knowledge of the country was reputed to extend only so far as the turf at Randwick. He wore suede shoes. He called himself a balletomane. What would he know about wheat and dairy, about farming and fisheries? Either he would work assiduously and do well, with McEwen's guidance, or he would flounder and do nothing. Considered in this light, the choice makes sense.

McMahon's new portfolio was cause for amusement, particularly in light of the other incongruous appointments Menzies made. Labor MP Fred Daly was scathing. McMahon's only connection with the land, he said, 'is a couple of pot plants on the window sill, a watering can, and one chook; yet he has been made Minister for Primary Industry!'[5] Daly called it a matter of 'square pegs in round holes', but McMahon was sanguine. 'Don't worry,' he would joke. 'I have two plants on my front balcony and I know a little bit about it.'[6] Whether McEwen knew it or not, McMahon did have familiarity with the country and rural matters, through his family's extensive landholdings. He had also demonstrated to Menzies knowledge of food and wool production, and their links to Australia's economy.[7] Soft though his hands might be, he was hardly going to do nothing in the portfolio. Nor was he likely to turn down an appointment that held the allure of a position in cabinet, which had suddenly become much more prized.

In addition to a reshuffle and reshaping government departments, Menzies cleaved the ministry in two. There would now be only twelve positions in the cabinet; the remaining ministers were simply excluded from it. 'Ministers not in Cabinet will be invited to attend and to participate whenever matters affecting their own department are under Cabinet consideration,' Menzies decided. 'I will also have the right to invite to a Cabinet discussion any non-Cabinet Minister who has special knowledge or experience on the particular under consideration.'[8]

According to McMahon, membership of cabinet was a part of the deal he struck with McEwen: 'He persuaded me to accept the portfolio of Primary Industry on the understanding that he would ensure I would be a member of the new cabinet.'[9] McEwen's regard for him had led them to be friendly, supposedly to the point of playing billiards, going to the theatre, and dining together. 'I became a very firm friend of John McEwen,' McMahon later said. '… There was nothing we would not do if we could find amusement and, above all, if we could find opportunities we would talk together about the world's problems.'[10] It would have been an incongruous sight to behold: the gadabout and garrulous McMahon, small and balding but flashily attired, and the dour, large-framed, and strait-laced McEwen, whose sombre visage was enlivened only by occasionally wearing a maroon-coloured tie.[11]

Yet McEwen could not promise that McMahon would be one of the twelve. That was Menzies' decision to make, and throughout the first weeks of January the decision was being constantly revised. On 5 January, Fadden met McMahon in King's Hall and told him he was in the cabinet. This news seemed confirmed when Eric Harrison said the same as they walked to the Hotel Canberra in the company of Philip McBride and Athol Townley. By the next day, however, Harrison was saying that it all depended on the Country Party. McMahon went to McEwen, who implied that Harrison was scheming against him. This, too, seemed confirmed when Fadden and Hugh Roberton, a Country Party MP and soon McMahon's successor in social services, told McMahon on 9 January that the Country Party had nothing against him at all. But the next day, McEwen came to McMahon and told him that it was in fact Fadden who did not want him in the cabinet. The motivation, according to McEwen, was jealousy. The repeated references in the press to McMahon's expertise in economics seemed an attack on Fadden's competence, one that would be magnified if McMahon were a member of the cabinet.

Fadden denied it, but McMahon did not believe him. Suddenly, he was out of the cabinet and in a portfolio he had not wanted. At

Government House on 11 January, when the cabinet was being sworn in, Harold Holt told McMahon that the decision to exclude him had occurred sometime after 5 January. State representation, Holt suggested, was the issue on Menzies' mind at that point.[12]

On 25 January, McMahon went to Harrison to find out what had happened. Harrison told him he had been excluded from the cabinet for reasons that seemed to have little to do with McMahon personally. There was the need to represent all the states in the cabinet, Harrison said. There was McMahon's relationship with McEwen. They were too close, and McEwen was untrustworthy, Harrison informed McMahon. 'I would be "drummed" out of the Liberal Party if the association did not end,' McMahon wrote later.

McMahon was angry. He had been the dupe in the machinations of others, and the manner in which it had all happened was insulting. Even the phone call from Menzies telling him he would be moved had been abrupt, he complained. 'Your time will come—let bygones be bygones,' Harrison told McMahon.[13]

The advice might have been well intended, but Harrison was not the one being pasted. The appointment made McMahon a political punch line, and his exclusion from cabinet furthered the humiliation. McMahon was part of the 'second eleven', as the ALP called the excluded ministers, apparently not good enough to work at the highest level.[14] The press seemed sympathetic, noting the importance of agriculture to Australia's economy, and McMahon's training in economics. 'Could you imagine anything more ludicrous than a country which depends almost entirely on primary production having a cabinet which doesn't include the Minister for Primary Production?' asked Frank Browne, author of the muckraking newsletter, *Things I Hear*.[15] In light of these arguments, McMahon could be forgiven for feeling that his exclusion was unjustified; but it is quite likely that McMahon's behaviour was among the reasons for his exclusion.[16]

Within the cramped, crowded offices of Parliament House and in the small provincial pond that was Canberra, gossip travelled quickly and character assessments were easy. This was to McMahon's detriment. Though admired for his work ethic, he was widely regarded as a leaker and grandstander, his self-interest operating to the exclusion of modesty and loyalty. 'McMahon, until he learned better, was over-eager, talkative, and almost clamorous in reciting the virtues that he considered fitted him for ever higher office,' Alan Reid wrote later.[17] The press found him as wanting as the bureaucrats did. 'Harold Holt made an absolute fool of himself in Cabinet this morning,' McMahon told the journalist Hal Myers one afternoon, while still minister for social services. The pronouncement was so abrupt and unexpected that Myers stopped speaking so as to hear more. McMahon's voice was loud, excessively so—a by-product of his hearing difficulties—and Myers, even as he marvelled at the tirade, could not help but wonder how it might sound through the thin walls of the adjacent office where Holt himself worked.

McMahon went on and on, ending only after claiming that he should be prime minister after Menzies. 'To me the idea of Bill McMahon as Prime Minister was ludicrous,' wrote Myers. 'He had ability; his weakness was character.' That weakness was on frequent display: seeking to cultivate the journalist Angus McLachlan, McMahon promised to support anything the *Herald* might want in cabinet. McLachlan was outraged: 'How can you respect a man like that?' he asked.[18] Graham Perkin, a tyro journalist working as the number two to *The Age*'s Ian Fitchett, could recall McMahon giving him a story while standing next to him at a urinal, and the next day joining Menzies in criticising Perkin for running it. 'I hope you are ticking him off for that appalling piece of reporting,' McMahon said to the prime minister, in Perkin's presence. 'It was irresponsible, not the sort of thing you would expect of a reporter from *The Age*.'[19]

Fred Osborne, still smarting from the way he had been betrayed five years before, was similarly unimpressed. He found it difficult to have anything to do with McMahon, he said later, and though counselled to patch it up, Osborne simply could not do so. He could not get past his disapproval of McMahon's character, the flaws of which seemed to be constantly on display. He knew this was a political mistake on his part. McMahon was entrenched in the ministry by now, and his seniority among the Liberals from New South Wales was improving. 'I should have made my terms with him,' said Osborne later, 'but I didn't.' Counselled to do so by William Spooner, Osborne tried, but felt repulsed. It was no good, Osborne decided. 'I can't have anything to do with him at all,' he said. 'No good.'[20]

Whatever the initial tenor of the relationship between McMahon and McEwen, it was fraught within a few months. McMahon was not content to be idle in Primary Industry or to be a substitute for McEwen. His resolve to exercise his ministerial powers brought him into conflict with McEwen, who was stung by what he saw as McMahon's overstepping of responsibilities and his foray into an area sensitive to the Country Party.

The first of their arguments, according to McMahon, came when he authored a cabinet submission on the dairy industry and butter production: 'On that matter Sir John McEwen and I had our first real quarrel.'[21] During the meeting, McEwen called him out of the cabinet room. 'If you go on with this submission,' McEwen said, 'I will fucking murder you.'[22] McMahon immediately sought advice from Menzies. Speaking outside the cabinet room, he told the prime minister what McEwen had said. Menzies told him to persevere with the submission, but when it was not reached at the meeting, McMahon decided not to persist with it—'at that time', he noted.

It was only then, McMahon wrote later, that he became aware that restrictions and caveats had been placed on his power as a minister. At a meeting prior to his appointment, McMahon wrote later, Menzies, Fadden, McEwen, and Holt had agreed that he 'would not have the power of recommending policy decisions made by Mr McEwen. This decision was never conveyed to me whilst I was Minister for Primary Industry.'[23] Was this true? Perhaps. Certainly, there was little clarity over how far McMahon's remit ran.

In April, McEwen and McMahon argued in King's Hall over the handling of a Fisheries Bill and a Dorothy Dixer on the likelihood of a stabilisation scheme for the dried vine fruits industry.[24] Tensions over the question of responsibilities were palpable. McMahon claimed later that in the confrontation in King's Hall McEwen said that if he was not allowed to have his way, he would do McMahon in. McMahon brokered a peace by getting McEwen to agree to have their respective permanent heads meet to sort out who had jurisdiction. But the tensions were still evident, even in the House a month later. 'I should like an assurance from the Minister for Primary Industry that he will put this on his plate or on the plate of the Minister for Trade, who has been handling this Bill,' said Hugh Leslie, a Country Party MP, during debate on the Fishing Industry Bill. McMahon moved to assert himself on this matter immediately: 'The administration of this Bill will be within the jurisdiction of the Department of Primary Industry.'[25]

Saying so was easier than doing it. The hazy lines of responsibility between Trade and Primary Industry, and the overlaps of their interest in policy, called for a close working relationship between McMahon and McEwen, which simply did not exist. McMahon wanted power for himself; McEwen was reluctant to allow him to exercise power in an area that had so long been his own.

The stabilisation plans that McEwen had worked on while minister for commerce and agriculture were a case in point. They ensured that producers of wheat, dairy, meat, and fruit remained viable and received equal recompense for their goods, whether sold abroad or on the domestic market. Despite the 'lot of torment' involved, McEwen believed they were among his 'more substantial achievements'.[26] Many of them involved Commonwealth guarantees, subsidies, and bounties intended to promote stability and greater economic efficiency; though these had been earmarked for progressive reduction, little had been done to enforce those reductions.

As the minister now responsible for these agreements—many of which were to expire in the next three years—McMahon was in a position to begin forcing reductions, or, at the very least, resisting requests to increase the generosity of the agreements. In June, McMahon took to cabinet the Dairy Industry Committee's request for a £100 increase in the owner-operator allowance for dairy producers, but recommended it be rejected out of hand. 'A favourable decision would immediately bring similar requests which would be hard to resist from other industries … This would further produce increased pressure on costs of living and add further to the inflationary pressures against which Government policy is being directed.'[27] At the same meeting, he recommended that the government begin reducing the bounty paid under the agreement.[28] McMahon had chosen his moment well. McEwen was in London, accompanying Menzies at the Conference of Commonwealth Prime Ministers. Without McEwen there, cabinet approved both recommendations.[29]

MENZIES was in North America when one of the great crises of the 1950s erupted: the nationalisation of the Suez Canal by president Nasser of Egypt. Motivated by the need for funds to complete construction of its High Dam at Aswan, aware of the anti-British sentiment that was leaching into the government, and mindful that British troops had just been withdrawn from the canal zone, Nasser saw an irresistible opportunity. Control of the canal could be taken from the remaining British civilian contractors, and the ensuing revenue from the canal's use could be diverted to ensure construction of the dam.

Planning of the operation was meticulous and the execution flawless: Egyptian officers were given sealed instructions that could only be opened when Nasser gave the code word. When he uttered the name of the canal's French designer, Ferdinand de Lesseps, thirteen times in a widely broadcast speech delivered in Alexandria on 26 July, his officers opened the envelopes and followed the orders they contained. Troops occupied the controlling offices for the canal. Martial law was declared in the canal zone. The company that operated the canal was dissolved and a new one, run by the Egyptian government, established in its place. The speed of Nasser's action stung the British and French governments, both of which regarded the nationalisation as the illegal seizure of a strategic and geopolitical resource.

Menzies received a cable from the British prime minister, Sir Anthony Eden: 'We cannot allow Nasser to get away with this act of appropriation.'[30] While claiming it was a last resort, taking the canal back by force was clearly on Eden's mind. Within forty-eight hours of Nasser's announcement, more than 20,000 British reservists had been called up, and British troops were being massed in Libya, along the Egyptian border. A joint communiqué from Britain, France, and the United States called for a conference to discuss the 'international management of the Canal'. Menzies decided he would be there for it.

The cabinet, with Fadden as acting prime minister, gathered in Canberra on Tuesday 7 August to discuss the crisis. McMahon was there. Many of his colleagues arrived angry and knowing little more than what they had read in the press. At the meeting, they were given copies of cables that revealed the situation to be more perilous than had been disclosed to the public. Belying their public show of diplomacy, the British seemed intent on using military force to retake control of the canal; the Americans were willing to apply political pressure to the Egyptians, but would not be involved in any military action; and, from the cables read by cabinet, Menzies seemed willing to countenance Australian involvement in military operations.[31]

The minister for external affairs, Richard Casey, presented a position paper that outlined Australia's limited options and, indeed, its limited involvement. No Australians held shares in the nationalised company. No Australian oil imports came through the canal. The canal's significance to Australia's commercial interests was 'important' but not 'vital'. Casey was not in favour of a British resort to military force, and his two years as the UK's minister of state in the Middle East had left him sceptical about British imperialism and its attitudes towards former colonies. He was critical of the nationalism and the fervour with which Eden had responded to the crisis. Publicly, Australia had to stand with the British, Casey said, but privately matters were different. 'Eden has to be weaned away from [the] threat of force,' he told the meeting.[32]

Casey's argument attracted only two supporters, no more: Philip McBride, the defence minister, and McMahon. McMahon was scathing about how things had unfolded and the current direction of events. He suggested that Menzies was 'out of place' in attending the conference, which had been called at a foreign minister level. 'Casey should go,' McMahon said.

He strongly supported Casey's position. The British could 'huff and puff', he said, but world opinion was against them, and even the assistance of the Americans would not help in the long run: the British would be back out again in a few months. 'We can't help militarily,' McMahon said. 'We must moderate the British attitude. Casey should do it.'

In response to the bellicose jingoism of his colleagues, McMahon was realistic. The US line was correct, he argued. 'Nasser won't agree to [an] international convention—he has just nationalised [the canal]'. The Suez Canal, McMahon went on, was too valuable to Australian trade to have it disrupted. He recommended Australia 'not get into any camp'.[33] McMahon's was a perceptive assessment, one that belied his inexperience with matters of foreign affairs. Much later, he claimed that it sprang, in some part, from his belief that Egypt had a right to control the canal: 'I couldn't understand how anyone could protest about Egypt taking over the Suez Canal,' he said later. 'The proper thing to do was to fit in with it, and see that you got a good deal from the Egyptian Government.'[34]

But his colleagues did not agree with this. Nor did they heed his assessment of the consequences. Like the public at the time, they were emotional, invested in the symbolic significance of the canal. 'Our reaction was predictably an angry one,' recalled Howard Beale, the minister for supply.[35] Informed by memories and tales of Egypt during World War II, their reactions were to support Britain come hell or high water. McMahon's arguments and opposition were discounted, not even rating a mention. Menzies received word of the cabinet's support for Britain while he was in London, where he was preparing for the opening of the conference on 16 August.

The conference and its somewhat arbitrary list of invitees resolved on a series of proposals devised by the US secretary of state, John Foster Dulles. In the main, they consisted of the establishment of an international board (on which Egypt was to have representation) to manage the canal, recognition of Egyptian sovereignty, a commission that would sort out issues of compensation, and enshrining interference with the canal as a violation of the UN Charter.

On 22 August, Menzies cabled his colleagues in Australia, telling them that he had been asked to join a committee that would present these proposals to Nasser. Then, joining the committee turned into leading it. Upon the receipt of cables from Dulles and Eden asking that Menzies be spared to 'give his personal help' to lead the meetings with Nasser,[36] an ad hoc committee meeting of the cabinet in Sydney on 27 August approved the requests. According to Menzies, his colleagues were 'delighted' by the request, regarding it as 'a compliment to Australia'.[37] Later, McMahon would claim otherwise: 'Unfortunately, Menzies happened to be in the wrong place at the wrong time,' he said.[38] The opposition leaked: papers like *The Argus* reported unrest in the cabinet over Menzies' 'intrusion' into a field better left to Casey.[39]

Menzies' talks with Nasser were a failure, foundering on a mutual inability to compromise or recognise the validity of the other's argument. They broke down completely when US president Dwight Eisenhower, with presidential elections scheduled for early November, scotched any prospect of the use of force against the Egyptians, which Menzies had suggested to Nasser might still have been in the offing. The prime minister left Nasser and returned to Australia, via Washington, on 18 September after sixteen weeks abroad—returning to the 'rather battered home front,' as he put it, of domestic affairs.[40]

Eight days later, there was a ballot for the deputy leadership of the Liberal Party. Eric Harrison, occupier of that position since 1945, had been angling to go to London for almost a year as Australia's high commissioner. On returning to Australia, Menzies finally signed the required papers. Four candidates stood for the vacancy on 26 September: Richard Casey, Philip McBride, Harold Holt, and senator William Spooner of New South Wales. Casey's elimination in the first ballot surprised some; Spooner's unexpectedly strong showing surprised others. Nonetheless, Holt, then aged forty-eight, was the victor and new deputy leader.

Harrison's departure, and the appointment of the attorney-general, senator John Spicer, to the newly formed Commonwealth Industrial Court, opened up two vacancies in cabinet. One of them, finally, went to McMahon.

McEWEN'S absence from Australia in June was followed by another in October. In that month, the minister for trade returned to Britain to re-negotiate the so-called Ottawa Agreement. Struck in 1932, the agreement set out the trading relationship between the United Kingdom and its autonomous dominions, including, at that time, Australia. In broad terms, Australian goods—mainly primary produce—received duty-free or fixed-rate entry to the UK market; in turn, British-manufactured goods that were exported to Australia received preference against those from other countries. Of great significance to Australian industry, the agreement also restricted the amount of protection that could be given, via tariffs, to Australian manufacturing that competed with those British imports.

Initially of benefit to Australia, the Ottawa Agreement was the target of sustained and growing criticism by 1956. The balance of trade had shifted in favour of Britain, which was pursuing what John Crawford, secretary of the Department of Trade, later called 'its traditional cheap food policy'.[41] Britain was using the abundant supply of meat, cheese, butter, and fruits from other countries to force prices down. Australian primary producers, unable to compete, were finding their share of the British market was shrinking. Not only did they therefore require alternative markets for their goods, but there was also a need to nurture and protect Australia's manufacturing sector, which McEwen regarded as vital to Australia's prosperity. Ottawa had to be retooled and revised, industry groups demanded: 'The time is long overdue for a complete review of Ottawa's outdated and now one way preferential provisions.'[42]

During McEwen's trip in June, the British had been intransigent. They had no desire to reopen Ottawa. 'For five weeks we tried to get useful talks started, but were told bluntly that our proposals left no scope for negotiation,' McEwen wrote later.[43] Only after McEwen delivered a blunt threat to abandon the agreement altogether did the British begin speaking seriously. The aim of McEwen's second trip was to finalise those discussions. He wanted a guarantee that Britain would take a quota of Australian wheat each year, and an agreement to reduce the tariff preference for British goods imported to Australia. 'The negotiations were very protracted,' McEwen commented, but eventually they succeeded. He and Crawford reached a deal. It was one of his biggest achievements, McEwen thought, one of the hardest earned and most valuable.[44] Importantly, it was the first step in a courageous process, pursued by McEwen, to open trade with Japan.

Both parties drafted a joint statement for the press, and arrangements were made for its simultaneous release in Australia and in Britain. On the evening of 12 November, though, prior to the agreed release date and time, the statement appeared:

> The Acting Minister for Trade (Mr William McMahon) announced today that the Australian and United Kingdom Governments had negotiated a new and comprehensive trade agreement which would replace the Ottawa Agreement of 1932.[45]

In the newspapers, the announcement was almost all in McMahon's name. 'Mr McMahon said two cardinal objectives sought by major Australian industry organisations had been achieved,' wrote *The Canberra Times*. 'Mr McMahon said the new agreement preserved the principle of mutual preference.' In much of the press coverage,

McEwen's role was downplayed, as though he had merely wielded the pen, as passive as the sentence itself:

> A detailed trade agreement based on these agreed principles will be drawn up early next year. They were initialed in London on November 9 by the Minister for Trade, Mr McEwen.[46]

McEwen was furious. The premature release had embarrassed him with the British Board of Trade, and the press reception was an insult to his considerable efforts negotiating the new agreement. Upon his return to Australia, he went to McMahon's office in the Commonwealth Bank Building in Sydney to demand an explanation. As McMahon recalled later: 'He was under very great emotional stress and accused me of "blacking him out" of the press on the UK–Australia Trade Agreement.'

According to McMahon, two officials from the Department of Trade had given him a copy of the press statement. His only role had been to suggest an alteration in the sequence of paragraphs in the statement, he said. He was not responsible for how the press interpreted or reported the news. Moreover, McMahon told McEwen that he had followed instructions: 'As the agreement between us was that I did what I was told by the officials I issued the document presented to me.' According to McMahon, McEwen accepted this explanation: the trade minister supposedly departed the office 'still in a rage', but saying it was 'not completely' McMahon's fault.[47]

Other accounts indicate that McEwen did not believe a word of it. 'A later investigation ordered by McEwen could find no record of the department having sighted the statement before it was issued,' wrote McEwen's biographer, years later. Moreover, it was the last occasion on which McMahon ever 'acted' for McEwen in any capacity.[48]

It was unwise to cross McEwen: he was a good hater. Though capable of sentimentality with those close to him, the tall Victorian was ruthless with opponents, prone to nursing grievances and exacting retribution. Evidence would suggest, however, that he did not view McMahon as worthy of the status of an opponent. He was a pest, yes—but an opponent? Informed that McMahon had dressed down one of his officials and declared him unfit for his job, McEwen was amused more than roused to anger. 'Well, you're in distinguished company,' he told the official.[49]

For his part, McMahon regarded this period as the formative phase of McEwen's dislike for him. This was the seed for their later feuds—and it all stemmed from McEwen's jealousy, anger, and pride. In McMahon's eyes, he had done nothing to earn this enmity. He was blameless in everything that went on. 'Continuous complaints were made to both Menzies and Holt about me,' McMahon wrote later. One complaint apparently occurred after McMahon had an eye operation:

> Menzies called me into his room and said that McEwen has complained that a great friend of his has informed McEwen that I had informed him that McEwen was suffering from cancer. Menzies suggested that I should go and see McEwen before Cabinet. I refused and said—'If that's the kind of friend he has and the kind he trusts I don't want to have anything to do with either of them. Anyway, why should I make explanations when I have never said anything like this at all.'[50]

The pettiness of the incident is palpable. The insecurity of the man who recorded it is evident. McMahon was sensitive to his status and his dignity as a minister. He would not respond to scuttlebutt. He wanted to exercise his power. It was McEwen who was causing problems, not him.

The conflict with McEwen was more than simply one of personality. The need to re-negotiate McEwen's industry stabilisation schemes saw them clash repeatedly, and exposed substantive, policy-based differences. These stemmed from 'the intention of Mr McEwen to exercise his influence on a Junior Minister in an area in which Mr McEwen's Country Party interests were involved,' McMahon wrote later.[51]

In January 1957, when McMahon mooted a five-year plan for the dairy industry, McEwen responded by referring to 'the issue of functional responsibility' between him and McMahon.[52] He perceived a 'real political consequence' in McMahon's recommendation that the Australian Dairy Industry Council's request for an increase in subsidies be rejected in the new plan; nonetheless, the request was rejected.

Three months later, the Dairy Industry Council had reviewed its case and McMahon took it to cabinet. 'In effect, [it] amounts to a request for substantially greater assistance than in earlier proposals,' he wrote. He noted why the industry wanted the subsidies to increase: the drought in northern New South Wales and Queensland meant dairy farmers there were doing it tough. But Victorian producers, he went on, had increased their production of butter to more than make up for it. And while the case could 'fairly be made out for additional assistance to some sectors of the butter industry', he wrote that 'it is quite impossible to devise a price stabilisation scheme which will give additional assistance to those sectors of the industry in need of it without giving the same assistance to others less in need of it'. Overall, McMahon's analysis was pessimistic.

The core problem, he wrote in his submission and reiterated in cabinet, was that there were areas of Australia ill-suited to butter production, and some producers' holdings were too small to allow for an economically efficient industry. 'The need is rather for greater efficiency and/or the retirement of some of the marginal producers ... If the government goes into a further five year scheme much on the same lines as the present one it will only serve to perpetuate the present state of the industry.'[53]

Cabinet approved his recommendation to reject an increase, but McMahon's wish to overhaul the industry went nowhere. The agreement he recommended to cabinet and presented to the House in May maintained much of the framework of the deal that McEwen had struck five years before. The subsidy for 1957–58 was maintained at the preceding year's level, £13.5m, and measures to address the problems of geography and weather were absent. The most notable and perhaps enduring of the features that McMahon introduced was to allow the Australian Dairy Produce Board to use stabilisation funds for research and 'sales promotion', in order to maintain and even expand the market for goods from the dairy industry—especially for butter producers, who faced competition from the increasing consumption of margarine.[54] Overall, however, the effects of his failure to overhaul the dairy industry would linger for another decade.

McMahon's work thereafter tended towards establishing and funding industry bodies that could increase efficiency and better promote the industries to the world. He was able to establish and fund the Australian Wool Testing Authority to assess and certify the quality of production;[55] he obtained renewed funding for the Wool Research Trust by proposing, and obtaining, a contribution from the industry itself to go along with the Commonwealth's pound.[56] Then he did the same for the wheat industry, establishing state-based committees to distribute research funds in order to draw on developments in soil fertility, field and crop rotation, wheat breeds, and mechanisation.[57] By 1958, after McMahon had negotiated a new stabilisation plan for the wheat industry, he had only to provide funding for a similar research body for the dairy industry, which he duly did in September.[58]

THE changes in the ministry that had begun with the departures of Harrison and Spicer continued during the remainder of the parliamentary term. Howard Beale left to become ambassador to the United States. Philip McBride and Arthur Fadden each announced they would not contest the next election. Both would retain their portfolios until then, but Fadden would resign the Country Party leadership in February 1958. There were replacements for each, but the most significant and notable was that of Sir Garfield Barwick, the lawyer widely lauded for his work on the 1945 Airlines Case, the suit against William Dobell, the bank-nationalisation case, and the Petrov Affair. His decision to stand for Beale's seat of Parramatta upended all ideas of seniority and hierarchy within the government—at least, according to the press. Frank Browne was particularly sweeping in his analysis of what it augured:

> For Harold Holt, it means no leadership. For the New South Wales cabinet aspirants it means no cabinet. All in all, to the Liberal federal politicians, the entry of Sir Garfield Barwick means exactly what the acquisition of a Derby winner means to the other stallions at a stud. Prosperity for the stud, but the first steps towards the boiling down for the other stallions.[59]

Labor made similar noises. When Barwick appeared in the House after winning the March by-election, Labor wit Jim Cope was heard calling across the chamber to Holt: 'Bad luck, Harold.'[60]

Not all such approaches were successful. Supposedly with Menzies' blessing, McMahon approached John Kerr during this period to see if he would be interested in seeking preselection for the Liberal Party for the Senate. Kerr thought little of the offer: he only wanted to be in the House.[61]

Throughout the year, the government seemed hardly troubled by the prospect of the pending election. It was happy with its record in office. Fadden's August budget—his last—contained few initiatives. It was all about maintaining growth and stability. 'We can point to a great estate, in good repair, amazingly developed, sensibly managed, respected and trusted all round the world,' Menzies said.[62] Yet unfinished business nagged. The Commonwealth Bank had still not been reorganised properly; a host of other Bills relating to banking were held up in the Senate. There were grounds for a double dissolution, but Menzies demurred. He would not allow any opportunity for Labor or its breakaway groups, such as the emerging Democratic Labor Party, to gain power in the Senate through the proportional voting system.

Nonetheless, the emergence of the DLP as a viable political force—fielding 113 candidates, all directing their second preferences to Liberal and Country Party candidates—cruelled any chance of the ALP winning office at the election, whenever it was called. The ructions from the split were persistent, and the divides too big to bridge. Even Evatt's offer to vacate the Labor leadership after the election, in exchange for those vital second-preference votes, could not do it. Senator George Cole, the putative leader of the DLP, wanted more: Labor had to abandon socialism, put an end to union unity tickets with communists, withhold recognition of Communist China, and end its opposition to the 'Industrial Groups' that Evatt so disliked.

All of these issues came up on 14 November, when one of the first televised election debates in Australia was held in the ATN Channel 7 studios in Sydney. Notwithstanding the criticisms of him, it was testament to his talents that McMahon took part. With him seated around a table beside Holt, opposite Evatt and Calwell, the debate was low-fi and adjudicated by Angus Maude, editor of *The Sydney Morning Herald*. None of the men was practised in television appearances, and their body language betrayed discomfort, wariness, and impatience. Evatt, recovering from a recent bout of pneumonia, was hunched over the table and made his arguments only to Maude, facing the editor's way so that he appeared, to the television viewer, in profile. Holt sat straight, visibly tapping a finger on his chair, glancing every so often at his wristwatch, which he had placed on the table in front of him. Calwell shelled the debate with coughs, folded his arms, massaged his knuckles, and spoke in an aggrieved rasp, usually to the floor.

Only McMahon seemed comfortable and confident.[63] His hearing aid disguised by the camera angle, McMahon spoke almost entirely to Calwell and Evatt as though trying to persuade them to his point of view. He tried forever to have the last word in any discussion, and was repeatedly cut off by Maude: 'No, I'm sorry Mr McMahon, no, I'm sorry, I can't accept another word on this.' McMahon constantly talked, protested, even called Maude's impartiality into question at one point: 'You said you'd give us a fair go!' His protests became boasts, of course: 'Can I speak here? Because if one person has taken a deep interest in financial and economic problems, I have.' Even Calwell found this humorous: 'So has Mr Holt.'

The debate was sedate until its end, when Maude brought up communism and its influence on the Labor Party. Evatt and Calwell bristled at suggestions they were soft, and McMahon overreached, declaring that the government would never recognise Communist China, as Evatt had promised.

Maude sensed the opportunity. 'You'll never recognise them?'

'Not until they've given up war as an instrument of policy. But if they give up war as an instrument of policy, then it'll be considered.'

'And how will you know they've done that?' Maude asked.

'... Well, I don't know,' McMahon bleeted feebly.[64]

The misstep hardly mattered. The 22 November election saw the government returned with the largest majority commanded by any since Federation; moreover, it had retrieved a majority in the Senate.[65]

Menzies drew up his new ministry quickly. The attorney-general, senator Neil O'Sullivan, resigned to open up further options. Allen Fairhall was dropped. Garfield Barwick became attorney-general. John Gorton, an obscure senator from Victoria who, until then, had been languishing on the backbenches, became minister for the navy. Men were shuffled along, moved around. The Old Guard that had so attracted the ire of the forty-niners was almost entirely gone.

With Fadden now retired, McEwen was leader of the Country Party. It was time to make his decision: Treasury or Trade? He doubled down and surprised many by taking the latter. 'This post was the one most central to Country Party interests and policies,' he wrote later.[66]

Officials within the Department of Trade were relieved. It was tomato sauce odds that if McEwen had left, McMahon would have replaced him—a prospect about which they were very circumspect. 'We in the Department had agreed to have a party once the new ministry was announced,' said Eric McClintock, a senior official within Trade at the time. 'We struck a deal with the people at Primary Industry. If we kept McEwen, and they [Primary Industry] got McMahon, we in Trade would pay for the drinks.'[67]

McMahon was angling for something bigger. He knew that Holt, as deputy leader of the Liberal Party, had the pick of portfolios, and he was aware that Holt held no particular interest in economics. In the face of Holt's vacillation, McMahon staked a claim for Treasury. He had a degree in economics. He had long been lauded as a 'financial backstop'. He was interested. Why not him?[68]

Few shared these opinions. Paul Hasluck, the minister for territories, thought the idea a non-starter:

> McMahon would certainly have had no hope of being Treasurer under Menzies for the simple reason that Menzies himself did not trust him and doubted whether McMahon had that high standard of incorruptibility that Menzies himself would set for the Treasury. Menzies said something of the sort to several of us at the time. 'You couldn't trust McMahon not to give away budget secrets if it suited him.'[69]

Menzies did not want him in Treasury, and McEwen did not want him in Primary Industry. *That* job was to go to a Country Party MP, which it duly did.

On 10 December, McMahon was sworn into his new portfolio: minister for labour and national service.

CHAPTER FIFTEEN

Perception

1984

Verification was a constant problem within the McMahon office. On a copy of an aide-mémoire that he had prepared in 1967, which addressed his difficulties with McEwen, McMahon had scrawled notes and added details, few of which could be substantiated. He claimed that he had been involved—along with McEwen and John Crawford—in the creation of the Department of Trade; and he claimed that his appointment as minister for labour and national service was made over the objections of McEwen and Crawford, who wanted him instead to be minister for supply.

His handwriting spidered across the pages, offering examples and asides to support his arguments and story. There was McEwen telephoning at two o'clock in the morning to complain about a cabinet submission on the stabilisation of the dried vine fruits industry; McEwen leading the charge against McMahon's attempts to reconstruct the butter industry in Western Australia; McEwen instructing Trade officials to withhold vital information from McMahon; and cabinet decisions made and undone against a background of threats and libellous accusations.[1]

McEwen was not the only person with whom McMahon recorded disagreements. Recalling the Suez Crisis, McMahon wrote that cabinet ministers had gathered in Sydney to discuss the British and American request for Menzies to lead negotiations with Nasser. Six ministers gathered, with Arthur Fadden supposedly chairing the meeting. Each minister had a telephone, and each minister told Menzies that the task was impossible and that the British and Americans were using him.[2]

Bowman checked other accounts and found differences. Menzies had said nothing like this in his memoir, *Afternoon Light*, he noted. According to that book, there were no telephone calls to Australia and no misgivings expressed. 'My colleagues were, as I now know, delighted,' Menzies had written. 'They regarded the appointment as a compliment to Australia, though they (and I) fully understood the immense risks, perhaps the certainty, of failure.'[3] Bowman did not point out that McMahon's account differed in another respect: Fadden had not been at the meeting, on the phone. He was in Brisbane, taking care of his son, who was grievously ill.

Bowman stapled his notes to the relevant page and delivered it to McMahon. 'Can these versions be reconciled?' he asked. 'Has Menzies got it wrong? Is he hiding something? I am looking for other sources, but perhaps you can settle the question immediately.'[4]

McMahon called him in to talk. After some discussion, the former prime minister told his ghost that it was a long time ago and perhaps did not matter much now.[5]

But other claims had been long repeated and *did* matter. One was McMahon's claim that Menzies had demanded he stand for the deputy leadership of the Liberal Party when Eric Harrison resigned.[6]

In the middle of the night, the story went, sometime after Menzies' return to Australia in September 1956, McMahon received a summons to the prime minister's office. He ran from his room at the Hotel Canberra with a raincoat thrown over his pyjamas, and arrived to find Menzies offering him a drink and the deputy leadership. Menzies intimated an opportunity to succeed him as prime minister, but McMahon refused the offer, concerned about his hearing problems.

'Well, that didn't stop Billy Hughes from becoming the leader of the party!' Menzies scoffed. The prime minister assured McMahon that he could do the job; moreover, Harrison would be able to get the New South Wales members on side and vote him in. He did not want Harold Holt to become deputy leader, Menzies continued, because he had not supported him in 1941, when Menzies had been forced to resign.

McMahon refused to go along with it. He cited his long friendship with Holt, with whom he frequently breakfasted at the Hotel Canberra and in whose company he regularly walked to and from Parliament House. He stressed the gravity of his hearing problems. To Menzies' consternation, McMahon said that it was neither practical for him nor loyal to Holt.

They argued, went back and forth, supposedly for two hours, until at last Menzies relented and McMahon departed.[7]

That, McMahon believed, was among the origins of his stormy relationship with Menzies. It was proof of his unwillingness to obey Menzies unquestioningly, to stay firm in what he believed and wanted, and it affected his standing in the party for *years*.

How to evaluate that story? How to verify it? How to write it, even?

All stories have dual landscapes. In one, there are the events of the real world; in the other, there is the perception of those events by the storyteller, the construction of their telling, the interpretation and meaning that is drawn from them. McMahon's work on his autobiography, and his work with his writers and researchers, made his perceptions clear. He was important from the beginning—why else would Menzies want him to be deputy? His judgement, plainly, was impressive from the beginning—there was proof of that in Suez. His ability was so great, too, that it demanded immediate recognition—why else the early promotions, the rapid rise, the attention of enemies? McMahon thought the setbacks and the antipathy of colleagues were the result of pettiness, malevolence, jealousy, and conspiracy. In his telling, *he* was the victim, the righteous one, throughout it all.

For McMahon, ensuring that people came to see him and the whole period of Liberal government as he did remained the constant goal; for Bowman, it was reconciling that goal with the events as they had occurred and how others saw them. Was it possible? Was there some middle ground?

CHAPTER SIXTEEN

War and Strife

1958–1964

McMahon had never forged particularly close relationships with the public service heads of his departments. He simply was not in his portfolios long enough to do so. But as minister for labour and national service between 1958 and 1966, McMahon's relationship with his permanent head would prove crucial to his biggest success and advancement in the Liberal Party.

Henry ('Harry') Bland had dominated the Department of Labour and National Service even before his appointment as its permanent head in 1952. Sydney-born but Melbourne-based, the tough former solicitor prized efficiency and possessed a marked intolerance for grandstanding. He could bash heads as readily as break bread; he had no compunctions about intervening in industrial disputes; he understood the labour scene, and was zealous about defending his department's role in it. Working with Harold Holt, McMahon's predecessor, had been productive and enjoyable for Bland; he later remarked that theirs was the 'apogee' of a relationship between a permanent head and a minister.

No such relationship formed with McMahon. Well-acquainted with the member for Lowe even before his appointment—the McMahon family stables were not far from where Bland lived in South Randwick as a boy; the two men had brushed in Sydney's legal scene in the 1930s; and Bland's father, Professor F.A. Bland, had lectured McMahon at university and, since 1951, as member for Warringah, was a colleague in the House—Bland knew enough to be wary from the outset. Time did not change his mind. Their relationship, he said, 'approached the nadir' of that between a permanent head and minister.[1]

Bland found his new minister difficult in almost every respect. He thought McMahon had 'absolutely no feel for industrial relations and he never understood them'. Moreover, McMahon told Bland's wife, Rosamund, that he was uninterested in industrial relations and did not intend to become interested. Why should he, McMahon said, when he had Bland?[2]

McMahon could always be counted on to read his papers: 'Probably no minister ever read cabinet papers so assiduously as he,' Bland conceded.[3] But he rarely seemed to evince a thorough understanding of them. They came back heavily underlined in all colours, like rainbows. Everything was critical, but nothing was absorbed. 'He used to be terrified of going to a meeting,' Bland said later. 'I'd spend a great deal of time briefing him, and no matter how far I went, he'd get his facts mixed up.'[4]

What most frustrated Bland, however, was McMahon's propensity for talking. The secretary preferred his minister to rely on him for information; McMahon favoured a wider harvest of knowledge. He was frequently in contact, via the phone, with business people and departmental officers, drawing on an array of views that could be at odds with his permanent head's. These contacts were not entirely new. Reginald Reed, the chairman of shipping company James Patrick & Co., recalled that he had first met McMahon a decade before:

> It was 1949 and I was picking up for a shift, and there were about 500 wharf labourers standing there, waiting for a job. And there was a young, good-looking fellow, well-dressed, standing in the middle. I thought, *God, he can't want a job down here.* When it was all over I introduced myself to him, and I found out that he was down there, making a study of industrial relations.[5]

By Reed's lights, this willingness to engage ensured that McMahon was well prepared for the position: 'When he became minister for labour, no one knew more about the waterfront than Bill.' One observer noticed at the time how this played out:

> McMahon is not disposed to accept Bland's advice as readily as Holt did. Furthermore, as McMahon resides in Sydney, Bland [based, as

the Department then was, in Melbourne] does not keep in such close contact with him except through McMahon's private secretary who is very close to Bland ... If McMahon wants to know anything about shipping he is disposed to ring [Joseph] Hewitt [chairman of the Australian Stevedoring Industry Authority] rather than Bland and this is causing some friction.[6]

His propensity for talking perhaps explains why McMahon seemed pathologically unable to keep a secret. 'There was probably never a more assiduous leaker of cabinet documents than Bill,' Bland commented.[7] He found it infuriating: loose talk impeded the work of the department and undermined relationships. Moreover, McMahon's stories were rarely accurate. 'He told you what he would have wished he'd said and done, and that varied even in the course of a day,' Bland said.

Bland's concern at these brazen, barely disguised indiscretions was hardly confined to him alone. In September 1959, Menzies caught McMahon leaking red-handed—and promptly put him over a barrel for it.

On 22 September, the South Australian Liberal Party MP Keith Wilson gave a speech on a government Bill that provided for a 7s. 6d. increase in the pension. A member of the social service committee, Wilson had a sustained interest in housing and pensions and, in the course of his speech, had referred to 'proposals recently placed before the government' to revise the means test. He referred to those proposals again and again, expressing a wish that they be considered closely.[8]

McMahon met Wilson the next afternoon. He had with him a copy of the cabinet submission prepared by the social services minister, Hugh Roberton, for the 1959–60 budget. That submission—which, among other measures, recommended a revised means test—had been only partly successful when it had been considered in July. The proposed revision of the means test had been deferred so that a report by government members of the social service committee could be considered.[9]

Word of McMahon's meeting with Wilson reached Menzies. He summoned McMahon to his office. What ensued was an interrogation, one that resulted in Menzies ordering a stenographer into his office. The prime minister recapped the conversation aloud, and the stenographer took it down and then typed it. Menzies handed the piece of paper to

McMahon and told him to check it. McMahon corrected the document in pencil. His changes related only to his intentions when meeting with Wilson. He left the rest of the document untouched:

> I [Menzies] said, 'Did you tell Mr Wilson the substance of the proposal made by Mr Roberton to Cabinet?'
>
> He [McMahon] said, 'Yes, because I thought it important to show Mr Wilson that such proposals were not new.'
>
> I said, 'That means that in substance you have conveyed to a private member the nature of a proposal made in Cabinet Room by a Minister, and have indicated that it was rejected by Cabinet.'
>
> He said, 'Yes.'
>
> I said, 'How long have you been a Minister?'
>
> He said, 'Eight years.'
>
> I said, 'This is an outrage. I will consider the position.'[10]

'I showed this note to W. McMahon who altered it as above!' Menzies scrawled on the bottom. The prime minister initialled the page, placed it in an envelope, sealed it, and dated it. 'Note of *private* conversation between P.M. & W. McMahon', he wrote on the front.

According to many, that note was Menzies' insurance: should he ever catch McMahon leaking again, the confession could be used to dismiss him from office. It was kept in a safe throughout the remainder of Menzies' time as prime minister, always available for use, its existence widely known.[11]

The question inevitably arose, however, why Menzies never used the letter. He certainly had no love or liking for McMahon, who regularly sat opposite him in cabinet.[12] In private, Menzies referred to McMahon as 'that little bastard' or 'Little Willie', and would mutter that he did not trust the little man.[13] But none of McMahon's failings, personal or political, was enough to warrant his dismissal. 'Perhaps I should have done something,' Menzies lamented later—but he never did.[14] Was he, as some suggested, susceptible to flattery? According to Dudley Erwin, McMahon would approach Menzies and praise his speeches: 'And you would hear this great man [Menzies] purring like a pussycat.'[15] Whatever the veracity of this explanation, it is undeniable that Menzies' failure to remove McMahon would forever perplex his colleagues.

For those in cabinet and the ministry, there was little liking for McMahon. Senator Shane Paltridge, the minister for civil aviation, disliked McMahon intensely. Paul Hasluck, who had initially thought of McMahon as a 'rather funny little man', regarded him with a contempt that only ever grew.[16] McEwen would frequently clash with McMahon, and he detested his inability to keep secrets.[17] 'Oh, Jack was in a foul mood in Cabinet tonight,' McMahon would say.[18] Country Party MP Doug Anthony, elected in 1957, initially respected McMahon for his position and seniority, but soon saw that McEwen 'had complete disregard and distrust of McMahon'.[19] Alexander Downer, who entered cabinet in 1958 and sat next to McMahon, admired his work ethic, but thought he lacked Holt's 'humanity' and could be irritating. McMahon spoke too much, on too many subjects, pontificating when he should have been quiet. 'Occasionally,' Downer wrote, 'he erupted into fits of temperament, gathering up his papers and leaving the room with merely a nod to the Prime Minister.'[20]

Garfield Barwick's dislike was sharp. He believed that McMahon had undermined him, had bet on him to lose his seat, and was a compulsive leaker of information. 'He couldn't keep a secret,' Barwick said. All sorts of measures had to be taken to counteract this, Barwick recalled. A cabinet discussion on commuting a death sentence had to be conducted late at night, without an advance submission, in order to prevent McMahon leaking it beforehand. 'So I brought the paper in,' Barwick said. 'The item came on somewhere about quarter to nine … And we finished somewhere about 11.00pm. *The Sydney Morning Herald* had it before midnight.'[21] Also of annoyance was McMahon's propensity to re-explain matters and his attempts to be friendly. When McMahon told Barwick not to be annoyed, that he was only trying 'as a brother lawyer' to be helpful by re-explaining something, Barwick was acerbic: 'Not so much of this "brother lawyer" please. There is a hierarchy in the law, you know.'[22]

Others, from further away, had a slightly different view. His 'party days' friend, Richard Kirby, now knighted and president of the Conciliation and Arbitration Commission, had watched McMahon's advancement with a recognition that there were qualities in the man—persistence, a readiness to fight, discipline, and a capacity for hard work—that others might not see:

People used to say 'Billy's far too well-dressed to be able to pass his exams'. When he did, they said, 'Billy will never get into politics—his manners are too good'; and later, they said, 'Billy will stay on the backbench. He's too much a dilettante ever to make the ministry.' Billy was a magnificent fighter—literally. He could box like a thrashing machine and he was game as hell. But people seemed to overlook that.[23]

McMahon was not unaware of the dislike that he attracted. 'In the early years, for nearly ten years, I think I felt a fair degree of antipathy or hostility,' he said later. But he attributed it to his propensity for work and preparation: 'I was a hard worker and I usually went into cabinet fully briefed about whatever paper was to be discussed and a lot of people didn't like it.'[24] The inability to recognise how and why people disliked him was a conspicuous failing, one that would become as pronounced as his need to secure acknowledgement of his merits and talents.

McMahon's new job required him to be game. It was important politically and economically. Industrial relations had been prominent in the government's agenda in the past decade. Its efforts to contain inflation and combat communism had been frequently directed towards the trade union movement, which the government believed had been infiltrated by communists intent on disrupting productivity and industrial peace by inciting strikes and unrest. Tension was particularly evident in the stevedoring industry, which had replaced coalmining as a hotbed of industrial disputes. Clashes with the Waterside Workers' Federation of Australia (WWF) had been perennial for Harold Holt and would be also for McMahon. The union was militant. Its general secretary, Jim Healy, was a communist. Combined with the ineptitude of some employers, the union's intransigence had helped to make Australia's shipping industry one of the most inefficient in the world.

Yet in the first decade of the Menzies government, Holt and Bland established a way of handling disputes. They had built up the Australian Council of Trade Unions (ACTU) as a key point of contact with the union movement, regularly consulting and pampering its president, Albert Monk, in a deliberate ploy to moderate union demands. They had worked in concert with the Conciliation and Arbitration Commission, which mediated negotiations or sat in judgement as an independent third party with powers to set awards, working conditions, and man-hours. They had used the pulpit afforded by Parliament and the information provided by the department and ASIO to pressure, influence, and intervene in the labour market. Importantly, Bland and Holt tried to be fair: they were as willing to 'clout' employers as they were to go after the unions in pursuit of what Bland defined as a 'test of public interest'.[25] They were an effective team, and their example showed that flexibility, toughness, and a capacity for negotiation were prerequisites for success in the labour field.

Ostensibly, McMahon was no different. His overriding concern was ensuring that industrial unrest was kept to a minimum. Holt had managed to keep the days lost to disputes low, so McMahon needed to maintain those low levels, if not do better, to be successful. Yet his willingness to trust his relationships with shipping representatives left him largely unsympathetic to the concerns and demands of unions, most of which he believed were controlled or influenced by communists. He often attacked any unrest as the work of communists.[26] Combined with his propensity to leak, this black-and-white view of the world caused Bland to keep McMahon in the dark about the relationship with Monk and, indeed, some of the policy aims that Bland was working toward. But the hurdles and difficulties would come thick and fast.

Amid a surplus of labour and the growing mechanisation of waterfront work in the late 1950s, the WWF began lobbying for the introduction of pensions and long-service leave for its members. After the Tasmanian state government decided to offer the latter in 1960, Bland saw an opportunity to deal with unpalatable problems.[27] He pressed for the Commonwealth to introduce its own less-generous scheme and, simultaneously, to extract a 'disciplinary *quid pro quo*' from the wharfies, as one historian later put it.[28] The stick to Bland's carrot of long-service leave was three-branched: first, the accrual of long-service leave would be suspended for up to a month for each day lost to port stoppages. Second, attendance payments—money paid to wharf workers for coming to work—could be automatically suspended for four days by the Australian Stevedoring Industry Authority (ASIA) should a sizeable stoppage occur in a port. Third, workers aged seventy and over would be automatically transferred to an 'irregulars' register, and workers over sixty-five would be offered the same opportunity, with the inducement that those workers could immediately access that accrued long-service leave.

McMahon received this proposal early in 1961. His response was guarded, cautious. He was unsure that public opinion would swing in behind the government, and he worried about the political implications of such a move when another election was imminent. Bland had to persuade McMahon and then assuage him again, buck him up and assure him of the pervasive problems and the ways that the new measures would address them. 'By legislating for long service leave you are in effect coating the real pill which is provisions to secure improved performance and better discipline,' Bland wrote to McMahon, early in March.[29] A fortnight later, he was writing again, this time rather tiredly, to outline his measures once more: 'The issues are very simple.' Increased indiscipline could not be addressed with the available remedies, he wrote. The ageing workforce was inefficient and could not be gotten rid of without inducements of the kind that the measures would provide. In the absence of action, long-service leave was inevitable—but inaction would ensure it came without *any* benefit to the government.[30] The argument eventually convinced McMahon. He came on board.

Other ministers also responded cautiously when the proposals were circulated before their submission to cabinet. The timing was bad and the measures seemed provocative. Holt disapproved; McEwen had reservations. But Bland pushed McMahon to override them. He pointed out the political benefits that the measures could bring: a chance to campaign on communism would be lost if the government delayed. McMahon vacillated, hesitated, and then managed to bring Holt and McEwen around. The submission was placed on the cabinet agenda, and was accepted on 19 April 1961, with a remit to get the measures on the statute book quickly.[31]

The WWF was stunned. It received news of the measures on the same day that it met employers to discuss the prospect of pensions. It quickly realised the outrageous hand it had been dealt. Its workforce would be winnowed; access to more generous, state-based long-service schemes would be blocked; the sanctions and penalties would dissuade protest actions. There were no bright spots.

McMahon introduced the legislation in the House on 10 May. He noted that in the time since he had taken on Labour and National Service the man-hours lost to strikes and stoppages had risen, from 345,000 in 1958–59 to 806,000 in 1959–60. His cause established, he blamed the most draconian measures on the WWF: 'It is they who must carry the responsibility for what is proposed.' Everything that was happening on the waterfront was the responsibility of its leaders: 'In truth, the leaders of the Waterside Workers Federation have been engaged in a prostitution of the very purposes of trade unionism.'[32]

Labor was outraged by the measures as much as it was by McMahon's handling of the Bill. The lack of warning, the failure to provide timely copies, and the abbreviated debate that McMahon enforced by use of the guillotine angered them greatly. Arthur Calwell—now leader of the opposition, after Evatt's ignominious appointment as chief justice of the Supreme Court of New South Wales—registered strong protests, but found it hard to avoid the decided notes of chaos.[33] He was wedged: unwilling to embrace the communist-tainted WWF, as some members of his own side wished, yet clearly wishing to protest the drastic action. He was not helped by a WWF strike, held in defiance of the ACTU. Between the unrest on the waterfront and the Coalition's freewheeling use of the communist brush, typified by Liberal MP Jim Killen's declaration that Jim Healy had 'the interests of Moscow at heart', the Bill seemed to work out entirely in the government's favour.[34] The only salve for the ALP was that it could needle McMahon for his reliance on Bland for information about the measures.

Nonetheless, McMahon won plaudits for the action, and the political dividends flowed throughout the year. A three-part series on thuggery and violence on the waterfront, written by Alan Reid for *The Bulletin*, reinforced the perception that Bland, McMahon, and the government had done so much to create.[35] Jim Healy's unexpected death in July and the subsequent election of an ALP-aligned successor, in Charlie Fitzgibbon, ensured that the WWF's ability to campaign against the new Stevedoring Act was limited. By August, almost half of the 1,844-strong workforce had taken the long-service leave benefits and transferred to the 'irregulars' register, improving efficiency. McMahon was triumphant.[36]

The efforts needed to convince McMahon to take on the WWF were dwarfed by those required to convince him to support the removal of the 'marriage bar', which forced women who married to resign as permanent officers of government workforces. In November 1959, a Menzies-appointed committee studying public service recruitment formally recommended that the bar be removed. In its reasoning, the committee cited international disapproval, the outdated nature of the bar—the UK, from whom Australia had inherited the bar, had removed it in 1946—and the discrimination against women.[37] But action was deferred until an inter-departmental committee could report on the consequences of the removal of the bar. It took until August 1961 for that committee to report back. When it did, Bland pressed McMahon to support its recommendation that the bar be consigned to the past. 'I hope ... you will support this. It is entirely right in principle,' he wrote. Removal of the bar, he went on, conceivably had a 'political value' that could be used as a trade-off for equal pay.[38] This was not enough for McMahon, and when the submission went to cabinet on 24 October he voiced no support. As the resulting cabinet decision noted, the recommendation was considered 'as a social question' only. According to the secretary of the prime minister's department, John Bunting, cabinet took the view that:

[I]t was against public policy to facilitate the employment of married women, and thus perhaps worsening a situation in which already there was too [much] neglect of children in favour of paid employment.[39]

The result, as well as McMahon's refusal to offer support, frustrated Bland immensely—but did not cause the permanent head to abandon his own views.

Throughout the year, McMahon wrote to Menzies—supposedly on the prime minister's invitation—with thoughts on the economy and the political landscape. He drew on departmental figures on employment and industry to fortify his analyses, and by mid-1961 they were leaving him equivocal. The government was short odds to win the election, yes, McMahon wrote, but there were problems. In its attempts to discipline the overly buoyant economy the year before, in 1960, the government had been forced to offer strong medicine, in three doses. The third had been conspicuous and severe: in order to mop up excess demand, reduce monetary liquidity, and reduce the high rate of imports, Harold Holt had introduced in November 1960 a package of measures collectively referred to as the 'credit squeeze'.

Earlier in 1961, as those measures bit, there had been murmurs of discontent. By June, McMahon was writing that criticism of the government was rife within the circles he moved, and spreading. He suggested that Menzies make a statement to restore confidence. A month later, he wrote to say that unemployment was growing and that school leavers would soon be entering the work force, affecting unemployment again. Industry was suffering, and business was growing ever more critical. 'What should we do?' McMahon asked. His answer, though, was *not much*. 'It is worrying, but not a cause for alarm. The theme [for the election] should be a sound and developing economy and we should certainly give up explaining away the past and rationalising about unemployment.'[40]

But it was unemployment, and the government's management of the economy, that turned out to be the biggest issue of the otherwise unremarkable election campaign. Replying to what he termed the government's 'stay put' budget in August, Labor leader Arthur Calwell outlined his own plans should Labor be elected: he promised to restore full employment within twelve months, and undertook to expand social services without increasing taxation. By November, he was making the government's economic performance the emblem of everything that was wrong with it:

> There was no valid reason for the credit squeeze which sent prosperous industries sliding down hill, and men and women cascading into the unemployment pool. That was a piece of high-handed economic bungling which only a reckless, power-hungry Government could conceive and carry out; and carry out against the warnings of the people, industry and the press.[41]

Calwell's mention of the press was hardly idle. At the behest of Warwick Fairfax, the soft-spoken chairman of John Fairfax & Sons, *The Sydney Morning Herald* was supporting the ALP's campaign with advice on economic policy and advertising, and by lending employees, including one Maxwell Newton,[42] as speechwriters. The munificence prompted Calwell to request an explanation as he was leaving the paper's Broadway offices. 'Well, it's a simple proposition,' Fairfax replied. 'If you were running a newspaper and you found that your classified advertisements had fallen drastically … you would want a change of government, wouldn't you?'[43]

Not the only explanation, it nonetheless had some force given the string of redundancies the paper had been forced to make earlier in the year. Fairfax and Menzies had long regarded each other with ambivalence if not outright hostility, with Menzies blaming the paper for his resignation in 1941. On the surface, the *Herald's* drift towards the ALP was circumspect and slow; realistically, given its material support, the paper's eventual advocacy for a Labor vote at the 1961 election was unsurprising.

Criticism from the *Herald* was countered by the support the government received from the Packer-owned *Daily Telegraph*. Sir Frank, as he had become known in the two years since his knighthood was awarded for his 'services to journalism', was an unabashed admirer of Menzies and profoundly disliked Calwell, who, as minister for information during World War II, had enforced censorship restrictions to the point of ordering seizure of newspapers. Importantly, Packer and McMahon were friends. They had become closely acquainted, thanks to the efforts of George Halliday, a surgeon with expertise in ears, noses, and throats who treated both for their various ailments. 'He succeeded in bringing his two patients together,' David McNicoll, one of Packer's favoured journalists, wrote later, 'and, in doing so, steered Packer to a political fixation about McMahon.'[44] The relationship was strengthened by their shared experiences at Abbotsholme, the connection of Allen Allen & Hemsley (which Packer kept on retainer), McMahon's investment in Sydney Newspapers Ltd, mutual acquaintances (notably, Jack Cassidy), and McMahon's defence, in October the previous year, of Packer's controversial attempt to buy publishing company Angus and Robertson, then chaired by McMahon's mentor and colleague, Sir Norman Cowper.[45]

Thus, in November, when Alan Reid bluntly informed Packer that he thought the government was going to lose, the press proprietor dispatched him immediately to Menzies with an order to repeat the warning and what Reid believed was the solution: a promise to restore full employment within six months.[46]

Menzies' subsequent promise that he 'would never rest content' until unemployment was eradicated was given splashy, prominent coverage in the *Telegraph*. Despite the absence of any kind of method or timetable, the words were enough for the front page and a subsequent editorial that Menzies had talked 'sense' on jobs while Labor played politics.[47]

In spite of the urgency of Reid's warning and the *Herald's* criticism, there was little awareness within the government that the election might be close. In mid-November, McMahon was writing to Menzies to tell him that he thought the government's prospects were improving and that 'another wonderful victory' was in the offing.[48]

It was nothing of the sort. The swing against the government on 9 December was emphatic. Fifteen seats were lost to the Labor Party. Fred Osborne, who had broken into the ministry in 1956 and since become minister for repatriation, was swept away, as were two other ministers. Alan Hulme, the minister for supply, and Dr Donald Cameron, minister for health, both lost their seats. Earle Page, a candidate despite lying unconscious in a hospital with cancer, was defeated: he died without knowing he had lost.

In Lowe, McMahon was staggered to find that he had to go to preferences to hold on to his seat.[49] For a few days, as the seat tallies showed the Coalition and the ALP neck and neck, a fresh election seemed possible.

It came down to Moreton—a Queensland seat held by Jim Killen. Initially written off as a Labor gain, Killen's slim chances revived in the drawn-out process of tallying postal votes and preference flows. But he was in need of help. McMahon claimed to have offered the decisive assistance, telephoning Killen to say that he would 'arrange for the best scrutineer in New South Wales to go to Queensland'.[50] It was a false claim. John Carrick, the New South Wales general secretary of the Liberal Party, had already moved. Bill Wakeling was already on his way to Brisbane to scrutinise the count. Decades of experience and practice came with him. His motto? 'There's no such thing as a valid Labor ballot.'[51]

The count in Moreton took two weeks, but the preferences shook out narrowly in Killen's favour. He was in, and the Menzies government was saved.

The close election was a shock, yet McMahon suggested later that it could have been worse. 'Had the election been held two weeks later we may have been beaten,' he told Packer journalist Dick Whitington. For McMahon, the result was an example of the importance of the press and powerful allies: 'One of the means by which the strong trend against us was slowed was the sustained support of *The Daily Telegraph*. I believe this to have been the decisive influence.'[52]

MANY things looked different on the other side of the election. The government had said during the campaign that the ALP's economic policies were a recipe for disaster; afterward, it co-opted those policies to stimulate the economy and demonstrate its sensitivity to public opinion. According to John Stone, the then-secretary to the Treasury, Sir Roland Wilson, was called down to Melbourne and told by Menzies that 'Treasury views would have to be "bent" for a time in a more populist direction.'[53] In cabinet, when McMahon realised what was happening, he protested the gall as much as the offence to Treasury orthodoxy. 'Sir, we can't keep on implementing Labor policies that we condemned at the elections,' he said. Menzies was cutting: 'If they were good enough for 50 per cent of the electorate, they should be good enough for you. Next item, please.'[54] The prime minister's authority saw these policies enacted, but there was resistance within the public service. 'We spent a lot of time during the next two years fending off a series of "bright ideas" emanating from McEwen's Department of Trade—on the whole successfully, but not wholly so,' said Stone later.[55] It resulted in a mini-budget in February 1962: unemployment benefits were increased, income tax was reduced, and sales taxes and import controls were lowered.

Menzies' position also looked different after the election. The close result prompted a recognition that the day would surely come when the Grand Old Man was no longer prime minister. Who would lead the Liberal Party then? With Holt's reputation damaged, some looked towards McEwen, whispering of his switching parties or merging them. McEwen later disavowed entertaining the idea at all: 'I am sure that if the Country Party were to disappear, if its members were to join the Liberals, then another Country Party would crop up almost the next week,' he said later.[56] Nonetheless, the shock result caused a low-burning tension and suspicion between the two parties.

The worth of the marriage bar also resurfaced. Liberal Party senators Ivy Wedgwood, Nancy Buttfield, and Annabelle Rankin, and Country Party senator Agnes Robertson pressed for its removal; in March 1962, amid a separate campaign for equal pay for women, Harry Bland saw an opening. Could removal of the bar be used as a trade-off to defeat the push for equal pay?[57] By May, Bland had succeeded in getting a submission prepared for cabinet. Again, however, McMahon was against the proposal. On a letter containing Bland's suggestion that he had come around on the marriage bar, McMahon was emphatic: 'No!'[58] Cabinet offered the same answer when it considered the matter again in August. There were too many objections to its introduction, McMahon told Bland afterward.[59] Unemployment was still high. The public service unions were against it. Bland was critical of his minister. On the removal of the marriage bar, he said later, there was 'no support' from McMahon.[60]

The changes that McMahon had made to the Stevedoring Industry Act also looked different after the election. Since the Bill had been passed, the WWF had been trying to draw McMahon's attention to what it saw as the manifestly unjust penalties that could now be levied on waterfront workers. The suspension of attendance payments lay at the heart of their objections. At Bland's urging, McMahon had turned a deaf ear to these efforts; now, with the government's political mortality on show, he became sufficiently concerned to begin listening.

For, after months of getting nowhere, the WWF had embarked on a public campaign against the Act. Throughout the early months of 1962, the union publicised its grievances in pamphlets and letters, at rallies, and on television. They told stories about workers showing up a few minutes late, being suspended and then penalised for up to five days' wages. They talked of arbitrarily applied penalties, unjust employers, and a government unwilling to listen.

By April, McMahon was concerned; by May, Bland shared that concern. After meetings with the new WWF general secretary, Charles Fitzgibbon, and Albert Monk of the ACTU, and liaising with employers, Bland understood the need for retreat. He counselled McMahon to do it artfully, to make it sound as though the changes rushed through the year before had always been subject to consultation.

The wording of the eventual cabinet decision echoed this approach.

At the end of a lengthy list of amendments adopted by cabinet was the crucial one: that 'the long service leave penalty in section 52A be removed'.[61] Bland and McMahon believed this was a substantial concession, yet the WWF continued to object. McMahon grew frustrated. He believed that the government had earned the public's admiration for how it had handled the waterfront, and was afraid that the dispute could spoil that. Telling Bland that the matter had gone on for far too long, he canvassed threatening to desist from the changes to long-service leave and demanded alternatives as well as further knowledge about strategy. Where, he wanted to know, was this all leading?[62]

The WWF was angry. It believed that the Stevedoring Industry Authority was biased against it, that waterside workers were more harshly dealt with than workers from other industries, that work opportunities were being squeezed by mechanisation, that employers were too quick to resort to expensive arbitration, and that they gained nothing from the constant demands for ever-greater efficiency. Its objections continued to the point that by the following year waterfront workers had been penalised more than £1m in attendance payments. Thanks to a provision that allowed those penalties to be levied against future earnings, workers were liable to pay them back. The sum was beyond repayment, to the point of meaninglessness, and its continued growth simply goaded the union movement to greater intransigence.[63] Its anger was exacerbated again when, in May 1963, a ruling from the Conciliation and Arbitration Commission excluded waterfront workers in Sydney and Melbourne from an increase in the hourly margin. They would receive the increase only when 'suitable assurances had been made about their future behaviour,' the commission decided.[64] It was a ruling made at the urging of the department, and it was an outrage too far. Waterfront workers throughout the country walked off the job.

McMahon's concern intensified. With Bland abroad, he convened a conference with the ACTU and WWF, and desperately looked for ways to pacify the waterfront without losing face. His department urged negotiation and compromise. Employers were resorting too quickly to sanctions, which 'should be used sparingly' and 'only as a last resort' after conciliation and arbitration had been exhausted, it noted.

Providing for additional conciliators, to step in before arbitration, was canvassed as an option.[65] The need to address concerns about pensions was observed. McMahon wrote to Halford Cook, the acting head of his department, to emphasise the importance of public opinion: 'We must watch the public relations angle *most carefully*. We just cannot afford to be called appeasers or gullible.' But there was more than a trace of fear and dread in his note: 'I don't want a repetition of the experience we had after the long service leave conference.'[66]

On 30 May, the WWF and ACTU accepted McMahon's proposal for a working party comprising representatives of the union movement, shipping owners, and the various regulatory bodies. Chaired by Cook, the working party would explore ways to restore peace to the waterfront.

The working party delivered an agreement at the end of July to suspend the attendance-payment sanctions and all debts incurred under the sanctions. While this amounted to a complete about-face by the government, McMahon quickly came around. The increased productivity and favourable press that resulted from peace on the waterfront was worth the retreat.[67] 'The long service leave has been a major achievement,' he said later. 'It has had a stabilising influence, particularly since we removed the penalties which were often used to justify stoppages and in any case were, for the older men, like a red rag to a bull.'[68] Along with the Conciliation and Arbitration Commission's decision to award another increase in the margin and extend an extra week's annual leave to wharfies, the lull in industrial hostilities was a welcome respite. By September, McMahon was writing to Menzies to say he was content and that the unrest had been dealt with:

> So far as matters in and around my own bailiwick are concerned the outlook has considerably improved and is now reminiscent of Primary Industry during 1958. By this I mean matters such as Margins; Public Service Salaries; Industrial Peace; the Waterfront and Employment—are all in a pretty good condition.[69]

A similar statement could be made about the government by 1963. The economy had recovered, and unemployment was falling. Holt's August budget had been warmly welcomed. A royal tour earlier in the year, to commemorate the fiftieth anniversary of the foundation of Canberra, had been capped by the Queen's decision to confer a knighthood on the prime minister, which he accepted in full regalia during a July trip to Britain. The public's hostility to the government had dissipated.

Moreover, the unity that Labor had forged in 1961 was dissolving. After the government's announcement that an American naval communications base would be built at North-West Cape in Western Australia, the Western Australian branch of the ALP called on the federal executive of the party to oppose the construction of any military base that could host nuclear weapons. That was a spur for a special federal conference, held in Canberra in March 1963, to clarify defence and external affairs policy. The conference culminated in a debate that was long and went late into the Thursday night. As they were not members of the federal conference, Labor leader Arthur Calwell and his deputy, Gough Whitlam, were excluded: they could only urge delegates to reject the proposal from Western Australia. Their arguments won the day, internally, but came at a bitter cost when a photographer snapped both men standing under a street lamp outside the Hotel Kingston, where they were awaiting the decision of the conference. The unflattering photographs subsequently accompanied a highly charged story that Alan Reid wrote for the Friday edition of *The Daily Telegraph*. Noting that thirty-six 'virtually unknown men' had decided the ALP's policy, Reid argued that Calwell and Whitlam had been 'publicly humiliated'. 'The conference,' he wrote, 'has demonstrated that it regards the federal parliamentary Labor leader, not as an alternative prime minister, a leader and an adviser, but as a lackey.'[70]

For the Coalition, it was a gift. Menzies made much of the thirty-six unelected 'outsiders' that he declared controlled Labor, and in doing so tarred the party for years to come. He made the most of the opportunity to divert attention from tensions within his own ranks—principally with McEwen.

Relations with McEwen had been fraught since the election, complicated by rumours about leadership and party supremacy. Moves to redistribute the electoral boundaries had been the first of it. McEwen lashed out at the initial proposal put forward by the minister for the interior, which would have seen the Country Party lose three seats. It was 'crazy' and 'cock-eyed', he declared, and made clear to Menzies that he would break the Coalition agreement to oppose the proposal should the prime minister give it the go-ahead.[71] As proposals went back and forth, the tensions aroused spread into other issues. In July 1962, the minister for air and minister assisting the treasurer, Leslie Bury, was forced to resign at McEwen's instigation after suggesting that the likely effects on Australia of British entry to the European Economic Community had been greatly exaggerated. Liberal MP C.R. 'Bert' Kelly was also criticising the government's tariff policy, embittering McEwen, and an old debate on whether three-way contests—where both Liberal and Country Party candidates competed against Labor—were damaging to the non-Labor cause broke out anew. When McMahon wrote to Menzies on 22 August 1963 in another of his missives, he noted that 'the appearance of unity is of major importance', but that not standing up to McEwen could also be damaging: 'If he keeps on getting his way he will remain insatiable.'[72] By September, as he wrote to assure Menzies that all was well in his bailiwick, he had to caution that success at an early election was contingent on McEwen's actions.[73]

In October, Menzies announced a snap House election, to be held on 30 November.[74] It was a year early, but he was motivated, Menzies suggested, by the need for a stable majority in the House during a time of potential crisis, most notably in Indonesia and Malaysia, to which Australia was now sending military aid. In his policy speech on 12 November, the first to a television audience, Menzies announced that he would amend the legislation governing redistributions to ensure that any surplus fraction of a quota would result in the award of another seat, and that there would be allowance made 'for some variation between compact metropolitan seats and very much larger rural areas', taking into account economic, social, and regional factors. It was a sop to the Country Party, but it eased the tensions.

More important than this, however, were the promises in education. Funding for schools was a state responsibility, Menzies had always held—yet, over the past term, successive influences had swayed the prime minister to liberalise his attitude. The sustained population growth since World War II and growth in retention rates for high school students were increasing pressure on the education system. The private school system, which did not receive government aid, made representations for help. As a result of negotiations between Menzies and the Catholic archbishop of Canberra-Goulburn, Eris O'Brien, the government introduced small measures that allowed it to gauge initial reactions. According to McMahon, it was the 1956 introduction of financial assistance to independent schools in the ACT that gave the government confidence to proceed further: this, he said later, was 'the real beginning and the critical breakthrough of aid to church and independent schools'.[75] The decisive, and most public, shift came in July 1962. New South Wales state authorities had declared that the toilet facilities at Goulburn's Our Lady of Mercy Preparatory School were inadequate and needed to be upgraded. Unable to afford to do so, Catholic schools in Goulburn opted to shut their doors and send their 2,200 students instead to the city's government schools, which could not cope. The protest drew national coverage, called attention to the lack of resources afforded to private schools, and to the outsized role that they played in the education system.

McMahon, along with colleagues John Cramer, Jock Pagan, and John Carrick, sought to persuade the party to adopt a policy of state aid nation-wide. The efforts were unsuccessful throughout the parliamentary term, until a cabinet meeting was held on 15 October 1963 to discuss the impending election. According to McMahon, he urged colleagues to support the idea. He found little response until Barwick observed that Menzies was soon to open a science block at Waverley Christian Brothers Secondary College in Sydney. A group of businessmen called the Industrial Fund had paid for the block, Barwick pointed out, and he wondered if the government could assist with similar projects elsewhere. This received wider support from colleagues; following it up, there was McMahon: 'All I say is make £5m available as scholarships for primary and secondary [school students],' he said.[76]

That is exactly what Menzies did. In his election policy speech, Menzies announced scholarships for secondary and technical school students, and yearly £5m grants for technical schools and to improve the teaching of science. All these, he noted, were available for government and non-government schools without distinction.

The beginning of state aid to non-government schools struck at a schism in Australia's culture that ran back to the days of Sir Henry Parkes. Politically, it was a masterstroke, one that delighted the DLP and Bob Santamaria.[77] The ALP had taken for granted the allegiance of Catholic voters; now the Coalition was openly bidding for that allegiance. Labor did not recognise the danger: though it also offered scholarships, Calwell was not prepared to provide direct aid to non-government schools.

The campaign was marked by two events, neither of which was to Labor's advantage: the death of Archbishop Mannix on 6 November, and the assassination of US president John F. Kennedy on 22 November. ALP federal secretary Cyril Wyndham was in no doubt about the effect. 'That's us, we're finished,' he thought when he heard news of the latter. 'No way, no way, can we win the election.'[78]

On polling day, the government was returned with a majority of twenty-two, including its Speaker. The uncertainty of 1961 vanished. In Lowe, a seven-point swing back to the Liberal Party saw McMahon return to his comfortable majority.[79]

INITIALLY, the National Service component of McMahon's portfolio did not occupy much of his time. But in 1963, concerned about the potential of conflict in Australia's immediate region, and conscious that full employment was dampening recruitment for the armed services, options to increase military manpower were openly canvassed in the defence committee of cabinet.[80] The army tried to resist any mention of conscription, objecting to the part-time nature of previous schemes and the inability to enforce an obligation for service outside Australia, but pressure for its reintroduction mounted nonetheless. Cabinet's concern at the gap between the army's targeted strength of 33,000 men and existing strength of 22,500 did not dissipate, especially as the visibility of Australian, British, and American involvement in South-East Asia continued.[81]

After the 1963 election, that involvement grew increasingly urgent. The United States was escalating its military presence in Vietnam to support the anti-communist government of South Vietnam against the threat posed by the communist North Vietnamese government of Ho Chi Minh. There was pressure from the US about military capability and requests for assistance; the new US president, Lyndon Johnson, spoke of his hope that 'some other flags' would soon appear alongside America's in South Vietnam.[82] The government's attitude hardened, prompted by concern among its backbenchers and criticism by the DLP. The Gulf of Tonkin incident in August 1964, persistent tensions with Indonesia over the newly-formed Malaysian Federation, and the detonation of China's first atomic bomb in October nudged matters further. Early in November 1964, the defence minister, senator Shane Paltridge, submitted to cabinet the army's grudging proposal for a selective national service scheme that could make up for a shortfall in voluntary recruitment. Paltridge, however, noted that responsibility for a national service scheme would be the responsibility of McMahon's Department of Labour and National Service—and that it was hostile to the idea, complaining of the political and administrative problems such a scheme would pose.[83]

Cabinet ignored the objections. It directed that a compulsory, selective national service scheme for the army be established immediately, to be legislated before the half-Senate election, pencilled in for the end of the year. To be composed of twenty-year-old males selected via ballot for two years' full-time service, with liability for overseas service 'as required' and three years' reserve service afterward, the aim of the scheme was to increase the army's strength to 33,000 by the end of 1966.[84]

It was a sudden, clumsy, and very public about-face. As late as 26 October, the minister for the army, the member for Barker, Dr Jim Forbes, had disavowed any intention of introducing conscription,[85] yet on 10 November Menzies had announced it, and the next day—ironically, Remembrance Day—McMahon was at the despatch box, presenting the legislation.[86]

The hurry was apparent. The poor preparation was obvious.[87] Questions about its scope, its exemptions, its reasons, and its injustices failed to receive satisfactory answers. Twenty-year-olds could not vote—yet they would be conscripted. There were suggestions that university students would be exempt, yet McMahon stated that students who 'failed to be diligent with their studies' could be forced to join.[88] Whether migrants would be subject to the call-up caused confusion even between McMahon and Menzies. 'We were at cross-purposes here,' the prime minister admitted in the House.[89]

The ALP's response was immediate. Calwell accused the government of 'torpor and smugness' in defence policy. He called the government hasty, confused, and inconsistent. He was scathing about the macabre lottery system that would select conscripts, and declared Labor's total opposition to the National Service Act.[90]

The government's move and Labor's bluster amounted to a stalemate at the half-Senate election held on 5 December 1964. Though the Coalition attracted a 4 per cent swing, both parties won fourteen seats, with two going to the DLP.[91] As a result, the government would lose its majority in the Senate after 1 July 1965. It would take time for the opposition to conscription to find its voice.

CHAPTER SEVENTEEN

Exposure

1984

Nothing delighted McMahon more in retirement than receiving attention. He was at his happiest when he could say something, and see it that evening on the news or the next day in the newspaper. He was always ready to comment, deride, or make a prediction—as he accurately did in March, saying that New South Wales premier Neville Wran would enjoy a comfortable win over Nick Greiner at the pending election. He was especially delighted with the reception to his remarks that Bob Hawke was the 'one who can do best in ensuring the foundations of the economic and financial system of Australia'.[1]

Exposure seemed to renew him, give him another burst of energy. Even the promise of it was enough for him to say yes. When, in March, a man with a video camera came to the office and asked him to tape a video for his father's sixtieth birthday, McMahon beggared his staff by agreeing. He smiled and waved into the camera, saying, 'Happy birthday, George.' Joyce Cawthorn sniffed at this silliness: McMahon didn't know the man from Adam, she told Bowman.[2]

At other times, McMahon's willingness to say yes led him to odd encounters. In May, while a royal commission studied the Menzies government's decision to allow British nuclear tests in Australia between 1958 and 1963, a television crew came to the office to quiz McMahon about Maralinga. McMahon allowed himself to be questioned on camera for an hour, but afterwards he had so little idea of the details that he had to ask Cawthorn when the programme would be shown. 'He didn't know which programme or who had interviewed him,' an astonished Bowman wrote in his diary.

Cawthorn was little help: despite the fact that the crew had come carrying video cameras, she had thought the interview was for radio. So did George Campbell. Bowman, perturbed but proactive, looked at the weekly television guide. Then he suggested that they check if the interview was intended for Terry Willesee's programme on Channel 7. Still marveling at the obliviousness of Cawthorn and Campbell, and worried by McMahon's tenuous grip on reality, he at least had the satisfaction of writing in his diary: 'Struck it in one.'[3]

CHAPTER EIGHTEEN

Preparing the Way

1964–1966

McMahon was a demanding and difficult man to work for. For his staff, long days were routine. Being bothered at home by him was ordinary. His whims were frequent. Pat Wheatley, who joined McMahon as an assistant private secretary in 1964, could recall being sacked and then reinstated within a matter of hours.[1] Unreasonable demands were par for the course. Overnighting in Orbost once, McMahon found himself without a toothbrush. He called his private secretary, Margaret McLean, and told her to obtain one for him. Somehow, she managed to convince a local chemist to come into town at nine-thirty on a Sunday night, open his store, and allow her to buy a toothbrush. McMahon's response? Discovering that the toothbrush was red, McMahon told her that he used yellow.[2]

Sir Richard Kirby observed that McMahon simply never let up about work, that he did not allow for much difference between work and relaxation. 'You'd be at some social gathering,' he said later, 'having a drink with Bill and he'd get you off in a corner and let you know the government's case backwards and sideways and why this should happen, why that shouldn't … He just couldn't restrain himself.'[3] Kirby spoke from experience. In 1963, when he deliberately neglected to inform McMahon ahead of time of that year's basic wage decision, Kirby was pestered all night by incessant phone calls from a minister unwilling to take a hint.[4]

Harry Bland found much the same thing. 'Daily, nightly, weekends and holiday; he would even follow me around the world!' he said later.[5] Evasions were necessary. Bland's secretary and wife were enlisted to relay excuses when McMahon telephoned: 'My wife became quite professional at telling him I was under the house repairing something or on the roof repairing something.'[6] Calculated rudeness could temper McMahon's demands, but inevitably the phone would ring again and his wavering voice could be heard down the line with fresh demands.

On one occasion, Bland was so pestered by repeated phone calls that he exacted revenge. McMahon had asked him to reconsider some advice, and Bland promised to do so. He said he would call back—late, probably, but he would definitely call:

> So I went on doing what I was engaged in and around about 11, 11.30, went to bed and set the alarm clock for 4 o'clock. I slept soundly until the alarm clock went off, whereupon I rang him in Sydney and said to him, 'Well, Bill, I've been thinking about this all night, and the answer is still *no*.' Well, it stayed *no*, and I don't think I got a call from him for another thirty-six hours.[7]

Peter Kelly, McMahon's press secretary from 1963, thought his boss 'intense'. McMahon did not make light-hearted conversation, and he was an inexhaustible worker. He had many acquaintances, but few close friends.[8] He rarely lightened up. In his regular games of squash, McMahon was combative, competitive. Kelly worked out that it was easier for all concerned if McMahon won the game: 'He just hated getting beaten,' Kelly said.[9] The hatred was such that it prompted Tom Hughes, a member of the House of Representatives from 1963 and an occasional squash partner for McMahon, to go to Kelly with a query. No matter how well *he* played himself, Hughes said, McMahon always seemed to win.

'I know what he does,' Kelly replied. 'He keeps the score.'

'Yes, he does,' said Hughes.

'Well,' Kelly said, 'he calls it wrongly, sometimes, so that you can never win. He cheats.'[10]

McMahon's competitiveness and intensity, his drive and discipline, never waned. His decision to employ Kelly was a part of that. Press secretaries were rare birds in ministers' offices. Many did without. Not McMahon. 'I do need one,' he said.[11]

A former journalist for *The Bulletin* specialising in industrial relations, Kelly became a political adviser as much as a press secretary. He was on hand to point out opportunities and options. Knowing McMahon's desire to be treasurer, Kelly encouraged him to canvass votes for the deputy leadership of the Liberal Party—a position that would become vacant when Menzies resigned and Holt took over, as was widely expected, before the next election.

Initially, McMahon did not understand. He asked about the leadership. Why could he not stand for that? Kelly pointed out that Holt had it sewn up. But no one would be thinking about the deputy leadership, he said. And why would becoming deputy leader make him treasurer, McMahon wanted to know?

'It wouldn't, not automatically,' said Kelly. 'But you'd have enough support within the party to suggest that you choose your portfolio — that is, Treasury. Especially with your background.'

Together, they began working through a plan. McMahon obtained a whip's sheet that contained the names of all Liberal members and senators. He altered it to have three categories—yes, no, and doubtful—and recorded the results of his canvassing of colleagues. Said Kelly: 'He'd go around approaching people, saying, "I'd like to stand eventually …"'

There were promises, intimations, bargains. William 'Bill' Aston, a former colonel in the army, the government whip from mid-1964, and member for the Sydney seat of Phillip, came to Kelly to tell him about an approach from McMahon. 'I asked him to make sure he gave me a ministry if I voted for him,' Aston told Kelly. 'He said yes to that. So, would you tell him from me that I'll cut his fucking balls off if he doesn't?'[12]

Kelly also suggested that McMahon speak with Maxwell Newton, the hotheaded, gap-toothed, and brilliant economics graduate of Cambridge University who had, on the strength of his letter writing, been made political correspondent with the *Herald* and *Australian Financial Review*.[13] A Hackett scholar, Newton believed that economics and politics were indivisible and that the protectionist policies pursued by McEwen were damaging Australia's economy. During his rise to managing editor of the *AFR*, he had repeatedly criticised McEwen's Department of Trade and the Tariff Board. Upon resigning from Fairfax in the wake of the 1963 election, Newton was snapped up by

Rupert Murdoch and appointed editor of his new national broadsheet, *The Australian*. Newton would be sacked from *The Australian* in March 1965, but a proliferating stable of newsletters ensured that he remained a key figure. Newton had contacts in the government and the bureaucracy, and his main newsletter, *Incentive*, was widely read. Kelly told McMahon that getting 'friendly' with Newton was in his interests. McMahon agreed, but it took some time for the relationship to warm up. Newton initially complained that McMahon did not really talk for long.

'Look, the best time to ring him is when he's got nothing on,' Kelly said. 'And that usually is on Saturday morning. Ring him then, and make it a regular arrangement.'

Kelly checked out that doing so was fine with McMahon—and it was. The relationship went from there.[14]

There were other actions required if McMahon's ambitions for elevation were to be realised. His hearing was one. His deafness caused problems in the House, where responding to interjections and colleagues was often necessary to winning debates. In the office, it could make the most casual discussion fraught. According to Bland, McMahon 'never heard intonations, so that when someone made a jocular remark about him, he often took umbrage. He just hadn't heard the nuance in the speaker's voice.'[15] At Bland's urging, McMahon went twice to the United States for operations. They resulted in a marked improvement, one that delighted his staff as much as him. 'I think anyone could understand it,' he said later, of the difference the operations had made. 'It brings you back into life and takes away the tension and irritation of not knowing what has been said.' The success was 'a god-send and a relief,' he added.[16]

It did prompt some adjustments. McMahon later said that after the operations he was woken by the noise of his Commonwealth car driver 'belting on his front door and shouting'. When McMahon demanded to know what on earth he was doing, the chauffeur said, apparently nonplussed, that it was how he always knocked on the door.[17]

Interviewing McMahon later, the journalist John Edwards wondered if it was fair to say that these operations had 'prepared the way' for his marriage. McMahon was curt: 'No.'[18]

Rumours about McMahon's personal life had long abounded.

His liking for fashion, the regular proclamations that he had been a 'balletomane', his light step, and his long-running bachelorhood, were all fodder for gossip. Stories that began with a nugget of fact were wound with scurrilous whispers. That he got on especially well with women was apparently suspicious. The women's groups in Lowe thought him charming, caring, a good local member—even though he did not live in the electorate.[19] Harry Bland's wife would receive deliveries of flowers from McMahon, as if to apologise for his arguments with her husband.[20]

Canberra 'is the Mediterranean of gossip,' wrote Jim Killen,[21] and McMahon, disliked by so many, attracted his own share. He was aware of it. After the end of one parliamentary session, McMahon asked Kelly into his office and asked what members of the Press Gallery thought of him. 'Hesitantly,' Kelly recalled, 'I told him that they regarded him as indefatigable, that he always appeared well-briefed, that he marshalled his facts well and was most persistent.' It was not enough. McMahon wanted more. He pushed Kelly, pressed him; eventually, Kelly told him that there were rumours and jokes of homosexuality. 'Oh. That again!' said McMahon. He was not fazed.[22]

His staff saw no evidence that could give the rumour a foundation. 'In seven years of working with him … I never saw one incident or example of homosexual behaviour,' said Kelly. 'Never. Not once.'[23] Observing that McMahon frequently went out with women, Pat Wheatley concurred.[24] 'I did not think he was gay,' said journalist Alan Ramsey later, but he understood how the rumour could arise.[25]

But McMahon told a much later staff member of an affair with a ballerina when he had been young, and both Kelly and Wheatley attested to McMahon's romantic involvement with a female member of his staff while minister for labour and national service.[26] 'She was his girlfriend, in a way,' Kelly said later. 'He used to occasionally have dinner with her, especially when we were away from Sydney. I was invited along, usually as a cover.'[27]

For whatever reason, that relationship was over by the time McMahon attended a charity function at the Argyle, a Sydney restaurant in the Rocks owned by Sam McMahon, who had lately moved into hospitality and the liquor trade.[28] There, McMahon met Sonia Hopkins.

Sonia was Lowe and Liberal. The daughter of a prominent textile merchant and grazier, she had been born on 1 August 1932 and raised in Strathfield and Killara. Educated at Methodist Ladies' College, Burwood, and then Ravenswood College, Gordon, she had joined the Liberal Party as a matter of course. 'There wasn't much going on in that area in those days,' she remarked later. 'You went to dancing class and joined the Young Liberals.'[29] Engaged at twenty, a marriage to her teenage sweetheart was called off close to the last minute. The benefits of a booming economy and full employment were evident in the course of her twenties: she had trained and practised as an occupational therapist at St Vincent's Hospital and in private practice, and then changed careers entirely in 1956. Three years as a colour consultant with the paint company Taubmans was followed by work as a travel consultant for cruises with P&O. Then, in 1963, a three-week holiday to New York became semi-permanent when she took a job in a news bureau attached to the Australian consulate. Another holiday, to Jamaica in the following year, resulted in a job as a film production assistant with 20th Century Fox. That work was brief: the film slated for production fell through, and Sonia returned to Australia early in 1965.

She was thirty-two years old, drifting and beautiful when she went to the Argyle on 3 April. McMahon was twenty-four years older, pre-occupied with politics, fit, but hardly handsome. He was apparently smitten from the beginning. He later said that Menzies had advised him to marry a long while before. 'I ignored his advice for seven years, until I met Sonia. That was it.'[30] Her feelings took longer to bloom. 'It was gradual,' she said.[31] Nonplussed, he pursued her over the course of the year. There were dinners and dances, many of them at the Coachman, a restaurant in Redfern. 'Moon River' became their song.

The fervour of the relationship was surprising. The speed with which it moved prompted suggestions that it was politically motivated. Kelly had once mentioned to McMahon that it would be very hard to become deputy, let alone leader, as a single man. 'Are you telling me I should get married?' McMahon asked.

'Well, I think politically it would help,' Kelly replied.

McMahon's response was firm: 'I'll decide that, and I don't need you to advise me.'[32]

Politics still remained in the front of his mind. Only four days after meeting Sonia, McMahon was in a vital cabinet committee meeting arguing whether to send a battalion of Australian soldiers to Vietnam. (After all but 'breaking his neck' to get on the committee the year before, the introduction of conscription had forced Menzies to invite him on.)[33] US delight at Australia's decision to introduce conscription in 1964 had now been replaced by an expectation that Australian soldiers would soon follow. Menzies was willing: as he said at another meeting, Australia was looking for a way into the conflict, not a way out.

McMahon, however, was not so willing. At the meeting, he aligned himself with Hasluck's position. He was in favour of delaying a decision on sending troops until American strategy became clear. Overruled by Menzies, McEwen, Holt, and Paltridge, the confidential decision was made to provide a battalion as 'an act of faith' once a formal request was received.[34] Three weeks later, only a day short of the South Vietnamese government making that formal request, Alan Reid broke news of the decision in *The Daily Telegraph*. Given his links to Reid and the relatively few people who knew of the decision, McMahon seemed a likely source of the leak.[35]

There were other issues, too. In the wake of the 1961 election, Menzies had promised to establish a 'Committee for Economic Enquiry', tasked with investigating 'proposals for major developmental projects'.[36] It was a way of answering the critics of the government's economic standing, but, dilatorily, Menzies failed to appoint its members for another year. It took until January 1963 for a chairman, in the form of Dr James Vernon, managing director of the Colonial Sugar Refining Company, to be appointed, with Sir John Crawford (formerly of McEwen's Department of Trade) as vice-chairman. Over the following two years, the committee provided confidential drafts of its report to the Treasury, which reacted warily to the growing scope of measures that the committee recommended. What most caught the Treasury's eye was the recommendation that a standing committee be created to review and advise on Australia's economic growth: unsurprisingly, the Treasury took a dim view of a body that could challenge it. John Stone, for example, thought the report and the committee was a 'naked grab for power' by Crawford.[37]

McMahon had been against the committee almost since the

beginning. In an unsent letter dated 15 January 1962, intended for Menzies, he wrote of his regret that he had been excluded from the committee, and criticised it on grounds that it would be uninformed by appropriate information and expertise.[38] Treasury was aware of his scepticism. In the lead-up to cabinet's consideration of the finished Vernon Report in August 1965, the secretary of the Treasury, Sir Roland Wilson, wrote to McMahon to enlist his help in opposing it. While the report looked reasonable enough, he told McMahon—moderate in tone, seemingly the work of sensible men—a little digging revealed questionable forecasts and defective predictions:

> I am therefore taking the liberty of suggesting … that you might, on this occasion, spare no effort to explain to your colleagues what the projections in Appendix N are all about, and where the Committee has gone seriously wrong in working them out and drawing conclusions from them.[39]

Wilson left no stone unturned. Peter Kelly recalled that John Stone, one of Wilson's 'bright young men'[40] in the Treasury, came to brief McMahon on the report. 'They [McMahon and Stone] were there for four or five hours,' he said.[41] Stone, however, has no recollection of meeting with McMahon to discuss the report. His views on the Vernon Report, he said, were set out in the cabinet submissions that were drafted for Holt. 'They gave credit where credit was due and derided factual or analytical sloppiness wherever they (not infrequently) occurred.'[42]

The efforts were effective. In cabinet on 12 August, Holt read a long submission attacking it. Peter Howson, the minister for air, believed that the report, through Crawford's part-authorship, presented affairs as McEwen saw them. 'This is a continuation of the battle between Treasury and Trade that has been going on for ten years,' he wrote in his diary. 'Harold feels his reputation is at stake, and therefore, to an extent, his chances of becoming Prime Minister.'[43] McMahon backed Holt up, homing in on the weakness of the projections that Wilson had pointed out to him. McEwen was not present to defend the report, which he regarded as 'a good objective analysis of the Australian economy'; he was overseas, and he and Crawford rued the missed opportunity to defend it.[44] Maxwell Newton, no doubt writing from McMahon's retelling, printed in his newsletter, *Incentive*, that McMahon had 'delivered a stinging attack' on the report.[45] Not long afterward, decrying the committee's supposed intrusion into political matters, Menzies rejected the report in a long, scathing speech in the House.[46]

Positioning for Menzies' retirement was going on in earnest throughout 1965. The prime minister was seventy years old and the unquestioned supreme chief of Australian politics. Rivals were gone, even rewarded: Richard Casey had retired in 1960 and become governor-general in July 1965. Harold Holt's succession was all but assured: Garfield Barwick had given up on hopes of succeeding Menzies, and departed to be chief justice of the High Court, with McMahon's urging,[47] and Paul Hasluck had not yet gained the prominence to be a strong candidate for the leadership. There were questions only about the deputy leadership and the rungs below that.

One opportunity for McMahon to begin laying claim to the deputy leadership lay in the public service marriage bar. Since its last consideration in cabinet, spurred as much by the lobbying of Bland and his understanding of the labour market, McMahon had begun moving in favour of its removal. In September 1964, he told a Brisbane audience that there were jobs 'women can do as effectively as men' and that it should be up to a woman individually to decide whether she should take a job.[48] 'The Commonwealth cabinet's perennial bachelor and the hope of single ladies in Canberra,' wrote *The Courier-Mail* the next day, was now 'gallantly carrying the lance for married women.'[49] A year later, following a public protest by Merle Thornton and Rosalie Bognor, who chained themselves to the bar of Brisbane's Regatta Hotel to protest against the marriage bar, McMahon told Bland he was now 'quite prepared' to press for its removal.[50] That same day, he publicly attacked the 'Victorian attitude[s]' held by industries and employers.[51]

Another opportunity for McMahon to gain the esteem of his colleagues began on 30 July, when the WWF announced its decision to carry out a series of twenty-four-hour stoppages, nationwide. Pensions were the union's principal grievance. Claiming that the regular pension was inadequate, the WWF argued that the highly profitable shipping industry had both the responsibility and ability to look after its workers, just as other countries did. The union's participation in the 1963 working party had come with some hopes of discussing pensions, but those hopes had been dashed. In October 1964, the WWF resolved to concentrate on the issue. Five months later, a delegation of workers and union representatives put their case to McMahon, but went away empty-handed. A series of small stoppages in April 1965 achieved nothing. Conferences initiated by the Conciliation and Arbitration Commission broke down in May. The government and employers blamed the WWF for not considering any proposals but pensions; the WWF blamed employers for their suspicious offer of permanent employment, which it called 'a smokescreen to cloud the issue'.[52]

Man-hours lost to stoppages rose, fuelled by the anger about pensions, protests against apartheid in South Africa, and military involvement in Vietnam. McMahon, angered and concerned that the waterfront could become unmanageable, announced on 22 June that an inquiry would be held into the stevedoring industry. To be conducted by A.E. ('Ted') Woodward, a Queen's Counsel who had acted as junior counsel for the Victorian and Commonwealth governments and opposed the ACTU in long-service leave and national wage cases, the terms of reference for the inquiry were wide-ranging. Efficiency, discipline, redundancy, industrial disputes, permanent employment—all the issues, in effect, that had proved nearly intractable on the waterfront for years—were to receive studious investigation. 'Mr Woodward will commence the inquiry as quickly as possible,' McMahon said.[53] Perhaps unaware that the most recent inquiry into the waterfront had taken two-and-a-half years, McMahon promised that Woodward would be finished 'in about three months'.[54] Woodward was unimpressed with the timeframe and the connotations it gave—namely, that the result was known in advance.[55] The WWF, neither unreasonably nor groundlessly, saw the inquiry as an attempt to provide cover for a punitive forthcoming attack by the government. ASIA chairman, Norman Hood, was of a similar mindset.[56]

They were correct. Bland had supposedly been laying the groundwork for a clash with the WWF for some time. 'I'd been waiting for years to go after the WWF,' he later claimed. Deciding that the employers could not be relied upon to 'stand firm' against the pensions campaign, he apparently told McMahon in March 1965 that it would be 'disastrous' to concede to demands for pensions without some quid pro quo on the part of the union movement. Seeing no special reason for a pension within the industry anyway, Bland argued that the WWF's demands were 'sheer industrial pressure' that could easily continue: 'What I am raising in effect is the fundamental issue—whether we should not resist the present claim, even if it means a head-on collision.'[57]

Bland's willingness to bring on that collision was spurred by a chance discovery. In a conversation with Hood, Bland learned that the Melbourne branch of the WWF had apparently recruited a number of men with extensive criminal records. In any dispute, Bland realised, this information could torpedo public sympathy for the union and help to isolate it. After all, how could the ACTU stand shoulder to shoulder with thugs and criminals?[58]

Sometime in the intervening months, without McMahon's knowledge, Bland supposedly went to Menzies for a meeting. He was mindful that the prime minister had won his spurs appearing as the sole advocate for the Amalgamated Society of Engineers in 1920, and was thus familiar with industrial relations; he was also aware that Menzies knew about McMahon's propensity for leaking. After briefing him on his proposal to tackle the WWF, Bland asked Menzies to put McMahon 'under proper control':

> I put it to R.G. [Menzies] that he ought to call a meeting of McMahon and me, tell us that he was concerned about the situation and that he thought that action should be taken, that is to say action on the lines that I'd indicated to him, and that he should say to Billy that the whole exercise demanded a higher order of secrecy and that if Billy was as much as to open his mouth he'd be fired from the cabinet.[59]

In what Bland described as 'a most remarkable exercise', Menzies supposedly went along 'with relish'. At the subsequent meeting between the three men, Menzies laid out the course of action, noted the stakes, and then waved his finger at McMahon: 'If there is any leakage of this I will assume that it came from you and I'll fire you.'[60]

According to Peter Kelly, however, McMahon's resolution to take on the unions had nothing to do with Bland. Kelly recalled bringing a departmental minute to McMahon's attention that, he said, recommended 'complete capitulation' to the WWF and its strikes.

McMahon agreed with his view—but asked what he suggested.

'I think the only way you can do this is to take the communists on,' Kelly told him. 'There's no way around it, because they'll just keep increasing their demands, in other unions.'

McMahon was initially hesitant and understandably wary, but he quickly came around once the political benefits were pointed out.

'Anyway, as you want to be treasurer,' Kelly told him, 'this would give you a lot more strength. If you're seen to be quite strong and take them on, it would advance things more considerably.'

According to Kelly, when Bland was told of McMahon's decision to take on the communists, he became completely unavailable to McMahon. He cut off contact. 'He hid from McMahon for about three or four weeks,' said Kelly. 'You just couldn't contact him. Couldn't find him anywhere.'[61] In his memoirs, McMahon would echo this: Bland disagreed with the idea of taking on the WWF. When McMahon insisted on persevering, Bland told him that he would wash his hands of the matter. The responsibility for it would be McMahon's.[62] Bland's claims—about initiating the moves himself—were simply false. 'That is complete bullshit,' Kelly said of Bland's claims.[63]

Whether he disagreed or not, Bland was still preparing the way. On 1 August, he wrote to McMahon to ask him to dissuade the Liberal MP Tom Hughes from debating WWF official Norman Docker on television. 'From now on we have to be sure that we win every battle,' he wrote. 'We cannot afford to lose one.'[64] He asked Hood to survey the kind of cargo that would be arriving in Australia in the next few months, and to check the criminal records of all people the WWF had submitted to ASIA for registration in Sydney and Melbourne.[65] He wrote to Ted Hicks, secretary of the Department of Defence since 1956, to request information on the availability of service personnel from mid-August onward, in case of a national stoppage on the waterfront.[66] Bland also harried departmental staff for ASIO intelligence:

> It is desperately important that we have the most up-to-date intelligence as to what the Communist Party is up to. We want to know why it has selected this time for a head-on collision with the government and what bearing this has on a general attempt to get control of the trade union movement. In short, we want every scrap of information that we can get

that has any relationship to the ultimatum the Federation has given us on the waterfront and to trade union activity at large.[67]

On 3 August, Bland prepared a long letter for McMahon to send to Menzies outlining in great detail the proposed course of action. In a separate letter to McMahon, sent the same day, Bland covered the possible consequences of the proposed action against the WWF. Those consequences could spread beyond the waterfront, he warned, and they could be dire. 'Sydney's gas supplies could be cut off,' he noted, by way of example. Throughout the letter, he fortified his minister. The showdown would pay off: 'It took six months of fearful disruption in New Zealand in 1951 to clean up the waterfront. But there has not been any worthwhile trouble since.'[68]

The same day, the Conciliation and Arbitration Commission rejected an ACTU application to reconsider that year's national wage decision, which had been all but frozen. The decision prompted an inept statement from Docker. He declared that there was 'no future' in the commission and that suggestions for further arbitration were foolish and misleading. 'We are fighting the government on these matters,' he said. 'They have mounted a vicious campaign against us, but we shall win.'

That quote was on the second page of McMahon's cabinet submission that was circulated at the end of August. Recapitulating the decades-long unrest on the waterfront, the submission pinned much of the blame on militant, communist-tinged leaders like Docker, who, it claimed, controlled the WWF. The submission was designed to anger, provoke, and stiffen the resolve of its small readership. There was no prospect of a deal 'on any reasonable basis', it claimed, and thus the government was at a 'crossroads':

Are we to keep on manoeuvring within the present system, with experience to tell us that no lasting solution will be achieved, that the Federation will, under its Communist controllers, continue to resort to direct action, that there will never be stability on the waterfront and that we will continue to face adverse effects on our economy and our overseas trade? Or are we now to attempt a radical solution of the difficulties, recognising the dislocation we may have to face?[69]

The submission recommended dramatic changes. It removed the WWF's power to recruit workers and gave it to ASIA. It mandated that employers appropriately supervise stevedoring operations. It strengthened ASIA's power to suspend and deregister wharf workers. These were but the stepping stones to the biggest changes: the minister would have the power to ask the Conciliation and Arbitration Commission to deregister the WWF, to strip the union of its rights and privileges under the *Stevedoring Industry Act*, to strip it of its rights to represent a member, to terminate any lease the WWF had with the Commonwealth or ASIA, and to register unions in place of the Federation.

Drafted in large part by Bland, McMahon contributed 'some deft touches' and, in the cabinet debate in the evening of 1 September, he won the support of his colleagues.[70] Holt congratulated him on the paper and the 'courage' of his approach, and told colleagues that he had known 'in his bones' that at some stage the government would have to act on lines suggested by McMahon. Menzies agreed: 'We don't avoid the ultimate conflict by evading the first—we tackle the first, but we must win the first.'[71] Cabinet approved the 'course of radical change' that McMahon's submission recommended. It asked that those changes be enacted quickly, that the 'public mind' be prepared, and that contingency plans be put in place for the disruptions that might occur.[72]

The latter was well underway, and McMahon and Bland worked quickly to meet the other requests from cabinet. On 14 September, Bland suggested to McMahon that Menzies invite the press barons—including Warwick Fairfax, Rupert Murdoch, Frank Packer, and Sir John Williams, of the Herald and Weekly Times—to Canberra to take them into his confidence, and that detailed briefing materials be prepared for the press to use once the government revealed its hand. Bland also spoke with Fitzgibbon, the WWF's general secretary: 'I floated what was happening on the waterfront and the sorts of things that the government might do in the circumstances. Before I'd finished that meal I knew what his attitude would be,' Bland recalled.[73]

On Thursday 23 September, McMahon presented the measures to the Coalition party room. He received a rapturous reception, particularly from the backbench, which had been itching for a fight with the WWF for years. The Bill, wrote Peter Howson that night, 'is, in essence, a declaration of war against the Waterside Workers' Federation. The party has never been so united.'[74]

On the same day, the WWF was holding a federal council meeting in Sydney. At midday, Fitzgibbon interrupted proceedings to report that he had been informed that legislation targeting the WWF and its right to recruit would be introduced to the Parliament that night.

That evening, staff of the Department of Labour and National Service began delivering a booklet detailing the new measures to newspaper editors around the country. At eight o'clock, following the dinner break, McMahon introduced the Stevedoring Industry Bill 1965 to the House.

He outlined the decline in man-hours on the waterfront throughout the country, and the costs that this had imposed. He set out the work stoppages and the burdens this had created. He set out the WWF's campaign and its intransigence. He recited Docker's denunciation of the arbitration system and subsequent lies. 'This is how the Federation works,' he said. 'It makes agreements and dishonours them. It defies the arbitration system except when it suits its purposes. It breaks the rules of the trade union movement and then, when it is in difficulties, seeks its support.' He noted that the WWF accounted for nearly a quarter of all industrial disputes, yet made up only one per cent of Australia's workforce. He argued that wharfies were not poorly paid by any standard. Most colourfully of all, McMahon told the 'sorry story' of the WWF's supposed propensity for hiring criminals:

A check of a batch of 990 names submitted recently to the Authority for recruitment in Melbourne revealed 260 men with criminal records. In Sydney a batch of 181 names included 33 with criminal records. In Gladstone 3 out of 12 had criminal records. There were men with long lists of convictions, up to the present time, of assault with violence, larceny, thieving and receiving; and this is an industry where pillaging is a problem. Some of the men whose names were submitted were actually facing criminal charges when they were nominated by the Federation.

'The Federation has been given opportunity to behave responsibly,' he said. 'It has betrayed its trust, not only to this Parliament but to the Australian people.'[75]

McMahon's speech was effective. Menzies called it 'masterly'.[76] Even Bland, so dismissive of McMahon, thought so: 'Billy played this up marvelously.'[77] The press latched onto the claims of criminality and came out almost entirely in favour of the Bill. It was a 'politically courageous decision,' wrote Maxwell Newton.[78] Labor listened to the speech quietly, cautious that it was prelude to a snap election.[79] It was only a week later, as the Bill was shuttled through the Parliament, that the opposition began to question it seriously. Most notably, and dangerously for McMahon, Labor picked up on the WWF's vehement denials about the character of its members, and began asking for further information.

Initially, at least, McMahon continued to play up this angle. Twenty-five per cent of WWF-nominated workers had criminal records, he said.[80] 'Large numbers of people with criminal records of larceny, receiving, consorting, procuring, assault and battery, and offences of that kind were being employed,' he said.[81] 'Cases of repeated convictions for such offences as assault and battery, thieving and receiving; such offences ... as sodomy and similar offences; repeated assaults on females and procuring. There were many other types as well. All of those offences were shown in the records I examined. This is enough to convince me that the government was fully justified in taking the action it did.'[82] The answers were sure and his performances sound. It was the confident, argumentative man his university peers had written about.

Labor could not lay a glove on McMahon. But boasts inevitably began to creep into his answers. 'I have mentioned the total number and I have personally looked at a great number of records; in the case of New South Wales I have looked at every one,' he said on 30 September.[83] A fortnight later, when Calwell pressed him on the records, McMahon went too far: 'I stand on the statement that these details have been checked and re-checked,' he said. When Calwell asked who had checked, McMahon replied that he, his department, and ASIA had checked the records: 'I repeat now that of the 990 named in Victoria, 260 did have criminal records.'[84]

The ALP's focus on the records, and Arthur Calwell's request to see them, prompted Bland to check them himself. What he found would have prompted a sharp gasp. The 260 men in Melbourne supposedly possessing criminal records had, in fact, not criminal records at all but merely police records. Some had been acquitted of crimes, or their cases had been withdrawn, or struck out, or adjourned. Some had been charged only with traffic offences. Perhaps worst of all, of the 260 'disreputable men' McMahon had decried, almost half had subsequently been accepted by ASIA as fit for work on the waterside.[85] Could they really have been so bad then? Or was ASIA at fault?

McMahon was in danger. If the true state of those records became public, it was certain that public opinion and the press would turn on him. The measures would be lost. The ALP would press for his resignation. The WWF would be emboldened. The months of preparation and secrecy would be for nothing.

But to Bland's surprise, McMahon seemed unafraid when he was informed. 'It is just no use crying over spilt milk,' he responded. He was serene. As he noted, he had met with Menzies and decided on a course of action that could deflect Calwell. The deficiencies of the records would remain secret. His rebuke, therefore, was mild: 'It seemed to me axiomatic that the most detailed check should have been made by the responsible officer at the highest level!' McMahon was all too aware of the debt that he owed to Bland. His standing within the parliamentary Liberal Party had soared. His reputation within its membership was at a high. His public profile had lifted. 'Secretary, the Stevedoring Bill was *the* most important we have introduced since I became Minister!' he told Bland. Amid all this, could McMahon really fail to be generous?[86]

Everything, it seemed, had worked out favourably—at least publicly. The contingency plans to use scab labour, service personnel, and volunteers to keep the waterfront operational never had to be put into action. Press support never turned against the government. Within the union movement, the legislation seemed to have its desired effect. The ACTU, trying to calm the waters, had first condemned the Bill, then called for delay, then sought support for an 'all-in' conference to discuss issues on the waterfront. Those in the WWF who might disrupt that conference were cowed and wrangled into participating, and Charlie Fitzgibbon was able to overcome the communist elements that had made the union such a target.

On 13 October, subject to a promise that there would be no further port stoppages and an understanding that the stevedoring legislation was non-negotiable, Menzies announced that the proposed conference would go ahead with Woodward as chair. That conference, which went on for several months, resulted in agreement on a range of issues that had bedevilled the stevedoring industry. To Bland's disgruntlement, a pensions scheme was designed and implemented.[87] Permanent employment was introduced. New approaches, to discipline within the industry, to recruitment, to long-service leave and redundancy, were accepted.

'Well, we won, hands down,' Bland later said, in a small triumphalist revision. 'Billy received the plaudits. The Federation capitulated. Peace returned to the waterfront'.[88]

That peace enabled re-consideration of the marriage bar. Agitation for its removal was coming from the Equal Opportunities for Women Association, which Merle Thornton had founded in the aftermath of her protest at the Regatta Hotel,[89] and from Labor member for Oxley, Bill Hayden, who was raising the matter repeatedly in the House.[90] In November, McMahon took a Bland-drafted submission on its removal to cabinet. This time, he spoke in support of it. Given his earlier opposition, there were questions about his change of heart. Writing to Menzies, John Bunting wondered if it was McMahon's advisers or his relationship with Sonia that accounted for his 'new view of things'.[91] Feminist activist Helen Crisp, who had pushed for the removal of the bar, similarly saw the coincidence.[92] Nonetheless, on 30 November, cabinet finally accepted 'the principle' of employing married women. But it added a rider: before this was translated to legislation, another inter-departmental committee was to report on the administrative requirements, consequences, and impact of the change.[93] Change, on some things, was slow.

McMAHON'S courtship of Sonia Hopkins continued. Her feelings for him developed as the dinners and dancing went on. 'I really liked being with him,' Sonia later said. 'He was very attentive and a very kind fellow.' McMahon had fixed on her. He proposed marriage early and, although he had to renew the proposal repeatedly during the year, Sonia finally said yes. 'He eventually wore me down by seeing me so often and constantly wooing me.'[94]

Apparently, making the proposal required some leeway from McMahon's colleagues. Bert Kelly, deputy government whip, recalled McMahon's staff telephoning to ask if McMahon could leave Parliament early. When Kelly refused, they came down to see him personally and ask again. Kelly refused once more, but, his curiosity aroused, asked why McMahon needed to leave. 'We think tonight's the night,' they told him. 'If you let him go we are sure he will pop the question, and he will come back properly engaged. And you know what this means to his office, this Parliament, and the nation.'

Whether the staff were being unduly dramatic or not, the explanation changed Kelly's mind. McMahon was given leave, and duly popped the question. 'I took all the credit for it,' Kelly joked later.[95]

On 24 October, McMahon announced that he and Sonia were engaged. The press was invited to his flat for photographs and a quick comment. It was soon established that the engagement would not be long: they would be married in December.[96] By all accounts, the difference in ages did not worry them. Nor did the quick development of their relationship: 'When my feelings for him deepened, I said yes,' Sonia said.[97]

McMahon was proud of himself and his fiancée, though he could be odd about it. In the days after his engagement was announced, he called Peter Kelly into his office and said, rather peculiarly, 'You know I'm quite well off.'

'Yes,' Kelly said, wondering what was happening.

'Well, Sonia is very, very, very, *very* well off,' said McMahon.

'Oh yes, that's good,' Kelly replied, still puzzled.[98]

Both parties were aware of the strengths and flaws of the other. McMahon discussed the pending marriage with Bland, and Sonia did the same when McMahon was in the House. 'The turning point was her conviction that one day Bill would be PM and she would be the châtelaine of the Lodge,' Bland recalled.[99]

The wedding was held in the late afternoon on 11 December at St Mark's Anglican Church, at Darling Point.[100] The night before, McMahon launched a book about journalism and toured Kings Cross, singing 'Get Me to the Church on Time' as he walked through the streets. He played squash in the morning, and arrived at the church in a morning coat and waistcoat, a white carnation bristling by a puffy white pocket square. The church was crowded with guests and well-wishers, and press thronged the streets outside. Sonia, in a high-necked, full-length lace gown, arrived at four o'clock in the company of her father. After the ceremony, it took almost half an hour for the couple to make their way to a waiting Commonwealth car barely thirty metres away. 'Good luck, dears,' one elderly lady called, grabbing McMahon by the sleeve.

A reception for their 300 guests followed at the Royal Sydney Golf Club, and then McMahon and his new wife departed for their honeymoon in the Pacific islands. They went to Tahiti, Mo'orea, and Pago Pago (modern-day American Samoa). While still on their honeymoon, McMahon received a phone call from Peter Kelly.

The prime minister had called a meeting of the Coalition parties for 20 January, Kelly told him. He was likely to announce his retirement. Holt would obviously stand for the leadership, and would almost certainly take it unopposed. The deputy leadership—the key to McMahon becoming treasurer—was about to become vacant. Kelly urged McMahon to return home, observing that although McMahon was well positioned, Hasluck was standing—with Menzies' backing.

It was unsurprising that Hasluck had Menzies' backing. Since 1949, there were clear, if subtle, signs of Menzies' preference for Hasluck. The former diplomat, historian, and journalist from Western Australia had been promoted to the ministry before McMahon in 1951, and his portfolios—territories, defence, and then external affairs—had given him an autonomy that McMahon had not enjoyed until he took labour and national service. He was senior to McMahon in the cabinet pecking order and had been appointed to the UK Privy Council on Menzies' recommendation on New Year's Day. As the historian Geoffrey Bolton later noted, the implication of this honour was that Hasluck was of 'prime ministerial quality'.[101]

McMahon returned to Sydney and immediately began to canvass for votes. He called everyone he could, drawing support from New South Wales and Queensland in particular. 'Billy lobbied furiously,' Tom Hughes recalled.[102] It was a marked contrast to Hasluck, whose preference that colleagues recognise his ability unbidden caused him to refrain from anything beyond an announcement that he would stand. Still basking in the favourable press from his fight with the waterfront,

McMahon worked his contacts within the media. In *Incentive*, Maxwell Newton covered the contest as if it was a commercial deal:

> The essential point to be considered by the Liberals in the choice between Mr Hasluck and Mr McMahon for the deputy leadership of the party is, in the view of those proposing the cause of Mr McMahon, whether the Liberal Party wants to have as its deputy leader a man from the politically relatively insignificant state of Western Australia or one from New South Wales, where so many of the big battles of recent years have been fought and won. There is also the point that in New South Wales lies much of the money backing for the Liberal Party and, on this view, a deputy leader from New South Wales could be able to give the party much greater high level contact with such financial resources.[103]

According to Gordon Freeth, minister for shipping and transport, and one of McMahon's critics, the contest was scurrilous, with whisperings, rumours, and behind-the-scenes machinations. 'The press were getting stories about how unapproachable Paul Hasluck was, how he lacked ability and this kind of thing,' he recalled. 'It was a very wicked campaign.'[104] This, the pressure of extra voices, and the brazen electioneering prompted disquiet. 'This was the first time I recalled the Party being subjected to high pressure voting tactics and people brought in from outside to exercise their influence,' Les Bury later said.[105]

Nonetheless, the tactics worked. At the party meeting on 20 January, Holt was elected unopposed to succeed Menzies. The soon-to-resign prime minister called for nominations for the deputy leadership. In the resulting ballot, McMahon narrowly defeated Hasluck, 37–33.

McMahon's success owed much to developments over the previous two years. The fortuitous timing of Menzies' resignation ensured that McMahon's clash with the waterfront was still fresh in his colleagues' minds; the favourable press he had attracted and engineered was still lingering. Bland was later scathing of McMahon's role in the whole affair—dismissing him as a figurehead who lied about giving years of thought to the problem—but he grudgingly saw that the clash was McMahon's 'greatest triumph' and that it made him in his party's eyes.[106]

McMahon's marriage to Sonia had helped. It had all but erased the stigma that McMahon carried as a bachelor. Even Menzies, as he gave his farewell press conference that evening, saw fit to mention it. 'I have one of my own [wife],' he said. 'Harold has his and Bill McMahon, God be praised, has one of his. We are not answerable for our wives. They, poor dears, are answerable for us.'[107]

McMahon's opposition had helped as well. Hasluck's refusal to lobby his colleagues allowed McMahon to cajole, flatter, duchess, and bargain with his peers almost without contest. However distasteful Hasluck may have found this kind of campaigning, it was an influential factor in his loss.

Yet there were signs in the victory that McMahon would have done well to heed. Peter Howson doubted that McMahon had got any votes from within the cabinet—a sign that close contact with McMahon did not breed admiration.[108] That Menzies had backed Hasluck and not McMahon was another sign that he was not a favourite of the party: should his ambitions extend further than the Treasury, he would have to work out how to placate his critics.

Nonetheless, for the moment, McMahon was happy. When the new Holt government was sworn in on a sunny Australia Day, McMahon attended in full morning dress, a red carnation in his lapel, an effusive smile stretched across his face.[109]

CHAPTER NINETEEN

Lauding the Headmaster

1984

McMahon's treatment of Menzies in his autobiography was a problem. Overly long and overly reliant on the public record, the section on Menzies had the effect of shunting McMahon off-stage. When he wrote to McMahon setting out his thoughts on the manuscript, Bowman couched this criticism carefully: 'To step aside is valid when the other character looms very large and the author is able to portray him *in the light of personal knowledge and experience* and to a lesser extent personal opinion.' But the present treatment was inappropriate, Bowman suggested. '[Menzies] should not be used as an umbrella or a prop, nor would any second-hand portrait of him be appropriate.'[1]

The advice was important and, indeed, went to the heart of one of the probable selling points of the book and its value as an historical document—the story of McMahon's relationship with Menzies.

The relationship was long. Speaking after Menzies' death in 1978, McMahon claimed an acquaintance that went back as far as the early 1930s. Menzies had given legal advice on Jack Lang's attempts to abolish the New South Wales Legislative Council, which Allen Allen & Hemsley had been involved in, and their paths crossed in another case on patents, McMahon said. 'I did not like him for a long period,' McMahon said. He had found Menzies arrogant and disrespectful, but subsequent events had forced him to swallow his pride.[2]

According to McMahon, their relationship while in government was harmonious, if marked by occasional problems. He believed that Menzies respected his abilities but disliked his iconoclasm. McMahon's public statements about him were admiring, but always tempered by declarations that he had never been an unquestioning sycophant:

> I would never call him a headmaster, but he loved to predominate. He
> loved to excel ... I never found him very difficult to handle. I always
> went my own way. I know that frequently he didn't like it, and that
> frequently [he] reacted. But that didn't stop me at all. I enjoyed myself
> whilst he was there.[3]

But there was a change in McMahon's approach, one prompted by
Menzies' remarks that the journalist David McNicoll had published in
1979. Drawing from an interview surreptitiously recorded in the face of
an express wish that McNicoll not do so, conducted when Menzies was
bedridden, depressed, and recovering from two strokes, the interview
had caused uproar when it was published, even though the background
suggested it should have been treated carefully.[4]

Menzies' remarks about the Liberal Party and his successors had
been withering. He had 'no respect' for Richard Casey. Garfield
Barwick had been 'a disappointing politician' and 'never any good in the
Parliament'. Harold Holt was 'dreadful', had mucked everything up.
John Gorton was just a 'mischief maker'. Billy Snedden was 'a hopeless
leader'. The greatest fire, however, had been reserved for McMahon:

> McMahon ... to me is a contemptible little squirt. He just looked
> forward to tomorrow's leading article. That's all ... McMahon, I think,
> is the most characterless man who was ever prime minister of Australia.
> A dreadful little man.[5]

McMahon had brushed those comments aside when they were
published. 'When I first read it, I just burst out laughing,' he said. '... I
don't think it served Sir Robert well.' But he did not intend to respond
further, he said. Throughout his life he had always avoided public,
personal recriminations, despite provocation, and he saw no reason to
change that now. 'In the seventeen years I served under Sir Robert, I
gave him undivided loyalty and he continued to promote me—which
was not his practice.'[6]

But when it came time to write his autobiography, McMahon,
it seems, decided that he would have to respond—albeit in a more

indirect fashion. He would admit to admiring Menzies and lauding his successes and his qualities. But he would attack Menzies, too. What he told Bowman, and what Bowman subsequently drafted on McMahon's instruction, showed this aplenty.[7]

First, McMahon would question Menzies' political success. The Labor Party that Menzies faced was weak and flawed, he would argue. Chifley was sick; Evatt was erratic; Calwell led a divided party. In McMahon's reckoning, Menzies was lucky to have had such opponents. Second, McMahon sought to claim credit for measures Menzies had taken. *He* had advised and, yes, he had warned Menzies about the economy in the lead-up to the 1961 election. *He* had drafted Menzies' policy speech in the lead-up to the 1963 election. Along with Garfield Barwick, *he* had been the one to convince Menzies to offer assistance to private schools.

McMahon could be quite bold. He wanted to tackle his reputation as an inveterate leaker and debunk the rumours that Menzies had extracted a signed confession from him. In McMahon's telling, the supposed confession that Menzies had extracted in 1959 was a fiction. His office had not even received the cabinet submission he had been accused of leaking, he claimed, but when he told Menzies this, the prime minister had been untroubled. Menzies showed McMahon a note that he had dictated to Hazel Craig. McMahon told him it was false, but Menzies did not reply. (There are obvious problems with McMahon's version of this story: in addition to confusing the dates—in the draft, McMahon claimed that this incident occurred while he was minister for primary industry—McMahon's version fails to account for his handwritten annotations on the confession.)

On Menzies' criticism of his relationship with the press, McMahon could hardly deny reality, so he sought to turn it into a positive. Of course he had been close to the press, he said. Why should he not be? The support of the media barons—Sir Frank Packer, Ezra Norton, and Rupert Henderson—helped the government, most obviously in 1961. What was wrong with it?

In McMahon's telling, Menzies was petty, vindictive, bitter—almost as bad as McEwen. Menzies had reneged on a promise to appoint him to a ministry in 1951; had berated him for leaking when he had done so at the request of Menzies' office; had panicked during the colours controversy; had been vainglorious and wrong during the Suez crisis; had nursed a grudge after McMahon refused the invitation to stand for the deputy leadership in 1956; had called his honesty into question over the leaked social services proposal in 1959; had attempted to take McMahon down, using senator Alister McMullin in 1965; had timed his retirement in January 1966 to coincide with McMahon's honeymoon, so that McMahon would not be able to stand for the deputy leadership; and had, in his retirement, made statements about McMahon that were ultimately more damaging to himself.

Nor was McMahon the only one to suffer unduly. Menzies' mercurial regard, McMahon would argue, extended to colleagues. Jo Gullett and John Howse, both Liberal backbenchers, had, like him, been promised ministries by Menzies, but were left to languish, McMahon claimed. But for his refusal to play along in 1956, McMahon said, Holt might also have suffered from Menzies' mercurial regard. Menzies would laugh at Casey's deafness, McMahon claimed, and had left Hasluck in the Territories portfolio as retribution for Hasluck's criticisms in the official history of Australia's involvement in World War II. Menzies had acquiesced in Barwick's appointment as chief justice of the High Court only under duress; had been supportive and then sharply critical of Gorton when his name was proposed as Australia's ambassador to the US. Menzies had wanted Gorton, McMahon told Bowman, but, the moment his name was put forward, turned wholly against him.[8]

It was an unflattering portrait, all the more so since it jarred with the laudatory glow that usually surrounded treatments of Menzies. And it was certainly deliberate. In order to salvage his reputation, in order to overcome the insults and disregard of his party, the press, and the public, McMahon had to make space where he could prove himself right, where he could show how others around him had faltered, been treacherous, been wrong.

The question that inevitably accompanied this, however, when Bowman set to rewriting, was simple: how much of it was true?

CHAPTER TWENTY

Protection (I)

1966

The lead writer for the newsletter *Inside Canberra* predicted it correctly: aside from foreign affairs, the factor that would most affect the Holt government was McMahon's appointment as treasurer.[1] In the short term, McMahon's appointment was to cause bitter disputes within the Coalition; in the longer term, it signalled the waning of protectionism and the ascendancy of pro-market beliefs in Australian economic policy-making.

These duelling ideological beliefs had been swirling for decades. They had defined political debate at Federation. They had been the faultlines in the governments of Barton, Deakin, and Reid. Eventually, protection had won out and been elevated to the point that it was, in W.K. Hancock's words, 'a faith and a dogma'.[2] Despite that triumph, the dispute about protection and free trade defined, albeit latently, the differences between non-Labor politicians from Victoria and New South Wales.

As the scholar James Jupp later noted, the differences between the non-Labor politics in both states and their capitals were most apparent at these ideological levels. 'Here the conventional contrast is between the cynicism and materialism of Sydney and the altruism and idealism of Melbourne. Sydney has been hard-nosed where Melbourne is softhearted. Sydney inherits market-oriented conservatism from the old Free Traders, where Melbourne espouses the welfare stateism of Deakinite Liberalism.'[3]

McMahon's appointment represented a geographic and ideological shift in this debate. His promotion to the Treasury elevated the visibility of the critics of protectionism, along with the state where those critics were most dominant. Moreover, McMahon's appointment gave the Treasury a minister who was much more aligned with its thinking and much more inclined to argue against the interventions of the Department of Trade and Industry.

This brought McMahon back into conflict with McEwen. As leader of the Country Party, McEwen had sought to broaden his party's base by attracting the support of Australia's manufacturing industries. Recognising that their viability rested on their being able to compete with imports, McEwen presided over the use of tariffs as a form of protection. He would recommend to the Tariff Board that it conduct an inquiry on the efficacy of tariff protection for a class of imports, and then see that the board's resultant reports—which inevitably recommended protection—were accepted in cabinet. 'It was my view that Tariff Board recommendations should be accepted wherever possible,' he wrote later.[4] Furthermore, to ensure that no Australian industry would suffer unduly while that inquiry was being conducted, McEwen oversaw the creation of the Special Assistance Authority, which had the power to impose tariffs as an interim measure. 'In my view there are few things I did in my period as a minister more important', he said.[5] The tariffs were to be a temporary shield for industries that were developing and growing, and were much in line with the strand of economics promulgated by David Syme and Alfred Deakin, itself inherited from Friedrich List's 'National System economics'.[6]

It was a precarious and audacious strategy. In advocating for the imposition of tariffs, McEwen was arguably acting against the interests of his core constituency. Tariff protection for the manufacturing industries increased the costs borne by the farmers, graziers, and pastoralists that the Country Party purported to represent. They had to pay more for the chemicals, clothing, and machinery that were necessary for business.

The apparent contradiction, and McEwen's skill in navigating it, caused some to scorn and others to marvel. Arthur Fadden, observing politics from retirement in Brisbane, was privately savage of McEwen's direction.[7] Alan Reid, watching from the Press Gallery, could only wonder. 'McEwen was like a rider in a Roman ampitheatre, riding upright with a foot on each of two horses,' he wrote.[8] But McEwen did not agree that these 'horses' were in any kind of conflict; he saw them moving towards 'common interests' of national development and prosperity.[9]

McEwen's approach had held sway for almost a decade. In that time, he had few critics and he could usually afford to ignore their criticisms. But by 1966, the ground was shifting. In Queensland, prominent graziers were voicing criticism of McEwen's approach and its effect on primary producers. Maxwell Newton was running regular tirades against McEwen's policies, and other members of the press were taking an interest in tariff policy. Godfrey 'Alf' Rattigan, the recently appointed chairman of the Tariff Board, was unexpectedly pursuing an increasingly independent line on tariffs, pushing not for blanket protection but for balancing protection with Australia's trade relationships. Liberal MP Bert Kelly's long-running criticism of tariff policy was beginning to attract an audience in Parliament and beyond. A farmer from Merrindie before entering politics, Kelly did not agree that Australia's manufacturing industries required the protection afforded by tariffs, and he repeatedly pointed out the burden that tariffs were placing on farmers. Though he had sometimes felt isolated, Kelly knew he was not alone in his criticisms. He knew that the issue was bound up in party politics. 'The Liberals were frightened of McEwen,' he said later, '[and] that's the truth of it. He was a bonny fighter and he could clobber you like hell.'[10]

But McMahon's appointment to the Treasury hinted at change in the landscape of the debate. 'McMahon knew the damage that was being done,' Kelly said. McMahon was surreptitious about it, but Kelly knew he was on his side. In 1962, they had run into one another after a debate on tariffs. At the time, Kelly had been frustrated, despondent about his lack of traction. 'I don't know why I stop here,' he said. 'No one takes any notice of me.'

McMahon told him to come to his office. Once there, he showed Kelly two copies of the tariff legislation that Kelly had criticised. The first was the legislation as it stood before it had been put to the party room; the second was the legislation afterwards. 'You're the only man who spoke,' McMahon said, pointing out the differences. 'It just goes to show that it's worthwhile. You know it can alter things.'[11]

BECOMING treasurer was the fulfillment of a dream. After six months in the portfolio, McMahon was proclaiming his comfort with it. 'I like it best because I feel I have trained myself for this kind of portfolio,' he said, 'and because I speak the lingo—and because I have had considerable university and practical experience in this field.'[12]

That experience ensured McMahon was willing to question advice.[13] Between this and his acknowledged propensity to telephone all and sundry, journalists wondered how the secretary to the Treasury, Sir Roland Wilson, would handle his new minister.[14] According to a popular story, Wilson did so without trouble: 'Bloody do what we tell you and you'll be fine,' the experienced mandarin told McMahon.[15] But Wilson did not tell anything for long. In October, three years short of his retirement, but three months after his appointment as chairman of Qantas, Wilson resigned—partly to allow his deputy and colleague Richard Randall to lead the Treasury, and partly to escape from McMahon, whom he held in some disdain.[16]

McMahon had taken over in favourable conditions. He and the Treasury were reasonably confident about Australia's prospects, despite a drought that had hampered growth in the previous year. The conversion from pounds, shillings, and pence to decimal currency on 14 February had gone smoothly. The economy was expanding. Employment had returned to the 'boom year' levels of 1960. 'There is certainly a strong urge for expansion within the economy and a wealth of opportunities for it,' the Treasury mid-year assessment read. 'The scope for it is bounded only by the limitations on our resources of capital and labour.'[17]

Conscious of those limitations, McMahon did the requisite job of a treasurer in this era, and scrutinised proposals for spending. He cut to pieces a request from the Queensland state government for financial assistance for its dairy industry, variously arguing that there was no precedent for assistance, that accepting the request would become a precedent, that a state-based policy would become a national policy, and that the request was not detailed enough to warrant acceptance.[18] Over the objections of Charles Adermann, the deputy leader of the Country Party and minister for primary industry, cabinet took McMahon's side.[19] When Adermann submitted a proposal to renew and increase the three-year-old superphosphate bounty, McMahon sought to reject it, then delay it, then scale it down. He was partly successful: it would be renewed, but there was to be no change in the rate, and he would be the one to announce it in the budget.[20] When cabinet considered a proposal to increase Commonwealth assistance to flying training, McMahon was simply dismissive: 'The proposals, in total, go beyond what is a reasonable measure of assistance.'[21]

There were continual skirmishes with McEwen and Trade, not all of which went McMahon's way. In February, McEwen succeeded in getting the government to accept a Tariff Board report on motorcars. It had heretically declared that 'no general increase in the level of protection afforded [to] vehicle production can be justified either by the recent level of imports or in terms of normal tariff making criteria'. The report also recommended, however, that tariffs on passenger cars and station wagons be increased if imports reached 7.5 per cent of new registrations.[22] That same month, a McEwen proposal to offer more capital investment to farmers was superseded by McMahon's counter-proposal that sought to meet McEwen's halfway.[23] In March, the two men clashed over rural finance, McMahon winning out and 'thrilled' by his victory.[24] Soon after that, when Holt presented cabinet with a long-in-the-works report on creating a system of grants to spur research and development in secondary industries, McMahon and McEwen argued again.[25] McEwen preferred that eligible research and development programmes qualify immediately, and McMahon argued for a scheme that would select the best research after evaluation by experts. Officials within the public service were alive to the 'sharply opposed positions' presented by the two senior ministers.[26] When they were discussed in May, cabinet referred the proposals to a committee for further consideration. It was a stalemate.[27]

Holt's elevation to the prime ministership saw the government turning in a new direction, with a new image. Fit, silver-haired, genial, and urbane, Holt's media image was much more relaxed and extensive than Menzies' had been, and the unexpected policy areas he began to stake out encouraged suggestions of a new era. Within weeks of taking over, Holt had disinterred a series of immigration reforms that had been buried by Menzies in 1964. Those measures relaxed entry and residency requirements for Asian migrants to Australia, and allowed eligible non-European migrants to become Australian citizens upon completion of a five-year residency. It was the beginning, Holt's biographer later wrote, of the 'formal deconstruction' of the White Australia Policy.[28] The reforms were widely welcomed in Asian countries that Holt toured during the early months of 1966, as he sought a closer diplomatic engagement with Asia—another of his shifts of policy.

The acclaim that greeted the Holt government matched McMahon's happiness in his marriage. In Sydney, he and Sonia moved to a flat in Point Piper with glorious views of the harbour. It took a long while to set up the flat properly—'I think it will take forever to finish at this rate,' Sonia was saying in March—but they were hardly deterred from buying property.[29] Early in May, McMahon finally decided to eschew the Hotel Canberra, where he had held a permanent booking for years, in favour of a proper home in the nation's capital. He and Sonia purchased a small modernist-styled unit in the leafy old-money suburb of Forrest. The unit, one of a set designed by the architect Roy Grounds, had ceilings made of compressed straw and a glass wall that allowed the northern sun to pour inside. It was beautiful, but decidedly different from the antique styling of McMahon's Sydney home. 'I think this one will be fairly contemporary,' Sonia said.[30]

It was just as well they had settled down for, by month's end, they had another reason: Sonia was pregnant. They found out in a manner that was, considering McMahon's reputation, faintly ironic. While Sonia was in hospital for a curette, a journalist rang McMahon to confirm that he would soon be a father. Surprised, McMahon demurred from answering and called Sonia's doctor. The doctor confirmed it. Someone in the hospital, he and Sonia deduced later, had leaked it. McMahon told Sonia, much to her surprise. 'We had never even discussed having children,' she said later.[31] McMahon was delighted by the news, with the proviso that his new Sydney flat might not suffice for long: 'I expect we will have to find a new and bigger home.'[32]

Despite the demands of his portfolio and his new home life, McMahon remained a regular dinner guest of Frank Packer's. David McNicoll recalled that if there were famous guests at Packer's table, the treasurer would be present. 'And he was impressive,' recalled McNicoll. McMahon would talk with dazzling detail and authority on all facets of international finance and economics. 'His grip, his absolute positive assertions, impressed guests greatly,' wrote McNicoll.[33]

McMahon spent the winter working on the budget. He immersed

himself in the Treasury throughout its preparation, reportedly to the point of occupying an office in the department.[34] Recognising that military commitments in Vietnam were taking up an outsized portion of expenditure, McMahon and his officials worked to reduce spending elsewhere. In mid-July, following three full days of cabinet meetings on the budget,[35] McMahon, Roland Wilson, and Peter Howson shared a bottle of champagne to celebrate their success in guiding the deliberations. As minister assisting the treasurer, the English-born Howson was well placed to appraise McMahon. What he saw left him enamoured, and would make him an admirer and confidant of the treasurer—a point reiterated in the diary that he diligently maintained in the ensuing years. McMahon, he wrote, 'had certainly done a magnificent job, with a complete mastery of each of the 107 Cabinet submissions'.[36]

Was it really so smooth? Later, McMahon claimed a completely different experience. While putting the final touches on the budget documents during a holiday at the Alexandria Headland, McMahon claimed that he came to believe that the budget was not economically or politically sensible. Sonia and Maurice O'Donnell, a deputy secretary in the Treasury, had agreed, with Sonia particularly pointed about the measures for families and children.[37] McMahon managed to persuade Holt to his view, but then had to run the gauntlet and, supposedly, get agreement to his proposed changes from Alan Hulme, Paul Hasluck, and John McEwen, with the latter bitterly denouncing the move in private.[38] Whatever the veracity of this claim, it points yet again to key characteristics of McMahon's: a belief that his grasp of politics and economics was far ahead of his peers'.

McMahon handed down the 1966–67 budget at eight o'clock on Tuesday 16 August 1966. Nervous, speaking flatly, and sipping repeatedly from a glass of water, the fifteen minutes that it took him to arrive at the budget's 'central problem' provoked a guffaw from Fred Daly that it was 'about time'.[39] Observing that military commitments required a 34 per cent increase in defence spending from the 1965–66 budget, McMahon argued it had required that 'difficult choices' be made in all other areas of expenditure.[40] Thus the absence of reductions in taxation, the small increase in spending on pensions—'Not enough,' Arthur Calwell called, after McMahon announced the $1 increase—and the careful caveat that only 'within limits' did the government want the budget to be 'expansionary'.[41]

Its reception was decidedly mixed. Outside of the 'quite impressed' coalition party room,[42] New South Wales Liberal Party premier Bob Askin suggested that state taxes would rise as a result of the token assistance given to his state. Manufacturing and employers' bodies made their disappointment clear.[43] Even the ever-reliable *Daily Telegraph* argued that while McMahon had 'done a good job' amid 'difficult circumstances', the pension increase was simply 'niggardly'.[44] *The Australian* suggested the budget was timid, and called it 'a half-speed-ahead budget'; *The Age* called it 'practical'.[45] Both papers gave faint praise for the government's resistance to election-year largesse.

McMahon might well have hoped for inclusion of another measure: the removal of the marriage bar. In April, aware that the inter-departmental committee was soon to report on the consequences of its removal, he had written to Holt to remind him that 'the submission is on the march again'. Assuming the committee reported in time, McMahon suggested keeping it for the budget, so that he could announce it. 'It is one I initiated personally,' he added, pointedly.[46] But the report had arrived too late for the occasion, and the minister for labour and national service, Leslie Bury, was only able to report to cabinet on the issue on 24 August. This time, with the support of Holt, McMahon, and Bury, the recommendation that the marriage bar be removed was accepted.[47] Legislation was prepared for October. The Bill was passed, and when it came into effect on 18 November it finally removed the outdated barrier to equal employment in Australia.

Almost immediately after the budget, tensions with McEwen flared again. At first, it was a request for a loan to assist the sugar industry. In cabinet, McMahon pointed out that the Commonwealth had provided assistance earlier in the year: '[I] don't believe we should go further.' The principle and precedent was at the top of McMahon's argument to refuse: 'If we agree and give $19m to bring them up to 1965 income, where do we stop and why not other commodities too?' The extended debate was fierce. Calling sugar 'a great national industry', McEwen argued it was a 'victim of US foreign policy'. To McMahon's 'query' about precedent, McEwen was forthright: if the same request were made the next year, his answer would be yes, again. 'We can't allow a great industry to die,' he said.[48] Liberals in the cabinet echoed McMahon's arguments, but this time Holt sided with the Country Party, accepting that sugar was 'an industry of such value that it has to be sustained'. McMahon and his officials were aghast, and in a subsequent cabinet meeting his submission sought to change Holt's mind. McEwen would have none of it: 'What I give you is my best and I consider well-informed judgment,' he said. 'Don't brush it aside—it's not a Country Party judgment, it's a best judgment on [a] wider canvas.'[49]

Then there were problems over tariffs. In October, the Tariff Board's proposal to introduce a system of bounties and a support price on industrial chemicals was submitted to cabinet, and McMahon and McEwen butted heads again. 'Our industry can be pushed out of [the] ring by giant competitors,' McEwen told cabinet. 'We decided by the terms of our reference [for the report to the Tariff Board] that we want the industry ... we must assist.'[50] McMahon disagreed with the main thrust of the report, believing that acceptance would result in inefficiency and that it should therefore be examined further. To this, McEwen was cutting: 'What that means is that we put T[ariff] B[oard] aside and set up an independent committee in its place—we can't do it.'[51]

McEwen's resulting victory in cabinet caused criticism from Newton, who echoed McMahon's line and assailed cabinet's timidity in accepting McEwen's policy. In *Incentive*, the journalist argued that 'there is virtually no possibility of competition from imports', and that Australia was going to be 'wasting increasing quantities of scarce national capital in an area of production where we are perhaps worse off, in an internationally competitive sense, than in almost any other area of national economic activity'.[52]

According to McMahon, this fight poisoned McEwen against him. 'When John McEwen went mad on tariffs,' he said, 'I opposed him bitterly. It was one of the reasons he became a bitter enemy of mine.'[53]

Fortunately for the government, attention to these divisions was diverted when United States president Lyndon Johnson visited Australia late in October. The relationship with the US had been on show throughout the year. Johnson's vice-president, Hubert Humphrey, had visited Australia in February and Holt had travelled to the United States in July, where he declared that Australia was 'an admiring friend' and 'staunch ally' that would be 'all the way with LBJ'.[54] The government's commitment to the US alliance and Holt's warm relationship with Johnson had also been evident in the February decision to support the US bombing campaign in North Vietnam, the March decision to treble Australia's military presence in Vietnam to 4,500 men, and Holt's tour of South Vietnam and South-East Asia in April. Johnson's visit, replete with a ticker tape parade and declarations of support, also helped the government overcome the increasingly vociferous criticism of conscription.

The government's view was that Australia's contribution to Vietnam was the premium to be paid for the ANZUS alliance, and was crucial to maintaining American presence in the Asia-Pacific. This won public support. Yet Peter Kelly, in the run-up to the election, asked McMahon if he thought the Americans would truly ever come to Australia's aid in the event of an attack. McMahon sat back and thought. Kelly, who had expected an immediate answer, was amazed—a feeling that was increased when McMahon eventually responded: 'No, I don't.'[55]

Australia's involvement in Vietnam became the principal issue of the 1966 election, called for 26 November. With the ALP still wholeheartedly opposed to the war, the campaign posed a sharp policy-based choice for voters. Moreover, Harold Holt's fresh and relaxed media presence gave the Liberals an advantage over the ageing, raspy-voiced Arthur Calwell, fighting his third election as the ALP's leader.

McMahon's stature as deputy party leader and treasurer meant that his voice was loud. He echoed the domino theory, and argued that conscription was the only way to fortify Australia's security.[56] He also provided his own justification for Australia's intervention in Vietnam. Alongside Australia's treaty obligations under SEATO, its alliance with the US, and the threat posed by communism to world peace, McMahon again voiced the liberal sentiments that had animated him back in 1954. 'Nations should have the right to freedom and independence,' he said. 'The individual should be free to determine his own form of Government. We believe all people should join in the benefits of modern scientific discoveries and technological developments. We do not believe that nations should resort to war to settle their political problems. These are the fundamental reasons why we are fighting with our allies in South Vietnam.'[57]

On the domestic front, he called the ALP out for its 'inaccurate, inept, irresponsible and deceptive' economic policies. 'He must think he is Father Christmas,' McMahon said of Calwell.[58]

But the campaign revealed divisions within the non-Labor party memberships. In New South Wales, a splinter group of supposedly disaffected Liberal members attacked the government over its support for the Vietnam War. Funded by Gordon Barton—owner of IPEC (the Interstate Parcel Express Company), McMahon's old university friend, and a critic of the government's 'two airlines' policy—the so-called Liberal Reform Group, organised only a few weeks before the poll, carried an anti-war message aimed at voters stranded in the policy divide between the Coalition and Labor.[59] McMahon denounced them immediately.[60]

Meanwhile, in Queensland, the graziers who had been criticising McEwen's policies on tariffs announced that they would encourage people to vote for Liberal Party candidates in five electorates where the Country Party was running against Liberal and Labor candidates. Funded by Charles Russell, a disaffected former Country Party MP, the Basic Industries Group (BIG) attacked McEwen for what it argued were the higher costs his tariff policies were imposing on primary producers. McEwen was not backward in taking them on: he called them 'faceless' and a 'distraction' from the message of the election.[61]

In spite of these divisions, the government was re-elected in stunning fashion. The Coalition's numbers in the House swelled from seventy-two to eighty-two, and the Coalition vote, expressed as a percentage, was its highest since 1951. The efforts of BIG came to naught. It barely affected the electorates in which it had campaigned. In Lowe, McMahon's majority went up by nearly 3 per cent. Francis James, the candidate for the Liberal Reform Group, garnered only 4 per cent of the vote—not that it would dissuade Gordon Barton from further involvement in politics.[62]

Triumph was supplemented when, two days later, at King George V Hospital, McMahon became a father. Born at seven-and-a-half pounds, Melinda Rachel McMahon had 'long slender fingers, beautiful blue eyes like her mother's, quite a lot of auburn hair and her mother's lips,' McMahon said to reporters. He was delighted enough to joke around: 'The only thing about her that resembles me is her voice—it's good and loud.'[63] When Melinda was baptised, Holt and George Halliday were present as her godfathers.[64]

For McMahon, 1966 was a triumph, strewn with highlights and achievements. Val Kentish emphasised this same point. 'You had just been married,' she told him, years later. 'You had just become treasurer. You were elected deputy leader of the Liberal Party. You had moved into a new home. You became a Privy Counsellor [on 14 June]. And at the end of the year you became a father. And everyone who ever knew you sent a congratulatory message. I know—because I answered them all!'[65]

THE year that followed revealed that the triumph had come laced with danger. Chief among them was the elevation of a new opponent.

Gough Whitlam's accession to the ALP leadership on 8 February 1967 was the most foreseeable outcome of the 1966 election result. Tall, erudite, eloquent, and quick-witted, with a compelling self-belief that could infuriate colleagues, Whitlam seemed nothing like ALP leaders of the past. He had a decidedly middle-class background: the son of a senior public servant, he had attended Canberra Grammar School; like McMahon, he had studied arts, then law at Sydney University while boarding at St Paul's College. When World War II broke out, Whitlam had interrupted his studies and joined the RAAF, serving as a navigator aboard Ventura bombers in northern Australia, attacking Japanese targets in the Timor Sea. When he arrived in the House of Representatives in 1952 as member for the Sydney electorate of Werriwa, Whitlam began setting out unexpectedly new directions for the ALP. He took an interest in housing and urban development, constitutional law, and Commonwealth–state relations. Serving as Calwell's deputy since 1960, in increasingly bitter circumstances, Whitlam survived fierce party infighting to consolidate a position as a party leader-in-waiting. He had evident appeal to the media and middle classes, represented (even more than Holt) a generational change in Australia's leadership, and possessed a formidable parliamentary presence.[66]

McMahon and Whitlam had clashed in the past, most notably in September 1957, while McMahon was minister for primary industry. A minor kerfuffle about the provision of a report on poultry saw the two exchange insults in the House. McMahon declared that his decision to withhold the report stemmed from his observation that Whitlam was unable to 'interpret facts correctly or to draw proper conclusions'. Menzies intervened to stop the matter continuing, but when McMahon tried to frustrate Whitlam's objection, the Member for Werriwa lashed out: 'You dingo! You stink and crawl away!' Whitlam withdrew the remark, but later in the day, when the matter came up in the adjournment debate, McMahon provoked him again. 'This is one more contribution by the honourable member to what can be regarded as a tissue of falsehoods and misrepresentation relating to this particular matter,' he said.

Whitlam's interjection was immediate and it was cutting: 'I would resent that from anybody but a quean like this.'[67]

The insult 'was too personal, too cruel and too precise,' wrote Whitlam's biographer, and Whitlam apologised when the House resumed on 1 October.[68] Whitlam had hardly calmed his temper in the years since this outburst, but he had certainly outgrown its juvenility, and over the year would establish a clear ascendancy over Holt in the House, exacerbating government difficulties elsewhere.

One of those was in the Senate. Special elections to fill six vacancies in the Senate had been held alongside the election in November. While the government won four of the six vacancies, one of those won by the Labor Party, in Western Australia, had previously been a government-held seat, and it thus emerged from the election one seat weaker in the Senate than it had been. In February 1967, its strength declined further when South Australian Liberal senator Clive Hannaford resigned his party membership and moved to the crossbenches to protest Australia's involvement in the Vietnam War. Hannaford's resignation meant that the government could only count on twenty-eight votes in the sixty-strong Senate, notwithstanding that he remained generally sympathetic. It was a weakness compounded by another problem: a sizeable and restless government backbench in the House of Representatives.

More fractious, less disciplined than those of the past, the government's backbench members and senators were keen to make their presence felt. As the Labor speechwriter Graham Freudenberg later observed, the new backbench knew nothing of opposition or defeat. The near-loss of 1961 meant little to them. 'They knew little about Holt and he knew little about them,' wrote Freudenberg.[69] In the Senate, the government's weakness was exacerbated by backbenchers willing to cross the floor, sometimes impervious to the consequences.

All of these factors would come into play over 1967—and turn it into a year that McMahon would come to rue.

CHAPTER TWENTY-ONE

Protection (II)

1967

The rivalry and antagonism between McMahon and McEwen reached into the public service. Their departments were in constant competition to stay ahead of one another. 'Again there is a battle with Trade, but at least we are trying to hurry Treasury to get their job done quickly so that we will be ready to deal with it in cabinet before Trade are ready to deal with theirs,' wrote Peter Howson, after a February meeting with McMahon.[1]

Throughout the early months of 1967, at the urging of their respective ministers, both departments were formulating proposals to strengthen—and, in McEwen's case, *protect*—investment opportunities in Australia. McEwen wished to create a government-funded corporation to raise money internationally and invest in new, large-scale Australian companies and projects. In his vision, the Australian Industry Development Corporation (AIDC) would allow Australian businesses to avoid trading away control of the assets that they built up in exchange for the investment necessary for success. He talked about it in terms of not 'selling off the farm'. The purpose of McEwen's proposal was not to eradicate foreign investment, but to narrow the open-door policy that he believed the Treasury was allowing.

McMahon's proposal was similar in purpose, but wholly domestic in nature. Arising from a document he found in his in-tray upon becoming treasurer, as he said later,[2] his Bankers' Development Refinance Corporation would draw from the trading banks and, with support from the Reserve Bank, allow Australian investors to access larger amounts of domestic capital than was then available. As McMahon

later argued, the benefit of the Treasury's proposal was that it would
not be competing with the Australian government—as McEwen's
proposal would—when it sought to borrow from overseas lenders.[3]
His corporation would give 'large new capabilities to the Australian
capital market,' McMahon said. 'It will enable Australian enterprise to
venture more boldly in the development of Australian resources on a
massive scale and will advance us, as a people, towards a fuller and more
productive use and control of the natural riches of our own country.'[4]

But the fights over these proposals and tariff policy worried the
prime minister. On 24 March, just before the proposals went to cabinet
and on the same day that his brother died, Holt expressed concern about
McEwen's reactions, and suggested that McMahon allow McEwen to
win a few of their debates.[5] Though angered, McMahon also realised
that it would be unwise to push McEwen too far. Bert Kelly, who had
been given a ministry after the 1966 election, recalled this awareness
after McMahon encouraged him to attend a cabinet committee
meeting on tariffs on stationary cars: 'Come along Bert, and carry the
argument against it.' When Kelly did so, and McEwen 'started to do
his block', McMahon told him it would be better to be quiet: 'You're
carrying things a bit far.'[6]

The rift between the men was verging unconscionably close to
being played out in public. During Question Time on 11 April, the
Labor member for Bendigo, Noel Beaton, asked McEwen whether he
agreed with McMahon's dismissal, made on television, of the effect
on Australia of the mooted British entry to the European Common
Market. McEwen did not rise from his seat. He made no move to
answer the question at all. He simply sat there, steadfastly ignoring
the waiting MPs and colleagues around him. Eventually, the Speaker,
William Aston, was forced to intervene: 'I do not think the Minister for
Trade and Industry is responsible for a statement made on television by
another Minister.'[7]

The dispute over the AIDC was a proxy for the longer, larger battle.
McEwen believed that McMahon's continued opposition to all that he
did went beyond any policy-based difference: 'I thought on a number
of occasions that he was attacking particular proposals simply because
I was putting them forward and not on their merits.'[8] He also believed
that it was fought over in a consistently scurrilous way:

McMahon did all he could to oppose this [the AIDC], even bringing in a Bill which he thought, incorrectly, would make the Corporation unnecessary. At one stage a paper attacking the notion of the AIDC and arguing that this body would be used to further Country Party interests was circulated in Cabinet ... It transpired that the document had been written by a Treasury official and that it was being circulated on McMahon's authority but not through the normal channel provided by the cabinet secretariat.[9]

Hasluck agreed, suggesting that McEwen was 'subjected to constant misrepresentation, disclosures to the press of departmental information, and attempts to rally various lobbies of opinion against him'.[10] For Hasluck, the method was bound up in character: 'By nature, he [McMahon] would prefer the devious route to the direct route.'[11] Was McMahon so devious as to leak? 'Undoubtedly,' said David Solomon, a journalist in the Press Gallery at this time. 'There wasn't anyone in the Press Gallery who didn't think so ... McMahon's principal target (of the leaks) was McEwen.'[12] Their relationship was heated: 'They hated each other like poison,' Don Chipp would later say.[13] 'It was a real, genuine hatred between McEwen and McMahon,' said journalist Alan Ramsey.[14] Their policy differences exacerbated their considerable personal differences, as Doug Anthony later argued. 'They were a bit like water and oil,' he said. 'They didn't mix very well. I think that over a period of time, McMahon told stories to the media that annoyed John McEwen.'[15]

However McMahon fought, no one could deny that he was doughty, even formidable, in cabinet. John Bunting, secretary of the prime minister's department, thought that McMahon's approach to that forum was key. 'He was tenacious in cabinet as a minister,' he remarked. 'More than anyone else, he used to regard it, if necessary, as a battleground.' This was an approach that had gone on for years. 'If he, as minister for labour, or the navy in the early days,' Bunting said, 'or foreign affairs, later, or Treasury—if he came in there as the minister for any of those, [then] he battled and if he didn't get total victory he went out wounded, and he seemed to think it was a point of honour.'[16] Richard Farmer agreed: 'McMahon showed much more strength in those internal debates than people give him credit for ... He fought his corner, and invariably won.'[17] Howson attributed McMahon's victories to extensive preparation, wide consultation, practised arguments, and hard work. 'The reason Treasury won,' he said, 'was because McMahon had done his homework much better than McEwen had.'[18]

It was undeniable that both men had supporters in the press. McEwen could usually rely on support from Rupert Murdoch's *Australian;* in *The Sydney Morning Herald*, he could count on Ian Fitchett, the moustachioed, aloof political correspondent, to echo his point of view. McMahon, in turn, could rely on Sir Frank Packer, Alan Reid, and Maxwell Newton. Farmer, a journalist who joined Newton's growing stable of newsletters, recalled that the relationship between McMahon and Newton occurred almost entirely over the phone, even though Newton worked barely a suburb from Parliament House. 'They'd talk for hours every Saturday.' Sometimes McMahon would call from his home, sometimes from a payphone. He would never say hello. Just: 'Is Max there?' Farmer invariably answered, and, upon hearing the recognisably 'squeaky voice', would get Newton. Overhearing Newton's part in the conversation, Farmer had no doubt what was happening: McMahon would be going through economic matters on the cabinet agenda, and Newton would provide advice.[19] McMahon's press secretary, Peter Kelly, concurred. Was there an exchange of ideas, information, and perspectives between McMahon and Newton? 'Yes, all the time,' he said.[20]

The proposals for McEwen's AIDC and McMahon's Bankers' Development Refinance Corporation (later known as the Australian Resources Development Bank) were put on the cabinet agenda for discussion on the same day. When McEwen saw this, he 'sniffed the air' and beat a tactical retreat.[21] McMahon's proposal was approved and the bank duly established. But McMahon was not content with this victory. When McEwen wrangled an agreement that 'a study' would be made of the practicalities of the AIDC, McMahon did all he could to see it killed off.[22] The Department of Trade just wanted 'an all day sucker' to keep it quiet, he said later.[23] Thus, on 15 May, he wrote to Holt to report the unfavourable findings of a Treasury officer who had sounded out overseas bankers about McEwen's proposal. In the process, he accused McEwen of impropriety for sending a public servant overseas on a similar mission:

Employing travelling salesmen to sell one Department's ideas in a field belonging to another Minister's responsibilities, and before Cabinet has reached conclusions on them, is carrying impropriety to lengths that should not be tolerated.[24]

On 16 May, with McEwen absent at trade talks, Holt revealed his susceptibility to McMahon's arguments. Holt criticised the Country Party minister for social services and acting minister for trade, Ian Sinclair, for a speech made two days earlier, which had suggested the AIDC was going ahead.[25] Calling the whole issue 'an embarrassment', Holt complained that 'the impression being spread is that we have taken [the] main decision and [that] only details [are] left for consideration'.

When asked to speak, McMahon gloated. He said that the continued references to the AIDC undermined the Treasury scheme. 'This [is] not permissible and I object,' he said. He expressed his 'surprise' and 'deep regret', and spoke of the 'impression' of 'hostility' between Trade and Treasury—and between ministers. He then brought up the reports of officials within McEwen's department canvassing reception to the AIDC: 'This [is] intolerable.' Sinclair denied any intention of an attack on Treasury, but defended the 'consulting' that those officials were doing. Holt tried to draw it all to a close: 'We've got [a] certain amount of water under the bridge.'[26]

But McMahon's and Treasury's lobbying against the 'McEwen Bank', as it came to be known, did not stop. It went on behind the scenes and in the press. 'We have here a plan for a Government bank,' wrote Maxwell Newton, the next day, 'under the control of the Country Party, to be known as the AID Corporation, under the mantle of Mr McEwen, going out to borrow money overseas on Commonwealth Government guarantee and then to relend that money to Mr McEwen's friends.'[27] Sir Richard Randall wrote to McMahon and Holt, arguing that the Department of Trade and Industry had 'no formal responsibilities in the area of public finance, banking, loan raisings, local or foreign, or for the regulation of investment', and yet had put forward its proposal without 'any consultation whatsoever'. Approval of the AIDC would challenge 'long established financial policies and procedures' and enlist the Commonwealth government as 'the guarantor of loans raised for investment in private enterprise', Randall argued. Most importantly and fundamentally, it was 'a challenge to the hegemony of the Treasury over one of its most important and difficult fields of responsibility'.[28] The advocacy from McMahon and Randall worked in pushing the AIDC off the agenda—which was just as well, for other, long-running issues were moving towards their climaxes, seemingly all at once.

One such issue was discontent over the findings of the royal commission that had investigated the collision in 1964 of HMAS *Voyager* and HMAS *Melbourne* and the subsequent deaths of eighty-two navy personnel.[29] Led by the former attorney-general and the then–chief judge of the Industrial Court, Sir John Spicer, the commission had criticised Captain John Robertson, commanding officer of HMAS *Melbourne*, in terms that implied negligence on his part, and apportioned him with the heaviest blame for the disaster. When the Naval Board subsequently failed to defend him or clear him of the imputation, and he was given an appointment that amounted to a demotion, Robertson resigned from the navy.

Politics entered the affair almost immediately. The minister for the navy and Liberal member for Perth, Fred Chaney, prevented Robertson from receiving a pension, and cabinet concurred. But John Jess, Liberal member for La Trobe, believed that the government's handling of the affair had been ham-fisted, and that the denial of a pension to Robertson was unjust. Jess had met repeatedly with Menzies to discuss the issue, and, in the lead-up to the 1966 election, had presented Holt with what he regarded as evidence that warranted another inquiry: chiefly, that the commanding officer aboard *Voyager*, Captain Duncan Stevens, had a history of being unable to exercise command due to inebriation.

By March 1967, Jess had enough allies on the swollen government backbench to force a reckoning on the issue. Despite the best efforts of the new minister for the navy, Don Chipp, to evaluate the veracity of the new evidence, Jess would not be persuaded to desist.[30] McMahon became involved as a relay between Jess and Holt. Jess wanted the royal commission reopened, the findings against Robertson and other officers re-examined, and the new evidence that related to Stevens examined. Jess stated that he was prepared to raise the matter in the House, resign from the party, and resign from Parliament altogether if his demands were not met. Support for Jess's campaign continued to grow, but cabinet held firm. McMahon advised Holt against any ex gratia payment to Robertson and, on 2 May, Holt delivered exactly that message to Jess. Within three days, news that there was a dispute had leaked to the press; within a few days of that, the issue at hand was widely known. Political pressure became immense: the press, the ALP, and the government's backbench were agitating for a new inquiry. Unable to withstand it, Holt agreed that the House would debate the affair on 16 May.

It was the same day that Holt had taken Sinclair to task over the AIDC, and, during the evening debate, he made an egregious error. The new Liberal member for Warringah, Edward St John, was making his first speech in the House. A Sydney-based QC turned politician who proudly noted his relation to Oliver St John, the counsel who had defended John Hampden from Charles I's attempts to collect ship money without parliamentary approval, St John had a wowser's propensity for disapproval and an ambition exceeded only by a zealous regard for the truth. He had decided to speak about the sinking of *Voyager*—a deliberately provocative matter to address. Holt attended the beginning of the speech, left, and then inexplicably returned to listen. After declaring his belief in the veracity of the new evidence, St John asked:

> Is it irrelevant that the captain of a destroyer in port is perpetually drunk, comes back every morning at eight o'clock under the influence of liquor, sleeps all day, and then starts drinking again? ... Is this irrelevant? Is not this one of the facts and circumstances leading up to the *Voyager*'s disaster? Or have I lost the meaning of the word 'irrelevant'? Are we playing a battle of semantics? What is the meaning of the word 'irrelevant'?[31]

Angry and red-faced, Holt was moved to interject: 'What is the meaning of the word "evidence"?'[32]

Holt's breach of courtesy was conspicuous. No one had interrupted an MP's first speech in more than a decade.[33] Holt's undisguised embarrassment pointed to his immediate regret at having done so. Some observers picked it as the moment that revealed 'how the pressures of his job were beginning to eat away' at Holt.[34]

When he summed up the debate the next day, McMahon tried to slap St John down and give the initiative back to Holt. 'The Government has not closed its options,' he said. 'The Prime Minister after considering all points that have been raised will take the matter back to the party room and then decide exactly what is to be done.' Nonetheless, it was evident that an inquiry would have to be held, which was exactly what Holt confirmed on 18 May.[35]

Nine days later, a long-gestating and repeatedly rescheduled referendum was finally held. The referendum posed two questions. The first proposed to amend section 24 of the constitution, 'breaking' the nexus between the House of Representatives and the Senate, which provided that the House should, 'as nearly as practicable', be twice the size of the Senate; the second question proposed the removal of discriminatory references to Aborigines from sections 51 and 127 of the constitution.

The timing of the referendum was poor. In blows to Holt's authority and standing, six Coalition senators declared their opposition to the first question, and it was resoundingly defeated nationally and in every state except New South Wales. However, the second question was carried overwhelmingly, with 90.77 per cent of the vote, in all six states. The margin of that result provided impetus for Holt to establish the Council for Aboriginal Affairs and to enlarge Commonwealth government involvement in Indigenous Australian matters.

Yet again, unhappily for Holt, the tensions between McMahon and McEwen continued to bubble and froth. In private, McMahon was critical of negotiations McEwen had undertaken on wheat prices at trade talks in Geneva. 'Bill McMahon tells me that it's going to cost us quite a lot in foreign exchange and is hardly worth our taking part in the agreement,' Peter Howson recorded.[36] McMahon's criticisms undoubtedly occupied some of the weekly telephone conversations he was having with Maxwell Newton, who recorded very nearly the same things in *Incentive*: 'Meanwhile, Mr McEwen has so far achieved virtually nothing in his negotiations in Geneva ... He has had to accept what he said he would not accept before he left Australia.'[37] By mid-June, McMahon and McEwen were arguing volubly: 'The row has been so fierce that Harold Holt himself has had to intervene between the two of them,' Howson wrote, after McMahon told him about it.[38]

An edge of their dispute was revealed to the public after McEwen made a speech at a convention of woolgrowers and graziers on 19 June. Responding to an earlier speaker who had criticised his approach to tariffs, McEwen defended himself and the policy he was pursuing. Then, he resurrected an old enemy, and argued that the criticisms he had heard were those of the Basic Industries Group (BIG):

[This is] a group, unseen and unknown—its members faceless and nameless but very real indeed—very rich, indeed, and very reckless in misrepresentation. It has one publicly avowed intention ... to destroy the Country Party in favour of the Liberal Party.[39]

The reference to the Liberal Party was not an accident. The mentions of BIG were a feint. This was an attack on McMahon, one that McEwen renewed two days later while addressing the Country Party's annual conference. The somewhat-beguiled BIG, gifted a notoriety far beyond its worth, held a press conference and announced that it would re-form.[40]

McMahon saw instantly what was happening. He sent a note to Holt, who was abroad: 'Just in case you get a question about this statement on your arrival. We in the Liberal Party have no association and never have had any with the Group.'[41] Advised by his colleagues to keep quiet,[42] he went to Sydney Airport on 22 June to meet the prime minister when he returned to the country. He denied having anything to do with BIG or knowing about them at all.[43]

The denial did not stop the controversy. On 26 June, *Sydney Morning Herald* political correspondent Ian Fitchett published a story with a knotty, if hardly subtle, accusation:

If Mr Holt raises with Mr McEwen the BIG question, Mr McEwen will be able to point out that while he himself has made no charge that a senior Liberal Minister was working with the group, everybody connected with politics had no doubt that such a Minister, even if he were not working with the BIG, was carrying out his own campaign against the Country Party.

Moreover, despite himself *not* making any such accusation, McEwen was 'bound', the article continued, 'to demand an assurance from Mr Holt that the senior Liberal Minister concerned clears himself and also gives an assurance that he will cease his alleged activities'.[44] It took no great deductive powers to understand that the senior minister was McMahon, nor that the attack placed him in an impossible situation. He could hardly prove a negative, nor could he attack an accuser who did not exist.

On 29 June, the spokesperson for BIG denied that they knew McMahon or that he had any connection to their efforts. Holt spoke on the same day. Trying to end the squabbling, he called criticism of the Country Party and McEwen's approach on tariffs unfair, and stated that McMahon had given him assurances that he had nothing whatsoever to do with BIG. Restoring the Coalition's unity was Holt's ultimate objective: 'The activity of any organisation which could be regarded as prejudicial to the harmonious working of the Coalition is certainly not in the interests of myself or any of my colleagues in the Coalition.'

Luckily, events moved on swiftly. When Britain announced it would withdraw its military forces from Malaysia and Singapore by the mid-1970s, Australia's defence policy was thrown into flux, prompting considerable dismay and anger. The British attitude, Holt told the British secretary of state for defence, Denis Healey, in a June meeting, appeared to be that 'the world east of Suez could go to hell'.[45] There were also Loan Council meetings to hold and the budget to prepare. Those meetings prompted more rows and more concern—particularly for Holt. On 26 July, over dinner at Government House, having heard the prime minister bemoaning the McMahon–McEwen feud, the governor-general, Richard Casey, offered to intervene. As he later explained, Casey believed that ensuring the stability of the government was 'one of his responsibilities' as governor-general.[46] It was an extraordinary offer in many respects, verging on improper, but Holt demurred on taking him up on it immediately.[47]

Casey's offer was a signal of just how serious the problems were becoming—and how much Holt needed to get control of his government.

AS treasurer, McMahon was always keen to reinforce perceptions that he had complete mastery of his portfolio. 'He was always trying to impress people,' recalled Alan Ramsey. 'Always.'[48] McMahon's way of doing so—by 'the numerical blitzkrieg', as journalist Maximilian Walsh called it—had remained the same for years. He would confidently bombard audiences with figures and statistics on every economic measure, and they were never, ever wrong.[49]

The reality was different, but it was hidden by the elaborate work of his office. While McMahon rained down numerical hell on the ALP in the House, a member of his staff would check his figures with Treasury officials. His office would then prepare copies of McMahon's answers—with the correct figures—for distribution in the Press Gallery. Unable to wait until the publication of *Hansard* the next morning, journalists would use those answers for the reports they filed that night.[50]

It would not have worked had journalists paid more attention. When he began work in the gallery, Robert Haupt observed that upon any question asked of McMahon, the pens in the gallery would go down. There seemed to be an unspoken consensus that it was time for a break. It took Haupt a little while, but soon enough he understood. *Why would you bother recording answers when you were going to have the full text soon enough?* Not quite so lazy himself, Haupt took notes and compared them to the daily and weekly *Hansards*. But he was boggled to find himself in the wrong. 'They invariably told the same story,' he wrote. 'McMahon right; Haupt wrong.'[51]

The reason for that lay again with McMahon's office. When *Hansard* extracts were sent to it for proofing, the figures would be altered to be true, to align with the answers distributed the day before. 'He [McMahon] was a devil with the way he used to alter *Hansard*,' Peter Kelly recalled. 'You're not supposed to alter *Hansard*, but he'd make all sorts of alterations and corrections.'[52]

There could be no such alterations to the budget speech. Because of its importance and high visibility, drafts of the speech were largely prepared within the Treasury. Stemming from Randall's pen, the 1967–68 budget speech, delivered on 15 August, was clear, punchy, and notably devoid of statistical blizzards.

It was a budget that again wrestled with defence expenditure. Despite the opposition of Allen Fairhall, Malcolm Fraser, and officials within the prime minister's department, McMahon managed to prune a mooted 24 per cent increase in the defence vote to 18 per cent. This 'dominant element' was allocated $1,118m, and McMahon offered self-congratulations for accommodating the substantial rise without 'distortion or disruption' of the economy. Nonetheless, he noted that similar escalations of spending could not continue. The example of Britain, then attempting to reduce the resources that it devoted to defence, was salutary. 'Seriously weaken the potential for growth,' he told the House, 'and the capacity to support an expanding defence effort is whittled away.'

Despite the expenditure on defence, the budget was notable for its spending on social services. There were measures to provide hearing aids for pensioners, benefits for people with disabilities, and an increase in child-endowment assistance for large families. The lattermost measure prompted laughter from Labor MPs: 'You are only looking after yourself,' Jim Cope called. Even McMahon could laugh: 'As I said at my Party meeting, it shows that I have other ambitions besides my political ones.'[53]

Reception to the budget was far better than the previous year's. *The Daily Telegraph* and *The Age* variously called it a 'no-shock' and 'no worry' budget that would aid the 'family man'. Though *The Australian* was more critical (once its striking printers returned to work), it, too, gave McMahon some praise.[54] Maxwell Newton, in an appearance in the pages of *The Age*, was also positive, arguing that McMahon's achievement was restraining the growth of government spending.[55]

The budget was a rare moment of good news and respite. Divisions within the government were never in abeyance for long,[56] and missives about its faltering support in the electorate were all too regular. The May referendum had been followed by a by-election in July to replace Liberal MP Hubert Opperman, who had resigned to become high commissioner to Malta. The loss of that seat prompted concern from many within the party;[57] the subsequent death of Labor MP George Gray augured another by-election, this one in the Queensland seat of Capricornia. Despite suggestions that it be delayed to coincide with the Senate elections due in November, the date was fixed for 30 September. An established Labor seat, the government nevertheless campaigned energetically. Holt declared that he wanted to win it. McMahon did not go so far, but he put his foot in it when he attacked the Labor candidate's atheism.[58] The press, not unreasonably, took a dim view of the overly personal criticism; and when the by-election was held, the

ALP candidate, Dr Doug Everingham, easily made it home. It was another blow to Holt and, according to Labor speechwriter Graham Freudenberg, the psychological effects were profound. The prime minister, he thought, had lost 'something of himself in Capricornia'.[59]

McMahon was not around to survey the damage. Accompanied by Sonia, he left Australia on 13 September to attend the Commonwealth finance ministers' meeting in Trinidad, which discussed the position of British sterling, the British application to join the European Economic Community, and the economic problems of the developing Commonwealth countries. Then he flew to Rio de Janeiro for a meeting of the International Monetary Fund (IMF). There, he spoke on the need to study gold production and its place in the international money market. From there, McMahon and Sonia flew to New York, where they received a summons from US president Lyndon Johnson.

Johnson apparently wanted advice on how to rid himself of US defence secretary Robert McNamara, whose differences over Vietnam War policy were growing. By chance, on the plane between Rio de Janeiro and New York, Sonia had been seated next to George Woods, the president of the World Bank, and he had informed Sonia that he intended to resign. 'So I told Bill, who told Lyndon Johnson, who then appointed McNamara as the head of the World Bank,' Sonia said later.[60]

This was not the only topic of discussion. Aware that McMahon was concerned about the economic strains caused by the rapid growth of military expenditure, the US president pressed him for more support in Vietnam. Johnson, McMahon wrote to Holt, expressed himself 'in strong and at times emotional language' on the matter, to the point that the Australian ambassador to the United States, Keith Waller, told McMahon afterward he could not 'remember stronger pressure being brought to bear'.[61] The same pressure was applied again when McMahon met McNamara. McMahon had been directed by cabinet to meet with the defence secretary to discuss the F-111, a long-in-the-works tactical strike and bombing aircraft that the Australian government had agreed to purchase in 1963. Delays, technical problems, and budgetary excesses had plagued the plane, and, despite the initial intransigence of the US defence secretary, McMahon managed to renegotiate the spread of payments for the aircraft. This was a win—but also a sop, as McNamara proceeded to lambast McMahon about Australia's contribution to

Vietnam. None of America's allies, McNamara told him, was 'bearing their fair share of the load'.[62]

Neither his success nor his absence from Australia had removed McMahon from criticism; if anything, in his absence, it spread and intensified—chiefly over news that Newton had accompanied McMahon on the trip. Rumours that Newton had gone at McMahon's invitation, and as an advisor to him, caused great unrest. When a journalist rang Liberal Party director Bob Willoughby to ask whether the party was paying Newton's fare, Willoughby 'nearly had a seizure'.[63] In the House, Labor Party frontbencher Frank Crean asked if Newton was now on McMahon's staff or writing for a newspaper.[64] The prime minister's office was sufficiently concerned to look into the rumour.[65] Supposedly at the deputy prime minister's instigation, McEwen's staff began gathering information on Newton and his relationship with McMahon:

> On being questioned as to why he thought NEWTON was dangerous, informant said that he was convinced that NEWTON was working to split the Liberal-Country Party coalition. In support of this view, he said that Mr McMAHON made great use of Maxwell NEWTON, and that he, Mr McMAHON, had arranged for Treasury to pay NEWTON's fare when he accompanied the Minister on a recent trip abroad.[66]

McEwen's staff made contact with all sorts and would continue to do so. The printer of Newton's newsletters was approached in March the following year, and his statements—that he had seen McMahon visit Newton's home repeatedly in 1967; that McMahon had even rung him, the printer, at home one night looking for Newton—were placed on file. The printer had seen Newton boast of his friendship with the treasurer and how McMahon had helped him. Sonia McMahon had also called Newton at the printery, either late in October or early in November, the printer said, to discuss changes in one of the newsletters.[67]

Ostensibly, McEwen's concern stemmed from the information Newton was printing in his newsletters and uncertainty about how close McMahon was allowing Newton to get. Was Newton being given confidential information? Was he the beneficiary of favoured treatment? People throughout the government knew how close the two men were: 'Everyone seemed aware of them!' Tony Eggleton recalled.[68]

Much later, Clyde Packer would claim that Newton had been arrested in Trinidad for swiping 'a British working paper' and was only freed on McMahon's intervention.[69] John Stone, part of the delegation in Trinidad, recalled it first-hand. 'Max turned up there,' he said later, 'to the dismay of Dick Randall and the Treasury team, but obviously by arrangement with McMahon, and in no time had been given copies of several documents to which he was not entitled and which could only have come from McMahon!'[70]

Being seen to be close to Newton was no way for McMahon to build bridges with McEwen. Earlier in the year, during his attacks on BIG, McEwen had intimated that the link between McMahon and BIG ran through Newton, who was widely (and correctly) suspected of authoring BIG booklets like *The Great Hoax*, which attacked the Country Party's advocacy and policies for the dairy industry.[71] To link up with such an avowed critic was provocative, if not dangerous.

The Press Gallery was apprehensive about the fierce dislike that McEwen had for Newton, but mindful that Newton was paying exorbitantly for a wide range of journalists to file reports for his newsletters.[72] Alan Reid disapproved of Newton's membership of the Press Gallery;[73] Robert Macklin, then working for *The Age*, found the gallery divided about him. 'It became a very vicious place to work,' he said.[74] Jonathan Gaul, the president of the gallery, agreed. 'McMahon was being blackguarded all the time by McEwen's people—as were we. We [those who worked for Newton] were put down as being in the pay of the Japanese, as though we were trying to undermine Australian manufacturing and jobs. It got pretty intense behind the scenes.'[75]

But nothing appeared in the public sphere. No newspaper ran a story on the matter. Alan Reid later suggested it was because the truth—when checked—was rather plain: Newton was paying his own airfares and enjoying no special treatment beyond the ordinary courtesy of a member of the press while covering a minister.[76]

McMahon arrived back in Australia on 22 October. The political landscape was tense, febrile, and shifting. Within the Liberal Party, MPs were suspicious and angry with McMahon.

But, notably, they were also uncertain about Holt. In McMahon's absence, the government's fortunes had slipped—mostly thanks to its own mistakes in an affair that was rapidly drawing to a climax.

IN November 1965, the Menzies government decided to overhaul the No. 34 Squadron of the RAAF, which transported government VIPs around the country.[77] For an announced cost of $11.4m, the government re-equipped the fleet with seven new aircraft. Exploiting the hazy guidelines on use of the fleet, politicians were soon bickering with one another for the use of a particular aircraft. The minister responsible, Peter Howson, recorded one instance of this wrangling on 11 March 1966:

> VIP aircraft: G-G, PM, and Treasurer all want Viscounts on Tuesday morning. WMcM asked me to get G-G to give way. John MacNeil sounded out Murray Tyrell [official secretary to the governor-general] and found G-G was adamant. So I put my problem to Jack Bunting [secretary to the prime minister's department]. He agreed that G-G should have preference. So rang PM, who agreed to give way, but asked me to inform WMcM. These VIP troubles take up a hell of a lot of time.[78]

McMahon was only too happy to use the planes whenever he could. Upon receiving a request from McMahon for use of a VIP flight, David Fairbairn pointed out that there was a commercial flight leaving only half an hour earlier. Surely McMahon could take that? McMahon's response was ridiculous: 'But I'm playing squash!'[79]

This kind of squabbling and largesse did not, initially, cause much alarm. What did cause embarrassment was the unconsidered cost of maintaining and running the fleet, which was eventually understood to be more than double than the announced expenditure. Holt decided on a strategy of obfuscation, and directed Howson to draft a list of rules to better govern use of the flights. Thus, in May, when questions about the fleet were raised by senator Vince Gair (DLP, Queensland) and the Labor member for Grayndler, Fred Daly, Holt and his department sought to deflect scrutiny by stating that little information about the fleet was available.[80]

The answer was inaccurate. Manifests were maintained and, though difficult to work out, the costs of an individual flight could be calculated. Howson recognised that the answer was inaccurate, but he was unwilling to force the issue. Mixed with cracks of responsibility within the public service and Holt's desire to deflect questions about the VIP fleet, the inaccurate answers stood.

They were suspicious answers, and they prompted further questions.[81] As the issue grew in prominence throughout 1967, the government's inability to command a majority in the Senate became increasingly uncomfortable. Late in September, there were fourteen questions without notice about the VIP fleet in one day.[82] Another sign of the government's weakness came when the president of the Senate, Sir Alister McMullin (Liberal, New South Wales), tried to proceed with further business and was thwarted when a dissent from his ruling was carried.[83] The next day, 27 September, the Senate leader of the opposition, Labor's Lionel Murphy, gave notice that he would call for all material relevant to the VIP flights to be tabled in the Senate.[84] On 5 October, following an ineffectual statement by Holt in the House, the Senate voted to compel the government to table the relevant papers.[85]

Holt was angry and embarrassed. On 12 October, the cabinet decided it would 'resist' the Senate's demands.[86] Nonetheless, four days later, Holt reshuffled the ministry and demoted Sir Denham Henty, the government leader in the Senate, who had announced that he was not seeking re-election in the November poll. Holt had recognised the need for a stronger hand in the now-restless chamber, and thus effected the elevation of the Liberal senator from Victoria and minister for education and science, John Gorton, to the Senate leadership.

Wiry and laconic, a loner by temperament and impulsive by instinct, with a charmingly battered face and raffish appearance, Gorton, born in 1911, was the illegitimate son of a Roman Catholic barmaid and a bigamist Englishman who tried to grow oranges near Kangaroo Lake, Victoria. His mother's contraction of tuberculosis when he was a boy resulted in their separation. When she died in 1920, Gorton's father could not bear to remain in the country house where the burgeoning family had been living. He handed his grieving son to a woman that Gorton, for much of his life, believed was his paternal aunt—but who was, in fact, his father's first wife, Kathleen Gorton, who had refused to divorce him. In her cool care, the young John Gorton also met his sister, Ruth, with whom he got along, but little more. He attended Geelong Grammar, gained second-class honours in history, politics, and economics at Oxford, and flew Spitfires and Hurricanes during World War II. While attacking Japanese bombers near Singapore in

1942, Gorton crash-landed after an engine failure, and emerged from the wreckage with his face wreathed in wounds that accounted for his rough appearance. A Japanese submarine torpedo then sank the ship on which Gorton was convalescing; the survivors were picked up by a passing corvette late the next day.

All this meant that Gorton had to develop a tough, self-sufficient exterior. With little time for pomp and waffle, he prized independence, loyalty, and honour. He rated himself highly, and judged others critically. 'Not much,' he said, when a friend sought his assessment of his parliamentary colleagues. 'I'm the best of them.'[87] Elected to the Senate in 1949, Gorton had spent the first nine years of his parliamentary career on the backbench. Menzies had left him there until 1958; Gorton had come into cabinet only at Holt's elevation in 1966. Coming from the Senate, Gorton had garnered few headlines, and there was little knowledge of him within the parliamentary party.

Gorton took a dim view of the intransigence that Holt seemed intent on maintaining. He perceived that the Senate was unlikely to back down on its demands for disclosure in the VIP affair, and believed that, unless the government changed its approach, the whole affair could become much more significant than it deserved. He told Holt as much, with some effect: Holt, Howson, and the secretary of the prime minister's department, John Bunting, decided to disclose some material.

On 24 October, two days after McMahon's return to Australia, Holt made a statement in the House about the VIP fleet. He denied any impropriety, and tabled records that showed he had flown some 250,000 miles as prime minister.[88] The statement, far from clearing up the matter, further inflamed it. In the House, Labor members seized on the disclosure that McMahon had often used VIP planes to travel between Sydney and Canberra despite the abundance of commercial flights on the route.[89]

In the Senate that afternoon, the minister representing the minister for air, Colin McKellar (Country Party, New South Wales), began to answer some of the Senate's questions about the VIP fleet when Clive Hannaford—the former Liberal, now independent, senator—collapsed in the chamber and subsequently died. The chamber was adjourned, giving the government vital time to regroup.

On 25 October, Gorton made his first move to retrieve the

initiative. He had learned there were some records in existence, and thus tabled a set of papers that gave the dates of VIP flights, the names of passengers, the names of applications, the authorising party, and the places of departures. Notably, he stated that if the Senate wished for more information, 'it could be provided'.[90] That afternoon, learning that it was possible to produce the authorisation books and passenger manifests, Gorton met with the secretary of the Department of Air, A.B. 'Tich' McFarlane, and asked him to bring the records. At ten minutes to nine that evening, Gorton returned to the chamber with the records and tabled them.[91]

His actions averted disaster. Murphy had planned to call McFarlane to the bar of the Senate for questioning over the records. There would have been substantial government embarrassment had this occurred: the failings of Holt, Howson, and the prime minister's department would have been on public display. With sudden, cool, and apparently nonchalant judgement, Gorton had put an end to it.

The fallout was considerable. One of the consequences of the about-turn and inconsistency was demands for Peter Howson, as minister for air, to resign. Howson, however, returning from a trip to Uganda, believed Gorton had acted 'abominably'. In his view, the Senate leader had broken cabinet solidarity, traduced a decision of cabinet, and exposed Howson considerably. Despite not believing he had done anything wrong, Howson offered his resignation.[92] Holt refused it.

Within the party, there was admiration for Gorton's actions. He had saved the government at a critical point, acted decisively and shrewdly, and demonstrated an unexpected adroitness in parliamentary proceedings. For a party beginning to appreciate that Holt's blunders were endangering the government, these were welcome skills to behold.

Ian Fitchett espied the admiration and the contrast. Writing on 31 October, Fitchett suggested that Gorton had emerged from the shadows as a potentially significant figure within the government. 'His leadership material is being remarked upon in a Liberal Party which is frankly worried about its future if anything happens to Mr Holt … If the occasion arose,' Fitchett went on, 'there could be a strong move to find him a seat in the House of Representatives with the party leadership in mind.'[93]

This was the spur to growing unrest in the ranks of government supporters, who wondered about Holt and his judgement, were troubled by the government's direction, and worried about tension between McMahon and McEwen.

ON 8 November, Holt questioned McMahon about his relationship with Maxwell Newton and the progress of Treasury advice on a minor cabinet matter. McMahon replied via letter the next day. He denied offering any assistance to Newton while he travelled to Trinidad and Rio de Janeiro, and denied responsibility for the delay.[94]

These answers did not satisfy anyone. The next day, Holt, McEwen, and McMahon met in the prime minister's office with other senior ministers—Paul Hasluck (external affairs), Allen Fairhall (defence), John Gorton, and, from the Country Party, Doug Anthony (primary industry) and Ian Sinclair (shipping and transport)—present. Supposedly frustrated with McMahon's misrepresentation of affairs, McEwen had refused to meet with him alone and requested that Holt arrange the meeting. Holt agreed, believing that it was the only way to handle the problems between the two men.[95]

McEwen accused McMahon of leaking information on tariff policy to people outside of the Parliament, and of working against cabinet decisions by leaking secret information to critics of Australia's tariff policy. McEwen soon brought up Newton. He demonstrated the clear bias that existed in Newton's newsletters. Then he showed that Newton was being employed by the Japanese External Trade Organisation (JETRO) to provide information about Australia's tariff policies. McEwen had a copy of Newton's contract, and quoted from it in detail. McEwen argued that Newton was, in effect, a 'paid agent' of a foreign government, hired to serve the interests of the Japanese and work against the interests and policies of the government of his own country.[96]

Gorton thought McMahon was rendered nearly inarticulate.[97] McEwen attacked McMahon 'horse, foot, and guns' during the meeting: 'You're just a bloody liar, McMahon,' McEwen said.[98] The treasurer's protests of innocence persuaded no one. And when he said that he had tried to talk with McEwen about it earlier, he was immediately shut down: 'I would not talk with you alone because I would not trust you not to spread a false account of what passed between us,' McEwen told him.[99] When McMahon subsequently bleated platitudes about coalition unity, Hasluck interrupted to say that it was an issue *not* about the two parties but about the whole government. Holt told McMahon to end his association with Newton immediately.

Little had been resolved. Afterwards, in the presence of Gorton and Hasluck, Holt 'spoke feelingly' about McMahon's disloyalty to him, and rued Menzies' inaction on McMahon: 'If only Bob had done something about it we all would have been saved a lot of trouble.'[100] Why, so many of them wondered, had Menzies not used the signed confession of McMahon leaking?

There was one clear outcome: McMahon did end his association with Newton. Tony Eggleton thought that McMahon backed off from Newton in the latter part of 1967.[101] Peter Kelly recalled the same: 'It would have been too damaging, and would have given McEwen a reason to demand he be sacked.'[102] When McMahon told Kelly about the meeting, he added that McEwen had pressed for Kelly's sacking: 'Jack wants you gone too,' McMahon said.[103] But if McMahon was cowed, his reaction quickly turned. Within weeks, he was spreading a different account of the meeting, most notably to Alan Reid.[104]

Soon after, McEwen departed Australia for meetings in Geneva. His decision to do so had been picked over in the press when it was announced late in October, most notably by *Inside Canberra*, which suggested his absence stemmed from a refusal 'to aid the government while Mr McMahon continued to undermine him'.[105] Whatever its spur—and it is likely that it had less to do with McMahon than it did with the need to attend the talks—McEwen's absence came at a critical time, for on 19 November the British government announced its decision to devalue sterling by 14.3 per cent.

McMahon was in Dubbo when he heard. He travelled to Sydney, and from there issued a statement to reassure markets about Australia's position. He wrote that Australia's external reserves were 'well spread' across multiple currencies, and that for the British decision to have its desired effect, no other country should follow it.[106] He was himself thoroughly in favour of the British decision, growling to one journalist that it was 'about time that Britain faced up to her responsibilities'.[107]

McMahon's statement—issued without clearance from

Holt—foreshadowed the line that the Treasury would take at the emergency cabinet meeting Holt called for the following day. Yet it could not hide the fact that, of the $1,170m Australia held in external reserves, $715m was in sterling and other foreign currencies that would be affected by the British decision to devalue. Cost pressures could rise and exports suffer if Australia did not devalue. The Country Party ministers would surely want Australia to follow the British devaluation: if Australia did not, its primary industry base would see its production costs rise, hitting farmers and seemingly validating the criticism of the Basic Industries Group.

Mindful of the opposition he could expect, McMahon rang Howson and asked him to come to Canberra. But the next morning, McMahon told him not to attend the meeting. Holt, McMahon explained, had been conscious of the likely party-based tensions that the issue would bring up: Howson's presence would 'upset the balance between the number of Country Party ministers present and the number of Liberal Party ministers present'.[108]

Holt was wise to be tactful. With McEwen in Geneva, Sinclair was acting minister for trade and industry. Though clearly adept and aware, he hardly had McEwen's stature or force. It was best to give the appearance—if nothing else—of a fair and open debate.

That afternoon, on 20 November, cabinet met to discuss its response. There were two submissions before it: one from Treasury, and one from Trade.[109] The former argued that Australia should not devalue; the latter argued that Australia should. Country Party ministers Anthony and Sinclair asked for an adjournment to think the decision over and consult. Holt refused: 'We can't put this discussion off.' The prime minister rubbished any prospect of getting a full devaluation through the IMF, and scorned suggestions that the government go halfway, saying it would look like a 'sordid political outcome'. The politics, too, he suggested, were obvious: 'We would be crucified by electorate if we went full 14 per cent.' Trying to forestall objections from Anthony and Sinclair, he promised that there would be assistance to primary industries.

The two Country Party ministers continued to voice their concerns and argue for devaluation, but they were wholly on the back foot. McMahon repeatedly countered that devaluation would bring its own cost increases and that inflationary reactions would be almost entirely at the expense of the primary industries that Anthony and Sinclair—and by extension, McEwen—were trying to protect. Sinclair tried to push for cabinet to wait until McEwen returned, but to no avail. Holt observed the tension the decision was causing:

> I recognise the grave problems for [the] Country Party—and for others of us. But we've had expert advice and as [the] Australian cabinet we reach a joint view. I appreciate in both sense[s] that you [Sinclair] and Anthony have argued not on party lines but on portfolio lines … Realise difficulty for Country Party—even to [the] point of its position in Coalition—not saying it does, but recognise that it could. But best we make announcement now.[110]

The meeting broke up at six o'clock. Twenty-five minutes later, Holt submitted a draft statement announcing that Australia would not follow the British devaluation.[111] When it was cleared, it was issued immediately to the press, to widespread praise. The decision not to devalue was welcomed almost unanimously, and fears that it would create divisions eased when McEwen issued a press statement from Geneva supporting the decision.

For McMahon, the decision was one of the most notable of his time as treasurer. While it owed something to McEwen's absence and Holt's chairmanship of that cabinet meeting, the credit was largely his to claim. The argument had been conducted almost entirely on his turf. It was his line that carried the day. It was his department that triumphed over Trade. And it was a decision that was ultimately vindicated. 'Politically, this was a major defeat for McEwen and a major win for McMahon,' said John Stone later. 'Economically, it was significant in breaking the relationship with sterling that had stood for decades, and beginning the long, drawn-out series of moves towards reorienting the dollar *vis-a-vis* other world currencies.'[112]

The triumph and acclaim was short-lived, however. Five days later, another half-Senate election turned disastrous for the government. A 2.9 per cent swing away from the Coalition left it clearly in the minority in the Senate. The government claimed three of five vacancies in Western Australia and South Australia, but the DLP took a seat apiece in Victoria and Queensland, and the independent senator Reg Turnbull was re-elected in Tasmania. In the new chamber, the Coalition held twenty-eight seats to Labor's twenty-seven, the DLP's four, and the single independent's. Overall, it seemed a rebuke to the prime minister and a spark for unrest.

Members met in Sydney and in Melbourne to discuss the election and what it meant. Word of these meetings leaked. Spying Alan Reid at the top of the stairs in King's Hall, Holt grabbed the journalist and asked what he knew. 'Oh, I know a bit,' said Reid. It was the wrong response. Holt wanted everything: 'What do you know?' he demanded. Reid told him the little that he did, but he neither possessed the details that Holt wanted nor was he willing to tell all that he knew. When Holt asked him to find out, Reid was noncommittal.[113]

The unrest prompted others into action. Dudley Erwin, the government whip, had been talking to backbenchers in the House and Senate for some time, and he drafted a letter to Holt about the disquiet. He showed the draft to Gorton, who suggested amendments to make it 'lower key'.[114] Gorton thought that Holt was off his game, but also believed McMahon was making trouble for Holt. 'He was being undermined all the time by McMahon, who was working around amongst members, trying to get rid of him,' Gorton said.[115] Some disagreed: 'It would have been a waste of time and effort and done him [McMahon] no good at all,' said David Solomon, later.[116] Journalist Alan Ramsey believed that McMahon was not performing the vital role of deputy leader—to protect his leader's back. Others suggested that Gorton was working against Holt. Years later, William Aston, the Speaker and Liberal member for Phillip, recalled Gorton telling him that he was working to become prime minister.[117] Most, however, concurred with Gorton: 'There was quite a clear emergence of a McMahon group who were obviously intriguing against Harold Holt,' said Gordon Freeth.[118] 'I know that McMahon was actively working against him,' said Sir James Plimsoll, head of the Department of External Affairs. 'So much so that … he was spoken to very severely by somebody who told him that he was destabilising the government. And McMahon's reaction was, "He had no right to tell me what I should do."'[119]

The meeting Plimsoll referred to was with the governor-general.

Hearing that Holt's attempts at reconciliation between McMahon and McEwen had failed, Casey renewed his July offer to intervene. This time, Holt accepted. Reasoning that McMahon was the most to blame for the dispute, Casey invited him to Admiralty House. They met on 8 December, and had a 'long and hard talk'.[120]

McMahon prepared an account of the meeting three days later and addressed it to Holt. It was explicitly selective: 'I do not think it is necessary to relate in detail the whole of the discussion with him, which must have taken close to an hour and three-quarters,' he wrote. The most important factors remained.

Casey, he said, had claimed a 'constitutional responsibility to serve the government … and see that the government functioned effectively'. McMahon, however, had taken umbrage at this, telling Casey that in doing so he was 'assuming the role of the Prime Minister'. He 'challenged' Casey's constitutional authority and 'denied' Casey's supposed 'constitutional right' to speak with him as governor-general—but also said he was willing to speak 'in a friendly way', as former colleagues. From there, according to McMahon, the discussion was straightforward. Casey asked him about the fight with McEwen, and McMahon's explanation and denial of any fault was satisfactory. It prompted Casey to admit surprise. 'God!' the governor-general supposedly said. 'I have been misinformed on this too.' Accordingly, Casey took McMahon's denials of impropriety in good spirit, laughing about the press and stating that he had 'a totally new insight' into the Resource Development Bank, once McMahon had explained it to him. Casey had said he would speak with McEwen about 'the sources of friction' between him and McMahon.[121]

Potentially unbeknownst to McMahon, however—for Casey had said that the meeting would remain between them—the governor-general had prepared his own account on 9 December and sent it to Holt.

According to Casey, he told McMahon that the meeting was occurring with Holt's blessing and that, in his interpretation of the constitution, he had a role to play in ensuring the government's interests and wellbeing were supported. The coalition between the Liberal and Country parties was 'essential', he told McMahon, and thus the 'present notorious relationship' with McEwen was a problem. Casey raised

McMahon's relationship with Newton, and Newton's considerable criticism of McEwen, noting that the journalist had accompanied McMahon on international trips. At this, according to Casey, McMahon interrupted to deny that he and Newton had anything more than the normal relationship between a member of the press and the government. Casey was sceptical: 'It was noticeable that he referred to Newton as "Max" throughout,' he wrote.

The meeting continued with a chorus of denials. According to Casey's account, McMahon denied saying anything about McEwen's going overseas, denied any animus towards McEwen, denied McEwen's suggestions that he was trying to become deputy prime minister, and denied doing anything to provoke McEwen at all. Casey could do little in response. He brought up the widespread beliefs, the images, the appearances, but McMahon did not allow even this to trouble him:

> I said that the 'image' remained in the minds of a number of people that he had an animus against McEwen, which, in the interests of Government harmony had not been dispelled. I suggested that he make efforts to dispel such an image. He said that he had made such efforts, to which McEwen had not responded. I suggested he keep on trying.

For Casey, the meeting was frustrating. McMahon 'threw a lot of flowers at himself' and denied all. The discussion over the Australian Industry Development Corporation (AIDC) and the Resources Development Bank went nowhere, though Casey wrote that McMahon did not disagree with the assessment that the Resources Development Bank did not have 'much scope'. Overall, Casey was unsurprised and unimpressed. He had known McMahon for a long time, and knew just how longstanding the animus with McEwen was. 'I remember a long talk I had with McMahon, about ten years ago,' Casey wrote, 'when the conversation was largely about his hostility to McEwen.' Nonetheless, writing from hope rather than experience, Casey told Holt that the meeting 'may have done some good'.[122] In reality, Casey had no confidence that it would do anything. 'The little fellow just sat there and told me one barefaced lie after another on things that he must have known I knew the truth,' he told Hasluck.[123]

Both letters were sent to Holt; in the meantime, McMahon

remained incensed about the meeting. He felt it was a slight to his dignity and a slur on his character to be summoned and thus accused. He certainly thought it was unconstitutional, and said as much to people who asked.[124] Peter Kelly recalled McMahon being annoyed and angry with Casey. The governor-general's intervention had been inappropriate. He was wrong to do it. 'He had no right to do that,' McMahon said to Kelly. 'He had no right at all.'[125]

Two days after the McMahon-Casey meeting, McEwen returned to Australia. Whether it was because he had been offered fresh information, or because the half-Senate election was over, or because he was concerned about the poor Country Party vote recorded at that election, McEwen issued a long press statement that called into question cabinet's decision not to devalue. Arguing that the action struck at the 'wealth-producing industries, both primary and secondary', McEwen called for an independent authority to recommend currency decisions. He called the decision not to devalue 'one of the classic deflationary acts open to a government'.[126]

Holt met senior Liberal ministers. In his eyes, McEwen's statement called into question the government's unity on the currency decision, and could undermine confidence.[127] He told McMahon, Hasluck, Fairhall, Bury, and Gorton that the problems created by McEwen's statement should be addressed without delay. According to Hasluck, McMahon egged Holt on, terming it a challenge that had to be met.[128]

On 12 December, McEwen came to Holt's office to discuss the matter. After forty minutes, McEwen emerged, looking tense. He slammed the door behind him and departed without a word to Peter Bailey, a first assistant secretary in the prime minister's department who had been assigned to work in Holt's office. A few minutes later, Holt buzzed for Bailey to join him. The public servant asked how it had gone. 'Well,' Holt said, 'the government is still there and we've [not] devalued and that's all right.' To Bailey's congratulations, Holt smiled. He had asserted the authority of his office: 'I now feel I'm really the prime minister.'[129]

A statement was issued immediately. It reaffirmed the decision not to devalue. By its emphatic language, the statement could be said to have implicitly called into question McEwen's judgement: 'Because of his absence abroad at the GATT meetings in Geneva, my colleague did not have the advantage of participating in the wide ranging cabinet discussions, nor did he have the detail before him of the latest appreciation of the likely effects of British devaluation on our own economy.'[130]

In the press, Holt's actions were praised and lauded, and widely called a win for him and his party. Holt had taken 'the tough line', wrote one journalist. 'He deliberately, calmly, and completely rebuked Mr McEwen in public and in private.'[131] Another suggested that McEwen and the Department of Trade and Industry had emerged diminished: 'The economic deficiencies of his department are becoming one of Australia's most serious handicaps.'[132] But, though important, it was hardly as triumphant or as pivotal a moment as the press was apt to suggest. Hasluck later argued that McEwen's statement was likely made in an effort to ensure that the compensation paid to rural industries was generous.[133] It is probable that McMahon viewed the affair as a boost for him just as much as one for Holt.

The rest of the week was spent in preparation for the Christmas vacation. Parliament had risen. Holt and his wife dined with Casey on Wednesday, and discussed McMahon, McEwen, and the year that had passed. Holt, according to Casey, said that 1967 had been a year 'he would not easily forget'.[134] He was looking forward to a break. The press attended drinks at the Lodge.[135] A final cabinet meeting on the Thursday night to discuss assistance to rural industries affected by the British devaluation ran late, but the next morning Holt was in his office early, as normal, signing papers and Christmas cards. He left Canberra at eleven o'clock, and boarded a plane to Melbourne, from where he would drive to his holiday home at Portsea. In his briefcase were the letters from McMahon and Casey about their meeting, and a new version of Dudley Erwin's letter about the disquiet of the government backbench.[136]

That afternoon, at the Treasury's Christmas party, McMahon met and spoke to Howson. He and the prime minister, McMahon said, were concerned about leaks from cabinet. He thought Gorton was responsible.[137]

CHAPTER TWENTY-TWO

The Story and the Fact

1984

Unable to trust the accuracy of McMahon's memory, Bowman found that arriving at the truth entailed finding a way through a labyrinth of mirrored walls. There were points of view and there were hard facts; there were sources that differed and sources that were in agreement. Understandably, he saw, McMahon often chose to cite as proof for his statements and point of view those works that agreed with him.

On chapter drafts and notes, McMahon would scrawl references to various books that were scattered around the office. Alexander Downer's *Six Prime Ministers*, Edgar Holt's *Politics is People*, Nugget Coombs's *Trial Balance*, a swag of biographies of Menzies, and the occasional memoir by a colleague were all well-thumbed, yet it was Alan Reid's *The Power Struggle* and *The Gorton Experiment* that were the most frequently cited sources.

Years later, Hasluck would call Reid a 'competent though somewhat venal purveyor of political gossip', and would scorn Reid's claims to writing history.[1] Drawing out the problems of Reid's accounts, Hasluck noted Reid's propensity for over-dramatising his work, and for filling in gaps with assumptions and hearsay. Hasluck would argue that Reid was a partisan, writing from McMahon's point of view.

Discussing Reid's account of a meeting between McMahon and senior ministers, for example, Hasluck was cutting:

I was present at the meeting throughout and very few, indeed scarcely any, of these things recorded by Reid were said by McMahon at the meeting at all. Any third party who was present could not have reported them because he would not have heard them. The man most likely to know what was in McMahon's mind was McMahon himself. The only person who would have a reason for representing that McMahon made these long and detailed accounts of his conduct, when in fact he did not make them, was McMahon himself. I can find no reason why any other informant would have dressed up McMahon's unspoken justification of himself in such terms as those that Reid sets down. Hence I deduce that Reid has depended chiefly on McMahon and perhaps solely on McMahon for his account of what was said.[2]

The close relationship between Reid and McMahon, and the problems of Reid's work, were well known within press and political circles, yet Reid's work nonetheless loomed over discussion of the inner workings of the Holt and Gorton governments. In the McMahon office at Westfield Towers, Reid's books were the clinching argument—a hardly surprising result, since they possessed the sturdy credibility of being sympathetic to McMahon.

Newspaper and magazine articles were accorded a high status. Few things are as dead as yesterday's newspaper, Churchill once said, but McMahon chose to treat clippings as if they were gospel.[3] When queried about a particular claim, McMahon would demand that an article by Fitchett, or Peter Samuel, or Reid be disgorged from one of the twenty-seven filing cabinets. Quotes were selectively drawn, stitched together, inserted into the manuscript drafts. How those articles had been written, what sources they relied upon, and whether McMahon himself had influenced the articles was never discussed. McMahon would not allow their reliability to be questioned.

At other times, McMahon drew on aide-mémoires that he had kept throughout his political career. A habit since his days as a solicitor, he had prepared them every single time a conversation of possible significance occurred. Yet they were hardly impromptu documents. 'He would repeatedly hone whatever he was working on,' Peter Kelly wrote later, 'sometimes making six or seven drafts. It used to drive his secretaries mad!'[4] The many drafts and constant revisions made their reliability suspect. As Kelly himself later said, McMahon's memory 'was always shaded to himself. Always.'[5]

However difficult his sources were to trust, the manuscript had information that was new—most notably, about the period leading up to December 1967. According to the draft, Holt was on McMahon's side in the disputes with McEwen and with Casey.

Perhaps most sensationally, McMahon told Bowman that Holt had agreed that the governor-general had overstepped the bounds of his constitutional role.[6] When Holt was told of their 8 December meeting in Sydney, he agreed with McMahon's assertion that Casey had acted inappropriately and that Casey should therefore be dismissed as governor-general.

'That would have been a giant upheaval,' wrote an astounded Bowman when he read this. 'It is difficult to believe now that it was ever in the realm of practical politics. I think the reader will need to be persuaded.' To this, McMahon wrote that the papers that provided for Casey's dismissal were in Holt's briefcase when he left for Portsea.[7]

Contemporaries of Holt and McMahon were dubious about the claim. 'I didn't hear any dismissal suggestion,' wrote Tony Eggleton. 'In my view, [it is] most unlikely that Harold would have acted against the GG, even if he felt that Casey had been indiscreet.'[8] Peter Kelly heard nothing of this at all. 'I couldn't confirm or deny it,' he said later. 'I wouldn't know.' But he was not confident: 'I doubt it went that far. I doubt it went that far.'[9] There were no papers to this effect in Holt's briefcase.

In McMahon's telling, Holt believed that by his statement on devaluation, McEwen was attempting to wreck the Coalition; that McEwen had realised his audacious ploy to straddle two separate, even duelling, constituencies was backfiring; and that McEwen was looking for a distraction to it all—and hence fixed on McMahon. In McMahon's telling, on 12 December, Holt had declared he had reached his end. There would be no placating McEwen. There would be no more mollifying. McEwen would be given the choice—to put up or shut up. According to McMahon, Holt was confident that if McEwen led the Country Party out of the Coalition there would be enough members who would stay. But then, in the meeting with Holt on 14 December, McEwen had backed down, had conducted himself professionally, and all had been saved.

McMahon also claimed that Holt was worried and paranoid in the days that followed. According to McMahon, on the morning of Friday

15 December—before he had left for Portsea via Melbourne—Holt had called McMahon and asked him to come to Parliament House. They met just as Holt was leaving and went back to Holt's office. 'He was just very, very anxious,' McMahon said later. 'He was more serious, more worried, than I've known him before.'[10] While they discussed the assistance to primary industries, looming in the conversation were reports that MPs were caucusing to remove Holt as prime minister. They had spoken on the Wednesday about the reports, but McMahon had supposedly known nothing. He was aware that Billy Wentworth was involved, that John Gorton was the likely beneficiary, and that Bill Aston, the Speaker, had stopped the talks in New South Wales. But that was all.

Holt suspected his involvement, McMahon wrote, and they had quarrelled about it. With Reid's help, McMahon had proved he was not involved, and Holt had apologised.[11] (Here, though, was a sticking point: on the draft, Bowman asked how Reid had been able to help—only for McMahon to deny that Reid *had* been helpful!) Then Holt asked McMahon to call him on Sunday morning so they could speak again. It would be proof of their reconciliation.

McMahon agreed, and the two men embraced. According to McMahon, the two men then shook hands and Holt asked why McMahon was not shaking hands with him. McMahon told him that he was—and that if Holt was unable to feel it, he must be grievously ill.

Bowman, making notes on the manuscript, asked questions: how could this be right? Holt could surely see, couldn't he? Wouldn't he see that they were shaking hands? *Seeing* was distinct from *feeling*, wasn't it? Why, if they had just hugged, would they suddenly shake hands?

McMahon's answers, scrawled in a violet pen, clarified nothing.[12]

Certainly, Holt was ill. During the Senate election campaign in November, he had complained of numbness in his hands,[13] and a Melbourne specialist had prescribed medication to combat the pain Holt was experiencing in his neck and shoulder muscles.[14] 'Harold was receiving medical treatment for shoulder pains,' Tony Eggleton said later.[15] Was this why he had not been able to feel the handshake?

In the manuscript, McMahon wrote that he had urged Holt to see a doctor, but the prime minister brushed him off, saying that even after all the years they had been friends, McMahon still did not appreciate how strong Holt was. He had then left, cheery and happy, and that was the last McMahon ever saw of him.

Was it true? Some were inclined to doubt. Eggleton could not recall McMahon meeting with Holt on the morning of 15 December.[16] Certainly, there was no other record of their meeting. Did it happen?

McMahon's manuscript contained further claims. When the time for his phone call to Holt came on Sunday morning, McMahon wrote that he had decided against calling. He was, he wrote, resentful that Holt had suspected him of intriguing against him. He repeated this publicly. 'On that occasion,' he said, 'because of the quarrels I'd had with him that week, I told my wife I wouldn't do it. She tried to persuade me to do it and I refused.'[17]

Bowman queried this when he came across it in the manuscript. 'After the scene in Parliament House, this is a little surprising,' he wrote. After all, they had reconciled. They had shaken hands. Why was McMahon still angry? McMahon did not respond.

Yet here was another contradiction. Holt's housekeeper, Tiny Lawless, recorded in her diary that McMahon *had* telephoned, and what she had heard of the conversation left her to wonder what had happened on the call. When interviewed, she elaborated:

Lawless: He [Holt] had a phone call, and I answered the phone call, and it was Billy McMahon from Sydney.
Interviewer: How did you know it was him?
Lawless: I'd known his voice. I knew him well, too. He said, 'Is that you, Tiny?' I said yes. And he said, 'Is Mr Holt there?' I said yes. I got him. He came to the phone, and coming back in, as Mr Holt was finishing his conversation, I just heard, 'That's that, Billy,'—to him—and he said, 'That's it, Tiny,' to me.

When this was put to McMahon later, he denied it: 'No, I did not.' But Lawless was not going to back down. She remembered. She remembered it clearly:

Interviewer: Mr McMahon says he never made a phone call on that day.
Lawless: Mr McMahon did make one … Absolutely certain, I am. Just as I came out looking at him, he [Holt] was saying goodbye to Billy and he said, 'Alright, if that's the way you want it, have it that way.'[18]

'In politics,' Hasluck wrote later, 'the story and the fact are not always the same.'[19] Working out what was story and what was fact in McMahon's autobiography was taking time—too much. And it was never really certain whether those facts were true.

CHAPTER TWENTY-THREE

Cold Water

1967–1968

The news flashes began just before two o'clock, Sunday 17 December. Jim Killen rang McMahon immediately. The deputy leader had not heard anything.[1] Then Peter Howson was calling to inform McMahon that it was confirmed.[2] Police, military, and lifesaving personnel, in helicopters and in boats, on foot and in the water, were converging on the shores around Portsea, Victoria.

The prime minister was missing—missing at sea.

'When I heard that he had disappeared,' McMahon said later, 'well, for me, it was just two or three days of agony. And I never wanted to think—and I never did think—I *stopped* myself from thinking—what might have happened.'[3]

Howson asked McMahon to spread the word. McMahon agreed, but he did not need to. Phones were ringing everywhere that afternoon. Down at his farm in Stanhope, Victoria, John McEwen heard the news from Lady Ansett, wife to Sir Reginald. McEwen had barely put down the phone when it rang again with official confirmation.[4] McMahon was soon on the line to inform McEwen, but the Country Party leader was already making his plans to travel to Canberra. John Gorton was sitting in his gardening clothes at his home in Narrabundah, Canberra, when Ainsley Gotto, a staff member attached to the office of the government whip, Dudley Erwin, called to break the news.[5] Paul Hasluck was at his duplex in Deakin, Canberra, when McMahon called at around three-thirty. Noting that the prime minister's wife, Zara Holt, and press secretary, Tony Eggleton, were on their way to Melbourne, McMahon asked Hasluck if he should travel to Melbourne, too. Hasluck thought not, and said as much.[6]

Meanwhile, Sonia contacted McMahon's staff and asked them to come to their flat in Darling Point. When Peter Kelly arrived at around half-past four, the place was excitedly busy. There was nothing concrete, Sonia said to him, but Holt was likely dead—drowned, most probably. Absorbing this news, Kelly noticed that McMahon, who seemed 'solemn', was packing a bag. He asked Pat Wheatley, also present, what was going on. 'We're off to Canberra in a VIP,' she replied.

Kelly was disbelieving. 'What! He must be mad.'

Kelly was thinking of the media fallout. With the controversial VIP affair barely beginning to fade from memory, McMahon was going to commandeer another VIP flight? More critically, was he really going to jet into Canberra to lay claim to the prime ministership with the search and rescue still underway? With his colleague, friend, party leader, and prime minister potentially dead?

Kelly hinted that McMahon should hold back, but to no effect. He told Sonia of his concerns, but she refused to intervene. So he decided to shock McMahon: 'Do you really want Fitchett to write in tomorrow's *Sydney Morning Herald* that McMahon arrived in Canberra before the body was even cold?'

This prompted a response. McMahon might have been grieving, but what he said revealed his uppermost concern: 'But Jack's already there!'

Kelly's droll reply that McEwen was, after all, the deputy prime minister, failed to dissuade McMahon. The treasurer was panicked by the political implications of Holt's likely death. With Holt gone, the Liberal Party leadership—and, with it, the prime ministership—would fall vacant. McMahon knew that as the Liberal Party's deputy leader he had the first claim to the job of leadership, even if only in a temporary capacity—and from there it was easy to foresee making it permanent.

But McEwen's presence in Canberra could upset that. Without McMahon around to contest advice or say differently, McEwen, as deputy prime minister, could take charge, possibly even be sworn in as prime minister. From there, who knew what could happen? McEwen could emulate Arthur Fadden and remain prime minister, with the Liberal Party acquiescing in a subordinate role under the Country Party, just as the UAP had in 1941. All the policies that McMahon had advocated would be overturned, replaced by policies he had resisted. The AIDC, the move to devalue, the support of economically inefficient industries—they could all come back.

Even if this worst-case scenario did not eventuate, an acting prime minister McEwen would have the clout to cruel McMahon's chances of becoming prime minister. He certainly had no liking for McMahon—this could be his way to exact revenge. McEwen would certainly know how to do so. He would not make the mistakes that Sir Earle Page had made in 1939. McEwen would know how to ensure he had his way.

Understandably, then, Kelly's warning did not immediately cause McMahon to drop the idea of going to Canberra. The treasurer did what he normally did when he heard an opinion he did not like: he rang around until he could find someone who had similar views to his own.[7]

Those calls went nowhere. A conversation with Gorton, in which McMahon raised the prospect of an immediate party meeting, ended with Gorton's demurral.[8] A talk with Eggleton, in which McMahon ventured going down to Melbourne, stymied McMahon. 'I discouraged him from joining what was already a full house,' Eggleton said later.[9] A steady stream of calls to the Liberal Party organisation, to state politicians, and to the press continued for the remainder of the afternoon.[10]

Cold-blooded as it might seem, McMahon was not the only one thinking of the consequences of Holt's probable death. Dudley Erwin had called John Gorton and delivered a blunt message to get over his shock at Holt's disappearance: 'I am afraid, John, that it is true and you must start to think what this means to you.'[11]

McEwen was similarly thinking ahead. His men in the Country Party—Ian Sinclair, Doug Anthony, and Peter Nixon—had been informed of the state of affairs and were on their way to Canberra. McEwen had called Peter Lawler, acting secretary of the prime minister's department while Sir John Bunting was on holiday, and asked him to be present at Canberra Airport when McEwen arrived. From the moment he stepped off the plane, Lawler thought, McEwen was in charge.[12] Moreover, it was obvious that McEwen was soon to appeal to the highest authority: at the Hotel Kurrajong, Lawler noted McEwen's secretary, Mary Byrne, putting out McEwen's formal clothes.[13]

Anthony went to see McEwen immediately upon reaching Canberra. In the hotel room, the two agreed that McMahon would obtain no benefit from the upheaval caused by Holt's death. 'McMahon's name never came forward from McEwen as a possible leader of the Liberal Party,' Anthony recalled. 'My thoughts were similar to McEwen's.'[14] They could not abide him, and they would not allow the Country Party to serve in a government led by him. To the inevitable question this raised—who, if not McMahon, would be acceptable as a successor to Holt—they decided on Gorton. Though a senator, Gorton's handling of the VIP affair, his wartime service, and his familiarity with rural matters were enough to win McEwen's approval. Hasluck—ostensibly Gorton's senior and, without McMahon, certainly the most experienced Liberal minister—was scratched.

At around twenty minutes past seven, McEwen called Hasluck. He caught the external affairs minister just as he was about to leave for dinner with New Zealand's high commissioner. McEwen informed Hasluck that the governor-general was likely to commission him as prime minister on a caretaker basis once he had been satisfied that Holt was dead. The commission would be temporary, to be held until the Liberal Party elected a leader to replace Holt. McEwen told Hasluck that he would inform Casey that he would not serve under McMahon. Nor would the Country Party serve in a government led by him. McEwen's question was whether or not he should let others know. 'I thanked him for his frankness,' Hasluck recalled. 'I said that, as he already knew, I myself would find it impossible to work with McMahon as prime minister.'[15]

In Yarralumla, meanwhile, Casey had taken care to be abreast of all the necessary information and to take every precaution. At three o'clock that afternoon, he had called Nigel Bowen, the attorney-general, for advice on Holt's commission as prime minister.[16] Judging that Holt was likely dead, Casey sought confirmation that forty-eight hours was 'about the appropriate period of time' to wait before swearing in a replacement. Bowen agreed, as did the man Casey telephoned next, the chief justice of the High Court, Sir Garfield Barwick.[17]

Casey also contacted Sir John Bunting, who had by now broken his holiday. Casey told Bunting that a 'personal and confidential letter' should be among the papers in Holt's briefcase in Portsea. It was the letter about his meeting with McMahon. It needed to be returned, Casey said.[18] Police were dispatched to Holt's home in Portsea to retrieve the letter. They marched straight into Holt's bedroom, where his briefcase was located, his housekeeper said later. With the letter in hand, they left via the window.[19]

Some time after seven-thirty, McEwen arrived at Government House to dine with Casey. 'We discussed all the matters involved and potentially involved,' Casey wrote in his diary, 'so that I knew his attitude in the circumstances that lie ahead.' Casey had already decided the person he would commission as prime minister to succeed Holt. When he had spoken with Bowen and Barwick, he had explicitly mentioned that it was McEwen who would be sworn in.[20]

Luckily, Casey found a willing audience. McEwen said that if Holt were dead, Casey would have to commission a new prime minister. But, McEwen went on, to commission any Liberal Party member as prime minister on an interim basis would give them an 'absolutely unfair advantage' in the leadership contest that would follow. Therefore, Casey should commission him as prime minister. But he would not accept any formal conditions to that commission, he said. His promise that he would hand it back once the Liberal Party elected a new leader should suffice. Casey agreed.[21]

From there, they discussed the Liberal Party. 'His attitude toward McMahon is a key matter,' Casey wrote.[22] McEwen informed Casey that neither he nor his party would serve under McMahon should he be elected leader of the Liberal Party. Moreover, he told Casey that he intended to make this fact known to McMahon and the Liberal Party.

At around the same time as McEwen told Casey this, Hasluck was speaking with Gorton at the New Zealand high commissioner's home. Around dinner and games of Scrabble, Hasluck told Gorton about his phone call with McEwen.[23] Gorton agreed that a commission for McEwen to become prime minister was appropriate. He mentioned that the government whips had been contacted by McMahon, who wanted an immediate party meeting. Both men disagreed with this kind of speed, mostly out of respect for the Holt family. Gorton let on that his aversion to McMahon was almost as strong as Hasluck's.

Later in the evening, Hasluck drew Gorton aside. Sitting on the sofa, Hasluck told Gorton that he should put his hand up for the leadership.[24] The contest should be between the two of them. The other potential contenders—Allen Fairhall, David Fairbairn, Les Bury, and Alan Hulme—were just not good enough. And he himself, Hasluck went on, had the disadvantages of age and a reputation rubbished by McMahon. 'Gorton gave no clear response except to say that he agreed that I was the only senior minister in the House of Representatives with "enough brains" to be prime minister,' wrote Hasluck.[25]

By half-past nine, Gorton had left the high commissioner's residence and thus was not present when Hasluck received a call from Government House, from which McEwen had just departed.[26] Could Hasluck meet with Casey the next morning at ten o'clock? Hasluck accepted.[27]

Returning to the Hotel Kurrajong, McEwen was joined by Anthony and Sinclair. After about fifteen minutes, Anthony emerged from the hotel and asked his driver to take him to Gorton's home in Narrabundah.[28]

The Senate leader was in his pyjamas when he heard tyres crunching outside his home.[29] It was Anthony. He came bearing word that Gorton would be the Country Party's preferred candidate in the imminent contest for the leadership of the Liberal Party.[30]

BY the time McMahon arrived in Canberra the next morning on a commercial flight, he had lost crucial time and influence. His absence from Canberra had left him unable to make the case to Casey that he should be commissioned as prime minister. It is likely that his argument would have rested on the events of 1945, when John Curtin died in office and Frank Forde, deputy leader of the Labor Party, was sworn in as prime minister by the governor-general, until a party-room ballot was held to elect a new leader—in that case, Ben Chifley.

There was another precedent, though, which was potentially more relevant—the death of Joseph Lyons in 1939. His death had ostensibly left a question about who the governor-general should commission. But a cabinet meeting had resolved the question: as leader of the UAP's coalition partner, the Country Party, and the highest-ranking minister after Lyons, it was Earle Page who received the commission.

But even here there were murky waters. At the time of Lyons' death, the UAP did not have a deputy leader in place, Menzies having resigned several weeks earlier. Yet at the time of Holt's death, there *was* a deputy leader in place—McMahon. Also, McEwen's assertion that neither he nor his party would serve under McMahon was, for the moment, irrelevant. Whether McMahon could command the confidence of the House was a moot point. Parliament was not in session, so a test of the government's numbers was not in the offing. Therefore, as Geoffrey Bolton later argued, 'custom dictated that, as senior partner in the Coalition, the Liberals would expect their leader to be selected'.[31]

Casey took a different view, one that drew as much on his experience in politics as a member of the Lyons and Menzies governments as it did on his knowledge of the personal dispute between McEwen and McMahon. First, just as Lyons had designated Page acting prime minister while he was away, so, too, had Holt designated McEwen. Indeed, McEwen was the first minister to be officially designated deputy prime minister. There were, therefore, grounds to suggest that McEwen should act as prime minister in Holt's now-permanent absence.

Second, Casey did not agree that McMahon's deputy leadership was relevant. A notable factor in the commissions to Page and Forde had been the order of precedence. In both cases, Page and Forde were the ministers ranking immediately after the prime minister. McEwen ranked above McMahon in the Table of Precedence. That McMahon was deputy leader of the Liberal Party was immaterial: his possession of the deputy leadership did not necessarily involve progression to leadership.[32]

Last, and most contentiously, the coalition between the non-Labor parties was all-important. It had been in the 1930s and it was still. Commissioning McMahon, while knowing of McEwen's warning, would endanger the coalition. 'Casey wanted at all costs to preserve the Coalition,' wrote his biographer.[33] This was perhaps the most partisan judgement Casey could make, and the one most open to question and criticism. Was it really within his role to facilitate a Coalition agreement?

By the time McMahon's appointment at Government House was fixed, a whole troop of Liberal Party MPs had already come and gone, and each had confirmed Casey's belief that, at least in this case, the deputy leader would not necessarily become leader. Hasluck had told Casey that he would not serve under McMahon; Fairhall had informed Casey that he might stand for the leadership; Gorton gave similar news; and Erwin, the Liberal Party whip, informed Casey of McMahon's 'increasing unpopularity'. By the time McMahon arrived to see Casey at four o'clock, his opportunity to put his case had been severely undermined. Casey had already resolved on commissioning McEwen.[34]

Even before he arrived at Government House, though, McMahon was aware that serious obstacles would have to be overcome if he was to mount a credible bid for the leadership. McEwen had spoken with Gorton and Hasluck in his office at Parliament House, and confirmed that he would not serve under McMahon. McEwen said the same to Erwin, and then to Fairhall, later that day. Erwin told McEwen he had to tell McMahon. 'Please, would you tell McMahon you are not prepared to do this?'

McEwen agreed, and immediately picked up the phone and asked McMahon to come to his office. Erwin was just leaving when McMahon arrived. His presence, immediately before a pivotal meeting, sparked considerable enmity from McMahon, who blamed Erwin for what followed.[35]

McEwen was direct. His words, he said later, were 'very heated', but they were also few.[36] He told McMahon that his party would not serve in a government led by him. 'Bill,' he said, 'I will not serve under you because I don't trust you.'

The explanation was simple, unadorned, and decisive. For some it was not enough. Much later, when Reid was researching the events that followed Holt's death, he asked McEwen what he had said. McEwen repeated the single sentence. 'And I waited for him to go on,' Reid recalled. 'He didn't go on. I said, "Yeah, go on, go on, go on." He said, "That's it."'[37]

McMahon requested no further information. He said nothing. He did nothing. 'He just sat there looking at me and then left the room,' McEwen wrote later.[38]

McMahon returned to his office. For a minute, he was alone, absorbing the news. Then he called for Peter Kelly. 'Jack has said he won't serve with me if I'm the leader,' he told his press secretary.

'Did he say why?' Kelly asked.

'He said he didn't trust me. That was all.'

'What did you say?'

'I said nothing.'[39]

This was the course of action that Kelly advised McMahon to take. A slanging match with McEwen—apparently McMahon's first instinct—would be impossible to win. Kelly perceived that McMahon had never had a chance of taking the leadership. Standing would not even be a gamble; he would lose. But in standing, Kelly thought, McMahon might also expose the paucity of his support in the party, and thus endanger his hold on the deputy leadership.

'I expressed the second dilemma as circumspectly as I could, adding that if he lost the deputy's job he could not be certain of even retaining the Treasury portfolio,' Kelly wrote later.[40]

McMahon's meeting with Casey that Monday afternoon did not cause the governor-general to change his mind. The next day, almost forty-eight hours precisely since Holt had disappeared, with his young lieutenants, Anthony and Sinclair, looking on, McEwen was sworn in as prime minister.

WORD of McEwen's veto of McMahon quickly became common knowledge among politicians, staff, and the Press Gallery.[41] Reporters battered McMahon with questions when he arrived at Parliament House on 19 December, and, despite repeated statements that he would not be commenting, the reporters persisted. Within the party, McEwen's veto apparently prompted colleagues to keep their distance from McMahon. The next day, when the swearing-in ceremony for ministers serving McEwen was held, McMahon arrived first, and he arrived alone. To questions about the veto, McMahon was evasive: 'It's Mr McEwen's business, not mine.'[42]

Was he an outcast?, a journalist asked him much later. 'I wouldn't use that phrase. Not an outcast,' he said.[43] In private, he was anxious. According to Hasluck, McMahon was 'very fluttery'.[44] Howson, the recipient of several calls from McMahon during these days, noted variously that the treasurer was 'extremely emotional', 'in rather an emotional state', and in 'a highly emotional state'.[45] Later, he would be more direct: 'McMahon was completely obsessed and incensed with what had happened. He just could not believe it.'[46] Certainly, McMahon was in a dire situation. The pressure on him was immense.

Later that evening, McEwen made the rumour public. At a press conference held in the government party room at Parliament House, journalists asked him to confirm it: 'Mr McEwen, are you prepared to say publicly, as you have apparently said privately, that you will not accept Mr McMahon as a prime minister, as leader of the Liberal Party?'

McEwen was blunt. Yes. The rumours were correct. He would not accept McMahon as leader. 'Mr McMahon knows the reasons,' he went on. 'My senior Liberal Party colleagues not only know the reasons, but knew the reasons before Mr Holt's death.' When another journalist asked if McEwen would make those reasons public, the Country Party leader said he would not. McEwen was aware that Earle Page's inflammatory accusations against Menzies in 1939 had caused much support to swing towards the putative leader, and had no intentions of repeating that mistake.[47] Therefore he cited a belief that quarrelling and politicking in the midst of funeral preparations would be intolerable.[48]

McMahon was in an invidious position. He was being impugned in public, yet could do little about it. What charges could he refute? What could he say? Moreover, any public spat between him and McEwen would likely see him emerge the loser. He would appear to be making political hay while a country mourned. His only option was to take McEwen on in private. His options were limited, however, to the one authority who had already declared his hand: Casey.

Nonetheless, McMahon rang and asked the governor-general to arrange a meeting with McEwen, with Casey to act as witness. 'I said I had no wish to be in a position, in the circumstances, to appear to be acting as umpire between them, which constitutionally would have been wrong,' Casey wrote to Buckingham Palace. The most that Casey would do was pass on McMahon's request to McEwen. The Country Party leader said he would meet McMahon, but only if a Country Party supporter was present. 'I passed this on to McMahon, with no result,' Casey recorded.[49]

Amid preparation for the memorial service for Holt, which government leaders from all over the globe were attending, the lobbying for votes began. Paul Hasluck would be a candidate, as would Les Bury, the minister for labour and national service. Billy Snedden, the minister for immigration, held off announcing his candidacy, but was nonetheless sounding out support. And then there was John Gorton. 'I'm not too good at this,' he said to Jim Killen, when he called to seek support for his bid.[50] Luckily for Gorton, he had proxies working on his behalf to gather support and clear obstacles, such as the need to transfer from the Senate to the House. To effect this, potential contenders for Holt's seat, which Gorton would require, were leaned on and urged to make way.[51]

McMahon was trapped. His peers were not standing by him. His ministerial colleagues were not offering him support.[52] They had little sympathy for him, and they held a high regard for McEwen.[53] Howson had already told McMahon of his belief that McEwen was not bluffing. Mounting a bid for the leadership, Howson intimated, would be futile. When McMahon asked for advice on confirming this, Howson advised him to turn to the people who had gotten him the deputy leadership two years before.[54]

Those people—most notably, the Packer press—were about to make their influence felt. Reid began to probe at the charges, still being made in private, about McMahon's connections with BIG.[55] Meanwhile, a holidaying Sir Frank Packer was ringing his trusted columnist, David McNicoll, to find out what was happening. On the first day, McNicoll recalled, Packer's first question expressed his preference clearly: 'What about Bill McMahon?'[56]

As the week neared its end, it seemed that McMahon would not have a chance. Certainly, he seemed to think so. On Friday 22 December, after the memorial service at St Paul's Cathedral, Melbourne, McMahon went to the Southern Cross Hotel, where many other MPs were gathered, and told Clyde Packer that he was not going to run. McEwen's veto, he said, was the reason.[57]

That same afternoon, a group of Liberal Party–machine people—including the federal president, Jock Pagan; the New South Wales president, Fred Osborne; the New South Wales general secretary, John Carrick; and the Victorian president, Robert Southey—were meeting in the party's headquarters in Melbourne to discuss the leadership. Some were of the view that McEwen should be persuaded to stay on as prime minister. In the evening, the talks shifted to Pagan's room at the Menzies Hotel. Members of the federal executive were in attendance. The talks were long, lasting until two-thirty in the morning, resolving only when the Victorian Liberals vehemently scotched any prospect of a merger between the Country and Liberal parties and any prospect of McEwen staying on.[58] Yet, even then, there was pressure to have the matter reconsidered. On 29 December, the Victorian MP Sir Wilfrid Kent Hughes, in a column for the Melbourne *Herald*, argued that McEwen should be invited to stay on. When asked to elaborate, Kent Hughes happily complied.[59] Privately, the idea also enjoyed the support of David Fairbairn, minister for national development.[60]

Over Christmas, the manoeuvring continued. Some sought to posture. Some sought to make deals. With McMahon apparently out of the race, Packer swung his support, on advice from McNicoll and Reid, towards Gorton.[61] But Packer was keen to see McMahon protected: 'Well, see Gorton,' he said to McNicoll. 'Ask him if he'll have Bill as Treasurer. Let me know how he reacts.'[62]

Gorton was spending the break at Billy Wentworth's Pittwater home. Of the three approaches that Packer emissaries made, it was the last that proved decisive.[63] In the New Year, McNicoll visited and had a chat with Gorton. If Gorton won, McNicoll asked, would he keep McMahon in the Treasury? Gorton got the message. He understood that the support of the Packer press was contingent on his answer. He told McNicoll what he needed to hear—and, according to a later aide-mémoire by McMahon, told McMahon that he would be retained in the Treasury.[64]

Menzies was roused to intervene. Supporting Hasluck's candidacy but despairing of his refusal to canvass for support, the retired prime minister perceived that McMahon was 'playing for preservation' and that there was an opening. He telephoned McNicoll, and urged him to support Hasluck.[65] When McNicoll pointed out that Gorton had all but guaranteed McMahon would stay at the Treasury, Menzies sought to say the same of Hasluck. 'Call him and say, "I've just been talking to Menzies and he says you're willing to have McMahon as Treasurer",' Menzies told him. 'I'm sure he'll say yes.'

Hasluck was called and, indeed, said as much.[66] It did not change anything. Gorton was the pick of the Packer press.

Back in Sydney, McMahon was contemplating his position. The urge to confront McEwen publicly had not wholly vanished. In the days following Christmas, Peter Kelly was summoned to McMahon's home. McMahon was having drinks with friends. He handed Kelly an eight-page aide-mémoire that detailed his feud with McEwen. Kelly was horrified. 'You're not going to release this, are you?' he asked.

McMahon told him just to read it. After he had done so, Kelly sat with McMahon and suggested changes. McMahon agreed to some, but declined others. Sonia asked Kelly if he thought McMahon needed to respond to McEwen's veto. Kelly knew his reponse would be unpopular, but stated it anyway. 'No,' he said, 'I don't.'

McMahon's friends were voluble in their disagreement. Notably, Norman Cowper and Jack Cassidy were both present, and both disagreed with Kelly. Not to be dissuaded, Kelly found the time to warn McMahon: 'You know if you release this you'll lose the lot, don't you?'

McMahon brushed him off. 'I understand you.' But it was not the time.[67]

'There was a lot of pressure on him to stand for leader after Holt drowned,' Kelly said later. 'A lot of pressure—from family, his doctor [George Halliday].'[68] But the pressure, Kelly thought, was misplaced. If McMahon stood for the leadership, and lost, the prospect that he could lose everything was very real. 'It was very strong pressure,' Kelly said.[69]

A few days later, McMahon telephoned Kelly to tell him that Sonia's advice was that he should stand. Kelly disagreed and said so. And when McMahon told him that Sonia was the best political judge he knew and that he felt bound to take her advice, Kelly gave up. 'If she's the best political judge you know, you should take her advice,' he said.[70]

Rumours that McMahon might stand in spite of McEwen's veto spread quickly. Press sympathy for the treasurer had been surprisingly generous, even outside of the Packer press. On 29 December, all newspapers gave prominence to a statement issued by BIG spokesman Colin Chapman that denied McMahon had anything to do with the group's work.[71] McEwen denied that BIG had anything to do with his veto. The coverage made the Country Party leader aware, nevertheless, that remaining silent about his reasons for vetoing McMahon could backfire just as easily as public accusations could. Moreover, the provocations of some journalists rankled. According to Fitchett,

McEwen told Angus McLachlan, editor of *The Sydney Morning Herald*, that he would not take any more attacks on his actions and character: 'I can, I'll take a lot as a minister, but I will not take this sort of stuff, my character, my reputation being impugned by men like Newton and *The Review* while I am prime minister, and I *am* prime minister. I might only be prime minister for a fortnight, but I am Prime Minister of Australia.'[72]

Cannily, shrewdly, McEwen decided to use his friends and the resources of his office. ASIO officers allegedly broke into McMahon's home in Sydney in search of 'politically damaging material';[73] on 4 January, on the same day that *The Daily Telegraph* ran an anonymously authored and immensely flattering profile of McMahon,[74] *The Australian* published an equally laudatory and anonymously authored profile of McEwen, contending that it was contrary to the public interest to deny McEwen the prime ministership simply because he belonged to the Country Party.[75] Suspicions spread quickly that the paper's proprietor, Rupert Murdoch, had written the editorial in aid of his friend McEwen. 'I remember Murdoch telling the editor of *The Australian* [Adrian Deamer], after Holt's death, that we had to support McEwen—and not McMahon,' recalled Alan Ramsey.[76] That regard for McEwen prompted a front-page article two days later, which offered a well-sourced explanation for McEwen's veto. 'It was a beat-up of immense proportions,' McEwen's biographer wrote.[77] Using ASIO-sourced intelligence, the article claimed that McMahon's 'close association with an agent of foreign interests' was the main cause. That agent—Maxwell Newton—had 'sought to constantly undermine Australia's tariff policy and Mr McEwen, as the man behind it, to the detriment of Australian industry,' the article stated.[78]

The accusations prompted public denials from Newton, and days of claim and counter-claim from all involved. He had attended these meetings as a working journalist, Newton insisted, and denied claims that McMahon or the Treasury had funded his trips to the IMF and World Bank meetings. Rokuro Sase, of the Japanese Trade Centre, wrote to newspapers to deny that any of Newton's work for it was of a political nature.[79] Newton's contract with the Japanese External Trade Organisation (JETRO) was leaked and published.[80] McEwen's hand in all this was never particularly hidden. His press secretary readily confirmed—both to newspapers and to government staff—that the allegations about Newton were the spur for McEwen to veto McMahon.[81]

Whatever their veracity, the articles had the effect of halting any kind of move from McMahon to contest the leadership and, in fact, exposed him to a last-minute danger that he might be removed from the deputy leadership. Could someone with these accusations against him really continue in the Treasury? Hasluck, writing later, thought that McEwen's actions should have finished McMahon forever:

> The decent thing that might have been expected of him, after having been placed under such a cloud, would have been to offer to stand down both from the Treasury and from the deputy leadership. In any case, he seemed bound to lose both offices.[82]

That McMahon remained silent seemed cause for suspicion, despite Reid's claim that any response would entail breaking cabinet solidarity—thus giving grounds for McEwen to seek his dismissal.[83] For others, the prospect that McMahon might stand for the leadership, and thus endanger his hold on the deputy leadership, raised the possibility of McMahon's departure from Treasury—which could leave McEwen with ascendancy in economic policy. This could not happen.

As the date for the vote drew close, the prospects of the candidates running became clear. Billy Snedden prompted ridicule with his announcement that he would be running 'as a leader on the wavelength of his era'.[84] Les Bury had announced he was standing—and then had gone hiking with his family in the Snowy Mountains. With undisguised support from Menzies and the considerable respect of many colleagues, Hasluck had resolutely refused to campaign for the leadership and sent only a typically understated letter announcing that he would put his name forward.

The contest, as Hasluck had suggested in December, was between him and Gorton. Building on considerable support from fellow senators and Victorian MPs, Gorton brightened his prospects by adept use of the media. He appeared on a quiz show with Barry Jones, was photographed swimming and lazing on a beach, and in television interviews on Channels 7 and 9 presented himself as a straightforward, wry, charming, and knowledgeable man. Gorton emerged a much-strengthened figure. The public liked him. His colleagues believed his natural talent for television and his laconic approach would ensure he was a potent political asset.[85]

THE date of the ballot, 9 January, arrived with little certainty about who would prevail. Consensus among the party and the press was that it would take at least two ballots for one of the candidates to acquire a majority. No one had such support that they could win immediately.

While meeting with MPs before the ballot, McMahon made no attempt to disguise the fact that he would be voting for Gorton. He thought Gorton would win. The extent to which McMahon's statements affected others is debatable, but certainly it is true that pro-McMahon MPs would have an important role to play.[86]

At two-thirty, the eighty-one Liberal Party parliamentarians assembled in the government party room. McMahon sat at the table at the front, pale, his arms folded, looking drawn and reserved. In front of him was the long statement he had drafted to read at the meeting. Also on the table were the ballot boxes. Behind him, on his right, Hasluck, Gorton, and Bury were squashed into a couch, facing the party. Tony Eggleton ushered the press in to take photos and record film. 'Only two minutes, chaps,' he said. 'That'll be all you're allowed.' The candidates and the members made idle conversation, affected nonchalance. The smoke from Bury's cigarette fluttered like a feather in the afternoon light. After two minutes, the press was sent out: 'Right,' called Eggleton. 'Thank you, gentlemen.'[87]

The doors closed, and McMahon opened the meeting. Some were surprised that he was chairing, and dissatisfied with the way he proceeded to do so. Kent Hughes believed that 'arrangements' had been made to smother all business besides the election of a new leader. Still wishing to see McEwen remain prime minister, he had asked Dudley Erwin to put a resolution to this effect on the agenda, ahead of a ballot for the leadership. The request had not been met: his resolution was set down the agenda.[88] Les Irwin's wish that the party discuss McEwen's press statements was similarly set down the agenda. According to Reid, there was the potential in this early stage of the meeting that a move would be made to spill the deputy leadership.[89]

McMahon moved a motion of condolence for the Holt family. After a minute's silence for Holt, he moved on. 'We come now to the purpose for which we were called together today. We meet to elect the leader of the Liberal Party, who under well-established Constitutional practice will be called upon by the Governor-General to become the Prime Minister of Australia.'

McMahon went through the areas and problems that he believed confronted the country, linking these with the need for effective leadership. 'Whichever one of the candidates who is elected will have our unqualified loyalty and support,' he said. Then, explaining that the coalition between the Liberal and Country parties might be at risk if he put his name forward for the leadership, he told the meeting that he was not standing. 'I do this with regret—but in what I hope is the best interests of the Government.' He finished by advising his colleagues to be careful with what they said. Leaks were inevitable, and the impression of division should be avoided.[90]

But just as McMahon called for nominations, two MPs raised the question of the deputy leadership. State considerations came into play, in questions of leadership—should the deputy leadership be spilled?

McMahon said no. There was no vacancy for the deputy leadership. Why should it come up?

Later, some of his colleagues would marvel at this response. 'It seemed to me to be quite illogical,' recalled Gordon Freeth, who believed that the runner-up in the leadership contest should become deputy leader. According to Freeth, it was McMahon's 'emotional speech' that ensured the matter was not pressed: 'The mob got up to their feet and applauded him for this great sacrifice he'd made.'[91] It was, however, understandable for others. Menzies, observing events from retirement, had already surmised that McEwen's veto and humiliation had given McMahon 'the aura of martyrdom', and McMahon took advantage of it.[92] 'That was the best favour McEwen ever did for McMahon,' said Don Chipp. '[It] won him a lot of sympathy.'[93] Tom Hughes recalled it similarly: 'I, probably within my own mind, was rather sympathetic to McMahon. I didn't know him then as well as I came to know him.'[94]

Any move to spill the deputy leadership was averted. McMahon called again for nominations.[95] Bury, Snedden, Hasluck, and Gorton all stood to nominate for the leadership. The party voted. As expected, it took two ballots. Bury and Snedden were eliminated on the first, and just after a quarter past three the whip announced that Gorton had triumphed over Hasluck.

McMahon vacated the chair for the newly elected leader. It took only a few minutes for Gorton to breeze through the remaining items on the agenda. Irwin and Kent Hughes both decided against discussing their resolutions.[96] The meeting broke up.

The images that appeared on the evening television news suggested harmony and unity. Footage of Gorton and McMahon shaking hands with well-wishers in King's Hall, smiling and happy, of the press conference where they sat side-by-side, would have suggested that all was well. Privately, however, no ballot could resolve the various bargains and deals that had been struck, the wounds inflicted, and the insults hurled around in the twenty-three days that had passed since Holt's disappearance and death.

McMahon, while certainly aggrieved, nonetheless had some reason for thanks. He had endured one of the most public humiliations possible in politics. He had kept his position. He was bloodied, yes—but he had survived.

Writing that night to Menzies to explain and understand his loss in the ballot, Hasluck admitted that McMahon—'the little man'—was a much more formidable figure than he had allowed himself to believe:

> In the outcome I think the result of the party meeting was far more a triumph for McMahon than it was for Gorton ... In my limited experience I have never seen anything done with such brilliant cunning and today I think he is in a stronger position than he was the day before Harold died ... In a wry sort of way I recognise McMahon now as being a more clever man than I thought he was, although my distrust of him is greater than ever and my contempt for his political methods is profound.[97]

The 'dark forebodings about the future' that Hasluck went on to note were apt—and would eventually be realised.

CHAPTER TWENTY-FOUR

Privilege

1984

For someone so well off, McMahon was singularly odd about money. Bowman had been told this when he first started, but as time passed he saw it for himself. At first, it was innocuous. McMahon was tight-fisted. He preferred $50 notes to $10 or $20 notes.[1] He juggled bills so that he would not have to pay until the very last moment. He was loath to waste cheques, on the grounds that each one cost him money.[2] He seemed forever insecure about his wealth. One week, he told an amused Joyce Cawthorn, 'I'm not a rich man, you know.'[3] A fortnight later, he came into the office boasting that he had recently had the contents of his home valued and that everything was now worth so much more than it was when he had purchased it. There was furniture worth $20,000! There were earrings worth $2,000! Paintings—'Some of them horrible,' Cawthorn said to Bowman—were now worth ten times their original value![4] Then, a few weeks later, he complained about not having enough money to pay his tax bill. At this, Cawthorn sighed: 'He always exaggerates.'[5]

At other times, the preoccupation with money seemed injurious. In mid-April, McMahon's housekeeper rang the office to say that she had received no pay and no allowance for the supplies she had used at work for the previous few weeks. Cawthorn was staggered. Each week, she told Bowman, she sent $484 to Sonia via McMahon's driver to pay the housekeeper and gardener. Where had it gone? The housekeeper was apparently scared: she had children at school in the United States, and was afraid of losing her job if she complained.[6] Yet, after a few days, she went to her agency to complain. They took it up formally with Cawthorn, who in turn took it to McMahon. 'He was unaware of whole thing,' Bowman wrote, after hearing about it from Cawthorn, 'and seemed thrown off balance to hear that the housekeeper had not been paid.'[7] It took a few days to sort out the mess, but eventually five missing pay packets were found in a room filled with junk in McMahon's house. There was no proper explanation, and it was not enough. On 1 May, Cawthorn told Bowman that the housekeeper was quitting: 'Not happy.'[8]

Money seemed to deepen McMahon's moods, make him fluttery and frantic, confused and uncertain. In June, the problem of paying staff apparently resurfaced when Cawthorn burst into Bowman's office again. McMahon had accused her of failing to pay staff at the farm that he and Sonia maintained near Orange. One man had left because of it, McMahon had said. At this, Cawthorn was indignant. It was *certainly* not her responsibility to pay them, she complained to Bowman. She had *nothing* to do with it. But then, when she telephoned McMahon's agent in Orange—an elderly man with emphysema and a rough tongue—he rubbished the story. The farmhand in question had left for an entirely different reason, he told her. Then he went on, with words that were music to Cawthorn's ears: 'What have you people done to deserve to work for a miserable old bugger like that?'[9]

As the accounts manager, Cawthorn saw how intent McMahon was on getting the most out of his entitlements as a former prime minister. Cawthorn told Bowman how McMahon had gone to the Melbourne Cup and kept a driver waiting all day. When he received the bill, McMahon took it to the 'top man', as he called the official in charge of his entitlements, and said, 'You take care of this.'[10] According to Cawthorn, the 'top man' did. Sonia and McMahon also put all their mail through the office, Cawthorn said, including the 500 or so Christmas cards they sent out each year. When they were away and had to contact the office, they would call and tell whoever answered to call them back so that the office would bear the brunt of the cost. 'We can't do that sort of thing,' Cawthorn told Bowman.[11]

None of McMahon's former colleagues would have been surprised to hear of any of this. There had been many sniggers and raised eyebrows at the way that McMahon went about ensuring he obtained the full perquisites of office. While a minister, he caused 'fuss and bother' to ensure he got a bigger and better office, and he insisted on getting a car more splendid than those used by his colleagues, recalled Paul Hasluck. 'And, of course, none of us was surprised when, the disciplines of Menzies being removed, at the coming into office of Holt, McMahon made excessive use of VIP aircraft—an abuse of privilege not fully disclosed in his case in the replies to the parliamentary questions in 1967.'[12]

But Hasluck, like others, struck a more serious note when thinking about McMahon and money. He wondered about McMahon's propriety in office, and suggested that Menzies had doubts about this.[13] For himself, Hasluck said that he would 'doubt his [McMahon's] basic honesty in money matters, but am confident that he would be most careful and watchful to protect his reputation, so this side of his life was never the cause of political anxiety'.[14] There were some, however, who were not so confident. There were rumours of McMahon playing the stock market while he was treasurer and prime minister, of him later betting on movements of the exchange rate, and whispers of him using his position unduly.[15] Speaking with the surety that McMahon would never hear it, Malcolm Fraser put this forward most confidently.

According to Fraser, it had begun when McMahon was treasurer. All the members of cabinet had been offered shares in a resources company, and in a cabinet meeting Gordon Freeth had raised the propriety of taking up the offer. Cabinet came to a decision that ministers would not take up the shares they had been offered. Some years later, Fraser mentioned this to a longtime friend. To Fraser's astonishment, the friend, who headed a stockbroking firm, knew already. The friend said to Fraser, 'Well, Malcolm, would you like me to tell you the sequel?'

The sequel was that one of the ministers who had received an offer went to the firm and said that while he did not think his colleagues would take it up—on grounds that they were strapped for cash—*he* himself would take it up, as well as all the shares that had been offered to his colleagues.

Fraser needed only one attempt to guess the identity of that minister. 'That was the treasurer, wasn't it?'[16]

Many people were sceptical about the suggestion that McMahon might have been corrupt. His inability to keep his mouth closed would have found him out, Alan Ramsey thought. Moreover, all of McMahon's work and ambition would have been for nothing had he been found out. 'He wouldn't have gone anywhere but out on his bloody ear,' said Ramsey later.[17] Would McMahon really have taken that chance? Would he have endangered all those years of work? Whatever the truth of the rumours—and it is notable that none of these were put on the record while McMahon was alive, when he could have responded to them—it was certainly the case that by 1984, as he worked on his book, McMahon was watchful with money, hated to spend it, was furious when he had to, and could be driven to great upset by it.

On 22 June, McMahon rang the office four times from Melbourne. He was panicked. 'Hopeless confusion,' Bowman called it. He wanted to know about his return flight to Sydney, and wanted the office to redirect his calls to the Ansett switchboard so that he would not have to pay. When this was said, all Bowman could picture was McMahon agonising over whether to drop another twenty-cent coin into the payphone.

When the office got an Ansett operator on the line and told him what was happening, he was incredulous. 'What? A former prime minister, and he can't get anyone to lend him a telephone?'[18]

CHAPTER TWENTY-FIVE

The New Man

1968–1969

Three days after the leadership ballot, McMahon sent his new prime minister a letter. 'So that you will be aware of the background of my recent problems with Mr McEwen,' he wrote, in a rather drastic understatement, '… I attach copies of some aide-mémoires and a document of a short history of my difficulties with Mr McEwen.' There was a lot of material in the package he sent. The 'history' ran to thirteen foolscap pages and the aide-mémoires to twenty-five. 'I think it is essential for you to know everything relevant to this problem,' McMahon went on, 'because, doubtless, other rumours will eventually circulate designed to exacerbate the tension between Mr McEwen and myself, and the tensions between the parties.'[1]

It was a defensive ploy. McMahon was well aware that with Holt gone, he would need Gorton's help to counter McEwen's influence and advocacy on matters of trade, tariff, and economic policy. He knew, too, that Gorton possessed considerable licence as a new prime minister and little liking for him personally. Gorton, recalled Tony Eggleton, who had been retained by the new prime minister, 'acknowledged McMahon's seniority and ministerial experience. But,' Eggleton added, 'like former leaders, he had reservations.'[2] Public support for the Victorian senator was strong, and there were calls for him to use his accession to break with the past. On the day of the ballot, *The Australian* editorialised that the first task of the new leader should be 'to make absolutely sure that Mr McMahon is not returned as Treasurer'.[3] The calls continued after the ballot, even while McMahon received favour for his decision not to stand. 'There is a chance for the new Prime Minister to give entirely new shape and direction to some key posts in the Ministry,' ran one editorial.[4]

Gorton did just this following his 24 February election to the House of Representatives as the new member for Higgins. Don Chipp, the minister for the navy, was dropped, as was Peter Howson, whom Gorton blamed for the VIP affair and had little regard for anyway. Chipp took the rebuff with good grace, but Howson felt deeply injured by it. He blamed Gorton for the VIP affair, and thoroughly resented the fact that the man who had embarrassed him so was now the leader of his party and his country's prime minister. From the backbench, Howson would become a trenchant and hostile critic.

Gorton filled the resulting two vacancies, and those created by Holt's death and the retirement of senator Denham Henty, with supporters. Senators Malcolm Scott and Reg Wright became ministers, as did MPs Billy Wentworth and Phillip Lynch.

Had Gorton been bolder, McMahon might also have been removed from the Treasury.[5] On taking office, Gorton had taken care to be briefed on McEwen's concerns about McMahon's relationship with Maxwell Newton, to the point that he even consulted the director-general of ASIO, Sir Charles Spry.[6] What he heard did not cause Gorton to think better of his treasurer, and he began sounding out the consequences of sacking McMahon. There was support within the party, as Robert Southey, the president of the Victorian Liberal Party, intimated in an April letter. But weighing against this were state-based factors. McMahon still enjoyed support among the New South Wales Liberal Party, Sydney's business community, and the Packer press. Moreover, to remove McMahon could suggest that Gorton was giving in to the Country Party on economic policy. Gorton pulled back.[7] It was better to maintain the still-fragile peace.

And it *was* fragile. The events of the summer were not going to be easily forgotten, no matter the number of paeans about unity. The rift with McEwen was still palpable. When Gorton opened a cabinet meeting on 28 February with a speech on proper process, McEwen followed with a spiel on propriety that was wholly directed at McMahon: it was important, McEwen said, to approach cabinet decisions objectively, without any 'earlier "lining up" of support'. At the same meeting, when tariffs on stoves arose, the two clashed again.

McMahon pointed out that the Tariff Board had taken no evidence on solid-fuel stoves, yet had recommended a duty anyway: 'Surely this should be non-protective.' As usual, McEwen reiterated that reports from the Tariff Board should be accepted—or what was the point of having the board?[8] Moreover, McEwen was quick to reopen old debates: within weeks of Gorton's taking over, McEwen had spoken with him about the prospects of the Australian Industry Development Corporation.[9]

There were other issues to tackle as well. The royal commission into the sinking of HMAS *Voyager* reported with a complete exoneration of Captain John Robertson. Whether to provide Robertson with compensation, and in what form, was the topic of several cabinet discussions. Reversing his earlier position, McMahon argued that an ex gratia payment was the best option.[10] The Tet offensive also brought up Australia's commitment to the US military efforts in Vietnam. Two months before his death, Holt had overruled objections from McMahon, Hasluck, and Fairhall, and had committed another battalion of troops and a squadron of Centurion tanks to the conflict. With Australia's contribution now at some 8,000 soldiers, Holt wrote to the US to advise that Australia had reached the 'full stretch of our present and planned military capacity'.[11]

Now, at Gorton's suggestion that Australia's commitment left little space for further contributions, McMahon noted that during his talks with Johnson, the president had said Australia would not be asked to contribute more unless it was able to meet the request. Moreover, mindful that public opinion was turning—he was telephoning 'a hell of a lot,' said pollster Roy Morgan[12]—McMahon was critical of the conflict. His longstanding reservations returned. He did not believe that South Vietnam was 'pulling its weight', and he urged caution. The government needed a 'reappraisal' of everything raised so far. It needed more knowledge of the US strategy in Vietnam, and to understand better the domestic and economic strain that the Vietnam commitment was imposing.[13]

Less than a week after that meeting, something of that economic effect was felt when the turmoil that had forced Britain to devalue sterling caused a run on gold and the failure of the London Gold Pool, which had helped balance demand since 1961.[14] McMahon led the cabinet discussion on the US proposal for a two-tiered market to govern gold sales—the first, in effect, for governments and central banking purposes, where gold prices would be fixed at $35 per ounce; the second, where the price would float, for speculators and industrialists—though he acknowledged that it was an interim measure only.[15] Not even two weeks after that came Lyndon Johnson's surprise decision to forego seeking a second presidential term and to immediately halt the bombing campaign in North Vietnam. This news, announced before the government was informed, prompted another scramble in the cabinet.[16]

Like many of his colleagues, McMahon came rapidly to realise that the prime minister was wholly his own man and apt to doing things in that vein. Gorton's attempt to depose Sir John Bunting, the longtime secretary of the prime minister's department, was glaring evidence of this. After reading all of the papers documenting the VIP affair, Gorton concluded that Bunting had allowed Holt to become vulnerable to charges of deceit and a cover-up. To prevent it happening again—to prevent it happening to *him*, even—Bunting had to go.[17] But opposition to such an ignominious removal welled within the public service, and Gorton was forced to devise a workaround.

Thus, taking a suggestion from Bunting that the functions of the prime minister's department should be reshaped, Gorton created the Department of the Cabinet Office, which would provide commentary on cabinet submissions and record cabinet decisions—and installed a shocked Bunting as its secretary. Bunting attempted to fight the move, but could not win. 'I have been in a fight and carry a few marks,' Bunting would soon say.[18] Observers were in no doubt about the effect on him. 'It was a body blow to Bunting,' said Peter Lawler, the deputy secretary in the prime minister's department, who opted to follow Bunting to the cabinet office.[19] Gorton's decision had the effect of putting the public service offside from the beginning of his government, and confirmed the wilfulness suggested in his January comments that:

> The Prime Minister ... is not to be chairman of the committee so that a majority vote in the committee says what's going to be done. He should put to the Cabinet or the committee what he believes ought to be done, and if he believes strongly enough that it ought to be done, then it must be done.[20]

For Gorton, this was the point of leadership. He was not prepared to be conciliatory about his beliefs, as he demonstrated when he appointed Lenox Hewitt as secretary of the prime minister's department. A former deputy secretary in the Treasury, Hewitt was formidable, intelligent, and blessed with a decisive grasp of issues. He was also divisive and fierce, undiplomatically intolerant of prattle or prevarication. These qualities caused Gorton to like him immensely and the bureaucracy to dislike him intensely.

Gorton also raised eyebrows by appearing to publicly question Australia's defence arrangements. Sceptical of the worth of Australia's military presence in Malaysia and Singapore, mindful of the strain that military commitments caused, and wishing to maintain some flexibility ahead of the pending British withdrawal from the Asia-Pacific region that had been announced by British prime minister Harold Wilson, Gorton questioned the doctrine of 'forward defence' supported by Hasluck and Fairhall. The inconsistency and apparent unpredictability of Gorton's public comments caused concern about the direction of Australia's defence policy. It even prompted McEwen to join McMahon and Hasluck over lunch to discuss how best to respond should these matters be raised in the House.[21]

Gorton's propensity for socialising with women and enjoying a drink also caused concern, particularly among more conservative members of the government. In the face of their grumbling, Gorton was defiant and blunt. 'I like a party where I can sing and dance and yarn,' he said. 'Yes, I even like talking to women! How else can I keep in touch with what people are thinking and saying? … Do they want me to live in an ivory tower and meet only diplomats and politicians? Well, damn it, I'm not going to.'[22] For some members, used to the portly dignity of Menzies and the urbane restraint of Holt, this was a decided change in prime ministerial behaviour.

All of this created concern within the government, though little of it was to McMahon's benefit. The treasurer was 'distrusted everywhere,' Peter Howson wrote in March.[23] It was as much to do with the events of the summer as his general modus operandi. McMahon knew it. 'It is true, I'm sure, that to a lot of members I lost a great deal of favour,' he said later. These months were 'a difficult period of readjustment,' he said.[24] Working with McEwen after the veto took conscious effort.

'I had to try to pretend to myself that none of it had happened. That was the only way in which it was possible for me to carry on.'[25] Howson thought McMahon 'lonely and anxious', that he was missing his typical 'happiness and self-assurance'.[26] McMahon was anxious, jittery, and suspicious that he was under surveillance by forces working on behalf of McEwen. 'McMahon was convinced that McEwen had used ASIO to tap his phone,' Alan Ramsey recalled. When he sought to speak with journalists, McMahon would do so from a phone box outside his home.[27] Concerned that reporters might be seen when they came to his home, McMahon would also turn off lights and usher them in via the back door.[28] His concerns were not without some warrant, and his suspicions were not entirely paranoid. In the absence of an official statement, rumours about why McEwen had rebuffed him were thick on the ground in Canberra, and could easily verge on the scurrilous. McMahon would recall the toll that these took:

> It was not easy after the McEwen episode putting up with journalists who would ring me late at night and tell me that I was supposed to have been seen entering a hotel on a certain date in the company of a nice-looking young man in blue pants or something like that and then to hear a demand that I should identify who that young man was. In fact, that actually was the story put to me on one occasion. When I thought back on the date mentioned I was in bed with my wife.[29]

But McMahon had not given up on his ambitions. By the end of May, he was 'starting to try to build up his own faction in the party'.[30] Surreptitiously, quietly, behind the scenes, he worked at rebuilding himself. He was aided in this by the rise of Eric Robinson, a businessman-turned-politician who was elected, in June, as the new president of the Queensland Liberal Party. A fan of McMahon and his close ties to business, Robinson presided over a new and divisive approach from the Queensland section of the Liberal Party. The division would become a foil for Gorton, working to oust him in favour of McMahon.[31]

On a personal level, McEwen's veto, marriage, and fatherhood had effected change in McMahon. Marriage, most of all, had calmed him, had given him more breadth. His staff saw it. 'It softened him in lots of ways,' said Peter Kelly. 'He became less engaged in his work, although he still worked long hours.'[32] So, too, did the public service. Peter Lawler, working in the cabinet office with Bunting, thought that McMahon was 'more concentrated, more serious, more on the job' after his marriage, but that it had 'humanised' him, too.[33] McMahon recognised that there was change. 'I've had to adapt myself to a different life and become much more tolerant of others,' he said.[34]

The demands he placed on his staff did not change. Kelly could recall McMahon keeping a public servant working late into the night with him and then calling for him to come back early the next morning. When Kelly made a small, gentle plea that it would be rough on the man, McMahon's response was blunt: 'Well, I'll be up, won't I?'[35] He was always demanding, brusque, and seemingly unaware of the toll that his incessant demands could exact. When the deputy secretary of the Treasury, Maurice O'Donnell, died in September 1969, some blame was levelled at McMahon. 'I know that O'Donnell served him so assiduously that when he died of a coronary, it was generally believed in Treasury that McMahon's demands had killed him,' John Stone said later.[36]

Nonetheless, McMahon was more expansive and reflective about the cost of his work. No, he did not get to go dancing, he said. Excursions to the theatre were 'a rare indulgence'. He did not listen to music. He read little but cabinet papers. He played squash twice a week to keep fit, yes, and could occasionally make time for golf, but that was about all.[37] Otherwise, McMahon's life was work and family—and his family was growing. Sonia was pregnant again, due to give birth at the end of July, and his daughter, Melinda, was growing up. Deciding that their flat in Darling Point was too small, he and Sonia scouted for a new home. They eventually bought a house at 18 Drumalbyn Road, close by Frank Packer's residence, 'Cairnton', in the affluent Sydney suburb of Bellevue Hill.

Meanwhile, there was instability in the ALP. Despite having established a clear ascendancy over Harold Holt the year before, Gough Whitlam found his authority within the party constantly in question. Tensions between the right and left wings were a recurrent source of angst, and, in the first half of 1968, they were exacerbated by the public support Gorton enjoyed and the party-reform agenda that Whitlam pursued. It became the subject of headlines in the lead-up to the April meeting of the ALP federal executive. Objections to seating the right-wing Tasmanian delegate, Brian Harradine, were the first challenge; second was the repeated and humiliating censures that the executive—outvoting Whitlam each time—imposed on the party leader.

Whitlam decided to go to the mat. 'Am firmly convinced that I cannot face the Parliament or the public with confidence unless Caucus shows its confidence in me,' he telegrammed his colleagues. He announced he would resign the leadership and recontest it immediately.[38] Jim Cairns, the left-wing opponent of Australia's involvement in Vietnam, reluctantly announced he would stand against Whitlam, and notably framed the leadership contest as a marker for the future: 'Whose party is this—ours or his?' he asked.[39] The resulting ballot was close—too close for Whitlam's liking, and it gave the government breathing space to develop its agenda.

One part of that agenda was Commonwealth–state relations. As the annual Premiers' Conference neared in June, McMahon and Gorton worked in concert to effect a decisive shift in those relations.[40] At issue were money and power. Since 1942, the Commonwealth government had held the power to tax income, the revenue of which it distributed to state governments according to a periodically adjusted formula. By 1968, the premiers were muttering about the injustice of that power, the formula, their own budgetary hardships, and the steps they would take if the Commonwealth did nothing. On 27 June, the premiers came to Canberra with tough talk, expecting a buy-off.

They were to have a rude shock. McMahon's preparatory submission to cabinet had argued that it was necessary to make a forthright declaration of what was acceptable and not in the taxation field. Prompted by moves in Victoria and Western Australia to introduce receipts taxes, he urged his colleagues to consider 'the likely effects of state tax on our revenues and its implications'. McMahon argued that the Commonwealth should veto moves by any of the states to re-enter the income tax or payroll tax fields. Furthermore, it should adjust the distribution formula to penalise those states that persisted with any such attempts. Believing that this would be 'strongly supported' by the public, cabinet accepted McMahon's submission, and Gorton duly informed the premiers on 28 June.[41]

A series of grants lessened the blow, but the premiers nevertheless all departed Canberra angry. Though McMahon, too, caught some of the stick, the premiers lashed Gorton most of all. They branded the prime minister a 'centralist' who was upending decades of understanding of Commonwealth–state relations. The meeting especially antagonised the Liberal premiers of New South Wales and Victoria, respectively Bob Askin and Henry Bolte. The latter, no fan of Gorton's already, was especially angered. 'The federal government's prestige has diminished since Mr Gorton became prime minister,' he remarked later that year.[42]

'From the beginning,' one observer wrote, 'the Commonwealth showed who was boss.'[43] For some readers, this would have sounded like criticism. For Gorton and McMahon, this would have been a compliment.

THERE was further change in McMahon's professional and personal life. Towards the middle of 1968, Peter Kelly decided to leave the treasurer's employ. He had made the decision the year before, but delayed his resignation in order to see through the 1967 Senate campaign.[44] Now that had passed, Kelly was out. 'I left him [McMahon] because, first of all, I wanted to go and work with Maxwell Newton,' Kelly said later. 'I thought I'd learn more.' But there was another reason, one that spoke to McMahon's still-evident ambitions and capacities:

> I also left, as a secondary motive, because I didn't think he'd be a good Prime Minister. I didn't think he could handle the work. I thought it'd be too big for him, as far as foreign affairs and managing men went. I didn't think he could handle the job.[45]

Once Kelly had officially joined his staff, as head of service in the parliamentary Press Gallery, Newton announced the news on the front page of the 1 July issue of *Incentive*.[46] Six months later, Pat Wheatley would also leave McMahon—and, like Kelly, she went to work for Newton.[47] She was surprised to find McMahon's reaction was far from congratulatory when she told him the news while he holidayed with his family at Surfers Paradise. 'He wasn't happy,' Wheatley said later. She realised only afterwards that news of her new employer might cause him embarrassment. Tensions with McEwen, after all, were still rife.[48] Newton's name was still poison. What kind of message did this send? McMahon's reaction was swift, unsentimental, and unceremonious. Wheatley was sent back to Sydney on the first available flight early the next morning, and immediately transferred from his office. The speed did not help. News of Wheatley's appointment caught the attention of the press, and McMahon issued a statement that was, soon after, contradicted by Wheatley herself. Newton, for his part, was cutting when asked to explain it: 'What do you want me to say? That I'm hiring her because she's going to bring me a big stack of secret Treasury files?'[49]

On 27 July, Sonia gave birth to a second child, Julian. Within weeks, McMahon was talking about how his two children had affected his life:

> Now I've got two children I'm developing an even more different attitude. Where I go they want to follow. They want to participate in everything I do, even reading the newspapers; they insist on eating my breakfast with me and drinking my coffee with me. Somehow it all adds up to making me accept some previously unbelievable aspects of life. So, in the long run, marriage and children have made me more adaptable and tolerant. Life is better and much happier.[50]

There were some hard decisions to be made. For a time following Melinda's birth in 1966, she and Sonia had accompanied McMahon between Canberra and Sydney. Sonia soon realised that the constant travelling was no good for them. They employed a nanny to look after Melinda and, subsequently, Julian, in Sydney, while she accompanied McMahon to Canberra and on the international trips his career required. 'It was a hard decision,' Sonia said later. 'Very hard. I loved being with Bill and I loved being a mum. But I knew I had to make a decision and I chose to be with my husband.'[51]

On 13 August, Parliament returned for the spring sittings, and McMahon delivered the budget. One might have expected it to be tough. As Treasury's analysis of the 1967–68 financial year noted, there had been 'more than the usual disruptive economic events' over the previous twelve months.[52]

In the face of all this, the 1968–69 budget was surprisingly generous. With only an 8 per cent increase in defence expenditure (in contrast to 18 per cent in 1967–68), the budget was defined by spending on social services. 'The Government,' McMahon said, 'has placed the objective of helping the aged, the sick, and the needy in the forefront of its domestic programmes.' Aided by a 'buoyant' economy with strong demand, McMahon announced increased spending on social services, housing, repatriation, and health by $111m. In the social services, that expenditure went to increases in the pension, health benefits for the chronically ill and aged, and repatriation benefits for war widows and invalids. There was extra spending in education: capital grants for school libraries and preschool teachers' colleges, and university scholarships for undergraduate and postgraduate students. In keeping with the new attention paid to Aboriginal affairs since passage of the 1967 referendum, the budget contained a $10m appropriation for assistance in housing, education, health, and enterprises.

To pay for this, McMahon drew on the growth in tax receipts—there was a projected $482m increase in receipts, attributable to the growth of the economy—and increases in company tax, sales tax, and television licence fees.[53] According to John Stone, these increased taxes 'were, in hindsight, undesirable; and to the extent that they were needed to pay for the (non-Defence) spending measures ... those measures were also wrong-headed'.[54]

Preparation of the budget was nowhere near as smooth as it had been under Holt. In July, McMahon had telephoned Howson to complain that Gorton could not understand 'the elementary facts of Keynesian economics', and felt he could print Treasury Bills without economic damage or inflation. 'This apparently led to an explosion on Wednesday [17 July], at which Bill finally stood him up,' Howson wrote in his diary, 'and for a time John went carefully.'[55]

Despite its fraught preparation and generous measures, the reception to the budget was decidedly mixed. Some observers noted that it reflected Gorton's preference for a 'full social programme', albeit in a 'give and take' fashion.[56] More generous observers suggested that it demonstrated 'a place for humanity',[57] but the voices of discontent were louder. Pensioners' groups thought the measures underwhelming. Education groups thought it patchy. Predictably, business groups criticised the increases in company tax—'Savage and unwarranted,' said one—and the state premiers continued to squabble about their own taxation powers.[58]

The journalist Maximilian Walsh, however, was suspicious that the budget was a prelude to an election. 'The very sectors where Mr McMahon and Mr Gorton have directed their attention—health, pensions, and education—are the three key issues selected by voters polled on the eve of the general election in 1966 and the Senate election in 1967,' he wrote. Nonetheless, he wondered if the efforts would pay off: 'Unfortunately, nobody has turned up a scintilla of evidence to show that such sentiments receive their just electoral reward.'[59]

Similar doubts were shared within the government. Gorton's appeal and the new directions he appeared to offer suggested that the gamble of an early election could well pay off. But there were some hard questions to be asked. Were health, education, and pensions really the best policy areas to fight on? Eighteen years of Liberal–Country Party rule had been won on the back of national security and opposition to communism. Were these reliable planks to be so cavalierly exchanged for areas where Labor had long held an advantage? Would holding off until 1969—when the economic headwinds could be stronger—be a safer bet? McMahon, according to Howson, thought it would be better to go,[60] and repeated this belief to pressmen right into October: 'I think that the early election is a certainty.'[61]

These questions were complicated by the existence of the DLP. Preoccupied with defence, and defined, to some extent, by its ardent anti-communism, the DLP had looked with concern on Gorton's statements about the role of Australia's military in Malaysia, Singapore, and Vietnam, and the budget's emphasis on social spending. In light of the close of Britain's open-ended commitment to the Asia-Pacific region, the DLP preferred to see defence spending increase. Amid speculation about an election, the DLP's attitude became a significant issue and its disquiet a portent of problems. In October, senator Vince Gair, the DLP's leader, had a meeting with Gorton, and informed him both of his concern and his decision that the DLP would preference other parties ahead of the government in certain seats, should an election be held that year.

Meanwhile, divisions were emerging and antagonism brewing

between McMahon and Gorton. Late in May, Fred Deer, the general manager of the Australian company Mutual Life and Citizens' Assurance Co. (MLC), wrote to McMahon to state his concern about an influx of foreign capital in the life-insurance market. Prompted by his desire to protect MLC, Deer asked McMahon and the Treasury to intervene. McMahon replied that he would watch the situation, but was otherwise noncommittal. His was an unsurprising response: as his debates with McEwen had demonstrated, he was open to foreign investment in Australia, and, if not necessarily in favour of a takeover, McMahon was wary of the consequences of legislation to limit overseas shareholdings. Come September, however, press reports that MLC was the subject of a takeover from unknown foreign interests prompted a wholly different response from Gorton, who was acting as treasurer while McMahon was overseas.

On 16 September, Treasury advised Gorton that caution should be heeded before stepping in, but that, if the government was intent on doing so, then a signal—a statement on the options present in the Life Assurance Act, for example—would be sufficient to deter the bid without deterring foreign investment altogether. But Gorton, concerned by the money involved, preferred to be more explicit about MLC and about foreign investment altogether. Six days later, armed with advice from attorney-general Nigel Bowen, Gorton issued a press statement announcing that the government would amend the ACT Companies Ordinance to remove any option of anonymity for shareholders and restrict the percentage of an Australian company that could be owned or controlled by foreigners. The statement was dressed in unapologetically nationalistic tones:

The Government believes this action will protect the interests of the policy holders [of MLC]. We also believe that Australians will share our determination that control over their Australian savings, and decisions on the investment of their Australian savings, shall remain in the control of an Australian company and will not be allowed to fall under the control of overseas interests.[62]

Issued while on a flight between Perth and Adelaide, without consultation with cabinet and with the barest knowledge of the Country

Party, the statement and the decision contributed to growing unease within the government. Privately, MPs were concerned by the prime minister's deviation from previous lines on foreign investment and his willingness to act unilaterally. That the move won public support did not ease their discomfort; if anything, it exacerbated their concerns that Gorton might repeat this kind of action.

Gorton had no compunction about the decision. He did not believe that Australia was so in need of foreign capital that it should greet it with an 'almost dog-like gratitude', as the Treasury seemed to believe.[63] Criticism of the speed of the decision was patently silly for the simple reason that speed was essential. 'Action had to be taken in a hurry,' he subsequently told cabinet. On unilateralism, Gorton was willing to admit the charge: 'I could have been accused of being a dictator,' he said.[64] But that willingness to make decisions came from his position: 'You [as prime minister] can make a decision and say that's it.'[65] The incident confirmed Gorton's inclination for decisive, immediate action and his dim view of Treasury and its orthodoxies.[66]

For McMahon, the decision on MLC was infuriating. He had found out by telephone while standing in a Zurich train station. The decision had been made in his absence. It was made over his objections. And, in spite of the fact that he had nothing to do with it, when he returned to Australia *he* was the one who had to sign the amended ordinance giving effect to the decision.[67] He made his feelings clear, but was in no position to overrule Gorton or to push him around. Further interference from Gorton, this time in negotiations on the International Monetary Fund agreement, rankled with McMahon, but the MLC decision always remained the key sore point.[68] 'I will not discuss the MLC action, nor its relationship to takeover bids by foreign organisations,' he said flatly, a few months later. Why? Because he was overseas when it happened and the responsibility was not his. It was for Gorton to explain, he said.[69]

McMahon returned to Australia well aware of the concern within the government—and the way that it was being muffled, for the moment, in anticipation of a snap election. All the circumstances seemed fortuitous. The ALP was still recovering from its April disarray. The economy was buoyant. Gorton enjoyed public approval for the strong, nationalistic appeals he was making. Why would he not go?

Press enquiries to the prime minister's office on the likelihood of an election in 1968 had been met with only one answer: 'No comment.' The refusal to confirm or deny was understandable, but the fervour of that speculation suggested that careful handling would be required should it be punctured.

Yet Gorton seemed oblivious to this. In a speech on 14 October, he called the speculation 'fascinating' and gave the impression that it had all been a game for him.[70] When he announced the next day that there would not be an election in 1968, observers in the press, the Parliament, and the government were dumbfounded. In searching for a satisfactory explanation, they seized on the DLP's threats to preference Labor ahead of the government in selected seats. It became common wisdom that Gorton's nerves, for once, had got the better of him. His subsequent statement that he had used the prospect of an election as leverage to force through redistribution changed no one's mind. 'His last minute retreat does not evidence that degree of strength that one expects as essential and exemplary leadership,' Arthur Fadden would note.[71]

McMahon was frequently butting heads with Gorton and McEwen. Yet there were times where friends and supporters of all three had significant stakes in the outcome of those debates, and the battles fought in cabinet thus echoed battles taking place elsewhere. One such battle occurred late in 1968. Rupert Murdoch, a friend of McEwen and a fan of Gorton, needed approval to transfer capital from Australia in order to take a controlling interest in the firm that published the British tabloid *The News of the World*. He was facing time constraints, and secrecy was essential to the bid. Murdoch was sure that the Treasury would oppose the request, just as it had in the past; moreover, he was sure that McMahon would leak it in order to satisfy the whims of Sir Frank Packer, an antagonist of Murdoch's who had once vowed to send him 'back to Adelaide with his fookin' tail between his fookin' legs'.[72] Only recently, Packer had managed to reduce Murdoch's ownership of various Sydney and Melbourne TV stations from 25 to 10 per cent.[73] Murdoch could not allow Packer to thwart him again.

Murdoch approached McEwen to ask what could be done. McEwen decided to work around the treasurer and Treasury. Deliberately waiting until a weekend that McMahon was not in Canberra, McEwen rang

Gorton and asked him to look at the paperwork on the application. At the Kurrajong Hotel, with Murdoch supposedly waiting in the garden, Gorton and McEwen went through the request together.[74] Gorton's support was a given. 'I was so much in favour of Australians owning overseas interests,' he said later. Moreover, he liked the young press baron. His support was a lock. 'I always liked Murdoch,' Gorton said later, 'and I started him on his way.'[75]

Thus, when the matter arose in cabinet, McMahon was destined to lose. His comments—that while the Reserve Bank appeared to agree with Murdoch's application, its advice was not 'a definite or precise recommendation' for approval—were discarded. His arguments for refusing the application fell on deaf ears.

Gorton stated that he was in favour of approving the request, as did McEwen and a host of other ministers. McMahon's argument that the current rules did not allow it and that approval would open 'an area we have so far refused to open' were trumped by arguments that to refuse the application would stifle enterprise. McMahon's was a lonely, dissenting voice. Absent a derisory comment from Hasluck that Murdoch was a 'brigand', other ministers in the cabinet were for approving the application. 'Consensus is *for*,' Gorton said.[76] The decision was made. And, with that, the prime minister had won himself a powerful ally and Murdoch could establish his beachhead in the British tabloid market.[77]

All this led McMahon to recognise that he would need to adapt to his new leader, on policy as well as political grounds. Though Gorton gave priority to economic growth, McMahon understood that the prime minister was less amenable to the belief that growth could better come through economic efficiency—a belief that was holding increasing sway within the Treasury.[78] More troublingly, McMahon perceived that Gorton's economic outlook was closer to McEwen's than his own. It called for adroit manoeuvring. Thus, by December, McMahon was reluctantly participating in Gorton's moves to restrict foreign capital, most notably in a measure that made it possible for shareholders to prevent a foreign takeover of a listed company unless it enjoyed the full support of every shareholder.[79]

McMahon's colleagues and the press reacted adversely to these moves. To those within the party, like Howson, McMahon could explain. 'He realises, above everything else, that the Treasury must keep control and not let Gorton get this into his own hands,' Howson wrote, after an explanatory phone call. With the press, however, McMahon had to defend the decision. 'We do want this large inflow of capital but we don't want unfair practices by financial and industrial interests overseas that are so powerful that, if they care to move in in strength, they can take over Australian companies,' he said in December.[80] The press was scathing. Even friends like Maxwell Newton attacked him for this heresy. The treasurer, wrote Newton, had 'abandoned any claim to be respected as a minister who stands for the implementation of sound economic principles [and] abandoned any claim to be the latter-day exponent of traditional Liberal policies'.[81] The *Australian Financial Review* similarly noted just how quickly the old shibboleths were being expunged:

> The consistently permissive, but clear-cut policies towards foreign investment in Australia sedulously built up by successive Liberal-Country Party governments over nearly twenty years of power-sharing are being shot to pieces by the Gorton Government.[82]

The treasurer was aware that his leader was pushing him towards areas and policies that he was averse to. He knew he would come under fire from the press for going along with it. And he knew, too, that Gorton was spreading the case against him. The prime minister's hostility was barely disguised. He disliked his treasurer almost as much as he disliked the Treasury.[83] It was obvious in private, palpable even in front of the press. In a briefing on 11 December, Gorton told journalists, on background, that the government had requested papers from Treasury on foreign capital in September, but that the papers had not been received. 'They seem to be taking a long time to do it,' he said lightly. 'I can only say I keep asking for it.'[84]

Nonetheless, McMahon was not willing to break ranks. He knew what was ranged against him. He knew that in an open dispute he had no chance of victory. Yet in spite of this he was also unwilling to vacate the field. He would not countenance retirement. He would not accept a diplomatic appointment. He would persist—in private and in public—and he would survive.

He would have observed that the political landscape was shifting. There were the concerns within the government about Gorton, yes—but there were other, more significant portents.

One of those was in tariffs. There was growing friction between McEwen and the chairman of the Tariff Board, Alf Rattigan, over tariff policy and levels of protection. Rattigan's increasing assertions of the board's independence saw him lead it towards a more stringent logic in its inquiries. To wit, a Tariff Board inquiry into the worth of hot-water bags—initiated by Australian rubber company Ansell, whose bottom line was being hit by the increasing prevalence of electric blankets—concluded that, on the basis of figures submitted to it by Ansell, it was doubtful whether manufacturing of the bags in Australia could ever be economic. The resultant report thus suggested that tariff duties on imported hot-water bags be removed so as to phase out an economically inefficient industry. In December, when McEwen took the report to cabinet for debate, he surprised some by seeking that it be rejected—and that, in fact, the industry should have the opportunity to request another inquiry. With Gorton's support, McEwen succeeded in having his way, though to McMahon's suggestion that the government 'should be calming down on tariffs', McEwen was sharp: 'What does that mean?'

'Means in public discussion,' McMahon said.

'This public debate started when Maxwell Newton fomented it for Japanese reasons—i.e. out of his secret contract with them,' the Country Party leader snapped.

Gorton intervened to cut off the argument, and Hasluck made a joke: 'We're supposed to be deciding with bags, not hot water!'[85]

The sharp exchange confirmed the continuation of the struggle over tariffs and the new direction of economic policy. The decision drew applause and derision, the latter most acerbically from Maxwell Newton, whose response would have surely provided some succour to McMahon. 'Mr McEwen is at pains to commit the government to blanket protection regardless of cost to the nation,' Newton wrote in *Incentive*. 'He is even prepared to commit the government to the ridiculous proposition that however much it costs the nation's pensioners, we must sustain a local hot water bag industry.'[86]

Less than a month later, McMahon received another reminder that he still had friends and allies when, a year to the day since Gorton had taken over, Alan Reid published his first book. Notable for popularising the writing of contemporary political history in Australia, *The Power Struggle* was a punchy and dramatic account of the summer of 1967—the infighting between McMahon and McEwen, Holt's disappearance and death, and Gorton's unexpected election. It contained a largely accurate summation of Casey's letter to Holt, and confirmed rumours that there had been unrest within the government before Holt's death. Since word of its composition began, the book had been keenly anticipated within government circles. It was, wrote one journalist, the 'most talked-about back-of-the-hand subject' in Parliament House, rumoured to contain information that could harm Gorton and the government both.[87]

After reading an advance copy, McMahon disdained the book in private conversations, describing it as 'rather sketchy and journalistic', but he nonetheless discussed it repeatedly and urged colleagues to read it.[88] Some of its contents were a surprise even for those who featured in it; to the public at large, the book added new dimensions to the events of the previous summer while remaining accessible, even exciting, to read. Upon publication, Gorton supposedly had a copy especially delivered to him while he attended the Commonwealth Prime Ministers' Conference in London; McEwen was alleged to be furious at the dark, vengeful pen portrait of him and the lighter, much nobler depiction of McMahon; and within the Press Gallery, the publication and impact of the book enhanced Reid's prestige perceptibly.

Most importantly, perhaps, the book was still relevant. Its protagonists and themes, the issues it sought to explain, the manipulation and manoeuvres that it described—all were still topical in January 1969. For McMahon, it would have been another reminder in a new year that he was not entirely alone.

EVEN without allies, McMahon was never entirely helpless. His nervy manner, which could suggest weakness and indecision, belied a resilience to withstand stress and setbacks, to endure pressure and political posturing.[89]

He was well aware of the currency that rumour could enjoy, the way it could harden like concrete and become, by repetition and invocation,

almost the same as evidence. Journalist Mungo MacCallum recalled
that McMahon was blatantly obvious about it: he would 'ring up to
try to have a chat and try and plant some idea in the reporter's mind'.[90]
Dudley Erwin, a critic of McMahon's, recalled that he was especially
good at starting rumours. McMahon would make a suggestion while at
a party or a dinner, giving just enough information for it to be credible
while remaining deniable, and allow those who heard it to carry the
rumour from there. 'All McMahon had to do was drop it in the right
place and the couriers were on it,' he said later.[91]

One such example came on 10 February 1969, when Gorton
announced the appointment of Hasluck as governor-general to succeed
Casey. Almost immediately, rumours began to swirl. Gorton had
appointed Hasluck in order to remove a potential rival for the leadership,
the main strand of them went, and to remove a dissident from Gorton's
thinking in foreign relations and defence.[92] Judged against the context
of Gorton's unilateralism and willingness to intervene over the heads
of his ministers, the rumour seemed credible, even satisfactory. But,
much later, Hasluck would write that he had decided long beforehand
to retire at the 1969 election, and that the appointment, therefore, was
untainted by any kind of conspiracy by Gorton. Hasluck pinned the
blame for rumours to the contrary on McMahon. 'I felt at the time
that McMahon was doing a great deal to denigrate me and to harm
my reputation and his only motive that I can see was to destroy me as
a possible rival,' he wrote. Gorton's supposed malevolence was likely
McMahon's, he thought. 'If I were seen by some to be a potential rival
to Gorton, by the same token I was no less dangerous to any ambitions
that McMahon might have had for the Prime Ministership.'[93]

Hasluck's appointment received an uneasy reception.[94] That a
contemporary politician was being appointed was some part of it.
The greater part of that unease was that while Hasluck may have
been Gorton's only possible choice, he was also one of the last of the
Menzies-era men, a bulwark of that stable, predictable, and prosperous
era—and was now departing the political scene. Moreover, for those
concerned about Gorton's instincts on defence and foreign relations,
Hasluck's appointment removed an obstacle to Gorton assuming
greater control. For the DLP, this was another cause for concern.

Other rumours circulated and were soon to be brought into public view, aided only slightly by touches from McMahon.

On 10 February, the same day that Hasluck's appointment was announced, Newton published a small note in his newsletter *Insight* stating that Ainsley Gotto—Gorton's young private secretary, who was the object of disreputable rumours and disdain from some ministers—had been making 'a valiant but unconvincing attempt to hide her dissatisfaction since an uncomfortable social occasion at the United States Embassy late last year'.[95]

That 'social occasion' had been a late-night visit to the American embassy in Canberra on 1 November 1968. At the invitation of the ambassador, who was seeking to assuage Gorton's anger that he had not been forewarned or consulted about the American decision to cease the renewed campaign against North Vietnam, Gorton went to the embassy after the conclusion of the parliamentary Press Gallery's annual dinner. It was after midnight, and he came with guests: Tony Eggleton and Geraldine Willesee, a journalist for Australian United Press, the daughter of Labor senator Don Willesee, and the only female member of the gallery. Little happened: Gorton spoke with Willesee, telling her that he had not been consulted about the cessation of the bombing campaign, and Eggleton spoke with the ambassador. By three o'clock in the morning, Gorton had returned to the Lodge and Willesee was at home. While perhaps unwise, there had been nothing egregious or wrong about the evening.

But rumours about what had happened were thick on the ground in Canberra within a day. Those rumours later prompted Australian United Press to sack Willesee on grounds that she was a liability, yet they intensified when Frank Browne—producer of the controversial newsletter *Things I Hear*—wrote repeatedly of an article, supposedly pending publication in the British magazine *Private Eye*, about the prime minister's behaviour while meeting with American singer Liza Minnelli.[96] Browne's writings prompted Labor MP Bert James to raise them in an adjournment debate when Parliament returned in March 1969. He sought an explanation from Gorton. 'I have no doubt that the Prime Minister could clear the air in regard to this shadow that has been cast on his integrity by this magazine,' James said. 'I have no doubt that the matter will soon be clarified to the satisfaction of all members of the House and those who had the unpleasant experience of reading this damaging article against our Prime Minister.'[97]

Government MPs Jim Killen and Tom Hughes gave an immediate reply. Killen called James's speech an attempted smear, and Hughes argued that James was 'giving wider publicity to the scurrilous emanations of this libeller Browne than they had otherwise obtained'. He called on someone from the Labor side to disown James's comments.[98] Having already spoken in the debate, Labor frontbencher Fred Daly sought leave to speak again so that he could reply to Hughes, but Dudley Erwin, the leader of the House, refused. Sensing an opportunity to divide the government, the ALP's former leader, Arthur Calwell, moved a suspension of standing orders in order that Daly might speak. Chaos ensued: bereft of ideas of what to do, Erwin followed McMahon's orders that he not back down, and, in the ensuing vote, fifteen government members crossed the floor to vote for the suspension, unwilling to gag Daly. The vote was tied at 42–42 and, in the absence of a majority, was declared defeated by the Speaker.[99] McMahon then sought to cover up the chaos for which he was partly responsible by attacking the ALP's leadership for not—in the twenty intervening minutes—disowning James's speech.[100] It was a clumsy attempt to regain the advantage, and the ALP's deputy leader, Lance Barnard, had no trouble turning it back:

> I have heard sufficient from the Treasurer tonight to convince me that what the Leader of the Country Party had to say about him some time ago is quite true. If these are the kind of tactics that the Treasurer adopts in this House and outside the House it clearly indicates what the Leader of the Country Party had to say about him about 12 months ago would not only be substantiated by all members of the Australian Country Party but by honourable members on this side of the House as well. It was a despicable attitude for the Treasurer to adopt. He knows that I was not in the House tonight and did not hear the debate.[101]

The next morning, responding to a motion to refer the matter to the House Privileges Committee, Gorton spoke shortly and sharply on the allegations raised by James. After declaring himself the 'subject of a scurrilous whispering campaign', Gorton dismissed them out of hand. Following speeches from Whitlam and McEwen, the government gagged debate and voted the motion down.[102] That afternoon, Gorton convened a special party meeting and asked for a vote of confidence from his party. He received it: all the government members stood and applauded him.

Except one. Edward St John, who had proved already that deference to the office of the prime minister came second to his iconoclastic views and judgement, remained seated and silent while his colleagues stood and applauded.

St John had voted for Gorton in January 1968, but had been rethinking his support. By February 1969, he had resolved that Gorton was a 'dangerous' and 'inadequate' prime minister who should be removed from the leadership. His concern was largely personal: he did not believe that Gorton had the fit character to be prime minister, and felt he could not conduct himself in a way that was above reproach. St John had already spoken with Gorton, but left unsatisfied. Thus he compiled material to support his arguments, made no secret of his discontent, and spoke with colleagues and peers. At McMahon's urging, St John read *The Power Struggle*.[103]

James's speech, the government's moves to gag debate, and the apparently senseless acclamation Gorton had received in the party room prompted St John to intervene. During the adjournment debate that night, speaking just after ten-thirty, St John raised his concerns about Gorton and his conduct in visiting the American embassy. Arguing that this conduct was intentionally calculated to 'prejudice' the Australian–US relationship, St John asked:

What would the American Ambassador and his wife think of a Prime Minister who being invited to a social or other occasion arrives at two-thirty in the morning or somewhere about that time with a young lady not his wife aged nineteen and stays for some hours?[104]

Gorton responded immediately, dismissing any suggestion of impropriety, and setting out what had happened in some (though erroneous) detail. With considerable support from the government benches, Gorton angrily bemoaned that a 'perfectly reasonable and proper thing can be twisted, turned, and slimed over'.[105] By the middle of the next week, following continued ructions and press conferences during which St John enlarged upon his grievances, Gorton's supporters were moving to force any concerned Liberal MP to choose between Gorton and St John. In the party room, a motion was proposed. It deplored St John's attacks, asked him to consider his place in the party, and expressed confidence in Gorton's leadership. The option was open to him, but St John decided against forcing a secret ballot in the vote on the motion, in which those of a similar mind might express their support. He departed the party room, thereafter sitting as an independent.[106]

The controversy over Gorton's actions at the American embassy marked a turning point. For while the prime minister's public approval barely seemed to dip in this period, the press regard for him changed decisively. They were now attuned to his behaviour, willing to write about it and interrogate it, and unwilling to accept—as had been the case for years previously—an absolute distinction between the public official and the private person. In many ways, this change was bound up in the generational shift then underway in the Press Gallery. Predominantly white, male veteran journalists were retiring, giving way to younger, tertiary-educated reporters, including women, who were less trusting of politicians, more open to new methods of reportage and to shifts in understanding, and attuned to public perception and moods.

None of it was to Gorton's liking. During the subsequent months, he grew increasingly critical of journalists, to the point of preparing a 'black list' of reporters that he tried to tell Tony Eggleton to have nothing to do with. Eggleton successfully resisted this—but he could not evince any change in Gorton's attitudes towards the press.[107]

Newton was one journalist who felt the force of this antipathy. Initially favourable to Gorton, Newton had turned on the prime minister with a dislike as marked as that which the prime minister's office, in turn, responded.[108] Tentative criticisms had become blunt and increasingly merciless. The note about Ainsley Gotto in the February issue of *Insight* was but one instalment. In December 1968, Newton published a verbatim transcript from a Gorton press conference, replete with statements that some material was off the record, not for use, and not for attribution.[109] The following April, he published a largely accurate summation of a late-1967 cabinet decision on assistance to Singapore, and boasted that his business was to 'penetrate the government'.[110] In May, another of his publications, *Management Newsletter*, contained a summary of a confidential cable between the Department of External Affairs and the Australian embassy in Paris, which discussed Australian ambassador Alan Renouf's meeting with the French foreign minister, Michel Debré.[111] Confidential but hardly of national importance, the leak nonetheless prompted a furious response.[112]

Nine days later, on cabinet orders, ten police officers arrived at Newton's home and office in Kent Street, Deakin, just after 12.30pm, to execute a search warrant to discover the source of the leak.[113] McMahon's former staff members, Peter Kelly and Pat Wheatley, were there. Kelly saw the police car turning into the driveway, and knew exactly why they were coming. He retrieved the copy of the cable, and hid it in the bottom of a large wastepaper bag. He then rang the parliamentary Press Gallery and invited reporters to come, witness, photograph, and report the search.

The police spent eleven hours going through everything from the filing cabinets to the toilet cisterns, the beds and cupboards, the washing machine and laundry. Newton's children came home from school to see their home ransacked, the press documenting it all. 'No words could describe the feeling of powerlessness,' wrote Newton's daughter, Sarah, later.[114] Police seized thirty documents relating to the Renouf-Debré cable, and left open the possibility that Newton could be charged.

By this time, Kelly had been out of McMahon's employ for almost a year. In that time, he had hardly exchanged a word with his former boss. If their paths crossed, McMahon would say hello—but otherwise McMahon kept to his promise to Holt, and steered clear of anything related to Newton. 'We had virtually little or no contact with him,' Kelly said.[115]

Nevertheless, some time after the raid, the phone in Newton's offices rang. Pat Wheatley answered and heard a recognisable voice. As usual, there was no greeting, and no small talk. She heard just five words before the line went dead: 'The warrants. Check the warrants.'[116]

She told Newton and Kelly, who followed up on the advice. Three months later, following an application by Newton, his wife, and three other associated companies, Justice Fox of the ACT Supreme Court ruled that the search warrants had not been properly executed and thus were invalid. The documents that had been seized had to be returned. Court action arising from the raids was halted.[117]

Small as it was, the phone call was a sign that McMahon was prepared to aid those whose work was destabilising Gorton. Aware that Gorton was suspicious of him, gauging that there was discontent within the party but uncertain about its extent and depth, and apprehensive about the security of his position, McMahon and his allies were working to ensure that his options remained open.[118]

McMAHON handed down his fourth budget on 12 August 1969. Designed with clear knowledge of the election pencilled in for the second half of the year, it was a budget that could afford largesse. As the Treasury noted in its mid-year assessment, the previous year had been one of 'exceptionally fast growth'. Rural production had recovered from the drought. Building and construction were high. Mining was expanding rapidly. Manufacturing was rising to meet domestic demand. Imports had risen, but exports were well up on the previous year. Australia was reaching the end of the 1960s with favourable prospects.[119]

'Again,' McMahon said, introducing the budget, 'social welfare has an honoured place in the proposals I make. They take us much further along the road the government is determined to follow in accordance with the policy it initiated last year.'[120] The references to continuity with the 1968–69 budget were deliberate—a signal to Gorton's pronounced influence over the budget process and its basic purposes. Echoing Treasury concerns that the booming economy brought with it dangers of inflation fuelled by rises in disposable income and growth in employment (itself caused by the increasing number of women in the workforce and the growing migrant intake), McMahon had sought to contain government expenditure during the budget sessions. Gorton, however, resisted this, and, aided by ministers with expensive proposals, forced a budget that was expansionary in nature, with a 9.6 per cent rise in total outlays, versus a 7.6 per cent rise in 1968–69.[121]

The prime minister and deputy prime minister were well able to get their own ideas included. The most notable and expensive of Gorton's was the introduction of a 'tapered' means test—another step in the long-running promise to liberalise it—which allowed 250,000 people to become eligible for the pension. Pensions and payments to widows without children were increased by $1 per week (just shy of $12 in 2018 values). There were increased benefits for people who became pensioners because of the increase in the basic rates, most notably in medical and hospital treatment. There were increases in allowances paid to aged persons living in aged-care homes; there were increases in unemployment and sickness allowances.

While spending on social services was the 'largest single item' in the budget, there was an obvious nod to Gorton's past as minister for education in the spending on schools, universities, and colleges. A total of $265m was appropriated for spending on schools—an increase of 38 per cent on the previous year's total. Funding for universities and colleges of advanced education was increased for the 1970–72 triennium. Places for Commonwealth scholarships would double, to 4,000 per year. Subsidies for independent-school students would be paid at $35 per primary-school student and $50 per secondary-school student. There was also money for teacher education and training.

McEwen, for his part, had forced the inclusion of a range of concessions to rural industries. The subsidy on superphosphate was increased for the second consecutive year. The subsidy on nitrogenous fertilisers was renewed. The government's contribution to wool research and promotion was increased, and the levy on woolgrowers reduced. The allocation for research and development grants in manufacturing and mining was doubled.

On the whole, as McMahon explained, the budget was designed to share the prosperity of Australia's economy with the less fortunate. 'It will be seen that humane values are in the forefront of the purposes this budget is designed to achieve.'[122]

The budget received a more positive reception than the previous year's. Much of the press echoed the lines about humanity and charity: 'It might be called a budget for the little people, the sick, the old, the pensioners, the low-income families, the widows, and children—and the Aborigines,' wrote *The Daily Telegraph*.[123] Yet close observers noted that while there were no explicit tax rises in the budget, the government was nonetheless relying on a growth in income-tax receipts—a natural consequence of prosperity, rising incomes, and a progressive tax scale that had not been revised in fifteen years.[124]

And yet, while quite plainly an election budget, it was hardly

McMahon's. In interviews with the press, and in discussions with his colleagues, he let slip that he did not agree with its measures. It was unsurprising, then, that the press leaped upon this point. The budget was an 'act of vandalism' that represented the 'biggest single defeat' of Treasury since the establishment of the Vernon Committee, Maxwell Newton wrote; it was a 'heavy blow' to a treasurer who, Max Walsh argued, had been 'soundly defeated' by Gorton and 'humiliated' by the concessions to McEwen.[125] Such statements might have hurt, but they had the benefit of allowing McMahon to duck responsibility for the budget's consequences. As *The Australian* editorialised: 'There are two sets of judgments operating within the Government and, not unnaturally, the Prime Minister's have prevailed. The direct result is that he alone bears primary responsibility for the results.'[126]

This responsibility was quickly felt. The 5 per cent reduction in defence expenditure had been glossed over in McMahon's speech, dismissed with the quick note that it did not amount to a reduction in Australia's defence effort, but it did not escape the wary eye of DLP senators. Their concern about the falling expenditure was compounded when, two days after McMahon handed down the budget, the new minister for external affairs rose in the House to present a statement on Australia's foreign relations.

Gordon Freeth—a West Australian, a 'forty-niner', an open admirer of Hasluck and a critic of McMahon, whose opinion of him was not improved by close contact, a rower and medallist at the British Empire Games in his youth who maintained his vigour with regular games of squash and golf, and otherwise boxed, ran, and swam—had been an unusual replacement for Hasluck.[127] Possessing little background in foreign relations, Freeth had queried the wisdom of it when he was appointed. The prime minister told him that he would hold the portfolio for only a year—just until after the election, at which point Gorton could shift Freeth back to a more fitting role in economics.[128] Accepting this, Freeth had worked quietly and without much visibility in the intervening months. Yet while the statement he proceeded to give displayed little of the hesitancy that might be expected of a novice, it would cause a political uproar.

After noting new US president Richard Nixon's statements on the need for Pacific countries to assert their security, Freeth emphasised that the way to prevent further Vietnams was to ensure that countries had 'sufficient strength' to protect themselves. But, Freeth went on, 'I do not only mean military strength. I mean decent standards of living, efficient and honest administration, harmonious relations with neighbours, and the easing of communal tensions within a country.' This was new, if unoriginal—yet when Freeth then discussed the Soviet Union, he seemed to display political naivety as much as naivety in foreign affairs:

> Australia has to be watchful, but need not panic whenever a Russian appears ... In principle, it is natural that a world power such as the Soviet Union should seek to promote a presence and a national influence in important regions of the world such as the Indian Ocean area.[129]

The apparent suggestion that there could be any kind of a rapprochement with the Soviet Union—which only a year before had invaded Czechoslovakia and reasserted its harsh line on dissent, and whose support for the North Vietnamese had ensured that military efforts there were continuing long after they might otherwise have—was met with some disbelief from Labor and outright anger from the DLP. Whitlam called it 'a striking and significant departure' from previous policy, and applauded the hope that Australia might engage with Russia.[130] His applause was a sure sign that the DLP would be absolutely opposed, which it duly was. The DLP thought the speech augured a decisive and radical shift, and, in his anger, Vince Gair repeated his threat to withhold the DLP's second-preference votes at the election. Within the government, the initial appreciation of Freeth's 'good speech' gave way to muted disavowals as it overshadowed the budget.[131] McEwen made his disdain well known, and McMahon put the word about, accurately, that Gorton and Freeth were the only cabinet ministers involved in the speech's preparation. Neither cabinet nor its foreign affairs and defence committee were consulted, he told Peter Howson.[132]

The damage was compounded when, five days after Freeth's speech, the minister for defence, Allen Fairhall, announced his decision to retire at the forthcoming election. Publicly, Fairhall attributed his decision to health reasons; privately, he believed that the government would win the election, but would lose the one that followed, in 1972. He wanted to go out on top—'decently', as he put it.[133]

Whatever the veracity of his reasons, Fairhall's retirement became another subject of rumour, discontent, and complaint. Concern at the rapid turnover of ministers deepened. Rumours of the prime minister's overt disdain of ministers and their departments rippled through the government. Whispers that Fairhall, like Hasluck, had been forced out, wound their way through Parliament House. Unrest over the prime minister's political wisdom and methods of work—exemplified in his tendency towards unilateralism, his unwillingness to observe the old faith of federalism, his emphasis on social welfare, and his happy antagonism of the DLP—fermented and grew within the party.[134]

The next day, Gorton informed the Coalition parties that the election would be held on 25 October. Whether he had picked up on the discontent or not, Gorton was aware that his party's belief in the potency of national-security issues needed to be addressed, just as the DLP needed to be assuaged. To this end, Gorton assured restless backbenchers that defence would be a major issue during the campaign. And while hardly disavowing Freeth or his speech, Gorton added forceful denunciations of Russian actions to his speeches. On 12 September, speaking to a Liberal Party rally in South Australia, the prime minister said that the establishment of any Russian naval or military base in Australia's region would be a threat, and that there was neither any 'intention' nor the 'remotest possibility' of a military understanding being reached between Australia and the Soviets. It was notable that Gorton allowed no time to speak on the 'other issues of significance and importance' in the campaign. Plainly, he was going to concentrate on what was most important.[135]

Yet the prime minister's lack of consistency was plain, and the pressure he was under evident. Four days after Gough Whitlam launched the Labor campaign with promises to introduce a universal health-care scheme, remove the means test, raise pensions, abolish national service, and withdraw troops from Vietnam, Gorton recorded a policy speech that sought to reassure the DLP and resurrect the worth of his incursions into health, education, and social welfare.

It made for a curiously extravagant and disparate pitch. Beginning with a warning that the public should not discard the progress of the previous twenty years, Gorton promised that if the government was returned it would not sign the nuclear nonproliferation treaty, and would retain national service, improve the air force, strengthen the navy, keep up the army, and maintain a presence in Vietnam, Malaysia, and Singapore. He suggested the government would reduce income tax, spend money on water, rail, and nuclear power, and invest in education at all levels. There would be assistance for parents of children with disabilities, a subsidy for Meals on Wheels, improvements to health care, and the scope of the Home Savings Grant Scheme would be increased. Immigration, trade, industry—all received a run in the speech. Perhaps most enduringly, Gorton promised to establish a film and television school and to provide a $1m grant to the Australian Film and Television Development Corporation to invest in Australian film production. While this grab bag was attractive, its effectiveness was undercut by the stilted, formal delivery. Gorton gave his speech in front of a lectern that inhibited any semblance of charm, familiarity, or engagement. The audience to which the camera occasionally panned was composed of decidedly underwhelmed Liberal Party figures, including McMahon, who watched without joy.[136]

The sections on defence were barely enough for the DLP. It had held off announcing a policy on preferences until it had heard Gorton's speech; now, once the speech was broadcast on 8 October, it decided to make good on the threat made by Gair the year before. The party's resolve had been fortified by an early intervention from Bob Santamaria, chairman of the National Civic Council, who called for someone to 'act effectively to bring the Government to a sense of reality'.[137] The threat did not extend to electing the ALP, but the DLP did give its preferences to candidates from other parties.

The campaign did not go well for the government. Three weeks out, a poll showed Labor leading the Coalition 45 to 42 per cent. Overcoming that disadvantage was hard fought, done in increments, bit by bit. Gorton spoke relentlessly on defence, trying to turn back the DLP's criticism and expose the gap between the government and Labor; McMahon attacked the opposition on its economic credentials.

In public, they were working towards the same end: victory. In private, they were backgrounding one another and manoeuvring to be best placed once the election was over.[138] Even those observing from some remove could see it. 'That untrustworthy little scamp McMahon is already, I think, on the warpath,' Menzies informed his daughter.[139]

The façade could not last. The divergence between public unity and private disharmony was too great, and the division between Gorton and McMahon broke through to the public. At first it was low-key: they could not agree on how much Labor's policies would cost.[140] Soon it was more serious. Barely days after appearing to gain ground on Labor, Gorton allowed his personal hostility towards McMahon to edge into public view. On 19 October, in a televised interview, he was asked to confirm that McMahon would remain treasurer if the government were re-elected. The most Gorton could bring himself to say was that McMahon would be a 'member' of the government.[141] It was an indulgent statement made worse by repetition: the journalists pressed him twice more for an answer, but Gorton would go no further than this.

It was a signal of the licence that Gorton allowed himself. He was going to do things his way, critics and enemies be damned. 'Gorton's handling of the question asked him about Bill McMahon,' Arthur Fadden wrote privately, 'was to say the least stupid and cruel. I have never experienced such a hopeless Liberal-Country composite government campaign.'[142] The opposition seized the opportunity to raise questions of division, to suggest disunity: 'The Prime Minister is openly humiliating and repudiating Mr McMahon,' Whitlam gloated.[143]

With only four days to go, McMahon publicly maintained his composure. In private, he was vituperative: 'Do you think the bastard would dare?' he hissed at one journalist, when asked about reports he would be shifted.[144] But publicly he was calm. His response was a measure of so much: his self-discipline, his calculation and self-control, his awareness of his strengths and those of his prime minister, his knowledge that this was a battle not to be fought right now. When the press asked him whether he would still be treasurer, McMahon did not lash out. He did not fight back. He deflected. Only a very close listener would have understood the message. 'It is up to Mr Gorton,' he said. 'I think you had better get an answer from him.'[145]

CHAPTER TWENTY-SIX

Fragments and Credit

1984

'There is no complete life,' wrote the American novelist James Salter. 'There are only fragments.'[1] To judge from the drafts that covered his time as treasurer, McMahon seemed to follow that pronouncement to the letter: his was a mess of short, fragmentary chapters, overlapping and disjointed, that prised apart all the interlocking circumstances, each setting out an event or person, a policy or development, as though they were all discrete entitities. There was a chapter on Lord Casey and his interference in 1967; two chapters on Harold Holt and McMahon's friendship with him; a chapter on the 1967 visit to Australia by American officials General Maxwell Taylor and Clark Clifford to discuss Vietnam; a chapter on the Resources Development Bank; a chapter on McEwen's Australian Industry Development Corporation; and more.

For Bowman's predecessor, Mark Hayne, this scattershot approach had been the cause of immense frustration and the result of McMahon's 'total lack of historical understanding and sense of chronology':

> Rather than working systematically through periods of his life, and placing them in ordered, coherent chapters, he [McMahon] would take ideas randomly. He would write two or three pages and then expect that they would be 'pasted' in an *ad hoc* fashion without any proper linkage with other sections.[2]

Repetition, as Bowman had observed when he first read the manuscript, was the most immediate consequence of this method of work. This could be addressed through careful editing—but a deficiency that could not be so easily repaired was the absence of context from all of the events, people, and policies that McMahon sought to discuss.

This was crucial. For the man who proclaimed himself to have been the country's best treasurer, the chapters covering 1966–69 were going to be at the heart of the autobiography. They would need to set out a credible and convincing argument that McMahon was as good as his boasts—that he really *had* been the country's best treasurer. An explanation of the circumstances, conditions, and his actions had to be detailed, logical, and credible if it was to convince.

He could not merely cite his credentials as the first treasurer with an economics degree—there were more than a few who knew of the circumstances in which he had obtained his economics degree in 1948, and knowledge of those circumstances would spread further when Heinz Arndt published his memoirs in 1985. He could not simply list his role as a governor of the International Monetary Fund (1966–69) and chairman of the board of governors of the Asian Development Bank (1968–69)—his critics would observe that these were hardly endorsements of him personally. Nor could he point to the buoyant economic conditions, the strong growth and prosperity, that Australia had enjoyed while he was treasurer. There were so many who dismissed his work, saying either that he simply did what he was told or that a drover's dog could have done the job.[3] Gallingly, many of *those* critics were on his side of politics. Dudley Erwin, admittedly a Gorton supporter, was derisory of McMahon: 'Whilst it went down that he was a great treasurer, I think anyone could have been a great treasurer in the days that he was treasurer.'[4] Billy Snedden ascribed McMahon's success to the 'fortunate era' in which he was treasurer,[5] and John Stone dismissed McMahon's claims as an economic sure-touch: 'Like many other claims by McMahon, his expertise in this area was considerably overstated.'[6]

Numbers would not be enough. If McMahon were to rebut his critics convincingly, he would need to cite specific measures he had initiated, and explain how they had contributed to Australia's wellbeing. Yet even this would be insufficient. For while such examples might prove McMahon's claims, they would not explain how and why he had aroused so much ire and controversy while he was treasurer.

He would need to explain the regular bouts of disunity and anger that had plagued the governments in which he had been treasurer—most sensationally, how and why McEwen had vetoed his candidacy for the leadership in the days following Holt's death; how and why he had become so mixed up with Maxwell Newton, Alan Reid, and the Packer press; and how and why Gorton had seen fit to eject him from his favourite portfolio.

McMahon was certainly aware of this, yet he was unable to work with the discipline needed to achieve the emphatic and convincing argument required. A draft that attempted to integrate the events, people, and policies of his time in Treasury was flat, lacking detail, and strewn with vast slabs of old speeches. Hayne had observed that these speeches were integral to McMahon's process: what the former prime minister called 'writing', Hayne wrote later, was to take those speeches and scrawl little notes and comments where there was space on the page.[7] He had refused to countenance removing or editing those speeches. To Hayne's suggestion that the general reader might find them boring, McMahon was adamant that they go in, word for word. By the time Bowman came to work on the chapters, McMahon was just as implacable: there was to be *no* change in the chapters he had drafted.[8]

That he had not actually written the majority of these speeches was of no concern to McMahon. The logical flaw in citing his own speeches as proof of his own brilliance failed to bother him. He wanted the speeches in; he wanted the chapters left untouched. They were good enough.

It was unfortunate. McMahon's time and significance as treasurer was already coloured by assessments of his character—the work of Alan Reid aside, *always* to McMahon's detriment—and not by his willingness to argue a perspective that was contrary to McEwen's. As John Stone later observed:

His [McMahon's] time in Treasury was principally consumed by his long-running battle with McEwen—a battle in which he was fully supported by the Treasury on the policy issues concerned, and which was very much to his credit (whatever his personal motives).[9]

McMahon's questioning of protection; his willingness to take on McEwen over the Australian Industry Development Corporation; his advocacy and victory in the decision not to devalue following the UK's devaluation of sterling; his reduction of the deficit, from $644m in 1966–67 to $30m by 1969–70; and his efforts, with Gorton, to set out the relationship between the Commonwealth and the states—all of these were significant, more than creditable to him.

Moreover, the repeated humiliations, the criticisms, and the hostility he engendered were, at least in part, caused by his willingness to force a debate on tenets of policy that had long been taken for granted. As one observer later suggested, for all of McMahon's many faults, he could be called a 'martyr' for the free-trade movement: 'Few (if any) suffered more, personally and politically, for their beliefs.'[10]

That was the story to tell. *That* was the story that might convince. But McMahon seemed unable to tell it.

CHAPTER TWENTY-SEVEN

Subsequent Plots

1969

'He says I can run!'

It was the afternoon of Monday 3 November. In the ten days since voters had delivered their verdict, government MPs had been scrambling—scrambling to understand, to contain, to address, to vent, to discuss, to simply *deal* with the fallout of the election. For although the government had been returned, a swing against it of 6.6 per cent and the loss of sixteen seats had dampened the joy of victory and quashed any suggestion that Gorton's approach had been vindicated.[1] The DLP's threats had paid off. Gordon Freeth, the target of their ire, was a conspicuous casualty: his West Australian seat of Forrest had been claimed by the ALP, thanks to discontent among farmers, the efforts of the far-right group the League of Rights, and the DLP's decision to withhold preferences.

Gorton had been unapologetic. Happy at least to see Edward St John bundled out of Parliament after running as an 'Independent Liberal', Gorton pointed out that the government had won. He argued that there was always going to be a swing towards Labor—a consequence of its new leader, its promises on pensions and allowances for families, and the reversion to normalcy after the 1966 election. Since that election, moreover, there had been a redistribution. That explained some of the losses, he argued. He therefore saw little rebuke in the election: when asked if he would do anything differently, Gorton demurred. He would not alter much of his campaign, he said.[2]

Understandably, Gorton's critics in the party were dissatisfied. Les Irwin, Liberal member for the New South Wales seat of Mitchell, had called for a party-room meeting to grapple with the result.[3] The party organisation in New South Wales was concerned.[4] The party's executive in Queensland stated that it would have to discuss the election.[5] David Fairbairn, the minister for national development and member for the New South Wales seat of Farrer, who had been aggrieved by Gorton's intervention in a matter involving oil companies Esso and BHP, met the prime minister three days after the election, and saw no sign of contrition. Nor was there any sign that Gorton's outlook had been shaken by the result. 'Absolutely none,' he told John McEwen.[6]

This proved decisive. In a two-line telegram he sent to Gorton on 30 October, Fairbairn informed the prime minister that he had 'reluctantly decided' that he could not serve in a Gorton-led cabinet.[7] Moreover, as he stated in a subsequent press conference, Fairbairn was considering standing for the leadership of the party at the next meeting.[8]

At first, Gorton thought it was a joke. Half an hour later, when he read Fairbairn's press release repeating the statements, humour gave way to shock. He was flabbergasted, he said. His supporters swung into action to back up their leader. Statements of firm support were issued both privately and in public. The idea of a leadership challenge, to them, was ridiculous. 'I was dead against it,' said Tom Hughes. 'Dead against it.'[9] Yet Fairbairn was not alone. Critics of Gorton were also mobilising. Kevin Cairns, the Liberal member for the Queensland seat of Lilley and deputy government whip, informed Gorton that, like Fairbairn, he was not prepared to serve, even in his 'humble position'.

Fairbairn's telegram and subsequent movements towards declaring himself were a jolt to McMahon. The treasurer 'felt a move should be initiated' within a day of the election,[10] but he was not prepared to lead a challenge unless he could be guaranteed a majority of support. He wanted to avert any situation in which McEwen could intervene and wreck his ambitions again. But things were not going to work that way, he was told. Howson, who had said publicly that he was uncommitted but pleased that someone with 'the guts to stand up for his convictions' was bringing the leadership issue on, told McMahon that he would need to declare his hand.[11] On the next day, 29 October, McMahon was vacillating. He wanted to challenge Gorton, but could hardly summon the courage to do so: 'It's still obvious he's going through an agony of soul,' Howson recorded.[12] By 31 October, Howson thought McMahon's chances were good, but that the treasurer needed to declare himself immediately.[13] Boldness was required—McMahon needed to gamble.

The next day, McMahon spoke with Frank Packer and said that he was seriously considering a challenge.[14] Packer was on board, and willing to provide encouragement as well as influence. Disillusioned with Gorton after he told Packer 'where to get off' during a debate on wool marketing, Sir Frank saw to it that an editorial ran in *The Sunday Telegraph* on 2 November applying the pressure where it would most matter:

> Mr McEwen should be able to see that if we are to have a new Prime Minister he must be chosen from those men who have commanded the respect of the Party, who have the capcity to rehabilitate its image in the electorate, and who—by seniority, experience, and accomplishment—have proved that they have the potential for the country's most important office.[15]

McEwen was way ahead of Packer. On 31 October, he had rung Sir Murray Tyrrell, official secretary to the governor-general, Paul Hasluck, to sound him out about meeting with Hasluck 'without it being known'. According to Tyrrell, McEwen mentioned that it was to be a 'penetrating conversation'. When Tyrrell questioned the wisdom of a meeting, specifically mentioning 'past history' (that is, Casey), McEwen conceded that he should not come to Government House. Nonetheless, McEwen kept talking. 'It looks as if McMahon will be a candidate,' he said. 'I don't propose to veto him. That would only help him and I don't propose to encourage him. But I would require a tight letter of understanding with him.'[16]

In a press conference on the morning of 3 November, McEwen responded to Packer's lobbying. Exasperated and concerned with Gorton, angered and clearly conscious of the groundswell of discontent enveloping the government in the wake of the election, aware that he would soon retire, and acknowledging that it seemed poor form to deny the Liberal Party the chance to elect its most experienced figure, the Country Party leader intimated to journalists that his refusal to countenance McMahon as leader was no longer in force.[17] 'Mr McMahon and I have been for years on an amicable daily relationship, working together as cabinet ministers on Christian name terms,' McEwen said. 'I am not playing any cat and mouse situation on an issue of such great importance to the stable government of this country. I am sure that if Mr McMahon is concerned to know my attitude he would come and see me.'[18]

McMahon was so surprised at McEwen's statement that he did not even question the clear power dynamic at play. He was so eager, so excited, so hopeful for what it might portend that he refused to countenance any delay. Already in Melbourne for the Melbourne Cup, which was to take place the next day, he did not wait for a Commonwealth car to be organised. It was a sure measure of his excitement and urgency that he paid for a taxi from his own pocket to take him immediately to McEwen's flat in Toorak, where he could bend the knee.

An hour later, he emerged from that flat radiating joy. Unbridled excitement, energy, hope—all of these were the result. 'McMahon was jubilant,' McEwen put it, tartly.[19] Everything had been overturned.

McMahon called as many journalists as he could. The news burst from him like laughter: 'He says I can run!'[20]

AT six-thirty that evening, McMahon issued a statement to the press. Negotiated with McEwen, it was carefully worded and notably bereft of the excitement that had characterised McMahon's earlier reaction:

> After reading Mr McEwen's statement this afternoon, I had a discussion with him. It was friendly and in general terms. I am sure that if I were successful in the ballot for the leadership of the Liberal Party, there would be no objection from him. It would, of course, be necessary to make the usual arrangements for co-operation between the two Coalition parties. I have informed Mr Gorton that I intend to submit my name to the ballot.[21]

Fairbairn had confirmed, earlier in the day, that he, too, would stand, and offered his reasons for doing so: the brawls with the states had caused ill-will and disunity, the prime minister's antagonism of the DLP had been unwise, and there seemed to be no prospect of change in Gorton's attitudes.[22]

In the ensuing melee of press coverage, the mention of coalition 'arrangements' in McMahon's statement nearly went unnoticed. As some observers saw, McEwen was, like Page in 1923, taking advantage of the upheaval in his coalition partner to strengthen his party's position within the government. As McEwen was soon to demand, the price of the continuation of the coalition agreement was an assurance that all major government decisions were first approved by cabinet; the appointment of another Country Party minister; and the inclusion of another Country Party minister in the cabinet yet again, in order to develop experience ahead of McEwen's anticipated retirement within the year. While a good deal for the Country Party, there were some who were concerned by the price. 'I can't say I was happy,' Doug Anthony said, of the lifting of the veto on McMahon.[23]

McEwen's stance was a blow to Gorton: his decision not to stand in the way of the challengers was conspicuous and, as Reid pointed out, gave an impetus to McMahon's candidacy.[24] Gorton clearly recognised the danger. Amid the continuing efforts of his office and supporters to consolidate a majority, the prime minister made conciliatory noises about the campaign, his government, and the future.[25]

But Gorton also had extensive support, most notably in the Senate. Within three days of the election, Victorian Liberal Party senator Magnus Cormack had organised a meeting at Melbourne's Australia Club to marshal Gorton's supporters and ensure that, but for four or five, all Liberal senators would vote for the prime minister.[26]

McMahon, meanwhile, began to canvass with the aid of his supporters and allies. Howson kept in touch with him, as did Alan Reid. Writing ahead of the ballot, but published after it, Reid told readers of The Bulletin that 'a new face' was necessary if the government wished to avoid annihilation at the next poll: nothing else would do.[27] In Queensland, Eric Robinson and supporters on the state party executive were agitating to deliver a rebuke to the prime minister in the form of a directive expressing dissatisfaction, disapproval, and distrust of him.[28] In New South Wales, a member of the Young Liberals from McMahon's electorate, Bruce MacCarthy, succeeded in having a

motion of no confidence in Gorton's leadership debated and passed at
the Liberal Youth Council. The finality of that motion was only halted
when a rescission motion held the matter over until the next meeting.[29]
McMahon also made time to quell a vocal critic. Responding to
demands from New South Wales premier Bob Askin that he declare his
position on states' rights, McMahon told the press on 4 November that
he was a 'confirmed federalist'. Askin's about-face was blatant. In the
morning, he had said that McMahon was the least sympathetic federal
politician he had worked with in five years; by the evening, mollified
and appropriately acknowledged, Askin was walking away from any
involvement at all: 'I now propose to leave the election of the prime
minister to the federal members.'[30]

Meanwhile, concerned that McMahon might fall short, his allies
lobbied Gorton to retain him as treasurer no matter what might occur.
Jeff Bate cabled the prime minister for this reason. Frank Packer ordered
David McNicoll to deliver the same message. At this craven bit of
politicking, Gorton deadpanned. After a long pause, he asked McNicoll
how he would feel if someone he worked with was undermining him.
To McNicoll's remark that it would be an unpleasant situation, Gorton
was straightforward. 'Well, that's how I feel about Bill McMahon. Tell
Frank I appreciate his loyalty to Bill, but I can give no guarantee of
keeping him in the Treasury.'[31] Said Gorton later of Packer: 'He'd do
anything to help McMahon.'[32]

For some MPs, the choice was simple. Gorton supporter Tom
Hughes was straightforward: 'Fairbairn didn't have the intellectual
capacity to be prime minister, nor McMahon.'[33] For others, the
choice came down to questions of character, and here memories were
long and reservations clear. On 31 October, from a sense of fairness,
Gorton informed Bert Kelly, the minister for the navy, that he would
be dropped from the ministry should Gorton win. The warning
offered Kelly the opportunity to line up behind a candidate who would
retain him. But even now, with the axe looming, Kelly's reservations
were sufficient to prevent him making an easy choice. Fairbairn,
he confided in his diary, 'didn't have the other qualities necessary
for leadership'. He was 'very tempted' to vote for McMahon—the
treasurer's economic principles were much in line with his own. But he
saw a problem: 'The point that was niggling me was Billy McMahon's

trustworthiness.' Kelly rang Freeth, newly defeated, and asked what he should do:

> He [Freeth] said he had very good reason for knowing that McMahon was still behaving in an untrustworthy manner and that, although he didn't hold Gorton in very high regard as an administrator, he himself would vote for Gorton because of Billy's (McMahon's) defects of character.

Freeth's advice confirmed what was already—thanks to Gorton's honesty—in Kelly's mind. Kelly would vote for Gorton.[34] For those not in the Parliament, the choices were not attractive. Observing the government from his home in Melbourne, Menzies wrote to his daughter that although Gorton had 'grave defects of mental equipment and hard work and experience', the treasurer was not a viable choice. 'McMahon is simply not to be trusted.'[35]

It was this kind of reservation that led the dissident MPs supporting McMahon and Fairbairn to give undertakings about preferences. Should the contest go to a second ballot, in the absence of an absolute majority, the loser's supporters would move en masse to the other.[36] Would this be enough? Publicly, McMahon was ebullient about his prospects: 'Yes, I think we will win,' he told reporters.[37] Privately, however, he knew that he would not.

When members and senators gathered at Parliament House on the wet Canberra morning of 7 November, it was clear that the challengers would fall short. For the past few days, Gorton supporters had been running the line that the public had only just elected Gorton—was the Liberal Party really going to overturn all that and elect someone else? According to Howson, McEwen called him fifteen minutes before the meeting was to take place to suggest that the insurrectionists 'cause a blue'. McEwen supposedly suggested that, if sufficiently provoked, Gorton might lose his temper and simultaneously lose support.[38] Whatever the truth of that advice, it was not to be. The anti-Gorton candidates and their supporters could not agree on tactics. While there were a few willing to bring on an open debate, no one made moves to force it. Chaired by the Speaker, Bill Aston, the meeting went immediately to a ballot.

The count took time—enough to suggest that the vote was closer than expected. Eventually, the three scrutineers returned to the party room and announced that Gorton had been re-elected to the leadership by an absolute majority. Because the Liberal Party did not disclose the figures, estimates of the count were rife. Gorton believed that he had received forty-five votes at a minimum, twelve more than necessary for a majority.[39] Others were less certain about the scale. Reid believed that McMahon and Fairbairn together attracted at least thirty votes.[40] Peter Howson thought it was along similar lines.

The ballot for the deputy leadership was not close. McMahon easily fought off Snedden and the surprise candidacy of Queenslander Alan Hulme; supposedly, it took only three minutes for the scrutineers to count the votes.[41]

The meeting broke for lunch, then resumed to discuss a proposal on electing the ministry. Following this, Gorton presented himself to journalists. Telling them he was pleased with the result, he was also clearly aware of the need for conciliation: he echoed his statements of a few days before, promising to discover the causes of the dissatisfaction expressed by electors. He refused to discuss whether McMahon would remain treasurer, and dismissed out of hand any suggestions that the government was losing too much experience and talent.[42]

Halfway through the press conference, McMahon appeared in the crowded room. He pushed his way through the press of bodies, at one point shoving a cameraman so as to get to the front before the radio and television coverage went off the air: 'Get out of my way!' When the press caught sight of him, they called out for photos of goodwill between him and Gorton. 'Why not!' McMahon said. 'Yes, why not!'[43] The two men shook hands and, when the press sought to ask him questions, McMahon took the seat that Gorton had vacated.

His answers were earnest, unctuous. He did not put a toe out of line. 'John Gorton has been elected the leader of the Liberal Party,' McMahon said. 'We in the party have given our unqualified allegiance to him as the leader, and there are no divisions in the party itself.'

Would he continue in his portfolio? asked a journalist.

'I won't express a view,' McMahon said. 'Of course it's always my wish to remain treasurer, but I do not wish to commit the prime minister.'[44]

Gorton was looking on icily—but on show, yet again, was the

determination, the professionalism, the cool calculation that McMahon brought to so many of his political dealings. McMahon had lost the ballot, but he was determined to wait for another opportunity.[45]

WHAT to do with McMahon figured large in many subsequent discussions. In the evening of 7 November, Gorton called upon Hasluck to 'talk things over'. Gorton was clearly angered about the actions of the malcontents and how McMahon had conducted himself. 'He recounted,' Hasluck wrote later, 'that Malcolm Mackay, the member for Evans—"that oily man of God"—had insinuated himself among Gorton's supporters and dropped hints as heavy as bricks.' When Gorton refused to make any promises about promotions or quid pro quos, Mackay went to McMahon and was supposedly promised a ministry. 'Gorton alleged that McMahon had made promises of portfolios to "all sorts of people",' wrote Hasluck.[46]

Hasluck's subsequent advice on how to tackle the problems exposed by the election was accepted, but soon Gorton was cutting to the real purpose of his meeting: 'You want to know what I'm going to do with McMahon,' he said.

It would be the happiest thing if he could get rid of McMahon, Gorton confided. But he knew he could not get rid of the treasurer entirely. Nonetheless, Gorton said, 'he was not going to have McMahon as treasurer'. The experiences of the past two years were enough. On McMahon's orders, according to Gorton, Treasury officials had withheld information. McMahon had misinformed him or hidden information in order to ensure that various policies failed. McMahon had told lies about communication between the state premiers and himself. Furthermore, 'a great deal of the difficulty in federal–state relations' was due to McMahon telling lies. He could not have McMahon as treasurer and simultaneously implement his policies and improve his relationships with the state governments, Gorton told Hasluck.

McMahon would go to external affairs, Gorton said. Unable to kick McMahon out of the ministry, he would instead consign him to a portfolio where he would be continually out of the country. When Hasluck mentioned that McMahon could use the change as an opportunity to gain sympathy for himself, Gorton cut across him again:

'That's what John McEwen thinks, too.' He was well aware of how the press had alleged divisions between himself, Hasluck, and Fairhall, and how McMahon could revive it for his own advantage. Hasluck thus cautioned Gorton that if he was set on transferring McMahon, he needed a 'stronger, more intelligent and more industrious' minister for defence—one who would 'not intrigue with McMahon'. Gorton, however, had it all worked out. Malcolm Fraser, minister for education and science, and one of Gorton's strongest supporters, would go to defence. Les Bury, the minister for labour and national service, would replace McMahon as treasurer.

For his part, McMahon was aware that his move to challenge Gorton had placed him in a precarious position. Worryingly, his standing among his allies had fallen. The manner of his losing, and the way in which the challenge had been mounted, had left McMahon exposed. Alan Reid felt that McMahon was finished as a leadership prospect.[47] Newton, too, thought McMahon was now naked: he had left his run too late, had worried too much about his future, and was again dependent on Gorton.[48] Howson was scathing: 'Bill McMahon has been shown to lack courage in a crisis, not having, therefore, the real material for leadership.'[49] McMahon could not have failed to be aware of these feelings; nor could he have been unaware of Gorton's deep antipathy and desire to remove him from the Treasury.

But willingly letting go of his prized portfolio was never in question. When he met with Gorton after 7 November and was told of Gorton's plans to move him, McMahon put up a fight. He raised objections, 'all sorts of pleas and arguments', as to why he should be left in Treasury, and only after a resolute Gorton refused to budge did McMahon give way. But, even then, McMahon tried to draw victory from defeat. He told Gorton that if he could not be treasurer, then External Affairs was the only portfolio he would accept. Gorton was nonplussed. 'It suited me all right so I let him have it,' he said later. The question Gorton wanted answered, however, was whether there would be any 'hitches' by McMahon or other ministers at the swearing-in of ministers. Would there be any problems, any shows of defiance, any scenes or outbursts? McMahon told Gorton that everything would be right.[50]

But Gorton had bigger dangers than McMahon. He had been wounded by the challenge. The fact of the government's re-election had been overshadowed by the contest. Even if they had reconfirmed Gorton's leadership, his colleagues were still doubtful about his abilities and his character. When McEwen met Hasluck on 11 November to discuss the agreement between the Liberal and Country parties, he was blunt. Gorton had not understood the problem of consultation. He had thought it meant some loss of his position as prime minister:

> But McEwen had told him that if he was making unilateral decisions it virtually meant that the Country Party was handing over its policy-making functions to the leader of another party. When he was slow to grasp this Mr McEwen had had to say to him: 'Well get this into your head. There will be no coalition at all if you insist on having the sole right to make decisions that bind the Country Party without consultation with them.' … The trouble was, McEwen said—and he spoke amusedly and without rancour—Mr Gorton had not the slightest idea about the system of cabinet government. We then discussed in a relaxed way the oddity that a man who had the advantage of a University education seemed never to have learned anything about the nature of political institutions or the conventions surrounding them.[51]

As ever, the conversation came back to McMahon. McEwen thought it a mistake to move 'the little man' from the Treasury, and told Hasluck that it was a pity Menzies had not got rid of McMahon when he 'had the wood on him'. The Liberal Party was 'foolish' for electing McMahon to the deputy leadership: 'That laid the scene for their subsequent plots.' And then McEwen wondered: had he acted unwisely back in 1967, vetoing McMahon's candidacy? It was a good question, but not now one that much mattered. Looking ahead, McEwen was fatalistic.

The Liberals, he told Hasluck, 'still have trouble ahead'.[52]

CHAPTER TWENTY-EIGHT

Loyalty

1984

Working to rewrite the memoir required Bowman to delve into the voluminous files that McMahon had assembled. Scattered through the dross and banal papers that filled those twenty-seven filing cabinets, there were documents that spoke to the unease and disputes with Gorton. Notably, they charted how disquiet had broken out in the course of the leadership challenge and been subsumed again in its aftermath. For all the caveats that had to be placed on their reliability, they portended a simmering and divided party.

According to the documents, McMahon had spoken with Fairbairn before his challenge and told him that he did not think Fairbairn would succeed against Gorton.[1] He had spoken with Gorton, too, about the demands McEwen made for extra Country Party representation in the ministry and cabinet. He had listened to Gorton wonder about defying McEwen. He wrote that Gorton believed the cause of the swing against the government had been Labor's promise to subsidise interest rates on homes. To McMahon's disagreement, and his suggestions that the DLP and Vietnam were the principal problems—foreign affairs, he told Gorton, needed someone with a political nose—Gorton was dismissive, and insistent on the centrality of housing as the issue.[2] In his note of the meeting with McEwen in Melbourne on 3 November, McMahon told McEwen that Gorton had decided to emulate the ALP, saying that Whitlam had won because of his policy of centralisation. Why couldn't he?

In his account of that meeting, McMahon had also given clear signs of ingratiating himself with McEwen. The demands McEwen had made for extra representation in the ministry were appropriate, he had said, considering the Country Party's numerical strength. So, also, was McEwen's wish that devaluation assistance for rural export industries, like wool, continue. McMahon said that an inter-departmental review should consider the problem. Only then, after this exchange, did the two men move on to discuss McMahon's prospective candidacy for the leadership.[3]

Other memos went into the contest and its aftermath. Robert Cotton—a senator from New South Wales and former president of the New South Wales division of the Liberal Party, who, during the race to succeed Holt, had declared that McMahon enjoyed neither his support nor that of the New South Wales Liberal Party—had told McMahon that a challenge in the wake of the election was hopeless. But, Cotton went on, matters might be different after the half-Senate election, due to be held by mid-1971. The deck would be loaded against Gorton, Cotton had said. See how he did until then.[4] The new treasurer, Les Bury, warned by McMahon that Gorton and Hewitt would erode his position if he were not careful, had said something of the same.[5] When he spoke with Dudley Erwin, soon to be returned to the backbench, McMahon said he had tried to keep Erwin in the ministry, but had advocated him losing his position as leader of the House, on grounds that it was too much for him to handle. Erwin's response to this was not recorded.[6]

Then there were other documents that, in their own way, were of special significance. A confidential three-page memo written days after the 1969 election was particularly significant, even incendiary. It was a tour-de-force argument that disloyalty to Gorton was, in fact, not disloyalty at all:

> If we accept the fundamental premise that the incumbent [Gorton] is a national disaster and grossly unsuitable for the job, there is an obligation on those in a position of power to have him removed for the nation's good ... More than the leadership of the Liberal Party is involved—we are toying around with the destiny of this country ... We are considering not only the re-election of a deficient leader of the Liberal Party—we are talking about the leadership of the country.

If Gorton was able to remain in office, the memo continued, losses in the next Senate election, due by mid-1971, would be the result. Was party unity really the reason to not move against him?

Declaring that McMahon was the only government member with sufficient stature to challenge Gorton, the memo went on to outline the extent of McMahon's support and how it could be enlarged—by 'overt and covert means'. McMahon would need a hard count of his supporters within the Liberal Party, first of all, but then he should endeavour to find out 'which newspaper proprietors would back you; what would be the reaction from the political writers; how far would leading industrialists, businessmen, etc. back you—to the extent of influencing members of threatening not to supply funds to the Party if you were not elected; the use of newspaper advertisements canvassing your support'. The leadership would be a messy one to fight, the memo conceded, and McMahon should be prepared to go to the backbench should a challenge fall short.[7]

Who had written the memo would clearly have been of interest. But its provenance was disguised: beyond the heading of confidentiality and the date, there was no author listed, no signature at its bottom.

No MP can be held responsible for the contents of their mailbag. The mere receipt of the memo could not be held against McMahon. He had not written it. But he *had* seen the memo. He had thought it necessary to annotate it: just to the left of the reference to 'the incumbent', he had scrawled, 'Gorton', as if it had been ambiguous. He had clearly, too, seen fit to retain it: 'Thanks,' it said at the top, in his distinctive, thick black handwriting. 'File.' And at the top was another piece of his handwriting—the name of the press secretary whom McMahon, a year and a half after his departure, had still not seen fit to replace: 'Peter Kelly'. Why was his name there? Did McMahon wish to hear his opinion of it?

Kelly had seen the memo. He was given a copy. McMahon sought his opinion on it, even though he no longer worked for him. Kelly could recall the memo because of the spelling mistakes. 'I remember reading it and thinking that this bloke [who wrote it] should have been a better speller than that,' he said later. 'I remember thinking that at the time.'

According to Kelly, the author of the memo was Eric Robinson, the then–state president of the Queensland Liberal Party. Later to enter the House of Representatives and serve as a minister in the Fraser government, Robinson was well known as a Gorton critic and McMahon confidant, the provider of a home at the Isle of Capri where McMahon would sometimes holiday and make use of the telephone. 'He was a very, very close friend of McMahon's,' Kelly said later. Robinson had left the memo unsigned because not to do so would have been dangerous. Had it ever leaked, it would have caused uproar within the party.

What was the memo's effect on McMahon? 'He would have been flattered,' Kelly said. 'But he also would have read it very carefully and thought about it a lot.'[8]

Evidently, McMahon did consider the memo closely. Only a few days after receiving it, he stood for the leadership of the Liberal Party. The question that mattered about the memo when Bowman encountered it was slightly different: had the memo sketched out a plan for what McMahon did afterwards?

CHAPTER TWENTY-NINE

A New Stage

1969–1970

The Gorton ministry that was sworn in on 12 November 1969 was conspicuously peopled by Young Turks. Four of the five new ministers—Don Chipp, member for Hotham and returning to the frontbench as the new minister for customs and excise; Tom Hughes, now member for Berowra and attorney-general; Jim Killen, member for Moreton and minister for the navy; and Andrew Peacock, member for Kooyong and minister for the army—were noticeably young, with thirty-year-old Peacock especially so. The vaulting promotions of Malcolm Fraser, to defence, and Billy Snedden, to labour and national service, were similarly notable. It was clear that the new ministry augured a shift within the government. By now, the Liberal-Country Party coalition had been in office for twenty years, and just as the 'forty-niners' had been blooded and risen to the ministry in the late 1950s, so, too, was another generation of Liberal-Country Party MPs beginning to take its place.

Some of the older ministers resented this. Although Malcolm Scott and Bert Kelly returned quietly to the backbench after their demotions, Dudley Erwin was less than amenable. Having waited thirteen years for a ministerial appointment, Erwin was aggrieved by Gorton's decision to dismiss him after barely eight months' service as minister for air. Speaking to journalists in the days that followed, he blamed Gorton's private secretary, Ainsley Gotto, and intimated that he had been sacked because he was not a member of the Mushroom Club, as the four Young Turks were.

Erwin's very public criticism brought attention to this benign, if widely disapproved of, group within the Liberal Party. So-called because, they said, they were kept in the dark and fed on bullshit, the thirteen members of the Mushroom Club were united only by the enjoyment of good food, wine, and discussion.[1] Other Liberal MPs, already suspicious of 'cocktail cabinets' and cronyism, felt Erwin's criticism keenly.[2] They regarded the Mushroom Club as a voting bloc for the prime minister, and Gorton, mindful of the perception, asked that the club dissolve.

Nonetheless, the damage was done. 'So Gorton has promoted his friends but left himself without any allies on the backbench and has made no attempt to heal the rift which is now so wide in the party,' Howson exalted.[3] Fresh from organising against Gorton, Howson must have been surprised by the prime minister's apparent obliviousness to the tension within the party. Gorton could not have been unaware: a report delivered to the Liberal Party's federal executive would soon comment that the 'road back' to success would be 'infinitely more difficult unless the Prime Minister, reaffirmed as Leader, is given full support and loyalty by the Federal Parliamentary Party and the Organisation, and unless the Government and Parliamentary Party work together as a team'.[4] Moreover, at a party-room meeting on 24 November, the day before Parliament's new session, an extended dissection of the election campaign and the government's policies dominated the day, with considerable, if indirect, criticism of Gorton from Fairbairn and Howson. It would have been uncomfortable for Gorton and delightful for McMahon. As the new minister for external affairs and Howson agreed that night over the telephone, the meeting was 'a most useful exercise' that would be remembered in months to come.[5]

Meanwhile, without much enthusiasm, McMahon started to delve into his new portfolio. 'I didn't want this job. I'm not interested in it,' he told C.R. 'Kim' Jones, an official at the Australian embassy in Tokyo who reluctantly came to Canberra to interview for a position as McMahon's principal private secretary. To Jones, McMahon made his concern for his new ministry abundantly clear: 'I want someone who will look after things for me.' Jones was startled, but not wholly surprised. 'He was angry he had been moved from Treasury,' Jones said later. The anger would not fade, but McMahon's antipathy for his new ministry would dissipate. 'He was aware that he would be judged as a minister on his performance there,' said Jones. McMahon would work to make the portfolio a success.[6]

Just as others had experienced, working for McMahon was not easy. 'I found him quite difficult, initially,' Jones said. It took him about six months to understand McMahon properly, to see his quirks and characteristics. McMahon was intelligent, in his own way, thought Jones. He was inclined to take advice and follow recommendations from the public service, but he also drew from views outside the public service. He was not much interested in people or things outside politics. His habit of underlining passages on briefing materials was unusual, but not necessarily indicative of an inability to absorb the content: 'It could sometimes seem as though it was a bit of a substitute for reading.' McMahon's demands could be unpredictable. He had a tendency to assume that if he had a thought, everyone would know of it. Therefore, staff had to learn to anticipate McMahon: 'You had to play a game of guesswork and assessment.' He was courteous, rarely rude, but he could be very brisk. He was still not considerate of how his working habits could affect his staff: 'He did his job, and felt they should do theirs.'

McMahon worked hard, and worked long hours. He was assiduous, but sometimes not as sharp as he thought: his tendency to provide detail when answering questions in the House meant that *Hansard* pulls still had to be scrutinised closely. 'Sometimes,' said Jones, 'I had to massage *Hansard* to correct—without substantially altering—his answers.' McMahon moved paper quickly, and was constantly on the lookout for more to do. 'He hated to have nothing to do at any point,' Jones said. 'At quiet moments—waiting at airports, on planes, travelling in cars—he would telephone somebody, or think up tasks for the department, or his office.' It called for some adroit management. To keep McMahon focused, to occupy him and, at times, to distract him, Jones made sure to always have a supply of written material on hand that he could give his minister to work through. McMahon's habit of producing aide-mémoires, and what was in them, was also notable: 'They were his version of what happened,' said Jones. 'Sometimes they were what he would have liked to have happened ... There was an element of wishful thinking in them.'

Sonia's effect on her husband was also noteworthy. Rumours that their marriage was a sham were rubbish. Jones saw a strong, loving relationship. 'She was a very positive influence on him,' he said later. 'Sonia was good at managing him, steering him, preparing him, keeping him in a good mood.' Travel was notably easier when Sonia was around; moreover, she could speak to her husband in a way that others could not. Averse to late nights, favouring a good night's sleep, disdainful of conversations without meaning or purpose, McMahon could be oblivious to niceties and leave a dinner as soon as dessert was finished. Sonia, however, could remind him to stay put.[7]

His new responsibilities also put to good use his talents in entertainment. For all the derision and dislike that McMahon aroused among colleagues, he was an immensely charming man. The qualities that saw him become a fixture at Sir Frank Packer's dinner table never went away, and, on the diplomatic circuit, he could be similarly attractive company.[8] At dinners and at parties, in meetings, and indeed in idle conversations, McMahon could be witty and lively, humourous and quick. 'He is a charming and generous host and a gracious guest and is surprisingly attractive to women,' Don Chipp would later say.[9] Fashionably dressed with expensive tastes—'Hunt, you're wearing the same tie as I am,' he told Ralph Hunt once, to which Hunt replied that McMahon's tie was likely three times the price—McMahon could strike those who met him as urbane and knowledgeable: in sum, the perfect dinner companion.[10] Others agreed, but placed a heavy caveat on this. 'He could be charming, but he was always trying too hard,' journalist Mungo MacCallum, nephew of Billy Wentworth, said later. 'His ambition always got the better of him. At that point (indeed, before it) he could become a crashing bore.'[11]

Despite his lack of experience with foreign affairs, McMahon had enough confidence in his abilities to appraise the department's strengths and weaknesses.[12] One of the earliest results of this was his effort to remove Sir James 'Jim' Plimsoll.[13] Secretary of the Department of External Affairs since 1965, Plimsoll had had a long career, glittering with achievement. He had supported Evatt at United Nations conferences in New York in the late 1940s; had been sent to Korea aged thirty-three to represent Australia on the United Nations Commission for unification and rehabilitation during the Korean War; had served as Australia's permanent representative at the United Nations in New York (1959–63); and had been Australia's high commissioner in India

(1963–65). Yet his management and administrative skills were lacking, and the reverberations from the advice he had given to Gordon Freeth, on the Soviet navy's presence in the Indian Ocean, were continuing.[14]

In this light, McMahon's decision that Plimsoll should go was understandable. But the ill feeling it aroused within the department was unfortunate, and McMahon's handling of it was clumsy. On 25 November, before even telling Plimsoll, he telephoned Arthur Tange, the former secretary of the department, now serving as Australia's high commissioner to India. 'I'd like to invite you back in Plimsoll's place,' McMahon said to him. While Tange believed the department 'needed attention', the request placed him in an awkward position. Only a few days before, Gorton had requested he take over the defence department from Harry Bland, who had decided he would retire.[15] 'Oh, oh, oh,' McMahon exclaimed, as Tange told him this, 'they kept me in the dark!'[16]

Denied his first choice, McMahon nonetheless remained interested enough to seek his opinions. After Tange reiterated that he thought the department 'very sick' and suggested a meeting,[17] McMahon sent him a cable seeking both his concerns and a recommendation for a successor for Plimsoll.[18]

On the requested recommendation of a successor, Tange was blunt. In a letter written by hand to escape the need for a stenographer, he ruthlessly assessed various officers of the department before landing on the ambassador to the United States, Sir Keith Waller. A former private secretary to Billy Hughes, Waller had decades of experience in the department and internationally. He had served in China, Brazil, the Phillipines, the UK, Thailand, and the USSR. The measure of his excellence was apparent in his appointment as Australia's ambassador to the United States: he was the first career diplomat to serve in the role. According to Tange, Waller was 'the only top quality man with indisputable capacity to be a good Sec. of E.A.'[19] McMahon took the advice. Waller was his man.[20]

Removing a permanent head can be fraught; but, luckily for McMahon, Plimsoll had already decided that he should move on. 'If a Minister and Permanent Head aren't getting on in a reasonable way,' he explained later, 'then the Permanent Head ought to go. There was no personal bitterness between us, but it just wasn't working out very well and he [McMahon] wanted Waller.'[21] Plimsoll did not much like his new minister, anyway. He thought him weak, uncertain, and craven. 'I found him so disorganised and he could never remember from one minute to another what he'd already decided,' he said. McMahon's tendency to intrigue and manipulate, to gossip and meddle, was another factor: 'I couldn't stand that,' Plimsoll said.[22] Thus he made it easy. When McMahon snapped at him that he did not care for Plimsoll's advice on what he could not do, Plimsoll ended it there and then. 'In that case I wish to resign immediately,' he told McMahon. 'This is no good.'[23]

The deck was shuffled to ensure it all worked and that everyone saved face. Cabinet decided that Plimsoll would be sent to Washington in June as Australia's ambassador to the United States. Gordon Freeth would become Australia's ambassador to Japan, replacing the former secretary to the prime minister's department, Sir Allen Brown.[24] And so, early in the New Year, Keith Waller was woken at four o'clock in the morning by a call from Plimsoll. Cabinet had appointed him secretary of the Department of External Affairs. Did he accept? 'Rather reluctantly I said yes,' Waller recalled.[25] His sorrow was immediate. When Waller informed his wife of the news, he felt moved to supplement it: 'What a fool I am,' he said.[26]

However Waller might have felt, his appointment would be one of the most influential actions of McMahon's time as minister, both in the effect on the department and its make-up and structure, and in the evolution of Australia's foreign policy.

AMONG the first dilemmas that McMahon confronted as minister for external affairs had to do with Vietnam.[27] US president Richard Nixon's announcements of American troop withdrawals had added considerable credibility to those calling for Australia to reduce its military commitment in the war-torn country. On 9 December, cabinet discussed a joint submission from McMahon and Fraser about a defence-committee report on Vietnam and the likelihood of America withdrawing further troops. The discussion resulted in a consensus that Australia's involvement was too heavily reliant on American decisions about its commitment; thus, at cabinet's request, Gorton wrote to Nixon, seeking an understanding that Australian withdrawals would be planned in tandem with American ones.

Nixon responded the next day through an intermediary. The US president suggested he was willing to have 'meaningful discussions' about the Australian and American military presence, but added his hope that any reductions in Australian troop strength would be offset by greater economic aid to South Vietnam. The Australian ministers did not recognise the opening that Nixon had left them to exchange a military commitment for an economic one.

What followed showed yet again the dangers of depending so heavily upon the Americans. On 16 December, at roughly the same time that Gorton announced Australian units would be withdrawn only in consultation with allies and when the military situation in Vietnam permitted, Nixon announced the withdrawal of 50,000 American troops. Gorton was forced to make a statement on radio and television that night reaffirming his statement of the morning. In doing so, he, McMahon, and McEwen had missed an opportunity to reset Australia's Vietnam policy, leaving it dependent on American developments. The political cost was high. Gorton's statement seemed inconsistent on an issue he had emphasised during the election campaign; Whitlam's approach, of not replacing a battalion as it returned from a tour of duty, appeared prescient; overall, it further undermined public confidence in the government's policy for Vietnam. The matter did not improve. In a January visit to Australia, US vice-president Spiro Agnew was unable to shed any light on his government's intentions for Vietnam. Of this, McMahon was scathing: he found Agnew 'naïve' and 'certainly unimpressive' when he spoke with cabinet.[28]

The need for a new policy was obvious, as was a better understanding of American intentions. But the difficult relationship between Gorton and McMahon impeded that. McMahon thought he was being bypassed, and, early in February, sent Gorton a short, sharply worded letter that sought advice about Australia's presence in Vietnam and the impact of the United States' changing policy. 'It is clear that the whole subject is still very closely held in Washington,' he wrote:

> For us to be fully informed, therefore, it seems to me that we need to give some thought about the next step and whether we should prompt the Americans to say something more.[29]

It was no use. Gorton had little time for it. He thought McMahon was 'like a little boy scuttling around—you know, peeking out from a crack in the rocks'.[30] A close relationship was not in prospect, for the simple fact that Gorton could not trust McMahon—and with some good reason, as debate over the Nuclear Non-Proliferation Treaty would soon show.

Long in gestation and negotiation, the treaty's progress towards fruition had become increasingly rapid over the previous five years.[31] But Australia's regard for the treaty was unmistakeably ambivalent and reflective of its continuing, quixotic efforts to possess nuclear weapons.[32] Driven by the pro-nuclear Australian Atomic Energy Commission (AAEC) and its chairman, Professor Philip Baxter, vice-chancellor of the University of New South Wales, those efforts had been initially directed towards acquiring nuclear weapons from abroad. In 1958, Menzies had pressed the British to share nuclear armaments with Australia; three years later, he had gone further, suggesting that Australia:

> [...] secure now from the United Kingdom recognition of an obligation to allow Australia the right of access to United Kingdom nuclear weapon 'know how' (or preferably ... the right to draw on the U.K. nuclear weapons stockpile) in the event of important countries in the general Pacific and Indian Ocean areas acquiring nuclear capability.[33]

Spurred by the proliferation of nuclear weapons (most notably, China's acquisition of nuclear capability in 1964), the imminent withdrawal of the British 'east of the Suez', and fear of an American retreat from the Asia-Pacific region, in the mid-1960s the government began to redirect its efforts. It aimed to develop nuclear weapons, or, at worst, to preserve its options to do so at a later date. In 1967, Sir Leslie Martin, a scientific advisor to the Department of Defence, confided to the visiting chairman of the US Atomic Energy Commission, Glenn Seaborg, that the Holt government was 'struggling with the decision of whether to produce a nuclear weapon', and three months later David Fairbairn, as minister for national development, was restricting exports of Australian uranium on grounds that Australia might need it.[34] Gorton's elevation had spurred efforts further.

As a senator, he had supported Australia's acquiring nuclear weapons; as prime minister, he was intent on preserving Australia's options for doing so.[35] He had pushed for construction of a nuclear-power reactor at Jervis Bay, was willing to allow the US to use nuclear explosives to blast a deep-water harbour at Cape Keraudren, in Australia's north-west, and he signed a secret co-operative agreement with the French in June 1969 that would ensure Australian access to nuclear technology.[36] Understandably, with these positions, Gorton was opposed to the Non-Proliferation Treaty; as Plimsoll said later, Gorton was 'very sticky' on it.[37] His opposition was aligned with the AAEC, defence personnel, and a broad coalition of bureaucrats scattered through the departments of Prime Minister, the Cabinet Office, Defence, Trade and Industry, National Development, and Supply—the so-called 'Bomb Lobby'—who used every argument they could to undermine the treaty.[38] As Lenox Hewitt had written to Gorton in 1968:

> Will the Americans come to our aid, under ANZUS, with nuclear weapons in the event of a threat to Australia by Chinese nuclear weaponry? This year; next year; in twenty-four years from now? Will they???[39]

This was not the view taken by officials in the Department of External Affairs. Aware of the vehemence that underlay international efforts to stem the proliferation of nuclear weapons, guided by knowledge of Australia's strategic position in relation to threats and allies, and already exercising influence on the treaty's negotiation, its officials had the intellectual heft to oppose the 'bomb lobby' and Baxter, an energetic advocate whom McMahon later recalled pressing 'strenuously' for production of weapons-grade plutonium.[40] But for a long time the department had been without a champion at cabinet level who could counter Baxter's opposition to the treaty. While he was minister, Hasluck had thought it should be ratified, but was unwilling to contribute to the department's policy-making,[41] and Gordon Freeth had not held the portfolio long enough to make a mark on the issue.

Thus the tide of events preceding McMahon's appointment had favoured the sceptics of the treaty. A working group convened by Gorton to recommend whether Australia sign had been loaded from the start. Its final recommendation, that the government hedge its bets by only indicating 'a willingness to sign the treaty subject to understandings, qualifications, and possible amendments', was of little surprise.[42] An intransigence that was cloaked in seemingly reasonable concerns was the modus operandi of the treaty's opponents, publicly and in private. During the election campaign, Gorton had emphasised that his government would not sign until it was assured that the treaty would be 'effective', provide 'real protection', and not endanger Australia's security.[43] As one observer noted later, Gorton's strategy to resist the treaty was 'simply not to sign the treaty rather than directly reject it'.[44]

Gorton's public and private opposition, and that of a majority of his ministers, could well have seen the battle won. But McMahon's appointment altered this. He was already a notable opponent of Gorton's strategy on nuclear weapons and power. As treasurer, he had opposed Fairbairn's 1966 proposal for a nuclear-power reactor and Gorton's push for the Jervis Bay reactor. His objections had chiefly been to the immense cost involved,[45] but he had also questioned the underlying rationale for both.[46]

Now, as minister for external affairs, mindful of both the diplomatic pressure that was building internationally for Australia to sign the treaty and the attitude of his department, McMahon saw that continued ambivalence and resistance would result in isolation. He came out in favour of signing the treaty. His department, finally, had a champion: one who was well-versed in how government worked, who was experienced with Australia's politics—and who would go to extraordinary lengths to have his way.

Without Gorton's knowledge, McMahon sought to involve the American government in the decision of what Australia would do. He wanted the Americans to change Gorton's mind. To that end, on 30 January, McMahon met with the US ambassador to Australia, Walter Rice, and discussed his colleagues' opposition to the Non-Proliferation Treaty. Then, according to Rice:

> He [McMahon] suggested that if US were to influence decision a private message from president Nixon to Prime Minister Gorton should be sent immediately—before Wednesday [4 February]. He indicated NPT was a hot political issue within the government. I reminded him that PM

had resented what he considered to be application of pressure by us a year or so ago and that Secretary [of State William] Rogers had assured Gorton personally that US would exert no pressure on Australian decision. McMahon felt that letter from anyone other than president himself would be resented.

Rice was not in favour of the idea. He told McMahon that the US would allow Australia to make the decision at its own initiative, and await the outcome. But he was in no doubt about what McMahon was suggesting: that if the US wished to ensure a favourable response, a message from Nixon to Gorton would be 'the only effective way of producing results'.[47] To involve a foreign government, even one as closely allied as America, in a matter soon to come under consideration by cabinet, was an astonishing step—yet Rice's hesitation did not dissuade McMahon from his efforts to turn Gorton around.

A few days later, McMahon spoke with Gorton about the treaty over the telephone. He followed the call up on 6 February, advising that the window for signing the treaty was closing and that the matter needed to be considered:

> In effect we have only three more weeks in which it will still be open to us to take two steps in regard to the treaty—first signature and later ratification. Once the treaty is actually in force it will be only open to us to decide whether or not we should finally *accede*.[48]

McMahon was bringing all the pressure he could to induce Gorton to back down. In his subsequent submission to cabinet on 13 February, McMahon argued that continued intransigence would be self-defeating. Japan and West Germany had now signed the treaty. It had garnered sufficient signatures to come into force in March. If Australia signed before the treaty came into force, it would have 'locus standi' to reserve ratification until its objections and concerns had been met. But once the treaty was in force, McMahon stressed, 'the successive steps of signature and ratification are no longer open to us'. Moreover, he went on, a failure to sign could have adverse effects—on the availability of equipment, material, and technical information necessary for Gorton's prized Jervis Bay reactor, on the attitude of the US, and on continuing stability in the Asia-Pacific region. His submission argued for the pragmatic course, emphasising that 'the critical problem here is the manner of public presentation'.[49]

Gorton was scathing about this reasoning and the submission. On the margins of his copy, he dismissed the arguments: 'This is just absolute blather,' he scrawled at one point. 'Gobbily gook [sic],' he wrote at another.[50] But when cabinet came to consider the submission on 17 February, McMahon had his way.

The debate was held almost entirely along the lines he had set. He made the argument over and over again: the government should sign the treaty now in order to avoid acceding to it later. Australia could sign, could fight its corner on interpretations and concerns, and only once they had been resolved would it consider ratification. Gorton thought signing would be 'going back' on the government's commitments. He thought the treaty was 'not effective', was not satisfied with progress safeguarding Australia's concerns, and did not believe the treaty would help Australia's safety. He claimed that US president Richard Nixon had admitted he could not 'see any point in signing' the treaty. But even Gorton backed down. He was, he said now, 'not strongly against signing' the treaty.

McMahon made it easier for him. He did not think that Gorton was going back on commitments, he said. Australia could follow the line adopted by West Germany, signing while reserving the right to not ratify. And to suggestions that ratification was inevitable once the decision was made to sign, McMahon was firm. 'The decision on ratification remains here at this table,' he said. 'And if we don't sign, there will be questioning overseas as to what this country is up to. The solemn and profound step of ratification is one to be considered when it comes but it is not inevitable.'[51] Cabinet agreed. Australia would sign, yes—but this would be '[O]n the understanding that signature does not in any sense commit the government to ratification, and on the further understanding that it would not propose to ratify until such time as the difficulties it now has with the Treaty are resolved to its satisfaction'.[52]

Neither this nor the clear signs that Gorton would not move for ratification were enough to distract from the obvious about-face. Within a few months, Gorton had gone back on an election commitment, Labor noted. What else could he go back on? It was a revelation of weakness compounded by the conspicuous decision to sign without ratification. As British diplomat Martin Reith observed privately:

> Mr Gorton has made nothing but losses out of the late decision to sign the Nuclear Non-Proliferation Treaty. The styling was so wrong—all the appearance of having been taken under pressure, Mr Whitlam's or worse still Mr McMahon's—and instead of killing it now, the implied unwillingness to ratify still leaves his opponents with the chance of a second go.[53]

It all served to overshadow the role played by officials within the department and, indeed, the scale of one of McMahon's achievements while minister for external affairs.[54]

While McMahon triumphed over Gorton this time, there were to be occasions when he lost—and not just to Gorton. Having nursed it for the two years since McMahon rendered it redundant, having spoken to Gorton about it in 1968, and no doubt aware that his own mooted retirement left a finite opportunity to get it through, John McEwen saw that the time had come to try again on his Industry Development Corporation—and, this time, to ensure that he would win. In January 1970, he wrote to Gorton suggesting that they co-sponsor a submission to cabinet to establish the AIDC. His language was grand, significant, heavy on nationalism. He knew how to attract Gorton's attention. The AIDC, McEwen suggested, had the potential to be the 'most fundamental breakthrough in development policy since 1949—a breakthrough with great national appeal and tremendous economic advantage'.[55] Lenox Hewitt's support, in his private advice, was coloured by appeals to Gorton's dislikes. Writing of McMahon's Resources Development Bank and Treasury's earlier opposition to the AIDC, Hewitt argued that it was 'difficult to avoid the conclusion that the attitude of the Treasury in this whole matter has been one of a dog in the manger determined to preserve a monopoly on borrowing abroad—perhaps because of a fear that the competitive institution might be a success'.[56] The appeals worked. Gorton was on board.

He and McEwen circulated the revived proposal on 23 January. The reasoning for the AIDC was much the same as before: there was 'a need and opportunity to develop policies aimed at encouraging industry growth and Australian participation therein'. The AIDC would facilitate the 'development and expansion of Australian industry'. It would have a particular emphasis on export-oriented industry and the preservation of maximum Australian ownership, they argued. By borrowing funds in international markets, the corporation would invest in and lend capital to Australian companies, allowing them to expand, resist foreign takeovers, and increase their ability to generate capital. Speed was of the essence: Gorton and McEwen wanted the announcement to be made 'as soon as Parliament resumes' so that the corporation could open its doors by the following year.[57]

But cabinet was not about to give the go-ahead quite so quickly, even with the prime minister and deputy prime minister urging approval. Despite the inclusion of a nineteen-page document rebutting potential arguments, the cabinet meeting on Wednesday 28 January was contentious. Ministers questioned the measure on philosophical and logistical grounds. McEwen, outlining the proposal, was not to be dissuaded. 'We are talking about something to operate 100 years,' he said, to McMahon's note that capital inflow was down and Bury's concern at the difficulties of raising funds abroad. 'Not [a] matter of now [current] international markets.' McMahon was unconvinced. He insisted that Treasury supply a 'special paper' on the AIDC.

In the face of these delaying tactics, McEwen was calm. 'I'm open minded on that.' But he wanted approval of the AIDC before the departments got their chance to weigh in. 'If Cab[inet] accepts principle then Treasury, Trade, and AG's [Attorney-General's] go through,' he said.

McMahon and Bury tried to forgo that. To McMahon's suggestion that the Department of National Development also contribute comments, McEwen was dismissive. It did not really concern the department, which did not really have the expertise anyway, he said. What he wanted was simple and straightforward: 'Would hope Cabinet approve in principle,' he repeated.

Gorton echoed him: 'I would hope Cabinet accept in principle.' The prime minister now came in to take over from McEwen and argue the case. There was a problem, wasn't there? If there was, what did the government lose by trying to fix that problem? he asked. 'I think it is something we ought to try.'

Bury successfully pressed for time for the Treasury to comment. His department had only received the submission on the Saturday night, he said, and the Australia Day holiday had drastically limited his department's scrutiny of the submission.

McMahon reiterated his wholesale opposition to the AIDC. There was no need for the corporation. Its certain failure would affect the government, he said. And the political consequences could be disastrous. 'I would like to leave matter to merchant banking. I'd hate to see Corporation in hands of Whitlam.' McEwen was happy to rejoin this battle. Their exchanges were sharp. There, again, was the gulf that had separated them for years. McMahon's stance reflected his longheld faith in markets, his belief in the orthodoxies dominant in his state. He wanted to see the problem—if it was really as bad as McEwen and Gorton suggested—handled by the Resources Development Bank or by the private sector. But McEwen's response was as it had always been, and again in conformity with the economic orthodoxy widespread in Victoria. Okay, McEwen replied. 'You said is there a demonstrated need for this Corporation to attack [the] problem. I go back and say here is a demonstrated need for some kind of protection.'

The debate continued after lunch. Gorton tried to move things along—'I still think Cabinet express desirability subject to paper from Treasury for next week,' he said—but McMahon was blunt: 'No. With weight of you and McEwen behind it [this] puts impossible burden on us.' Nonetheless, McEwen and Gorton pressed for a result then and there. 'I should like decision,' Gorton said. He wanted initial approval, but his ministers were ready to quarrel over that, too. Fraser wondered if initial approval could be conveyed 'more strongly' to Treasury, so that its comments were more helpful. Other ministers wondered if 'approval' was too strong. Should the decision say that cabinet was 'strongly attracted' to the proposal? Gorton and McEwen would have none of it.[58] Pending comments from the Treasury and the Attorney-General's Department on the establishment of the corporation, cabinet gave its 'initial approval', said the resulting minute.[59]

When Gorton and McEwen fronted cabinet on 5 February, they were able to secure firm approval. Cabinet decided to establish the AIDC 'along the lines' set out in the original submission.[60] But this meeting was even more contentious than the previous one. The sceptical Treasury comments that McMahon and Bury had wished to present were met with a determined rebuttal from both Gorton and McEwen. 'I'm astonished at paper,' Gorton said. McEwen thought it dishonest and a distraction, intended 'to make bloody fools of [the] PM and myself on something we never suggested,' he said. '... I'm outraged by this paper.' McMahon, fighting a losing battle, nevertheless continued to press for the primacy of the Resources Development Bank. McMahon's opposition required Bury to be effective; he was not. Bury could not push back on Gorton and McEwen. 'What in hell has this got to do with proposal [the] PM and I put up?' McEwen demanded to know, to one of Bury's concerns. 'Nothing!'[61] The fervour of the prime minister and the Country Party leader was obvious. 'They both regarded this almost as an act of faith,' Bury said later.[62]

Gorton, for his part, admitted that the proposal was divisive: 'It [the AIDC] quite clearly had very strong opposition.' Malcolm Fraser pointed out that the submission enjoyed the support of only two people, but McEwen had a ready answer: 'Malcolm, there are times when you need to understand that it's the weight and not the numbers that counts.'[63] Gorton concurred with this: 'It's quite a thing, I think, to expect a Cabinet to knock back something that's strongly approved by both the Prime Minister and the Leader of the Country Party,' he explained later. To Gorton, it was evident that it was his advocacy that made the difference: 'It [the AIDC] wouldn't have been set up but for me.'[64]

News of the decision was leaked to the press by the weekend, and, in a subsequent cabinet meeting, the suspicion for the leak fell on McMahon. 'I want to say again that [journalist Max] Walsh called me,' McMahon protested. 'He *had* the story—if you read what he said, he talked about the eclipse of McMahon. Is that something I would have been likely to give him?'[65] But McMahon was certainly spreading stories. When he rang Howson on 8 February, McMahon was suggesting that Gorton had thrown his weight around to ensure the AIDC was approved. 'Apparently in Cabinet eight Ministers voted against it,' Howson wrote in his diary, 'but, after lunch, led by Ken Anderson, five Liberal Ministers changed their minds and voted with the PM and Jack.' In the same conversation, McMahon also deliberately moved to sabotage the cabinet decision: 'Bill has asked me to try to gain some support from other Liberal backbenchers to oppose it in the party room.'[66]

Those backbenchers duly did so. Early in March, when the AIDC was brought to the party room, up to twelve Liberals spoke against it, and Gorton was left to defend it on his own. For critics like Howson, the meeting was another opportunity to show that the party was divided, that there was a gulf between the prime minister and his dissatisfied backbench.[67]

Yet a similar gap could be said to exist within the ministry—between the old, practised hands, like McMahon, and the new ministers rising to prominence under Gorton. The tall, aloof, and habitual pipe-smoker Malcolm Fraser was the most conspicuous of these. An Oxford graduate and grazier, Fraser had been elected as the member for the Victorian electorate of Wannon in 1955 when he was but twenty-five years old. He had then spent ten years on the backbench, ostensibly in obscurity, but with the growing recognition of peers and observers that he was a formidable presence.[68] Fraser's ministerial career had only begun when Holt appointed him minister for the army in 1966, yet from there it developed quickly—to minister for education and science, in 1968, and then minister for defence, in 1969. Fraser was ambitious, intelligent, and, in the coming months, would demonstrate an unexpected toughness: first, by successfully renegotiating the terms of the delivery of the F-111 with an intransigent United States; second, by standing up to McMahon.

McMahon and Gorton had agreed in December 1969 that McMahon would make a ministerial statement about his new portfolio early in the parliamentary session. When McMahon discovered that Fraser also intended to make a ministerial statement, he became adamant that as the senior minister his should go first.[69] His anger when that was refused was nothing, however, when he read the draft of Fraser's statement late in February.[70] It seemed a clear trespass into McMahon's portfolio of external affairs, with an extended opening statement on the 'broad picture' of world relations and how they related to defence needs. McMahon told Plimsoll to speak with Tange and have the sections removed. In this, Plimsoll was unsuccessful, and he advised McMahon to speak with Fraser himself.[71]

McMahon did so on 6 March. Their meeting was heated.

McMahon demanded that Fraser remove the first sections of the speech. He threatened to brief colleagues and the press that Fraser was 'overstepping the line' if he refused. But McMahon's bluster went nowhere. The much-younger Fraser would not be cowed, even by a colleague as senior as McMahon. He refused to remove the sections, arguing that they were important to the substance of the speech, and appealed to Gorton. The prime minister backed his defence minister, and McMahon fumed.[72] The slight was obvious, well known to many, and a decided rebuff of McMahon's authority.

At other times, however, there was clear cooperation within the ministry. One such occasion was the joint cabinet submission that McMahon made, with Bury, to explore what it would mean for Australia to seek membership of the Organisation for Economic Cooperation and Development (OECD), an organisation designed to foster better economic growth and trade through the exchange of ideas and policies among governments.[73] Concerned by the possible influence it might have on Australian and international trade, McEwen found the OECD's emphasis of free trade extremely troubling, and believed that Australia's proper place did not lie with the largely industrialised countries that comprised the OECD's membership. 'Australia will only join the OECD,' he said, 'over my dead body.'[74]

Nonetheless, to officials within the Department of External Affairs and the Treasury, the OECD was worth joining. As the departments said, the OECD was 'the major forum for consultation on economic matters among Western governments at a high policy level'. Moreover, 'it is in the OECD that the formative (and often decisive) discussions take place on many important matters—including financial matters (such as the position of sterling) which are of importance for our general relationships with the major countries of Europe, the United States of America, and Japan'. The departments never left it alone, and a working party in 1969 that included McEwen's Trade and Industry continued to discuss whether Australia should join. They were helped by McEwen's eventual decision to be flexible: in exchange for conditions that would allow Australia to maintain its tariff system and the Department of Trade and Industry's input over matters of direct concern, he agreed not to oppose another submission recommending that Australia consider joining.

As one who had absorbed the arguments of Treasury and, now, External Affairs, McMahon wrote to Gorton to argue that the option be explored. 'The arguments for Australian membership of OECD are based on an assessment of the widest financial, economic and political benefits as the Treasurer and I see them[,] which would derive from our membership of what is essentially the main organ for economic co-operation between countries of the Western world,' he wrote, on 2 April.[75] It was a moment when coordination paid off. On 30 April, cabinet approved the submission from McMahon and Bury, and resolved to explore the possibility of Australian membership of the OECD.[76]

CHAPTER THIRTY

Le Noir

1984

Given their long, fractious, and well-publicised relationship, a question of interest for the book was what McMahon might say about John McEwen. McMahon would surely have special words for the man who had speared his hopes of becoming prime minister after Harold Holt's death, and he would surely feel some urge to air their many heated clashes in cabinet.

Ostensibly, McMahon would write his story of these battles; he could respond, too, to McEwen's dour, spare autobiography, which a Canberran economics historian had put together from a series of interview transcripts after McEwen's death in 1980. Privately printed by McEwen's widow, a copy of *John McEwen: his story* had been sent to McMahon's office upon publication, with a note that the book was for those 'likely to be interested in John McEwen's "own story"'.[1]

McEwen's comments about McMahon in his book had been largely benign. Though he had strongly implied that McMahon was an inveterate leaker to the press, and suggested that McMahon was out to sabotage McEwen, there was little in the manner of blunt criticism. The most strident accusation he had levelled was that McMahon 'did not impress the House or the country with his strength of character' while prime minister, and had not learned when to exercise his own judgement about questions of policy.[2]

Whether because of this or some feeling of restraint about the treatment of the dead, what McMahon had to say about McEwen was unexpectedly soft. He echoed much of what he had already said in public. There were few denunciations, and little gloating. He wrote that McEwen had been mistaken on questions of trade and tariff policy, occasionally vindictive in his conduct, and had strongly wished to become prime minister properly, whether by transferring to the Liberal Party or with its acquiescence. McMahon was also generous. Just as he had when McEwen died, McMahon had called McEwen a giant of Australian politics, a much admired and respected figure.[3] He even admitted to some feelings of pity. Recalling both McEwen's battles with neuro-dermatitis—which occasionally left McEwen with bleeding, bandaged feet[4]—and the death of McEwen's first wife, Ann, in 1967, McMahon wrote of once seeing the Country Party leader standing alone, and feeling profoundly sorry for him.

And yet, just as with Menzies, McMahon's treatment of McEwen—where he would fit in the memoir—was a problem. Bowman was quick to diagnose the issue: skipping over McMahon's early time in politics meant that their relationship was difficult to understand. 'Like Menzies,' wrote Bowman to McMahon, 'he [McEwen] will appear and reappear in season until the time comes to deal with him thoroughly.' Discussions of McEwen were slotted in around the 1967 devaluation debate, the problems with Newton, with Gorton, and with McEwen's decision to rescind his veto in 1969.

For Bowman, rewriting the manuscript and trying to fit it all together in a way that was understandable and comprehensible meant a considerable re-adjustment. The time to deal with McEwen, he wrote to McMahon, had to be 'when, after Holt's death, he says he and his party will not serve under the Liberal Party's deputy leader if he [McMahon] is elected Prime Minister', in the eleventh chapter.[5] McMahon had agreed to the solution Bowman proposed, but, as ever, it was a shaky agreement. There was no telling whether it would hold when Bowman reached it.

CHAPTER THIRTY-ONE

Battles

1970-1971

When he rose in the House on 19 March 1970 to deliver his ministerial statement, nine days after Fraser's well-received one, McMahon was well aware of the dangers that could befall him. What had happened to Gordon Freeth was not going to happen to him.[1] He was determined to avoid any such mistakes.[2] Speaking quickly and without some of the panache of his past performances,[3] McMahon said he would set out a candid assessment of Australia's foreign-policy objectives amid a world in a profound state of change.[4] What followed mixed the obstinate with the clear-eyed, and hardly suggested a new course for Australian foreign policy. Yes, the USSR had engaged with the West, signed the Partial Test Ban and the Nuclear Non-Proliferation treaties, and, yes, it had agreed to a ban on the use of outer space for nuclear war—but apart from disarmament, there were no signs of détente, he argued.

On China, he held to the attitudes he had stated back in 1958. China could not forever remain on the periphery of the international community, but, in the absence of evidence that China was prepared to comply with 'the broad rules of international behaviour', he could not countenance change. 'Consequently we still regard communist China and other communist regimes as a central obstacle to peace, stability, and ordered progress throughout Asia.' The Guam Doctrine, enunciated by US president Nixon in July 1969 and confirmed again in February 1970, ensured Australia enjoyed the support of the US, and this was welcome news, particularly since the British were to be gone from the Asia-Pacific by December 1971.

From there, McMahon moved to Japan, to note its ever-increasing significance to Australia in trade—and stressed its importance to stability and prosperity in the Asia-Pacific region. That was something new: no external affairs minister since World War II had given Japan such prominence. McMahon was recognising Japan's ability to assume a role much broader than its trade status. Within the Asia-Pacific region, he said, Japan had an important role to play, diplomatically and politically. Meanwhile, on Vietnam, he argued that the situation was improving: 'I have no doubt that our common objectives in Vietnam are capable of being achieved.'

Yet just as important, and problematic for the central thrust of McMahon's statement, were the sudden shifts and turmoil that had engulfed Laos and Cambodia in the days and weeks preceding his speech. In Laos, North Vietnamese soldiers had launched an offensive across the Plain of Jars. In Cambodia, on the day before McMahon's speech, the head of state, Prince Norodom Sihanouk, had been deposed. Sihanouk's fraught pursuit of neutrality in the Vietnam conflict had weakened his political position and become impossible to maintain, especially as North Vietnamese and Vietcong forces used Cambodia's neutrality to occupy and operate from within its borders. The prime minister, General Lon Nol, had been convinced to lead a coup and establish a new government that would abandon neutrality and become a pro-West state.

McMahon was aware of the implications for Australia. As he noted that night, the Asia-Pacific region and the Middle East were the two places where crises affecting world peace and stability were likely to arise.[5] Those implications became urgent in the weeks that followed McMahon's speech.[6] Taking advantage of the turmoil of Sihanouk's deposition, and provoked by Nol's pro-West regime, the North Vietnamese and Vietcong rapidly expanded their control of Cambodian territory, spurring calls for diplomatic talks. Indonesia's foreign minister, Adam Malik, called for a regional solution that would preserve Cambodia's independence and neutrality, prevent a foreign military intervention, and re-activate the International Control Commission, established in 1954 to implement and monitor the Geneva Accords that had ended the First Indochina War.[7] After hesitating initially, McMahon came out in support of a diplomatic conference to discuss a solution. He soon convinced Gorton and McEwen that Australia should take part, should it be held.[8] 'Australia is ready to take part in such a meeting and believes it should convene at the earliest possible date,' he said, on 27 April.[9]

Inevitably, however, the problems of consultation and reliance on American decisions rose again. Without forewarning Australia, Nixon announced that American and South Vietnamese military forces would be ordered into Cambodian territory with a mission to destroy the strengthening communist threat; at around the same time, the new Cambodian government made an appeal for military and economic assistance to respond to the communist aggression.

The Gorton government had a dilemma. If it voiced support for Nixon's decision and agreed to provide military assistance, it could fairly be said to have undermined the conference before it even began. But silence, too, could be as damaging to its relationship with the United States. In cabinet on 1 May, McMahon argued that while Australia might 'applaud' what the US was doing, it should be quiet about it in order to preserve its options for the future. 'Least said the better,' he said.[10] Cabinet agreed: Australia would continue to support and participate in the conference, but it also acknowledged and sympathised with the American decision to intervene in Cambodia. It was a difficult position to balance, was unlikely to win favour with anyone, and the government did itself no favours by not announcing it until 5 May. When he did so, speaking in the House, Gorton committed to 'try by diplomatic means' to ensure Cambodia's neutrality, but soon swung towards attacking the Labor Party. Responding to Whitlam's criticism of Nixon and the 'widening' of the war, Gorton pointed to the North Vietnamese and Vietcong violation of Cambodia's neutrality and the necessity of a response. Arguments like Whitlam's, Gorton said:

[...] are for the theory that Communist forces should be allowed to operate as and when they like; that they should be excused for invading and occupying neutral countries; and that it is wrong for action to be taken to stop them and that such comments by giving that support, to me, Sir, show a willingness, even a desire, to accept defeat or surrender of Allied forces in South Vietnam.[11]

Rhetorically it was a strong response, but there was little denying that Gorton spoke from a position of weakness. Nixon's announcement, on 20 April, that America would withdraw another 150,000 troops over the coming year was a blow to the Australian government's efforts to sustain flagging public support for the war. Cabinet's response to Nixon's announcement was uncertain. It recognised the need and desire to withdraw Australian troops, but had little inkling of how to present the decision. McMahon told Howson later that an initial draft, which had announced that a battalion would not be replaced when its rotation ended in November, was 'a terrible hash', and cabinet had forced Gorton to rewrite it.[12] Left only with a 'form of words' for 'guidance', Gorton announced the decision in the House on 22 April, retaining a caveat that further withdrawals within the next year were possible.[13]

Labor was now set to reap the rewards of its implacable opposition to the war. Whitlam pointed out that the government was reactive. He argued that its policy for South-East Asia was 'in ruins', that its rationale for its policy had 'crumbled', that the premise of Australia's involvement in Vietnam was 'false and untenable', and that the regularly invoked objectives were 'unattainable'. 'It is time to end trying to save face and start trying to save lives,' Whitlam said. The war in Vietnam, he said, 'is the war of a party; it is not the war of this nation.'[14]

The lethality of Whitlam's rhetoric was sharpened by his awarenesss that public opposition to the war was reaching a critical mass. The visibility of the protest movement in the United States, the growing toll of killed and wounded soldiers and civilians, the scandals and horrors of My Lai, and the repeated inconsistencies of the government's policy towards Vietnam were difficult to ignore—and about to become impossible. Inspired by similar marches in the United States, preparations were underway for a 'moratorium' campaign to protest against Australia's involvement in Vietnam. Whitlam, therefore, could not have felt more confident when he replied to Gorton.

If the government hoped that its announcement would cool the fervour of the protesters, it was to be sorely disappointed. To opponents and supporters both, the reduction seemed uncertain, a bastardised compromise; for some, it suggested that further action could be spurred by more protests, more public pressure. More than 200,000 people turned out throughout the country to protest on 8 May, with Labor frontbencher Jim Cairns, the member for Lalor, a prominent leader of the campaign.

There was, therefore, a charged backdrop when McMahon left Australia for Djakarta, Indonesia—the site of the conference—on 14 May. The foreign ministers of Indonesia, Japan, Korea, New Zealand, the Philippines, Singapore, Thailand, South Vietnam, and representatives of the Laotian government were in attendance, but the absence of the United States, the USSR, and communist countries caused many to dismiss the conference as irrelevant. McMahon said otherwise, but there was no doubt that the potential for agreement on a workable solution was low.[15] In spite of this, as McMahon's private secretary, Kim Jones, said later, McMahon was 'very keen' on the conference. He took an active role in it: 'McMahon put his heart into participating.'[16]

Conducted under the Indonesian *musyawarah* system, in which decisions could only be reached by consensus, the conference was almost certainly a failure as far as solutions for Cambodia were concerned.[17] The joint communiqué issued at the end urged cessation of hostilities and withdrawal of foreign forces from Cambodia, stated that the Cambodian people should control their own problems, and that the International Control Commission be re-activated in order to arrive at a 'just, peaceful and effective resolution of the present situation'.[18] The last proposal received a cool reception: few had any confidence in the commission's ability to ensure future agreements were kept, and the inability to isolate Cambodia's problems from those of the region meant that little could be done otherwise. Within three days of the conference's conclusion, the main proposals had been firmly rejected.[19]

In spite of this, the conference was among the highest points of McMahon's time as minister for external affairs.[20] In lending support to Indonesia's efforts to hold the conference, McMahon ensured Australia maintained good relations with its neighbours and strengthened the willingness of Asian-Pacific countries to work for regional solutions.[21] By remaining involved after the US and UK declined invitations to attend, he ensured that Australia's foreign policy could not be said to be defined by its alliances with both. By remaining involved in spite of Australia's support for America's action in Cambodia, he ensured that Australia's commitment to diplomacy remained evident. McMahon's encouragement of Japan's involvement was also important, particularly as Japan agreed to serve, alongside Malaysia and Indonesia, on a task force that consulted with the United Nations on ways to implement the conference recommendations. It was an opportunity for Japan to exercise the broader role McMahon had encouraged in his statement of 19 March. He had managed to balance Australia's alliance with and support of the US with its involvement in regional diplomatic efforts for peace and stability. In sum, McMahon had put the statements of his speech into practice.

Back home, however, the government had plunged into fresh turmoil. On the same evening that Gorton announced the government's position on the Djakarta conference and Cambodia—that is, 5 May—McEwen had introduced legislation to establish the AIDC. The shouts and yells of a 'vociferous' opposition during McEwen's second-reading speech had not provoked an outpouring of support from the government's side of the House. The Liberal-Country Party backbenches, Howson observed giddily, had been 'completely silent'.[22] Beginning on 14 May, and continuing over the next week, Howson led a sustained attack on the AIDC. 'Is this Corporation really needed? Is there a firm demand established by the Government for this Corporation and for the tasks that it is expected to perform?' he asked. 'So far in this debate, I do not believe that a full and sufficient case has been made out for this Corporation.'[23] Fellow backbenchers described the AIDC as socialistic, and suggested that those within the government supporting it were not real Liberals. There was, however, no disguising the fact that Gorton was as much a target as the legislation. During the drawn-out debate, Howson and his allies sought to make amendments, to make a general nuisance and disrupt Gorton's plans. Even Labor could see it. 'It is now 12.45 a.m.,' said Fred Daly wearily, on 21 May, 'and we are debating in this Parliament not the provisions of this legislation but the machinations and hatreds in the once great Liberal Party and the feeling against the Prime Minister.'[24]

The AIDC was but a background drama to further, more serious, trouble. In January, cabinet had decided that the Commonwealth should assert its jurisdiction over offshore areas, clarifying that its sovereignty ran from the low-water mark—that is, the level reached by the sea at low tide—to the edge of the continental shelf.[25] The move had been made in order to end a long-running dispute and ambiguity over which level of government possessed sovereignty over these offshore areas. At stake was potential revenue, via mining permits and royalties, and the implementation of environmental protection.

The state governments had been involved in negotiations on the matter for the previous two years, and, when the cabinet decision was announced in March, they reacted with scorn, anger, and full-throated criticism. In addition to arguing that the decision was an infringement of states' rights, premiers argued that it broke an undertaking for consultation and discussion that Fairbairn had given while minister for national devlopment. Criticism of Gorton and his approach was everywhere in the media, in the state and federal parties. McMahon was aware of the discontent, and concerned by where it could lead. Howson, recording that McMahon believed public opinion against Gorton was 'getting restive', thought that McMahon was also wondering about his position and his future.[26] Others, like Snedden, thought that 'there was a conspiracy going on', the chief beneficiary of which would be McMahon.[27] Matters were serious—and becoming more so by the day. On 30 April, Reg Swartz, the minister for national development, tabled all correspondence that had passed between Fairbairn and the states; on 8 May, with Gorton in Japan, Fairbairn decided to speak in the House.

Feelings about it were high. Having briefed journalists about the issue for days, Howson was confiding in his diary that 'things are brewing up toward a crisis'. After Fairbairn spoke, Howson was sure that one was imminent.[28] The thrust of Fairbairn's speech was simple. He accused Gorton of failing to honour a commitment that he, Fairbairn, had given on behalf of the government. A commitment had been made, Fairbairn argued, and now—since Fairbairn's resignation from the ministry, since the cabinet decision to assert Commonwealth sovereignty—it had been 'dishonoured'.[29]

The seriousness of Fairbairn's attack was evident to all but McMahon, who initially failed to perceive its significance.[30] As Howson told him, the charge against Gorton was searing, all the more for the reputation of the man making it. Howson's hopes for an imminent crisis—potentially within the next week of the parliamentary session—were sustained by his subsequent conversations with colleagues[31] and further fortified by conversations with McEwen, whom, he suggested, should consider whether he would be willing to take on the prime ministership in a caretaker mode.[32]

Gorton replied to Fairbairn on 15 May. According to him, Fairbairn's understanding of matters was mistaken. Cabinet had decided in February 1969 to legislate to assert Commonwealth rights over the seabed outside the three-mile limit, and Fairbairn had been deputised to inform the state ministers of that decision. Fairbairn's belief that a commitment had been given to undertake prior consultation was incorrect. 'The discussions which had been suggested were not discussions on whether or when we should legislate, but discussions on the administrative and other consequential effects of our legislation on what is called the regime.' Gorton had examined the record, and regarded it as failing to support Fairbairn's charges. 'I believe that that seems a flimsy ground on which to accuse the government of dishonour and it is not supported by the record.'[33]

The matter might well have rested there had Labor not intervened to exploit the tensions that were still swirling. Citing Fairbairn's accusations and Gorton's response, Rex Patterson, the Labor member for Dawson and a former officer in the Department of National Development, moved an amendment of no confidence in Gorton's leadership and his cabinet.[34] Once Whitlam had seconded the amendment, Gorton moved immediately to bring the debate on as a motion of censure.[35]

However his critics might denigrate him, Gorton still possessed shrewd judgement and an ability to make quick decisions. Bringing the debate on immediately was evidence of this. It raised the stakes. The 'termites' undermining Gorton's leadership, as Hughes called them, had a choice. They could support the motion, and thus bring down the government, or part ways with Fairbairn's criticism and vote with the government. Howson saw this immediately, particularly after Fairbairn declared that, as it was a matter of his honour, he would vote against the government on the issue.[36]

It was only half-past twelve: there was plenty of time in the day for the debate to go on. Yet the whole affair was given an additional urgency by the government's unexpectedly small majority. Labor only required a few Liberals to support the motion in order to win. It had one already, in Fairbairn, and critics like Jeff Bate were intimating that they, too, would cross the floor. Exacerbating matters, Labor decided to cancel all pairing arrangments but for the one concerning McMahon. Absent Labor MPs were called to Canberra; when word of this leaked, Gorton's office began making urgent calls to missing Liberals to return to Canberra immediately. There was an air of panic throughout the building. The whip's office thought that a vote taken at twelve-thirty would have been equal, which would draw the Speaker and his casting vote into play.

Clearly aware that the government could fall should the motion succeed, McEwen approached Howson and Fairbairn with a draft amendment to Patterson's motion, seeking their support in order to ensure that the overall censure was defeated. Howson insisted that there be an understanding that the offshore legislation be delayed until the next parliamentary session. McEwen took it to Gorton, and Howson began negotiating with his colleagues to ensure they would support it. State politicians rang in to lobby and pressure both sides. In New South Wales, the general secretary of the Liberal Party, John Carrick, 'put the bite' on New South Wales Liberals not to vote against Gorton.[37] In the House, some saw the opportunity for amusement. Jim Killen, the minister for the navy, passed Whitlam a note. 'It's going to be alright,' the note said. 'McMahon is on his way back from Djakarta.' Whitlam's reponse was pointed: 'Is that so? I understood he was going to join Sihanouk.'[38]

By five o'clock, having gone back and forth on a draft that would satisfy Howson and his rebels, McEwen managed to extract an agreement with Gorton on a draft amendment. Gorton had reason to be satisfied. He had stood his ground, accepting only the most inconsequential of amendments. He had forced the malcontents to expose themselves, and they were found wanting. He had won. The rebellion faded, faltered. And when word of that leaked, the heat went out of the whole debate. Howson introduced the agreed upon amendment, toothless as it was. Labor quarrelled with the Speaker over a ruling. With the exception of Fairbairn, who abstained from the vote, the dissenters fell into line to support the government. The motion failed. It was over.

That evening, Gorton was scathing about the rebels and buoyed by his victory. To Hasluck's guarded queries about the day's events, the prime minister grinned and suggested it all was 'perhaps just as well'—an assessment that staggered Hasluck.[39] When Hasluck mentioned the possibility that the rebels might, by pairing with Labor, force the government to defer the offshore legislation for six months, Gorton was adamant that he would do no such thing. 'I'll take them to an election! It would be the best thing.'[40]

The day's events had not prompted any new caution in Gorton. But it had revealed how deep the antipathy to his policies ran, how much the party festered with tension and dislike. McMahon was on the phone, eager for news from all and sundry, and old enemies were in the mood to take up their own arms. Fred Osborne, president of the state Liberal Party in New South Wales, rang Howson to accuse him of disloyalty. Howson gave no quarter and dismissed Osborne entirely. It was all due to the way that McMahon beat Osborne back in 1951, he decided.[41] The possibility that Osborne might not still be nursing this grudge did not appear to have occurred to Howson; nor did the possibility that Osborne might have good reasons for supporting Gorton over the minister for external affairs.

When McMahon surveyed the political landscape after his return from Djakarta, he was delighted. Howson's actions had been 'useful', he said over the phone. Gorton's mood since had been murderous. The party was febrile, much more divided than it had been in the leadership challenge only six months before. What a week it had been.[42]

'OF course, there was persistent tension in the cabinet,' said Tom Hughes, later.[43] Serving as attorney-general—the pinnacle of political life for a practising lawyer, as he was—Hughes was well-positioned to observe how that tension and division cut across the government, and how often it centred on McMahon.

For there was the obvious enmity with Gorton. Mutual, personal, and professional, that enmity had not changed in the time since McMahon moved to external affairs. Gorton did not respect McMahon's handling of the new portfolio[44] and still distrusted his propensity to leak, which prompted him to avoid passing on his correspondence with Nixon to McMahon or the Department of External Affairs.[45] The prime minister thought McMahon bent on treachery and disloyalty.

'All the little bastard is interested in is promoting himself,' Gorton had declared within earshot of journalists, while visiting Tokyo that April.[46] McMahon, in turn, disliked Gorton. He was still angry about his move to the external affairs portfolio, seeing it as a 'dirty move' to sideline him.[47] There was the enmity with McEwen, still deep despite suggestions of a thaw. There were the inter-party suspicions of Anthony and Sinclair. There was the generational divide and dislike of Fraser, Chipp, Killen, and Peacock. But these were not the only causes of discord: there were clear philosophical and ideological differences as well.

The most notable and important of these was on federal and state government relations and powers. Gorton and his supporters emphasised nationalism, and, perceiving the limits of state-based action, saw the virtues of a strong federal government. Neither Gorton's nor his supporters' views about this were new: Menzies and Holt had recognised and presided over the steady accretion of power towards the Commonwealth. But both of Gorton's predecessors had downplayed it, even as the reliance of state governments on Commonwealth-collected revenue increased. Gorton's forthrightness, however, inhibited him from following the Menzies and Holt line. In his dealings with the states, Gorton had been blunt. There were no platitudes from him about where the real power lay.

But such talk was anathema to the state governments that heard it and to the generation of Liberals—generally 'forty-niners'—that had entered politics to fight against the perceived socialist powers of the federal government under Labor. That the current federal government was, for now, Liberal-controlled did not weaken their objections to Gorton's approach. The state governments, with their various powers and influences, were bulwarks against the growth of a centralised, all-controlling, Canberra-based federal government. They were to be strengthened, not denigrated or overpowered. As one anonymous state Liberal party official put it to the British diplomat Martin Reith:

> The Federal Government may come and go; it may be Liberal and a friend one time, it may be Labour [sic] and an enemy the next. We dare not put into the hands of the present Government in Canberra powers that could be used by a Labour Government to bring socialism into the States.[48]

Thus, Gorton's efforts on the offshore legislation exposed fissures that ran through the government and cabinet—and, indeed, through the wider party organisation and membership. By declaring that the Commonwealth possessed powers that were, in large part, assumed to be held by the states, Gorton was forcing his party towards a fundamental reckoning—to choose between the 'horizon' he could see, as Don Chipp put it, and the *status quo*.[49]

McMahon hewed to that *status quo*. In keeping with his long-held beliefs about the necessity for power to be diffused, beliefs that had characterised his election to Parliament in 1949, he did not agree with the continued accrual of power to the federal sphere. In the face of Gorton's push for this power, his preference was for inaction. Gorton's allies saw this position as cowardly, political, calculated to avoid controversy. They did not see the philosophical belief underlying McMahon's position. 'If there was a choice between action and inaction,' said Hughes, 'he [McMahon] was quite often in favour of inaction.' On the question of offshore legislation, Hughes said, McMahon's response was 'to leave it alone'. This never held weight with Gorton or Hughes.

'I believed that the prime task of an attorney-general—I'm talking about myself, as attorney-general—was to explore the limits of Commonwealth power and act within them as established,' said Hughes later. 'Hence, I was entirely in favour of having the High Court determine who owned the territorial sea—[the] Commonwealth or the states?' McMahon's willingness to avoid that determination was simply untenable. 'One had to know who owned the area,' said Hughes. '… It had to be settled.'[50]

Nonetheless, the events of May had left the party's divisions exposed. In June, the Liberal Party's federal council met to discuss a timely internal party report on federalism. Gorton, reckoning with the anger of delegates from Victoria and Western Australia, had to defend his trespasses.[51] 'We need a large and continuing infusion of capital from overseas to sustain our growth,' Gorton said, on the AIDC. 'If this is a departure from Liberal principles, a foray into socialism, [then] so is the TAA [Trans Australia Airlines], the Commonwealth Trading Bank, the Australian National Line, and a myriad of other ventures.' The offshore legislation, meanwhile, 'is intended to discover who has the legal responsibility for control of the seas around Australia, who has the legal right to control areas which are at present in dispute.'[52] The defences were of little use. What Killen later called an 'inexorable gathering of political forces' had been unleashed.[53]

McMahon, observing it all as the deputy leader of the federal parliamentary party, could not have failed to perceive the deep disharmony. It would have been a hint of Gorton's increasingly precarious footing; moreover, for a man as familiar with the Liberal Party as McMahon, it would have been easy to perceive the ways that disharmony could be used to his advantage.[54]

Through his time working with the Policy Research Group and his involvement with the New South Wales party organisation, McMahon possessed an intimate knowledge of the federal Liberal Party machine. From his years as a minister, where he had travelled broadly to campaign for colleagues, he had developed contacts and links that went across the nation. From his years as deputy leader, he knew his parliamentary colleagues, their weaknesses and strengths. From his years as an MP, he knew what it augured within the party membership. Bruce MacCarthy, still prominent within the Young Liberals in Lowe and Sydney, thought McMahon 'was someone who actually listened'. McMahon would regularly telephone MacCarthy, and ask him to come to see him in his office in the Commonwealth Bank Building in Martin Place. They would sit—the minister for external affairs and the 20-year-old MacCarthy. And then McMahon would speak. 'Well, okay, what's going on?' he would say. 'What's happening? What are people saying out there?'[55]

Alongside his attention to the party's base, its networks, and outposts of power, McMahon was sure to keep tabs on the press. 'He accorded a high priority to contacts within the media,' Kim Jones said later. 'He kept in frequent close touch with Press Gallery journalists and senior editorial staff, sometimes on a daily basis.' Of course, it went higher than this. 'He was close to [Sir Frank] Packer,' Jones recalled. 'There was no doubt about that.' The relationship was broad: when McMahon decided he needed a press secretary, he rang Packer for a recommendation. And although Packer had pulled back from outright public opposition to Gorton, Alan Reid was still involved in fomenting unrest.

As well as giving advice to Howson and Fairbairn, Reid was working on a sequel to *The Power Struggle*. His still-unnamed book, largely toiled over at night, was to chronicle the path from Gorton's accession to the rebuke of the 1969 election. Given Reid's connections and propensity to retail gossip and insider information, it promised to be much in the vein of its predecessor, with revelations that could destabilise the government. Meanwhile, in the pages of *Incentive*, Newton was hammering at Gorton with a fervour that was both desperate and angry. Still stinging from the raid upon his offices, he ran regular criticism of the government's handling of the economy and Gorton's policies. The AIDC was 'another nail' in Gorton's coffin, he wrote in June, and treasurer Bury was lacklustre and 'passive' in the face of the problem of inflation.[56] This was an attack that McMahon was happy to echo in private, despite entreaties of confidentiality and discretion.[57] Speaking with Howson repeatedly throughout July, McMahon talked freely about preparations for the upcoming budget, so much so that when Bury delivered it, late in August, Howson saw no reason to change the judgement he had formed in the weeks beforehand.[58]

THROUGHOUT these months, there were issues that rose to prominence, fell away, and swelled again. For the government, the most serious were the continued ructions between Gorton and the state governments, exacerbated now by litigation over the levying of the receipts tax and the pending offshore legislation. For McMahon, there were intermittent questions about the whereabouts of Francis James, the former editor of *The Anglican* who had stood against him in Lowe in the 1966 election on behalf of the Liberal Reform Group. Rumours were rife that James had been arrested on espionage charges after illegally entering mainland China, and Labor and Liberal MPs pressed McMahon about what he was doing to locate James and bring him home.[59] McMahon was also contending with the needles and barbs of Bill Morrison, the new Labor member for St George. A former diplomat with experience in London, Moscow, Washington, Thailand, and Malaysia, Morrison was quick to point out the flaws, inconsistencies, and mistakes of McMahon's conduct of foreign policy.

Then there were the global tides. The June election of Edward Heath's Conservative Party in the United Kingdom, and its decision to retain a token British military presence in the Pacific under the new Five Power Defence Arrangements (with Australia, New Zealand, Malaysia, and Singapore), meant McMahon had simultaneously to welcome the news while making clear that Australia could cope without the British. It was a line he failed to walk convincingly, with some observers remarking of McMahon's public comments that he was still living in the 1950s.[60] Furthermore, even on such important occasions as this, the rivalries of domestic politics were undisguised to international observers.

'Mr Gorton's isolation from his colleagues was clearly brought out,' wrote the British high commissioner in Canberra, Sir Charles Johnston, after the British defence secretary, Lord Carrington, visited Australia for talks on the British presence. 'His Ministers of External Affairs and Defence, Messrs. McMahon and Fraser, although inclined to be jealous and suspicious of each other, were united in the way in which they spoke about him—or rather did not speak about him.' Both men reassured Carrington that any attempt by Gorton to make troops unavailable for use in East Malaysia would be prevented, and urged the British to hold the next Five Power conference anywhere but in Canberra, where Gorton would have to chair sessions. Their reason, they said, was that Gorton had been needlessly provocative by speaking of 'Malaya' at the previous year's conference in Canberra.[61]

When not speaking ill of their prime minister, McMahon and Fraser did ensure that the new Five Power Defence Arrangements were realistic and useful. They successfully pressed for inclusion of 'externally promoted subversion and insurgency' among the causes that would activate the agreement for the countries to consult. As McMahon put it, 'if insurgency were not covered … the commitment would be virtually useless in military terms since insurgency was the only real threat.'[62]

Cambodia continued to occupy much of McMahon's time.[63] Early in July, as fighting in the country continued, McMahon travelled to Saigon to attend the SEATO (Southeast Asia Treaty Organization) conference of foreign ministers, which was set to discuss the crisis. Defending the organisation from charges that it was obsolete and unable to deal with the instability resulting from the upheaval in Cambodia, McMahon attracted both plaudits and ridicule for suggesting that SEATO's worth rested on the promises of a renewed

British presence, the American assurance it would honour its treaty obligations, Thailand's readiness to consider intervening in Cambodia, and the 'spirit of goodwill at the meeting'.[64] Another result of his efforts was the increase in foreign aid to Cambodia. In September, he announced that Cambodia would receive $2m in aid for 1970–71, to be made up of arms, transport, and communications equipment. The purpose of the additional aid was clear: to help Cambodia survive the onslaught and fighting.[65]

This was one part of a bigger victory, but it came laced with its own troubles. After pressing Gorton to increase foreign aid to South Vietnam,[66] McMahon managed to obtain a substantial increase in the overall foreign-aid appropriation in the 1970–71 budget: the $126m set aside for Papua New Guinea represented a 9.8 per cent increase on the previous year's sum, and the $57.8m set aside for other countries was 13.9 per cent higher. Coming in the face of opposition from the Treasury, which had sought to contain the aid appropriation to a 7 per cent rise, the increase was marked and the victory significant, a validation of McMahon and his department, and of their equal ability to argue their corner.[67] But the press reports that publicised this victory gave ample ammunition to Whitlam. While congratulating McMahon's efforts, the Labor leader pointed out that if Papua New Guinea was excluded from consideration, Australia's overseas-aid programme would amount to a miserly 0.2 per cent of gross national product, well short of the 1 per cent ambition recommended in a major report produced under the auspices of the World Bank, which cabinet had itself endorsed.[68] Moreover, as Whitlam pointed out later, McMahon's announcement on Cambodia was a reversal of earlier promises, sustained for the five months since Sihanouk had fallen, *not* to provide military aid. The inconsistency gave Whitlam the opportunity to lambast the government's foreign policy and its inability to extricate itself from the tragedy of Vietnam: 'Cambodia is the proof, as it is the product, of the colossal blunders of Vietnam.'[69]

But McMahon was not present to hear the criticism: he was abroad. Accepting an invitation that the Japanese ambassador had extended in April,[70] McMahon left Australia on 7 September to visit Japan and the United States in a trip as memorable for his conduct as any foreign-policy achievement. In Japan, following a speech on

Australia's aid policy, McMahon staggered Australian officials who were accompanying him by insisting that they join him for a workout in the gym and a Japanese massage. 'They will walk on your back,' he told them. 'This really strengthens your back muscles.' After the massage, he strode back to his hotel wrapped only in a towel.[71]

Things were no less odd when McMahon arrived in the United States ten days later. For although the catalyst of the trip was meetings of the ANZUS Council and UN in New York, McMahon ensured there was room set aside for pleasure. During his time in the US, he was to watch Sir Frank Packer's second attempt to win the America's Cup.

During his quixotic quest, Packer had attracted a large amount of press attention, both at home and abroad, and garnered high-level government support. The Australian embassy had rented a home in Newport for the entirety of September in order to observe the race; had held a costly reception for guests at a Victorian-era chateau; and when shipping delays caused concern that *Gretel II*—the yacht Packer had built to lead the challenge—might miss the challenge, Gorton had intervened to ensure it arrived on time.[72] Documents suggest that Packer might even have attempted, via McMahon, to enjoy further, more explicit, support in the form of a diplomatic passport. But, as Phillip Lynch told McMahon's secretary, following a conversation with Billy Snedden, 'no promise was made concerning a diplomatic passport for "Mr Packer" ... Secondly, in his present position he would have no entitlement for one.'[73]

A plane delay prevented McMahon from arriving in time for the second race of the America's Cup on 17 September, but it was cancelled 'for lack of a dependable breeze' and re-scheduled. Australia's ambassador, Jim Plimsoll, picked McMahon up at Boston airport and, the next day, watched as McMahon and Sonia joined Packer aboard *Pearl Necklace*, Sir Frank's chartered ship, to observe the race.[74] But that, too, was not an ideal day for yachting. Rain and fog led to cancellation of the race after the third mark, and that night McMahon, Sonia, and Kim Jones departed Newport for New York. Sonia returned to Newport the next evening, and was there to see *Gretel II* finally defeat the American-crewed *Intrepid* on 20 September. Her return was lucky—it was the sole victory that *Gretel II* enjoyed in its overall unsuccessful challenge.

McMahon spent four days in New York, meeting with the US

secretary of state, William Rogers, and the British foreign secretary, Sir Alec Douglas-Home.[75] Between calls home to Howson to enquire about domestic politics, he spoke at a luncheon of the American Australian Association and addressed the United Nations General Assembly, where he criticised the UN for its failure to debate the Vietnam War and argued that Asia received far less attention than its due in world deliberations.[76] The next day, on 24 September, he travelled to Washington by train. Plimsoll had arranged a black-tie dinner to be held in McMahon's honour at the ambassador's residence, and invited high-ranking government officials to attend. New Zealand's ambassador, the US undersecretary for political affairs, the director of the Arms Control and Disarmament Agency, the assistant secretary of state for near eastern and south Asian affairs, and the wives of all were in attendance.[77]

The evening ran smoothly until just after the dessert. With guests still sitting at the table, McMahon stood up and left the room. Plimsoll followed to find out where he was going. To McMahon's explanation that he was tired and going to bed, Plimsoll reminded him that the guests were important people who had deliberately come to meet and speak with him. This did not cause McMahon to change his mind. 'Some other time,' he said, and turned to go. Plimsoll had to do what Sonia might normally have done: he grabbed his minister by the back of his coat and prevented him from going any further. 'All right,' cried McMahon, 'I'll stay.'[78]

BY the time McMahon returned to Australia on 5 October, Gorton had decided upon the next test: a half-Senate election would take place on 21 November.[79] With five seats at stake in each of the six states, and two further seats contested in New South Wales and Victoria, thanks to deaths of two senators, it was not to be an election that favoured the government. Nor was it a particularly auspicious time to be out campaigning. A by-election in the Liberal-held seat of Chisholm, in Victoria, to replace the deceased Sir Wilfrid Kent Hughes, augured no great fortune. Quarrels with the states were still making headlines in the press. Bury's 18 August budget had been received with a mix of praise and damnation, the latter focusing particularly on its paltry

50c per week raise in the pension. Whitlam had harnessed the energies and goodwill of a party that believed itself set to make government, and successfully pushed for reform of the intransigent Victorian and New South Wales branches of the ALP, ensuring that they were modernised and integrated to follow the policy platform of the federal party—including, most crucially, support for state aid to independent schools.[80]

The government had its answer to these issues, but persistent protest action had encouraged it to focus on questions of law and order before anything else. Though there was justification for this—protesters had demonstrated outside the home of attorney-general Tom Hughes in August[81]—the situation was overheated, and inflammatory comments, like those of Billy Snedden, who had described the organisers of protests as 'political bikies who pack rape democracy', were not helpful.[82] In October, cabinet retreated from rushing into legislation, but specifically noted that Gorton would continue to discuss law and order issues in the campaign.[83]

The possibility that the Senate election might prompt unrest in the party had to have been a consideration for McMahon. Gossip about it was everywhere. On 13 October, Howson heard, from a third-hand source, that Snedden had suggested the possibility of a 'palace revolution' if the government's vote took a hit.[84]

Where *he* might stand in the event of such a revolution would have occupied some of McMahon's thinking. He would not have been too concerned by Fairbairn: the former minister for national development had garnered much esteem for his resignation and challenge of Gorton, and for his opposition to Gorton within the party room, but Fairbairn had also been damaged by the debate over the offshore legislation. There was also widespread suspicion that Fairbairn's assertive and ambitious wife, Ruth, wielded too much power in their relationship.

McMahon would, however, have had reason to be concerned by the growing regard for Malcolm Fraser. In spite of his youth, the minister for defence was increasingly mentioned as an imminent contender for the leadership. His work in the defence portfolio, dealing with the F-111 and Australia's commitments in Vietnam, had caused his stocks to rise. That his relationship with Gorton had very obviously deteroriated—especially after an episode of civil unrest in Papua New

Guinea—had, remarkably, broadened his appeal, to the point that Howson told Bert Kelly that McMahon and Fraser could well be the leadership team to 'unite the various factions that are all dissatisfied with the present leadership'.[85]

To what extent McMahon was concerned by Fraser's increasing stature is unknown; nonetheless, following McMahon's return from the United States, he and Gorton both concentrated their fire on Fraser during the course of an evening cabinet meeting. At issue was a proposal that Fraser had submitted in May to establish a single academy for the education of officer cadets in all three armed services. The proposal ostensibly enjoyed the support of the ministers for air, the army, and the navy, as well as their respective chiefs of staff. But by the time the matter was finally considered, in October, Gorton had become aware that this support was not necessarily sound; moreover, he questioned whether the proposal would divert resources from officer training. Following his department's advice, McMahon likewise expressed serious reservations about the proposal. Both he and Gorton questioned the stated costs and their efficacy, and in the cabinet meeting on 13 October the weight of their criticism was sufficient to see the proposal set aside. Fraser was told to come back with answers to the questions that they had raised, and the resulting cabinet minute summarily deferred any further discussion of the proposal until he had done so.[86] News of the rebuff quickly made its way into the press, with many observers linking it to leadership tensions and personal rivalries.[87]

Gorton's critics, meanwhile, watched the government's falling popularity with a glee that was tempered by awareness of Labor's potential to post a strong vote at the Senate election. When McMahon discussed a late-October Gallup poll with Howson, he was mindful of the dangers that a poor Senate result could present: 'We could well find ourselves with an election in a year's time,' Howson recorded of their conversation.[88] The up-and-down polling in the weeks leading up to 21 November gave critics like Howson moments of panic. On 12 November, thinking that Gorton might use a good result as a pretext to move against McMahon, Howson asked Alan Reid to speak with Frank Packer about persuading McMahon to stay in the Parliament, even if he was sent to the backbench.[89]

If Gorton had been considering this, the result put the kybosh on any such move. The government had an especially poor showing. Its primary vote fell dramatically, from the 43.4 per cent it had recorded a year before, at the 1969 election, to 38.9 per cent. The DLP, meanwhile, took 11.1 per cent of the vote, and held two seats and won another, for a total of five Senate seats. It was the minor party's best-ever performance, and one of the Liberal Party's worst.[90] Gorton's critics were gloating. 'Overall, it's been a disaster for the government,' wrote Howson.[91]

After campaigning widely himself, McMahon was keen to pin the blame on Gorton. On 22 November, he claimed to have urged Gorton to 'unite the factions in the party' and that 'big changes' were necessary if the government was to win another term in office.[92] Five days later, he was telling Howson that the cabinet's discussion of the campaign had been little more than a 'mass of sycophantic adulation of Gorton', with no one—not even McMahon, it would seem—prepared to tell the prime minister that he alone should supposedly bear the brunt of the criticism.[93]

If there had been any abatement of the tension between McMahon and Gorton, it was short-lived. Four days before the Senate election—that is, 17 November—the British prime minister, Edward Heath, had confirmed that the British government would resume arms sales to South Africa, in accordance with an agreement it had struck for use of a naval base at Simonstown. Opposition to resumption of sales immediately materialised in the form of the presidents of Zambia, Tanzania, and Uganda. In Australia, the Department of Foreign Affairs, as External Affairs was now known, prepared advice that Gorton and McMahon should express opposition to the arms sales at the next Commonwealth Heads of Government meeting to be held in Singapore in January. McMahon was receptive to the advice, but Gorton was not. Long a sceptic of the Commonwealth, he believed that it was not its business to tell another government what to do.[94] The argument was uneasily echoed within the prime minister's office and public service, all of whom could anticipate the line that the prime minister of Lesotho, among others, would model in two month's time in Singapore: while the British government might well have the right to make its own decisions on what it saw as a matter that affected British interests, the decision to sell arms was also 'an unprincipled act in support of South Africa and its *apartheid* policy'.[95]

There were other issues to be dealt with. Late in October, before the Senate election, John McEwen finally confirmed what had long been rumoured: that he would retire early in 1971. Now aged seventy, with thirty-six years in politics behind him, McEwen invoked the Roman senator Cincinnatus to declare that he would return to his humble Sabine farm.[96] Colleagues lauded his contributions to Australia's prosperity, particularly his advocacy for the trade treaty he had forged with Japan in 1957, and they noted his personal stature and convictions. But McEwen was not yet a spent force, and in the short time left before his departure, the aged Country Party leader set himself for one last battle—on tariffs.

Concerned by the Tariff Board's adoption of new principles for its decisions on tariff-making; worried by the confirmation, via a legal opinion, that the board could carry out reviews without government approval or references; and determined both to stop these and ensure continuation of the tariff policies he had spent the entirety of his career advocating, McEwen worked in secret to devise a cabinet submission that would all but eviscerate the Tariff Board as it existed under Alf Rattigan.[97]

The submission declared that the Tariff Board as it operated was not appropriate: the board, McEwen argued, was playing 'the role of an economic planning agency with the task of allocating resources within the economy', and was putting at risk investments totalling over $3,000m and the employment of 600,000 people. To prevent it doing so, McEwen's submission recommended that the government prepare a set of guidelines that the Tariff Board would be required to follow at all times when it considered tariff reviews. Those guidelines would include requirements that the board compare the cost of production in an Australian industry with the cost of production in another country of similar living standards—that is, a Western country—and that the board recommend levels of protection whereby the industry would be 'secure against damage from import competition'. Notably, the submission also proposed that the Tariff Board rely for information and expertise on the Departments of Trade and Industry, Customs and Excise, and Labour and National Service.[98]

But when the submission came up on 15 December, cabinet

unexpectedly decided to postpone its consideration. McEwen would have been surprised: his office had intimated to journalists that a statement on the Tariff Board would be issued that day after the cabinet meeting.[99] In the new time between the submission's circulation and its consideration, McEwen's opponents went to work. A copy was given to economics journalist Kenneth Davidson, of *The Australian*, who understood the landscape of tariff debates, the politics of that debate, and the likely effects of McEwen's proposal, should it be approved. Whoever leaked it knew what they were doing. Calling the submission one of the 'crudest economic arguments' he had ever seen, Davidson published a story on it on 18 December, and suggested that the public exposure meant the submission's chances of receiving approval were slim.[100]

The outcry that greeted news of McEwen's submission was loud. Financial journalists were scathing about the proposals, and industry groups mobilised to defend the Tariff Board. During the Christmas holidays and into January 1971, opponents and critics worked to see it defeated. The president of the Associated Chambers of Commerce said it was 'gravely concerned' at the threat to the Tariff Board's independence, and, like Bert Kelly, pressed cabinet to knock back the proposal.[101] McEwen's own statements raised the stakes. Arguing that 1.6 million people depended on the income of the 600,000 workers who would supposedly be affected by the Tariff Board, he dismissed criticism that his approach was hamfisted and inappropriate. 'To put under question, or in jeopardy, the livelihood of more than one fifth of the Australian population is certainly not a matter to be left light-heartedly to the Tariff Board.'[102]

'There is something almost heroic in the posture of that grand old warrior, Sir John McEwen, rising on the eve of his retirement to strike out against the Tariff Board,' *The Age* editorialised, on 26 January. But, however admiring it might have sounded, McEwen was, to many, completely in the wrong: 'His struggle to subdue the Tariff Board looks like being Sir John McEwen's last great battle. Sadly he deserves to lose it.'[103]

Duly, he did. When cabinet considered the matter on 27 January, it decided that there would be a 'progressive review' of tariffs, as McEwen had recommended—but the question of criteria and guidelines would be 'the subject of further examination' by the government. When would that occur? The cabinet decision did not say.[104] McEwen left the cabinet meeting 'visibly upset'. The circumstances of the defeat were humiliating. Undoubtedly, publication of the submission was the cause of the opprobrium and outcry; without it, as one journalist suggested, cabinet would likely have approved it without rancour. Who leaked it, then? 'The material came from the enemies of McEwen and McEwenism and they were myriad in the government,' Davidson said later. 'You can be fairly sure they came from the Liberal side of politics … It was somebody who was highly placed in the government.'[105]

Nine days later, McEwen tendered his resignation as deputy prime minister, as minister for trade and industry, as leader of the Country Party, and as the member for Murray. Farewelling him, the press could not help but note that his time was over. 'A great many of the things he held to be natural truths have come to be questioned with increasing frequency and growing effect,' wrote one journalist.[106] Colleagues thought his views were outdated. Hearing that cabinet had 'knocked out' McEwen's 'final flutter to hobble the Tariff Board' and that he was now soon to be gone, Bert Kelly was simply and completely relieved. 'If only he had been thoroughly done a long while ago by more courageous Prime Ministers or Cabinets, Australia would have been a lot better off.'[107]

ENSURING that *he* was better off had also motivated McMahon to restructure the Department of External Affairs, a process that culminated as 1970 ended. The afflictions Tange had diagnosed in 1969 had been largely confirmed in a subsequent departmental review, and since then McMahon had begun looking for ways to address them. He had made his views well known throughout 1970: since January, the journalist Bruce Juddery had been writing of McMahon's preference that the department be restructured to include a policy planning group that could study options for Australian foreign policy.[108]

On 6 April 1970, barely days after Waller commenced his tenure as secretary, McMahon wrote to him to outline the deficiencies of the department as he saw them.[109] Noting that his experience indicated that 'the lack of co-ordination is little short of alarming,' he told Waller that a deputy secretary who could co-ordinate the policy of the department's various divisions needed to be appointed. Next, he argued that there was clear need for two deputy secretaries: the first, with responsibilities for policy; the second, to oversee administration, defence, consular relations, aid, and other matters. The functions of the department needed to be allocated among the department's divisions 'on a more logical basis'. A 'critically important' matter was on policy itself. 'I have been informed that former Ministers have taken the view that it is not the function of officers to initiate policy or policy changes,' McMahon wrote. 'I do not agree with this. They have every right to do so and should be encouraged.'[110]

Moreover, cross that there had been no more than 'one or two occasions' when he had been advised to make a statement on television or the radio, McMahon told Waller that he wanted 'a different approach to public relations'. He wanted first assistant secretaries to discuss important matters with him, in person or over the telephone, rather than by minutes and memos. He wanted co-operation and goodwill with other departments—without, of course, 'subordinating the Department to the whims of others'—and he wanted the amount of administrative work that crossed his desk to be reduced. Some of these echoed recommendations that Waller had already made, in March; nonetheless, they soon saw results.

Late in April, at Waller's instigation, longtime diplomat K.C.O. 'Mick' Shann was promoted to deputy secretary, succeeding Jim McIntyre, who in turn was appointed Australia's permanent representative to the United Nations.[111] Promotions for sixty-three diplomats followed and, early in September, McMahon took to cabinet a proposal to rename the Department of External Affairs. Arguing that the name was anachronistic and, among other foreign ministers, unusual, McMahon sought to change it to the Department of Foreign Affairs. Some thought this Waller's idea, but McMahon had expressed his desire for the change as far back as June, when he called himself the minister for foreign affairs during a meeting of the federal council of the Liberal Party.[112] Kim Jones attributed the change entirely to McMahon. 'The name change was McMahon's initiative,' he said later. 'As he [McMahon] travelled, he saw that other ministers around the world were called ministers for foreign affairs, and he was minister for external affairs. He wanted the name to be the same.'[113] Gorton had no problem agreeing. 'Billy will be the head of the department of F.A.—fuck all,' he quipped.[114] Cabinet approved the change on 3 September, though it held off announcing the news until November.[115]

In Waller, McMahon had found someone who knew how to manage and administer. Waller could see the need for change within the department, and drove those changes while being careful to give McMahon the public credit he desired and loved.[116] On 20 December, after approval from the Public Service Board, McMahon announced a restructure of the Department of Foreign Affairs. 'I have been keenly aware since taking office of the need for a radical reorganisation of the Department of Foreign Affairs,' he said. The department's four divisions were to become seven, and renamed with their titular responsibilities. A second deputy secretary's position was established, as was a policy-research branch containing planning and liaison units. The first would 'prepare policy papers and proposals on any area or situation of current or potential interest,' according to McMahon, 'thus ensuring that a programme of forward thinking and planning is constantly in progress, and will act as a sort of "fire brigade" unit which can be injected into any part of the department which is dealing with a matter of major concern at any given moment.'[117] The Post Liaison Unit, meanwhile, to be headed by the diplomat Richard Woolcott, was intended to involve overseas-based departmental officers in the process of policy formulation—to make them 'feel less "out of sight, out of mind",' as Woolcott later put it.[118] Both were innovative moves, and, for McMahon, they were proof of his good work as minister. Alongside recent expansions to Australia's foreign-aid programme, he was winning plaudits for his handling of the portfolio.[119]

But there were still more issues to deal with, more changes to be made. Since returning from the United States, Waller had been pressing for reconsideration of Australia's policy towards the communist-governed Peoples' Republic of China (PRC). It was, he said later, 'the first thing' he wanted to do.[120] Apart from matters of trade, Australia had followed America's lead, and had recognised only the Nationalist-governed Republic of China (ROC), based in Taiwan. Notwithstanding that any prospect of the Nationalists returning to mainland China had long been extinguished, the fiction that it was the legitimate and sole government of China had been furiously maintained, aided and abetted by heated rhetoric—usually from Liberal or Country party members and senators—about the PRC's subversive actions in Vietnam and its international recklessness. For its part, the United States refused to allow any possibility that the Chinese communists might replace the ROC in the United Nations, which led it to using a series of procedural motions in the General Assembly to obstruct moves to the contrary.

Nonetheless, by 1970, the stalemate that had characterised international relations with the PRC—which in turn refused to countenance diplomatic relations with any country that recognised the ROC—was beginning to give way. The Cultural Revolution was drawing to a close. Amid tensions with Russia, the PRC was showing signs of engagement with other countries. Nations across the globe, including respectable allies such as Canada and Italy, were recognising the PRC and establishing diplomatic relations with it.

Within the Department of External Affairs, there had been disquiet about Australia's seemingly frozen position for some time. In March 1969, Australia's ambassador to Taiwan, Frank Cooper, had written of his belief that Australian policy on China appeared to be too much in thrall to America. Moreover, since that US policy represented probably 'the biggest blunder the Americans have ever made', Australia needed to do 'its own thinking on China'. Cooper had enclosed a prescient warning with this letter:

> In any event, one of the lessons of Vietnam is surely that we cannot assume that the Americans will always consult us if and when they decide that the time has come to attempt to settle the China problem.[121]

But the department's deputy secretary, Jim McIntyre, dismissed the warning, writing that it was 'irrelevant' if America's policy on China represented a monumental blunder. 'The policy exists. It sets the framework in which we have to operate.'[122] Nonetheless, there were continued attempts by diplomats to prompt a reconsideration of the government's policy, particularly as signs emerged of a change in America's policy. In October 1970, Waller received cables from Plimsoll, in the US, from the new ambassador to Taiwan, and from the acting first assistant secretary, all of which noted that recognition of the

PRC by Canada, Italy, and Belgium were sure to prompt uncertainty about Australia's policy—and cause problems.[123] Another letter, from Australia's ambassador in Paris, Alan Renouf, argued that Waller should know that 'if and as the pace of recognition increases, Australia should re-consider its own position'.[124] To this, Waller was straightforward: he was aware of the 'China problem', and had been working on it. 'The time before the Senate elections is hardly a propitious one for directing Ministers' attention to this problem,' he went on. 'But come December, we shall try to get things moving.'[125] He knew that there had to be some urgency: 'By the end of 1970,' Waller wrote later, 'it was quite apparent that this strategy [to prevent the PRC's admission to the UN General Assembly] would no longer work; the numbers simply weren't there, it was patently a device, no one could pretend to regard it as a sincere argument, and something new would have to be done.'[126]

McMahon was already aware that China was a political issue. In October, he had received notices from various committees and groups within the Liberal Party membership supporting recognition of the PRC.[127] In the September and October parliamentary sessions, Labor had questioned the government over the lucrative and long-running export of wheat, iron, and steel to the PRC, asking why it continued despite a US-led trade embargo. Labor also pressed the government over its refusal to recognise the PRC amid the tide of other countries that were moving in the opposite direction. McMahon's answers were an echo of his comments from the 1950s. Nothing, for him, seemed to have changed. He was anxious, still, to speak of the PRC as a looming and aggressive exporter of violence and communism:

> Our position is clear. We do not necessarily follow what other governments do. We have stated ... that of course we would like Red China to be in the United Nations provided only that it accepted the Declaration of Human Rights and abided by it and provided it was willing to abide by the principles of the Charter itself. The condition would be that Red China renounced the use of violence and force in an attempt to ensure its political objectives. Secondly, we have stated that if Red China does live up to its obligations we would be prepared to reconsider our position.[128]

Late in October, undeterred by comments such as these, the department sought direction from McMahon on a study of Australia's options regarding the 'China issue'. The preparatory paper specifically pointed out that cabinet had not formally considered diplomatic and political policy for China since 1958, and that public opinion within Australia was shifting markedly. To this request, McMahon was guarded, cautious about change, and unwilling to confront the need for urgency. To the note that Australia's policy had always been based on the needs of the US alliance in the short term and that US policy was 'changing', McMahon made clear that he had no desire to pre-empt or get in front of a shift in US policy:

> We must proceed on the basis that we review all the circumstances in order to decide what action should be taken in our best interests—no change may be needed and there may be variations between the extremes.

To the suggestion that Australia might encourage the 'emergence' of a 'two China solution'—that is, simultaneous recognition of the Taiwanese Republic of China and the Communist Peoples' Republic of China—McMahon was swift in his appraisal of its connotations. 'This savours too much of the Plimsoll/Freeth statement,' he wrote in the margins. 'It is politically unwise and I doubt if we could "facilitate the emergence". Handle this with sensitivity.'[129]

In December, as McIntyre wrote from the UN to concede that it would not be viable to continue to obstruct the PRC in the next year's sessions of the General Assembly, and as the press reported rumours of a reappraisal of Australia's China policy,[130] the Department of Foreign Affairs' Policy Planning Group sent McMahon a long, detailed, and fleshed-out draft policy paper. This time, urgency was emphasised. The acceptability of the PRC both domestically and world-wide; the absence of any Australian review of its policy since 1958; the definite beginning of a US shift in its relationship with the PRC; and—importantly—a potential breakdown in Australia's 'traditional trading patterns' meant that there was 'now an urgent need to review our policy towards China'. The submission bluntly echoed Cooper's warning from two years before:

[T]he United States, as a super power, will tend to move at its own pace, and that pace will largely be dictated by the desire on the part of Washington and Peking to achieve some accommodation of interests … Australia should clearly make every effort, first, to discover the guidelines of American assumptions and, second, and no less important, to impress our own fundamental interest upon the United States, before the latter commits itself to any particular course of action.[131]

McMahon's response to the paper was again circumspect, and betrayed his ideological blinkers. Stating that his changes were of 'crucial *political* importance', he redrafted a paragraph on Australia's aims to include a caveat that a relationship with the PRC hinged on its willingness to live up to the obligations of the UN Charter. He recast another paragraph to state that Australia needed to discuss the inevitability of recognition of the PRC with the US—not, as the draft had it, that recognition of the PRC was Australia's 'ultimate objective' and that it was in Australia's national interest to exchange diplomatic recognition with the PRC before its entry into the UN.

The comments that he sent to the department's deputy secretary, Mick Shann, revealed McMahon's view of the China problem. To him, time was hardly pressing: 'There is no desperate urgency,' he wrote, 'and I do not think a submission could be dealt with by Cabinet before February.' He believed that a submission that was as direct and blunt as this would be counter-productive: 'I do not want the impression to be created that I am trying to ram the Department's views down Cabinet's neck. A persuasive approach is, I think, better.' Finally, there was the transparent political calculation: 'Remember please that we have a DLP—and that its reaction must be considered!' More than a little hint of fear was conveyed in his postscript decision to attach to his comments a series of press cuttings 'which reflect the DLP views'. Variously noting the government's political reliance on the DLP, and the DLP's preoccupation with defence matters and foreign policy, those cuttings were further confirmation of what had motivated McMahon all year: the desire to avoid the kind of outcry that had seen Gordon Freeth lose office and the DLP win further seats in the Senate.[132]

According to Kim Jones, however, McMahon had not always been so mindful of the DLP when considering diplomatic recognition of

China. 'It was clear that McMahon was in favour of it,' he said later. 'Serious work on a proposal was done, and then stopped, put on hold.' The turning point, Jones recalled, came when three men in dark suits arrived in McMahon's office for a meeting. Not informed of the meeting, Jones did not know who they were. It was only afterward, when momentum on the issue of recognition stopped, that Jones understood: the three men were from the DLP.[133] Waller agreed that McMahon was very conscious of the DLP. 'They had a hypnotic influence on him,' he said later. Moreover, McMahon was aware of the need to engage with China. He told Waller much later that he should have taken the chance and recognised China. 'He knew this was the logical thing to do.'[134]

THE tension with Gorton persisted. In January 1971, following the good press that had greeted McMahon's reorganisation of the Department of Foreign Affairs, Gorton wrote him a cutting letter: 'The manner in which the press recently described your Department's reorganisation suggested to the uninformed reader a major expansion of staff ... It is, of course, inappropriate for this belief to be fostered in the community in the circumstances which the government now faces following the recent wage increases in the private and public sectors of the economy.' To this rebuke McMahon was perplexed: 'I think the reports did a lot of good for the Government,' he told his staff. 'Unless it is nitpicking again I can't understand it.'[135]

On 12 January, when McMahon and Gorton left Australia for the Commonwealth Heads of Government Meeting (CHOGM) in Singapore—leading a large delegation that included Sir Keith Waller, newly created knight Sir Lenox Hewitt, Sir Alexander Downer, and Nicholas Parkinson (respectively Australia's high commissioners to London and Singapore)—they travelled on separate planes. McMahon took a scheduled Qantas flight and Gorton a VIP aircraft that was not filled to capacity. Staying at the same hotel in Singapore, they took rooms on separate floors. It was a point that Alan Reid saw fit to make much of. 'McMahon,' he wrote of this, 'was treated in a humiliating fashion'.[136]

Gorton's return from Singapore was not a happy one. Amid a spike in inflation, he had to front the Liberal party room on 2 February to discuss the Senate election results. McMahon would have been aware that the anti-Gorton MPs had arrived at that meeting well prepared. Howson had been meeting with dissidents like Harry Turner, David Fairbairn, and Jeff Bate. The discontent and its causes had been well traversed.[137]

The meeting was predictably heated. When Fairbairn, Turner, and Jess criticised the campaign and Gorton's performance, Gorton answered them himself. He was more than willing to confront his critics. Howson, appraising it from the safe view of a chair, thought Gorton was using the meeting to establish his authority over the party.[138] Undoubtedly, Gorton was. Perhaps no moment showed this better—and, by corollary, the weakness of the anti-Gorton forces—than when Queensland senator Ian Wood rose to speak.

A travel agent who had gravitated to conservative politics for what he belived was its better policies for the poor, a 'forty-niner' who had entered federal politics out of horror at Labor's attempts to nationalise the banks, and an instinctively independent character undeterred by threats who would, in the course of his Senate career, cross the floor on 130 occasions, Wood was deeply concerned by the government's performance at the half-Senate election. For weeks, too, he had heard colleagues talk about how something had to be done—how some move had to be made to force the issue of leadership. Standing up, he took it upon himself to do so.

He told the party room that Gorton was the issue. With Gorton as leader, the Liberal Party would lose the next election. That could not happen. The party needed a new leader. Gorton had enjoyed three years in the position and had been found wanting. He should resign, Wood said.

Gorton was cool. 'Would you like to move that as a motion?'

'Yes, I would,' Wood replied.

Gorton looked around the room. 'Is there a seconder?'

Silence followed. No one rose to support Wood. No one spoke up to second the motion. All those who had spoken so heatedly about Gorton's flaws and failings had suddenly lost their voices. There was, Wood said later, an embarrassed quiet. 'It was a warm, sunny day in Canberra,' he recalled, 'and when I looked around all the snowmen had melted in the summer warmth, and they weren't there to support me.'[139]

After a tense second or two, Gorton moved on, and called for another speaker.

Watching that day in the party room, McMahon could not have failed to perceive that, even with all the obstacles ranged against him, Gorton was a formidable man, able to lead, willing to fight. Again, the prime minister had forced his critics to the precipice—and seen them pull back. He had shown nerve, courage, discipline.

Should McMahon ever wish to become prime minister, at some point, he would have to reckon with that.

CHAPTER THIRTY-TWO

A Transient Phantom?

1984

What could McMahon say about his time in the foreign affairs portfolio? What legacy could he say he left? From the vantage point of retirement, his short time in Foreign Affairs—just sixteen months—seemed an interregnum that was barely relevant, quickly forgotten. Certainly, McMahon had been no Percy Spender, devising the Colombo Plan and negotiating the ANZUS Treaty, all within a sixteen-month tenure. Was he, as one historian would later suggest, a transient and embarrassed phantom?[1]

In the view of officials within the Department of Foreign Affairs, this description was perfectly apt. To many of them, he had been a meandering disaster as minister. Their assessments, to be expressed in oral histories and memoirs, were unvarnished by diplomatic niceties. Their opinions were harsh.

Plimsoll had been blunt. McMahon was one of the weakest foreign ministers he had worked with.[2] Jim McIntyre, who had worked with McMahon for only a few months, was simply scathing. 'Bill McMahon,' he said later, '… I'm afraid, brought me no joy. I have to say quite frankly that, in my view, Bill McMahon is really just a rather vain and silly little man, not notable for integrity or truthfulness, I would say … He was really out of his depth in foreign affairs.'[3] Philip Flood, who would years later become secretary of the department, made a similar assessment. He found McMahon an uninspiring minister, thought him difficult to respect, and believed that McMahon enjoyed the apppearance of credibility only by the hard work and graft of others.

Equally offensive was McMahon's proclivity to preen himself, to meddle, and to manipulate. 'He also spent an inordinate amount of time cultivating journalists,' Flood wrote later. 'His tenure as minister seemed to be one continuous press conference.'[4] Certainly, there were moves, like his attempts to pursue a new policy with Japan, where McMahon seemed to chase a headline more than follow-through.[5] Others in the department were dismissive. McMahon was the stupidest foreign minister Australia had ever had, said one; he was ambitious and unscrupulous, said another; one more said that McMahon was the least effective, least interested, and least intelligent foreign minister he had ever served under.[6]

Waller was torn. He thought McMahon had an unusual memory: notoriously fallible with names, but astoundingly good with 'unlikely' bits of information. McMahon was a hard worker, if somewhat illogical in his methods: 'He dealt with it entirely as the spirit moved him.' McMahon's tenacity in cabinet was without equal, but he could be utterly unpredictable sometimes, to the point that the department had a special writing pad printed to record conversations with him. 'As soon as the telephone rang and [you realised] Billy was on it,' Waller recalled, 'you grabbed your pad and started writing furiously in the hope that you could make some sense out of what he was saying. I got through a pad every couple of days.' McMahon had perceived Plimsoll's failings, Waller noted, and he was useful with the entertaining that accompanied diplomatic life. McMahon was indiscreet, often did not know as much about a subject as he thought he did, and was 'desperately afraid of the DLP'. In sum, according to Waller, McMahon was 85 to 90 per cent good.[7]

McMahon hardly viewed his period as foreign minister in the same way as his critics. To judge by the length of the draft he compiled on it, it seemed that he accorded it much value. At some 18,700 words, the chapter on his time in that position was the longest of any in the manuscript that Bowman worked on—longer, even, than the chapter on McMahon's time as prime minister.

Some of it was misplaced material. McMahon had included lengthy digressions into his experience as minister for the navy and air, apparently arguing that this had given him an apprenticeship that was integral to his success in the foreign ministry. It left Bowman unconvinced. 'This really doesn't belong here,' he scrawled in his notes, and made plans to cut it.

But there was justification for writing at such length about his time as minister for foreign affairs. Despite the abbreviated time he had spent in the portfolio, McMahon *had* some worthy achievements to highlight: cabinet's acceptance of the proposal to join the OECD; the signing of the Nuclear Non-Proliferation Treaty; the better tenor of regional relationships following the Djakarta Treaty;[8] the broadened relationship with Japan; the expansion of Australia's aid programme; and the name change of the department, and the reorganisation that Waller and Shann, with his support, had driven.[9] None of these was insignificant. What they showed was that, as Kim Jones later noted, McMahon's initial antipathy to the portfolio had dissipated and he had become interested in it, even enjoyed it. The role gave McMahon 'a world stage to tread', Jones believed. Moreover, his status as a high-ranking, long-serving minister gave him great clout within the government. 'McMahon was very experienced in getting what he wanted,' Jones said later. 'He was relentless in cabinet, and he could win issues for the department. He won often, even though he had no background in foreign affairs.' That lack of background made those successes all the more notable. 'I believe he did make a substantive contribution on some issues.'[10]

Journalists who were normally critical could see this, too. Bruce Juddery, who had written closely about McMahon in his time at the department, was positive, if careful to note the important support role played by the department during McMahon's time. 'The main result of the McMahon years as Minister for Foreign Affairs ... was a rapid growth in the Department's influence, and the use of that influence particularly to demonstrate to the Government and the country that the world had changed.'[11]

There were inevitably failures: on Vietnam, McMahon had been able to do little, despite the clear and unambiguous evidence that the US was withdrawing and that Australian public opinion was virulently turning against it. On Cambodia, he had failed, along with many others, to find a workable solution to the turmoil and fighting going on there. And on China—an issue of extreme importance, to his embarrassment—he had failed in every sense of the word.

Even beyond a tally of successes and failures, McMahon's discussion of his time as minister for foreign affairs was important because it had a direct bearing on how he had conducted and, indeed, controlled, foreign policy while prime minister: his voice had certainly spoken louder than his two foreign ministers.[12] As Alan Renouf had remarked, Australian prime ministers tended to assume that they were particularly skilled in the field of foreign relations, and approached it with confidence. 'Menzies, Holt, Gorton, and McMahon so assumed,' wrote Renouf, 'each wrongly.'[13] McMahon was unlikely to agree. And he was not without grounds for argument: had he not voiced prescient concerns about Menzies' involvement in the Suez crisis in 1956? Had he not also identified the lack of an American strategy in Vietnam, when the first commitment of Australian troops was considered in 1965?[14] An explanation of what he had confronted as minister for foreign affairs; what he had tried to do and why; where he had failed and succeeded; what he had learned—all these were integral to the understanding McMahon was seeking to find by writing his book.

But again, as with so much else, the task seemed beyond him. When Bowman read this long, disjointed chapter, he found it disconcerting to read. The overview of foreign affairs that opened the chapter was poor. The effort to discuss Vietnam was 'no good'. The passages on the Djakarta conference were particularly bad: 'Doubtful if any of this is worth using,' Bowman wrote. A section on Japan was potentially salvageable, but even here there were 'obscure' passages that were just 'incomprehensible.' The only highlight, it seemed, was the 6,000-word section that McMahon had devoted to discussing China:

OK in parts. Note confusion between PRC and ROC. Good outline of cabinet submission of 9/2/71 on recognition of China (PRC). Q: When did Whitlam make his trip??—and McM his ill-timed criticism?[15]

How to pull the chapter together? How to explain and understand all that had happened?

CHAPTER THIRTY-THREE

A Natural Development

1971

McEwen's retirement necessitated another trip to Government House for John Gorton. He watched Paul Hasluck swear in the four Country Party ministers—Doug Anthony, Ian Sinclair, Peter Nixon, and Ralph Hunt—to their new portfolios. Anthony, the new leader of the Country Party, stepped into McEwen's shoes as deputy prime minister and minister for trade and industry; Sinclair took over as minister for primary industry; Nixon was sworn in as minister for shipping and transport; and Hunt became minister for the interior. It was a decisive shift in the leadership of the Country Party, from a generation that had witnessed Depression and then war to one that had known mostly peace and prosperity. It was, in its own way, comparable to the Liberal Party's transition from Menzies to Holt six years before.[1]

As in that case, the Country Party's new leader was well prepared for his new responsibilities. Still only in his early forties, Anthony had had thirteen years' experience in Parliament, and could count, thanks to his father—who had served as member for Richmond until 1957 and been postmaster-general from 1949 to 1957—a lifetime's immersion in politics. Blonde, bluff, and plain speaking, Anthony shared McEwen's toughness, pride in the strength of Australia's rural areas, and, just as crucially, his independence.

That independence had led him to differ from McEwen in several respects: Anthony had not supported the creation of the Industry Development Corporation and, while he shared McEwen's dislike of McMahon, had not agreed with the decision to rescind the veto. Despite this, Anthony knew there was no question it could be brought

366

back. 'I had no thought about reinstating a veto against McMahon,' he said later. 'I was a very new leader, and that sort of action would only lead to destabilisation and disaster.'[2]

But Anthony also knew that these could occur without his intervening: should the anti-Gorton forces move to spark a confrontation, Gorton could very well find himself facing a second challenge. And there were tests ahead that would help to bring on such a challenge.

One such test was a special conference of the state premiers. Called in the wake of the national wage case, which had resulted in a 6 per cent rise in the basic wage, the state premiers had come to Canberra in that first week of February crying poor. Led by the redoubtable Henry Bolte and Bob Askin, they argued that their states would incur substantial budgetary deficits without some form of Commonwealth assistance. Again, they insisted that the states be allowed to re-enter the income tax field. Gorton refused to offer any kind of leeway or money, instead urging the state premiers to cut expenditure, just as the Commonwealth had done. None of the premiers departed Canberra happy.

A little mollified by Gorton's agreement to provide funds for flood relief, Askin, facing an election in less than two weeks' time, was notably angered by the refusal of help. It was a 'very disappointing' conference, he said publicly, and insisted that in April he would return to argue again for the introduction of a state-levied income tax. 'This is the only permanent answer, and we will always be in this position if something like a growth tax is not introduced,' he said.[3] *The Sydney Morning Herald* was hardly restrained: 'Mr Askin is entitled to feel that he has been badly, almost unforgiveably, let down by the federal parliamentary leader of his own party, and even by the party itself,' it editorialised shortly afterward.[4]

Sir David Brand, the Liberal Party premier of Western Australia, was more reserved in his response, unwilling to draw too much attention in light of his own election, due for late February. When McMahon spoke to Howson the next day, he could easily see the politics at play. 'He feels that this could well lead to our losing the state election in Western Australia,' Howson recorded, 'though probably not in New South Wales.'[5] As it happened, McMahon was proved right: in Western Australia, Labor turned out the twelve-year-old Liberal-Country Party government and, in New South Wales, Askin managed to eke out a victory that owed nothing to Gorton and everything to Askin's own ingenuity and hard campaigning.

Barely a few days later, there was another test, another opportunity. Gorton's fights with the Australian Medical Association had been going on for a year, ever since he had unveiled his plan to reform the health care system. Again, McMahon was calling Howson with the inside story: 'Bill says Gorton is likely to antagonise the doctors, the business community, and the Premiers. My own feeling is that it would be good for him to antagonise as many people as possible, as the quicker we can precipitate these matters the better.'[6]

There was still the issue of China to consider. On 4 February—the day before the swearing-in of the new Country Party ministers—McMahon wrote to Gorton to broach the issue of Australia's relationship with the PRC. He pointed out that policy towards the country was now adversely affecting Australia's trading position. With a record harvest and anger over Freeth's comments about the morality of trading with communists, the PRC had decided not to renew a contract with the Australian Wheat Board for the import of some two million tonnes of Australian wheat. That decision, of some harm to Australian exporters, underlined McMahon's letter. 'As you know, the great bulk of our exports [to the PRC] consists of wheat and wool, which, though of only marginal significance to the Chinese economy, are a valuable source of foreign exchange to us,' he wrote, adding that that market could grow or diminish should Australia not be wary. Noting, too, that Australia and the United States were now the only countries that had a policy of treating the PRC differently from other communist countries, and thus refrained from exporting a range of materials, McMahon argued that Australia's policy was 'highly anomalous and may be imposing unnecessary hardships on Australian exporters for little purpose'. Looking towards the future, McMahon wrote that he saw a need to be flexible and responsive to change, but that—crucially, for him—trade policy had to be 'subsidiary to our actions in the domestic and international political sphere with regard to China'.

No action on the economic problems, McMahon finished, should 'anticipate our consideration of the whole problem' of China.[7] Five days after this letter, he circulated a long, detailed cabinet submission calling for a review of Australia's policy.

Emphasising that the PRC was soon likely to win admission to the UN, and that Australian policy could be thrown into disarray by the ROC being excluded from the world body, McMahon argued that there was also an economic consideration to the problem. While Australia's trade with the PRC had been previously unrelated to the question of diplomatic relations, recent events suggested that the PRC was ready to exploit the leverage that better trading opportunities might give it. 'Our immediate concern is therefore basically twofold,' he wrote. Australia should consider

> whether and at what pace we should introduce changes of substance in our policy toward the PRC, including the timing of recognition, and at the same time, whether and how to contribute to the continued existence of Taiwan as a separate entity, so long as it desires, and its right to remain a member of the United Nations.

He recommended that Australia begin consultations with the US, Japan, the ROC, and New Zealand in order to inform Australian decisions better; that the government make it known publicly that it had an interest in normalising bilateral relations with the PRC; and that ministers should, henceforth, refrain from 'hostile references to the PRC' and 'excessively warm or laudatory references to the ROC'.[8]

These recommendations were but a stopgap. McMahon was still not moving to broaden Australia's relationship with China beyond trade. Nor was he moving to countenance change beyond the lead of the United States. Diplomatic recognition was not in the offing. It was a failure of the department that McMahon headed—a department that was without China specialists to enhance its understanding and knowledge.[9] It was a failure of McMahon's, personally and politically—one that arose from a fear of change and a fear of the DLP, which on 17 February had reaffirmed its blanket opposition to any recognition of the PRC.[10] And when cabinet considered the submission on 23 February, McMahon's colleagues came to share in that failure.

McEwen's absence was sorely felt that day. Early in the 1960s, he had overseen the growth of Australia's trading relationship with the PRC, as it bought ever-increasing amounts of Australia's wheat exports—from the one-half of Australia's wheat exports that the PRC purchased in 1962–63, to the one-third of Australia's *total* wheat production it was purchasing by 1969–70. Moreover, as minister for trade and industry, McEwen had overcome significant internal opposition and the risk of arousing public opprobrium to negotiate a trade treaty with Japan in the 1950s. While there is little to suggest his own position on China was any different from McMahon's or Gorton's in 1971, McEwen had both the stature and the vision to perceive what might have been possible.[11] The delay that McMahon had urged in December—his comment that cabinet could not consider policy on China before February—had the effect of removing the possibility that McEwen might move the discussion beyond the myopic and fearful eyes with which McMahon saw matters.

Cabinet accepted McMahon's submission. It acknowledged that the PRC would soon likely enter the UN and take the permanent seat assigned to China on the Security Council. It accepted that this would call for a reappraisal of Australia's policy on China. But, as had been the case for so long, cabinet agreed that Australian policy had to follow the United States'.[12]

'A new power struggle has developed inside Federal Cabinet', wrote Maxwell Newton, late in February. According to him, McMahon was 'up and fighting again'.[13]

He was writing only days after McMahon had conspicuously thrust himself into the political limelight. When Whitlam attempted to bring a no-confidence motion against the government—for its 'failure to report to the House on the details and purposes of its monetary, fiscal, constitutional, and industrial policies for curbing inflation'[14]—one might have expected treasurer Les Bury to reply. The economy was, after all, *his* turf. But it was McMahon who responded to the Labor leader's half-hour speech. With Gorton looking on, McMahon spoke for an equal amount of time about the government's measures to fight the resurgence of inflation.[15]

To Newton, the context of the remarks was key to understanding them. 'Mr McMahon is taking no risks with his political position at the present time,' he wrote. McMahon's decision to detail the government's anti-inflation policy was all to do with politics: 'He wants to be seen to be a leader in that policy.'[16]

Whether or not it stemmed from McMahon's desire to shine in a field he knew well, the intervention appeared to be one hint of McMahon's willingness to work for the government. Gorton had come back from Singapore grudgingly admitting to Hasluck that McMahon had 'behaved well' at the conference; though he continued to have 'no illusions' about the foreign minister, he nonetheless wondered whether McMahon had given up on supplanting him.[17] By the end of the month, it seems, that view had settled: his regard for McMahon was benign, if still derisory. 'Don't worry, Billy big ears isn't trying anymore!' Gorton told the Young Liberal federal president.[18]

Gorton had reasons to feel confident. His critics within the party were quietening down. Plainly, his willingness to confront them, as he had in the party room following the half-Senate election, had worked. They were muting their public disapproval, in part because of their own need to survive preselection committees. Kevin Cairns, the Queensland member for Lilley, was talking of giving up on destabilisation, 'if only because of his large family and his need for economic security' as Peter Howson put it.[19] Dealing with issues in his own electorate, Howson was writing late in February that he and his band had 'done as much' as they could. Events would have to play out.[20]

Others were less sanguine about the state of affairs. Still working by McMahon's side, Kim Jones had no doubts about McMahon's ambitions: 'I think he had been ambitious to be PM for the past 25 years.' Much of what McMahon did as minister for foreign affairs emanated from his desire to build on his status within the party, the media, and the country. McMahon, said Jones, 'believed it was his destiny to become prime minister'.[21] Tom Hughes concurred. He had no doubts about McMahon. 'I don't think he ever gave up,' he said later. He also had no doubts about the number of the Gorton critics and their potential to cause harm. 'There were lots of white ants,' he said. 'Howson, Cramer, and people of no account like Leslie Irwin.'[22] Faraway observers also thought Gorton should not let his guard down, and were happy to point towards McMahon. 'You must promise me one thing, Mr Brown,' Sir Alexander Downer, Australia's high commissioner to London, told Victorian MP Neil Brown, in January: 'Never let the prime ministership fall into vulgar, Sydney commercial hands.'[23]

Whatever the level of vigilance these sentiments speak to, whatever the caution these warnings must have caused, the protection offered by Gorton's supporters and Gorton's own defences self-evidently failed. The eventual attack on Gorton came from an unexpected source, on an unexpected issue. But it also came through a wholly predictable cloud of intrigue at a time when the government was near breaking point. Was it inevitable? Potentially. 'Something,' Malcolm Fraser said later, 'was bound to be the last straw.'[24]

In May 1970, cabinet had approved a three-year civic-aid package to South Vietnam.[25] To fund construction of basic infrastructure—including homes, a hospital, and stable, safe supplies of electricity and water—the package was large-scale and intended to facilitate 'Vietnamisation', the policy whereby the South Vietnamese government and military would assume greater responsibilities as foreign troops were withdrawn.[26]

Fraser thought highly of the policy, but its noble intentions complicated the tasks of troops on the ground in Vietnam. Lieutenant-General Sir Thomas Daly, the army's chief of general staff, worried that civic-action teams would be vulnerable to attack from North Vietnamese and Vietcong guerillas if they were without the protection of troops. Therefore, as the government prevaricated over how best to extricate itself from a war that it now recognised was a liability, and how best to co-ordinate its withdrawal with an American administration that was secretive and distant about its intentions while itself moving to get out of the country, Daly counselled his commanders in Vietnam to be cautious about new, large-scale aid projects. His view, widely shared within the army, was that Australia should avoid beginning projects that might have to be abandoned should a sudden withdrawal take place. It was with this background that new guidelines on budget planning for civic action for 1971–72 were issued on 3 February. The guidelines were unintentionally blunt and easily misinterpreted: according to them, projects were to be 'expedited', efforts in the medical and educational fields were to be 'vacated', agricultural activities were to be transferred, and there were to be no entries into 'new areas of military civic action'.[27]

Within two weeks, a copy of the guidelines had been leaked to a journalist, who published it on 19 February. Newsworthy because it appeared to contravene oft-stated government policy that civic aid was continuing, the press reports that followed scratched at the suspicions of Fraser, who had thought the army intransigent, and had believed for some time that it was not keeping him wholly informed. He made an attempt to correct the reports by reaffirming that it was still government policy for the Australian army to maintain its civic-action activities. If there were any order suggesting it should be reduced or wound up, he said in a press statement, it was 'contrary to government policy'.[28] A subsequent statement suggested, correctly, that the guidelines had been misunderstood.[29]

These efforts, however, seemed to be in vain. Two days later, amid continuing press stories that suggested he was not in control of the army's activities, Fraser decided to brief several journalists from the Press Gallery about his frustrations with the army and its progress on Vietnamisation. One of them was David Solomon, who, on 22 February, published a story suggesting the army was sabotaging the government's efforts on civic aid.[30] On 24 February, amid parliamentary attacks from Labor about his handling of civic aid and the Australian presence in Vietnam, Fraser also briefed Peter Samuel, a journalist for *The Bulletin* who was known within government circles for his support of Australia's presence in Vietnam.[31] The defence minister also arranged for people within the army and the Department of Defence to speak with Samuel for the story he would publish in *The Bulletin* the next week.

Then something unexpected happened: the head of *The Daily Telegraph*'s bureau in the gallery, Robert Baudino, caught wind of the story—and not from Fraser. What he heard was similar to what Fraser had told Solomon and Samuel, but there were some differences and additional snippets that the two others had not been briefed on. Wondering what to do, Baudino spoke with Alan Reid on 25 February. Suspecting that the story could not be held over the weekend, as Fraser was briefing other journalists, and not querying whether Baudino himself had been briefed by Fraser, Reid advised that Baudino should check what he had heard with Gorton.[32]

Meanwhile, Fraser continued with his briefings, speaking with *Australian* journalist Alan Ramsey. In the main, Fraser's briefings had been the same for Solomon, Samuel, and Ramsey. His complaints centred on his belief that he was not receiving all the information necessary for making decisions, and that this affected his ability, as minister, to control the armed services. Given on background, whereby journalists could publish information without identifying its source, Fraser's view animated the article that Ramsey published on Sunday 28 February.

When he read Ramsey's article, Daly decided that he needed to speak with the press himself. He invited two other journalists to meet him the next afternoon for a briefing. But, late that night, Daly received a phone call—from the prime minister.

Baudino had followed Reid's advice and checked in with Gorton about what he had heard. He had revealed that he planned to publish an article of much the same ilk as Ramsey's, but with some important differences. He intended to claim that the Joint Intelligence Organisation (JIO) was reporting on the army's activities in Vietnam, and that Fraser had told colleagues he did not trust the reports he was receiving. Moreover, Baudino had told Gorton that the stories about civic aid were being fuelled by leaks and unofficial briefings from the Department of Defence. Gorton had made no comment on the allegations when they were put to him, but he did tell Baudino that if there were any attacks on the army or on Daly, he would come to their defence. After writing his story, Baudino had sent proof copies of it to Gorton's office. They had been returned, in Baudino's judgement, 'seen by the Prime Minister and photostated'.[33] Now, over the phone, Gorton asked if Daly was aware of the rumours flying around. When Daly said he was not, Gorton asked to meet him at his office at Parliament House at four o'clock the next day.

Gorton had already tried to speak with Fraser: he had called at the Melbourne Club, but had been unable to reach the defence minister, as Fraser had left for a meeting. Aware that Baudino's article was to be published on 2 March, wishing to clarify what was happening, and wishing also to let Daly know of his support, Gorton met with Daly on 1 March. The meeting lasted fifteen minutes. According to Daly:

John Gorton said to me, 'I don't even know whether the rumours are correct. But,' he said, 'they are emanating from the Press Gallery. Selected journalists are being briefed by somebody in the Defence Department.' I mentioned the article in *The Sunday Australian* the previous day by Alan Ramsey, and he [Gorton] said, 'Well, if these attacks continue, the army and its leaders will have my fullest support.'[34]

Fraser's name, according to both Daly and Gorton, was not mentioned in this portion of the discussion; they did, however, discuss Daly's difficult and contentious relationship with Fraser. Daly left, assured of Gorton's confidence in the army and of Gorton's support.

Daly told only three people of his conversation with Gorton: the secretary of the Department of the Army; his minister, Andrew Peacock; and Peacock's wife, Susan, whom he had telephoned because Peacock was convalescing in hospital with a serious sinus infection. However, word of Daly's and Gorton's meeting was hardly a secret. Daly had entered Parliament House through King's Hall, and he had been observed going to the prime minister's office.

The next day, 2 March, saw publication of Baudino's article. Fraser immediately prepared a response, denying that the JIO was specifically reporting on the army's activities, and also denying that he did not trust the army's briefings. The story was 'wrong and a nonsense,' he said later.[35] Gorton, who was consulted on Fraser's response, insisted that the statements to the press go out under Fraser's name—but he did not inform Fraser that he had spoken with Daly. He then departed Canberra for Shepparton, in Victoria, to campaign in the by-election being held to replace McEwen. 'Throughout the Shepparton trip,' Alan Reid wrote later, 'Gorton showed signs of being pleased with himself and life in general.'[36] To the press accompanying Gorton on the plane, the inference was clear: the prime minister had decided to use the incident for his own ends—as a rebuke to Fraser. Certainly, this was the view of Tony Eggleton, Gorton's press secretary:

I think there were people around John Gorton at that time who thought that Malcolm Fraser was getting too big for his boots and needed cutting down to size. And it may well be that it was felt that an article of

the kind that Alan Ramsey was writing might contribute to that. I think
that what they had in mind was some sort of a controlled burning-off
exercise which unfortunately became a bushfire.[37]

The smoke from that bushfire now attracted McMahon's attention.
In an unusual telephone call the next day to Jim Killen—unusual
because Killen was an avid Gorton supporter who made no secret of
his disdain for McMahon's undermining—McMahon dismissed the
reports about Fraser and the army. 'There's nothing in it,' he said.

Killen was not convinced. He thought the reports had the potential
to cause 'enormous fuss', and said as much. 'It'll be over in a day—it's a
matter of personalities,' McMahon told him. 'There is nothing political
involved ... This is just a little conflict of no consequence.'

But McMahon, thought Killen, did not seem completely
transparent. Before he rang off, the foreign minister asked him, out of
the blue, 'Did you see the report on Fraser and the Army in yesterday's
Daily Telegraph?'[38]

That day, the new issue of The Bulletin, carrying Peter Samuel's
article, 'The Australian Army's "Revolt" in Vietnam', went on sale.
Drawing on briefings from the defence department, the article retailed
how 'senior ministers' were concerned about the observance of cabinet
decisions by army personnel in Vietnam.[39] The implications of Samuel's
article were sufficiently serious that Daly went to Fraser and told him
that the press attacks had to be stopped. He wanted Fraser to issue a
joint statement refuting the suggestion of a revolt and the suggestion
that the Joint Intelligence Organisation had been ordered to report on
the army's activies in Vietnam. Fraser complied.

In the meantime, however, Alan Ramsey had heard about Daly's
meeting with Gorton. Telephoning Susan Peacock on 1 March to see
how her husband was, Ramsey heard that Daly had accused Fraser of
disloyalty to both the army and to Peacock. Having only spoken to Daly
within the last hour, Susan Peacock, according to Ramsey, was angry,
believing Fraser was 'doing a number' on her husband.[40]

Ramsey thus requested a meeting with Gorton to get a confirmation
or denial of what he had heard. 'Oh no, not you, too,' Tony Eggleton
said, when Ramsey approached him. Eggleton advised Gorton to refuse
the meeting, but Gorton overrode him. The best Eggleton could do was

get Ramsey to submit his questions in advance. The questions were on Gorton's desk at two o'clock on 3 March, when the journalist arrived. Reading through the five questions, Gorton answered some of them, but told Ramsey that he could not comment on what had been a private conversation with a third party. He was willing to tell Ramsey what *he*, Gorton, had said. He would not, however, speak for Daly. Ramsey decided that silence was an implicit confirmation that Daly had said it. He wrote his story for the next day's *Australian*. It was the front-page story, and its opening paragraph was incendiary:

> The chief of the army general staff, Lieutenant-General Sir Thomas Daly, has accused the defence minister, Mr Fraser, of extreme disloyalty to the army and its junior minister, Mr Peacock. He has told the Prime Minister, Mr Gorton, he believes the army, its department, and its minister are being discredited by Defence sources as part of a political campaign against Mr Peacock.[41]

By now, the press coverage and implications were becoming troubling. What had been a story of crossed wires now took on a far more significant weight; what had seemed innocuous now seemed to be deliberate; what seemed to be about chains of command was now all about politics. Fraser was being disloyal to the army and to a colleague: 'That, essentially, was the story,' said Ramsey later.[42] In Melbourne, Howson heard of it, and snickered: 'This could be quite an excitement for the weekend.'[43] Fraser was in Hobart when Ramsey's report was published. He phoned Daly, in Canberra, who told him that the story was untrue. 'Now, this is absolute rubbish,' Daly said later of the allegation. 'Complete nonsense. In my interview with the prime minister, Malcolm Fraser's name did not come up. Nor did Andrew Peacock's.'[44] Then Daly was asked to see Gorton again, this time at the Lodge. Daly's arrival, midway through a sitting for Gorton's prime ministerial portrait, caused a stir. The Lodge 'exploded into activity' as Gorton and Daly worked on a statement denying that Daly had said anything about Fraser being disloyal in the course of their meeting on 1 March.[45]

Denying that charge, however, was also an attack on Ramsey's work as a journalist. On Friday 5 March, Ramsey fought back. In *The*

Australian that day, he outlined how he had come to write the story. He disclosed that he and Gorton had a meeting, and that the prime minister had had the opportunity to deny the central allegation—that Daly had said Fraser was being disloyal—before it went to press. Gorton had not attempted to 'discourage' him from publishing it, Ramsey wrote.

Fraser, who had not known of the meeting between Daly and Gorton, was now profoundly unimpressed. He believed that Daly had accused him of disloyalty; he believed that Gorton did not support him; and he believed that the army was following its own whims and desires on civic action, irrespective of what he might order. Most concerning of all, to Fraser, was that all this enjoyed the apparent imprimatur of a prime minister who had committed—before consultation of any kind with the responsible minister—his unqualified support to the army. He spoke with his wife, who agreed with his tentative belief that he should resign. He spoke with Menzies, whom he saw on a semi-regular basis, and told the aged patriarch of the Liberal Party that his position was 'intolerable'.[46] By Saturday, Fraser had made up his mind: he began drafting a resignation speech.

Telephones were ringing everywhere. From Sydney, Sir Frank Packer decided that Gorton's failure to back his minister for defence provided grounds for intervention. It was time to come out and call for Gorton to be deposed and replaced. To that end, he telephoned his trusted lieutenant David McNicoll, and ordered him to break his holiday on the south coast and return to Sydney, where he would write an editorial for the *Sunday Telegraph* calling for Gorton to go. 'After sticking with him through times of mounting and sustained criticism,' McNicoll wrote later, 'we abandoned our support.'[47] In Melbourne, Howson was taking calls from Bert Kelly and John Jess, the latter having also received a call from Fraser. 'It's obvious that he's having to make a decision over the weekend', Howson wrote.

But the most important call Howson took that Saturday was from Sydney. McMahon, as usual, was on the line. Wanting to discuss the row, but also wishing to be kept 'as far removed from it as he possibly can', the minister for foreign affairs was 'most cagey' about it all, though he could have been forgiven for feeling some sense of being proved right. 'He'd warned me that this row could possibly be brewing,' Howson wrote afterward.[48]

In Yarralumla on Sunday afternoon, governor-general Hasluck was alarmed by developments and what he was hearing in the press. In a conversation with Gorton, after discussing what might happen in the Parliament, the governor-general ventured the opinion that McMahon was 'still at work':

> Mr Gorton agreed with alacrity and spoke of the 'whole thing' as contrived by the *Telegraph*. All the journalist [sic] who had been making up these stories were 'out of the same stable'. He spoke bitterly of 'planned attacks'. I suggested that, in the criticism of Fraser, there might be some comfort for him because the opposition to him in the Liberal Party was divided … I ended by saying that if he thought a conversation with me would be helpful I was at his disposal at any time. He thanked me and concluded by saying: 'I think we will have the usual trouble in the party room.'[49]

The editorial that had alarmed Hasluck would have delighted McMahon, especially its headline: 'Time for a change of leader.'[50] McMahon would have been even happier with the article that Alan Reid had written for that day's front page. Under the headline, 'Resign call to Fraser,' Reid reported that there were Liberal members who hoped Fraser would resign and make a statement to Parliament in the coming week about the crisis. The clear hope—that it would precipitate Gorton's fall from office—was evident throughout the report.[51]

The press was now providing the main impetus and fuel for the crisis, a point that Howson picked up on after speaking repeatedly during the weekend with Alan Reid. 'The important thing is to keep it going as long as possible and to delay any discussions in the party room until the last possible moment,' he wrote.[52]

Clyde Packer, Frank's son, managing director and chairman of GTV-9, and joint managing director of TCN-9, was aware of the importance of the press to the situation. Like his father, he, too, sensed that the crisis could precipitate action. 'I said to Alan Reid we should do something to get McMahon into office,' he said later.[53] The opportunity came that night: in what he called 'riveting television', a special broadcast of *Meet the Press* was arranged to discuss the crisis, with the participation of the journalists whose work had brought it on.

David McNicoll, besuited and moustachioed, opened the programme, and moderated the discussion with Robert Baudino, Peter Samuel, and Alan Reid.

Reid was asked whether anything would happen to Gorton's position as prime minister. Reid was blunt: 'I replied that this depended on what Fraser did. If Fraser resigned and stated the reasons for his resignation—and I believed there was a strong possibility that Fraser would do this—there could also be a successful revolt against Gorton's leadership,' Reid explained later. This straightforward analysis was followed by a description of a choice. Would Fraser be strong and take a stand?

> The test here will come with Mr Fraser. If Mr Fraser accepts this, he becomes henceforward a puppet in the same way as—I don't say this offensively—the treasurer, Mr Bury, has been reduced to a puppet.[54]

The pronouncement was enough to trouble all of the political insiders watching. Gorton telephoned Fraser, concerned by what he had seen and seeking reassurance. Reid's analysis had been clear, but Gorton told Fraser that the show was vicious and distorted. Privately, the prime minister believed that *Meet the Press* had done 'everything possible … to play on Fraser's vanity and conceit'.[55] He wanted to know Fraser's reaction. Fraser extended the prime minister the same courtesy he believed he had received: with a draft of his resignation on the table, he lied. 'Don't worry about it, boss,' he told Gorton. 'Just have a good night's sleep.'[56]

In Fraser's mind, the lie was justified. He feared Gorton would have dismissed him had he been given any further cause for concern. 'I think that was legitimate,' he said later.[57] The likelihood of this eventuating was not, apparently, considered. 'The prime minister's office was taken by surprise by the Fraser strategy,' Tony Eggleton said later. There was no expectation that Fraser would resign.[58] Moreover, Fraser seems not to have considered that any move by Gorton to remove him would surely have precipitated a crisis of its own—possibly one that would have been worse.

Nonetheless, events were moving in only one direction. Reid's pronouncement on *Meet the Press* may not have confirmed or been formative in Fraser's decision to resign, but it certainly prevented him from retreating from it. The press—almost uniformly, from Fairfax to the Packer stable—was certain that the coming week would bring change.[59]

ON Monday, Fraser made his moves to bring about that change. Just before one o'clock, he telephoned Hasluck and told him he wished to hand in his resignation as minister for defence. When Hasluck advised that he should, really, speak with Gorton before doing so, Fraser interrupted to ask whether a prime minister who wished to dismiss a minister would ask for that minister's resignation. Hasluck said that would be the courteous and customary way of doing things. Then Fraser said he wished to resign. He had discussed it, and had been over it thoroughly with people whom Hasluck would, apparently, respect. He would not be dissuaded from it. But Hasluck was not about to rush matters and, while clearly conscious of Fraser's future, was also considering the implications of Fraser's resigning:

> I could only counsel him to consider very carefully the possible consequences of his actions on the government, on the party, and on his personal future. He should not assume that a resignation would advance his own future prospects. Mr Fraser interrupted to say that he was not looking for any personal 'dividends'. He just felt someone had to do something to bring back a little bit of order and decency into government. I asked if he considered whether his action might only open the way for someone who might have lower standards than the present Prime Minister. Mr Fraser said somewhat ruefully (judging from his voice) that he had thought of that. I asked him if he had thought of the outcome in the party room. He said he could not help that; the trouble was there already.[60]

The prospect that McMahon might become prime minister self-evidently horrified Hasluck, but it would not dissuade Fraser. He was not to be moved. He had thought of the consequences and, plainly, he accepted them as the price for his subsequent actions. They were not his responsibility.

Due to attend a cabinet meeting at half-past two, he did not appear at Parliament House. Gorton tried to reach him by telephone, but Fraser had taken his home phone off the hook. Alan Hulme, the postmaster-general, left to find Fraser and try to reason with him, but it was too late. A letter, hand-delivered to the prime minister's office, was given to Gorton just after three o'clock. It was short, to the point: Fraser advised that he had considered the recent events 'carefully and deliberately', and regarded Gorton's conduct as indicating 'significant disloyalty'. He resigned, would deliver a letter to the governor-general to that effect, and, in the House, would seek leave to make a statement.

Reading this note, Gorton asked his ministers in the cabinet room whether they would support him, support a challenge to his leadership (should one eventuate), or themselves challenge his leadership. It was a political exercise: Gorton wanted to be able to say he had the unanimous support of his ministers. One by one, Gorton went around the room to ask each minister individually. Chipp observed that Gorton sat for a moment in silence after receiving all the assurances but one. Then Gorton turned to his left, where McMahon sat. Eyebrows slightly raised, Gorton asked, 'Will you be standing against me, Bill?'

McMahon did not hesitate. He looked up. 'No, absolutely not.'[61]

News of Fraser's resignation leaked quickly. Just after four o'clock, Fraser telephoned Hasluck to ask if he could come immediately to hand in his resignation. 'I wrote a letter to the prime minister and said I would call on you tomorrow and that no announcement would be made until I had seen you,' he said. 'I now find that already an announcement has been made from the prime minister's office. He refused to see me.'[62] Hasluck said yes. Within ten minutes, Fraser was at Government House, his resignation letter and a copy of the letter he had sent to Gorton in his hand. 'Well, how do you feel now?' Hasluck asked him.

Fraser told him he was relieved, and again Hasluck began to probe why Fraser had resigned. Throughout the conversation, Hasluck sensed that Fraser was thinking much further ahead than the present parliamentary term. Was he thinking of the leadership, after 1972? Potentially. But on the whole, Fraser seemed calm, Hasluck thought. Fraser 'expressed concern at the general deterioration in politics and administration'. The ill-feeling in the party had grown. The methods of working in cabinet had deteriorated. The public service was in confusion, and its morale was low. Standards of behaviour had fallen.

What, Hasluck asked him, would he do now? Fraser said he would speak in the House: 'His statement ... would be brief and to the point and would deal mainly with his views on the defence structure, and relationships between Defence and the service departments, and his views on the relationship between a Prime Minister and his Cabinet.'

It was by now almost six o'clock. Fraser left. Hasluck telephoned Gorton and told him that Fraser had resigned. 'We had a conversation,' Hasluck told Gorton. 'He gave me his reasons for resigning and said that those reasons were known to you.'[63]

FRASER'S resignation was the blow that left the government teetering—and Alan Reid was determined to keep it that way. In Canberra, he met David Fairbairn and John Jess. They had decided that they and Howson should say publicly that they were willing to cross the floor and vote with the opposition, should it move a vote of no confidence in Gorton in the next day's sitting of the House. Telling Howson this in a telephone call after midnight, Reid ensured that Howson understood the consequences of such a move: the three of them would give the opposition a victory, should it get so far. The success of that motion could bring down the government and force an election—which the Coalition would, on its present polling, lose. Liberal MPs would be forced towards a choice: to remove Gorton, or to go the country with the likelihood of defeat.[64]

A meeting of Liberal Party members was scheduled for 11.30am, but it was delayed as Gorton prevailed on Fraser to meet and discuss his resignation. Gorton wanted him to withdraw it, and offered to apologise in the presence of cabinet ministers should Fraser agree. Bert Kelly, who went to Fraser's office following this meeting, found the 'poor beggar' in a state, apparently agonising over whether to accept. Kelly, and then Tony Street, told Fraser that he should refuse. 'This papering over the cracks wouldn't carry conviction,' Kelly decided.[65]

Fraser refused the offer. At 12.30pm, the party meeting began. Gorton spoke about Fraser's resignation and the events leading up to it—'with considerable restraint', Kelly thought—and admitted he had erred in not defending Fraser. He apologised in front of the whole party room. Then Fraser spoke, giving his view of events, but adding that there were other cases where Gorton had been unwilling to listen and consult cabinet.[66]

But there was not to be a resolution that day. Following Fraser's statement to the party room, the Tasmanian senator John Marriott tried to move a vote of confidence in Gorton's leadership. The idea was quickly scuttled when the anti-Gortonites said that they wanted to hear Fraser's statement to the House.[67] The meeting broke for lunch. 'He's still in,' MPs told the press.

At 2.30pm, when the House convened, Whitlam moved a suspension of standing orders to allow Fraser to speak. There were to be no petitions or questions just yet. Fraser stood from his new position on the backbenches and quietly, calmly, proceeded to outline the circumstances that had led to his resignation. Considering the near-labyrinthine circumstances that had provoked it, the account of the press stories about civic aid was persuasive. Gorton's assurance of support for Daly was 'an impetuous and a characteristic action'. His refusal to deny that Daly had called Fraser disloyal was, itself, disloyal. 'One sentence would have killed this report,' Fraser said. That this might be a gross oversimplification received not a mention: 'The Prime Minister, by his inaction, made sure it would cover the front page.'

But this was not the main cause of Fraser's resignation. According to him, it was merely the latest example in Gorton's 'obstinate determination to get his own way'. Fraser now cited an attempted call-out of the Pacific Islands Regiment that had occurred in July 1970. He regarded this as proof of Gorton's disinclination to accept cabinet governance and of his wilful unilateralism. To those listening in the House, learning of the matter for the first time, it was persuasive. To those who knew, however, it was anything but. Tom Hughes, afterward, would follow Fraser from the House and demand to know how, since Gorton *had* acquiesced and held a cabinet meeting on the matter, this example could hold water. To this, Fraser said nothing.

The most damaging part of the speech came at its end. In what Kelly thought 'unfair', and Killen 'unnecessarily brutal', Fraser declared:

> The Prime Minister, because of his unreasoned drive to get his own way,
> his obstinancy, impetuous and emotional reactions, has imposed strains

upon the Liberal Party, the Government and the Public Service. I do not believe he is fit to hold the great office of Prime Minister and I cannot serve in his Government.[68]

Gorton's response, immediately following this peroration, was another demonstration of his control under pressure. Despite what some observers called a lack of fire, his reply calmly dissected the case that had been made against him. Fraser had not been obstructed in his work as minister for defence. He did not believe Fraser had planted the story on civil aid. Fraser had been a 'good' minister, too. It was a 'tragedy' that he was resigning. Gorton admitted that he had been wrong not to deny that Daly had called Fraser disloyal, but he observed that 'an enormous amount [has been] built on that particular point'.

Whether this would have persuaded his critics would not be known. As Gorton detailed the course of his meeting with Ramsey, the journalist—watching in the Press Gallery—interjected.

'I,' Gorton was saying, 'therefore replied to that question: "Had General Daly said what it was claimed he did say?" by saying that I thought it wrong to discuss or comment with Mr Ramsey on what a third party had said and Mr Ramsey replied: "Fair enough."'

'You liar,' Ramsey yelled from the Press Gallery, above and behind the Speaker's chair.[69]

To the Speaker's cry for order, Arthur Calwell could be heard growling that the Speaker should 'deal with the animal'. Ramsey, embarrassed by his interjection, hurried from the gallery to find Tony Eggleton, Gorton's press secretary, to apologise. Labor, meanwhile, offered the opportunity to exploit the moment, moved to have Ramsey called to the Bar of the House, where he could be made to testify about what had happened during his meeting with Gorton. After twenty minutes, Gorton intervened to cut off the debate. Reading from a note delivered from Eggleton, he told the House that Ramsey had apologised for losing control of himself, and that was enough for him.

Faced with the surety that Ramsey would not elaborate further, Whitlam withdrew the motion. The House proceeded to Petitions and Questions.[70]

THAT night, supporters and rebels canvassed for votes. Gorton supporters Don Chipp, Andrew Peacock, and Jim Killen did a count, and finished happy. 'We came back and said, it's no worry,' Chipp said later. 'He's home and hosed.'[71] That confidence spread. When Jim Plimsoll telephoned the prime minister's office to discuss a matter to do with the National Gallery, he heard Gorton calling out in the background: 'Tell Jim that it will be alright, I've got the numbers.'[72] The confidence enjoyed by Gorton's supporters was such that they told Robert 'Duke' Bonnett, a Gorton supporter from Queensland, not to bother leaving his sick bed in Townsville. His vote would not be needed.[73]

Those on the other side were likewise inclined to think Gorton had it. 'I don't know that McMahon was confident of coming out on top,' Kim Jones said later.[74] 'I thought that there was no way in which we would win the vote,' Fairbairn said later.[75] Howson thought it was 'even money', and, while hosting a pre-arranged dinner for English stockbrokers, was nearly staggered to observe that all McMahon wished to discuss was the economic situation in London.[76] The press, staking out Parliament House and its surrounds, were able to catch McMahon and Sonia leaving for the dinner. Sonia's dress, black, with a plunging neckline and a split up the left leg, ensured that they were a conspicuous pair.

At 7.45pm there was another meeting in the party room, to discuss Fraser's charges about the call-out of the Pacific Islands Regiment. Gorton's reply was convincing, as even Howson grudgingly admitted.[77] It was clear that the day's events, and those to come, were overshadowing everything else. 'The real problem is now pretty well obvious that we can't hope to succeed in the next election under Gorton as presently discredited,' Bert Kelly recorded that night. But, if not Gorton, who then should lead the party? Would that affect how people voted in the event of a challenge to Gorton? Kelly spoke to fellow South Australian and minister for health, Jim Forbes, and found out:

He was undecided about what he ought to do about Gorton … Anyhow, after some hesitation wh[ile] Forbes asked for some time to think it over, he eventually came back and told me he is going to vote for Gorton, mainly because he's certain about the alternative. Anyhow, he is not going to put up with having the government dictated to by the press.[78]

All manner of decisions were made overnight. Victorian members Tony Staley and Tony Street decided that they were prepared to vote against Gorton, but not for McMahon, who himself rang Howson early the next morning to say that ministers were starting to shift, that the prospects of success were improving. Alan Reid in turn told Howson that he thought they might just have the numbers, but that he could not be sure.[79] Neil Brown, filing into the party room that day and apparently still torn, asked the president of the federal Liberal Party, Robert Southey, what he thought the party should do. After an initial refusal to answer, Southey bluntly echoed Forbes' arguments. 'He said that we should remember that if we removed Gorton, the press, which had been baying for Gorton's scalp for months, would claim it as a victory for the power of the media to remove the elected leader of a political party anytime it wanted to.'[80] Had Brown been from Queensland he might have received different advice, and without hesitation: Queensland Liberal Party president Eric Robinson had already declared on radio that the party would be better off with a change in leadership.

The meeting began at ten o'clock. Les Irwin, a tried-and-true Gorton critic, told the prime minister he should stand down and avoid an acrimonious debate. Gorton, neither out of character nor unreasonably, refused the request of a man he regarded as a treacherous leak.[81] Then, in a move that appeared unplanned and was certainly mistaken, the Victorian backbencher Alan Jarman moved a vote of confidence in Gorton's leadership. Another backbencher, Len Reid, seconded the motion. They may have been acting with the best of intentions, but as junior members they were not the best advocates to lead the debate. Nor was the motion itself wise. In addition to throwing the onus on Gorton's supporters to prove that they were in the majority, it removed the need for Gorton's critics to prove their possession of a quality they had long been shown to be wanting: courage.

Fairbairn followed Jarman and Reid, and said he would cross the floor to vote against Gorton in the House, should it come to that. Malcolm Mackay said much the same. John Cramer was less forthright, but no less critical. And though Bert Kelly—acting in the belief that putting everything out would hardly help—suggested stopping the deluge of criticism, the anti-Gortonites refused. 'I felt we needed to make it clear to the Ministry that the rift was in the party room and so encourage some of the swingers to veer towards us,' Howson wrote.[82]

The cause was helped by a question from avowed Gorton critic, Kevin Cairns. He asked Gorton whether, if he were defeated in a vote of confidence, he would recommend that the governor-general dissolve the House, or recommend that he send for a successor. Gorton was honest enough to answer. No, he would not recommend that there be a dissolution. He would recommend that the governor-general send for whoever was elected to replace him as Liberal Party leader.

The answer was a pivot point: like the motion of confidence, it gave some security to those undecided members that they could vote against Gorton's leadership without an immediate cost.

What followed from that was a procession of Gorton's critics. John Jess, Jeff Bate, Alexander Buchanan, Harry Turner, and Peter Howson—among others—spoke, berating Gorton and his leadership, and stressing that he needed to go. Their number was such that Ian Wood, the senator who had attempted to topple Gorton five weeks before, could not himself speak this time, Gorton telling him that his colleagues probably had the case covered.[83]

Gorton's defenders were not lining up to support him. Two ministers, Nigel Bowen and Bob Cotton, spoke, as did senator Marriott and Bob Solomon, but Gorton twice refused to allow Killen to do so. 'I do not want you to speak,' he said.[84]

'It went on and on,' Bert Kelly recalled. 'I must admit that Gorton behaved magnificently in the chair and gave all his detractors free rein.'[85] It was almost midday before the party decided to take a vote. Again, the Gorton camp made a tactical mistake by allowing it to be a secret ballot. Members could vote for whomever they chose, free of any obligation but to that of their conscience.

The votes were tallied at the front, before everyone. Papers were sorted into two piles—'Yes' and 'No'—that grew evenly as each vote was sorted. It was tense. Chipp thought that there was a distinct smell of blood in the air. Nervous smiles from Gorton supporters and critics faltered as the piles grew at the same rate and the number of votes remaining to be counted dwindled.[86] Hughes, sitting next to Gorton, was not certain what would happen. 'I don't think I'd addressed my mind to the outcome,' he said later. 'It was obviously going to be a close-run thing.'[87]

McMahon had spent the entire time in one of the large green armchairs at the front of the room, hand capping his eyes, trying to look uninterested in what was happening. He could not have been anything but apprehensive, especially once Gorton's scrutineer for the vote, the member for North Sydney, Bruce Graham, withdrew the final ballot paper and allocated it to its proper pile.

'Prime Minister,' he said, 'the vote is thirty-three all.'

It took a moment to digest the news and work out that, of the sixty-seven people in the room, one had cast an informal vote. What were they to do? Western Australian senator George Branson suggested holding another ballot, in the hope that the informal voter might make up his mind. Gorton scotched the idea immediately. 'Well,' he said, 'that is not a vote of confidence, so the party will have to elect a new leader.'

To some, Gorton's pronouncement was mistaken, the product of haste. 'It all happened in a rush,' Hughes said later.[88] Chipp had visions of adjourning the meeting for half an hour so Gorton could think and decide on tactics.[89] But the party, as Howson saw, was in no mood for prevarication.[90] By the time that Gorton might have had second thoughts, it was too late. He was finished as leader of the Liberal Party, and had agreed to go.

In only a few moments, the Liberal Party's leader had been deposed, and the party was moving on to choose his replacement.

John Cramer sought to nominate McMahon, but was argued down. Gorton turned to McMahon. 'Will you stand, Billy?' Upon McMahon's confirmation, and Snedden's decision to nominate, too, the party went to a ballot. Now, as ever, was the choice. McMahon was one of the last of the Menzies men. He had the most ministerial experience of all the parliamentarians assembled. He had proved himself competent in his portfolios. He had been there for a long time. Who else could it be? Why would they not vote for him?

'I voted against Gorton and of course McMahon for leader,' wrote Bert Kelly that night, 'as I am certain Snedden hasn't got the ability.'[91] Neil Brown, regarding Snedden a 'much more pleasant person', decided that he would vote for him. But then Malcolm Fraser, striking a match to light his pipe, sat down next to him. When Brown mentioned that he did not really know who to vote for, Fraser was dismissive. 'What do you mean, you don't know?' he asked. 'It's blindingly obvious that McMahon is the only choice.'[92]

Much of the party seemed to agree. The count of the ballot papers did not take long. Within minutes, McMahon was declared the victor, with Snedden later claiming that it was by a margin of three to two.[93] Finally, McMahon was leader of the Liberal Party.

His triumph was immediately scarred by an act of political madness. Alan Hulme, calling for a round of applause for Gorton's now finished leadership, suggested that Gorton nominate for the vacant deputy leadership. Gorton went along with it. He agreed to stand. The sympathy and respect he had gained—in his conduct of the meeting and his loss of the leadership—gave him an overwhelming sympathy vote. With Fairbairn and Fraser standing against him, Gorton won easily.

There were immediate signs it was not going to work. McMahon told Gorton he would vote for him, but Gorton watched him fill out the ballot and spied that his name was not written there. Nothing less than what Gorton expected, the deceit hardly augured a fresh start or an attempt to heal wounds.[94]

Gorton critics thought that it had been planned all along, just in case the confidence vote went against them. Others saw it as a snap decision. 'That was Gorton acting *ex improviso*,' said Tom Hughes.[95] Nobody saw it working out. 'It's a pity,' wrote Howson, 'as it will make it so much more difficult for us in the weeks ahead.'[96] Hughes was dismissive of the whole idea. 'I voted for Gorton, but it wasn't going to work. Nothing was going to work once McMahon took over.'[97] 'It is going to be terribly awkward to work a Cabinet with an unwillingly deposed Prime Minister in it,' Bert Kelly wrote.[98]

Outside the party room, Tony Eggleton had been given news of the leadership change to McMahon. His reaction, and that of the parliamentary staff and Liberal Party officials, was 'surprise and dismay'.[99] Nonetheless, he announced it to the waiting press and went back to the government lobby for further news. Then he heard that Gorton had been elected as McMahon's deputy. His earlier reaction was echoed when he announced it to the press. 'You must be joking,' said Allan Barnes, of *The Age*, in the circle of reporters.

'I don't joke on such matters,' replied Eggleton.[100]

The party-room meeting broke up. MPs left, went into the lobbies and offices to talk to press, to commiserate, and to celebrate. Scrums of reporters waited for McMahon, prepared for the inevitable press conference that had to follow.

Soon enough, it did. McMahon sat at a hastily prepared table festooned with fifteen microphones. Sonia was by his side, calm and, for the most part, unsmiling. In every way, McMahon gave off the image of the professional he claimed to be. His suit was dark, conservative. His red tie was simple. His arms were folded. He made eye contact, spoke clearly. He restrained his smiles. He tried not to allow the scale of the moment to overwhelm him.

'I don't want to say a great deal to you today other than this,' he said.[101] 'I am a party man. I believe in the Liberal Party and I believe the Liberal Party is the organ by which the national will and consciousness can be put into effect. I am a very great believer in the system of cabinet government, in full discussion in cabinet, with every member having the opportunity to express his views, and only when political matters of the highest moment are involved, should the prime minister feel that he should intervene ...'

He told the press that his aim would be to ensure cohesion, so that by the time the government went to an election it had enough of the public's confidence to warrant a bigger majority. To questions, he said little. He was not sure of the procedure, but the House would meet at half-past two and likely be adjourned while he and Gorton went to see the governor-general. He was sure that he and Gorton would work together in the interests of the Liberal Party and the interests of the country, despite their antipathy. His ministry would be announced in due course. No, the press could not ask a question of Mrs McMahon. Asked if he would be prime minister and treasurer both, McMahon said he would consider it, but it was unlikely.

'What do you see as the main problems confronting the government today?' one journalist asked.

'Don't ask me that at this moment,' McMahon replied. 'As soon as I have had time to settle into the leadership of the Liberal Party, then of course I will have another conference and you can ask me all the questions you want then.'

There were some small moments of levity. When asked if he would send a telegram to John McEwen, McMahon said he would. But, he added, 'I haven't thought out the contents yet.'

At another point, a journalist asked if McMahon had thought he might finally win the leadership that morning. 'Sir, the prime ministership has been your goal for a long time … Were you surprised and how do you feel personally now that you have attained it?'

'It is a strange thing, but everyone seems to think I am a person of tremendous ambition,' McMahon replied. 'I don't think I am … I don't feel the slightest bit excited or emotional … I have taken it in a composed way because I have been here a long time.'

WATCHING McMahon's press conference in Whitlam's office was a host of Labor parliamentarians and staffers. Some were nervous about seeing Labor's best asset—Gorton—gone. Some wondered about McMahon, whether Whitlam would be able to grapple with a *third* Liberal Party leader, whether his rise would engender a public desire to give him a fair go. 'He has to be given a fair chance,' Clem Lloyd later explained.[102] Others were completely unruffled by the idea. Seeing the new Liberal Party leader in his first televised outing, Graham Freudenberg thought he was doing well. 'It was a competent performance,' he wrote later, 'during which only a slight tremor of the upper lip and later, to an observant journalist, a wet patch on the table where his hands had rested, betrayed his nervousness.'

Fred Daly, the Labor frontbencher, told Whitlam, also watching, not to underestimate McMahon. The caution was unnecessary. Like his colleagues Tom Burns and Mick Young, soon to shout celebratory drinks in the Non-Members Bar until it closed for the night, the Labor leader believed he had McMahon's measure. He was confident. Seeking to reassure his colleagues, he was blunt.

'Now listen,' Whitlam said. 'If there had been an open contest after Holt went, who would we have wanted? Not Gorton, certainly not Hasluck. We would have wanted them to choose Bill McMahon …'[103]

THAT night, television viewers saw their new prime minister and his predecessor—the new leader and deputy—making their way through spectators and press at Parliament House to the prime minister's black Bentley. They saw footage of McMahon, Gorton, Anthony, and Hasluck standing on the portico of Government House, smiling and shaking hands.

It was, as ever, a façade. Gorton, sworn in as minister for defence, had no respect for his successor. Anthony did not trust his new coalition partner. Hasluck did not esteem his new prime minister: 'He was an awful little tick,' he said later.[104]

But McMahon, throughout it all, appeared untroubled. He smiled, chuckled. Made small talk. Laughed with unfeigned delight. Savoured the moment of triumph, of realising an ambition that had been years in the making. As one of his staff would later say, McMahon walked into the job as though it was a natural development, the next inevitable step.[105]

Twenty-one years of experience lay behind him. Twenty-one months in which to use it lay ahead.

CHAPTER THIRTY-FOUR

Activity and Responsibility

1984

Even thirteen years after Gorton's downfall, there were questions to be asked. How had it happened? Why had it happened? Bowman, swimming through the files and poring over the documents in the autumn of 1984, could not have failed to wonder about how Gorton had come to such an inglorious end. McMahon's becoming prime minister was a pivotal moment in his life. It would be in the autobiography, too. How to explain it, though? How to understand it?

In 1971, it did not take long for the finger of blame to be pointed at the Packer press.[1] Within days of Gorton's deposal, theories about a 'Packer plot' to unseat him were rife. Most were based on the high visibility of the Packer-owned Australian Consolidated Press in the days preceding Gorton's fall. Certainly, the involvement of the Packer-employed journalists Robert Baudino, Peter Samuel, and Alan Reid—the latter notoriously anti-Gorton—gave those theories credibility. *The Daily Telegraph*'s editorial calling on Gorton to go lent them the veneer of possibility. Reid's pronouncement on *Meet the Press* about Fraser's position lent the theories solidity. Finally, that McMahon, the most evident beneficiary of it all, was known to have been close to Packer, made it inevitable that the theory—for some people—would become fact. 'The Prime Minister is Prime Minister as the result of a co-ordinated campaign mounted originally by Sir Frank Packer,' the Labor member for Fremantle, Kim Beazley Snr, said within a few days.[2]

In the months that followed Gorton's fall, there were many who saw proof of it everywhere. Labor, most pointedly, made much of Packer's involvement. It dug up evidence of McMahon's long relationship with the press tycoon, noting their association through Sydney Newspapers Ltd. Labor accused McMahon of leading a government subservient to Packer's outside influence, of allowing the prime ministership to be but a bauble.[3] 'To Sir Frank Packer,' Beazley said, 'the Government of the Commonwealth is another one of his personally owned projects, like the yachts *Gretel* or *Dame Pattie* in the fight for the Americas Cup.'[4]

For those 'inside' Canberra, the theory that Packer had been the principal cause of Gorton's fall became even more interesting when, in June 1971, *The Australian Quarterly*, a political science journal run from Sydney, published an anonymously authored article that betrayed an insider's knowledge of Packer's ACP and canvassed Packer's involvement.[5] 'Mr Y', as the author was called, was generous to the suggestions, noting that the idea of a 'Packer plot' had some plausibility. There was highly centralised editorial power within the Consolidated Press, he wrote; there was considerable co-operation between its publications; and there was Packer's love for exercising political power. These were reasonable grounds for thinking that Gorton had been felled by the machinations of the Packer press and Packer himself.

And yet, Mr Y said, the suggestion of an orchestrated, top-down plot was far-fetched. It would have barely concerned Packer that Fraser had fallen out with the army and felt the need to brief the press. Moreover, Packer had nothing to do with the row between Gorton and Fraser, let alone Fraser's resignation and unprecedented attack.

The only point that Mr Y would concede warranted consideration of Packer's influence was *The Daily Telegraph* article written by Robert Baudino. Everything beyond that was either out of the hands of the Packer press or exploited by the Packer press, just as any press organisation would. The Baudino article was the important point. According to Mr Y, Alan Reid's recommendation that Baudino check his story with Gorton—*not* with Fraser—was key. 'Reid must have known that to "check" the [Peter] Samuel story properly the person to go to was Fraser not Gorton,' wrote Mr Y.

> But apparently on Reid's suggestion, Baudino went to Gorton. Reid must have realised that Gorton was likely to act impetuously and fall into serious political error. He knew Gorton loved a fight and was in a mood to fight Fraser, so it seems likely he encouraged that process

by sending Baudino to Gorton. Even if he did not foresee precisely
Gorton's reaction, it turned out to be the first of two fatal false steps. In
his impetuous anger Gorton called the Chief of the General Staff, Sir
Thomas Daly, and sided with him, making only the most perfunctory
effort to contact his responsible minister. Reid had led Gorton into his
first error. He had provided the first opportunity for the Prime Minister
to demonstrate 'significant disloyalty' to his colleague, Mr Fraser.[6]

Reid, for his part, would deny that this was in any way his intention,
writing later only that he believed Gorton 'could have [had] an angle'
that put a 'different emphasis' on Baudino's story.[7] Was it merely
accident, then? Was it simply a case of a breakdown in communication
between Fraser and Gorton? In spite of his point about Reid, Mr Y
certainly thought so. Claims of a Machiavellian scheme that was
calculated and deliberate were overblown, he reckoned. 'To depict the
fall of Gorton as merely a "Packer plot" is to overlook the extent to
which Gorton himself contributed to his own demise.'

On this, Mr Y was correct. Gorton had endured many attacks from
the press, some of whom had acted outrageously. As Edward St John
would write, Reid had 'not infrequently played an active political role'.
His deliberate building up, with Peter Samuel, of David Fairbairn's
stature as a critic following the 1969 election; his advice to Peter
Howson about tactics to weaken Gorton; his gratuitous advice to
Whitlam on how best to exacerbate Gorton's woes—in all of these,
Reid had exercised 'power without responsibility', as St John argued.[8]

Gorton had, too, come under a harsh attack from Fraser. And
while arguably provoked by Gorton's refusal to deny a charge of
disloyalty, Fraser's resignation and bitter denunciation in the House of
Representatives was founded on sandy grounds of propriety. As one of
Fraser's biographers noted later, Fraser had 'initiated a campaign against
the army through unattributable press leaks, assured his prime minister
that he had not made the leaks, denied them when they were published,
asked one journalist if he would deny having a briefing at all, and finally
misled his Prime Minister about his intentions to resign. This,' finished
the biographer, was 'a poor basis upon which to demand proper and
appropriate procedures in government.'[9]

Nonetheless, all of these were but secondary factors in Gorton's fall. Gorton's battles with the state premiers had alienated parts of the Liberal Party machine, its base, and its parliamentary members. His contravention of Liberal Party shibboleths had turned colleagues against him. And though his critics were almost certainly intractably opposed to him, Gorton had not gone out of his way to convert them into allies. The fault, as Gorton's biographer was later to note, lay largely with Gorton and the Liberal Party: 'Elements of the Liberal Party brought John Gorton down, ably assisted by Gorton himself.'[10] The latter point had been predicted: the general secretary of the Liberal Party in New South Wales, John Carrick, had told the British high commissioner to Australia in May 1970 that Gorton might, 'in a blaze of frustration', decide that he 'would give the whole bloody thing away'.[11]

But what of McMahon's role? Had he been involved? When asked by the press at the time, McMahon had been absolute and unequivocal in his answers: no. 'I never took any action to do anything else but to treat Mr Gorton as the leader of the government and give him my devoted loyalty,' he said.[12]

Almost certainly, however, he had been backgrounding against and undermining Gorton. As the journalist Laurie Oakes later wrote, 'McMahon waged an unrelenting campaign against Gorton to further his own ambitions. McMahon rang journalists at all hours of the day and night leaking information extraordinarily damaging to the prime minister and the government.'[13] Alan Ramsey thought the same: 'He flattered journalists by telephoning at any time of the day or night, usually at weekends, to chat about some alleged outrage or other committed by McEwen or Gorton in cabinet, then left you with the problem of sorting fact from fantasy.'[14] Lenox Hewitt had seen it first hand. 'As I moved around business circles in Sydney,' he said later, 'I'd be asked questions. *Wasn't Gorton financially unsound?* Thoughts that had been planted in the business community by Billy.' McMahon was unscrupulous. 'He would say anything at all that suited his needs of the moment,' Hewitt said later. 'He would say anything that was in his own interest, no matter what else got in the way.'[15]

Nonetheless, McMahon's absence from the events that ultimately sparked Gorton's resignation was unusual. Was it really the case that he had, as Alan Reid later put it, 'had the office [of prime minister] virtually handed to him without him lifting a finger'?[16]

There were some who scoffed at this. Robert Southey, the president of the Liberal Party, had suspicions that he could never confirm. 'I couldn't describe Bill McMahon's role in Gorton's downfall in any coherent, connected, analytical fashion,' he said later, 'because that's not the way Bill McMahon worked. It was rather hole and corner. It was a smile here, a nod there, a wink there.'[17] Howson, too, wondered about it. Noting from his diary a prediction from Alan Reid that there could be a change of prime minister in March, he found himself questioning McMahon's involvement with Packer. 'I feel that they had been planning, knowing that some crisis would develop, and knowing that there were people in the party room who would be prepared to act along similar lines. It will be interesting if in the history books we can see the full planning that led to the March crisis.'[18]

Jim Killen thought similarly, but he, too, could only wonder. McMahon's telephone call to him on 3 March was 'unusual', he thought, and his unexpected reference to *The Daily Telegraph* article authored by Bob Baudino was troubling. It convinced Killen that McMahon had a 'far greater interest in the reports of conflict between Malcolm Fraser and the Army than he affected to have'.[19] But what problem was there in being interested? Was that good cause for some suspicion? The subsequent editorials in *The Daily Telegraph*, calling on Gorton to go, brought McMahon back to Killen's mind; then Gorton's resignation had left a dumbstruck Killen wondering how it had all happened. 'It had only been a week,' he reflected, 'since McMahon had said to me, "There's nothing in it."'[20]

There was one figure who was certain that McMahon was involved. By 1984, when Bowman was working on McMahon's memoirs, Fraser was a year out of office, dethroned by Bob Hawke in an election that would see the Liberal Party consigned to opposition for thirteen years. Fraser had long intimated his suspicions about McMahon to people, and within the next three years would record them fully.[21]

In Fraser's reckoning, like Mr Y's, Baudino's story in *The Daily Telegraph* was the beginning of it all. Fraser regarded it as 'the most damaging' piece of reportage to have come out of the whole affair. Unlike Mr Y, however, Fraser did not regard Reid's advice that Baudino consult Gorton instead of him as the pivotal moment. For Fraser, it came earlier.

Fraser believed that McMahon was the one who had set the wheels in motion. The key detail, and the foundation for Fraser's belief, was the mention, in Baudino's article, of the Joint Intelligence Organisation reports. Those reports, Fraser said later, 'presumably went to John Gorton, [and] they would have to Billy McMahon'. From there, Fraser had no doubt about what happened. McMahon had given word of these reports to *The Daily Telegraph*'s Baudino, made them sound more sensational than they were, and thereby prompted the story that appeared on 2 March. 'I have always believed,' Fraser said, 'that it was Billy McMahon who provoked the *Telegraph* into reporting the way it did—which was quite deliberately designed to achieve that … to cause friction between myself and Tom Daly in the army'.[22]

In Fraser's telling, the subsequent events were merely guided along to their inevitable, calamitous conclusion: Daly's accusation, Gorton's demurral, Fraser's resignation—and Gorton's demise.

Was McMahon involved? There was no paper trail to help answer the question. Nor was Bowman ever likely to hear a confession. The trail simply ran cold.

CHAPTER THIRTY-FIVE

The Crumbling Pillars (I)

1971

The work began immediately. McMahon knew there was no time to be wasted in drawing a line under Gorton's prime ministership and establishing his own. The distinction needed to be made at once. In the car back from Government House after the swearing-in ceremony, 'reflecting on the many issues he had to deal with', McMahon told Tony Eggleton that he would need his help. One of the first tasks he gave Eggleton was to speak with Lenox Hewitt, the Gorton-appointed secretary of the prime minister's department. He was to be removed, McMahon said, and replaced by Sir John Bunting, who would be brought in from the cold of the cabinet office.[1]

Hewitt expected the move, but it came at a wholly inopportune time: his mother-in-law was being buried that day. Asked to wait for McMahon's call, he eventually left for the funeral, arriving late. Then, after as brief a period as he could afford to be away, he returned to his office, where Tony Eggleton informed him that he was sacked. 'I accordingly made the changes to my office as quickly as possible,' Hewitt said later, 'in order to rejoin the mourners still at my mother-in-law's house.'[2] It was, he would say, the 'first public execution of a permanent head,'[3] and he was not impressed that the news had come from Eggleton rather than the prime minister.[4]

McMahon's decision to remove Hewitt and place Bunting back at the prime minister's department was inevitable. Bunting's reappointment was a deliberate signal of the restoration of government in a Menzian ideal: party consultation, cabinet process, respect for the public service. Hewitt's removal would emphasise Gorton's fall.

Policy would alter. Policy-making would change. It was the first of many actions McMahon would take to present himself as an orthodox, professional politician, and it was meant for many audiences: his party, the public service, the states, and the media. But Bunting expressed some indecision about returning. *You would be mad*, he told himself. It was only after a 'thoughtful lunch' and family meeting that Bunting agreed to the move.[5]

Almost immediately, however, the plan hit an obstacle. As Gorton had found, removing a permanent head is almost impossible. To rid himself of Hewitt, McMahon initially sought to offer him a series of diplomatic posts. 'I explained that I did not wish to accept an appointment,' Hewitt recalled. 'But we went around, one by one, through offers of various posts in this rotation of countries.' Eventually, Hewitt was offered an appointment as head of another department.[6] The way was clear to reappoint Bunting. Though McMahon would later say that he had erred in doing so, the move helped to heal the discontent that had existed within the public service.[7] 'Bunting had reason to be grateful,' Peter Lawler explained later. 'McMahon returned him from exile.'[8]

There were other personnel moves to consider. McMahon needed to fill key positions within the prime minister's office. According to Kim Jones, who stayed with McMahon for the following six months, there was no help on this from Gorton's office. 'They just decamped,' he said later.[9] Val Kentish came with McMahon to serve as his personal secretary. Ian Grigg, an official from the prime minister's department, became McMahon's principal private secretary (in modern parlance, his chief of staff). Keith Sinclair, a former editor of *The Age* who had worked part-time in the prime minister's department as a speechwriter, would be on hand. Then there was the need for a press secretary. McMahon asked Eggleton—who had recently accepted a job with the Commonwealth Secretariat—if he would stay on, but he demurred, committing to stay only to oversee the transition and recruitment of a replacement. 'I had already worked for three prime ministers, and it was time for a change,' Eggleton said later.[10] Eventually, journalist Reg MacDonald, from *The Advertiser*, who had already been interviewed to replace Eggleton, would be appointed to the position.[11]

McMahon also began turning his attention towards the ministry. Plainly, there was going to be a high turnover. David Fairbairn was likely to be restored to the ministry, potentially even to foreign affairs.[12] Peter Howson believed he would return, but denied any hope of it in order to preserve the appearance that he had worked against Gorton for principle's sake.[13] Certainly, there would be change at Treasury: McMahon was not going to leave Les Bury in the portfolio. He also had promises to keep to those who had beat the anti-Gorton drum. How would he keep those promises? Who would go in the ministry? These questions occupied his thoughts all night, McMahon told journalists the morning after he was sworn in. 'I kept waking up during the night thinking about it,' he said. 'I didn't get much sleep.'[14]

The press reception to his accession was largely favourable. *The Daily Telegraph*, now with its favourite politician at the top, was exultant. 'Salute to the future,' its front page said. In an editorial, the paper intoned that McMahon would 'restore dignity and deep thought to the government of Australia and he will undoubtedly have the support and respect of all members of the Coalition … Mr McMahon is the right man to handle the hard tasks that lie ahead.'[15] Others were less effusive, more circumspect about what lay ahead. 'A tough role for a tough pro,' said the Murdoch-owned *Daily Mirror*, noting that McMahon could be said to have the support of only half of the Liberal Party room.[16]

Shying away from controversy was one of McMahon's goals. The party had turned to him as a professional, someone who could put an end to the instability and division. 'He seemed to symbolise the old order to those people who didn't like these ventures into new and unknown territories,' recalled Edgar Holt, an *éminence grise* of the Liberal Party. 'He was a proclaimed federalist, he was careful and cautious, and the emotionally exhausted Liberals weren't looking any more for a visionary or a romantic. They settled for what they thought was McMahon's realism and pragmatism.'[17] Calming the waters, being seen to be safe and sound, was McMahon's priority.

He would need all the help he could get. His government was not falling quietly in behind him. Doug Anthony admitted that the crisis had 'done great harm' to the government's cause,[18] and Robert Southey, the Liberal Party president, was lashing out at Eric Robinson for his call for Gorton to go.[19] Bob Askin was also not about to allow his dispute with the Commonwealth to be forgotten. Though happy that a New South Welshman now held the prime ministership and Liberal Party leadership, Askin was not going to offer his support unduly: 'My main test will be Mr McMahon's capacity to work out a solution to the crisis in Commonwealth–state relations,' he said.[20] Nor would Malcolm Fraser's actions be easily forgiven. Despite Menzies' commendation of Fraser's maturity and DLP leader senator Vince Gair's advice to 'bring him back', McMahon had no intention of putting back into cabinet the man widely blamed for sparking Gorton's downfall. Gorton, no more or less than any other, would not abide it.[21]

What to do with Gorton was another problem. Restrained when asked how he felt about his removal, Gorton made it plain that he thought his critics were at fault and that his election as deputy leader was demonstration of the party's preference. 'Well, Mr Fraser and Mr Fairbairn stood up,' he said, when asked to explain why he had put his name forward. 'I had been attacked by both these men. I believed it would be a fair thing to find out what the party thought of me in relation to those two.'[22] As deputy leader, Gorton had some latitude in choosing his portfolio. Sworn in as minister for defence to replace Fraser, there was every chance that Gorton would choose to change when McMahon shuffled the ministry. Initially, McMahon was inclined to allow Gorton this option.[23] But not for long: when Gorton said he might move to Treasury, McMahon told him that he had been given his first choice, and that defence was where he would stay.[24]

The problems of the ministry and personnel did not augur well for what would follow. On Friday 12 March, Doug Anthony, the deputy prime minister, and Alan Hulme, vice-president of the Executive Council, came to Government House to present Paul Hasluck with two proposals for his signature.[25] One proposal would remove Hewitt and replace him with Bunting; the other would abolish the prime minister's department and the cabinet office, and establish in their place a unified Department of the Prime Minister and Cabinet, headed by Bunting, and a new department, that of the Vice-President of the Executive Council, headed by Hewitt, designed to take on various ancillary functions largely from the prime minister's department.

Hasluck immediately raised objections to the final change. Was it desirable to establish a new department with that name? The Executive

Council—the body that, in advising the governor-general, oversaw cabinet decisions and statutory instruments—had no administrative functions, and the position of vice-president of the council existed in practice only as means to allow the council's business to go on when the governor-general was unable to attend meetings. Why did it need a department?[26] Was the role of the Executive Council about to change? Hasluck also questioned the administrative-arrangements order that had accompanied these proposals. Why—and, just as importantly, *how*—was the Department of the Vice-President of the Executive Council to be given the secretariat responsibility for the Executive Council? Were these proposals, he asked pointedly, the result of a considered examination of the position?

The two ministers were uncertain, and telephoned McMahon, who came to Government House to find out what the problem was. The prime minister was a 'little fussed', but did not comment when Hasluck explained his objections. McMahon took a pen and began making edits to the proposals, then told Hasluck he would not change the name of the new department 'because it would be embarrassing to do so'.[27] Hasluck cottoned on almost immediately: McMahon had already issued a press release on the matter, announcing it.[28]

Was McMahon becoming overwhelmed? Was there too much to do? Was it happening too quickly? According to Kim Jones, the answer was no. 'He moved in quite smoothly,' Jones said later. '… He had plenty of things in mind that he wanted. He had a clear agenda in place.'[29] Nonetheless, McMahon's promises to announce the new ministry had to be revised three times. It would be done over the weekend. It would be announced on the Monday. Then McMahon abandoned a date altogether: the ministry would be announced in due course.

During the weekend, McMahon began preparing for Monday's meeting of Parliament. Labor's motion of no confidence was going to be the first test of his prime ministership. Intent on meeting it, he worked with Keith Sinclair and Peter Bailey, from the newly restored Department of the Prime Minister and Cabinet, to prepare a speech rebutting Labor's inevitable criticisms. But shortly before the debate, McMahon decided that he could not read the speech. He preferred to speak from notes. He tore the speech up, went into the House, and brought the debate on.[30]

'The aim of the motion,' said Whitlam, who had come with a well-prepared speech, 'is not just to let the people pass judgment on the extraordinary events of the last week but to give them a voice on who should govern them. The clean air of public opinion should be allowed to flow through Canberra's musty corridors of power.' Whitlam's speech was eloquent, calm, prickling with sharp lines: 'The very malaise that was at the heart of last week's convulsion—the bypassing of Parliament and its proper procedures—continues unabated. The Bourbons have learned nothing. They will never learn. The sickness is too far advanced.' Whitlam homed in on the turmoil that had crippled Gorton and caused Fraser's resignation. He satirised McMahon's declaration that all government policies were open for review. He painted McMahon as a stooge of the press and a man of the past:

> To fill his [Gorton's] place the Press proprietors and the Establishment have nominated a man whose ability and application no one doubts but whose style, rhetoric, and attitudes are part of the [19]50s. His title deeds are doubtful and by whomsoever they have been conferred, they have not been conferred by the people of Australia. The only unity he can offer temporarily is the unity of exhaustion. He offers, in the long term, unity around reaction.[31]

McMahon's response was feeble. His own side was beggared to hear it. He sounded nervous, uncomfortable. To Whitlam's criticism of the lack of an election, McMahon quoted a constitutional scholar who had been dead for over a decade. His attempts to criticise Whitlam over national service and inflation were lacklustre. Trying to describe the philosophy that would guide his government, McMahon harked back to the days of 1949:

> We are dedicated to political liberty and the freedom and dignity of man; safe from external aggression and playing our part in a world security order which maintains the necessary force to defend the peace; looking primarily to the encouragement of individual initiative and enterprise as the dynamic force of progress; to make just provision for the aged, the invalid, the widowed, the sick, the unemployed, and the children.[32]

As an exposition of McMahon's beliefs it was substantial, but in the circumstances it was flimsy. It did little to rally his side. Worse still was McMahon's announcement, towards the end of his speech, of a $1 rise in the pension for married couples and of 50c for single persons. Canvassed in cabinet barely three hours before, on grounds that the costs of living was rising and the government would do this in the budget anyway, the announcement was not—as some in the press suggested—an act of generosity spurred by the needs of the moment.[33] But that was how it appeared. The speech was 'one of the worst' of McMahon's career, Howson thought.[34] Clem Lloyd's fears that McMahon might find favour were immediately dispelled: 'It [his speech] was a poor response.'[35] The dynamic between the government and Labor was set then and there. Whitlam had the ascendency. It left the government disheartened. 'Everyone is going round gloomily prophesying imminent disaster,' Bert Kelly wrote.[36]

ON 21 March, McMahon took the list of his ministry to Government House for Hasluck's approval. There were predictable names on the list: David Fairbairn had been restored to cabinet as minister for education and science; Malcolm Mackay, Kevin Cairns, and senator Ivor Greenwood had been given junior ministries. There were also notable absences: Malcolm Fraser had been left on the backbench, and senator Annabelle Rankin, who had burst into tears when told she was out, had a diplomatic posting to New Zealand as consolation.[37]

Other changes were more spiteful but no less expected. Jim Killen had known he was in for demotion; immediately after Gorton's demise, he had begun packing up his office in anticipation of it. Confirmation came on 18 March, when McMahon summoned him and said, 'I want you out—right out.' Killen was more amused than aggrieved during the encounter: he saw a nervous man with sweating hands who could barely clear his throat to speak.[38]

Tom Hughes, who was aware that he was synonymous with the measures on offshore sovereignty, the territorial seas, and the growth of Commonwealth power at the expense of the states (this most evident in what became known as the *Concrete Pipes* case, which was being heard in the High Court), also knew what was coming. McMahon called him in after Killen, and said that he wanted Nigel Bowen to be his attorney-general. 'Well, that means you want me on the backbench,' Hughes replied.

'Yes,' said McMahon, not so nervously this time. 'I've been under great pressure in the party to get rid of you.'[39]

But McMahon would not be rid of Hughes so quickly. Until McMahon went to Hasluck on 21 March, Hughes remained in the ministry as attorney-general, contributing to debates, responding to McMahon's request for advice on the controversial establishment of assistant ministers and parliamentary secretaries—positions that McMahon would use as reward for those who had supported him.[40] It was 'quite bizarre', Hughes said later. 'I was there for a fortnight, sitting in cabinet and advising on outcomes. He *still* wanted my advice. He was a dreadful little man.'[41]

Les Bury, too, knew that he was not going to remain in the Treasury, especially once Billy Snedden staked a claim. Accosting McMahon almost immediately after he had been elected, Snedden told him that Bury was not capable of doing the job and that it should be Snedden's. When McMahon demurred and replied that he would think about it, Snedden pressed his case. 'Don't think about it, Bill. You will agree to it now because there is going to be bloody trouble if it is not agreed.'[42] Snedden got what he wanted. Bury was moved to Foreign Affairs—but even here there was room made for humiliation. McMahon let it be known that his first choice had been the Country Party minister Ian Sinclair.

This was not all. The list of ministers that McMahon handed to Hasluck contained some extra, vindictive flourishes. Where Bury had been sixth in seniority under Gorton, he was now eleventh. Alan Hulme, keeping his portfolio as postmaster-general and vice-president of the Executive Council, went from fifth to tenth. Reading the new list, Hasluck was surprised. Did Bury and Hulme know of this? he asked. Was there any risk of 'unseemly objection, argument, or withdrawal from the room' by any of them? He also queried McMahon about the appointments of parliamentary under-secretaries. Might those who had been appointed think themselves entitled to a promotion, the moment one became available?

At this, McMahon looked startled, said he would have to be careful about it, and made a hurried note. Then he began complaining. 'He said further that he expected Sir Alan Hulme to retire from the Ministry but not from Parliament at the end of the year and that he did not know how long Bury would last,' Hasluck recalled:

> There seemed to be something wrong with his [Bury's] health. He seemed to have lost energy and never joined in any discussion. We discussed Treasury briefly. He [McMahon] was aware that departmentally its strength had diminished. He was not sure how Snedden would do. He 'knew nothing about economics'. Mr McMahon also told me other stories about his difficulties in making the Ministry but as some of them did not square with other accounts I had heard, I doubt very much whether he was speaking the truth, so I will not record them.[43]

In the days and weeks that followed, rumours abounded about the ministry. There were whispers that McMahon had originally intended to dismiss ten ministers, but that Anthony had intervened to prevent it, asking if McMahon really wanted to have a whole cabinet's worth of ex-ministers on the backbench.[44] Whatever the veracity of these rumours, few were happy about the ministry. Fairbairn was not pleased to have education and science, dismissing it as hard and unrewarding, and would depart the portfolio after five months, noting that he had not really achieved anything.[45] After taking a telephone call from John Jess, an anti-Gorton MP who raged that Malcolm Mackay had been promoted over him, Howson judged that McMahon had attempted to placate his enemies rather than help his friends.[46]

If this was so, McMahon's critics had no knowledge of it. Only a few days after the new ministry was announced, Gorton freely told Hasluck that he would support McMahon so long as he did not 'get up to any of his tricks'.[47] But, Gorton went on, if McMahon tried to do anything funny, Gorton would 'smash' him: 'And Billy ought to know that I can smash him,' he said. There were seven or eight other members who would do the same, Gorton added. When Hasluck asked what he meant, Gorton told him that 'the little bastard is already working against me in my constituency, spreading lies and trying to make me lose the party endorsement for the seat so that he can get me out of the road. If he goes on like that I will smash him even if I smash the party too.'

Sentiments like this prompted some to wonder about McMahon's prospects of surviving as prime minister until the election, let alone whether he could win it. In his favour, Hasluck thought, McMahon had no obvious internal rival, had been greeted with a wave of favourable opinion, could play on a public not yet 'wholly committed' to Labor, and was unencumbered by 'ideals or principles' that could lead him into danger. Weighing against that was Gorton's attitude, generational shifts within the Liberal Party, tensions with the Country Party, a deteriorating economy, McMahon's physical health and his 'defects of character', the DLP's attitude, and the potential for a lacklustre electoral appeal. McMahon would survive to the election, Hasluck thought, but that was almost wholly contingent on any decisive shift in the state of affairs.[48]

John Bunting expressed a similar view. Observing McMahon up close, he saw McMahon's propensity for hard work and his efforts to fit the mantle of the office. As he would write in June, McMahon was 'excellent in so many respects. Instinctively wanting and trying to be statesmanlike rather than merely political.' The pressures that came with that office, however, would not allow such disguises to be long maintained. McMahon, Bunting wrote, 'is, in fact, the most political of all politicians'.[49]

There were few expectations that McMahon would be a transformative prime minister. 'We [in the Packer organisation] at no stage thought that enlightened, stable, progressive, and relatively uneventful government would ensue under McMahon,' Peter Samuel said later.[50] 'The possibility was nil that he would, in any way, prompt the Australian people to create better than they knew,' wrote Donald Horne, Samuel's editor at *The Bulletin*.[51]

Most appraisals of McMahon were merely amazed. 'Who, with any experience of him and with him,' Arthur Fadden wrote privately, 'would have ever thought he would live to see Billy-the-flea Prime Minister of Australia?'[52] He was no less caustic when writing to Bunting to congratulate him on his reappointment: 'I hope that during the 12 some years that have elapsed since I had experience of McMahon that his loyalty and stability has most vastly improved. He will, even if he does not vainly make himself Treasurer as well as PM, make himself an intolerable nuisance ...'[53] International observers were more amused than anything else by McMahon's accession. As Morrice James, the British high commisioner to Australia, was to appraise that year:

Mr McMahon is a small, shifty, but dogged and resilient man whose Victorian appearance (bald head and muttonchop whiskers) belies his gift for a highly contemporary brand of political slickness. He seems perennially surprised to find himself Prime Minister of such a solid and substantial country as Australia. Both his countrymen, and—to an embarrassing extent—he himself, know that he is not much good in the part.[54]

Menzies was cautiously optimistic about McMahon. In a letter sent the day after McMahon's swearing-in, he wrote that he was 'delighted' to hear of Bunting's restoration, whom he called 'the Prince of Civil Servants'. But it was clear that he thought the strength of McMahon's government would be his cabinet:

You have my warm wishes ... You will, of course, have the aid of a team of able men of your own choice. You will also, having regard to your current circumstances, be able to exercise to the full your own uncommon knowledge of economic and financial matters and to feel assured of the co-operation of the business community. Cabinet decisions on matters of moment, decisions which are those of the whole cabinet, are of the essence ... Prime Minister, you will undoubtedly maintain the closest contact with your Ministers so that they all feel that they are members of a team of which you are the chosen Captain and the authoritative spokesman.[55]

Menzies' words were hardly a tonic. In the weeks that followed, it was clear that McMahon's cabinet was divided, antagonistic, with tensions over personality and policy. The new captain could not wrangle his team. 'Whatever the circumstances,' Anthony said later, 'one has to make adjustments and try to make things work.'[56] Gorton, however, seemed to make no attempt. His derisive regard for his successor was always on show. When McMahon resisted allowing Gorton to retain

Ainsley Gotto, the deputy leader supposedly told Tony Eggleton that his new boss could 'go to buggery'.[57] Moreover, in cabinet, between interrupting his colleagues and allowing the smoke from his cigarettes to blow into McMahon's face, Gorton was apt to puncture a vainglorious announcement with a blunt question: 'That's got to be fucking stupid, doesn't it?'[58] McMahon, supposedly exasperated by Gorton's habitual lateness and interference, began shuffling cabinet agenda so as to dispose of more difficult items before Gorton showed up.[59]

But there was neither time nor room to dwell on the divisions. Change of an urgent, challenging, and prevailing kind was underway. Old eras were closing; new ones were opening. The economy was changing, presenting inflation problems and exacerbating the difficulties of state budgets. The changes wrought by American intervention in Vietnam, and Britain's indecision over its role in world affairs, would present dilemmas and demand answers. Australia's policy towards China was in need of attention and decisions. Unrest over freedoms and equality was becoming manifest in protests over rights for Aborigines, and over charges of racism and sexism. The government would need to grapple with pressure for environmental conservation, for championing the arts, for increasing educational opportunities. In short, the government would need to respond to the new country that Australia was becoming. Personalities would have to wait.

FOLLOWING his reconstruction of the ministry, McMahon's first move was to mollify the state premiers. Ahead of a premiers' meeting in April, he sought advice from the Treasury about the state budgets and what the Commonwealth could do. He had no intention of allowing the premiers to become antagonistic: he wanted them sated and happy. The premiers, too, were aware that McMahon represented a chance to press their claims, and thus made nice in the weeks preceding the meeting. After suggesting that McMahon's support from the Liberal Party was dependent on his grasping 'the nettle' and developing a 'new-look scheme' in the federal-state sphere,[60] Bob Askin said he thought McMahon would be more sympathetic to the states than Gorton. Henry Bolte said that he believed a new era was imminent in Commonwealth–state relations. All of the premiers came to Canberra with different methods for the same goal: they wanted money to help with their deficits.[61] McMahon made almost no attempt to resist them or their demands.

After only a few hours of meetings on 5 April, McMahon announced that the Commonwealth would provide a special-assistance grant to the states totalling $43m in 1970–71, with the only condition that the money be used to reduce deficits, not increase expenditure. 'I welcome the degree of co-operation shown between all the premiers and the Commonwealth,' McMahon said. 'I feel it was an example of the sensible working of Commonwealth–state relationships.'[62] A few months later, there was another buy-off when McMahon offered the premiers access to the payroll tax.

The appeasement was transparent. The premiers gushed. 'Mr McMahon has passed his first test as prime minister with flying colours,' said Bolte afterward, in an assessment that Askin soon echoed: 'I would say he gets honours.'[63] It was an obvious about-turn, particularly when Askin's critical comments about McMahon were recalled, but there was also a hint that buying the states off would only encourage them. 'One swallow does not make a summer,' Askin said at a press conference afterward.[64]

And then there was Parliament. Eager to clear the notice paper ahead of the winter recess, McMahon took advice to pack the last week's sittings, limiting the amount of time that was available for debate. Thus the government scheduled only nineteen hours and ten minutes to debate seventeen Bills on matters as complicated and diverse as superannuation, communications, the wool industry, defence, state grants, Papua New Guinea, and income tax. If it were to work, the schedule would require a sharp use of the guillotine, a refusal to be shamed, and complete party unity. The latter was missing. Adding his voice to Labor's loud objections, Harry Turner, the Liberal member for Bradfield, told the House that Parliament was being treated 'with utter contempt'.[65] Killen, freed from the obligation of a ministerial line, was especially aggrieved: 'This is a disgraceful proceeding. It is a proceeding unworthy of the national Parliament and a proceeding which does great affront to this country.'[66]

It was an all-round mess, undignified and ignominious. During the sitting, the Speaker, William Aston, had to throw a pencil at

Billy Wentworth, minister for social services, to stop him snoring on the frontbench. The press were aghast. It was rush and chaos all over again. The arrogance and ineptitude was startling. It undid all the work McMahon had done since taking over. 'Mr McMahon became Prime Minister with a reputation as a systematic, deliberative, and shrewd politician,' *The Australian* editorialised two days later. 'The Liberal Party must now be questioning his political judgment.'[67] But McMahon saw no fault on his part. Amid 'the worst press he had received during his forty days and forty nights', he had a row with his staff and colleagues about it. Alan Reid, keeping in touch with all that he could, put it pithily: McMahon was blaming everyone but himself for the debacle.[68]

While upset, McMahon soon recovered his equanimity and by the end of the month was telling the governor-general that his ministry was 'working together very well'.[69] Cabinet business was 'now proceeding more smoothly than ever before, and there was no back log of delayed submissions'.[70] Certainly, there had been a lot of work done: among other things, cabinet had resolved that Australia would join the OECD; had approved the site for the new National Gallery and a scheme to provide $30m per year for rural reconstruction; and progress on self-government for Papua New Guinea was accelerating.[71] Moreover, McMahon was also now ready to rename the Department of the Vice-President of the Executive Council to which Hasluck had objected. It would now be the Department of Environment, Aborigines and the Arts, and its minister would be Peter Howson.[72] The appointment was a reward for an ally and vindication for Howson, who McMahon believed had been treated unfairly during the VIP affair. 'You ought to read the file,' McMahon told Hasluck. 'It's a shocker. Other people should have taken the blame.'[73]

But Howson's was very much a chance appointment. McMahon had been vacillating for a month over whether to bring him off the backbench at all. 'Had a quick talk with Bill McMahon this evening,' Howson wrote on 29 April. 'He tells me now that he doesn't think that he will make me the twenty-seventh Minister.' A week later, McMahon rang to offer Howson a ministry, only to rescind the offer the next day.[74] On 23 May, McMahon rang to offer a ministry once more, but delayed announcing it until the following week.[75] Finally, on 27 May, McMahon announced it. But, as Howson recorded:

Unfortunately he forgot to tell me to which portfolio, and ... we never got around to that particular part of the subject ... I got back to Kensington Road just in time to hear the 4 o'clock news, at the same time as Peter Lawler rang to tell me of my appointment. Not only have I got Environment, Aboriginals and the Arts [sic] but also twelve other important departments or committees. It's certainly going to keep me busy.[76]

Rumour abounded of Howson's displeasure at his new portfolio; according to a popular story, when he found out the precise details he snarled that 'the little bastard gave me trees, boongs, and poofters'. Whatever the truth of his initial reaction, by the following week, Howson was writing that McMahon 'had been wise' in giving him this 'wonderful opportunity'.[77] No doubt Howson was aware of the irony when he discovered that his new permanent head was none other than Lenox Hewitt.

Howson's appointment came at a precipitous time in Aboriginal affairs. On 27 April, Justice Richard Blackburn had ruled that the Yolngu people, living in Yirrkala land in the Gove Peninsula, in the Northern Territory, had no right to prevent mining by the North Australian Bauxite and Alumina Company (Nabalco) on their traditional lands. Their claim—that they held a 'communal native title' to the land that the court should recognise—was rejected. Blackburn found that native title was not part of Australian law and that, if it had existed, any native-title rights had been extinguished. But while Blackburn made clear that he was interpreting the law as it stood, his judgment made an implicit plea that there were grounds for the government to change the law:

> I am very clearly of the opinion, upon the evidence, that the social rules and customs of the plaintiffs cannot possibly be dismissed as lying on the other side of an unbridgeable gulf. The evidence shows a subtle and elaborate system highly adapted to the country in which the people led their lives, which provided a stable order of society and was remarkably free from the vagaries of personal whim or influence. If ever a system could be called 'a government of laws, and not of men', it is that shown in the evidence before me.[78]

The ruling caused an outcry, and thrust land rights for Aborigines onto the political agenda, a point confirmed when representatives of the Yolngu plaintiffs petitioned McMahon on the matter,[79] and by Blackburn's decision to write a confidential memorandum to cabinet urging that a system of Aboriginal land rights be created. To Nugget Coombs, now chairman of the Council for Aboriginal Affairs (CAA), these circumstances and McMahon's succession to the prime ministership seemed an opportunity for real progress, especially after the frustrations he had experienced under Gorton. 'While McMahon knew as little about Aborigines as Gorton he was a kindly and humane person and I had found him open-minded and easy to work with,' Coombs wrote later. 'I was aware that he would welcome help from me in a personal way and I believed that a deal could be done.'[80] Flattery was not beneath Coombs: within two hours of McMahon's becoming prime minister, the chairman of the CAA was in his office, offering 'a vision of a historical role for himself in Aboriginal affairs and the Arts'. How did McMahon react? 'Mr McMahon,' said Barrie Dexter, executive member of the CAA, 'was sympathetic and attracted, and asked Dr Coombs to commit his thoughts to paper.'[81]

McMahon's subsequent decision to remove responsibility for Aboriginal affairs from Billy Wentworth was not a blow, in Coombs's eyes, since Wentworth seemed to have little power within the ministry. But moving responsibility for Aboriginal affairs out of the Department of the Prime Minister and Cabinet and into its own department was a disappointment, since it distanced the prime minister from the issue.[82] Trying to salvage the situation, Coombs managed to strike a deal with McMahon: in exchange for agreeing to act in 'a kind of advisory role' and partnering the prime minister in games of squash, Coombs would have a direct line of responsibility to McMahon, should he require it. 'Without some new source of political initiative we were unlikely to fare better with the new Ministry, especially if Aboriginal Affairs was to be entrusted to some junior minister,' Coombs wrote later. 'Only the authority of the Prime Minister could achieve a significant change of direction.'[83]

An address to a conference of state ministers responsible for Aboriginal affairs on 23 April—before the Blackburn decision—had augured well. Using a draft prepared by Coombs, Wentworth read a statement in McMahon's name that declared that the goals of the McMahon government's policy were to encourage and assist the preservation and development of Aboriginal culture, language, traditions, and arts, 'so that they can become living elements in the diverse culture of the Australian society'. The statement dismissed the words 'assimilation' and 'integration' as inappropriate descriptors of government policy, and promised to consider appropriate policy for Aborigines and the land, economic development, and erasing discrimination against Aborigines from the statute books.[84]

But the ruling on the Gove Peninsula case was a test for how these words would be translated into practice. To the public criticism of the judgment, McMahon asked Coombs and the Council for Aboriginal Affairs to draft measures that would address the land-rights issues. It was a heady list that the council recommended exploring:

> [...] policies designed to give Aborigines protection for the use and benefit of reserve lands for ceremonial, religious, recreational and productive purposes; to establish a Land Fund to acquire land for Aboriginal groups outside reserves; to enable Aborigines to participate profitably in mining ventures[;] to be compensated for disturbance of their traditional way of life; and to provide grants-in-aid for Aboriginal commercial enterprises.[85]

The scope of those measures soon brought up tensions with the Country Party, the bureaucracy in the Department of the Interior (now responsible for administration of the Northern Territory), and the states. Cabinet ministers were sceptical of the CAA and suspicious that it had an agenda; as Snedden was to say in August of one of its papers, 'It is got together by people with strong views for Aborigines, but are not in normal character of [the] p[ublic] s[ervice].'[86] When the measures were referred to an inter-departmental committee for comment, it became clear that any action on them would be hard-pressed to succeed without McMahon's personal intervention.

Equally unexpected matters also reared up. In the three years preceding McMahon's succession, the opprobrium directed towards South Africa's apartheid regime had begun to be targeted at its sporting teams. But, attracted by the prospect of crowds and exciting cricket, and undeterred by the possibility that similar protests might occur in Australia, the Australian Board of Control for International Cricket (ACB) invited South Africa to send its cricket team to Australia for a tour in October 1971.[87] Another tour, by the South African rugby union team, was scheduled to precede the cricket tour in June and July.

Sir Donald Bradman, the chair of the ACB, had approached Gorton to learn his attitude to the invitation. Gorton told him that his government had no wish to prevent a South African cricketing tour taking place. When Bradman reapproached the government after McMahon took office, the assurance was repeated. McMahon had good reason to go along with it: a Gallup poll taken in March 1971 found that almost 85 per cent of Australians thought the South African cricketers and rugby players should come. Moreover, the tours enjoyed the support of most of McMahon's party: Menzies had suggested that the English, in cancelling the 1970 tour, had bowed 'to the threats of a noisy minority' and denied people 'their lawful right to go and see a match, whoever is playing'.[88] Why would McMahon get involved or cause a fuss?

It was in this context that when the South African government decided that there would be no blacks selected in its teams, McMahon wrote to South African prime minister, B.J. 'John' Vorster, to register his disappointment, but nothing else. As he told the House on the same day, 'We believe that sport should be left to the sporting associations themselves.'[89] His view was that apartheid was a matter for the South Africans—not him and not Australia. As he told Bunting privately:

This is a question internal to South Africa and for the people there, including the sporting people, to settle. The teams are doing what they can. It may be that the people are not in favour of Government policy in this respect. We believe that the policy in respect of the teams is unfortunate, but it is nevertheless a South African matter, and not our matter.[90]

A cabinet decision affirmed the stance: 'Sporting exchanges between countries should be conducted with as little political interference as possible.'[91] Fears from South African authorities that the tour might embarrass the government were waved away with notes that McMahon had expressed his attitude publicly.[92]

However fervently McMahon might wish otherwise, sports *were* entwined with politics. The protest campaign in England that had led to cancellation of the South African tour in 1970 proved it. Additional proof of the growing abhorrence of apartheid was evident in the UN's decision to deem 1971 the International Year for Action to Combat Racism and Race Discrimination. Nonetheless, McMahon was not willing to change his mind, even when the UN secretariat unit on apartheid circulated a paper pointing out that Australia had never expressed concern about or opposition to apartheid's practice at an international sporting level.[93] Nor was McMahon willing to allow measures that might compromise the government's position: he reiterated his abhorrence of apartheid, but Australia would abstain from voting on a UN resolution that condemned its application in sport.[94]

As the June rugby tour and the October cricket tour approached, the popular and political pressure for overcoming McMahon's position began to grow. Unions imposed so-called black bans on the South African teams, swearing they would not supply services to them.[95] On 13 May, the ACTU, led by Bob Hawke, pressured South Africa for a 'non-discriminatory' selection policy in its touring sporting teams and threatened to 'withhold their services from any activities directly associated with these proposed tours'.[96] Hawke, who had won the ACTU presidency on a platform that argued unions should be involved in social-justice issues as well as industrial ones, subsequently asked McMahon to cancel the rugby tour. 'Should these representations prove unsuccessful,' the ACTU executive decided, 'we advise our affiliated unions to take whatever action is necessary as an act of conscience on their part to withhold their services from any activities directly associated with these proposed tours.'[97] It was enough to prompt the president of Australian Rugby Union (ARU), Charles Blunt, to seek a meeting with McMahon to discuss ways of overcoming the boycott. But the message from the ARU was consistent: while it was determined to press ahead with the tour, it would reconsider it if the government advised otherwise.[98]

By late June, McMahon was saying that the government had made its decisions. 'We are not going to be beaten here,' he told Bunting.[99] He came through for Blunt with an announcement that the government would make RAAF transport available to move the Springboks around Australia, should it be required.[100] It was a decision made against the advice of the public service, but McMahon had now seen that there was political mileage to be made from intervening.[101] The rugby tour, McMahon said, should not be 'prevented or prejudiced by some groups within the trade union movement'.[102] The Labor Party's support for cancelling the tour gave McMahon licence to link the ALP with the protesters, whom he called a 'force hell bent on tyranny'.[103] However attractive it might have seemed tactically, the decision was plainly a strategic mistake. It had the effect of aligning McMahon and the government entirely with South Africa, as Whitlam pointed out,[104] while simultaneously undercutting his earlier statements that sport should not mix with politics. As Hawke asked, 'How more completely can you bring politics into sport?'[105] It also led to the easy quip that the RAAF should be known as the 'Royal Apartheid Air Force'.[106]

The protest campaign was well prepared, particularly in the eastern states. In Melbourne, Sydney, and Adelaide, activists harassed the South African team and interrupted matches, provoking violent clashes with police and fans. Premiers across the country were loud in their criticism: Henry Bolte said the campaign was the work of 'louts and larrikins',[107] and in Queensland, on 14 July, premier Joh Bjelke-Petersen declared a state of emergency to crack down on protests. That action gave the campaign against the tour another facet to attract followers—the importance of civil liberties. It also became linked with Aboriginal rights when activists decided to connect the protests against apartheid with awareness of racial discrimination endured by Aboriginals in Australia.

The tenor of the protest campaign, its successes and failures, as well as the language used by McMahon and the state premiers, led some to wonder whether it had been deliberately orchestrated as a lead-in to an election. As journalist David Solomon wrote on 6 July, the tour had 'turned into just the kind of riotous clash between demonstrators and police that a proponent of a law-and-order election would dream about—or try to bring about'. Publicly, McMahon speculated about calling an election, musing that he could win an additional five seats in a campaign framed around the question of who governed Australia; privately, he was circumspect.[108]

It was not to be. The highly visible protests, the harsh treatment meted out by police, Bjelke-Petersen's over-zealous reaction, and McMahon's provision of RAAF aircraft—not used, in the end—combined to diminish support for further South African tours, and weakened the government's standing in the polls. Press criticism almost certainly played a role, with *Age* journalist Bruce Grant writing that McMahon, by pursuing 'shrewd politics' and 'bad government', had opted to divide Australians rather than unite them.[109]

And there was the cricket tour to consider. In August, with the South African rugby team safely departed from Australia, Bradman approached McMahon again seeking advice and views.[110] After fobbing off the cricketing great, McMahon took the matter to cabinet. Demonstrations on the scale of those during the rugby tour would be near ruinous in a Test match: the length of games and style of play would be easily disrupted by protesters. If the tour went ahead, the Commonwealth would almost certainly have to intervene. Was the cabinet willing to do that?

McMahon was of the opinion that the government gained 'politically' from the tour. 'Are we to allow [a] small anarchist mob to run the community?' he asked.[111] But while his ministers were sympathetic to this point, they thought the government could not go through another furore. Anthony put this forthrightly. 'Don't want a repetition of [the] rugby [tour]. Did well with public, but public doesn't want a repetition.'[112] Don Chipp thought pragmatism was paramount: 'It is the practicality [of the tour],' he said.[113] Plainly, the easiest option would be to recommend to Bradman that the tour be cancelled. But to reverse a position in this way would have been an embarrassment for McMahon. Therefore, cabinet opted to remain neutral, and leave the Board of Control, already split on the question, to judge for itself.[114]

Bradman was not much impressed by cabinet's decision to make no decision. He had spoken with all those who would have to stand by him, should a tour go ahead. He had attended the rugby test match between the Wallabies and Springboks in Sydney. 'The ground was protected by barbed-wire barricades, and the police were ready for things such as smoke bombs and flares,' Bradman said later. 'But the barricades didn't stop the protesters. They invaded the arena.'[115] It was no good. The conditions were impossible. Bradman persuaded the Board of Control to cancel the tour.[116]

When the decision was announced, McMahon made shows of sympathy and invoked the 'great majority' who doubtless wished the tour to proceed. Whitlam was derisory: 'Well played,' he said.[117]

There would be no more tours until South Africa chose its sporting teams on a non-racial basis.

CHAPTER THIRTY-SIX

The Crumbling Pillars (II)

1971

Then there was Vietnam. Again, pursuing a strategy to quieten conflict and solve political problems, McMahon continued efforts to withdraw from the intractable conflict. In March, Gorton went to Saigon for meetings with South Vietnamese president Nguyen Van Thieu and the commander of American forces, General Creighton Adams, to discuss a withdrawal of Australian troops that had been approved by cabinet while Gorton was prime minister. On 30 March, McMahon was able to announce that Australia's forces would be reduced to 6,000 men within the next four to six months. He tried to dress the announcement up in terms that suggested Australian troops had made a difference. 'It is undeniable that there has been satisfactory progress towards the objective of establishing the circumstances in which South Vietnam can determine its own future,' he told the House.

> But perhaps more than ever before, the government of the Republic [of Vietnam] acknowledges that getting on top of the internal threat to security and the development of progressive government in the provinces are tasks best performed by themselves once a sufficient degree of security from massive external attack has been established.[1]

Implicit in the announcement was some recognition that Australia needed to make its decisions independently, and not in reaction to American ones. There were signs that it was a good strategy to pursue further. When, nine days later, US president Richard Nixon announced another American troop withdrawal, McMahon came under little pressure to modify the government's policy: he could point to the 30 March announcement as an indication that Australia was already moving to withdraw.[2]

Nevertheless, McMahon knew that there had to be some kind of change. Late in April, he was canvassing ending conscription once troops were withdrawn from Vietnam; early in May, he told Bunting that he wanted 'new thought to be given' to the strategy of Australia's commitment in Vietnam and conscription; by June, he was concerned that Australia's policy of withdrawal was not in 'drift'.[3] Changes that he pushed for would, eventually, lead to Australia's extrication from the conflict; but the successive Moratorium marches on 30 April, 30 May, and 30 June would ensure that they were considered under the pressure of substantial public protests.

The past continued to haunt the government. In June, the *New York Times* began to publish leaked extracts of a US Department of Defense report on America's political and military involvement in Vietnam. The Pentagon Papers, as they came to be called, soon caught the attention of the Australian press, which focused on the origins of Australia's involvement. Very quickly, opponents of the war pointed out that the public justification for joining the conflict—that Australia had done so at the request of the South Vietnamese government—was questionable, if not a lie. The furore prompted Menzies to make a rare public intervention and deny that he had misled Parliament when announcing Australia's commitment; meanwhile, the government, under McMahon, was forced to publish the South Vietnamese government's 1964 requests for military assistance.[4] But the conclusion was clear: the Australian government had decided to commit its military in advance of a request that it had sought to bring about in response to pressure from the United States. Though McMahon had, at the vital meeting where that decision was made on 7 April 1964, expressed his doubts about it, he was now the one who took the brunt of criticism. He did not aid his cause by pointing out that he was the only person at that meeting who was still in government.[5] It harmed the image that McMahon sought to create: of a calm, wise politician who was keeping up with the times.

By the winter of 1971, McMahon was tense, tired, and moody. He was arguing with Anthony and Sinclair. He was suspicious of Gorton.

He was critical of his ministers.[6] He was frustrated with the amount of work he was doing, weighed down by the pressure on him. Could his department help? he asked John Bunting. 'It was my belief that the first and principal step for him,' Bunting wrote of this conversation, 'was to put more responsibility on the relevant Ministers but I knew that in some cases this would cause him anxiety and that in a few matters the handling would not in reality greatly satisfy him. But this was the price he would have to pay for the shifting of the load from himself.'[7] As Bunting had seen, the cause of McMahon's angst was as much his own frustration with himself. Before leaving to take up his position in London, Tony Eggleton thought McMahon appeared 'uncertain and disappointed in his own performance.'[8]

Howson believed that McMahon needed 'encouragement', and thought he had a 'tremendous load'.[9] In May, McMahon was 'extremely tired' and in 'need of a rest', a point emphasised when he sat down for an interview with two journalists from *Time* magazine.[10] Appearing distracted throughout, McMahon spent the interview leafing through a voluminous briefing file and reading verbatim answers to the questions, which had been submitted to him in advance. His reliance on the material was such that when he was unexpectedly asked about Australia's future, he began to look concerned. There was no note about Australia's future in the file. After humming and hawing, he told the journalists he had to catch a plane and would send them his thoughts later.[11] 'Is the situation that he needs briefing before he can deal with a subject?' Alan Reid asked incredulously, when he heard. 'No piece of paper, no answer?'[12] Nor did McMahon ever provide that answer.

McMahon was indecisive. His propensity for telephoning around—'I get too many calls,' he complained to Bunting on 6 June[13]—saw him constantly revising his opinions, shifting his stance depending on what each new caller said. He buried himself in detail, but rarely seemed able to settle on a course of action. Speaking later, Bunting observed that McMahon worked hard but was 'somehow insecure':

> There was a real enigma there ... He had undeniable abilities, undeniable. He was very active, very hardworking. He started early and he finished late and worked, as far as I could observe, all the time in between ... He was nervous to a degree about any decision, and

he worked hard towards getting decisions, ceaselessly, relentlessly ...
McMahon—having decided that such and such was the right line—was
likely not to have second thoughts, but, more public service style, to be
seeing the other side of the case all the time and, in some ways, to be just
that little bit edgy, insecure; and sometimes of course it led to changes
in decisions.[14]

In June, he was 'vastly overworked', in Howson's opinion, and
despairing of the qualities of his staff.[15] When he gave a speech on tariff
policy to a Chamber of Manufacturers dinner in late July, Frank Packer
was blunt: 'Bill, that was a bloody awful speech.' The criticism—from
perhaps the only person McMahon could not brush off—prompted
him to begin talk of employing a full-time speechwriter who could
work alongside Keith Sinclair.

Was McMahon out of his depth? Was he failing? After a dinner
with McMahon at the Lodge in July, Bert Kelly certainly thought
so: 'I must admit that I am becoming acutely despondent about the
standard of leadership that we get nowadays. I never thought much
of John Gorton as leader and I don't think much of McMahon either.
There is far too much of the politician in him and too little of the
statesman.'[16] McMahon would never admit that. He would only say
that being prime minister exhausted him. There was so much work, so
many responsibilities. It was a totally preoccupying position, he would
say, with recurring deadlines, commitments, functions, and roles that
left little time to rest or think. 'The job is a man-killer.'[17]

Gorton, in particular, vexed McMahon. Much as he might think
wistfully of his deputy accepting a diplomatic appointment, there was
little prospect of Gorton giving McMahon the clear air that McMahon,
as his deputy, had never given him. At least there were regular breaks
when Gorton went abroad, such as in April, when he attended the
concluding talks on the Five Power Defence Arrangements in London.

Ostensibly, the talks should have been uncontroversial, something
McMahon could leave to Gorton to handle. Progress had been swift
since Lord Carrington's visit to Australia in July 1970. Australia, New
Zealand, Singapore, Malaysia, and the UK had established an air-
defence council; in February, Malcolm Fraser had announced that
Australian, British, and New Zealand armed forces would be organised

as a single force commanded by an Australian. The talks in London would see the final understanding hammered out. Assuming this occurred, the agreement would represent a substantial triumph for the government, one for which McMahon could claim credit.[18]

But another problem was brewing, one that would exacerbate the tension between McMahon and Gorton. Earlier in the year, Lee Kuan Yew, the prime minister of Singapore, had decided that the Australian and New Zealand governments should pay rent for the facilities their military forces used in Singapore, on the grounds that they were there for their own national interests. An *ad hoc* committee of cabinet considered the matter on 7 April. '[The] man is serious and would like to twist [our] arm,' McMahon said of Lee.[19] Nonetheless, cabinet decided to play for time and sought greater detail about Lee's demands while not conceding any obligation.[20] On the same day, however, McMahon sent Lee a cable. Australia, McMahon told the Singaporean leader, would contest any suggestion of payment of rent. Furthermore, there could surely not be any understandings made at the London conference when the financial consequences were so unknown. There was a warning note throughout the cable: mention of how soon the conference was to be, of the late stage that this proposal was coming up—and the prospect that an agreement at the talks might be prevented 'by differences of this kind.'[21] Lee's reply five days later was silky. It was 'unlikely' that the matters could be settled before the conference, Lee agreed, but the position shared by Australia and New Zealand was different from that of the British, which had built the facilities it sought to use and 'have always been and are here'. Despite entreaties for Australia and New Zealand to stay in Terendak, Malaysia, both had decided to move to Singapore, and had conceded that rents would be negotiated. What, then, was the reason for refusing to pay?[22]

McMahon cabled Gorton, now in London with Bury, to suggest that he might talk with Lee himself about the matter. Gorton cabled him back immediately to point out that there might be some confusion if McMahon were conducting a negotiation while his ministers did the same half a world away. 'You will of course be the best judge,' Gorton said, which prompted McMahon to complain about confusion and clarity. 'Regret if there should have been any grounds for confusion at your end,' he scrawled on his copy.

Meanwhile, Gorton managed to close off the differences that Lee had suggested existed between Britain, Australia, and New Zealand, and was pressing the issue of rents with the Singaporean minister for defence. Nonetheless, he was clearly worried about McMahon.[23] Gorton appended another warning to McMahon in a cable sent the next day. 'In view of the fluidity of the present situation, I strongly urge that no discussions of any kind be held either in Singapore, or between Canberra and Singapore until conclusion of London talks.'[24]

McMahon, aware of Gorton's anger, had several drafts—variously grovelling, pedantic, nitpicking, and indignant—prepared to rebuke his deputy. 'It would be a pity if the sense of my cable has been misunderstood,' ran one suggested line. The same tone ran through all of his subsequent communications with Gorton in London. When McMahon suggested that Gorton express confidence in the overall arrangements and say that any problems could be worked out, Gorton replied that this was unnecessary, unless McMahon wished to give away all of Australia's negotiating power on the rents and 'sign a blank cheque'. He urged that Australia be straightforward about the lack of resolution on the issue.[25] McMahon's response was petulant and seemingly intent on reminding Gorton that he was not prime minister anymore:

> I cannot let your 7232 [cable] go without comment. First, I have to say I find its tone surprising. In fact, I had the same reaction to your earlier cable but I decided to let that aspect of it pass. But getting back to 7232, it seems to leave out of account that I was responding to your cables. In the first place, you asked for response and, in the second, there are in any case always final responsibilities residing here in Canberra.[26]

There is little doubt that the matter would have been best left to Gorton: he was the minister on the ground. But McMahon's distrust of Gorton, as well as his understandable concern that the Five Power Defence Arrangements might be 'falling through over marginal issues', spurred him to intervene.[27] The successful conclusion of the arrangements did not make matters better for McMahon: he continued to regard his deputy with suspicion and dislike. His fear that his own power might be traduced or impinged was always palpable.

Attempts by Howson and Jess to upset Gorton's preselection for his seat of Higgins thickened the tension; equally to blame was what was later called 'de-Gortonisation', in which McMahon undid measures and initiatives that Gorton regarded as close to his heart. In June, McMahon deferred a decision on whether to cancel the proposed nuclear-power reactor at Jervis Bay;[28] later, he would cancel it entirely, saying that he was 'never convinced that the amount of money spent on it, and the work done, [was] sufficiently justified'. In his view, the project was 'moving too quickly and in the wrong way' with substantial problems of cost and viability still to be considered.[29] At other times the tension between McMahon and Gorton arose from understandable differences of opinion over matters of policy, such as when Gorton spoke to the Imperial Services Club on 18 June on the ideas of 'forward defence' and 'fortress Australia'. Gorton knew well that the matter was politically sensitive, given his own problems with defence matters while prime minister and McMahon's sensitivity to controversy. Nonetheless, in his speech, Gorton appeared to question the orthodoxy of forward defence when he emphasised the costs associated with maintaining Australian military forces in the Asia-Pacific region. Being clear about those costs and Australia's capacity to meet them lay at the heart of his concerns, as he made plain: 'The inexcusable action would be to pretend to the people of Australia that full and adequate defence was being provided when it was not.'[30]

For McMahon, this step off the orthodox line was simply too much. When he read of the speech, he told his staff that Gorton was 'a nasty bit of work' and had breached cabinet confidentiality by speaking about a matter that had been discussed in cabinet only days before.[31] He had a point: Gorton's advocacy in that meeting was much in the vein of his speech, and he had gained little support from his colleagues for it.[32] Yet McMahon refrained from confronting Gorton directly. Alan Reid was blunt about it: 'McM[ahon] as usual when Gorton is involved over-reacts. He gives the impression that he is frightened of the man.'[33] McMahon called Howson and told him the speech could provide the catalyst to get rid of Gorton altogether. He wanted to know what opinion was on the backbench.[34] By the next day, Howson could report back that McMahon should use Gorton's speech to mobilise opinion in his favour, both within the party and the press, in order to prepare

THE CRUMBLING PILLARS (II)

the ground for 'the next incident' that would inevitably occur within weeks.[35] It was not enough to reassure McMahon. The next day, his worry and dithering was palpable to Alan Reid:

> Gorton is rattling McM[ahon]. His nerves seem to be reaching breaking point. He is asking what he should do with Gorton. One suggestion was that he should be shoved upstairs, appointed to London in succession to Downer, whose term is up. McM[ahon] says that Gorton wants to go to London but he is suspicious of him. London is not as important as it was. But Gorton could still do considerable harm. But later when he offers the job to Gorton [he] knocks it back. As McM[ahon]'s stocks decline, G[orton] can probably see his rising. He undoubtedly nurses the thought that he can make a comeback, either before or after the next elections.[36]

A few days later, Reid was sick of it. When McMahon telephoned again to complain about Gorton, the journalist was extraordinarily blunt: 'For God's sake behave like a prime minister. If you want to take him on, take him on, but don't keep complaining about him behind his back. All that does is give the impression that you're dead scared of him.'[37]

A confrontation between the two would come in a matter of weeks. But what would throw McMahon into immediate despair was the crumbling of an old certainty: the palatability of communist China.

DAYS before taking over from Gorton, McMahon had authored a cabinet submission recommending that the restrictions on Australian trade with the PRC be removed, so that there would be 'as few restraints as possible' on the trading relationship.[38] In May, the McMahon cabinet agreed to relax controls of strategic exports—'My point is to screw everything out of [the] Chinese we can,' McMahon said during the cabinet meeting[39]—but in the intervening period there were clear signs that the parameters of Australia's relationship with China were beginning to change.[40] On 2 April, Jim Plimsoll sent word that the American National Security Council—comprising, among others, Nixon, his vice-president, the secretaries of state and treasury, and the attorney-general—had considered the PRC's representation in the UN.[41] It had not come to any decision, but the mere fact of the meeting made clear that the US would not consult Australia about a change in policy: it would *inform* Australia of a change in its China policy. When McMahon read of this meeting, he immediately sought to ensure that the White House heard Australia's views.[42] He was unaware that Nixon was not going to be listening: early in March, the president had directed that matters to do with Australia be handled by others. Only matters that required a 'presidential decision and can only be handled at a presidential level' would be presented to him.[43]

Advising McMahon on foreign relations, Richard Woolcott recalled advising McMahon that Australia should recognise China. The prime minister would not countenance it. 'McMahon said that he couldn't do it because his party wouldn't accept it,' Woolcott recalled.[44] Keith Waller thought similarly. 'I think the attitude of the DLP was a major factor … The McMahon government in particular was very timorous so far as the DLP were concerned. McMahon was in constant touch with B.A. Santamaria, and tended to check his moves before he made them.'[45] McMahon was caught in a bind. Labor was pressing the government over China's suspension of wheat sales, a sore point that led Doug Anthony to declare his bitter opposition to any rapprochement with the PRC. 'I wouldn't recognise Red China just to sell wheat,' he said, '[and] I wouldn't sell my foreign policies or my philosophies just to try to do a trade deal.'[46] Labor was also reaping the rewards of Whitlam's longstanding advocacy for the diplomatic recognition of the PRC—an advocacy that went back over sixteen years, to 1954:

> We must recognise the fact that the Government installed in Formosa has no chance of ever again becoming the Government of China unless it is enabled to do so as a result of a third world war. When we say that that Government should be the Government of China we not only take an unrealistic view but a menacing one. The Australian Government should have recognised the Communist Government in China.[47]

Showing what McMahon had called 'its smiling face', China was moving to engage with the international community. Most notably, in what the press soon termed 'ping-pong diplomacy', the PRC sent invitations to table tennis groups around the world to participate in the thirty-first World Table Tennis Championships in Peking, to be held during April and May. Encouraged by this move, hopeful that Labor's policy of recognition might give it some credit, and looking to embarrass the government further over the cancelled wheat sales, the federal secretary of the ALP, Mick Young, suggested that Whitlam seek an invitation to visit China.[48] It was a risky proposal, but one that Whitlam took up. On 14 April, he sent a telegram to Chinese premier Zhou Enlai:

> Australian Labor Party anxious to send delegation to People's Republic of China to discuss the terms on which your government is interested in having diplomatic and trade relations with Australia.[49]

Whitlam announced his move the next day, hoping to contrast the ALP's initiative with the government's inertia. The risky contrast was immediately palpable. Despite his awareness that there had to be change and advice that he not respond,[50] McMahon reacted with the same instincts that had guided his actions while foreign minister: political self-preservation. From a perspective of domestic politics, he could not afford the kind of criticism that had led the DLP to withhold preferences at the 1969 election. Moreover, he could not allow his own, barely healing party to fracture again, a possibility that a radical departure from long-drawn battlelines might provoke. McMahon thus seized upon Whitlam's telegram to go on the attack. Still speaking of the PRC in the 'red' language of the 1950s, he told the National Press Club on 15 April that China should not be admitted to the UN without an assurance that it would not pursue political objectives through force or insurgency operations and that the retention of a seat for the ROC was a paramount goal.[51] In the House, he suggested there were parallels between the telegram and Evatt's letter to the Soviet minister Molotov during the Petrov Affair. He said that Whitlam's attempts at engagement would fail. He called it all just politics.[52]

But then Whitlam announced that the ALP had received a response. On 10 May, a telegram from the People's Institute of Foreign Affairs—a front for the PRC to interact with nations that did not recognise it—invited an ALP delegation to visit the country. The risks of acceptance were quickly apparent. What some in the ALP had believed was a political stunt was now very real. Whitlam hesitated about going, but soon concluded that the risks were worth it.

McMahon was not nearly as daring, but he was aware of the politics involved. In a domestic sense, he saw that Whitlam's decision to accept the invitation to visit afforded him space to begin shifting the government's policy towards engagement with the PRC. After a cabinet discussion held at his initiative, McMahon gave a speech to the Citizens Club in Sydney on 13 May, announcing that the government would 'explore the possibilities of establishing a dialogue with the People's Republic (of China)', with a view to normalising bilateral relations eventually.[53] It was 'indication of flexibility' only, and limited in scope: an expansion of cultural exhanges, changes for visas and entry permits, and visits by sports teams, press, and artistic groups. The core issue, of diplomatic relations between Australia and the PRC, was completely separate.

The announcement was all politics, an attempt to show that his government was not following a trail blazed by the ALP, that it had its own initiative. But it was not well received. McMahon, apparently speaking from a rewrite of more conciliatory papers from the Department of Foreign Affairs, had appeared to suggest an almost total change in policy, particularly towards the Soviet Union. When he finished, the room stayed silent but for one person. Sir Frank Packer was the only person to applaud.[54]

McMahon was trying to find some political advantage, hoping to have the benefits of recognition and attack at the same time. He was also anxious to ensure that he not get out of step with the US. On the same day as his speech, McMahon sent a letter to Nixon seeking 'an indication of your present thinking' and reiterating that time was running out for a solution to the problems posed by the PRC's inevitable admission to the UN and the ROC's likely ejection from the Security Council.[55] Nixon did not trouble himself to respond until mid-July.[56]

Meanwhile, hampered by lack of contacts within the Chinese government, Australia's ambassador to France, Alan Renouf—McMahon's old flatmate—was told to 'make the initial move' and approach the Chinese ambassador to France, Huang Chen.[57] Renouf met the ambassador on

27 May. But upon being told that Australia sought, in the long term, to normalise relations with the PRC, Chen replied that obstacles to recognition were solely of the Australian government's making. Australia followed the US, had participated in the 'aggressive war' in Vietnam, had diplomatic relations with Taiwan, advocated the 'two-China' or 'one China, one Taiwan' formula, and had acted in a 'hostile way' towards the PRC, he told Renouf. Until Australia removed these obstacles, no relations could be normalised.[58] Subsequent meetings proved that matters would go no further: the PRC was not interested in discussing anything less than diplomatic relations.[59] 'On this I had nothing to say,' Renouf cabled to Canberra.[60] They were at an impasse.

Matters were still there when Whitlam, leading a delegation that included nine handpicked journalists, departed Australia for Hong Kong in late June. Arriving in China on 2 July, the Labor leader announced that Australia would 'learn more about China in the next fourteen days than it had ever previously'.[61] He was more correct than he could ever have thought.

As McMahon frustratedly declared that Australia could not get 'any common sense' out of the Chinese in its talks in Paris,[62] Whitlam and his party proved the opposite. They had meetings with the acting foreign minister, Ji Pengfei, and the minister for trade, Bai Xiangguo. Then, on 5 July, Whitlam was granted an audience with Chinese premier Zhou Enlai.

Conducted in the East Room of the Great Hall of the People, this was no benign photo opportunity. Zhou's invitation for the press to witness the meeting ensured that it was fraught with dangers that were amplified by Whitlam's being the first Western political figure to visit the PRC. Whitlam was not now playing only to an Australian audience: this meeting would have international significance. The political risks were immense.[63] Navigating those risks required finesse and firmness. After discussing ALP policy, Zhou sought to induce Whitlam to denounce Australia's alliance with the US. Zhou invoked SEATO: 'You cannot call SEATO a defensive treaty,' the Chinese premier joked, but Whitlam was forthright: 'It is moribund.'[64]

Zhou spoke of the Chinese relationship with Russia, via the Sino-Soviet pact, and how it had soured, what kind of a warning it could serve. 'Is your ally very reliable?' he asked. He moved on to Australian politics. The present government 'is not friendly' to China, he said, and cited McMahon's remark that diplomatic relations with China were 'far off now'.

Whitlam remained silent. Refusing to enter into any party politics, he would only promise that diplomatic relations would be pursued should the ALP win the election due the next year.

Zhou seemed to shrug. 'They do not want to establish diplomatic relations. He [McMahon] seems to be quite confident. It is probably because your party is in China.'

'This may be,' Whitlam replied cautiously. 'I must say, even to the credit of my opponents, they are catching up with the realities of life on China, to a certain extent. They know Dulles' politics have failed dismally, and if president Nixon says he wants to visit China, can Mr McMahon be far behind?'

Zhou did not wait for the translation. He began to laugh heartily. Soon, he moved to wrap the meeting up. 'What is past is past and we look forward to when you can take office,' the Chinese premier told Whitlam, 'and you can put into effect your promises.'

It had been a good meeting, but the memory of Zhou's laughter was to linger with Whitlam. Why had the Chinese premier laughed so? Whitlam had no inkling as to its cause. 'I was not in on the joke,' he later remarked.[65]

When McMahon heard news of the meeting, he seemed to be staggered. Then he seemed hesitant, unsure what to make of it. 'He is obviously concerned,' Alan Reid observed. '… There is almost a jealousy about it. But he clearly does not know what to do about China.' McMahon wanted to claim credit for driving the review of Australia's policy towards China, but 'the real story', in Reid's opinion, 'appears to be that the Department [of Foreign Affairs] did it of its own volition.'[66]

The prime minister was indecisive, blowing in the wind. He had his spine stiffened by a meeting with the DLP leader, senator Vince Gair, on 7 July, and then the next day met Harry Bland. He told Bland that Whitlam had 'goofed' on China, but it was clear that he was trying to convince himself, that he was trying to preserve his hopes: 'He probably believes that Whitlam has scored a major political point but he just doesn't want to admit it even to himself,' thought Reid.[67] He was hardly going to find direction from the press: the reception to the news was neither gushing nor harsh. McMahon decided to rely on the old touchstones. After checking his speech with the United States embassy in Canberra, he spoke to an audience of Young Liberals in Melbourne on 12 July:

> It is time to expose the shams and absurdities of [Whitlam's] excursion into instant coffee diplomacy ... He went on playing his wild diplomatic game, knocking our friends one by one until he was virtually alone in Asia and the Pacific, except for the communists ... I find it incredible that at a time when Australian soldiers are still engaged in Vietnam, the Leader of the Labor Party is becoming a spokesman for those against whom we are fighting.

McMahon's audience was favourable. His speech was punchy. His attack hit all the right notes—notes that had worked for twenty years. And the memorable metaphor ensured that the peroration of McMahon's speech would haunt him. 'In no time at all,' McMahon said, 'Zhou Enlai had Mr Whitlam on a hook and he played him as a fisherman plays a trout.'[68]

The affair made the Liberals excited. The opening and the prospect of an easy attack led some to have visions of victory and glory. Fraser told Howson that the government should call an election and capitalise on Whitlam's visit.[69] McMahon felt confident enough to declare, to another gathering of Liberal Party members, that 'China has been a political asset to the Liberal Party in the past and is likely to remain one in the future.'[70]

But that future was extremely short. On 15 July, McMahon received word that Nixon was about to take a decisive step on US-China relations.[71] Within two hours, Nixon appeared on television to read a statement that was, simultaneously, being broadcast in Peking. His assistant for national security, Henry Kissinger, he announced, had just returned from a secret diplomatic trip to China, where he had met with Zhou Enlai between 9 and 11 July. He himself, Nixon said, hoped to be able to accept an invitation to visit Peking by May 1972. He looked forward to meeting with Chinese leaders. He hoped to normalise relations between the US and China, to exchange views on questions of concern. 'I have taken this action,' Nixon said, 'because of my profound conviction that all nations will gain from a reduction of tensions and a better relationship between the United States and the People's Republic of China.'[72]

When he heard this, McMahon was aghast. He had, at least, avoided the fate of the tearful Japanese prime minister, who had heard of it via the press, but this was small salve to the considerable embarrassment and sense of betrayal he felt. Only the day before, Nixon had written to him and said *nothing* of Kissinger's visit, *nothing* of Nixon's willingness to go to China. If anything, that letter had indicated that Nixon had come to no firm decisions on *nothing* whatsoever. McMahon could not have failed to feel humiliated by the Americans. As he sadly told Graham Freudenberg much later, 'We thought we were being helpful.'[73] So much for that. 'He was, in a sense,' commented Richard Woolcott later, 'unlucky on it.'[74] But luck did not explain it all. McMahon had repeatedly failed to heed warning signs that the US would make its own decisions on China; he had repeatedly failed to seize opportunities for himself to recast and solve the problem. He had made his own luck—and lost.

When Whitlam learned of Kissinger's visit, while in Japan, he could not help but be amused. Now he had an explanation for Zhou's hearty laughter. Of course, after that visit, McMahon would not be far behind. Surprised and stunned by the news, he felt 'extraordinary vindication', he said later.[75] The joke was now his to share in, and it augured well for him: 'The mandate of heaven had clearly been withdrawn.'[76]

In public, McMahon tried to hide his discomfort. He told unconvinced reporters that 'normalising relations with China' had been Australia's policy for some time, and refused to answer questions about it. He was 'shaken and embarrassed', wrote one journalist; Labor was gleeful, happy to rub salt in McMahon's wounds.[77] When Lance Barnard, Whitlam's deputy, was asked to provide a memorable line, he invoked a fish: McMahon was like a stunned mullet, he said.

Stunned though he might be, McMahon made no secret of his anger in private. The editor of the *Canberra Times*, John Allan, who had received a telephone call from McMahon complaining about an editorial on his 'prime ministerial clangers', told the US embassy that McMahon was 'almost psychotic' about his humiliation. The Americans were unsurprised: they had already assessed that McMahon was 'on

edge and almost frenzied in trying to stay on top of his job'.[78] When
McMahon wrote to Nixon on 18 July, he complained that Australia was
'placed in a quandary by our lack of any foreknowledge' and continued,
sharply, that 'it should have been possible to advise your friends and
allies of the broad trends in your thinking.' But the most pressing cause
for McMahon's complaint was the damage that Nixon had done to
McMahon's politicking:

> Our relations with the People's Republic of China have in recent weeks
> been a matter of deep public controversy in Australia following a visit to
> Peking by members of the Australian Labor Party, including the Leader
> of the Opposition Mr Whitlam. We have felt obliged to criticise many
> of the things which Mr Whitlam said and did in Peking including some
> quite gratuitous attacks and criticism of our friends and allies including
> the United States ... Some of it would have been cast differently had we
> been given an indication of changes in American policy along the lines
> I have mentioned.

Reasonable as it was for McMahon to write it, the complaint surely
undercut his admonishment that, by Nixon's secrecy, there existed the
assumption that 'our relations are not as close as they should be'.[79] A
meeting between Jim Plimsoll and US secretary of state William Rogers,
in which Rogers explained his government's reasoning, failed to placate
McMahon. Rogers' suggestion that 'it had just not been possible to let
many know' had McMahon seething. 'But they trusted the Pakistanis!!
[sic]' he scrawled on the report of the meeting. 'Not us!! Or Japan!!'[80]
Two days later, McMahon canvassed making a national broadcast on
China to wrest back the initiative, to elevate these developments to
'national matters', outside the sphere of domestic politics.[81] But with his
colleagues, McMahon's frustration was clear. His disappointment was
palpable. It was a 'failure' of his prime ministership, he told Howson
over dinner on 20 July, and for that he blamed Nixon and his secrecy.
Howson tried to coax McMahon to move on. 'The main task is for him
[McMahon] to get some rest, because he certainly looks tired and is
a little tense and terse. He must also learn to delegate responsibility a
little more; he wants to do everybody's job himself.'[82]
    All McMahon could do was continue to criticise. All he could do

was hope that there were enough people who did not trust Whitlam, the ALP, or China, but who would trust instead in his own government's close relationship with the US. 'Whitlam did not even know that Kissinger was there,' he said. 'That's how much the Chinese trust him. It makes a mockery of the man.'[83]

It was feeble. McMahon was the man who had been made a mockery. If Australia looked 'less flat-footed, less ignorant, less obscurantist, less imitative' because of Whitlam's visit, as the Labor leader declared on his return, then domestically, it was the McMahon government that looked all of these things.[84] McMahon was flailing, blaming anyone he could. In a speech to the American National Club, he was sarcastic and meddling. 'I wouldn't be surprised if Zhou Enlai didn't get the best of president Nixon [when they meet],' he said to a startled audience, 'which in turn will adversely affect Nixon's election chances in 1972.'[85]

But McMahon was not going to stop trying to resolve the issue. At Frank Packer's suggestion, he explored trying to accompany Nixon when he visited China, but was told that the Chinese would be unlikely to accept this without some material change in Australian policy.[86] Looking for a scapegoat and a new change, he decided to remove Les Bury as minister for foreign affairs. Not offering any reasons, he told Bury late in July that he wanted him gone. On 30 July, when Hasluck queried this—having already heard the news from an outraged Bury—McMahon said that he had little confidence in Bury's ability to handle the House 'convincingly' when questions about China inevitably arose:

> He (the P.M.) seemed to be worried at the possibility of criticism of him over China. He then said that Bury was tired and sick and seemed to be running down. He (McMahon) himself had to 'do everything in Foreign Affairs' … If it was not for McMahon himself nothing would be done. He told me of the 'simply colossal' job he was doing in foreign affairs but he seemed to me to be trying to reassure himself as much as to give information to me. In short, he wanted a new Minister for Foreign Affairs before Parliament met.[87]

McMahon announced on 1 August that Bury had resigned for reasons to do with his health. Bury would have none of this pretence:

McMahon had sacked him and, furthermore, cabinet had 'leaked like a ruddy sieve', he told press and colleagues alike. The former foreign minister was angry. As he had told Hasluck when McMahon told him that he was to go, his departure had been inevitable: 'Of course,' said Bury, 'it was obvious he had it in for me since he lowered the seniority of Alan Hulme and myself when forming his cabinet and that he would try to get rid of me when he could.'[88] Nigel Bowen would be Bury's replacement, and would offer vital support for McMahon. But, simultaneously, Bury's sacking did not help McMahon. It simply created one more enemy on the government backbench. 'I have an intense antipathy towards McMahon and I don't like anything about him,' Bury said later. 'That's the truth of the matter.'[89]

The favourable press that Nixon received from his move to engage with China did, however, encourage McMahon to continue trying to resolve the China problem. On 28 July, he told the Liberal Party Council in Victoria that dialogue with the PRC was continuing, still aimed towards an eventual diplomatic recognition. He was trying to find another way forward by introducing distinctions in Australia's relationship.[90] Cultural exchanges should be the first steps towards a diplomatic relationship. Recognition could not be 'the first result of the first dialogue'. The ALP's position, of an immediate recognition along the lines of the Canadian formula, was reckless and tantamount to abandoning 'old friends' like Taiwan.[91]

It was a position that would find McMahon no allies, no friends. The Chinese did not see diplomatic recognition as a mere formality. For them, it was necessary. It was a prerequisite for China's involvement in the international community. It was a first step for normalisation. Anything short of that was worthless.

More troubling, for McMahon, was the criticism of Vince Gair. Nixon's move to engage with China had not been to the DLP leader's liking, and now, to McMahon's proposal, he was scathing. 'A new pattern of foreign policy now seems to be taking shape,' Gair said on 30 July, 'not based on the objective merits of the question under discussion, but as part of a popularity contest between Mr McMahon and Mr Whitlam as to who is more "ahead" on the China issue.'[92]

It made McMahon supremely cautious, unwilling to entertain any radical new approach on the scale of Whitlam's. The point was most evident when Andrew Peacock, as minister for the army, received a private invitation in October for him and his wife to visit Beijing. The invitation had come via Melbourne businessman James Kibel, a frequent visitor to China who had been sounded out by Chinese officials in Hong Kong about whether he knew any Australian ministers. Though it would not be an official trip, it was intimated that Peacock would have talks with premier Zhou and other senior officials.[93] When McMahon first heard the idea, he reacted cautiously, and suggested instead it be a trade delegation that included businessmen alongside government officials.[94] The Chinese renewed their offer to Peacock, but McMahon vetoed it completely: a visit had to be official, and certainly it should be at a senior ministerial level. That left the prospect of a trade mission, which gained some traction when Doug Anthony—discovering the proposal after a Labor member questioned him about it in the House—angrily insisted that he, not Peacock, should lead it.[95]

But amid the fallout from China's entry to the UN General Assembly and its assumption of a seat on the Security Council on 25 October—displacing the ROC, over the objections of the US and Australia—the proposal went cold. It would go no further. The government judged that the Chinese government was responsible. As Australia's representative in Hong Kong wrote, the Chinese were probably influenced by the belief that Australia 'did not accept the political implications' of the canvassed visit by Peacock, and that victory at the UN had strengthened China's hand. 'We would thus appear to be back in much the same position we were after the breakdown of the ambassadorial talks in Paris earlier in the year.'[96]

The government tried to suggest further dialogue with the PRC. China saw no point. Nothing had changed, and McMahon was left to make a lonely, sad admission in December that he had thought the government was on its way to some sort of success. 'But the Chinese acted in their own inscrutable ways and suddenly they cut off [talks], without rhyme, without reason, and we do not know when they are likely to resume again.'[97]

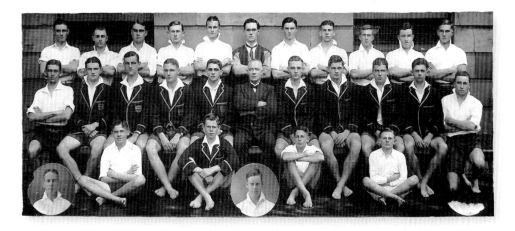

ABOVE: McMahon as part of the Sydney Grammar School rowing team. He is seated, second from the right. *Sydney Grammar School*

RIGHT: The new back-bencher: McMahon, June 1950. *NLA PIC/7122*

ABOVE: McMahon as Minister for the Navy and Air. *AWM HOBJ3783*

ABOVE: As minister for social services, McMahon made sure to publicise the government's contributions to the construction of aged care homes. Here, he presents the first grant, of £10,000, to the Whiddon Group. *Whiddon Group*

LEFT: The 'confession' Menzies purportedly kept in his safe, to be used if McMahon leaked again. McMahon's annotations are in pencil. *NAA: M2576, 2*

Note of conversation between the Prime Minister and the Minister For Labour and National Service, 23 September, 1959.

The P.M. "I asked Mr.McMahon whether he had seen any member of the Government Members Social Services Committee this afternoon"

He said "Yes, he had seen Mr.Wilson".

I said "Was any officer of Social Services present?".

He said "Not at the beginning, but there was one later on, with the consent of the Minister".

I said "Did you have with you a copy of the Mr.Roberton's Budget submission to Cabinet ?".

He said "Yes"

I said "Did you show it to Mr,Wilson"?"

He said "I dont think so."

I said "Did you tell Mr.Wilson the substance of the proposal made by Mr.Roberton to Cabinet?"

He said "Yes, because I thought it important that to show Mr.Wilson that such proposals were not new."

I said "That means that in substance you have conveyed to a private member the nature of a proposal made in Cabinet Room by a Minister, and have indicated that it was rejected by Cabinet."

He said "Yes."

I said " How long have you been a Minister ?"

He said "Eight years."

I said "This is an outrage. I will consider the position."

RIGHT: McMahon, with Menzies and McEwen, 1960. *News Ltd/Newspix*

ABOVE: McMahon, as
sketched by Paul Hasluck
in a Cabinet meeting. *NAA:
A2668, 1*

LEFT: McMahon and
Sonia, 29 November 1966.
News Ltd/Newspix

ABOVE: McMahon, at the swearing-in of the Holt ministry at Government House, 26 January 1966. *NAA: A1200, L53612*

ABOVE: Commonwealth police raid the home and office of Maxwell Newton on 23 May 1969. Newton looks on; behind him stands Peter Kelly, McMahon's former press secretary. *Herald-Weekly Times/Newspix*

ABOVE: McMahon, as foreign minister, speaks with Major John Bertram while visiting Phuoc Tuy province, South Vietnam, in April 1970. *John Fairley, AWM FAI/70/0253/VN*

ABOVE: Paul Hasluck and William McMahon at Government House, Canberra, after the swearing-in of the McMahon ministry, 22 March 1971. *NAA: A1200, L94978*

The McMahon ministry. CLOCKWISE FROM FAR LEFT: Senators Robert Cotton and Sir Kenneth Anderson, Dr Jim Forbes, Billy Snedden, Sir Alan Hulme, Doug Anthony, McMahon, John Gorton, Ian Sinclair, Nigel Bowen, Peter Nixon, Ceb Barnes, Senator Thomas Drake-Brockman, Phillip Lynch, Ralph Hunt, Andrew Peacock, David Fairbairn, Leslie Bury, Billy Wentworth, Reg Swartz, Don Chipp, Dr Malcolm Mackay, Kevin Cairns, and Senator Ivor Greenwood. *NAA: A1200, L94982*

ABOVE: McMahon, Sonia, and US President Richard Nixon, Washington DC, 3 November 1971. *News Ltd/Newspix*

ABOVE: McMahon, with drafts of his autobiography, in his office at Westfield Towers, July 1986. *Robert Pearce, Fairfax Syndication*

CHAPTER THIRTY-SEVEN

The Crumbling Pillars (III)

1971

The confrontation with Gorton finally came in August. McMahon had been agonising for weeks over what to do about his deputy and the pockets of support he still enjoyed in the party. After meeting with the Victorian division of the Liberal Party, McMahon was heard to say that Robert Southey was a Gorton man: 'I don't trust Southey.' McMahon was, Alan Reid believed, 'obsessed with Gorton'.[1] Bede Hartcher, the Liberal Party's federal director, told McMahon to have a face-to-face confrontation with his deputy and to bury the hatchet, but McMahon would have none of it.

The catalyst for Gorton's removal came, inevitably it seems, from the Packer Press, with the publication of Reid's new book.[2] *The Gorton Experiment* had been completed and sent to its publisher a short time before Gorton's fall in March, but had been supplemented by a fifty-four-page postscript following Gorton's fall. It was, again, punchy and dramatic, and its narrative stressed—as though to contrast with the image that McMahon was trying to create—the turmoil rife throughout Gorton's prime ministership. It told of Gorton defenestrating his government's best talents, of Gorton promoting his cronies, of Gorton endangering the whole of the government by his wilful recklessness. As with *The Power Struggle*, Reid was no impartial observer, and, while he mentioned his own part in several of the events, there was no acknowledgement of the role of the Packer press. Nor was there an acknowledgement of his own involvement in destabilising Gorton's leadership. Moreover, Reid's reportage was occasionally overly personal, as when he described Gorton on the opening page: 'A bastard by birth, gregarious by habit, distrustful by nature, wilful by temperament, Gorton was Prime Minister by accident.'[3]

Understandably, Gorton felt compelled to reply to Reid's account, not least because of the errors it contained. Speed, too, was a consideration. Thus Gorton negotiated an agreement to write a series of autobiographical articles for Rupert Murdoch's *Sunday Australian*, to be published under a song title that *This Day Tonight* had suggested encapsulated Gorton's style: 'I Did It My Way'.

Gorton's style was as punchy as Reid's. In the first article, Gorton defended his government and gave his own pen portrait of the journalist known to colleagues as the Red Fox:

> He is a slightly-built, balding man with little darting eyes and an expression of perpetual cynicism. When talking to one he tends to stand slightly turned away, peeping under a drooping eyelid from the corner of one eye. There is a knowing, downward twist to his lips as he speaks from the corner of his mouth. One expects momentarily to be nudged in the ribs with a confidential elbow and given a hot tip for the 3.30 at Randwick.

Moreover, Gorton continued, with a barbed flourish, while he was a bastard by the actions of his parents, Reid had achieved that status himself by following the riding instructions of Sir Frank Packer. In sum, Gorton argued that Reid's book was no good: reliant on backstairs gossip, leaks, partial and misleading accounts, and almost totally inaccurate. *His* articles, Gorton said, would show 'what really happened'. In doing so, Gorton could not resist slighting his colleagues. As he wrote, 'From time to time cabinet ministers have shown themselves so uncertain of their own opinions that they have chosen to canvass the value of impending legislation far beyond the cabinet room, indeed beyond the confines of the Parliament altogether. Others are afflicted with a compulsion to try out ideas on their wives.' The BHP-Esso matter, for example, 'had to be treated very circumspectly'.[4]

In writing this, Gorton set the scene for his final fall. By suggesting that his cabinet had leaked, Gorton had also leaked—and, furthermore, cast aspersions on his colleagues. It was ironic to a large degree that the man most notorious for leaking from cabinet would engineer the removal of his deputy for the same act.

McMahon heard of Gorton's article two days before it was published, while holidaying at Eric Robinson's home at the Isle of Capri, in Queensland. The holiday had come at Howson's urging, but McMahon was hardly upset that it was interrupted.[5] He recognised almost immediately that the articles provided him with cause to seek Gorton's resignation from the ministry and, hopefully, the deputy leadership as well. Predictably, given McMahon's angst and prevarication, he was both afraid of and delighted by the news.[6] The next day, having travelled to Adelaide to watch a game of Aussie Rules, he grew so impatient and anxious that he left at half-time to return to his hotel and pore over extracts that had been sent via teleprinter. Sonia, according to Reid's information, told her husband that Gorton had to go, but McMahon was uncertain. He returned to Queensland and began the rounds on the phone, canvassing opinion from colleagues, the public service, and the press alike.[7]

John Bunting provided advice on 9 August. It was circumspect and hesitant. There was no precedent for a minister writing while holding office, he argued, and Gorton's article did not breach any rule against disclosure of formal cabinet or government papers. 'But there is an atmosphere about the article which might be said to be in breach of standards,' Bunting went on. 'Also, the article could seem to offend against "collective responsibility" conventions.' Bunting suggested that subsequent articles might provoke other colleagues to reply, which would undermine unity and responsibility. Whether there was a fee involved (as there was), 'would be another factor at a judgment on propriety,' Bunting wrote.[8] Peter Bailey, the first assistant secretary, had also been asked to provide advice. He saw no legal offence or overt breach of cabinet secrecy, he wrote, but suggested that the real questions were whether Reid's book 'represents a sufficiently specific attack to permit a riposte on a series of fronts' and whether Gorton's articles were a 'reasonable defence against attack'. But his advice was similarly equivocal: the prime minister would be wise to discuss [the matter] with at least one or two of his colleagues.[9]

McMahon did exactly that. He spoke, at least, with Eric Robinson, Nigel Bowen, senator Kenneth Anderson, Neil Brown, Billy Snedden,

Robert Southey, Peter Howson, Jim Carlton (general secretary of the New South Wales Liberal Party), Alan Hulme, and Alan Jarman.[10] Opinion within the party coalesced. So, too, did opinion in the press. Sir Frank Packer, accepting an invitation from the ABC to appear on its *PM* radio programme, made a conspicuous contribution to the discussion about Gorton. Asked about Reid and his motives for publishing *The Gorton Experiment,* Packer said that Reid probably wished to make some money, and denied that the book—which had been published by a Packer-owned company—had been published under anything other than a standard publishing contract. Then Packer went on: even if the book were only 50 per cent true, it was 'a very strong indictment of Mr Gorton', who was a 'great embarrassment' to his successor, who was himself already 'an infinitely better' prime minister.

> *Packer:* I have no doubt there is squabbling in the cabinet, and in my view Mr McMahon ought to get rid of Mr Gorton out of the cabinet—not because of his ability but because of their inability to get along.
> *Interviewer:* What do you think he should do with him?
> *Packer:* Oh, well—retire him to the backbenches.[11]

But even this was not enough for the matter to be certain. Bert Kelly was so well aware of McMahon's tendency to back down that he sent him a telegram expressing support for sacking Gorton. 'You can't help feeling that Billy is a bit like the churchmouse who didn't want to get out into the middle of the room because he was a bit timid,' he wrote in his diary. 'So just in case he is like this I thought I'd send him a telegram.'[12] It was wise. When McMahon travelled back to Sydney on 11 August, he heard that Gorton might be at the Commonwealth Parliamentary Offices in Martin Place—so, instead, he went to his home to continue calling colleagues.

It was on Wednesday 12 August that McMahon finally sought to confront Gorton, asking him to call at his office at around three o'clock. Scuttling about to find all the details he could, Reid heard that McMahon had been 'whitefaced, tense' and that his staff were 'afraid of him fall[ing] to pieces' if there was a fullscale row.[13] But Gorton was not particularly interested in a fight. Like Killen, he was amused to see McMahon sweating and shifting in his seat, his resolve seemingly draining away as the meeting went on. McMahon told Gorton that he had given consideration to the articles he was writing. He had concluded that the first article infringed the conventions of cabinet solidarity and unity, largely because Gorton had reflected on other ministers who would not be able to reply. In another vein, McMahon suggested that there was a problem of incompatibility.

When Gorton replied that he believed he had a right to defend himself, and that he was surprised McMahon would suggest otherwise, McMahon told him that a public argument would be damaging. Cabinet solidarity was the overriding principle. Gorton did not question anything else. He would resign. The two agreed to exchange letters. Gorton asked about his entitlements as a former prime minister, and McMahon told him they would be the same as those enjoyed by Menzies and McEwen.[14] Then, no doubt hoping to be rid of Gorton altogether, McMahon asked whether he wanted a diplomatic appointment. As Gorton remembered it:

> He said, 'Would you like to go to London as the High Commissioner or something like that?' And I said, 'No. I want to stay here,' and he said, 'You'll have to be sacked,' and I said, 'All right, but you write to me and tell me that you're sacking me,' and so he did that and I had that in writing and I was happy to get out.[15]

That evening, McMahon—with the help of his colleagues and staff—drafted a letter to Gorton setting out his reasoning for seeking his resignation. Gorton's reply reached McMahon that night, and, by mutual agreement, both letters were released the next day.[16]

McMahon could have been forgiven, now, for breathing a sigh of relief. The confrontation was over. His antagonist was vanquished. There were some who saw it as proof of his resolve and as an opportunity for the government to make another clean start. Others were more withering. Maxwell Newton's sarcasm was barely disguised:

> It must have taken a tremendous personal effort for Billy to screw himself up to sack Gorton. In the past Billy has always got other people—myself, Alan Reid, Sir Frank Packer, Warwick Fairfax, and many others—to

stab his enemies for him while Billy waited in the background until the crisis which others had precipitated came to a solution.[17]

But what about the deputy leadership? At a press conference the next day, Gorton made no mention of resigning; instead, he held it over to the next instalment of his series in *The Sunday Australian*. Writing that it would be 'absurd' for him to remain deputy without also being in the cabinet, he said he would resign so as not to create division in the party.[18]

Thus, the race began for the deputy leadership. McMahon, according to Peter Howson, supported Reg Swartz, the leader of the House and minister for national development.[19] But it was a race for all comers. David Fairbairn was lobbying for votes, Billy Snedden had put his hand up again, Jim Killen's hat was in the ring, Don Chipp was putting himself out there, Billy Wentworth was on the phone, and Malcolm Fraser, too, was attempting to overcome the venom of Gorton's supporters by putting himself forward. It took a few ballots, but, with a considerable bloc of support from the Senate, Snedden won the post. It was, in many respects, his proper due as treasurer. A loss would have been an unprecedented rebuke. But it was hard not to see the result as a rebuke for McMahon. Quite plainly, the Liberal Party was not about to heed his preferences.

Amid this, watching with equal parts of disbelief and disgust, was the Labor Party. Whitlam gave notice that he would move a motion of censure: 'That, in the opinion of this House, the Prime Minister's methods and motives in removing his Ministers and his subservience to outside influence have destroyed trust in his government at home and abroad.'

It was the day of the budget, 17 August. Aware that the motion was coming, McMahon sought a meeting with Gorton to ensure that he would not embarrass the government during the debate. According to Gorton, McMahon told him that Packer had no influence on him at all and that he had an independent mind that ensured he was in and out of favour with the press. Most importantly, he wanted Whitlam's motion gone, dealt with before the dinner break, so that it would not impede or interrupt his government's first budget. Therefore, while agreeing to a suspension of standing orders in the House, he wanted only two people to reply: himself and Anthony. If the opposition criticised Gorton, then, yes, he 'might come in' to the debate. It was clear that McMahon was nervous, worried that Gorton might cross the floor or divulge details and information about the travails of recent years.[20] After Gorton left, McMahon set to work on Killen to find out what he would do during the debate.[21]

But it was neither Gorton nor Killen that McMahon should have been worried about. The real threat was Whitlam, whose ascendancy over McMahon in the House of Representatives was established and the object of entertainment for both sides. Whitlam's preparation was thorough. His argument was crisp. His lines were sharp.

McMahon, he told the House, had been duplicitous about the circumstances in which he had sacked Les Bury. McMahon, he told the House, had held Australia up to ridicule by his actions as prime minister. McMahon, he said, was now again under censure. 'No Prime Minister in the history of Federation has had this experience.' And both motions, he said, had one point in common: 'They spring directly from the conduct of the Prime Minister.' McMahon had lied about Bury's health; he had worked in tandem with the Packer press to ensure Gorton's downfall. The devastating and memorable point of the speech came as Whitlam canvassed how McMahon had reacted to news of Gorton's article in *The Sunday Australian*. 'He did nothing on the whole of the late afternoon and the night before the article appeared in the newspaper,' Whitlam said:

He did nothing between that Sunday and the following Thursday. He was spending the time with his great friend, Mr Eric Robinson, President of the Queensland Branch of the Liberal Party on the Isle of Capri at Surfers Paradise. There are 100 businessmen and journalists around Australia who could give evidence that they received calls from the Prime Minister at that time. Some were asked for advice; some were asked for help. The advice sought was how to get rid of John Gorton. The help sought was how to pour a bucket on him ... He [McMahon] was determined, like other Little Caesars, to destroy the Right Honourable member for Higgins and he sat there on the Isle of Capri plotting his destruction—Tiberius with a telephone.

From there came a detailed explication of McMahon's relationship with Packer. From there came an argument that McMahon was simply not good enough for the 'great' Liberal Party. From there came an argument that McMahon was a politicking, venal man looking to take advantage of the protests over the South African tour, including pressuring Bradman. From there came his indictment of McMahon for his dismissal of ministers, 'men of considerable skill', who now sat on the backbench. Perhaps a little weakly, from there came Whitlam's plea that those former ministers cross the floor and vote with the Labor Party—and, in doing so, give the Liberal Party 'a lease of life'.[22]

McMahon's response was not wholly inept, but he was certainly outclassed. A point-by-point refutation of Whitlam's motion would not be convincing, especially when so many of those points were plainly correct: the relationship with Packer, the relationship with Reid. On the whole, McMahon's argument was thin: the ALP was of no substance. The government—as it would prove in the budget it would hand down that evening—had substance. His government had been working for just five months and 'brought down a solid list of domestic legislation'. But, beyond this, McMahon flailed. He was scattered: he brought up tariffs, price controls, pensions. He tried to turn the suggestion of subservient influences back on Whitlam. 'Who is really speaking for Labor? It is not a question of who runs the country,' he said, 'it is a question of who runs the Labor Party.'

'Ask Frank Packer,' yelled ALP wit Ralph Jacobi, the member for the South Australian seat of Hawker.

The attack collapsed in an instant. McMahon was left defending the change of leadership, making loud proclamations of unity and purpose. 'You will find that the Liberal Party which I lead, with the Country Party standing behind us, will give to this country the kind of government that it needs and which will take it to a very much higher destiny than we know at the moment or that the Labor Party could ever think was realistically possible.'[23]

In the opinion of Bert Kelly, McMahon would have done far better if he had made a ten-minute speech, rebutting some of the personal attacks and nothing else.[24] Howson thought the entire debate had fallen flat.[25] He was wrong: Whitlam's attack would live on in the popular memory, and his sobriquet for McMahon—'Tiberius with a telephone'—would become famous.

TWO hours after Whitlam's motion was voted down, Billy Snedden rose to present the McMahon government's first budget. It was a document framed almost entirely against the backdrop of rising inflation: as Snedden said that night, 'Australia is in the grip of inflationary pressures.' Over the previous two years, he said, average weekly earnings had risen by 8.9 per cent and 10 per cent respectively; the consumer price index had risen by 3.2 per cent and 4.8 per cent. Wage increases—most notably in a 9 per cent increase granted under the Metal Trades award—were ominously large, and the slow uptick in unemployment, towards 2 per cent, posed problems for the government.

In Snedden's mind, it was a 'difficult time' to be treasurer. Though he and McMahon agreed on much, they differed on the degree to which political expediency should affect economic policy. McMahon, according to Snedden, was keen to take any advantage he could to earn plaudits, to pursue the short term in order to recover the government's position. His approach had long been transparent. To Bert Kelly, McMahon's announcement of the pensions increase, in the censure motion he had faced in March, was a disappointing move:

> This comes badly from Billy who knows better than anyone of the necessity for sitting on the economy's head and is evidently determined to be popular at any price, and to make his new image glow a bit.[26]

Kelly's misgivings proved, temporarily at least, unfounded. McMahon would not yet be quite so craven. For the 1971–72 budget, he wanted to be 'tough' and find a new rigour in the budget. According to Snedden, however, this was only so that in the following year, right before the 1972 election, the government could afford to be generous. Snedden disagreed with the strategy. He wanted to allow the economy to 'develop', as he put it, and manage problems as they arose. He also preferred to control the flow of information: he disliked McMahon's propensity for seeking to speak with officials from Treasury and requesting papers from the department.[27] None of these were new or unforeseeable conflicts—just the traditional tension between a prime minister and treasurer—but divisions within Snedden's staff at the Treasury exacerbated the disagreement between the two men. According to Snedden, both the secretary of the Treasury and the deputy secretary, Richard Randall and Jack Garrett, wanted a 'tight' budget that would impose taxes; the head of the Financial and Economic Policy division within Treasury, Frank Pryor, and his deputy, Bert Prowse, were against it.[28]

When the budget strategy was discussed in a cabinet sub-committee, Snedden found himself overruled, with Anthony taking McMahon's side, who in turn was joined by Randall and Garrett. Snedden began looking at cutting expenditure, hassling and driving unwilling colleagues to prioritise their spending. Their task was given additional urgency by world shocks, most notably when US president Richard Nixon decided on 13 August that the United States would suspend the conversion of the American dollar into gold, a decision that had seemed in the offing since gold prices had collapsed in 1968. This was, in effect, the end of the Bretton Woods agreement, which had underpinned world economic stability since the late 1950s; in Snedden's words, this 'undid everything'.[29] The need to diversify reserve holdings became paramount. The need to set currency exchanges became fraught. The systems of clean and dirty floats started to take shape.

Thus the budget that night sought to slow down the rate of growth in Commonwealth expenditure. Taxes were increased on company income and personal income. Excise duties on petroleum products and tobacco were increased. There were increases in licence fees. The charge payable under the Pharmaceutical Benefits Scheme was doubled from 50c to $1.[30] McMahon regarded the budget as an opportunity to recapture the agenda: he asked his officials to prepare a speech for the budget debate that emphasised the government's approach, the 'sense of sanity and leadership' that the budget provided, and its work to contain expenditure and inflation.[31]

Overshadowed by the turmoil of Gorton's resignation, the contest for his replacement, the need for a cabinet reshuffle, and by international reactions to Nixon's decision, the budget was tough, rigorous, and deflationary, all of which ensured it went without many admirers. 'This is not going to make us loved in the electorate,' Bert Kelly wrote in his diary that night, 'but it had to come.'[32] John Stone, observing the budget's preparation and strategy in the Treasury, agreed that it was designed to contest the inflationary forces that were reshaping the world, and, on the whole, 'was more or less successful from that viewpoint'.[33]

For Snedden, however, the budget was an example of how he was obliged to wear criticism for decisions that others had made. When the press criticised it as too tough, it was he who took the blame. The extent to which this contributed to his adverse regard for McMahon is difficult to tell, but there is no doubt that he believed his prime minister made life impossible. 'McMahon was mercurial, like quicksilver,' Snedden said later. Nervous, unpredictable, shifting his positions constantly, the prime minister 'could not have led a trail of ants to a fallen ice cream.' It was the difference between McMahon's idealised self, and what he really was. McMahon, Snedden thought, believed himself to be wise and cautious, even constant when he was wavering. 'He was never consistent and did not understand that he was being inconsistent; he simply did not understand consistency.' Keeping the record straight was another problem: after meetings, McMahon would call in a typist and dictate an aide-mémoire of what had happened. 'Bill, that wasn't said,' Snedden would invariably say, and the whole process would begin again. On one particular occasion, it led to a back-and-forth of rewritten versions:

> Every time he started to write it down he got it wrong. Ultimately I dictated it but it was expunged and he dictated his own version. It was not very accurate. It seemed to me that he wrote things down as he would have wanted them to have happened, not as they did happen. He had reconstructed them after the event.[34]

It made life difficult for all concerned: cabinet decisions had to be re-drafted and re-discussed, and what McMahon said of his conversations with industrialists and businessmen could never be trusted. Combined with his propensity to use the phone at all hours, and his willingness to telephone Treasury officers directly for information and advice, Snedden found himself fighting McMahon for consistency and control of his bailiwick.[35]

Bury's removal, Snedden's election to the deputy leadership, and Gorton's resignation, required successive reshuffles of the ministry: David Fairbairn was moved into defence; Nigel Bowen was moved into foreign affairs; and Malcolm Fraser came back into cabinet to replace Fairbairn, taking up his old portfolio of education and science.[36] Senator Ivor Greenwood became attorney-general, and senator Kenneth Anderson became minister for health. McMahon's new 'assistant ministers' were sworn in following a debate in the House about their positions, responsibilities, and accountability to the Parliament.

But there were always problems, and indiscipline was constant. Government backbenchers John Jess, Harry Turner, Bert Kelly, and Tom Hughes had all threatened to cross the floor if the subject of assistant ministries were not debated, and Hughes had pointed out that the success and failure of this 'experiment' would be all McMahon's.[37] The Senate president, senator Magnus Cormack, had already been quite clear about his regard for a 'covey' of ministers in the Senate: 'I am quite willing to support the Bill,' he said, '... provided we do not get any more cuckoos in the nest here.'[38] Such divisions continued to undermine attempts at unity and professionalism. 'The government's immediate as well as long-term concern must be to offer convincing proof that it can give the assured, stable, forceful and creative leadership that alone will retrieve the electoral confidence it has jettisoned,' the Canberra Times editorialised, on the day of the budget.[39]

Could McMahon harness the energies of those around him to do that? Could he lead a government that would retrieve that confidence? Certainly he was trying. Aware that Vietnam continued to be a millstone around the government's neck, he seized an opportunity to loosen it. On 18 August, he announced in the House that all Australian combat troops would be withdrawn from Vietnam, with a great number of them to be home by Christmas 1971. 'The combat role which Australia took up over six years ago in Vietnam is soon to be completed,' he said. Moreover, in the same speech, McMahon announced that the period of national service would be reduced, from twenty-four months to eighteen. Prompted by the government's sensitivity to domestic political pressure, the defence committee of cabinet had initially recommended withdrawal of Australian forces by August 1972. The shock of Nixon's rapprochement with China, however, had caused cabinet to re-evaluate and then accelerate that withdrawal: quite plainly, Australia could not assume 'that the United States would not now speed up its own programme of withdrawal'.[40]

However the decision came about, it was surely to McMahon's credit that he was extricating Australia from a conflict that had taken a tremendous toll, caused extraordinary upheaval, and appeared to be a near failure in attaining its strategic goals. But McMahon could not, and would not, escape the political cost of the decision to commit Australian forces in the first place. Nor would he receive the credit for ending Australia's involvement. To McMahon's statement that it was 'the Government's conviction that the decision I have announced tonight is a mark of the success which has attended our policies and actions in Vietnam over the years,' Whitlam's response was simple and immediate: 'There is one reason and one reason only why Australia is now getting out. We are getting out because the US is getting out.' McMahon, Whitlam said, 'is the sole survivor of the guilty men who sent us there in 1965'.[41]

Was McMahon rattled? Was he overworked and flailing? It seemed so. Alan Reid heard rumours that during a cabinet meeting McMahon was told that he needed 'vision and a blueprint for the future'. The prime minister's response? 'Get Bunting on it.'[42] On the same day that McMahon supposedly said this, 27 August, Parliament was adjourned for lack of a quorum, a failing that only added to the aura of disorganisation that was taking hold. The quest to regain the initiative, to overcome Labor's ascendancy in the Parliament, led McMahon into errors and made him suspicious. On 7 September, amid questions about the call-out of the PIR in 1970, Whitlam asked McMahon about his visits to Papua New Guinea. Was the last one he had made back in 1952, while he was minister for the navy? Had he stayed on Manus Island for less than twenty-four hours? McMahon's response was cavalier:

> If the honourable gentleman had been cautious enough to obtain information from the Department of Air as well as from the Department of the Navy he would have found that I visited Papua New Guinea on several occasions and not one. But I will try and obtain the details for him if I can … I went to Papua New Guinea on several occasions as Minister for Air, flying in a VIP aircraft, which in those days was most unusual.[43]

Peter Bailey, the first assistant secretary in the department of prime minister and cabinet, had his staff check to ensure the answer was accurate. Although they could verify that McMahon had visited Papua New Guinea once, they could not be certain about further visits. There were no records for it. Trying to be diplomatic, understanding that he could hardly call the prime minister a liar, Bailey drafted a minute noting that the department could not find documentation of a further visit. A few weeks later, once the parliamentary session was over, Bailey joined a few officials at McMahon's home in Sydney for drinks. At one point during the evening, Bailey had the uneasy feeling that McMahon was looking at him. *What's going on here?* Bailey thought. Then McMahon hoisted a glass of beer. 'You called me a liar!' he yelled at Bailey—and threw the glass at him.[44]

For the public service, managing the work with McMahon was impossible. McMahon would read and underline his memos and briefing materials, but fail to indicate decisions; he would harass public servants for material constantly.

Peter Lawler felt that there 'was a frenetic quality in McMahon's work as prime minister.' But all that business, all that work, seemed futile, Lawler thought. 'The McMahon show was tired, rambling, and had lost its way.'[45] Bunting found similar problems. Telephone calls with demands for information were frequent, and questions about unexpected topics made the veteran public servant uneasy. 'Although it was a pleasant and effective working arrangement,' Bunting said later, 'there was some degree of wariness in it.' He could 'never [be] quite sure' of his ground.[46] McMahon's relations with his colleagues complicated matters. 'I don't know that he commanded the authority that the others [prime ministers] had,' Bunting said later. '… He was first among equals, but only by a short whisker, a short half-head.'[47]

It was certainly the case that McMahon did not like working with the Country Party. In March, amid falling wool prices, there was a long back-and-forth with Doug Anthony and Ian Sinclair over the Australian Wool Commission, with McMahon suspicious of attempts to trick him. He thought the commission was being profligate, and that the leaks that followed the debate were being orchestrated by the Country Party in order to pressure him.[48]

But there were other, more serious problems that the Country Party brought McMahon that he needed to heed. Following the Conservative Party's victory at the 1970 UK general election, John McEwen had secured an agreement from the British to allow Australian agricultural suppliers 'the longest possible transitional period' to adjust to the new conditions that would result from Britain's fresh attempts to enter the European Economic Community.[49] After almost a decade in which Australia had been buffeted and disappointed by Britain and the EEC, it seemed that McEwen's actions had ensured there would be space for Australia to re-calibrate. But in mid-1971, while on a tour of EEC capitals, Anthony found out that Australia had been deceived: while Britain had secured a three-year transition for its own industries to adjust to its entry, it had not secured the same for Australia. As one later observer put it, 'While the British had obtained breathing room to allow their own industries to adjust, Australian primary producers would be subjected to the full blast of internal EEC preferences from the very day of Britain's accession.'[50]

Anthony greeted this news with profound anger. At best, the British had neglected to tell Australia of this change; at worst, Britain had deliberately deceived Australia. When he met with Geoffrey Rippon, the British minister overseeing the country's negotiations with the EEC, Anthony did not hold back. As he recalled, 'Rippon opened the discussion by making some derogatory and insulting remarks about things I had said and about Australia's attitude to Britain entering the EEC. I bristled and reacted in an equally brusque tone.'[51] The British gave equal serve, both to Anthony and Australia's high commissioner to London, Alexander Downer, who recorded Rippon telling him:

> We were, he [Rippon] said, a selfish country. We contributed little to international aid. We cared nothing for Britain. 'It would matter nothing to you if this country sank under the North Sea.' We thought of our own interests, and nothing else ... 'You cannot,' he proceeded, 'continue to live on England's back.'[52]

When McMahon heard of this from Downer and Anthony, he sent prime minister Heath a letter demanding the British go back and secure the transitional arrangements they had promised. There was little chance of this happening. Heath's reply was to the point: the negotiations were done. Britain would enter the EEC on 1 January 1973. Australia would have to make its own way. Aware that Australia's exports would be greatly damaged, Anthony pushed to have more trade commissioners overseas in order to find and develop emerging markets elsewhere.

Dealing with the Country Party was also fraught for McMahon because of the promises he had made to others. Nugget Coombs, writing in October to seek McMahon's intervention on the inter-departmental committee that was supposed to be discussing Aboriginal land rights, told him that the Department of the Interior—headed by Country Party minister Ralph Hunt—was recommending a 'continuation ... of policies which have been followed in the Northern Territory for the last twenty years'. The department 'opposed the Council's proposals to lease for general purposes to Aboriginal communities "land with which they have association by tradition or long occupancy"; for the purchase of land for communities outside reserves; and for support for Aboriginal enterprises.'[53] Coming after budget cuts, hostility from other departments, interference, and deliberate non-co-operation that had left him and his colleagues in the Council for Aboriginal Affairs immensely frustrated, Coombs was ready to make a big gesture. If McMahon did not intervene, Coombs intimated, he would resign.

McMahon's response was to duck the issue: he wanted Coombs to join him on a planned trip to the United States and London in November, and he wanted him to assist McMahon with 'special assignments', including writing speeches about the future and Australian society.[54] Hoping that he could still keep McMahon onside and involved in Aboriginal affairs, Coombs agreed, cautiously, but stated explicitly that he would not be a part of McMahon's official party on his trip and that any work for him was dependent on decisions about Aborigines going 'the right way'.[55] It was no matter. McMahon subsequently told a press conference that Coombs would assist him 'not in matters that involve him in the Arts and similar matters but as a kind of guiding philosopher'.[56] Whether it arose from some hope of political mileage, as a statement of fact, or even as a mischievous way of preventing Coombs's resignation, the statement caused many raised eyebrows. What kind of prime minister needed a 'guiding philosopher'?[57]

Even as this was happening, Howson was attempting to deal with the haphazard lines of responsibility in his portfolio. Coombs's licence—as chairman of the Council for Aboriginal Affairs and chairman of the Australian Arts Council, with a direct line to McMahon—and his advocacy for land rights for Aborigines grated on him, especially as he simultaneously sought to formulate a new arts policy. But he soon found that he had his own problems with McMahon.

In September, Howson announced that the film school Gorton had helped to initiate would be deferred for twelve months because of costs. That decision sparked a public intervention from Gorton, his first since leaving the ministry in August. Using Question Time as his stage, Gorton pointed out that the school was far cheaper than what Australians spent overseas for films each year. Howson, clearly aware that he was out on a limb and would be attracting press attention, told the House that it was being deferred in order to develop 'a better series of proposals than the original proposal'.[58] Within the week, Phillip Adams, an advertising executive who sat on the film school's council, resigned from it while appearing on ABC current affairs programme *This Day Tonight*. He followed up with a public and memorable quip that Howson was 'a pain in the arts'.[59]

The next day, Adams received a series of phone calls, each telling him that the prime minister would be calling in a successively shorter time frame. Finally, Adams heard McMahon's 'shrill, pipey' voice coming over the line to apologise for the furore about the school, to bucket Howson, and to promise that the whole problem would be solved.[60] Howson was none too impressed: 'He seems to have forgotten that he authorised me to defer the school for twelve months and is now talking of accelerating a decision,' he wrote in his diary. '... At the moment he can only see it as a row between Gorton and myself and is therefore trying at the moment to stifle criticism.'[61] McMahon subsequently told the House that Howson would present a proposal for the school before the next budget.[62] An argument with McMahon about it, Howson later noted in his diary, 'could well happen'. As he complained late in October, the problems were:

Coombs trying to advise the PM, Coombs and Len Hewitt fighting each other, the PM being always apprehensive or sceptical of Len Hewitt's advice, and Gorton wanting to fight us all. It is a time in which one can trust only one's self and take every precaution to record everything that is said or written.[63]

The chaos that had seemingly beset Gorton at every turn was increasing for McMahon. There were constant problems, and McMahon seemed unable to rise to the challenge of meeting them.

CHAPTER THIRTY-EIGHT

The Crumbling Pillars (IV)

1971

On 27 October 1971, McMahon left Australia for the United States and the United Kingdom. He was making the trip solely for political purposes. The visit to the US was almost entirely motivated by his wish to recover from the embarrassment over China; the leg to the UK, hastily arranged in mid-October,[1] was designed to prevent the appearance that Australia and the UK were not close, and to increase McMahon's stature by association with a successful conservative political leader in Ted Heath.[2] As the British high commissioner in Australia, Morrice James, wrote privately to London, McMahon 'wanted some of Mr Nixon's and Mr Heath's prestige to brush off onto himself'.[3] The desire was acute and it was transparent. The visits to Washington and London were 'first and foremost undertaken in search of credibility and reassurance,' wrote James. 'He [McMahon] was quite unabashed about this.' At least it was entertaining: 'The unconcealed gusto with which Mr McMahon plots his not-very-Machiavellian gambits is one of the engaging things about him.'[4] Few observers thought that McMahon would be able to earn the esteem of his allies: Menzies wrote privately that McMahon would 'provoke many unspoken questions in the minds of the people he meets'.[5]

For those accompanying McMahon, the trip was a succession of bewildering decisions, embarrassments, and mishaps. First was the considerable mirth that greeted the biographical notes McMahon's staff distributed to the press, which described McMahon as a 'soldier, barrister, economist, and Parliamentarian.'[6] Then there were the accidents on the squash courts. Nugget Coombs, joining McMahon's party partway through the trip, was roped into playing with the prime minister one morning, and was hit in the mouth by a forehand drive from McMahon's racket. The injury left Coombs requiring stitches.[7] 'That's no way to treat your guiding philosopher!' he joked to the press; but if Coombs had any wish of returning the injury, Richard Woolcott, in the delegation as foreign affairs adviser, soon satisfied him. Roped into playing with McMahon in New York and London, Woolcott accidently hit the prime minister with his racquet on each occasion, the second time inflicting a cut above McMahon's nose.[8]

The oddities continued. When Woolcott and two other diplomats arrived at McMahon's New York hotel room to brief him one morning, they found the prime minister clouded by shaving soap and clad only in a towel. He did not get dressed: the three diplomats sat down in three chairs that had been positioned in the middle of the room while McMahon plonked himself onto a large lounge chair, wrapped in the towel, to listen. They had some serious matters to talk about—namely, the speech-cum-toast that McMahon would give at a dinner in his honour at the White House. Their recommendation was that McMahon should avoid the obsequious overtones of Holt's 'All the way' comments. Instead, he should speak for fifteen minutes, at the most, on an independent foreign policy conducted within the framework of Australia's alliance with the US. They provided him with a draft.

But then they were interrupted by Sonia, who entered the room to model the dresses she had brought from Australia to wear to dinner with Nixon. One was white, long-sleeved, began at her throat, and came down nearly to her ankles. It would have been elegant, modest, and otherwise wholly unremarkable had it not been for the splits, held together by diamante bands, that ran up from the waist and down the length of her arms. Though on first glance it seemed anything but demure, the presence of flesh-coloured organza meant that it revealed nothing inappropriate. Was it all right, she asked her husband. McMahon told her it was fine.[9]

The Americans were well aware that McMahon was seeking reassurance and a show. They went some way to giving him what he wanted and needed. They made sure there was an appropriate amount of pageantry and a good stretch of red carpet for him when he arrived in Washington. They arranged for him to stay at Blair House as a token of their appreciation, organised meetings with members of their cabinet, and planned a dinner in his honour.

But McMahon wanted more than this. In a meeting with the secretary of state, William Rogers, he told the Americans that the best thing Nixon could do for him was 'to declare that [the] ANZUS treaty is as important as [the] day it was signed'. But Nixon, in his private talks with McMahon, would not do this, would not go quite so far. Moreover, McMahon seemed intent on handling everything himself. Bunting and Plimsoll, the ambassador, arranged with McMahon that they would join his meeting with Nixon after a brief discussion. But McMahon failed to make a signal, causing the meeting to continue without their presence. Afterward, when McMahon was leaving, Bunting grabbed Woolcott and told him to find out what had happened. As Woolcott recalled, McMahon's account was sketchy. The talks had been useful. Nixon had 'reaffirmed the validity of the ANZUS Treaty'. McMahon seemed attached to this point, thought it important, but Woolcott had a question: why had McMahon not made the signal for Plimsoll and Bunting to join the meeting? McMahon said he had forgotten. What happened after Kissinger joined Nixon, Woolcott asked. 'It was good,' said McMahon. 'We had a real meeting of the minds.'[10]

On his return to Blair House, ebullient and happy, McMahon told reporters that while his talks with Nixon were private, he could say that 'they could not have been put more frankly and in complete detail and I have no reservation whatsoever in saying that this is the kind of consultation we like and I doubt whether it could have been better'. He tried to wave away the US failure to inform Australia about China, and he sought to make as much hay as he could about ANZUS:

> One point I can mention to you because I think that this is of great importance to Australians was that he did agree with me that the phrase could be used that the United States Government, from the president down, recognised, or were prepared to confirm the unqualified and unconditional assurances that had been given to us in the ANZUS Treaty were as relevant and valid today as they were at the time the Treaty was negotiated.[11]

He wanted, he said to the press, 'to get the strongest affirmation' about ANZUS and he had got that. (He had also secured an agreement for a secret 'hot-line' to be established between the White House and the Lodge; it was, however, used for only a year and mostly to exchange birthday greetings.)[12]

And then there was the dinner at the White House, a night marked by three memorable moments. The first was Sonia and her dress: 'My god, I'll have her at my side!' Nixon exclaimed, when he saw her coming up the steps of the White House. 'My photograph will be in papers all across the country.'[13] Second was Nixon's repeated query of how to pronounce McMahon's name. Was it McMann? Mac-Mahon? Mic-Mann? The final highlight came when McMahon decided to imitate Nixon and speak off-the-cuff for his toast. For the Australians listening, what followed was a sustained embarrassment. From beginning to end, McMahon rambled, letting his sentences drift and becoming overladen with extravagances and asides. Trying to remember his Shakespeare, he became waylaid and stricken: 'I take as my text a few familiar words. There comes a time in the life of a man in the flood of time that taken at the flood leads on to fortune …' The American journalists listening in another room began to chuckle. Then McMahon began to talk of how he had sung *Fascination* to Sonia, in order to woo her. The American chorus of chuckles changed to 'hoots of laughter', recalled Alan Ramsey. The contingent of Australian journalists felt ashamed. 'I wish I was Italian,' one muttered.[14]

By the time McMahon arrived in London, the press was openly ridiculing him and the trip. Any chance of political gain was gone. McMahon was being lambasted for being ignorant of a request to train troops in Cambodia; for his criticism of Gorton and American senator and former vice-presidential candidate Edward Muskie; for his proud declaration that he liked the shape of his wife's legs and the look of her face; that he had chosen her dress because two slits in a dress were better than one. He sounded small, silly. When he met Ted Heath on 9 November, he spent the greater part of the meeting telling Heath all about his time in the US. 'Mr McMahon was clearly delighted with the treatment he had received in Washington, especially by the dinner and reception at the White House,' Heath recorded. 'He added that the president did inquire on five different occasions how to pronounce his name; this was counter-balanced, however, by the fact that "for the first time ever with a visiting Head of Government" the president said goodbye at the portico of the White House in front of the TV cameras.'[15]

McMahon did have several important points to talk about with the British. One was its entry to the EEC. Whether or not McMahon was tailoring his remarks for Heath or had changed his mind, he informed the British prime minister that he—McMahon—had told Australia that there had never been any undertaking from the British about safeguards for Australia in the EEC negotiations: 'This was absolutely clear and everyone in Australia understood it,' McMahon said. It was something of an about-face on his letter, but McMahon had already signalled that he would not traverse the criticisms Anthony had made: what was needed now was thought for the future.[16]

Therefore, in a subsequent meeting at which officials were present, McMahon told Heath of his belief that British–Australian consultations 'had been neither as continuous nor as frank as was desirable in the mutual interests of both countries'. What was to be done? McMahon had a ready answer: official, regular bilateral talks. It was a point that Morrice James had alluded to and which McMahon 'seemed keenly interested in' developing, very likely to use as a symbol of his government's close relationships abroad. Along with a proposal for another 'hot-line' between the leaders, nothing was to be resolved on the trip, but for months afterwards McMahon would continue to pursue it: 'We would like to establish regular bilateral talks of the kind we now hold at official level with Japan, India, and the United States,' he would write in December.[17] Heath would rebuff the move within the month: 'I doubt whether there is need for any new machinery for consultation "across the board".'[18]

There was also the proposal to move responsibility for the running of Australia House—Australia's high commission in London—from the Department of the Prime Minister and Cabinet to the Department of Foreign Affairs.[19] This proposal had originated with Keith Waller, who had argued that the need to mark relations with Britain as something special—by retaining the prime minister's personal control of policy for the UK—no longer existed.[20] Britain's turn to Europe, its disengagement from the Asia-Pacific, and the implications of its entry to the EEC meant that the handling of the Australia–UK relationship was best done by the Department of Foreign Affairs, in much the same way as relationships with the US and Japan were. The British saw no particular problem with the proposal, but McMahon would dither and prevaricate over it for the next year. It would exacerbate the anger of some and arouse despair in others. When hearing of a fresh round of McMahon's reservations, Waller would storm out of meetings, such was his anger.[21]

Despite his warm treatment from the British, McMahon's hopes that he might attract some gloss from the trip were dashed. The steady stream of dignitaries visiting London while he was there meant that journalists who accompanied him saw that his visit was not particularly special. In conjunction with the coverage from the US leg, their reportage was critical. It prompted Anthony to defend McMahon: he issued a statement saying that there had been 'almost a deliberate campaign to denigrate and undermine' the trip. Anthony was doing his duty. Even those sympathetic to McMahon had to admit that it had been a failure. When McMahon read Reid's critical coverage in *The Bulletin*, he declared that the journalist was a 'treacherous bastard' and promised to complain to Packer.[22] Reid, however, would not take the criticism. 'Forget I'm a newspaperman,' he said to McMahon. 'I'm an Australian. When you stand up before an assembly such as you had at the White House—and that's a very important forum—you are representing me and fourteen million other Australians. I can't speak for the other fourteen million Australians but I should imagine that they expect you to come up with something better than an account, however romantic, of your own domestic affairs. I know I expect more.'[23]

McMahon would not listen. He did not agree. Speaking to cabinet on 19 November, McMahon told his colleagues that the trip was 'very successful in terms of close relation[ship] w[ith] Nixon and Heath — especially Nixon'. He believed that the poor press reception was only because 'we don't do enough backgrounding'.[24] He would not give up hope that there could come a breakthrough, that the reception would turn around.[25] After making a statement to the House about his visits to the US and the UK, he decided to make a broadcast on national television. 'Both performances,' reported the British high commissioner later, 'were depressingly pedestrian.'[26]

THE problems continued. Amid further ructions with Nugget Coombs, Gorton, and the government's new arts policy, McMahon could be heard expressing doubts about Howson's handling of his ministry. 'For on[c]e [he] blames himself,' Alan Reid noted. 'Says he made a mistake.' Then he was embarrassed when Labor backbencher Norman Foster, citing three instances of it happening, pointed out McMahon's penchant for altering *Hansard*.[27] McMahon was angered and upset when he heard this. In a performance that left the crew of the plane he was flying on 'staggered', he lashed out at his principal private secretary, Ian Grigg, and Reg MacDonald, his press secretary, blaming them for the mess. 'I will now go through an hour of anguish on Tuesday,' he said. Gleaning the story afterward, Reid heard that McMahon:

> [...] would not listen to anyone and was highly emotional. He wanted the greens retyped before they were issued to the press. MacD[onald] said that this would draw attention to the fact that they were being changed. McM[ahon] wouldn't listen. According to crew, [he] told both Grigg and MacD[onald] to shut up.[28]

Then there was a scandal in miniature early in December. Amid efforts to secure a pay rise and an increase in the allowances offered to parliamentarians, following the issue of a report authored by John Kerr, McMahon intervened for what seemed mostly to do with his vanity, and turned it into another example of his panicky leadership. Telling Bunting that he would not consult Whitlam on the deal, McMahon declared, 'I'm the PM—I make the decisions.' Then the deal collapsed, and McMahon blamed everyone but himself. 'Well, the little fellow has made a mess of it again,' Anthony sighed as he left McMahon's office, aware that it had set off a fresh round of questions among his backbenchers.[29]

Then there were world problems. The government's efforts to present itself as united, professional, and in command of the economy were rebuffed when, in December, the so-called 'Group of Ten'—Belgium, Canada, France, Germany, Italy, Japan, the Netherlands, Sweden, the United Kingdom, and the United States—struck what became known as the Smithsonian Agreement. Intended to allow the world's

industrialised economies to reassess their exchange rates following
the August collapse of the Bretton Woods agreement and Nixon's
decision to suspend converting the US dollar to gold, the Smithsonian
Agreement posed, for the McMahon government, a diabolical problem.
While Australia had not followed the British pound in its devaluation
in 1967, its dollar was still pegged to it. Since, under the Smithsonian
Agreement, the British pound would rise 8.57 per cent against the US
dollar, the Australian dollar would likewise appreciate. McMahon,
Snedden, and the Treasury were in favour of allowing this because of
its anti-inflationary effects. However, like McEwen had in 1967, the
Country Party, under Doug Anthony, wanted the Australian dollar to
be devalued, potentially to even remain at parity with the US dollar: as
ever, a lower Australian dollar would help the party's constituency.

What followed was a long, exhausting debate. The discussion went
on for three days. Treasury officials, including the newly appointed
permanent head, Sir Frederick Wheeler, went in and out of the meeting.
The press was excited, its appetite stimulated by wild speculation and
a steady stream of leaks and counter-leaks. Trying to prevent this,
McMahon forbade his ministers from leaving the cabinet room during
his repeated consultations with Snedden and Anthony; trapped inside,
bored and tired, ministers gambled and played poker to pass the time.[30]
The first meeting lasted deep into the morning of 20 December, and
left McMahon 'grey with fatigue'.

Anthony and his colleagues were resisting McMahon's arguments
that Australia had to be part of a concerted world action; concerned by
the effect on rural industries and exports, they maintained a consistent
opposition to McMahon's statements. When McMahon suggested that
very few people disputed the correctness of the government's actions in
the 1967 devaluation decision, Anthony cut across him immediately:
'I do.' When McMahon, pressing for Snedden's position, said that the
government 'couldn't survive' if it stayed with the US dollar, Anthony
was blunt: 'Done like a dime [too] if we went with Treasurer.'[31]
According to Alan Reid, this kind of intransigence left McMahon:

> [...] nearly incoherent. He is reported as having said to his intimates,
> 'Christ, Christ we're in a bloody terrible mess—the coalition could
> be gone. What can I do? If I give in to Anthony I'm gone, finished.

If I don't, we split.' Asked if he thought the CP [Country Party] was bluffing he said, 'No, they're not—they're determined to get their way.' … McM tore into Fraser. 'He is no bloody help at all. He's in the CP camp.' Anthony, Sinclair, and Nixon kept storming into McM's office. There were numerous conferences between Anthony, Sinclair, McM, and Snedden.[32]

By the end of that first meeting on 20 December, cabinet agreed on a 6.32 per cent appreciation against the US dollar, but decided to hold over a final decision until the International Monetary Fund could give its approval. A draft statement was prepared: cabinet had 'reached certain general conclusions', but 'technical arrangements associated with these conclusions must be completed before a decision can be announced'.[33] But now there was a problem with Snedden and the Treasury, which had pushed for a full 8.57 per cent appreciation. According to McMahon, Snedden told him privately on 21 December that the governor of the Reserve Bank had said that the decision was disastrous and that an 8.57 per cent appreciation was necessary.[34]

When cabinet resumed, the argument began again, exposing further rifts and driving colleagues further apart. Fraser was sympathetic to the arguments coming from Anthony, Sinclair, and Nixon, and Snedden was growing frustrated with McMahon's attempts to broker a compromise. A conference in McMahon's office with Anthony, Snedden, and McMahon appeared to succeed, but the cabinet meeting had to be adjourned so McMahon could go to Victoria to avert a move by the Liberal conference in the Wimmera to run a candidate against Country Party member Robert King, who was also minister assisting the minister for primary industry. It was the last fight that McMahon would have wanted at that moment, and he returned to Canberra at two-thirty in the morning, exhausted and grey.[35] Only a few hours later, in the morning of 22 December, cabinet met again.

The agreement on a partial appreciation, struck in that private meeting, came undone as Anthony, McMahon, and Snedden debated over information and the Reserve Bank governor's real position. According to the cabinet notebooks, Anthony persisted with his desire for parity with the US dollar. McMahon advocated an 8.57 per cent appreciation on the basis that 'if we go lower [we] will be forced higher', but, clearly aware of the divisions with the Country Party, wanted a 'genuine compromise' even more. 'What we do is in nation's interest,' he told cabinet. 'I put those interests above everything. [We] have to look at whole thing hard and cold.' McMahon admitted that the collapse of the coalition was entirely possible. 'If we have to divide we just have to divide,' he said.[36] The debate went back and forth, breaking for further private conferences between the parties. But they seemed to get nowhere. Eventually, Anthony stood up and declared that the government was finished. 'That was a fairly traumatic moment,' Nigel Bowen said later, 'and he was chancing his arm a bit.'[37] Anthony began to walk out. It took a snide reminder from Snedden, that if the Country Party left there would be no devaluation whatsoever, to bring him back to the table and begin to compromise.

In press reports, the concessions that cabinet eventually hammered out represented an almost complete capitulation to the Country Party. 'McM[ahon] surrendered,' Reid wrote. '… Undoubtedly a win for the Country Party.' It was a compelling perspective: the long, very public wrangling for control of policy in an area where the two parties so sharply diverged ensured that any kind of compromise would have had to be seen as a victory for Anthony and his ministers. In reality, however, the decision was not as bad as made out. The Australian dollar would now be pegged to the US dollar: sterling would be abandoned once and for all. The Australian dollar would appreciate 6.32 per cent against the US dollar, and there were suggestions that the government—as it had when the Holt government resisted devaluation—would offer assistance to primary industries. Those within the Treasury were not much upset. 'The Treasury was well satisfied with the outcome, which indeed did McMahon and Snedden credit,' John Stone said later.[38]

Economically, the decision was sound; politically, it was disastrous. The length of time it took to reach the decision spoke to everything that was wrong with the government: a divided cabinet, an antagonistic coalition, stubborn ministers, and a prime minister, in McMahon, who was indecisive. The contrast between how Holt had handled the currency-exchange issue in 1967 and how McMahon had was sharp, and reflective of McMahon's parlous political position. The press that followed the decision was caustic, critical of both McMahon and the Country Party. 'All the ingenious verbiage,' *The Sydney Morning Herald* editorialised, 'all the facile explanations cannot hide the fact that, after twisting and turning for three humiliating days, the PM submitted to extortion and allowed government policy to reflect narrow sectional interests. He did himself great harm.'[39]

But McMahon was never one to be down for long. Two days out from Christmas, on the same day that a bomb was discovered at the Lodge and the press wrote headlines about assassination plots, he was on the phone to spread his side of the story. 'McM[ahon] phoning everyone, including me, to tell me about his great and glorious victory in the currency battle,' Reid recorded. 'If he goes on long enough he'll convince himself that he had such a win.'[40]

It had been a long year, full of turmoil and upset, upheaval and change. 'Every day a crisis,' Bunting had written in June.[41] As Graham Freudenberg would later suggest, the pillars that had held up the government for so long were crumbling, falling down.[42] In a short space of time, the certitudes of the past—the suspicion of Red China, the rightness of the war in Vietnam, the dependable relationship with the US, the gospel of cabinet solidarity, the line of Liberal unity, the talk of Coalition principles, and a heavy degree of support in the press—were giving way. Everything was in flux; everything was changing.

Would McMahon be able to salvage something in the year that followed?

CHAPTER THIRTY-NINE

The Stories Told

1984

As the autumn of 1984 grew colder, McMahon became noticeably more jittery and anxious. His demands, and his expectations of Bowman, already inconsistent and frantic, were suddenly edged with worry and anger. 'The Howson diaries have caused this flutter,' Bowman decided, when he came to write in his diary.[1]

News had recently broken of the imminent publication of the voluminous diaries of McMahon's former colleague and intimate, Peter Howson. Over 1,000 pages long even when edited, *The Life of Politics: the Howson diaries* documented in minuscule detail Australian political life from the final years of the Menzies government until the end of McMahon's. As with any diary, the events referred to alternated between the prosaic and the sensational, the revelatory and the mundane. An indicative example of all of these was Howson's record of McMahon's use of the telephone; as one observer would soon write, 'The phrase "Bill McMahon rang" punctuates the diary like a Greek chorus.'[2] Now, as the bleak months bled on, extracts of the diaries were beginning to leak, and journalists were calling McMahon's office in Westfield Towers for comment and interviews.

Initially buoyed by the attention, news of the pending publication soon caused McMahon to be anxious. Asked what he should do, Bowman told McMahon not to make any response to the newspaper extracts. McMahon heeded the advice, but would not ignore the reports. When *The Sydney Morning Herald* reported Howson's views of McMahon—'Quite accurate!' Bowman noted—the former prime minister took immediate issue with the detail.[3] He never had dinner

470

at the Melbourne Club, he said. Howson, therefore, was wrong.[4] A day later, he obtained a copy of the book and went off again. McMahon immediately saw two occasions in which Howson said they had been together when they supposedly were not, and thereafter told the office all about how wrong Howson was. 'In each case Howson was a *liar; emphatically a liar,*' Bowman wrote in his diary.[5]

McMahon could not dismiss the diaries and leave them alone. He returned to them again and again in conversation, unprompted—but now increasingly with anger. 'WM's vituperation about the Howson diaries is extraordinary,' Bowman observed. Having discarded his ghostwriter's advice and talked to a journalist, McMahon told Bowman that there was as much truth in Howson's diaries as there was in Anthony Grey's account of Holt's disappearance in his book, *The Prime Minister Was a Spy*. It was laughable, thought Bowman: 'McMahon hasn't even read the Howson book!'[6]

McMahon seemed unable to perceive that Howson's diaries might be more accurate than he thought. One night, Ruth Fairbairn, David Fairbairn's wife, spent an hour and a half on the phone with Sonia. She asked about Howson's diaries. Was it true that McMahon had called every night from Washington and from London, while he was prime minister, as Howson had recorded? Sonia told Fairbairn that it was not true. But then Sonia pressed McMahon the next morning about the matter. 'Did you make those calls?'

McMahon, telling Bowman about this the next day, seemed not to realise that his answer undermined all his vituperation and anger about Howson's book. Was Sonia right to deny that he had made the calls? Had he made the calls?

He did not remember, McMahon said.

It was a rare admission. Despite many occasions that should have disabused him, McMahon was always as bullish about his memory as he was about his abilities. What Bowman had experienced in the six months he had spent working for McMahon was as nothing to those who had worked with and around him in Parliament. McMahon's memory and his claims to greatness had become fabled there. McMahon had Munchausen Syndrome, Jim Killen used to joke to press and politicians alike, after McMahon had become prime minister. The reference, to the German nobleman satirised by Rudolf Erich

Raspe for the fantastical stories and exaggerations he habitually told at the dinner table, in absolute belief of their veracity, was no accident: the scrutiny that McMahon received as prime minister showed that the gulf between his claims and his conduct was gaping.

It was so egregious that the journalist Maximilian Walsh said there were two William McMahons: a 'public McMahon' and a 'private Billy'.[7] The former was the myth, the reputation, crafted through these boasts and exaggerations, these stories and impossibilities. The latter was the reality: the mistakes in Parliament concealed in altered *Hansards*, the private confusions and reliance on briefs, the claims for credit during success and the disavowals of responsibility during failure, the divergent recollections of those who had known better.

The dramatic gulf between McMahon's claims—what they suggested of his talents and qualities—and the reality of his actions led some to wonder about his mental state while prime minister.[8] Was there a reason, beyond incompetence, that explained his difficulties as prime minister? Did his problems in the job stem from an illness, a disorder, a diagnosable condition, perhaps? At its most ugly and insensitive, was he in some kind of mental decline?

Most people were uncertain. Journalist Alan Ramsey said later that McMahon was a fantasist who might well have been paranoid, but certainly did not have Alzheimer's. To Ramsey, McMahon's failings, inconsistencies, and lies were simply a matter of character: 'That was just the manner of the bloke.'[9] Laurie Oakes told Susan Mitchell that McMahon was a 'pathological liar' who bordered on the edge of having a disease.[10] And if he once thought McMahon was 'half way around the bend'—to the point where comparisons with Evatt were not unreasonable—Mungo MacCallum was later less certain.[11] 'I don't believe there was anything pathological about it. He was just a not very bright politician who had gone well past the Peter Principle and was scrabbling for purchase in any way he could.'[12] Those who had worked with McMahon saw no evidence for it. Kim Jones saw no basis for it at all.[13] Ian Grigg and Jonathan Gaul said the same: 'Not at all.'[14]

An absolute answer—both at the time that Bowman was working for McMahon, and in the years since—was unlikely to eventuate. But it is more plausible, and more consistent with his behaviour over a long period, that the gulf between reality and McMahon's claims stems from his repetition of stories over the years. Those stories had, like stones in a fast-moving river, become worn and smooth in their constant retelling; the facts that countered them, or which might have suggested alternate interpretations, had been forgotten—completely. McMahon had told his stories—of great victories, of expertise, and excellence, of fighting his way all on his own—so often, to himself and to others, that he had come to believe them absolutely.[15] By the time he became prime minister, McMahon lived as though he was recounting those stories, believing himself far more ready and capable in office than he actually was. He had become his image of himself.

And when reality seemed to diverge from this—as Howson's diaries chronicled, in detail—McMahon could not comprehend it, could not fathom how it might be right, had to dismiss it as lies, lies, and more lies. To do otherwise might be to suggest that his story was wrong. But that could not be. His story was the real story. His story was the right one.

As his staff in Westfield Towers continued the work on that story, McMahon remained obsessed by the diaries and by Howson. After comparing the Howson diaries with the theory of Holt's defection to China, McMahon returned to his office. The former prime minister, Bowman recorded immediately afterward, was glued to the radio, waiting for the broadcast of Howson's speech to the Press Club.[16]

CHAPTER FORTY

Survival Mode

1972

In November 1971, Menzies had emerged from retirement to speak at a Liberal Party fundraiser. Referring to the turmoil of the year, he had cautioned the party against concentrating on personalities; then, referring to the narrowed polls and the certainty of an election in 1972, the aged statesman went on to say:

> We have been here a long time, and we can be there much longer. But only if we can recapture that first, fine, careless rapture: if we can get back to that feeling that the whole world is in front of us, and that we have a continent to save, to lead, to inspire.[1]

By January 1972, McMahon knew that if the Coalition was to retain any chance of holding office, the turmoil of the previous year could not be repeated. There would have to be leadership.[2] There would have to be some consistency. There needed, too, to be innovation, fresh ideas. 'He was in survival mode,' recalled Ian Grigg, McMahon's principal private secretary at this time. 'He knew that the government had been in office for twenty-three years. He knew that the polls were not favourable for him. He knew that the electorate was probably due for a change.'[3] Polling bore this out. McMahon had finished 1971 with a 37 per cent approval rating, marginally above that of Gough Whitlam.[4] Beyond the small solace of that small advantage was a clear imperative that it be extended. The government's standing had to be retrieved.

As the new year began, McMahon sought to initiate the recovery with a flurry of decisions designed to make it appear that the government

474

had control of the agenda. McMahon announced moves to reorganise the command and organisational structure of the army; announced that pensions would be paid overseas; announced a minor cabinet reshuffle following the retirement of Ceb Barnes; commended his government's efforts in the release of Sheikh Mujibur Rahman, who would become the president of Bangladesh; announced that archival records from World War II would be released; and lauded US president Richard Nixon's proposals for peace in Vietnam.[5] With the last of Australia's combat troops having arrived home on 8 December, McMahon was not shy about hinting that withdrawal of the Australian Army Assistance Group, engaged in training South Vietnamese and Cambodian troops, could soon follow and that Australia's involvement in Vietnam would be ended once and for all.

But his efforts to regain control were hampered by the economy. Excessive wage increases in the latter half of 1971 had accompanied rapid price rises; now, in the new year, figures showed that unemployment had jumped to above 120,000, or 1.6 per cent. By the standards of the time, when long-term unemployment averaged 1.4 per cent, the rise in unemployment was abrupt and worrying, no matter how much McMahon tried to downplay it. Shortly after that, figures released for the December quarter showed a 2.3 per cent rise in the consumer price index, the highest jump recorded since the 1950s. This 'really bad news' left McMahon spooked and the object of considerable criticism from the state premiers, who continued to complain about budget deficits and a parsimonious Commonwealth.[6] He knew that he could ill-afford headlines that tarnished the government's reputation as a competent economic manager. Thus, when he heard of the consumer price index figures, he panicked. 'McMahon rang me where I was holidaying near Palm Beach,' Snedden recalled, 'screaming about how terrible the figures were.'[7]

McMahon's worry led him to turn on Snedden and the Treasury. Throughout January, he complained that Treasury did not pay attention to what mattered; in February, he told Paul Hasluck that he thought Snedden was 'hopelessly at sea' as treasurer and that he distrusted Sir Frederick Wheeler, who had been appointed secretary to the Treasury at McMahon's insistence.[8] Already 'greatly concerned' that there could be further bad economic news in the future, McMahon had decided that the economy was a matter for 'political decision'.[9] He told Hasluck that he was considering holding the election in November, 'before the figures for the seasonal decline in employment could be published.'[10]

By early February, McMahon was spreading word among the press that he was taking personal responsibility for the economy, in the belief that public knowledge that the 'best treasurer in Australia's history' was at the helm would help to restore confidence. 'In my view [he] is taking wrong attitude,' Alan Reid sighed, when he heard this. '[He] is not seeking to find out what would be best for the economy. [He] is seeking to find out what would have the best and most effective electoral impact.' Nonetheless, McMahon persisted with it: a week later, he was suggesting 'to various pressmen, facetiously but with underlying seriousness, that the line they should take was "the old master is back".'[11]

Soon he had substance to accompany the line. Measures that he claimed were all because of him were announced at a meeting of the state premiers on 14 February.[12] McMahon called for wage restraint, and announced almost $86m in increased spending, including an increase in the funds available for Commonwealth grants, so as to alleviate rural unemployment; an increase in the unemployment benefit; and restoration of an investment allowance for the manufacturing industry that had been suspended the year before.[13]

The measures might well have helped economically and satisfied the premiers, but in publicity terms they foundered. Sceptical journalists exposed the pantomime of Commonwealth–state conferences. 'The premiers come to Canberra on Sunday night, breathing fire and brimstone,' Richard Carleton said to McMahon, in an interview for *This Day Tonight*, after the conference. 'They come and meet you in the cordiality of the cabinet room, and it's all over. The Commonwealth makes a concession ... They will be back in June, and apparently the same thing will be played out again.' *Is this all just a charade?* Carleton wanted to know. Was there ever going to be a solution to the problems of Commonwealth–state relations? McMahon's response—that he had outsourced the question to a group of experts at the ANU (the Centre for Research on Federal Financial Relations)—was not particularly satisfying.[14]

The day after the conference concluded, the good news about the extra assistance was wiped away by BHP's announcement that it would raise prices on steel by 5.3 per cent. That news threw the government onto the back foot, as demands that it do something came up against the difficulties of doing so.[15] The matter was made worse by the fact that BHP's share price had risen by 45c, to $12.20, after restoration of the investment allowance, and the government's admission that it had known about the likely price increase for some time. As the ALP was to ask when Parliament resumed, should the government have restored the allowance, knowing it would benefit a company about to raise its prices?[16] McMahon *had* sent a letter to BHP's chairman on 23 December advising that the government would be concerned by any price rise, and Snedden had reiterated that message on 26 January. But the government seemed shocked by the news anyway.

Reid was beggared by the lack of preparation: 'If McM[ahon] knew about the price rises a fortnight previously then he was in a position to evolve how to deal with it … He's got me baffled.'[17] Privately, McMahon considered intervening and pressuring BHP to reduce its prices. 'He said there has to be leadership,' wrote Bunting, after a late-night telephone call from the prime minister. 'The Government must do something—that means it is up to him.'[18] By the next day, however, McMahon was backing off on grounds that he had been 'pre-empted' by a speech from Snedden.[19]

The signs of troubled economic waters, and McMahon's conduct, caused the concerns that were rife among his colleagues to deepen further. The Liberal Party was 'in deep disarray and was just disintegrating,' Snedden believed.[20] By the time Parliament resumed on 22 February, almost everyone on the government benches was glum. Bert Kelly approached Parliament House with apprehension. 'There is a feeling of imminent decay about the place,' he recorded.[21] MPs were worried, caucusing about their prospects in an election. Bill Aston, the Speaker, was especially concerned. As he told colleagues, he had sold his millinery business in order to concentrate on holding his marginal seat of Phillip. 'I have to try to stay in politics,' he said. 'But I'm being placed in a situation that I have no chance.'[22]

Matters did not improve. Amid talk of introducing controls over prices and wages, mooted as solutions to the economic turmoil, McMahon told the House of Representatives that price fixations should not 'be made a political football'. As he continued with talk of the welfare of the Australian people, a Labor MP beggared by the statement interjected: 'What is politics about?' McMahon replied without hesitation or a trace of irony: 'Politics is about trying to get into office!'[23] His allies were left cringing.

Frustration among steadfast supporters was growing. McMahon was putting people offside, causing them to question him. In January, he had 'spoken in strong terms' to Bunting about the failings of the Department of the Prime Minister and Cabinet.[24] The secretary was 'hurt, and angry', claimed Alan Reid. 'With rare indiscretion [he] claims that Bill only half listens to advice. Speaks to too many. Is most influenced by the person with whom he spoke last, particularly if that person flatters McM[ahon].'[25] Don Dobie, a McMahon supporter and assistant minister assisting the prime minister, warned McMahon that he was 'in for trouble' if his image did not improve.[26] Howson was also despairing:

Bill McMahon is not an easy Prime Minister with whom to work. How often one would like to be firm and tell him what one thinks, but then one has to remember that we put him there, that he's got to be supported. Half the time one spends trying to help him get over his own foibles and weakness of character. He is not good at building up a team spirit; he doesn't really know how to delegate; he likes to feel that he's doing everything himself.

'These,' Howson went on, 'are some of the problems that have caused me so much trouble over the last few weeks.'[27] But Howson's trouble with McMahon stemmed from his interventions in policy as much as his character.

Jolted by Nugget Coombs's threat to resign from the Council of Aboriginal Affairs, McMahon had taken an interest in the land-rights issues that had been successfully bottled up in the cabinet committee to which they had been referred. Late in September 1971, McMahon made clear to Howson and Ralph Hunt, the minister for the interior, his support for applications from Aboriginal communities in the Northern Territory for leases on consolidated lands, provided they could satisfy criteria related to their association with the land, their proposed use of it, and the effect of a lease on the interests of other

Aborigines.[28] Had it been enacted, this would have been a step forward, an acknowledgement that traditional associations with the land should be a basis for land-rights claims.

But McMahon was not constant in his views,[29] and his interference frustrated Howson, who knew that the dominant view of those who sat alongside him on the committee was diametrically different. While Billy Wentworth thought any decision that did not mention traditional associations would be 'meaningless', Malcolm Fraser was 'disturbed' and 'concerned' by it, and Hunt was 'very reluctant' to include it as a criterion.[30] Howson told McMahon, but the prime minister was unswayed: 'He's firmly convinced that this is an election winner and that we're just a lot of reactionary Ministers who can't see the problem as clearly as he can.'[31] When the cabinet committee met in December to make a decision, without McMahon present, it stripped out any acknowledgement of an association with the land. No minister attending the meeting was prepared to acknowledge this as a criterion.[32]

The measures left for McMahon to announce in a statement that he would make in January were small, and their formulation was fraught. McMahon abandoned a draft statement hammered out in December and asked Coombs to write him another; then he had Coombs rewrite it with Keith Sinclair; then he had Sinclair 'put it all together'.[33] The task was complicated by vacillation over its content and the need to consult with the state governments. Already disappointed by the committee's December decision, the Council for Aboriginal Affairs (CAA) was further troubled by the decision to release the statement on 26 January. 'We tried, without success,' recalled Barrie Dexter, of the CAA, 'to dissuade [McMahon], since we felt that a statement of new policies as niggardly as those now adopted by the government was hardly appropriate on Australia Day—the anniversary of the dispossession of the Aboriginals.'[34] Howson, McMahon, and his office seemed oblivious to this concern.

McMahon's statement outlined five objectives for the government's policies in Aboriginal affairs. The first was to assist Aboriginal Australians to have 'equal access to the rights and opportunities' that Australian society provided, while simultaneously encouraging the preservation and development of Aboriginal culture, languages, traditions, and arts, 'so that these can become living elements in the diverse culture of the Australian society'. Second, while acknowledging that assimilation and identification with Australian society was now a matter of choice, the government rejected any 'concept of separate development' as 'utterly alien'. Third, the government believed involvement of Aboriginal Australians in housing, education, and employment was a necessity for the objectives to be reached. Fourth, the strategy of overcoming problems faced by Aboriginal Australians required collaboration with the state governments, greater economic independence for Aboriginal Australians, and elimination of provisions in the law that discriminated against Aboriginal Australians. Fifth, special 'temporary and transitional' measures would be necessary to overcome problems faced by people of Aboriginal descent. The objectives were laudable, clear, coherent, with a progressive bent. But the crucial sections on land rights—the sections on which attention would be focused—were yet to come.

The government had decided to create a new form of lease in the Northern Territory, McMahon announced, to be called 'general purpose' leases, that would endure for fifty years and be granted if applicants could satisfy two criteria: an intention and ability to make economic and social use of the land, and use that would not conflict with another Aboriginal group or community. 'We decided to create this new form of lease,' McMahon said:

> [...] rather than attempt simply to translate the Aboriginal affinity with the land into some form of legal right under the Australian system, such as that claimed before the decision of the Supreme Court of the Northern Territory, because we concluded that to do so would introduce a new probably confusing component, the implications of which could not clearly be foreseen and which could lead to uncertainty and possible challenge in relation to land titles elsewhere in Australia which are at present unquestioned and secure.[35]

In effect, the government refused to change the law because it did not know what the consequences of those changes might be. It was a timorous argument, turgidly expressed. The refusal to acknowledge an association with the land as a basis for land-rights claims was an egregious hole in the statement, and guaranteed to win no support from any quarter. Equally outrageous was McMahon's statement that, in spite of opposition from the Yirrkala people, it was in the 'national interest' for the Nabalco mineral exploration and mining to continue.

The statement was heavily criticised. As the *Canberra Times* editorialised, McMahon had missed an opportunity to 'right a great wrong' in how Australia had treated Aborigines. While commending the objectives that would now guide government policy, the editorial bluntly called out McMahon's failure on the land-rights issue: 'It is probable that the government found it politically unfeasible' to introduce uniform land-rights laws, it argued.[36] An editorial in *The Australian* was ominous: 'To choose that day [26 January] as the occasion to announce a Government decision on the intensely felt issue of Aboriginal Land Rights is to invite the full judgment of historical perspective on the decision … What is missing is the guts of a historic act.'[37]

The statement incensed Aboriginal activists around the country, but it was younger activists who decided that an immediate and strong response was warranted.[38] After debating several ways of doing so, a few Sydney-based activists, some affiliated with the Redfern-based Black Power group, settled on giving that response outside Parliament House. 'Billy McMahon works in Canberra, down there,' they reasoned. 'We've got to go to Canberra'.[39] Four activists—Michael Anderson, Billy Craigie, Tony Coorey, and Bert Williams—left Sydney in a car that night, borrowing a beach umbrella and materials for placards on the way. At 1.30am on 27 January, they erected the umbrella on the lawns outside Parliament House. They used a shoelace to string up a sign reading 'Aboriginal Embassy'. And they sat beneath the umbrella and sign with placards in their hands. Expecting to be promptly arrested, the four were surprised when police informed them that there was no legislation under which they could be removed. The four were thus still present on the lawns when the sun rose. That vital reprieve gave time for more protesters to join them, and allowed reporters to record Aboriginal Australia's response to McMahon's statement.

McMahon's reaction to the embassy was delayed. Initially, he thought all was well. He told Howson that he had 'solved' the Aboriginal statement, and, preoccupied with the economy, he made no response for several days.[40] That lag, and the inability for police or the government to find grounds to remove the embassy, meant that it gained valuable publicity and support. The National Council of Aboriginal and Torres Strait Island Women was holding a conference at the ANU, and a contingent came to the embassy to offer their support. On 28 January, they issued a demand for McMahon, Howson, and the cabinet to resign. From a group that could hardly be attacked as radical, the statement was devastating about McMahon: the council was 'disappointed' at the 'token gestures' he had made on land rights, and 'disgusted' by his 'incompetent, uninterested, and unsympathetic handling of what should be treated as an important portfolio'.[41] Howson, for his part, responded in kind, telling one newspaper that he saw 'a disturbing undertone in the use of the term Aboriginal Embassy' that 'cut across the government's expressed objection to separate development and was kindred to apartheid'.[42] Over the days that followed, the embassy attracted more and more support, making McMahon's failure to address the issue conspicuous.

And yet there were those who did not think McMahon was without credit. Having successfully disassociated the CAA, Coombs nonetheless admitted, later, that he thought the prime minister 'had done his best', trying to overcome opposition from within the government to 'force through a decision which for the first time in Australian history made some acknowledgement of Aboriginal traditional rights in land, and provided a means whereby they could have obtained a limited title to it'—namely, the leases.[43] The Australian correspondent for the London *Times*, Stewart Harris, who took a strong interest in Aboriginal affairs, judged that McMahon had 'in fact done more for Aborigines than any other Australian Prime Minister, but in the context of their need nothing like enough.'[44] Few in the Aboriginal community would share this opinion. Sammy Watson, who manned the embassy in its early days, met McMahon and was blunt: 'He talked down to me as though I were some tribal fellow who only understood pidgin English. He was patronising to a sickening extent. I think he completely lacks any understanding of us.'[45] Charles Perkins, an officer on the staff of the Council of Aboriginal Affairs, and later the first Aboriginal secretary of a Commonwealth department, thought along the same lines. McMahon's attitude did not fit with the times, Perkins thought: 'In this day he has no place ... He is out of date and out of touch.'[46]

Amid press coverage, the embassy turned an initially hazy set of demands into a five-point plan for land rights, and sought to broaden its protest to a campaign. A placard at the embassy on 7 February called out the Labor Party: 'Whitlam: when you change McMahon's Govt will it make any change to the suppression of Aboriginal people?'[47] Whitlam's response was quick. The next day, he visited the embassy—now consisting of eleven tents and sixteen activists—and talked. When he emerged, he made an immediate and public promise to grant full freehold title to Aboriginal tribes and clans, should his party win government.[48]

Much to the chagrin of McMahon, this was a promise that increasingly looked as though it would have to be fulfilled.

AS the one-year anniversary of McMahon's becoming prime minister approached, gloom within the Liberal and Country parties continued to deepen. McMahon's reputation was shrinking. The government's standing in the polls was dismal. Labor had the upper hand in Parliament and in the media. Gorton looked to be more popular than ever. And every new day seemed to bring another unexpected problem to the fore. The government was consistently buffeted, unable to gain any semblance of control. 'I think it has been the hardest and most unpredictable year I've known since I've been in politics,' McMahon lamented. 'I've found it a very difficult year.' But he would not admit publicly that it was his fault. The poor polls, he insisted, were the result of 'so many crises of a kind over which we've had no control'.[49]

The government's lingering embarrassment over recognition of China flared when, amid US president Richard Nixon's visit to the People's Republic of China, the Chinese government's attempt to solicit a visit by Andrew Peacock arose in Parliament. There was also uproar when McMahon's answers about the matter were contradicted by television appearances by James Kibel. On 29 February, Labor launched a no-confidence motion over the matter. Whitlam was caustic and, in his speech, homed in on McMahon's relationship with the truth. 'The truth has caught him up and caught him out,' Whitlam said. McMahon had presented to the House 'an utterly false story—a fantasy, a fairy-tale, mischievous in its intention, mendacious in its substance'.

What was most devastating about Whitlam's argument was that

he placed the Kibel matter in a context of other questionable answers and explanations. He cited contradictions between public statements and answers from McMahon and Snedden on the BHP price rises, and McMahon's shifting answers on whether he had sent a letter to the South African government criticising its apartheid policies. The portrait Whitlam painted was one with which many in McMahon's own party agreed: that of a dissembler and liar, of a prime minister ill-prepared and unwilling, or unable, to state the truth.

When he rose to reply, McMahon sought to duck the topic entirely; then he sought to shift the issue; then he all but admitted errors in answers he had given in earlier debates.[50] McMahon compounded the awful optics when, as the House divided to vote, he approached Gorton. He had barely spoken to his predecessor since sacking him; now, though, he put his arm around Gorton and said he would like to sit and speak with him during the division. Gorton's response was blunt: 'Go to buggery.'[51] The motion was defeated, but afterward Reid heard that people were telling McMahon he had dealt with the debate quite well. Reid all but rolled his eyes: 'God protect me from my friends and keep me aware that reality is not what you want it to be but what it is.'[52]

Opinion polls recorded the drops in McMahon's popularity with increasing frequency. By March, he had a 28 per cent approval rating, according to Gallup. The multiplicity of such polls—from Gallup, the *Sydney Morning Herald–Age,* and ANOP—were by themselves a new phenomenon to grapple with: where Menzies had been the subject of only three opinion polls on his performance in his second prime ministership, McMahon would be the subject of twenty. They were a stark and regular demonstration of the government's declining standing, and a prompt for questions and whispers about McMahon's leadership. 'What the devil do we do next?' Bert Kelly wondered on 8 March. 'We've got Billy McMahon elected as our leader and obviously he is not doing it at all well and everybody knows this. What we can't think of is, how do we get rid of him? I suppose the only hope we have is that he suddenly drops dead one day.'[53] Word of the despair reached the governor-general's ears. Meeting with senator Robert Cotton on 9 March, Hasluck was told that the McMahon government's fall in the polls was prompting some members to consider radical measures:

They were in the mood of thinking that nothing could be worse than what they had and that they should change the leadership of the party once again and try to have a general election deferred until May, 1973, in the hope that they might have time to recover favour ... I asked whether this was a move to restore Gorton to the leadership. He [Cotton] said he thought some might think that way but he doubted whether it would work. I expressed the view that the Liberal Party would expose itself as completely confused and silly if it swung back from McMahon to Gorton after so many of its members had declared by a vote only a year ago that Gorton was unfit to be Prime Minister.[54]

Was the party really considering replacing McMahon? Despite initially dismissing murmurs to this effect on grounds that there was not enough time, Reid thought it plausible enough to be alert, particularly to a Gorton candidacy.[55] Press reports noted that the former prime minister was regaining popularity and eclipsing the government. As *The Age* asked, 'Who is that man flying around the country, talking to company directors, university graduates, and schoolchildren; opening fetes, libraries, and motel wings? Is it a Prime Minister, or a party leader? No. It is the super-backbencher.'[56] Meanwhile, Peter Buff, a Melbourne businessman and self-described chair of the 'Get Gorton Back Committee', was agitating for Gorton's return by stirring up the Victorian division of the Liberal Party. Within the parliamentary Liberal Party, McMahon's parlous standing gave the idea the whiff of a possibility.

The threat of being deposed did not provoke the best in McMahon. He continued to blunder, sometimes so poorly that his party had cause to call much more than his political judgement into question. That March, while commenting on reports about Chinese overtures to Kibel, West Australian Liberal senator Peter Sim was quoted as saying that Australia's foreign policy should not be left 'in the hands of two Manchester Jews'.[57] In Parliament on 23 March, West Australian Labor MP Joe Berinson called on McMahon to repudiate Sim, the statement, and its connotations. However, instead of answering with a straightforward repudiation of Sim's statement, McMahon handed the question to Nigel Bowen, the minister for foreign affairs. Concerned that McMahon had passed on the opportunity to disavow anti-

Semitism, the former attorney-general Tom Hughes rose from the backbench:

> Will the Right Honourable gentleman assure the House that neither he nor any member who sits behind him on the Government benches would ever wish it to be thought that he or any of them would endorse, or would wish to be associated with, an expression of anti-Semitic sentiment or any sentiment based on religious or racial grounds made by any member of the Government parties, if it were made?

McMahon's answer was perhaps worse than his handing it to Bowen. After a laudable declaration that the government believed in religious freedom, he told the House that 'a question of the kind asked by the honourable member for Perth [Joe Berinson] raising a sectarian issue of this kind is to be deplored ...'[58]

The House went into uproar. As Labor MPs were quick to point out, Berinson was a practising Jew with quite reasonable grounds for seeking a repudiation of anti-Semitism from the prime minister. McMahon refused to recognise this. He refused to rephrase or withdraw his answer. When Whitlam moved for the House to repudiate Sim's statements, McMahon tried to amend the motion so that it repudiated and condemned 'any anti-Semitic attitudes wherever expressed or implied'. This was, as Whitlam said immediately, 'too clever by half', and again there was great furore. Government members were visibly angry, and four appeared ready to cross the floor to vote for Whitlam's motion. McMahon was forced to back down. He removed his amendment.[59]

What was he doing? What had he hoped to gain by his actions? According to Reid, McMahon knew the question was coming, but had gone 'off the rails'. Bill Aston, whose electorate had a sizeable Jewish population, was scathing about McMahon's behaviour. 'What is wrong with him?' he asked. 'What has happened?' The Liberal member for the Queensland seat of Griffith, Don Cameron, was similarly disbelieving. 'I'll be loyal to him because he is the leader,' he told people. 'But, Christ, he must be mad.'[60] Howson was astonished, too, and lamented what it had done: 'It has had the effect of setting back all the good work that we've been doing in the last three weeks, it's depressed morale among the whole of the backbench, and altogether the press are going to have a field day.'[61]

McMahon was certainly aware that things were not going well. There had been more problems with Snedden, over the workings of a family unit tax and the appointment of Vic Garland as assistant treasurer; Gorton was continuing to draw headlines and attention; and good economic news was thin on the ground. Dining with McMahon two days before the brouhaha over his response to Berinson's questions, Howson found the prime minister 'tense'. He thought McMahon was 'finding the strain of office bearing heavily on his shoulders'. McMahon was hearing of moves against him and worried about unrest in the DLP, whose preferences he would need at the election.[62] Problems with the Liberal Party organisation were also causing McMahon concern. Already of the opinion that electoral defeat was inevitable, organisation members were making no effort to disguise their derision of their leader. As one told Reid:

> McM[ahon] talks all the time, makes extravagant claims about his ability and what he intends to do, and it has reached the stage that [no]body in the organisation believes either him or his claims. Their cry is, 'If he would only listen.' [Federal Liberal Party director Bede] Hartcher has complained bitterly about the cavalier way he treats the organisation, and the manner in which he won't listen to the state presidents and secretaries but 'just rambles on'.

McMahon was just as frustrated. 'What do they know?' he would say, when speaking about the organisation. His scorn and aversion to hearing criticism made him reluctant to attend meetings with the organisation, further reinforcing the problems and potential of a breakdown.[63]

Disquiet within the party over McMahon's leadership grew. A few days after his statements on the 'sectarian issue', McMahon's critics put pressure on him to call a party-room meeting to 'deal with the question of leadership'.[64] Killen, whose call for McMahon to restore Gorton and Bury to cabinet positions as 'a gesture of goodwill' had been rejected, was among those critics. 'Having regard to the extreme political crisis and its far reaching implications for the country and the party,' he wrote to the whip, 'I request a Liberal Party meeting of all senators and members to be called for next Wednesday.'[65] McMahon, realising that the moves were serious, reached for the telephone to firm up his support. 'It is touch and go,' Reid wrote at the time.[66] Others looked for more creative decisions. Bert Kelly, despairing of McMahon's performances and aware that he was manifestly distrusted by his ministers, rang the president of the Liberal Party, Robert Southey:

> [I] suggested that perhaps he ought to consider coming in and taking a strong stand, advising McMahon that he ought to leave the position and see if we couldn't arrange some kind of a take-over by a person selected by a small number of the party organisation and a number of senior ministers.[67]

And yet, even then, Kelly was not certain of the solution. The problem was not that critics of McMahon were rare: the party, almost as a whole, was 'disenchanted' with him.[68] The problem was that no one could agree on a replacement. Despite his popularity with the public, Gorton was still anathema to the conservative wing of the party; Fraser was still the object of antipathy from Gorton's supporters; and Snedden refused to allow himself to be considered. (According to Snedden, he also resisted pressure from Anthony to support Bowen in a bid.)[69]

By the time of the party-room meeting on 29 March, Reid believed that a spill was in the offing. 'McM[ahon] still unsure of his numbers … Position dangerous even though the rebels cannot be sure of the numbers.'[70] But the meeting came and went without a sound. The critics stayed silent. McMahon's position never came up. 'For the time being,' wrote a satisfied Howson afterward, 'it has headed off any threat to his [McMahon's] leadership.'[71]

TWO weeks later, on 12 April, Snedden announced that the government would introduce measures to improve public confidence and support consumer spending. The 'mini-budget', as it came to be known, had been developed only during the previous ten days as a response to 'changing social and economic circumstances'. Amid what Snedden deemed improving economic conditions that were nonetheless short of their potential, the treasurer announced that he and McMahon had agreed to reduce the levy on personal income tax from 5 per cent to 2.5 per cent (wholly reversing the rise they had instituted in the 1971–72 budget), increase the standard rate of the pension by $1 per week and the married rate by 75c per week, ease the means test on pensions, and allow small investors to treat profits on shares held for more than eighteen months as a capital gain. Snedden also announced that the government would move to set up an inquiry into the taxation system.[72]

The move was unusual, as Snedden himself admitted that night, but McMahon regarded it as absolutely necessary. As Bunting recorded of their conversation on 20 March, 'No matter where you looked, industries were depressed … People who spoke to him frankly were pessimistic. Gloom was still there.'[73] McMahon was concerned to act. He wanted the economy on a sound footing. 'The economy was his agenda,' Jonathan Gaul recalled. 'He paid more attention to that than anything else. Every day.'[74] Not everyone was convinced that action was necessary, though. *The Australian* wondered if the government would have anything left when the time came for the budget. 'With tax cuts, a tax review, and a pension increase now, what will Mr Snedden do for an encore in August?' Most believed it was a politicking move from a government keen to ensure the economy was growing by election time. Labor frontbencher and future treasurer Frank Crean called it a 'sordid political gesture', and even Anthony appeared to concede that it was thus: 'I wouldn't be honest if I said that this isn't in the back of our minds … We're very conscious that at the end of this year the economy has to be buoyant and moving along.'[75]

What no one could deny was that it was confirmation of a major change to the economic strategy announced in the 1971–72 budget. The rigour of that budget, and its attempts at deflation, were to be abandoned. Instead, the government would spend money to ensure that totemic issues such as employment, the cost of living, and pensions would play well for it in an election campaign.

But the spending would not solve the government's problems, largely because McMahon seemed unwilling to assess those problems realistically. When he met with Hasluck on 2 May, McMahon blamed his colleagues for the government's poor standing in the polls and its economic problems. 'He said that the main causes of their fall in popularity had been the mistake in the 1971–72 budget, the arguments over rural relief, the delay in making a decision on revaluation, and the handling of the postal strike last Christmas.' Whether this was wrong had not appeared to concern McMahon. 'In discussing each,' Hasluck recorded, 'he [McMahon] represents himself as having been right and the faults as being due to his colleagues or to the supplying of false information to him. He spoke very critically of the Treasury.'[76]

This was true. In what had become a fixture of inter-office memos and telephone calls, McMahon railed against the Treasury's estimates, forecasts, work, and ideas. He was scathing of its co-ordination of other departments and what he believed was its unwillingness to share information properly. In March, he was sceptical of Treasury advice on unemployment. He could not go on accepting suggestions that 'everything will come right'.[77] Treasury, he said a few days later to Bunting, 'have been consistently wrong'.[78] In June, he was saying that the stimulus had gone out of the economy: 'The mini-budget had not had the effect intended.' The Treasury needed to examine the situation and do so immediately. 'September would be too late for action.' There was more than a hint of his frustration evident in his request that Bunting tell Snedden to take it up with Treasury. 'Unless the treasurer himself did so, and with emphasis, Treasury would not take it seriously.' When he spoke to Sir Frederick Wheeler, the Treasury secretary, that day, McMahon was blunt in his opinion: 'He said that Treasury had been testing the situation at regular intervals since the last budget and had always been wrong so far.'[79]

Another element in McMahon's frustrations were problems with the Department of the Prime Minister and Cabinet. Its expanded list of functions, as well as restoration of its secretariat functions for the cabinet, was an enormous tax on the department's resources. Lenox Hewitt, who had carried a heavy load while he was secretary, believed the added work would be too much, especially alongside a prime minister so temperamental, self-interested, and exhausting. 'I would have thought it an absolute nightmare,' he said later. 'Bunting must have had a hell of a time with McMahon.'[80]

The secretary had foreseen the mounting work toll early. He edged away from participation on inter-departmental committees of cabinet, and he pressed for more resources from the Public Service Board.[81] The weight of work done by his department, Bunting wrote in June 1971, 'is not merely a five day a week weight, but a day and night weight, often of seven days.'[82] But the problems persisted, to the point that the department's failings became, in McMahon's eyes, Bunting's failings. That same month, McMahon told the secretary that the draft record of a cabinet decision was 'bad', that Bunting was not carrying out 'team work' with him, and not consulting properly.[83] He was still critical six months later. He lectured Bunting and Sir Frederick Wheeler for what he saw as their failures in co-ordination and staff work. He wanted better briefings and he wanted for them to be ahead of matters, so that he in turn could be as well.[84] He was still aggrieved in March. 'He said he should be getting more lead and more discussion of current matters,' Bunting recorded. The secretary had a different idea. He did not think it should be his department's mission to offer competing advice to that of other departments. As he said to McMahon, there were 'limits of time to what the Department can do'.

But to McMahon's offer to call the chairman of the Public Service Board and demand better resources, Bunting demurred. He did not want to use McMahon 'as a lever', he said. McMahon agreed to let the matter go, but added a condition. Bunting had to get results.[85] 'Bunting was at his wit's end with Billy,' Jonathan Gaul recalled, 'because he was always on his hammer. John Bunting was a gentleman. He didn't know how to cope with this sort of treatment.'[86]

McMahon's criticism of Bunting and the department was not unfair: McMahon was prime minister at a time when the demands upon him and his office were outstripping resources. McMahon himself was wilting under the pressure of work. He frequently complained to Bunting about the amount of paper crossing his desk and the problems of consultation.[87] He wanted the department to step up, possibly by emulating the British cabinet system, and he wanted there to be fewer matters on his plate.[88] 'He wanted to make progress in this direction so as to achieve a new basis in the new year, so that he would have more time available for forward thinking,' recorded Peter Lawler in late 1971.[89]

'Last week was chaotic,' Bunting recorded McMahon telling him, in a late-night call in May 1972. 'Papers kept rolling in.'[90] The problems were not solved by September. Whatever PM&C were doing to reduce his workload, they had to do more. 'He said that if we did not conform, he would simply send the papers back un-dealt with,' Bunting wrote, after a telephone call from McMahon.[91] But when Bunting sought clarification on the cause of the problem, McMahon's own staff told him that sometimes it was just a matter of accumulation.[92] McMahon did not believe it. He thought that it was 'laziness' on the part of the department.[93] Trying to explain and understand, Bunting sent McMahon figures the next day. The department received some 3,000 papers per month. Roughly 400 of those went to McMahon, he said. Half of those were letters to ministers, members, senators, premiers, and constituents, or matters relating to parliamentary questions. Of the remaining 200 papers, 150 were unavoidable: they were cabinet documents, Foreign Affairs cables, Treasury papers. The remaining fifty papers—two per day, Bunting pointed out—'are sent only after judgment in the Department that you would want to see them.'[94] Did McMahon really not wish to see them? The complaints subsided, but a month later, McMahon was ringing again:

> He said he would just have to ask me once more about the amount of work. He would just have to plead with me. Had he got an election or hadn't he? He would crack up if he went on with the work at the present rate … Take yesterday—he had all that work. It took all that time.[95]

The work was immense. But McMahon's problems were, in no small part, of his own making. As McMahon's principal private secretary, Ian Grigg, recalled, McMahon's demand for material meant that there was a large amount of paper coming into the office. 'He complained about it, but if he did not get a paper on something that he wanted, or thought he should see, then he would complain about that, too. He was demanding paper, he was getting paper, but then he didn't like the amount of paper that was coming through. It was Catch-22.'[96] Moreover, McMahon hoarded papers. Using a peephole in Grigg's office, staff would watch him hide files in his drawers. Between this and his unwillingness to delegate, McMahon's office was a bottleneck. The problem was exacerbated by his fervent belief that his personal involvement equated with success. All this ensured that McMahon took on far more work than he needed.[97] Suggestions that he delegate more, and allow his ministers to do more, would be accepted, then forgotten. It was McMahon's nature to try to control things himself.

This was evident in the way that he continued to meddle in Howson's portfolio. Already hampered by crossed lines of authority within the bureaucracies of his unwieldy ministry (nicknamed by some the Ministry for Bits and Pieces), Howson's work was incremental and frustrating, even without McMahon's involvement. 'I think that Bill McMahon didn't realise when he handed me all those things on my plate how big a job it was,' he would say later.[98] On the environment, for example, Howson was trying to develop an office that, as one writer put it, was little more than a 'postbox for communications between the state and Commonwealth governments'.[99] Whether the Commonwealth's role could be developed, and what part it would play amid the work of the state governments and Commonwealth departments, was a long-running problem. Howson's permanent head understood this. 'I always felt, for my minister, that he was at a disadvantage,' Lenox Hewitt said later, 'in that there was already people responsible for the matters in hand.'[100]

Matters were hardly going to be made easier by a prime minister who felt that taking action on the environment could offer some political traction. Throughout Howson's tenure, McMahon continually sought to involve himself, often frustratingly, in developing the government's environmental policies. Late in November 1971, cabinet decided against establishing a committee that could advise on a national approach for the environment, on the grounds that there were too many such committees and councils already.[101] 'Must say advisory councils haven't helped us—they create problems,' McMahon said, during the debate.[102]

Just after Christmas, however, McMahon telephoned Howson to say that he had changed his mind. The government 'needed' an advisory committee at Commonwealth level. Could Howson prepare another cabinet submission accordingly?[103] When Howson brought that proposal to cabinet late in January, there was another change. 'Half-way through the discussion it was obvious that most of the cabinet were against the proposal,' Howson recalled, 'and the PM proceeded to dump me, saying that the proposals I'd put up were nothing like what he had envisaged.'[104] Cabinet ordered instead that an inter-departmental committee be established to advise it on alternatives.[105]

By March, the work of that inter-departmental committee had wrapped up, with the same result that Howson had originally sought: an advisory committee on the environment. When that recommendation came to McMahon, he could not make up his mind whether to return to cabinet or make the decision himself. Then he argued with Howson over who should make the announcement. A week later, McMahon had decided that he would announce the committee, but that Howson could deliver a ministerial statement on the environment in the House.[106]

Drafting of the statement was just as difficult. An initial draft prepared by Keith Sinclair was reworked so as to be less 'negative', but then McMahon got involved, seeking to make it less 'low key' and more positive about the environment and what the government was doing. When Howson explained that the draft followed the line of cabinet discussions and thinking, McMahon said he would overrule the cabinet. Wary that changes of the sort McMahon wanted would involve significant expenditure, Howson made some changes only to be told again that it was still not positive enough: 'I had not seized enough of the glamour of this subject.' Conscious already of McMahon's tendency to take decisions without consulting cabinet, Howson saw similarities to Gorton, and he worried about the effect of cutting out vital input from other departments. 'He still doesn't realise that if he is going to make this a glamorous statement, he's also got to be prepared to pay for some of the promises that he's bound to make, and I don't think this has been accepted by the Treasury.'[107]

Four days later, to the horror of staff surrounding the prime minister, McMahon was taking over both the drafting and the announcement.[108] That decision would be reversed and the low-key approach would be restored, but McMahon continued to hound Howson for better news. When an article in *The Sydney Morning Herald* featured Howson's descriptions of the highly circumscribed role that the Commonwealth could play in environment policy, McMahon telephoned his minister to complain that he had not mentioned the possibility that the Commonwealth could give grants to the states for environmental purposes under section 96 of the constitution.[109] 'If the cabinet had ever told me that Section 96 grants were feasible I would have mentioned it,' an astonished Howson wrote in his diary, 'but I would have been in much more trouble if I had been too imaginative.'[110] Then McMahon and Howson were at loggerheads over who should head the advisory committee that McMahon had announced.[111]

At least Howson was able to make his statement, on 24 May. Stating that his purpose was to 'emphasise' the government's interest in the problems of the environment and its determination to do what it could to solve those problems, Howson stressed the need for co-operation and co-ordination with the states. The still-developing role of the Commonwealth was evident in what he proceeded to outline as the achievements and progress of the McMahon government's environment policy. Administrative machinery to deal with environmental matters had been set up, Howson said, and state ministers were meeting regularly, via the Australian Environment Council, to consult. There were also innovations: from now on, Howson announced, government proposals with any relevance to the environment would have to carry an explanation of their impact on the environment. That would prove contentious and difficult, but eventually would become a valuable and standard practice. The government had also adopted the OECD principle of 'the polluter pays', where the costs of pollution control were recognised as a part of the cost of production. There were initiatives underway to address water, air, and carbon monoxide pollution, and the government would continue to participate in international efforts to address pollution.[112]

Howson was pleased by the press reception the statement received, and by the apparent paucity of Labor's response, announced immediately by Tom Uren, the member for Reid. But it was always necessary to consider McMahon. The next day, amid the favourable reports in the morning's newspapers, the prime minister telephoned Howson to say that he was worried he had not made the statement himself.[113]

CHAPTER FORTY-ONE

On Edge

1984

'WM under strain today,' Bowman wrote in his diary, on Monday 10 March. Due to go into hospital on the Thursday for tests and treatment for a patch of skin cancer on his left ear, McMahon had been 'on edge, urgent, incoherent, memory gone, rambling', wrote Bowman. Though exasperated, Bowman had now had enough experience of McMahon to realise that it was not entirely normal behaviour for the former prime minister: 'For the first time I understand that this must be a manifestation of pressure.'[1]

But the behaviour tested McMahon's staff nonetheless. Three days later, Bowman was withering, calling McMahon 'jumpy and silly this afternoon'. He had especially upset Joyce Cawthorn. She had made out three cheques to meet McMahon's doctors' bills, but when she presented them to McMahon for his signature, he decided to up-end that approach. He came up with a complicated plan that saw him spend an hour on the phone with Medicare, the AMA, and his health insurer, getting advice about sending bills one way and cheques another. His purpose, Cawthorn vented to Bowman later, was to avoid paying the bills until the last possible moment. 'He never tears up a cheque, because of the 10 cents [cost],' she said, 'but now he's going to tear up three and ruin my accounting system!'[2]

By the Thursday, McMahon's staff was happy to see him go. McMahon had been petulant, brusque, rude for too long. 'Stop talking when there's so much to do!' he was saying, barging into conversations. He was annoyed that there was not a suite available at the hospital, he was annoyed about money, and he was annoyed about the prologue yet again. He had called Bowman to his office to discuss it, but had been too fluttery to talk properly. 'Quite unintelligible,' Bowman wrote after this latest waste of time.[3]

McMahon's presence in hospital prompted calls from the media. Sonia had told Bowman that the office was not authorised to say anything, but when the ABC telephoned the next week, Bowman decided to ignore her. He told George Campbell, who had answered the call, to say that he could not comment but to add that, to the best of knowledge, McMahon was fine and that if they called St Vincent's they might even be able to speak to him.[4]

Bowman kept working on the prologue—'or trying to', as he wrote. His opinion of it slipped the more he worked on it, and McMahon's interference, from his hospital bed, did not improve Bowman's mood or appreciation of it:

> It is abysmal; actually, far worse than that. I expected to finish it today. Then George came in to say WM had called and wanted him at the hospital at 2pm. He wanted the start of the prologue rewritten; he had some very good stuff from *The Economist*...

Bowman was profoundly unimpressed with this new development. Angered, he delivered a detailed opinion of it and of McMahon himself. 'How much longer did we have to suffer this childish nonsense?'

Campbell's response was dark: 'There's a chance the test will prove malignant.'

Time did not improve Bowman's mood. By the end of the day, he had decided on a course of action, McMahon be damned: 'I shall proceed with the editing and decline to look at the new material until the next round of editing, if there is a next round.'[5]

CHAPTER FORTY-TWO

Constant Threats

1972

A repeated theme of the McMahon government was the tension and division it found when moving to address new issues on the political agenda. Loosening censorship in Australia was a complete example of how conservative members of the government resisted attempts to have social changes reflected in public policy. To Don Chipp, the minister for customs, the need for change was obvious from the moment he took office. 'I inherited a censorship system which was secretive, archaic, and illogical,' he recalled.[1] Taking the view that censorship was thoroughly undesirable—even evil—if nonetheless necessary, Chipp had tried for the previous three years to liberalise the system gradually, arguing that 'a plurality of community standards' should prevail over those of one minister in one government. Ostensibly, Chipp had support for this from McMahon; after all, the prime minister would soon say that 'there has to be an overriding national interest' before censorship should be imposed.[2] Where the national interest figured in the case of *The Little Red Schoolbook* would soon take up considerable time—and provoke schisms within the government.

Written by Danish schoolteachers Søren Hansen and Jesper Jensen, and intended for young people, *The Little Red Schoolbook* had been controversial the world over for its frank treatment of sex, drugs, and alcohol. Notwithstanding that these were clearly discussed in an unenticing way, the book had been the cause of considerable angst among conservative members of the Parliament and government when its importation had been announced. Chipp had decided against prohibiting the import of the book on grounds that its section on drugs was anti-drugs, that its discussion of sex could be easily obtained elsewhere, and that its anti-authoritarian bent—summed up in a suggestion that adults were untrustworthy—was disagreeable but not objectionable.

Within the government, Chipp's action was cause for anger, and not only from members of the backbench. On 11 April, the assistant minister assisting the minister for civil aviation, John McLeay, criticised Chipp for allowing the book on grounds that it could undermine the morals of schoolchildren; on 17 April, government backbencher Les Irwin called for the book to be banned, saying that it would lead young people into 'misbehaviour'.[3] The continued controversy led to a summons from the prime minister, who told Chipp to change the decision. When Chipp refused, McMahon declared that it would go to cabinet. In the days that followed, McMahon worked through the press to try to have his way. Cabinet would force Chipp to back down, stories suggested, and *The Little Red Schoolbook* would be prohibited. Chipp retaliated in kind. He would resign, he intimated, if his decision were overturned.[4] Chipp was betting everything on his belief that McMahon could not afford a ministerial resignation that year, and would himself back down. He was gratified to find that when the matter came up in cabinet on 18 April, McMahon's first words were, 'We must support the Minister on this question.'[5] Cabinet thus agreed with Chipp's decision not to prohibit the book on legal and regulatory grounds.

But the controversy continued. The Catholic Archbishop of Melbourne called it a dogmatic work, and questioned why the government had allowed it in when the English and French governments had not. The minister for housing, Kevin Cairns, a very conservative Catholic, stepped into the fray, describing the book as 'gross, crude, and frightful'.[6] The minister for the navy, Malcolm Mackay, a Presbyterian minister, argued that Australia's morality was in danger: 'The nation is under siege right now from moral aggression by literature, drugs, and psycho-political mass communication.'[7] Doug Anthony told an audience of Young Australian Country Party members that the book was subversive—'a handbook for juvenile revolution and anarchy'—and DLP senator Jack Kane speculated about whether the book's communist provenance was evident in the supposed ownership of its copyright by the 'Radical Action Movement'.[8]

The optics—of government ministers disagreeing with cabinet decisions, and appearing to align themselves with political opponents—were poor. It highlighted, yet again, the ructions within the government. When *The Sydney Morning Herald* ran a story implying that Howson, Robert Katter, Wentworth, Mac Holten, and senator Robert Cotton—ministers all—had disagreed with the decision to allow *The Little Red Schoolbook* to be imported, McMahon insisted on reminding each of them of the principle of cabinet solidarity. 'Once a decision is taken it is binding on members of the Ministry and personal differences are not to be revealed,' he wrote.[9]

Similar attempts to shut down areas where tension and division could be found were constant. They were especially obvious in McMahon's uneasy handling of the offshore legislation that Gorton had championed before his downfall. Despite receiving its second-reading speech two years before, by April 1972 the Territorial Sea and Continental Shelf Bill was buried at the bottom of the House of Representatives notice paper. Knowing that there was pressure for it to be dealt with, and all too aware that Gorton would vote for it regardless of the government's position, McMahon, at a party-room meeting on 29 March, successfully persuaded his colleagues to make no decision on it before further discussions with the states. By mid-April, however, there was pressure for McMahon to hurry. Speaking with the prime minister for a 'solid hour' on 18 April, Gorton put a deadline to him: McMahon could have some time to consult with the states, but if he was not 'getting anywhere in a month', Gorton would cross the floor to bring the Bill on for debate.[10] In a letter sent to McMahon the next day, Tom Hughes threatened to do the same.[11] Shortly afterwards, Whitlam—correctly suspecting that there was pressure to be found on this point—gave notice that he would seek to suspend standing orders during debate on the government's Marine Science Institute Bill in order to bring on a debate on the offshore legislation. Quite plainly, he would invite Gorton to vote with the opposition, and challenge Jim Killen and Tom Hughes to join their fallen former prime minister.

McMahon sought to divert Killen and Hughes from doing so. In a meeting on 9 May, a 'terribly dejected' looking McMahon asked Killen not to support Whitlam's motion. 'I do not want anybody crossing the floor on that,' he said. The request outraged Killen. Eventually,

McMahon sought a promise that Killen would at least approach the motion with an open mind. 'You'll make up your own mind, won't you?' he asked. Killen slammed the desk with his fingers, so hard that they began to bleed, and told McMahon that he would never do otherwise. He thought McMahon was confused, uncertain of his authority, and unable to understand how the irresolution was damaging the government and the Liberal Party. Killen wrote later: 'I was convinced the office of Prime Minister was beyond him.'[12]

On 17 May, when the party room returned to discuss the issue, McMahon continued his attempts to bring Gorton, Killen, and Hughes on board. He told the party room that passing the Marine Science Institute legislation was necessary if Robert 'Duke' Bonnett, the member whose Queensland electorate would host the institute, was to hold his seat at the election. Delay could imperil Bonnett's efforts, he said. An unconvinced Gorton, Killen, and Hughes nonetheless struck a deal with McMahon: in exchange for voting against Whitlam's motion, there would be a debate on the offshore legislation the next day.

The backdown from the trio was a victory for McMahon.[13] Party unity would be maintained, at least on the floor of the House, and the issue could be defused by dragging it out until time ran out—as, indeed, it eventually did.[14] The Territorial Sea and Continental Shelf Bill would not be voted upon in the life of the McMahon government.

BELEAGUERED as the government was, it was able, on occasion, to assert itself in the Parliament and in national debate. The Whitlam-led opposition did not have the upper hand all year round. In February, the government was able to make much hay over Labor's candidate for the Victorian seat of Hotham. Barry Johnston, a primary school teacher who had received his national service call-up, had defied the orders and 'gone underground' in an effort to dodge authorities. The attorney-general, senator Ivor Greenwood, called for Whitlam to repudiate Johnston immediately. 'Failure to do so is to give support to those who defy the law,' Greenwood said, 'and the ALP, as a party seeking office, should unambiguously show whether it encourages lawlessness.'[15] When, three weeks later, Greenwood accused Labor of being in a position to assist the police track Johnston down, he managed to ensnare

Whitlam himself. Speaking on the radio, the ALP leader explained the situation by saying, 'Well, draft-dodging is not a crime. I am not going to assume that this man has broken any law.' *Are you saying that draft-dodging is not a crime?* asked his incredulous interviewer. 'How do you define draft-dodging?' Whitlam replied. 'Look, cut out all the nonsense about this. After this next election there will be no draft.'[16]

The government went immediately on the attack, and in the House of Representatives on 2 March homed in on the statement, attempting to portray the ALP as the party of lawlessness. What was notable, and perhaps why its attacks were most effective, was that Hughes and Killen spearheaded the debate. Hughes told the House that he had admired Whitlam's courage elsewhere. But: 'Why, on this occasion, has his courage failed him?' Hughes asked. 'Why has he not denounced the candidature of Mr Johnston? Why has he not denounced the methods by which Mr Johnston is promoting his candidature?' Killen, meanwhile, caught attention with a quip that Whitlam was the only man of whom it could be said that 'his Achilles heel is in his mouth'.[17]

Other elements of the ALP also caused problems. In April, the Victorian division voted to express its 'satisfaction' at successful advances of North Vietnamese forces into South Vietnam, prompting a pointed rebuke from Whitlam that the Labor Party's policy was to get a political settlement to end the war—not to applaud either side. There were problems with the party's immigration policy. In March, former ALP leader Arthur Calwell was the cause of consternation when he suggested his opposition to the ALP's policy for sponsored immigration. If 27,000 coloured immigrants came to Australia each year, he said on radio, in a decade they would number 270,000, and 'it wouldn't be very long before they would be taking the jobs of the Australian-born, even the Aboriginals'.[18] Then, in May, Fred Daly lost responsibility for the immigration portfolio when he publicly suggested retaining parts of the White Australia Policy.[19]

Contentious debates over preselections and whether to retain an 'inner cabinet' also caused problems. Later in the year, Whitlam's suggestions that he would revalue the dollar were he in power caused open disputes with his own shadow ministers. The decision by the People's Republic of China to resume buying wheat from Australia also undermined Labor's claim that diplomatic recognition was the only way to resume the sales. None of these was beneficial to the ALP, and they gave the government a boost—albeit a small one. 'I believe that morale is now starting to impove, and that we could well have turned the tide that has been flowing against us so much in recent weeks,' Howson wrote, after the debate on draft-dodging on 2 March. By the end of April, he was satisfied by the government's supposedly 're-established ascendancy' over Labor. 'It's had the effect of improving the PM's own morale,' he observed, 'and once he gets into good spirits he makes wiser and quicker decisions.'[20]

But, as journalist Bruce Grant had pointed out in March, the mere presence of problems for the ALP was not enough for the government. Its own problems—its confusion over direction, its manifest disunity, the steadily eroding loss of public confidence in its economic management, and the negative image of McMahon himself—would not be overcome without enormous effort. And even that might not be enough. 'The problem of legitimacy for this Government,' Grant wrote, 'is that even if, by some stroke of luck or brilliance, it were to remove unemployment, stop inflation, establish industrial harmony, demonstrate that Australia was defensible and, a week before the elections and just a few days after Mr McMahon had returned from a bigger banquet than Mr Whitlam was given in Peking, have Queen Elizabeth and president Nixon as simultaneous guests, the Australian people might still decide that, after all, it is time Labor had a go.'[21]

THE press was a persistent problem. Poor headlines proliferated, and McMahon's efforts to address them were inadequate. He believed his government had a good story to tell; in interviews, he always invoked the tremendous amount of work that was going on. 'I've always been a hard worker,' he said, '[but] never as hard as I work now because I have very little time for myself or, for that matter, my family. I work even in the car when I'm going back to the Lodge or I'm going home in Sydney and I get along with probably four and a half to five hours sleep a night.'[22] He sought to emphasise that he was taking 'decisive' action: 'Wherever a decision has to be made, I think I'll make it.'[23] His poor poll numbers, McMahon thought, were caused by a lack of knowledge among the community: 'I think the biggest problem we face is one of communication ... I think that if the people know the reasons [for government actions and policies], they will be satisfied and quickly our popularity will be restored.'[24]

This led McMahon to concentrate on media management as the solution to his ills. In January 1972, frustrated by leaks and hopeful that more engagement with the press would result in better headlines, McMahon had cabinet agree that he would speak about its decisions with the Press Gallery heads of bureaux.[25] 'I hope this is what you want,' he said to reporters, at the first briefing; the journalists were unimpressed. 'When do you think it will be likely we could have a full-scale press conference?' one asked.[26] McMahon's refusal to schedule such a conference rankled. Then it occupied precious column space, feeding the perception that McMahon was secretive, scared, and that his words never matched reality.[27] 'He has a communications gap,' one journalist said tartly, on the anniversary of McMahon's becoming prime minister. 'He declared this day a year ago he wanted the Australian people to be informed of what the government was doing, and why ... and has held few press conferences since.'[28]

McMahon would not accept this. He criticised the efforts of his press secretary, Reg MacDonald, both to his face and behind his back. Late in February 1972, he decided that he wanted MacDonald re-assigned and to replace him with a new press secretary.[29] Then he wanted MacDonald to stay, but with restricted, 'administrative' duties.[30] His discontent continued, leading to the farcical situation of MacDonald submitting, and then rescinding, his resignation in August.[31] Journalist Mungo MacCallum thought McMahon and MacDonald were both responsible for the problems. McMahon told MacDonald nothing, interfered in his work by ringing up journalists and complaining, and insisted on promulgating an image clearly at odds with reality. MacDonald, meanwhile, 'had no idea what the job was about,' said MacCallum. 'He played favourites among the Press Gallery [and] he told you things that in fact weren't so, simply just because he wanted to appear informed when in fact he wasn't.'[32] Howson thought McMahon himself was more to blame—an assessment echoed by Reid, who argued that suggestions to the contrary were 'a lot of rot'.[33] Writing in his diary, Reid was forthright: 'There is no love lost between McM[ahon] and working pressmen. But McM[ahon] provides them almost daily with the pegs on which to hang criticism. It is his performance that is key.'[34]

In an effort to address this performance, McMahon sought out Coombs to provide him with speeches on various aspects of Australian life.[35] They would be written, but not used. In February, McMahon had been persuaded to hire journalist Jonathan Gaul in a speechwriting role.[36] But McMahon would never be happy with the words that were written for him. 'They are a disgrace,' he would say, in late May, of one set of drafts. 'If I used these I would look as if I were blowing wind into a balloon. Not a single word of commonsense.'[37]

Gaul soon came to take on more and more of the duties of a press secretary. Long familiar with McMahon through his time working for Ezra Norton, Rupert Murdoch, the Fairfax group, and Maxwell Newton, Gaul believed that McMahon's relationship with the press was terrible. 'The media and McMahon had a symbiotic relationship,' he said later. But that changed. 'When he became prime minister, that started to fall apart.' A part of it lay simply in the restrictions on McMahon's time and position: he could not have the confidential conversations with journalists that he had had in the past. Another part of it was the media's sceptical regard for McMahon, and their sense that the long afternoon of Liberal and Country Party dominance was drawing to a close. Then there were the problems with McMahon's public performances. 'He hardly held any press conferences, because of his disabilities and his long tradition of one-to-one dealings with journalists,' Gaul said later. 'As press secretary I thought that McMahon was least effective on television, and not effective in press conferences or doorstops.'[38]

McMahon's relationships with the press would not improve. He regarded reporters as deceitful, critical, and biased in favour of Labor. This could lead him to over-react. When he bumped into Whitlam in the *This Day Tonight* studio for an appearance on 11 April, McMahon believed he had been had. The ABC's intention for Whitlam to appear on the same programme as him was insulting, and the manner by which it had been arranged was underhanded. Gaul agreed with McMahon. 'It was an ambush by Richard Carleton,' he said later. '... That was a set-up.'[39]

The next day, Labor questioned whether McMahon or his office had made a complaint about the incident. McMahon denied all, but a well-informed and mischievous speech from Gorton drew attention to it, fuelling speculation that McMahon had lied in the House.[40]

Unable to win journalists to his side, McMahon went over their heads. He was constantly in touch with editors and news proprietors alike to seek better coverage. In March 1972, McMahon convinced the chairman of the Melbourne *Herald* and *Sun* newspapers, Sir Philip Jones, to run articles praising the government. Jones, as Richard Casey wrote of him that year, 'was only too ready to be helpful' and 'very much' on McMahon's side.[41] McMahon was able to make use of an offer from the Macquarie Radio Network—not, initially, offered to Whitlam—to make a weekly broadcast entitled 'Report to the Nation'.[42] This was Gaul's idea. 'McMahon had more control over it, and interviews were usually with one presenter ... We would put McMahon on a few times each week.'[43] He also had a natural ally in Sir Warwick Fairfax, the proprietor of John Fairfax and Sons, who had privately confessed in December 1971 that, as an organisation, 'we do not usually support the Labor Party and certainly not in its present condition'.[44] Using that friendship, McMahon prevailed upon Fairfax to axe Killen's column in *The National Times*, and thereby subdue the critical backbencher. But that reprieve lasted only a few hours, until Killen accepted an offer to author a column for Rupert Murdoch's stable of newspapers.[45]

There were also rumours of McMahon's ability to pressure editors and proprietors on stories. In early May, Alan Reid heard that a journalist from the *Canberra Times* had asked some potentially embarrassing questions about McMahon's travel allowance. Rumours emerged that McMahon had made claims for travel outside of Canberra, including in Sydney and at the Gold Coast. McMahon seemed concerned, and while he left Bunting to deal with the question of repayments, he also 'contacted A.T. Shakespeare [owner of the *Canberra Times*] and virtually pleaded with him' to have the story quashed.[46]

The support that McMahon enjoyed from Packer's ACP and *The Daily Telegraph* had not waned since he became prime minister; indeed, until June 1972 it remained the one constant in the McMahon prime ministership. In March, when Snedden and McMahon found themselves enmeshed in controversy over a tax on the family unit, sharp-eyed observers noted that *The Daily Telegraph* had contorted itself in inextricable ways to produce favourable coverage of the prime minister. An early edition editorial argued that McMahon 'certainly has his problems when his treasurer flies a kite like that'. A later edition was different: 'The Prime Minister, who revealed last night he had not been consulted about the speech, would be justified in taking strong action against Mr Snedden.'[47] Moreover, despite the extensive coverage of McMahon's failings that he documented in his diary, Reid did not see fit to include criticism of McMahon in his columns. In public, as Reid's biographers later wrote, the journalist 'loyally upheld the corporate line', and focused his attention on Labor and the supposedly adverse effects of its new, voguish policies on a hypothetical 'Mr and Mrs Average'.[48]

But this long period of mutual protection came to an end on 4 June. For years, *The Daily Telegraph* had been a loss-making newspaper, unable to compete against *The Sydney Morning Herald* and its dominance in the classified markets. For a long time, the ACP-owned *Australian Women's Weekly* had effectively subsidised the paper, a state of affairs that caused no small deal of angst for Sir Frank's sons, Clyde and Kerry, who were well aware of the windfall that could come their way by selling the *Telegraph*. In the aftermath of a printers' strike in May, their argument that the paper should be sold began to gain force with their father, who was ageing and sick with lumbago. Finally, Sir Frank gave way, and Rupert Murdoch, who was looking to consolidate his position in Sydney's newspaper business, made an offer. On 31 May, Murdoch and Kerry Packer agreed on the 'broad outlines' of a deal; by 3 June, Murdoch had agreed to pay $15m for *The Daily Telegraph* and *Sunday Telegraph* mastheads.

Well aware of Murdoch's derisory regard for McMahon—a regard not improved at an earlier meeting in 1971—and given his own support for his old friend and prime minister, Sir Frank invited McMahon and Sonia to come up the road to his home, Cairnton, to meet with Murdoch, and have a drink. According to McMahon, the meaning of the sale was immediately apparent. 'Well,' he said to Packer, once he had heard the news, 'that just about ends our prospects in New South Wales'.[49] Nonetheless, Packer bade McMahon and Murdoch shake hands. As they did so, Murdoch told McMahon that he would correct any errors and, outside of the editorials, be fair. It did not assuage McMahon's misgivings. Neither he nor Sonia departed Packer's residence consoled by the meeting. 'Bill knew that was disaster as far as the election was concerned,' Sonia said later.[50]

The McMahons were right. Labor Party figures greeted the news of the sale with unalloyed joy. The sale of the *Telegraph* meant that the ALP would no longer have to contend with an unabashed enemy in New South Wales. It removed 'a constant threat' whereby every story about the ALP was presented in the 'most unfavourable light possible'. In an election year, this was an unexpected boon for Labor, and a blow to the government.[51]

DEFENCE and foreign policy had long been reliable electoral strengths for the government. Australia's military involvement in Vietnam had been electoral gold during Harold Holt's 1966 campaign, and it was the emphasis on Australia's security that had retrieved John Gorton's standing at the tail end of the 1969 campaign. McMahon had certainly made efforts to emphasise foreign relations throughout 1971, but after the embarrassments of the US rapprochement with China and his disastrous visits to the US and UK, it seemed there was little traction to be had. Thus he turned his attention to defence, attempting to establish it as an issue on which the government could campaign.

This first surfaced on 28 March, when defence minister David Fairbairn tabled the *Australian Defence Review*. A project initiated before McMahon became prime minister, the *Review* was originally intended as—and, until the last moment, was—a white paper that would set out the government's future defence policy. The government viewed it as an opportunity to draw discussions of Australia's defence away from the Vietnam conflict and to emphasise its strength and expertise in Australia's security.

But the secretary of the Department of Defence, Sir Arthur Tange, saw the paper somewhat differently: as he was to write, it was an opportunity to 'present new ideas and a more realistic view of what we [Australia] needed to do for ourselves'.[52] Thus, under Tange's supervision, the paper emphasised 'self-reliance' as a guiding strategic concept, and pointedly discussed Australia's capabilities and interests, framing these as considerations in any decision about Australia's defence policy. The paper stated that the fundamental objectives of such a policy were the 'independence and security of Australia'. In so stating, as Tange's biographer was to point out, the paper elevated independence to the same status as security and, by eschewing mention of any alliance, established a new direction for Australian strategic thinking.[53] These were significant departures from the orthodoxy.

After it was finalised, McMahon decided that it could not be published as a white paper. Rather, it should be given a lower status—that of a departmental review. It is highly likely that the new ideas Tange had worked to include were to blame for the downgrading of the paper. McMahon had no appetite to embrace them, particularly in an election year.[54] Certainly, he made his feelings clear when he left the House midway through Fairbairn's statement, which in and of itself appeared to downgrade the review further.[55] This was, perhaps, a mistake: the paper's emphasis on a policy that would become known in shorthand as the 'defence of Australia' would dominate official strategic thinking for the next thirty years.[56] Had the government seized this opportunity, it might well have shaped that thinking and forced debate onto the future of Australia's defence, instead of allowing the debate to centre on the ignominious past of Australia's involvement in Vietnam, which received fresh attention when a series of successful North Vietnamese offensives caused fears that the South Vietnamese government would be overrun. Calls from the DLP to re-commit troops to the conflict were loud, but McMahon and Fairbairn would stand firm on refusing to do so, even as the US responded with massive bombing raids and a naval blockade.

Another opportunity to highlight defence came in June. Two days after *The Daily Telegraph* was sold, McMahon left Australia for Indonesia, Singapore, and Malaysia. As with his visits to Washington and the UK, the ten-day trip was mostly for the sake of optics, for showing that the government could manage Australia's defence and foreign relations better than the ALP, which had undertaken to withdraw the Australian troops stationed in Singapore under the Five Power Defence Arrangements. The political dimension was never particularly disguised. Journalists drew attention to it repeatedly: 'Mr McMahon hopes to gain domestic political kudos for his test at the polls in November or December,' wrote one reporter.[57]

Given the continuing commitment to the arrangments, there was some logic to these hopes. But even before McMahon's departure there were signs that realising those hopes would require more finesse than McMahon had thus far demonstrated. Malaysian moves towards a 'neutralist' foreign policy, based on regional co-operation and the ASEAN community, meant that it had no wish to draw attention to the Five Power Defence Arrangements, though it would work to support them. Singapore's aversion to being used for a domestic political campaign—to the point that Singapore's prime minister, Lee Kuan Yew, had cancelled a proposed visit to Australia that year[58]—made it sensitive to any discussion of the arrangements. McMahon had a difficult task should he wish to return with a statesman-like glow: to show off the achievement of the arrangments without being seen to do so.

The trip started reasonably well. McMahon made a gift of sixteen superseded Sabre fighter planes to the Indonesian air force, held talks with Indonesian president General Suharto, talked of economic opportunity, and lauded Australia's closer relationship with Indonesia. He managed to avoid contentious discussions on the sea border, and he announced a three-year, $75m defence and civil-aid programme, the costs of which were to be borne by Australia.[59]

And yet, inevitably, there were gaffes. Shortly before he left Indonesia, speaking in a television interview with the ABC, McMahon appeared to downplay the importance of the Five Power arrangements. Explaining why there was no need for a similar defence arrangement with Indonesia, McMahon said that the arrangements were based on historical realities, and related only to the obligation to consult. 'You wouldn't like that with the Indonesians as well?' asked his interviewer. 'No,' McMahon said, 'there's no necessity for it. Nor do I think that there was any real necessity to have a Five Power Defence Arrangement so far as the UK, New Zealand, Singapore, [and] Malaysia are concerned. But it's there, and it's only an obligation to consult.'[60]

The pressmen accompanying McMahon leaped on the admission, arguing that it directly contradicted the rationale for Australia's contribution to the ANZUK forces stationed in Malaysia and Singapore. News of the statement shocked Fairbairn, who had spent weeks touting the arrangements and criticising Labor for its promise to withdraw the Australian infantry battalion that was stationed in Singapore under the arrangements. Initially, Fairbairn questioned the accuracy of the transcript; then he offered an anguished explanation for McMahon's statement: 'I believe that what Mr McMahon was saying was that because the five powers are so friendly, close together in every way, there was not the real necessity to have things in writing as well as to have the understanding.'[61] McMahon's protests—that he had only repeated what the arrangements actually said—did not convince anyone. He knew it. Aware of the damage being done, McMahon issued a statement making clear that the government considered the arrangements to be of great importance and that his comments had related only to an Australian–Indonesian context. Flying into Singapore shortly afterwards, he then had to explain himself to an unimpressed Lee Kuan Yew.

By the time McMahon arrived in Malaysia, any possibility that he could avoid drawing attention to the arrangements was gone. Bob Bowker, a diplomat in Australia's mission in Kuala Lumpur who was assigned to look after McMahon during his stay, found that McMahon was frustrated and incensed by the press coverage of his mistakes. Bringing the prime minister his newspapers and orange juice in the mornings was a memorable experience for the young diplomat. 'I would sit on the bed beside him,' Bowker recalled, 'as he told me what a bunch of bastards the press were.'[62]

Worse was still to come. While McMahon met the Malaysian prime minister, Tun Razak, the deputy secretary of the Malaysian Foreign Office told the party of Australian journalists that the Malaysian government would not be concerned if Australia withdrew its troops from the Five Power forces stationed in Singapore. Then McMahon emerged from his meeting to declare how much Malaysia appreciated the arrangements. To the press, the contradiction was renewed: the discrepancy was gaping; the problem was obvious. 'With a normal prime minister, with reasonable relations with the media, this could have been managed,' Bowker said later. 'But with McMahon, the press drew the conclusion that McMahon was seeking to mislead the public about Malaysia's support for the Five Power Defence Arrangements.'

When McMahon found out about the briefing, he was furious. He telephoned Tun Razak to complain, and Razak was persuaded to issue a clarifying statement that welcomed the presence of Australian military forces in the area. In the meantime, however, the press had questioned McMahon about the matter, provoking a strong reaction. 'McMahon did what McMahon did best,' Bowker recalled. 'He panicked.'

McMahon sent foreign affairs adviser Richard Woolcott and press secretary Jonathan Gaul to the ABC office in Kuala Lumpur to ensure that the statement from the Malaysian government was transmitted to Australia. It was an attempt to pre-empt news of the first briefing, and in their efforts to do so the two allegedly ordered a trainee Malaysian journalist to telephone the ABC's Sydney newsroom with the statement. The Sydney office refused to kill the initial story, allegedly prompting Gaul himself to telephone and read the new statement through the phone.[63] But it was no use. 'The ABC felt that we were trying to put the prime minister in a better light than he was meant to be,' Woolcott said later. Noting that it was his job to make McMahon look good, Woolcott felt the action went too far. 'As a public servant,' he reflected later, 'I should not have done so.'[64] Gaul had no regrets for the incident: 'My first loyalty was to McMahon.'[65] The damage was done. The next day, news of Woolcott's and Gaul's actions were in the newspapers, and the ABC's manager in Asia had made a complaint about interference, intrusion, and improper use of ABC equipment.[66]

'It was a complete catastrophe, an utter debacle,' Bowker recalled.[67] The headlines that eventuated were worse than scathing: they lampooned McMahon. The chance of some gain in stature was gone. 'Mr McMahon's journey to South-East Asia has become an excursion into blunderland,' argued one journalist.[68] 'Today Kuala Lumpur is full of red faces; they are all Australian and the reddest is Mr McMahon's,' wrote another.[69] Labor was joyful, happy to take its shots. 'The whole purpose of Mr McMahon's visit overseas was to use foreign affairs again as a domestic issue,' Labor MP Bill Morrison charged. 'This has now blown up in his face—and rightly so.' Even the DLP piled on: 'This is the second occasion on which an Australian Prime Minister has gone to Malaysia and confusing statements have harmed our image among Asian people.'[70]

McMahon continued to press his point of view in spite of the headlines. 'There are no differences whatsoever between Australia and Malaysia, or between Australia and Singapore, under these arrangements,' he said, in a nationally broadcast statement.[71] But it was no use. His hopes of highlighting defence and foreign relations, and using them to his benefit, had been extinguished.

CHAPTER FORTY-THREE

The Unequal Struggle

1984

McMahon was in hospital and then at home for two-and-a-half weeks, but his absence from the office meant neither less work for his staff, nor less frustration. McMahon was telephoning Cawthorn with demands that she had no idea how to meet, and complaining about his operation. From his desk, Bowman could hear Cawthorn crying, 'Oh, he's an impossible man. Impossible, impossible. Why don't I just go home?'[1]

The staff inevitably gossiped. When talking about why McMahon was in hospital, Bowman said that he had never noticed McMahon's left ear—'i.e. the rear-side door of the VW'. Cawthorn was surprised he had been able to miss it. The ear was horrid, she told him. It smelt and would drip on McMahon's shirts. Apparently, McMahon blamed his doctor for scraping it, but Cawthorn had her own conclusions: 'I bet he went out in the sun with it.'[2]

'WM says it is bloody awful being confined as he is,' Bowman wrote in his diary the next day, after speaking with McMahon on the phone. Bowman had sent him another draft of the prologue, but McMahon seemed little interested in discussing it. He much preferred to tell him about the flowers filling his rooms. There was a bunch from Bob Hawke, he told Bowman, and Hawke had even telephoned! McMahon was buoyed by the attention. He was especially delighted that Hawke had recalled his remarks on radio, praising him. 'Hawke thanked him for his public support recently,' wrote Bowman. 'Hawke [also] remarked on [Liberal Party president] John Valder's much-publicised remark that it would need a miracle for the Lib-CP to gain government, and said, "That should be worth 10% to us, shouldn't it?"'

Of course, McMahon's staff thought little of it. When Bowman recounted this conversation to her, Cawthorn was scathing. 'Come on!' she said. 'Hawke didn't call him—*he* called Hawke.'[3]

The work on the autobiography continued. McMahon was still intent on working, even from his bed. His efforts were not much good. 'George pretty disgusted with material WM is giving him and talks of finishing up soon,' Bowman noted, on 28 March. Five days later, it was the same: 'George continues to be overwhelmed by flow of rubbish from WM.'

Campbell was pessimistic about the book and about McMahon. On the same day that Bowman had the third chapter sent out to McMahon, Campbell came in to tell him about the British writer Leonard Woolf and his long-in-the-works autobiography and 'history of our own times'. The successive volumes had taken longer and longer to write, Campbell said, and the attempt to catch up to the present day had eluded him: 'By 1906 reached 1902, by 1912 reached 1907, by 1914 … etc.,' Bowman noted.

After saying all this, Campbell put it bluntly: 'He gave up the unequal struggle.'

The parallel with McMahon was impossible to ignore. Bowman, surveying the edits and corrections that McMahon had made to the latest draft, was despairing. 'He has entirely ignored my comments about ephemera …'[4]

CHAPTER FORTY-FOUR

Dither and Irresolution

1972

Over and over again, there were problems. Some were of the government's own making. Others were bad luck. All, however, added up to a sense that the McMahon government was inept, bungling, lurching.

Late in March, Sir William Owen, a justice of the High Court, died unexpectedly. Rumours about who would be appointed to his seat were galvanised by speculation that the foreign minister, Nigel Bowen, was a candidate. But there were compelling reasons to not appoint Bowen: McMahon relied heavily on him, had appointed him to many cabinet committees, and summoned him repeatedly for meetings and counsel. Nor could the government afford a by-election, particularly in a seat that, as Maximilian Walsh was to say, was 'ripe picking' for Labor.[1] Nonetheless, McMahon allowed the speculation to go on for some months. When he finally appointed Justice Anthony Mason, a judge of the Court of Appeal in New South Wales, to the seat on 24 July, it gave the appearance that the government had been too scared to appoint Bowen.

In June, with its usual antipathy towards international criticism, the French government decided it would proceed with a series of nuclear weapons testing in French Polynesia. Protests about the tests had been continuous since they had begun in the Pacific in 1966, but the latest round came at an especially inopportune time for the Australian government. When a virulent press reaction to the news began to swell, the government's ability to respond was hampered by the absence of so many ministers from Australia. McMahon was on his trip through

Indonesia, Singapore, and Malaysia; Nigel Bowen was abroad; and Peter Howson was in Stockholm for a UN conference on the environment.

According to Howson, the advice from officials accompanying him was to treat the tests in a low-key manner. But outrage from the New Zealand government would prevent that from being a viable course. In addition to renewing its calls for the tests to be postponed, the New Zealand government had decided to make use of its presence at the UN conference to criticise the French. Howson was asked by his New Zealand counterpart to support that criticism, and then to co-sponsor a resolution on the tests. His reluctance to support New Zealand without an explicit directive from Canberra caused reporters to speculate about the existence of a rift between the Australian and New Zealand governments. What followed bore out that speculation: in the series of mooted amendments and votes on resolutions between 9 and 13 June, Australia and New Zealand repeatedly ended up on different sides.

Press criticism ran hot in Australia. 'What is the real motive behind the government's inactivity on the French nuclear tests in the Pacific?' asked one reporter.[2] The next day, however, the instructions from Canberra suddenly changed. Howson and his delegation were to vote with New Zealand. The government had decided—embarrassingly, humiliatingly—to do what it had spent the past few days trying to prevent New Zealand from doing.

It was a blunder. The government had positioned itself against the tide of public opinion in Australia, and in moving to reverse course had seemed to be acting only so as to go along with that tide.

McMahon did what he could when he returned to Australia and found sixty protesters demonstrating outside his Bellevue Hill home. He had a letter of protest sent to the president of France, Georges Pompidou; he canvassed sending Doug Anthony to Paris to protest in person; and while appearing at the opening of a critical facility at the nuclear reactor in Lucas Heights, which had been built by French engineers, he told the French ambassador that 'none of the explanations you have given would in any way, in any shape at all, change my or my government's attitude, or the Australian people's attitude, to the atmospheric testing by any country'.[3] The government had to be seen to be going into the test matter thoroughly, he told Bunting.[4] But he could not dispel the distrust the incident had caused. Duplicitous suggestions that Australia had simply not thought the Stockholm conference the appropriate place for issues of disarmament and world peace would not do it.[5] Nor would an admission that 'we came in a little, a very little, slowly at Stockholm'.[6]

Problems with the states also claimed a part of McMahon's attention. Amid continued gloom over the rate of unemployment, the premiers came to Canberra on 22 June for another conference. They arrived, as usual, with complaints about their budget deficits. It was an uneasy meeting for McMahon: he was anxious to avoid the infighting of previous conferences, but also intent on preserving his options and viability at the upcoming election. He wanted no increase in taxes whatsoever, a desire shared by Robert Askin and Henry Bolte.[7] By the standards of their past behaviour, the two Liberal premiers were relatively muted in their criticism, but the presence of three Labor premiers in Don Dunstan, John Tonkin, and Eric Reece ensured that the federal government did not emerge unscathed. As Reid wrote of the proceedings, 'Dunstan took a lump out of McMahon.'[8] Again, the federal government opened its chequebook: financial-assistance grants to the states were increased by $112m for 1972–73, and $90m was provided for works and housing grants. Though Askin still made noises about returning income tax powers and the press continued to bemoan the state of Commonwealth–state relations, the outcome of the conference was about as good as McMahon could have hoped for.

But there were clear portents of change and declining confidence in his leadership. One sign of this lay in the retirement speculation that followed Henry Bolte from the moment he arrived at the conference.[9] In power since 1955, the irascible Victorian premier wished to depart politics on top—not in the wake of a likely federal election defeat, nor too close to the next Victorian election, due early in 1973. The idea of Bolte's departure worried McMahon enough that he beseeched Bolte to not retire. He wanted to ensure that he had some of the premier's earthy charm to use during the federal campaign. 'But I couldn't see why I should look a fool after he'd lost the election,' Bolte said later.[10]

Bolte's pending departure at least freed McMahon from a campaign to have the Victorian premier made a life peer. The idea of 'Baron Bolte' was clearly out-of-step with public attitudes, and Bolte had been awarded a GCMG only in January that year. Was it not too soon for another honour? When McMahon raised the issue in May, Hasluck asked who was driving the campaign. 'Bolte himself,' McMahon answered. 'He's pressing for it.' At the time, McMahon was inclined to give it to the Victorian premier in order to keep him 'on side'. It was worth doing even if it lost him support in the electorate, McMahon said. 'I must do something,' he told Hasluck. 'I must make some move. He keeps asking me what I have done about it.'[11]

In the end, nothing would come of it. McMahon would not propose a peerage for Bolte. When the Victorian premier retired in July, McMahon would lose a valuable campaigner in the state—but he would be free of the 'down-to-earth' premier and his demands.[12]

MOVEMENT in Aboriginal affairs was also slow. There was no progress on addressing the concerns of the activists encamped outside Parliament House, and even the government's own initiatives were gaining little traction. Coombs wrote to McMahon in April to note that the government had not issued any general-purpose leases for Aborigines and that the Northern Territory administration was granting only small, special-purpose leases. What was the government doing, Coombs wanted to know. An offer for the government to lease land from Lord Edmund Vestey, owner of a vast cattle station at Wattle Creek, for use by Aborigines had gone unanswered. 'Surely this is throwing away the opportunity for a significant initiative!' Coombs wrote.[13]

The tabling of the report of the Gibb Committee, set up in 1970 to investigate conditions on pastoral properties in the Northern Territory, did not induce the government to act quickly. Its recommendation that the government seek to buy various sections of pastoral lands for use by Aborigines only saw fruit in August, when a cabinet committee, in a deliberately 'low-key' announcement, agreed to accept Vestey's offer for thirty-five square miles of land at Wattle Creek for use by Aborigines. But at the same meeting, the cabinet committee decided not to pursue an acquisition of 1,500 square miles of land at Wave Hill for use by the Gurindji people. It was 'not practicable and should not be pursued', cabinet decided.[14]

What eventually did receive attention and movement was the

Aboriginal embassy. An inter-departmental committee set up in February recommended that the government amend the *Commonwealth Lands Ordinance* to create a legal basis for removing the embassy, but movement to act on that advice was slow. The proposal that McMahon took to cabinet on 2 May was approved with the clear caveat that the removal should occur 'tactfully and with the least disturbance'.[15] The need to create as little disturbance as possible was doubtless the source of the government's continuing inertia. In June, Ralph Hunt sent McMahon a 'pros and cons' list on removing the embassy that nonetheless made a clear case for its removal. The five months that it had gone on for was 'long enough'. The embassy had had a 'fair go'. Some of the people in the embassy were potentially targets of police. 'Proposed action is tactful,' the briefing went on. 'Directed at tents not the individuals.'[16] The government wanted the embassy gone, and was not about to hold back, but it was now conscious of timing. 'It has also to be remembered that it is now not long until National Aboriginal Day (14 July) and, after that, to the beginning of Parliament (17 August),' Peter Bailey wrote to McMahon. '… Also to be taken into account is your visit to the Northern Territory.' Essentially, Bailey continued, 'the decision is a political one'.[17]

On 17 July, a copy of the new ordinance that provided for the embassy's removal was delivered to the embassy. Hunt promised to give two weeks' grace before enforcing the law, but the activists were suspicious, and established a vigil to protect the embassy. On 20 July, aware that police were massing, the activists sent a message into Parliament House, intended for McMahon, explaining the situation and urging him or another minister to come out and talk. 'With the Prime Minister [inside] were three other ministers,' wrote *Times* correspondent Stewart Harris. 'Anthony, Snedden, and Sinclair. Not one of them emerged. The budget, a material thing, remained more important than a unique human need which they must have seen from their window.'[18] Ten minutes after the message was sent, sixty police officers marched on the embassy and, amid violence that saw eight people arrested and many injured, ripped the tents from the lawns and tore down the Aboriginal flag. It was a debacle conducted within full view of cameras and the Parliament. In the aftermath, Whitlam praised the activists sincerely and the government sarcastically:

The men and women who established the embassy should be congratulated on their initiative and self-discipline ... I suppose the government must be congratulated upon the dispatch it showed against these Aborigines in contrast to its impotence in the face of travel swindlers, international gangsters, and fascist bombers, and tax racketeers.[19]

There was criticism from McMahon's own side. After initially saying that he had been 'far too busy' inside Parliament House to watch the removal of the embassy, Hunt backtracked and said he had only seen it for a moment. Labor MPs present at the time 'should have used their influence to make the protesters conform to the law,' he argued.[20] It was a pathetic argument, and Queensland senator Neville Bonner, who was both the first and sole Aborigine elected to the Parliament, was scathing about how the whole matter had been handled. McMahon and Hunt knew his feelings on the matter, he said. He had wanted to have the ordinance debated in Parliament. 'In this instance the Executive Council should not have exercised that authority. I categorically state that I am disappointed with the government to the point of being disgusted by its action on this issue.'[21] There was widespread disillusionment over the government's handling of it. Letters flowed into McMahon's office decrying the move. 'I wish to register my strong protest concerning the treatment of the Aboriginal Embassy affair yesterday in Canberra,' ran one such letter:

Although I have voted Liberal in the past, my frustration with the cumbersome progress toward continued development for Aboriginals [means] that I can no longer vote, nor encourage others to vote, for your party. Australia surely has the resource[s] and determination to involve Aboriginal people in political action. Provoking violence by industrial or political self-interest must lead to chaos, and further de-humanisation.[22]

Undaunted by removal of the embassy, the activists launched court action calling into question the gazetting of the new ordinances. Three days after it had been torn down, the activists re-erected the embassy amid another police move to intimidate and disperse them. 'Girls were knocked to the ground and kicked, and men were smashed in the face and groin,' recalled Bobbi Sykes, one of those in the melee that followed. 'I was hurled to the ground on several occasions, and walked over by heavy cop boots. "The whole world's watching, the whole world's watching," we chanted. Police dragged people along the ground by their hair. We lost ... but we won.'[23]

McMahon would seem, in the days that followed, to grow concerned by the violence, but there were no regrets within the government more generally.[24] Believing the activists to be militant and radical, Howson scotched suggestions that the government offer the embassy's personnel a club or meeting place in exchange for complete removal of the embassy, and attended a meeting with them on 29 July with little interest in dealing with the issues they were raising. 'It was mainly a public relations exercise to show that we are prepared to talk to them,' Howson wrote later. 'We were patient and got rid of them after about two hours.'[25] It was a phrase that summed up the government's approach to Aboriginal affairs.

But there would be controversy over the government's handling of the removal of the embassy. In the House of Representatives on 15 August, the opposition moved a motion of no confidence in Ralph Hunt, the minister for the interior. Hunt would make no apologies for his actions: 'I held firmly to the view that the continued presence of scruffy tents outside Parliament House was not serving either the interests of the Aboriginal people or the Parliament in a dignified way.'[26] The motion failed, but just under a month later, on 12 September, the ACT Supreme Court ruled that the ordinances providing for the July removal of the embassy had not been appropriately gazetted, and were therefore inoperative. The embassy was re-erected outside Parliament House, but now the government gazetted the ordinance again—this time, at around midnight, after Parliament had adjourned. The embassy was removed less than an hour later.

On 13 September, the government moved to retrospectively restore the ordinance allowing for the embassy's removal. Labor castigated the government for the 'sloppy drafting', and called its tactics those of the 'Tcheka and Gestapo', but the most damaging interventions came when Jim Killen spoke on the motion. Believing that the embassy should be removed, Killen was nevertheless disgusted by the way the government had handled the matter, and its determination to charge the protesters who had been arrested. The prospect of Killen voting against the motion caused consternation. Fears that other members could join Killen and cross the floor prompted Sinclair and Chipp to canvass 'capitulation' on the question of prosecutions. That would not happen—Anthony would counsel against it, and McMahon, in Melbourne but in touch via the telephone, would agree—but the division was again in the headlines.[27]

Killen was unrepentant. The government had had six months to deal with the embassy, and in a mixture of 'dither and irresolution' had failed to do so properly. It had then resorted to an inappropriate gazetting, which Killen likened to Caligula's practice of depositing criminal edicts atop monuments, so they would not be seen and could not be known. 'What is the difference between what Caligula did and what happened last night?' he asked.[28] The motion would pass, and the collection of tents that constituted the embassy would, for a short time, be gone. What would remain, however, was the moral victory that the embassy represented for the rights and dignity of Australian Aborigines.[29]

A potential strategy for regaining the government's standing was considered, and indeed pursued, all year. There were many within the government who hoped that highlighting industrial relations, and the dangers of electing a union-influenced ALP, could provide a path to victory. The year had opened with a strike by the Australian Postal Workers Union and concern that union demands for excessive wage rises were a threat to the economy. Intent on showing that the government was concerned about this, McMahon canvassed inviting ACTU president Bob Hawke in for a meeting, then scotched the idea, saying that Hawke would 'use it politically'. Nonetheless, he added, 'We must be taking leadership somewhere.'[30] Over a dinner on 1 February, Bolte suggested that McMahon emphasise industrial trouble, and blame Labor and Hawke. But, as Reid judged it:

> I for one simply don't believe Hawke is such an ogre in the public mind as McM[ahon] makes out. Hawke too Australian in his manner and speech and approach to be such an orgre [sic]. And he achieves results and takes action which is more than government does.[31]

Legislation announced in December 1971 by the minister for labour and national service, Phillip Lynch, would ostensibly have aided the government. The package would have outlawed political strikes, done away with compulsory unionism, encouraged secret ballots before strikes, and altered the way that the Commonwealth Conciliation and Arbitration Commission dealt with cases—most particularly by compelling it to 'have regard to the likely national economic consequences' of its decisions.[32] The political intent was naked, and, in a lengthy and virulent speech immediately afterward, Labor's spokesman on industrial relations and former union official, Clyde Cameron, called the proposals 'notice of an early election next year', and accused the government of deliberately creating industrial unrest.[33]

The government would have expected nothing else from Labor, but the opposition of the DLP was surprising. On grounds that the proposals endangered 'moderate' unions while doing nothing to prevent supposedly communist-dominated unions to amalgamate, a process then underway within the metal trades, the DLP threatened to withhold its support.[34] This argument was felt most keenly among backbench government members, such as Dudley Erwin and senator Ian Wood, who believed the government should intervene to prevent the amalgamations.[35]

Amid widespread discontent with his leadership in the early months of 1972, McMahon had to tread warily: as Howson was to write, it was a 'test of firmness' for McMahon.[36] But McMahon would not necessarily hold out. Snedden and Chipp both recalled that McMahon used to meet regularly with the DLP senators, and would even try to second-guess the party's attitude on matters. It became a source of angst. 'Oh, I feel between a shit and a shiver,' McMahon would say of the tension between the DLP and the government.[37]

After two nights of party-room meetings on the amalgamations legislation, during which ministers pointed out the lawfulness of the union amalgamations and the need to resist the DLP's demands, the prospect of a revolt was headed off. But the DLP continued to withhold its support, and, while the government refused to consider retrospective changes to the laws relating to amalgamation, it was, by the end of March, making conciliatory noises about future amalgamations. Then came a victory for the DLP: the government decided to offer financial aid to two unionists opposing the amalgamation of the AMWU.[38] A few days after this came a headline victory: the government agreed to remove the proposed abolition of compulsory unionism, as the DLP had demanded, and agreed that future amalgamations could only go ahead so long as 51 per cent of the union membership agreed to it in a court-controlled ballot.[39]

McMahon was unrepentant about the concessions. As he said privately, there was no point in bringing a Bill into Parliament that could not be passed. 'To that extent we've had, therefore, to submit to pressure from the DLP,' Howson explained.[40] But McMahon was certainly frustrated by the process. When Lynch received the congratulations of colleagues for getting the Bill through, McMahon could not help but spread word that Lynch had initially refused to take the Bill to the party room and had asked for his help to do so.[41] Notwithstanding a largely positive reception from the press, what became clear afterward was the diminished attraction of an industrial-relations campaign. One newspaper editorialised that it did 'not look so certain an election-winner' as it had in December 1971.[42]

But industrial relations could certainly be an election loser. Nowhere was this better demonstrated than in a protracted series of oil strikes in the winter of 1972. In June, hoping to emulate the success of workers in the coal and shipping industries, oil-refinery workers in Victoria renewed longstanding calls for a thirty-five hour workweek and increases in their benefits. When employers, at the government's urging, refused to enter into discussions on the matter, the oil workers went on strike. Breakdowns in negotiations resulted in further stoppages that rippled throughout the industry and the country.

By 14 June, some 14,000 oil refinery workers and 1,500 tanker drivers and aircraft refuellers were striking.[43] By 21 June, crude-oil production in Bass Strait had dropped from 300,000 barrels per day to 10,000, sparking talk of petrol rationing.[44] On the same day, the deputy president of the Conciliation and Arbitration Commission, Justice Moore, agreed to requests from the oil companies to insert a clause in the award covering oil-refinery workers that would ban strike action.[45] That ban failed to compel the workers to back down, and by July the strikes had become serious. Newspapers led with stories about schools without heating and hospitals without power, about petrol rationing and the prioritising of essential services.

It was a perfect opportunity for Bob Hawke. Simultaneously swatting suggestions that the thirty-five-hour workweek would spread beyond the oil industry while elevating his profile as a dealmaker and advocate, the ACTU president seized the initiative and sought talks with the oil companies, positioning himself as a moderate between left-wing unions and the employers. Others made moves to lower the temperature. Justice Moore began hearing the strikers' claims on 14 July, but made this conditional on striking workers returning to work.[46] In return for them doing so, he promised to give an interim decision on their main wage claims within two hours.[47] The workers narrowly voted to return to break the strike, but divisions within the unions about observing the vote provoked sharp criticism from Moore, who nonetheless gave his decision on the wage claims and backdated it to 5 June. But both sides were unhappy, and, amid tit-for-tat claims and counterclaims, the strikes continued.

The government did little to intervene. It was occupied with preparations for the budget, the planned retirement of Reg Swartz, consternation over the Aboriginal Embassy, and another rise in the rate of unemployment in June. But its absence from the debate was also driven by its rigid belief that events still had to play out and that the Conciliation and Arbitration Commission was best equipped to handle the matter. This, along with a ban on ministers speaking out, was a serious error. By mid-July, the government's silence was conspicuous, and Hawke's star was all the more lustrous for his unerring advocacy.

On 22 July, McMahon began looking at ways to intervene. He told Bunting to assemble an inter-departmental committee to 'examine what the government can do and what it should do'.[48] Around midnight, four days later, McMahon phoned Bunting to say 'there was a need to move quickly. Action might be necessary in the next 48 hours.'[49] Cabinet met the next day. Believing that the ACTU was trying 'to divide the unity of the employers' in the dispute, the government decided it 'could no longer stand aside'. Senator Ivor Greenwood (attorney-general), Peter Nixon (minister for shipping and transport), and Phillip Lynch (labour and national service) were tasked with meeting with employers and the ACTU to find ways to resolve the matter.[50] It was an idea that McMahon would claim to have been against from the beginning.

The ministers proceeded to call upon Hawke at the ACTU office in Trades Hall, Melbourne. 'You've never seen such embarrassed people as those three as they walked into the old ACTU building, past the media,' Hawke later said. 'But they faced up to it. And we just belted at them that what they were doing was totally unacceptable.'[51] The meeting was fruitless, and Hawke now took aim at the government, whom he said had 'applauded' as the oil companies cheated and reneged on agreements.[52]

Hawke's involvement was paying off. While McMahon blamed the strike on left-wing unions determined to destroy the industrial relations system, Hawke was winning credit for successfully steering the dispute towards a point where it was possible to envisage a resolution. It jolted McMahon again. 'He had decided to go ahead with something decisive,' Bunting wrote, after another telephone call on 29 July. The decisive act that McMahon had in mind was to announce his intention to call Parliament together to resolve the dispute.[53] Should it come to this, he would be prepared to legislate to de-register the responsible unions and freeze their funding, much as he had threatened the WWF in 1965. McMahon believed that time was of the essence in all this. 'I must be saying something tomorrow night,' he told Bunting.[54] 'We need the facts and the issues set out. Deceit and disunity must be exposed,' he told Bunting the next day, Sunday 30 July.[55]

McMahon broke into national television programming that night. Declaring that the arbitration system 'can and must' settle the dispute, McMahon threatened to call Parliament together if the dispute were not resolved; then he telegrammed the state premiers to say that he would need their co-operation to alleviate the difficulties caused by the strike.[56] With his own side down two senators for health reasons, McMahon set his ministers to determining the likely numbers for a sitting of Parliament. The numbers in the Senate would be close, relying on the DLP and independents joining the government in any vote, and the House would require at least two days' sitting in order to overcome Labor's expected procedural obstruction.[57] McMahon would not be dissuaded from acting; as he told Bunting in another midnight phone call, 'The feeling for drastic action is unbelievably strong.'[58] Certainly he had plentiful support. Howson thought the 'strong showing' would be well received and of 'great electoral value'.[59]

But McMahon had not yet said publicly what he would do. This left an opening for criticism that his threat was inappropriate, and that over-the-top action might lead to a much larger and more dangerous confrontation with the unions. Rumours that he intended to de-register unions also opened the government to criticism that it would be the one usurping the role of the Conciliation and Arbitration Commission. 'The interests of the nation, the oil industry, workers, and the public may have been better served if the government had had nothing to do with the dispute,' Hawke said.[60] Labor, which had remained mostly quiet throughout the dispute, now gave notice that it would move a motion of no confidence in McMahon's leadership if Parliament were recalled.[61]

Within the government, there was now concern about the idea. Would Parliament still be recalled if the dispute was resolved? Uncertainty about the wisdom of the move grew. Searching for options, drawing on his experience as minister for labour and national service, McMahon telephoned Bunting in the morning of 1 August to refer him to section 29A of the *Conciliation and Arbitration Act*, which would allow Justice Moore to call together the parties for negotiation. Could Bunting telephone the secretary of the Department of Labour and National Service, Dr Halford Cook, and tell him to pass on the option to Justice Moore? Bunting did so.[62] By the evening, McMahon was still intent on pushing ahead, but was making clear intimations that developments in Melbourne could avert Parliament being recalled.[63] Reid was certain that McMahon did not want Parliament to meet at all. 'Obviously fearful of a motion of no-confidence,' he wrote in his diary. 'Fairbairn and the others forced him into it. He kept hoping for a miracle—for Hawke, Moore, God, anyone to solve his problem.'[64]

The end came quickly. At 6.30 that evening, a meeting of the legislation and programming committee of cabinet signed off on proposals for legislation, modelled on that used to break the coal strikes in 1949, that would de-register the unions involved in the dispute.[65] Emerging from the meeting, McMahon announced that Parliament would return on Friday 5 August.[66] But within minutes of his statement came news of an announcement from Justice Moore. 'Acting on my own initiative, I have today had informal discussions about the oil dispute and in the result I have made the following recommendations,' Moore said, in a statement issued to the press. Striking workers would resume work on 3 August, and employers would seek an adjournment of the proceedings listed for 4 August in the Industrial Court. 'In the event of these two conditions being complied with I will call a conference for Monday, August 7,' Moore said, 'to fix a timetable for the final resolution of this matter by a date to be decided by me.'[67]

Moore's statement ended the matter then and there. Hawke, who had made noises for several days about showing proof of the government's intransigence on national television, cancelled his appearance on grounds that he might prejudice an early settlement, and, instead, agreed to debate Lynch on the ABC's *This Day Tonight*. The unions, apprehensive about the effects of a full-bore attack in the Parliament, were ready to negotiate, as were the oil companies themselves. It was over.

'French champagne called for,' Reid wrote, of events in McMahon's office after Moore's announcement. 'They sat in PM's office drinking it. As Hawke debated with Lynch, [Don] Dobie said, "That's the finish of Hawke," as fine a political *non sequitur* as anyone could produce at that time.'[68] Dobie was wrong, and, though the crisis was certainly finished, it was not long before McMahon again began to attract criticism. Fraser thought it embarrassing that Lynch, Greenwood, and Nixon had gone 'crawling' to Hawke, prompting McMahon to say that he had disagreed with the idea.[69] Sinclair thought that McMahon's handling of it had been inept. McMahon had rushed out of the cabinet meeting on 1 August to take a 'telephone call every five minutes,' Sinclair would say later. 'Everybody accepted that the meeting was a disaster.' To Sinclair, McMahon's handling of the matter was proof that he could not fit the mantle of prime minister. 'The job was beyond him.'[70] Snedden had a similar view. 'That was the beginning of the end of the McMahon government,' he would say.[71]

There was also criticism of McMahon's announcement that Parliament would be recalled. As he told Bunting on 2 August, 'it was being said that he should not have issued his statement.' He had butted in on Moore, apparently. McMahon told Bunting he had not been aware of Moore's statement.[72]

The confusion continued. By Thursday, journalists were questioning McMahon, and Bunting was counselling the prime minister to move on. One reporter, *Sydney Morning Herald* journalist Brian Johns, accused McMahon of being a liar. He had spoken with the prime minister on 1 August, and, in that conversation, McMahon had said he had no knowledge that Moore was about to intervene. But then, in an interview that Thursday morning, McMahon had been asked whether he knew before issuing the statement. This time he said he did know. 'It may not be a case of lying,' Alan Reid wondered, when he sniffed out this story. 'It might be another example of memory going.'[73]

McMahon may well not have been aware that Moore was going to involve himself—but he certainly was aware that his suggestion Moore do so had been passed on. This was the basis for McMahon's later attempts to claim the credit for the end of the dispute. He had acted to end the strike, he would say.[74] He was right: he had made moves to do so, and his pointing out of section 29A of the Act may have been influential in Moore's actions. Few, unfortunately, would believe him.

SNEDDEN delivered the 1972–73 budget on 15 August. It was, as the treasurer said, designed almost wholly to 'step up' the rate of economic growth after a year of uncertainty and crises, of unexpected developments both domestic and international. Total Commonwealth expenditure, therefore, would rise by 11.6 per cent while simultaneously returning more money to Australians on predominantly middle and low incomes. Pensions would increase; the means test would be further eased with a goal of abolishing it, within three years, for those aged 65 and over; exemptions from estate duties would double to exempt 'modest estates'; people earning under $1,041 would be exempt from income tax; changes to the income tax rate would see the average wage earner's tax bill reduced by 17 per cent. 'The briefest portrayal of the Budget is as follows,' Snedden said. 'Taxes down; pensions up; and growth decidedly strengthened.'[75]

Was it? Commentators at the time noted that the 1972–73 budget was the culmination of a marked turn from the strategy laid out the year before, and the evidence that Snedden cited to justify that change was thin. Inflation had abated only modestly, and the rise in the consumer price index for the June 1972 quarter, at 6.1 per cent, was not much below the 7 per cent rise that had so troubled McMahon and Snedden at the start of the year. Snedden could not appreciate it at the time, but the conditions were a sign of a shifting economic order: slow economic growth and high inflation, nicknamed 'stagflation', would soon come to bedevil governments the world over. In a political sense, too, the change in budget strategy left the government open to charges of inconsistency. While it had been generous, it also ran counter to any sense of a consistent and steady government with a developed policy. As Whitlam observed, 'Last year, all brakes were on; this year, in the words of the Prime Minister, all stops out.'[76]

Preparation of the budget had, again, been difficult. The most contentious and long-running issue of difference had been Billy Wentworth's well-publicised proposal that cabinet abolish the means test for people above the age of sixty-five. 'The means test could turn out to be a killer,' he had said.[77] McMahon had been broadly in favour, claiming it could be an election-winning issue. But Snedden had been utterly opposed on grounds of the enormous cost—estimated to be between $400m and $600m—and the inequities of allowing the wealthy to access what, in his view, would become a supplementary income. Cabinet compromised by deciding to phase the test out over the following three years.[78]

McMahon continued to have problems with the Treasury. Throughout the course of the budget preparations in July and August, he peppered Bunting with notes to record what he regarded as the department's obfuscation, wilfulness, deceptions, and mistakes. Its attempt to have social service and welfare budget submissions circulated among all ministers was 'another Treasury stunt', likely designed to ensure the submissions would be heavily criticised, he said.[79] 'Treasury was seeking to lay down policy in areas belonging to other Ministers,' he told Bunting later.[80] He was 'amazed' at the papers coming from Treasury. 'He said they were putting the papers forward as if they were the policy makers,' Bunting recorded. 'They should not do this.'[81] McMahon found it 'strange' that the Treasury was suggesting across-the-board tax cuts of 10 per cent when they were saying only in February that 2.5 per cent was too much.[82] He returned to the topic not long afterward:

He again expressed surprise at the 'big turn-around' by Treasury. They had been telling us five or six weeks ago to stand fast. Now they were saying there was scope for significant stimulus.[83]

All of this turned McMahon completely against his old department. He was angered by it, antipathetic towards it—and towards his treasurer.

There was bitterness between them both over leaks. Appearing on television on his new programme, *Federal File,* on Sunday 13 August, Alan Reid had appeared to forecast many of the budget measures.[84] That it was Reid doing so ensured that McMahon was quickly suspected as his source. In a telephone call with an angry Snedden on 14 August, McMahon conceded that Reid had visited him on the evening of 12 August and asked about the budget's contents. But he had sent Reid packing, McMahon told Snedden. Furthermore, what Reid had said about the budget was, in fact, incorrect. Snedden's persistent anger over the matter, and the subsequent rumours rife among cabinet colleagues that McMahon had leaked the budget measures, caused McMahon to become so aggrieved with Snedden that he considered removing him as treasurer.[85]

Labor assailed the budget and the leaks, but within days it became clear that the tax cuts, education spending, and pension rises, had made an impact. Most important, it seemed, was its reception within the government. Just over a month earlier, a group of cabinet ministers—including Anthony, Sinclair, Snedden, and Fraser—had supposedly discussed in the cabinet anteroom whether it was still possible to remove McMahon from the prime ministership. 'The idea was that [Robert] Southey would persuade McMahon to have a diplomatic illness and then Anthony would take over,' wrote Reid, once he heard. 'Then after elections [the] diplomatic illness would turn into a mild heart attack and other arrangements [would be] made about the succession.' Was it true? Was it even possible that they could think McMahon would let go so easily? 'Pipedreaming,' Reid called it, but even a week before the budget he was returning to the question: 'Is it too late to replace McMahon?'[86]

Thus the favourable reception to the budget was of larger significance than it might have seemed. 'Rebels jammed,' wrote Reid. 'They'd still like to get rid of McM[ahon]. But they can't in the light of what he has done.' An 'ecstatic' McMahon believed he was 'over his final hurdle'.[87] But his advantage over the malcontents quickly evaporated. A favourable press reception and awareness that the budget could be a campaign issue caused Snedden and Anthony to wonder whether the government should call a snap election. Whitlam, after declaring the budget 'the last gasp' of a twenty-three year-old liberalism, had even said, 'By all means let us have an election on this budget; the sooner the better.'[88] Why not take him on, force him to oppose the budget in an election? At the very least, Snedden and Anthony thought, it would allow the government to avoid a presidential-style campaign where the merits of McMahon and Whitlam would be thrown into stark comparison.[89] It took a week for the idea to spread, but when Anthony and Snedden put it to McMahon he would not consider it. His need to protect his status and authority caused him to resist, to be utterly opposed. 'He exploded and shouted us out of his office,' Anthony said later.[90]

To those inside Parliament, McMahon's objection stemmed from the implied reflection on his abilities and the sense of being pressured by his own ministers. He decided that the ministry should be consulted, but this was seen as his way of playing for time. Snedden called around to find out what other members thought. Bert Kelly remarked:

> Billy Snedden asked me what I thought and I told him I thought it was a good idea. The chief reason is that I am frightened of two things, first, that the more Billy McMahon exposes himself to Parliament, the more shallow and unprepossessing does he become. Secondly, if we have a policy speech in the proper sense of the word, following this budget we will probably have to have another auction sale which we can't afford.[91]

When it came to ministers, however, there was no unanimity. While Fraser, Forbes, and Nixon were supportive, Bowen—whom Snedden and Anthony believed was in favour—turned against the idea after talks with McMahon. Lynch and Chipp were in favour of an election later in the year. Fairbairn said he would accept McMahon's judgement on the matter.[92]

That ended it. McMahon guarded his prime-ministerial prerogative zealously. He wanted a later election. It was not an unreasonable decision; in fact, it might very well have been a correct one. The logistics of a snap election were daunting, with neither the Electoral Office nor the Liberal Party organisation in any state to take on the strain of an election.[93] Moreover, as the subsequent publication of Gallup and ANOP polls suggested, the payoff for the budget measures was slight, with only a 1 per cent swing towards the government discernible.[94] Holding out, and hoping, was the government's best strategy.

CHAPTER FORTY-FIVE

Tributes

1984

McMahon returned to the office on Wednesday, 11 April. He was pale, his hair lacked 'its usual dark tints', and there was a little blood on his shirt collar. But he seemed happy, Bowman thought, and noticeably less stressed.[1]

But his memory was still failing, and his mind was playing tricks on him. That Friday, McMahon put a letter from a local pharmacy onto Cawthorn's desk. 'Get me James Clancy,' he told her, pointing to a handwritten annotation on the letter. Cawthorn called the pharmacy, but they had never heard of a James Clancy. When Cawthorn told McMahon this, later, he grabbed at the letter again and pointed, this time to the letterhead, to the pharmacy's address. 'Get me George Street!' Cawthorn was boggled. When McMahon asked, later, if she had contacted Street, she deflected the question: 'He's not available.'[2]

Easter and the ANZAC Day holidays allowed for a much-needed break. McMahon went to his property at Orange and came back 'a good deal quieter and saner'. Bowman made good headway on the book. By 27 April, he had finished chapters four and five, the latter on the economic problems in 1960–61 and McMahon's letters to Menzies.[3] But there were distractions over and over again. Three days later, Bowman had to set aside the manuscript to edit a letter that McMahon wanted sent to the *Sydney Morning Herald*. He had spent a week on it, and had sent George Campbell running around Sydney doing research for it. The letter was a gargantuan 1,500 words—too long to run in the newspaper—and in Bowman's opinion it was terrible. 'Hopeless,' he remarked, and cut it down to 500 words.[4]

And yet there were occasional glimpses of McMahon's ability to pull himself together when the occasion warranted. The next day, he taped a video address for a Masonic charity that provided homes for the elderly and infirm. The remarks were clear, lucid, and characteristically immodest: 'A tribute to those who first saw the need for proper care of the aged...' McMahon said.

In spite of himself, Bowman was impressed: 'Voice like Gladstone!'[5]

CHAPTER FORTY-SIX

'Where We Are Heading'

1972

McMahon had recognised early in his tenure that the government needed to refresh its agenda and policies. Whitlam had staked out ground in urban development and housing, had made forays into censorship policy and open government, and the government had allowed him to do so almost without contest. To have any chance of winning the election, McMahon decided, his government needed to demonstrate that it too had policy in these, and other, areas. To find this new agenda, McMahon turned to the Liberal Party organisatioin.

'Party policy needs restatement in fresh terms and in a contemporary environment,' he wrote, in a letter sent in August 1971. 'We should be able to state where we stand and where we are heading.'[1] In response to his request, the Liberal Party's joint standing committee on federal policy established twelve sub-committees to report with policy recommendations for education, social welfare, urban development, health care, arbitration and industrial law, law and order, immigration, rural issues, defence, and foreign policy, and 'national goals'. The remaining two sub-committees were to be purely oppositional: one was to study Labor's 'socialist objective' and its implications for voters, with the aim of 'destroy[ing] Labor's known policies'[2]; the other was to look at the ALP's power structure.[3]

By the end of May 1972, federal president Robert Southey was lauding the work as 'more far-reaching than any other undertaken since the formation of the Liberal Party'.[4] Aware that the need to counter the advantages held by the ALP was pressing, the decision was made not to hoard the policy recommendations but to use them before the election. What followed, throughout 1972 but most particularly in the latter half of the year, was the fruition of that policy work. It surfaced in a flurry of ministerial statements, a bevy of white papers, and a litany of reports, all of them aiming to demonstrate the existence and superiority of government policy—or, as Snedden was to put it, 'good reasons not to change [government]'.[5]

Some were in areas where there was little chance of movement. Suggestions that the voting age be lowered from twenty-one to eighteen were heard but then ignored. Attempts to have it lowered through court action were struck out. McMahon, who, two years before had told the Liberal Party's federal council that Liberal MPs in marginal seats would never agree to the idea, on grounds that 'it would tip the balance against them', would soon move to explore it, only for the Country Party to resist.[6] Suggestions that the government do something on superannuation were similarly considered but eventually forgeone.

Attempts to devise a policy on secrecy and transparency in government were similarly hampered. Catalysed by publication of Jim Spigelman's *Secrecy: political censorship in Australia*, which argued that the McMahon government was secretive and McMahon himself deceitful, McMahon harried the public service and his ministers to come up with a response.[7] By the time the response could be drafted, it was nearly too late. On 25 October, cabinet deferred the submission.[8] There would be no other attempt to address the matter. An attack on Labor for its support of the thirty-five-hour workweek came under the guise of a ministerial statement and with pointed reference to the economic cost. Senator Thomas Drake-Brockman, the minister for air, told the Senate, on McMahon's behalf, that, 'The sum of it all would be a serious assault on our standard of living.'[9]

Attempts to counter the Labor Party's policies in health bore mixed results. Under the gentlemanly minister for health, senator Kenneth Anderson, a wrangle with the Pharmacy Guild in April had been resolved with little criticism from Labor. There was a similar result in a debate in the second half of the year over reforming the funding of aged-care homes. But the government did not win plaudits for these successes, Anderson would say. Because the matters had Labor's support, they seemed uncontroversial, uninteresting, and thus media interest was limited. 'We got about as much publicity as you'd get if a dog bit a man,' Anderson said later.[10]

But there was relentless criticism from Labor, and considerable publicity, for problems associated with the common fee. In March, in response to questioning from Whitlam about overcharging by GPs in New South Wales, McMahon announced that there would be an enquiry, with details to be announced by Anderson that day.[11] The speed with which this moved was too fast for Anderson. After a cursory survey of candidates to lead the enquiry, McMahon selected John Kerr, only for Kerr to pull out when he was named chief justice of the Supreme Court of New South Wales. McMahon had known of this possibility before Kerr's appointment, Anderson said later, yet he had picked Kerr anyway. 'The anguish and concern we had in relation to that was unbelievable,' Anderson said.[12] Never particularly healthy, Anderson also became very ill in August, and was away from the Senate until October. In combination with his unprovocative manner, Anderson's absences in the vital second-half of 1972 meant that the government was unable to gain attention for its measures on health.

In other areas, the government's attempts to refresh and find new, appealing polices were more successful. Under Fraser, education received some of the most significant attention and action. In July 1971, the government had more than doubled—from 1,500 to 4,000—the number of scholarships for students attending colleges of advanced education;[13] in 1972, responding to increased demand and competition, Fraser gained cabinet's approval to expand the number of scholarships, this time also including those available to students attending, and about to attend, university.[14] After establishing the Commission on Advanced Education as a statutory body, cabinet accepted recommendations from both it and the Australian Universities Commission for a large expansion of funding for advanced-education providers and universities across the country.[15]

Changes in secondary education were no less remarkable. In December 1971, the government had increased the rates of per capita assistance to independent schools and announced $20m worth of capital grants. In May 1972, it went further: McMahon announced that the Commonwealth would provide $167m in capital grants over the years 1973–78 for construction of libraries and science laboratories in secondary schools; would provide $48m over the same period for building classrooms and facilities in independent schools; and would, with the states, commit to making per capita grants to independent schools at a rate of 40 per cent of the cost of educating a child in a government school—an extra \$14.3m per year.[16] Two months after this, cabinet agreed that the Commonwealth should partner with the state governments and provide \$1.5m over five years to 'stimulate' the teaching of Asian languages and cultures in schools.[17] Cabinet also agreed to provide 25,000 scholarships for the final two years of secondary schooling.[18]

By August, the government had committed to an extra \$72m in Commonwealth spending on education—a 20 per cent increase on the previous year's appropriation. It was an eye-catching sum, and belied suggestions that the government was doing nothing. But amid the continuing economic unrest, there were questions to be asked about the prudence of these increases. *Was all of this affordable?* one interviewer asked McMahon. Was there a risk in all the 'larger social service Bills' the government had committed to? 'No risk whatsoever,' said McMahon, 'because the Commonwealth always has the power to be able to pay for the promises it makes and the legislation it introduces ... I believe what we have done is just about right, and I think it will turn out to be right in the long run, too.'[19] McMahon was quite aware of the importance of education in public opinion; it was another of the ways that he attempted to regain the government's standing.[20]

Another area where the government made a significant change was in childcare. In the 1972–73 budget, the government announced its intention to provide assistance to non-profit organisations to establish and operate childcare centres for children of working and sick parents. Building on a promise made by Gorton in the 1969 election campaign,[21] the McMahon government passed the *Child Care Act 1972*, which offered money for the building and maintenance of childcare centres, the training of qualified staff, grants for centres to offer lowered fees to needy families, and funding for further research into childcare.[22] Though the test providing for lowered fees was criticised for discouraging mothers from working, the Act's significance lay in the changes that it augured.[23] Childcare became a public responsibility, and the Act created a basis for Commonwealth governments to continue intervening. It was implicit acknowledgement of the need for

Commonwealth involvement to ensure that high-quality childcare was available; it also opened the doors for professionalisation of the early-childhood education and care industry through training, qualifications, and continuing research.[24] McMahon, who had pushed to take up the issue and for its inclusion in the budget, was aware of its significance and, crucially, that it was only a beginning. 'I believe it is a very, very good start, but of course we would only regard it as the beginning of a process,' he said.[25]

The movement towards independence in Papua New Guinea had also been given fresh impetus by the McMahon government. Since taking over the external territories portfolio in January, Andrew Peacock had largely continued his predecessor's policy for a self-governing territory that would, after a suitable interval, become independent. But Peacock's conduct meant there was a key change. He was able to revitalise the process with his enthusiasm, charm, and willingness to engage; as one observer was to say, he 'animated' the government's policy.[26] Engendering goodwill over the course of seventeen visits, Peacock impressed upon Papua New Guinean officials the need to make their own decisions; back in Australia, he nudged the government's policy closer to Labor's by insisting on the reality of the move to self-government. He pressed colleagues to hasten their handover of vital infrastructure and civil responsibilities, such as control of civil aviation, and he was deeply involved in the considerable legislative and administrative changes that would need to be made in Australia and Papua New Guinea for self-government to work.

'Creating a nation out of 500 tribes, 700 languages, trying to draw them together and setting up a representative government for this diverse country, was a huge challenge and I loved it,' Peacock would say later.[27] After elections in April saw Michael Somare become chief minister, Peacock won cabinet approval to urge Somare to lay the 'sound groundwork' for the steps towards self-government, a point quickly taken up in the decision to hold a constitutional conference in Port Moresby on 1 August. Peacock also managed to nudge his colleagues in cabinet to accept that a request for independence might be made before the next scheduled elections in Papua New Guinea.[28] Peacock was not a McMahon supporter, but he offered his support to get the government moving. 'I did my job,' he said later.[29]

At other times, however, the McMahon government's moves to chart new policies was prompted less by purpose and more by accident and embarrassment. In a year characterised by pre-occupation with the economic downturn, poverty was an area where the government did itself no favours, yet managed to initiate worthwhile action.

On ANZAC Day, the Anglican Archbishop of Sydney, Dr Marcus Loane, called for the government to deal with unemployment and price rises. The archbishop observed:

> The April mini-budget does not solve these problems nor does it adequately take into account the fact that pensioners have to make ends meet at a time when they face the same cost structures as every other Australian ... Every winter in Australia welfare agencies, both Church and private, are inundated with pleas from those who have reached desperation point. It is a pity that this human need is not made obvious to those who hold the economic balance of power.[30]

The next day, when Bert Kelly brought Loane's statement to McMahon's attention in Question Time, McMahon said, 'It is obvious to me that the Archbishop does not have a very great knowledge of the problems associated with inflation and unemployment,' he said. '... I shall make certain that His Grace the Archbishop is informed of what the government has done and that he has every opportunity to form a better view.'[31] While a rebuttal of Loane's statement was quite reasonable, the suggestion that Loane had little knowledge of the problem was not; if anything, it was gratuitous and insulting.

Labor made moves to exploit the matter. Lionel Murphy, the ALP's leader in the Senate, resurrected his long-running motion for an enquiry into poverty by the Senate's Standing Committee on Health and Welfare. The DLP joined the government to delay the motion, but it was clearly well disposed to the idea: it had acted only to allow the government to consider initiating its own. Billy Wentworth now made a suggestion that the government hold an enquiry, but cabinet was 'not disposed' to do so.[32] Word of Wentworth's support for an enquiry leaked, ensuring that the matter continued to bob up in press reports. When McMahon was asked about the prospect on 25 June, he scotched it entirely. 'My own belief is that on social services and poverty it is up to the government to find out what is wrong and when it knows what is wrong, or when it even regards there are difficulties, to solve them itself. And that is my attitude and I believe it is the one we will take.'[33] By July, McMahon was 'pretty certain' there would not be any such enquiry.

Pressure continued to mount. Wentworth's support—in another letter to McMahon—saw the possibility of an enquiry return to the cabinet agenda, where it was once again shrugged off.[34] Religious and charitable groups called for the government to act; Gorton thrust himself back into debate with his opinion on the idea. 'The time has passed when we can give $1 or $1.50 or, if it's election year, $2 to pensioners,' he told a Liberal Party meeting on 28 July. 'The time has come for a proper public enquiry into these areas of poverty.'[35]

Eventually, the pressure grew too much. On 15 August, the day of the budget, cabinet met again and decided that, after months of delay and 'growing public concern about poverty and growing pressure', the government should 'take an initiative' and institute an enquiry. Cabinet had been forced to the decision. As the resulting minute noted, Murphy's motion for an enquiry would very likely have succeeded that week, and the government would have no control over its terms of reference. Thus a question was arranged in the House, so that McMahon could cut the pressure off immediately and announce the enquiry.[36] The terms of reference were narrowly drawn: the enquiry would consider the extent of poverty in Australia and its levels, the demographics of poverty, the factors that caused it, and what government could do to alleviate it. There were restrictions: among them, a statement that the 'poverty line' that had been devised by Professor Ronald Henderson, the foremost expert on poverty in Australia, should not be introduced, nor should the government subscribe to it.[37] Five days later, however, cabinet agreed that Henderson should be appointed to conduct the enquiry.[38]

In public, McMahon did his best to conceal the fact that the government had been forced into the decision. He believed it was the responsibility of government to find out where the poverty line was, he said, and thus it had decided to hold the enquiry.[39]

TERRORISM would also draw the government's attention. In the early hours of the morning of 5 September, eight members of the Palestinian terrorist group Black September stole into the Olympic Village in Munich, Germany. By dawn, they had murdered two members of the Israeli athletic team and taken nine further members hostage. Twenty-one hours later—after protracted negotiations, a bungled attempted rescue, and an airfield firefight—all of the hostages, a German police officer, and five of the eight hostage-takers were dead. Ten days later, on 16 September, an explosion in the General Trade and Tourist Agency, on Sydney's George Street, injured ten people, two of them seriously. Another explosion occurred on Parker Street, after a bomb was recovered from the George Street Adria Travel Agency. Both of these attacks were thought to have targeted Yugoslavian migrants who occupied and operated the agencies. A week later, Australian authorities intercepted two letter bombs, posted from Amsterdam, intended for the Israeli consulate in Sydney. Three further letter bombs, intended for the Israeli embassy in Canberra, were intercepted on 25 September.

Collectively, these attacks elevated terrorism on the political agenda and brought to the fore significant tensions within the government. Initially, those tensions centred on appropriate ways to register sympathy. McMahon's quick condemnation of the Munich attacks on 6 September was followed by questions over whether to follow it with a condolence motion in the House.[40] In light of the Israeli government's subsequent strike on Palestinian positions in Syria, Lebanon, and Jordan, which had caused 200 fatalities, Keith Waller advised McMahon's office that such a resolution would be 'badly received in the Arab world'.[41] McMahon would move the resolution, on 12 September, but only after clear pressure from Labor MP Barry Cohen and representations from prominent Jewish Australians to do so.[42]

Then there were divisions over how best to respond to the domestic terrorism of the Sydney bombings. Clearly, these were targeting Yugoslavian migrants, and were connected with a long-running campaign of violence by Croatian extremists. McMahon was not unaware of this campaign, nor of the long-running failure to take action over it: in December 1969 he had written to the attorney-general, Tom Hughes, of his worry that Croatian extremists had 'come to believe that they can act with impunity and that they can, therefore, without risk to themselves, step up the level and frequency of violence'.[43]

A possible reason for the failure to take action lay in the considerable support the government enjoyed among Eastern European migrant communities, and the sympathy for these stridently anti-communist communities within ASIO and the Commonwealth Police. Why irritate those supporters, or draw attention to the Liberal Party's association with less-savoury elements of those communities? In August, then, after security and militia forces killed six Australian-Croatian members of the Utaše terrorist group while repelling a failed incursion into Yugoslavia, attorney-general Ivor Greenwood told a disbelieving Yugoslavian ambassador that there was no evidence of Utaše terrorist groups operating in Australia.[44]

In the wake of the September attacks in Sydney, Labor leaped on the government's apparent indifference to domestic terrorism, and drew attention to the likely explanations. Accusing Greenwood of failing to act, Clyde Cameron noted that Croatian terrorist groups were, like Greenwood, to be found 'on the extreme right of the political spectrum'.[45] Lionel Murphy, meanwhile, used the attack to criticise the government's security credentials. 'How is it possible,' he asked, 'with the resources at the disposal of the Attorney-General, that after these warnings came and after the complaints were made to the Australian Government, so little is done that we have people able to be bombed in Sydney on Saturday?'[46]

The criticism was a jolt to action for McMahon. Keen to be seen to be doing something, he began to voice thoughts about a royal commission to investigate violence among migrant communities, potentially even among the more militant unions as well.[47] His thoughts about action coalesced with the international pressure, in the wake of the Munich attacks, for greater government attention to terrorism. But there was immediate opposition to the prospect of a royal commission within the bureaucracy and government. In a meeting with the secretary of the attorney-general's department, Clarrie Harders, Bunting noted that there were constitutional problems that needed to be considered: the government could investigate violence against migrants, yes, but 'violence generally in the community was another matter', potentially one that would require joint action with state governments. Moreover, a royal commission should be reserved as a 'last resort' for 'major investigations'. Harders did not debate this: he said that he hoped McMahon would not 'bolt', though it was clear that the prospect of a royal commission would be discussed by cabinet.[48]

When cabinet met, on 19 September, it provisionally decided against any action that might interfere with the police investigation underway in Sydney. Greenwood's subsequent submission to cabinet on 29 September continued to hold the line against a royal commission, variously arguing that nothing had changed since cabinet's original decision; the constitutional problems were near insurmountable; the government might appear to be overreacting, and to be doing so for political advantage; if a commission were established in time for the election campaign it could become a 'forum for unsubstantiated allegations involving political prejudice'; and a royal commission solely into the Yugoslav migrant community would not be advisable. McMahon was not inhibited when he read it: 'I don't agree,' he wrote repeatedly.[49]

If McMahon had hoped that he could wield a royal commission as a sign of his government's determination to act (however belatedly), or to fuel a campaign based on law and order, he was to be disappointed. Cabinet would not agree with him. When it met on 10 October, it directed instead that an inter-departmental committee be established to ensure greater co-ordination with the states 'in relation to political and industrial violence and terrorism in Australia'.[50] That committee would meet four times before it was disbanded. Its work would be palpable only in the future: in a disastrous raid on ASIO, and in a much-later royal commission into ASIO.[51]

ONE area that received a significant amount of McMahon's attention in 1972, in a clear demonstration of his attempts to steer the government towards new ideas and policies, was that of urban and regional development. The Commonwealth had long regarded involvement with urban affairs as beyond its remit, but in the previous seven years—amid calls for a national approach to urban affairs from academics and planning professionals—there had been pressure for this to change. Whitlam was soon aware of the opportunity that the issue presented, and had foreseen an accompanying push for decentralisation and rejuvenation of regional centres. His 1969 prospectus, *An Urban Nation*, had set out plans for a new Department of Urban Affairs to provide a way for the Commonwealth to play a role in urban and regional development, with provisions for sewerage, rehabilitation, and area assistance. There had also been pressure for action in the states: officials with Commonwealth and state governments had worked for seven years to produce a report on decentralisation that would become public in October 1972.

Labor's long interest in the policy, and the government's long antipathy for the area, was quite evident in the way it approached urban affairs throughout 1972. In March, the minister for housing, Kevin Cairns, bemoaned the fact that state and local governments had failed to attend to quality-of-living issues in cities, thus 'causing the public to direct its attention to the Commonwealth Government'. From a political perspective, this attention necessitated a response. As Cairns pointed out:

> It would seem that there is a general absence of anything like an urban policy at all levels of government. Nor are we likely to have the framework for urban policy formulation whilst a variety of institutions at different levels operate in relative isolation. Moreover, as long as there are no agreed-upon goals, there can be no meaningful co-ordination. This submission suggests that our first priority is not to try to determine urban policy, but to seek agreement at all levels that an urban policy is needed and to establish the facts on which a sensible urban policy may be based.[52]

Cabinet deferred a decision, but the next month McMahon was pushing for action: he wanted a special decentralisation unit set up in his own department.[53] He knew that it was both new and that there was a clear requirement for a response. As he wrote to Anthony on 15 May, his 'firm view' was 'that portfolio authority in relation to what would constitute major new initiatives by the Commonwealth touching state responsibilities must, for the time being at any rate, remain with me'.[54]

The secrecy and careful handling was deliberate. McMahon was coming up against concerted scepticism within the bureaucracy over decentralisation and urban affairs: only recently, the Treasury had 'poured cold water' on a mooted scheme from Hunt's Interior department to develop regional centres.[55] Attempts to push a policy along were constantly hampered and slowed. Sir Frederick Wheeler

regarded one draft of a new policy as 'a somewhat dangerous document
... particularly as to urbanisation', namely for the expenditure that
could be involved.[56] Approaches were made to Sir John Overall, the
head of the National Capital Development Commission in Canberra,
who agreed to give advice. By mid-September, cabinet had agreed that
a National Urban and Regional Development Authority (NURDA)
should be established, with Overall as its first head.[57]

McMahon announced the decision five days later. The authority
would be tasked with 'fostering a better balance of population
distribution and regional development in Australia,' he told the House,
and would back the growth of regional centres and sub-metropolitan
areas around existing cities. As with the environment, there would need
to be consultations and close co-ordination with the state governments,
and legislation for establishment of the authority would soon follow.[58]
It was a start, however belated, but it was immediately clear that the
ALP, by virtue of its long-developed policy, had the upper hand. What
about local government, Whitlam asked of McMahon. What about
pollution, education, health care? Where would they figure in all this?
Whitlam had specifics to offer, too. Noting that McMahon had been
'coy' about which regional centres would receive backing, the Labor
leader was straightforward: 'There should be no coyness about this. The
obvious first centre at which to start is Albury-Wodonga.'[59]

There were others who wondered whether McMahon knew what
he was doing. Reid received an 'incredible' briefing from McMahon
that same day. He was amazed. 'McM[ahon] didn't seem to know
what he was talking about,' Reid confided in his diary. 'Anthony was
present. He was grimfaced. He raised his eyes to heaven as he left.
Understandable.'[60]

But there were still problems. Coming amid a rush of other
legislation that the government wished to introduce, the drafting of the
legislation for NURDA took until 10 October, and required McMahon's
personal intervention to see it finished. When McMahon did introduce
the legislation, on 11 October, it was amid some embarrassment for his
mixing it up with other Bills that the government was working on. It was
'interim' legislation only, but McMahon was proud of it nevertheless. It
fulfilled his promise to tackle the issue; moreover, the Bill, in his eyes,
was 'amongst the most important legislation introduced into the Federal

Parliament during the post-war years'. It was an important about-turn on previous views of Commonwealth power and responsibilities. 'It marks our recognition that there is a direct contribution that the Commonwealth Government can make in national urban and regional development for the benefit of all Australians.'[61]

Importantly, for the campaign to come, it was also a move to engage with Labor. 'In making its late run,' *The Sydney Morning Herald* editorialised afterward, '… the government is ensuring that the Labor case will not win by default, and for the first time on record the two major political groups will present competitive policies on the problems of the cities and on decentralisation.'[62] But it was very late in the year, very late in the political cycle. As Jonathan Gaul was to say, 'It didn't get much attention.'[63]

Amid these efforts on decentralisation, the government worked to address areas of palpable commercial concern. The High Court's decision to strike down the *Trade Practices Act 1965–69*, in the so-called 'Concrete Pipes' case, had overturned decades of understanding about the corporations power.[64] The ruling would eventually provide for a great expansion of Commonwealth power, including the ability to regulate the trading activities of trading organisations, but, in the short term, the ruling left no valid trade practices legislation in operation. This ended when the government passed the *Restrictive Trade Practices Act 1971*, but it made clear at the time that this was interim legislation only: there would be more to come. Amid concern over competition and monopolies in Australia, this turmoil caused trade-practices legislation to become the object of a significant amount of scrutiny—more, in fact, than there had in quite some time, as the surprised commissioner of trade practices was to write.[65] In May, attorney-general Ivor Greenwood declared that the government would introduce new legislation that would, most notably, widen the scope of existing provisions within the interim Act so as to investigate monopolies and mergers (including takeovers) when they were judged to be against the public interest, and establish a Monopolies Commission that could investigate monopoly conditions.[66]

But the complexities involved, as well as the degree of attention given to different parts of it, caused the government to forego introducing all-encompassing trade-practices legislation. In the same month as

Greenwood made his statement, the DLP sought to halt all foreign takeovers and, pending a report from a Senate committee, demanded that the government initiate legislation to maintain Australian ownership of Australian companies.[67] Although it appeared to be an issue of cynical nationalism, the concerns raised about foreign takeovers were not without foundation. Capital inflow to Australia had increased dramatically over the preceding three years, from $797m in 1969–70 to $1,841m in 1971–72, and foreign takeover bids for Ansett, Kiwi, Fresh Foods, and Australian Frozen Food Industries had been controversial. Pressure within the Liberal Party caused the government to address the issue. But where McMahon felt the pressure to do something, Snedden was less than lukewarm. He believed that any action could be damaging to Australia's development.[68] McMahon grew frustrated. 'He wants Treasury hurried up on foreign investment and unemployment,' Bunting wrote, after a hectoring phone call from McMahon. 'Do they and I understand the importance?'[69] Snedden's reluctance, along with that of Treasury, meant that it took considerable time for the government to find solutions—and for indecision to hamper those solutions when it did.

In September, a cabinet meeting concluded that 'it would not be practicable' in the remaining parliamentary session to pass legislation that would prevent foreign takeovers. Time was running out too quickly.[70] But then, while announcing the government's policies on overseas investment, McMahon stated that 'the right balance between our desire for an Australian Australia and for greater growth and prosperity must be struck'. The time was right, he said, to begin trading off some of the benefits of overseas capital for a greater share of Australian industries and resources.[71] Speaking on the Macquarie Network the next day, McMahon stated that there should be a consideration of how Australia's interests figured in takeover bids from foreign companies. 'The point is that we have an abundance of overseas reserves and, much more importantly, Australians want to own Australian companies and they want an increasing share of ownership in overseas corporations.'[72]

But the lack of an immediate follow-through and the diminishing days in the parliamentary calendar led to suggestions that the government had no intention of acting. In an effort to counter those suggestions, when he returned for another interview with Macquarie on 5 October, McMahon stated that he had given directions to his department to prepare legislation to establish the vetting he thought necessary for foreign takeover bids. 'The Bill has been completed now, and I put the final touches on it yesterday with the technical experts, and I very much hope I will be able to introduce it into the House in the coming week,' he said.[73]

McMahon was either mixed up, or he was lying—for he was wrong. There had been no preparations made for a Bill on takeovers. 'It just was not in existence as yet,' Bunting would write.[74] This would not dissuade McMahon. The next day, 6 October, he told Bunting that 'strenuous efforts' were needed to get a Bill ready for Parliament. He believed that his statements had to be backed up with action. But there were problems. Bunting was uncertain whether a Bill could be drafted in time. Moreover, cabinet had decided against any kind of interim legislation. Would instructions for a Bill go against what cabinet had decided? McMahon was critical of Bunting's suggestion that he consult with colleagues about the matter. He wanted to know why Bunting was 'resisting' his line of action; Bunting must understand that he was making 'his own political judgments,' McMahon said. There had to be a statement of action. He needed to be able to say that the government was moving—on foreign takeovers, on urban and regional development, on restrictive trade practices, and on monopolies.[75]

Time would force hard choices on the government. Legislation for the Monopolies Commission and restrictive trade practices were introduced with a clear intention that they would not be passed: there was not enough time to force them through. This left the foreign takeovers legislation, introduced on 24 October. It was piecemeal, and meant only as an interim measure. It gave legal backing to proposals McMahon had announced on 26 September, but did not establish the independent authority that McMahon had proposed would vet takeover bids (that, McMahon announced, would occur in the next session). Nor would it have a long life: the operation of the Bill would cease on 31 December 1973, or by proclamation once another Bill had been passed. But the *Companies (Foreign Takeovers) Bill* would set out a policy, and it enshrined two powers to prevent injurious takeovers. A minister would be able to prohibit takeovers on grounds of the national interest, and the minister could limit the beneficial interests in a specified company for foreign interests. Moreover, there were penalties to ensure it was no figleaf.[76]

Labor called it a 'death-bed repentance', but was much in agreement with the Bill, a point borne out when it offered only minor amendments before it was passed the next day.[77] Given the late timing, it is doubtful that the Bill made much of an impact on the electorate, but for McMahon it was proof that the government was following through, that it was alive to public concerns, and acting in a responsible way. Ominously, however, in the view of a prime minister overworked and tiring, the problems and delays that had surrounded the Bill's drafting were also proof of lack of co-operation from colleagues and the bureaucracy.[78]

FOR every achievement and move towards new policy there was another fight, another muddle, another problem that should never have been cause for concern. Taken individually, each one could appear insignificant; in a series, however, each mishap upended McMahon's attempts to show that his government was professional, unified, and getting on with its job; each mistake reinforced the sense of chaos, of lack of control, of ineptitude, and even deception. One example had roots that went back to McMahon's time as minister for foreign affairs—what became known as the Jetair affair.

In 1969, just as McMahon had taken over as minister for external affairs, his department had decided to make a gift of five DC3s to the Nepalese and Laotian governments as part of its foreign-aid programme. Surplus DC3s were purchased from the RAAF in November 1969 and April 1970 for a total cost of $60,000. The need to convert the aircraft for civilian use, however, meant that the cost of the gift would be much greater and the delivery date of the aircraft much further away. When, on 5 December 1970, the struggling Australian airliner Jetair advertised that it had six DC3s for sale—a prelude to the company's imminent demise—the Department of Foreign Affairs realised it could purchase, convert, and deliver the Jetair aircraft for $360,000—some $65,000 less than the total cost of doing the same with the ex-RAAF aircraft. At around the same time, the department learned that it could provide, as part of another aid package, the five already-purchased ex-RAAF DC3s to the Cambodian government, which was seeking military-configured aircraft. After performing inspections on the Jetair aircraft, the department decided to make an offer to purchase them. With McMahon's approval on 1 January 1971, the department paid Jetair $275,000 for the six DC3s.

Almost immediately, however, there was concern within the bureaucracy. Normal purchasing procedures—namely, the calling of a tender—had not been followed. As Department of Foreign Affairs secretary Sir Keith Waller was to admit, there had been a 'technical breach' of Treasury regulations when the department agreed to purchase the aircraft from Jetair.

Labor senator George Georges spoke about the deal in the Senate on 12 September 1972. The breach of regulations was not the point of his scorn or enquiry; rather, it was McMahon. Georges wanted to know if there was any patronage involved in the deal. Had McMahon altered or tailored it to help a friend, who was a director? Did the deal represent true value for money? Georges would not allege improper conduct, but his insinuations were too cute by half. Eventually, accepting the challenge of government senators to put his charge explicitly, Georges was straightforward: 'I am accusing the Prime Minister of patronage.'[79] The Senate voted immediately to suspend him, but the damage was done.

Two weeks later, in the face of continued questioning, the government tabled a selection of papers related to the deal, only for Whitlam to raise further questions and call for more documents to be tabled.[80] Evasive answers from McMahon, and attempts by him to pass the matter to Nigel Bowen, in his capacity as the minister for foreign affairs, did little to deflect Labor. On 12 October, Whitlam sought to suspend standing orders to have all of the documents relating to the deal tabled.[81] The motion was handily defeated, but the issue refused to go away. Five days later, McMahon tabled a copy of the minute that Waller had sent recommending the purchase and a letter from Sir Kenneth Bailey, the former head of the attorney-general's department, who had advised McMahon on the legality of the deal at the time.[82]

The tabling of these papers, and others, disproved the charge that McMahon had exercised patronage in the deal, but left him exposed in other ways. Why had he not ensured the deal followed proper procedure? And why had he not immediately moved to dispel the issue by tabling the papers a month earlier? Whitlam cited these very points on 19 October, when he moved an unsuccessful motion of censure against McMahon 'for his incompetence and concealment in relation to Jetair Australia Limited'. Once again, Whitlam homed in on McMahon's suitability for his office and his truthfulness in the Parliament. 'Can this nation afford a Prime Minister who is pathologically incapable of admitting that he erred?' Whitlam asked. More critically, too, he noted that McMahon was shifting the blame for the matter to others. 'He has passed the buck to public servants who cannot defend themselves.'[83]

This was the most conspicuous outcome of the affair. McMahon's willingness to use the public service and individual public servants as means to deflect criticism was an embarrassing abnegation of ministerial responsibility, a reversal of the convention that a minister takes responsibility for the actions of his department. Certainly, Waller felt this way, particularly after he was named in the ALP censure motion: 'All this is wildly in breach of what [Erskine] May lays down [in *Parliamentary Practice*] and I felt pretty savage about it,' he wrote privately.[84] Journalists were scathing about McMahon's conduct, but with an additional note to their criticism. 'From now on,' wondered David Solomon, 'what senior public servant will not take account of the possibility that the advice which he gives, in writing, to a minister, might not be tabled in the House or the Senate, shortly afterwards, with his name attached?'[85]

Other problems of administration and division surfaced when cabinet decided against adopting the recommendations of a joint committee on retirement benefits for the armed forces. Despite agreeing that the retirement schemes for Australian military personnel were a mess, defence minister David Fairbairn believed that the committee had been set up to make trouble and that its proposed scheme was 'excessively generous'.[86] Labor and dissident members of the government backbench, especially the committee's chair and loud critic, John Jess, wanted the matter dealt with before Parliament rose for the election, and they had assurances from McMahon and Fairbairn that it would be. On 25 October, believing that McMahon had evaded questions about the matter and hoping to entice government dissidents to cross the floor, the ALP deputy leader and member for Bass, Lance Barnard, moved to suspend standing orders so as to adopt the recommendations in full. The motion was averted when Fairbairn undertook to provide a statement before the House rose.[87] Half an hour later, a hurriedly organised meeting in McMahon's office between McMahon, Fairbairn, Snedden, officials from the public service, and the dissident Liberal MPs, including Jess, negotiated a way out.

McMahon presented the results the next day. Seven of the committee's recommendations were accepted, he said. Six were adopted in part, two were referred for independent investigation, and two more were rejected. Labor, as was its wont, attacked the government, and Jess all but begged for the government to introduce legislation that day to get the changes through before Parliament adjourned. But the most ignominious part of the matter was Jess's subsequent attack, not withstanding its support for his scheme, on the Department of Defence. 'I am not impressed one iota with the support that this scheme has been given by the Department of Defence, whose job it is to stand and speak on behalf of the defence forces,' he said.[88] Fairbairn, unable to reply during the debate that followed, thought it singularly ungracious and politically self-defeating. 'From the point of view of the government,' Fairbairn said later, 'nothing could have done more to undermine its support amongst the services for the coming election.'[89]

UNDENIABLE throughout the year was the existence of a vigorous public-relations contest between McMahon and Whitlam. That contest focused as much on their personalities and appearances as it did on their respective policies. In appearance and manner, McMahon was always playing a catch-up game. After Whitlam returned from China, fluffy-haired without his Brylcreem, McMahon also began to eschew hair oil. He allowed his sideburns to grow almost to his jawline, and the koala-like tufts of hair around his head to grow long and curl on the nape of his neck.

But there was no way to disguise the larger differences. He was short where Whitlam was tall; thin where Whitlam was broad-chested. He was faint-voiced where Whitlam's was sure; bald where Whitlam sported a full head of hair. Abuzz and flighty where Whitlam was deliberate, McMahon simply could not help but appear a pitiably small figure by comparison. His image was not aided by his name: in spite of his preference to be called Bill, McMahon was popularly known by the diminutive Billy. In sum, McMahon always appeared the smaller, less impressive figure.

'Whitlam was the better speaker, had the better voice, and had a dominant physical presence,' recalled the journalist David Solomon.[90] Alan Ramsey agreed. 'Gough was in command of the way he spoke. McMahon was never in command of the way he spoke.'[91]

McMahon was always conscious of how he sounded and looked, but he could rarely appreciate how he was perceived. At an annual meeting of regional daily newspapers in March 1971, McMahon had shown up wearing an urbane dinner suit, a velvet bowtie, and patent-leather shoes with bows on them. He was thoroughly outperformed by Doug Anthony, whose bucolic presence and appearance was much preferred by the audience. McMahon's attentiveness to his appearance—always ducking into bathrooms to check his reflection, applying ointments, colognes, and lotions—was excessive. He was so fond of rubbing Nivea cream into his skin that Sonia had to tell him to stop: 'You're slipping away from me, Bill.'

McMahon could be acutely sensitive when informed of the problems of his appearance and manner: 'Why don't you stop criticising me?' he would usually say to staff who ventured suggestions. 'You're always nitpicking!' He wanted praise, not advice. He resiled from admissions of weakness. During a period where his deafness made it hard for him to hear his own voice, his press secretary, Reg MacDonald, suggested letting a few journalists know, in order to garner sympathy. McMahon would not consider it.

At other times, attempts to solve his problems went awry. After his staff noticed that he sweated profusely under the heat of studio lights, McMahon accepted their suggestion that he use amputee stump powder on his face. The powder worked—but it gave him a pale, sickly pallor that looked almost as bad as the sweating.

At a time when journalists such as Mungo MacCallum and Bob Ellis were exposing the follies of politics, all this made McMahon an easy target of ridicule. Cartoonists, too, delighted in McMahon: they found a fitting, comic essence in depicting him as a gnome-like figure,

short and weedy, a big-eared, ageing dwarf. Folk singer Eric Bogle
lampooned him in the same vein:

> Ah, poor wee Billy McMahon, he's certainly no Superman,
> He tries to be with it, and he dresses quite moddy,
> But with his big ears, and his skinny wee body,
> He looks like a cross between Big Ears and Noddy,
> Poor wee Billy McMahon.[92]

Quips and jokes about McMahon—that he looked like a
Volkswagen with both doors open, that his accent was 'Bhowani chi
chi', that he was literal old age creeping up on Sonia—were rife, an
influence on day-to-day reportage. The birth of McMahon's third
child, Deborah, on 28 September, for example, was greeted with both
congratulations and suggestions that her birth had been orchestrated as
an electoral ploy designed to attract support and aid McMahon's image.
Sonia McMahon would deplore this: 'It was just the luck of the gods.'[93]

But coverage of the image was not just superficial: it spoke to
deeper issues, ones that could not sometimes be stated explicitly. Few
journalists in the Press Gallery judged that McMahon could lead the
government to victory at an election, and fewer still thought he was in
any way up to the job of being prime minister. But they never stated
so. Why not? Mungo MacCallum reasoned that there were three
principal reasons. 'Anybody who tried to even hint at the fact that he
[McMahon] was incompetent was greeted with howls of "Bias," and
"You're prejudiced," and "We can't believe anything you write because
you take sides," and "You're a Labor Party stooge," and so on and on.'
And yet, when MacCallum would reply to these critics that McMahon
was incompetent and the critic knew it, suddenly a sense of decorum
would take over. 'Yes, of course he's incompetent,' MacCallum recalled
critics admitting, 'but, you know, he's the prime minister. You're not
meant to say that.' Then there was the threat of legal action: 'The laws
of libel at the time prevented one telling anything like the whole truth
about McMahon.'[94]

McMahon and his office were certainly aware that there were image
problems. They accepted offers of help from everyone they could. In
December 1971, the newsreader for Frank Packer's GTV-9 Melbourne,

Eric Pearce, offered advice on McMahon's 'television technique[s]', and an American management consultancy, McKinsey and Co., was called in to offer advice.[95] The following June, the chairman of Channel 10, Ken Humphreys, was offering suggestions and facilities so McMahon could practise his television appearances. 'This is a very important issue and will become more so,' Humphreys said of the new medium.[96] Humphreys would renew the offer again in August, just as another Frank Packer employee, TCN-9 producer and director Brian Morelli, was engaged by McMahon's office to provide advice.[97] Observing that McMahon performed better when he was relaxed, Morelli sought ways to ensure the prime minister could be comfortable. Some of his solutions were simple: when McMahon was interviewed by British talk-show host David Frost a few days after the budget, Morelli insisted on McMahon sitting to Frost's right, where his hearing was better.[98] In response, McMahon turned in a performance that was both amusing and revealing. To Frost's question of whether he prayed for things, McMahon cautiously admitted yes. 'Would you pray for something like victory at an election?' Frost followed up.

McMahon shrugged, grinned, and sheepishly said, to considerable laughter, yes.[99]

It was a 'magnificently direct answer', Frost told him, but there were others who thought it a wretched thing to say. 'Personally I thought it was in deplorable taste,' Reid wrote. 'I don't believe in bringing either God or wives into political wrangles.'[100]

Whitlam, for his part, knew that there was more to McMahon than the comic image; indeed, Whitlam offered one of the most pointed and accurate assessments of McMahon's character. When his turn came to speak with Frost, Whitlam precisely identified one of McMahon's defining qualities and admitted it was one he admired: McMahon's persistence. 'His persistence ...' Frost repeated. 'In the face of ...?'

'He stuck to his guns when he was very badly treated by Mr McEwen and he won, he broke through,' Whitlam elaborated. 'Some other people who would have had it like Barwick, if he'd stayed, or Hasluck, if he'd stayed—they missed out, they didn't have the persistence. McMahon did.'[101]

Whitlam's ability to recognise this quality also allowed him to perceive how McMahon was positioning the government, to see through the noise and chaos to the strategy McMahon was pursuing. The Labor leader understood that McMahon's persistence had ensured the coming election would not be a landslide for the ALP. Whatever the optimism of those who surrounded him, nothing could be taken for granted. 'McMahon was an extraordinarily skillful, resourceful, and tenacious politician,' Whitlam would write, later. 'McMahon tried, not altogether without success, to bestride two horses. He claimed to be the real heir to Menzies, yet he claimed to recognise and accept the need for change in a changing world. This balancing act,' Whitlam thought, 'he did with some skill.'[102]

And yet there was no doubt that McMahon was straining, almost desperately, to keep himself and the government afloat. 'In his little lonely office the once dapper, fighting-fit McMahon began to look pale and harassed,' recalled Edgar Holt, a Liberal Party public-relations officer with experience going back to Menzies. 'The effort of making decisions, the big ones, making or breaking his future, seemed to draw hugely on his physical and mental reserves. Often, members of his staff would look anxiously through the peep-hole that overlooked the prime minister's room and see him sitting at his desk, pale, head back, knuckles white as he gripped the arms of the chair.'[103]

AROUND 9 October, McMahon began writing to his ministers to say that the government should now avoid new major policy measures. It was time for the election. He sought from Bunting clarification over possible election dates, when the governor-general would be available, and a memo on how supply would be ensured through an election period.

Speculation about the election date had been lively for a considerable time. As Whitlam was to joke, there had even been speculation about the date that the election date would be announced. The dwindling number of possible dates narrowed the possibilities, but there were still difficulties and pettiness involved. Seeking to get his party ready, Anthony went to see McMahon to ask him when the election would be held. McMahon refused to tell him. 'There were only three people who would know, and I wasn't one of them,' Anthony said later, of the conversation the two had. It was a sign of how much McMahon distrusted Anthony and how zealous he was of his prerogative to call an election when he saw fit.

Exasperated, Anthony saw that it was no use arguing. He decided that the electoral officer would have to be aware of the date. So, too, would Sonia McMahon. Neither of them was likely to tell him, so Anthony gave thought to the third person. Eventually, he decided that it must be Jack Marshall, the relatively recently installed prime minister of New Zealand. 'I had a very good relationship with Jack, and the two countries had been having elections on the same day for a few years,' Anthony said. 'So I rang him and asked about his election date.' Marshall told Anthony that his election would be held on the same day as Australia's. Anthony thanked him and began to organise his party.[104]

Anthony made no secret of his belief that the election would be called for the same day as New Zealand's—25 November—so he could not have been happy when McMahon rose in the House on 10 October to announce the election date as 2 December. Whitlam, when he replied, mocked them both: 'Certainly one now has a magnificent example of the trust, the confidence, the comradeship between the two leaders of the coalition.' Declaiming that he was assuming the mantle of Napoleon, Whitlam could not help but note that the election date would be the anniversary of the Battle of Austerlitz: 'A date on which a crushing defeat was administered to a coalition—a ramshackle, reactionary coalition.'[105]

The next two weeks of Parliament ran with the spectre of the imminent campaign hanging over all parties. Howson was optimistic, reasonably confident, even. 'It's been a good session,' he wrote. 'We've certainly come out of it with a much higher morale than we started, and all of us feel that we're ahead of the opposition. If we can maintain this momentum, we should have no difficulty in winning the election.'[106] Bert Kelly had completely the opposite view. 'It hasn't been a great session … I would think, for the good of the country, Labor ought to have a turn.'[107] Most within the party, the opposition, and the media concurred. Published polls agreed that the government would lose, though a poll commissioned in Melbourne suggested that it might be otherwise with Gorton as leader. But there was not enough time to act. McMahon would take the party to the election.

On 1 November, McMahon came to Government House to advise
Paul Hasluck to dissolve the House of Representatives. The two talked
for about forty-five minutes. According to Hasluck, the prime minister
believed that the Coalition would pick up two seats in Western
Australia—Forrest and Stirling—and two further seats, those of
St George and Eden-Monaro, in New South Wales. 'Some people
had told him that he would also win three seats in Victoria, including
Bendigo,' Hasluck recorded, 'but he "did not know about that".' The
Coalition would not lose any seats except, potentially, that of Evans,
held by Malcolm Mackay. If McMahon was simply putting on a brave
face, Hasluck could not tell. The prime minister was making plans for
the future, patting himself on the back. He talked of the good reception
he was getting, and expressed confidence in the strength of the
economy. He gave himself 'personal credit' for the recent good economic
news. He told the governor-general that party meetings would be
held on 14 December and that a new ministry would be sworn in on
18 December. Parliament would resume in February the next year. 'He
expressed complete confidence in victory,' Hasluck recorded.[108]

CHAPTER FORTY-SEVEN

Finishing

1984

McMahon's moods grew worse. He was increasingly irascible, petty, and mean. He was horrible to his staff and visitors. A casual typist who arrived in the office to type Bowman's drafts was quickly sent on her way. Bowman was disgusted. When the typist had arrived, McMahon had murmured to Bowman that she was not the one he had wanted. And when the typist off-handedly mentioned that the work was going slowly, the former prime minister had all the reasons he needed. 'He was dissatisfied with her output in the morning and fired her,' Bowman wrote in his diary. Bowman thought the typist's work was perfectly fine, and to make amends he tried to have Campbell ring the typing firm to explain. In the meantime, Bowman fumed. 'He [McMahon] really is a dreadful old turd.'

That same day, McMahon called Bowman into his office to talk about an invoice that Campbell had handed him the day before. It was for three months' work, and was accompanied by a request for an advance on any future work. Bowman backed Campbell. His understanding and observation over these past months, he told McMahon, had been that Campbell was working full-time. He reminded McMahon that the job he had originally been hired to do was nothing like the job he was doing—and that it would take longer than the six months he had been hired for. Campbell was integral to getting the job done. It was imperative that Campbell be kept on so that Bowman could use him. McMahon seemed to accept this. But then, as always, came a quibble: 'I'm not paying him $4,000 and more.'[1]

The office was filled with tension again—over how long the next typist would last, whether Campbell would get paid, on the progress that Bowman was making. It took over a week for it to begin to dissipate. McMahon got the next arriving typist to accept a payment of $8 per hour, instead of her agency's $15, and Campbell gave McMahon a note stating that his bill was 'not a gun' at McMahon's head.[2] But the third cause of the tension could only be delayed, not resolved. On 18 May, McMahon went to the Gold Coast with new, Bowman-authored drafts of the first four chapters, the last chapter not so secretly copied by the new typist on McMahon's orders. 'It's another of his monkey tricks,' Bowman all but sighed in his diary.[3]

When McMahon returned, he was upset. He did not like what he had read, did not like the structure of the chapters, and he was panicking about the lack of progress. Bowman had his own schedule in mind—a chapter a week, he had decided—and was by now working on the seventh chapter. But this was not quick enough for McMahon. Bowman reminded him of their conversation the previous week, emphasising that the job had turned out not to be an editing job, but a writing one. 'I refused to say when it [the book] might be finished; I said that it had been clear from the outset that it could not be done in the six months I had been willing to give to editing. It would now require months more.'[4]

Blunt talk like this provoked McMahon. He told Bowman that twenty people were pressing him for the manuscript. If the book did not come out by the end of the year then he would be forgotten, he said. It needed to be published in September—barely four months away!

Bowman was incredulous, but McMahon was still going. Bowman should go back to editing the manuscript. Richard Smart had been looking for him to do just that, after all.

Bowman cut in. 'Fine, let Smart find someone to edit it.' He was unable to do so, he went on. The work was of an impossible standard.

'That's an insult,' McMahon said.

Bowman ignored this, and McMahon suggested they meet with Smart. Bowman agreed wholeheartedly. 'He rang Smart—tried to get him to agree that the MS needed only a bit of improvement for easier reading,' Bowman wrote in his diary. But on the other end of the telephone call, Smart wisely kept his distance. When McMahon mentioned a meeting, the conversation ended almost immediately. 'He doesn't think a meeting now would serve any purpose,' McMahon told Bowman, after hanging up.

Bowman was satisfied: 'An excellent outcome! It shows WM that he is on very shaky ground.'

The to-ing and fro-ing went on. Bowman reiterated that everything he produced was a draft—if McMahon wanted more of the 1961 letters to Menzies, they could be added in an appendix; if he did not want Holt praised so much in the chapter on labour and national service, then he could cut it out later. It was a draft. Moreover, Bowman said, McMahon's going through the draft and rewriting it, *after* Bowman had drafted it, was perfectly agreeable. These statements resolved nothing.[5]

The difficulties could hardly be said to have been unexpected. For all of McMahon's idiosyncracies and demands, he was hardly different from other politicians. The former British prime minister Anthony Eden famously gave his ghostwriters hell as he worked on his autobiography. Unsatisfactory drafts would be the subject of fierce, detailed, and harsh critiques; efforts that Eden found especially wanting would be hurled out the window, onto the flowerbeds outside.[6] Churchill, too, could be sharp with assistants who were short on facts, and was not above marking up drafts five or six times over.[7]

Nonetheless, by Friday, the tension in the office was thick again. Bowman and McMahon were not talking, and McMahon was trying to keep Bowman and Campbell from speaking, too. This latter effort was unsuccessful: Campbell told Bowman that McMahon had paid him $2,000—not everything he was owed, but enough that Campbell was willing to stay on until the end of June.

Things had not improved by the following week. McMahon was muddled, tired, and flustered. On the Monday, he called Bowman into the office and demanded to know what he was working on. Bowman told him that he was up to the Treasury period—he had stated this in a note that he had given to McMahon on Friday, along with a completed draft of the seventh chapter. Bowman told McMahon he was reading McMahon's original draft on the Treasury at that very moment:

> He then in an extremely muddled way began to talk about some aspects of Chapter 7, without actually referring to the chapter. He sought from George some file material which in fact I had affixed to the draft chapter

for reference and George was unaware of the material. When I referred
to other aspects of the chapter it was clear that they had gone out of his
mind, and he had only the vaguest notion of what was actually in it.

The conversation was directionless, trailing into irrelevancies and
questions, claims, and sources. Midway, with Bowman still there in
the office, McMahon called his brother, Sam. He wanted to know all
about when Roland Wilson, the secretary to the Treasury, telephoned
Sam for information about McMahon, who was apparently being
very tough on Roland. Sam promised to put some thoughts down
on paper, and rang off. A subsequent tangent, on Sonia's family and
her background and where to place it in the book, prompted 'real
enthusiasm' from McMahon: 'He seems to envisage acres devoted
to it.' But this, too, fizzled. Then there was another spurt of activity.
Campbell was hauled into the office and questioned whether Menzies
had made an announcement about state aid while at Waverley College
on 20 October 1963. To his cautious answer that, yes, Menzies had
made the announcement, at least according to one source, McMahon
seemed satisfied: 'It was good enough.' But then Campbell returned to
announce that his source had just telephoned to say that she had not
been present herself at the announcement, but that she knew of another
person who had been. McMahon told Bowman and Campbell to check
with that source. The ghostwriter was exasperated. Already certain that
McMahon was wrong, he just saw further wasted time.

After Campbell left, the conversation about the book resumed as
though it had never been interrupted. McMahon seemed not to have
deviated from his original line. He kept telling Bowman that Smart had
said that all that was necessary was to make the manuscript a bit more
readable. The book had to be in *his* style, he said. The thought seemed
to agitate him. It *had* to be in *his* style.

And then, from there, McMahon seemed just to give way. As
though his moods and demands had stemmed wholly from this one
cause, he deflated. He began talking about his general state of being, his
health, and his mind. 'I'm nearly seventy-seven,' he said plaintively. The
previous week had been dreadful. A trip away, over the weekend, had
been too much for him. He *had* to have a private secretary to take care
of things for him.

The opportunity was too good to pass up. He had had enough, Bowman decided impulsively. 'Well, Bill,' he interrupted, 'would you like me to finish up?'

McMahon did not respond. Ten minutes of idle, rambling conversation followed. But then, soon, in a roundabout way, he mentioned that, well, yes, he would like to get a secretary. Bowman could finish up. Yes. The two men agreed that Bowman would finish up his work at the end of June—in three weeks' time.

'For the rest of the day he was quite communicative and friendly,' Bowman recalled. And so, for a short while again, all seemed well.[8]

CHAPTER FORTY-EIGHT

In Calm and in Crisis

1972

McMahon was starting from behind. He knew it and he felt it. Once Parliament was dissolved and the election campaign began, the pressure upon him became immense. In spite of the confidence with which he had fronted Hasluck, McMahon was on edge. Edgar Holt, who had been dragooned into McMahon's office once the campaign started, found the prime minister 'tense, highly strung, and looking for signs and portents'.[1] John Howard, the metropolitan vice-president of the New South Wales Liberal Party, had joined McMahon's office in October with the task of building better links between the office and the party organisation. Howard thought McMahon embattled, 'nervous about his prospects and suspicious of the MPs around him'.[2] This impression did not change during the campaign. Bad news and criticism took a toll on McMahon. As Peter Howson was to say, 'As soon as he gets depressed, he shows it, and one has a continual state of troubles. Therefore, as much as one would like to criticise him at various times, one always has to remember the long-term effect of criticism.'[3]

From the outset, there seemed rarely a prospect that McMahon would be able to hold Whitlam back. There were few omens that he might pull off a miracle. The struggle was constant. 'The campaign was very difficult,' Jonathan Gaul would say.[4] On the first weekend, 4 November, a Gallup poll showed that the government's support had fallen, down from 45 per cent to 42 per cent, against Labor's 47 per cent. It was a 'bombshell', and in the party there was a 'fair bit of gloom' about.[5] Then there were problems putting together the policy speech that McMahon would give on 14 November. When McMahon

566

gave a draft of the speech to Doug Anthony, essentially as a gesture of goodwill, his deputy reacted immediately. A proposal to establish a Department of Secondary Industry received short shrift: it had to go, he said. Anthony was also concerned by the proposal to give eighteen-year-olds the right to vote; after consultations with the Country Party organisation, Anthony insisted that it also come out of the speech.[6]

No one knew what would make it in. It was a 'scramble', Edgar Holt recalled. Drafts were written, revised, cut apart, and stitched back together. 'For incomprehensible reasons, unless it was because Menzies wrote his own policy speeches and revealed them like Holy Writ,' Holt would say later, '... McMahon preserved the traditional exercise of policy-speech production without any of Menzies' feeling for words'.[7] The problem of McMahon's facility with words was exacerbated by the need to deliver the policy speech on television.

McMahon had practised delivering the speech for more than a week. Concerned by the prospect of hecklers, the decision had been taken to eschew a public delivery; aware that there might be need to break up the taping into segments, McMahon's office also decided to tape it without an audience. In his office in Sydney, McMahon practised again and again, receiving feedback from his staff and Sonia. But their well-meant criticism began to grate. His temper frayed. Eventually, he was heard to mutter that if he could not please anyone he might as well record the speech with his head in a toilet bowl.[8]

When the time came to tape the speech, on Sunday 12 November, McMahon was tired, moody, frustrated. It took four hours to tape all of the segments to a standard that Brian Morelli—seconded from TCN-9 for the duration of the campaign—was satisfied with. Screened on 14 November, the speech outlined a substantial programme in domestic policy issues, with a particular focus on 'young Australians'. The government would help young people buy land for houses by guaranteeing loans, and by paying half of the annual interest on a housing loan, up to a limit of $250, in the first year, and $25 less for each year that followed. McMahon lauded the significant increases his government had made in education spending, and announced plans to provide $25m to expand pre-school education, to double the number of technical scholarships to 5,000 per year, to offer an allowance of $400 per year for students in isolated areas, and $10m spending per year on primary school libraries. There would be a free, nation-wide dental scheme for school children; the government would match state government spending on community health services; and it would peg increases in the aged, invalid, and widows' pensions to the consumer price index.

McMahon also spoke about urban affairs and the National Urban and Regional Development Authority, highlighting that the authority would begin its work in land acquisition and building with $80m per year. He promised to spend $1,250m on roads over five years, $330m on improving public transport, and to link all state capitals and Alice Springs with the standard-gauge railway system. McMahon reaffirmed the selective immigration system and, because there was now a need to 'identify in positive terms the role of women in our society', said that a re-elected Liberal-Country Party government would hold a royal commission into improving the status of women in Australia.[9]

McMahon emphasised the government's economic record, and argued that the fight against inflation was close to won. Buoyed by that day's release of the unemployment figures, which showed a drop from the high of 1.96 per cent, McMahon pledged that his government would continue its 'responsible, sound policies'.

There was criticism of Labor in the speech, most notably in the sections on foreign affairs and defence. But Vietnam did not rate a mention. Nor did communism. The absence of these issues, and the brief discussion of foreign affairs and defence, was a clear sign of the government's awareness that these would not work in its favour. Perhaps acknowledging that his age and image might count against him in a debate with Whitlam, McMahon framed the election as 'a contest between two teams':

> Judging them man for man and collectively, my team is younger, better qualified and more experienced than the Labor alternative. Half my cabinet is forty-five or under. The Opposition's Shadow cabinet has only one man of that age ... We have the ability to manage your nation responsibly and well, both in calm and in crisis.

The government, McMahon stated, stood for a balance between the federal, state, and local government spheres, decentralised power, law and order, freedom and liberty. Labor stood for lawlessness, industrial unrest, profligate spending, and was governed by a non-elected machine.

The speech was not acclaimed. Criticism of McMahon's manner on television—'This was the best we could have expected,' Howson wrote, after watching—was abundant, as was derision for its production value and staid format. The manner of its delivery was, if anything, evidence of another gulf between McMahon and Whitlam. The latter had delivered his policy speech on 13 November from the Blacktown Civic Centre, before an audience of nearly 1,500 people. Howson thought it something akin to an American-style election speech.[10] He was correct. There was buzz, excitement, glitz, and drama in Whitlam's confident and proud delivery. As Whitlam's speechwriter was to remark, 'It was not so much a public meeting as an act of communion and a celebration of hope and love.'[11]

But the contents of the two policy speeches were remarkably similar. Their focus—both on domestic policy issues, committing to new spending in new areas—had considerable overlap, a point not lost on the journalists and newspapers reporting on the speeches. It had to be emphasised, argued *The Sydney Morning Herald*, that 'there are few of Mr Whitlam's practical proposals which are not matched by the government'.[12]

For McMahon, that was a win—and, indeed, proof of the value of the work that had been pushed through over the year. By the Wednesday, he was boasting about his speech's reception. When he taped an appearance for *A Current Affair* with Mike Willesee, McMahon said that he hated praising himself, but that he had to give a direct answer on how his speech had gone. 'The response has been remarkably good. I don't think it could have been better … I'm happy about the performance, and if I could take notice of what's been said to me, there is no doubt that it won votes.'[13]

THE autocue was big, boxy, and, for all its state-of-the-art pretension, hopelessly clunky. Taking the place of a lectern, the autocue hid McMahon from his audience at Sydney's Town Hall. Hired for the campaign in the hope that it would encourage McMahon to stick to a prepared text, the autocue was operated by a staffer seated at a table on the side of the stage, who would speed up, slow, or stop the scrolling text by using a pedal. McMahon thought it wonderful: he boasted of taking to the autocue like a duck to water, and relished being able to speak without wearing his glasses.[14] But using the autocue had its drawbacks. For one, it removed McMahon from his audience, distanced him, made him 'a bald head instead of an animated face', as Edgar Holt put it.[15] The autocue also had the effect of deadening McMahon's tone and intonation. Although McMahon would never claim to be an orator, the autocue left him without spontaneity. He would read in metered phrases, stilted and slow.

It was the object of much criticism. 'Disgraceful,' Killen said, when he saw it.[16] 'It'll be government via teleprompt,' Whitlam joked. Nonetheless, in repeated meetings and town halls across the country, McMahon would continue to use the autocue, reading his speeches dutifully, carefully. He rarely departed from his prepared texts. Protesters and rowdy attendees could not disrupt his progress, and the autocue's operator would turn up the volume to drown out shouts and yells.

Town halls and meetings, like that at Sydney's Town Hall, were reliably rowdy. Hecklers yelled at McMahon, tried to interrupt him. Liberal Party supporters would shout them down, or create human walls between McMahon and protesters. At one stop, protesters threw jelly beans at McMahon; at another, elderly ladies pricked balloons that had been inflated by Labor-supporting students. McMahon was never particularly effective in these situations. He did not have Menzies' wit and capacity for repartee, and questions and insults could leave him flustered. 'It was a very difficult ask for McMahon,' John Howard thought.[17]

It was not all his fault. The noise could be staggering, as it was in a meeting at Randwick Town Hall. A young woman who held up her Liberal Party membership card to prove her bona fides demanded to know what McMahon would do about French nuclear-testing in the Pacific. McMahon did not hear her properly. 'What I can say to you is this—that the whole question of taxation and the scale of taxation, the various methods of taxation ...' He could not continue: scornful laughter rippled over the room as McMahon's colleagues on the stage hurried to tell him he had misheard.

Meetings could be hostile, frustrating. Insults were frequent: 'Hello Big Ears! Come on, Baldy! Let's watch Billy boil!' Statements of pure scorn were par for the course: 'Bullshit! Bullshit, Billy!' Boos could suffuse applause with a sense of menace. In Adelaide, as McMahon left the town hall with Sonia, someone threw a smoke bomb. 'I saw it coming and pushed Sonia back,' McMahon said later. 'It landed well in front of us. I didn't even smell the smoke.'[18] At the Springvale Town Hall the police turned out in force to prevent any moves for violence. Protesters dominated the audience with 'It's time' signs and chants of 'We want Gough', and when McMahon and his party left, they were confronted by a crowd of shoving, screaming youths. The police had to form a barricade around McMahon to force a way through. Coverage of the evening's events made headlines and prompted the Labor Party to plead with its supporters to restrain themselves.

Advertising from both sides was caustic. The Liberal Party advertised its budget with an inopportune quote from Arthur Calwell: 'It was a wonderful budget!' The government also ran ads showing a man pulling away a mask of Whitlam's face—to reveal Bob Hawke. 'When Labor speaks, who's really talking?' it asked. Labor made use of television to advertise policy and Whitlam's biography, and encouraged a sense that the time had come for a change of government. 'It's time,' ran its slogan and song, the latter of which was played over video of well-known entertainers and personalities singing along. Labor's slogan was not particularly well countered: 'Not yet,' was the Liberal Party's reply. Other players were also getting involved. Promising to spend up to $40,000 to defeat the government, Patrick Sayers, chairman of the so-called Business Executives for a Change of Government, ran advertisements showing enormous pictures of John McEwen and the headlines that had followed his veto of McMahon in 1967. 'Is McMahon's leadership good enough for Australia?'

There were clear signs that McMahon's ministers had answers to this question—and not answers that he would much like. On 14 November, newspapers in Victoria ran stories suggesting that ministers were shunning McMahon, distancing themselves.[19] On 22 November, while speaking on talkback radio in Perth, Billy Snedden was moved to discuss leadership within the Liberal Party. Noting that he had opposed John Gorton when Gorton first became leader, in 1968, and that he

had similarly opposed McMahon when McMahon became leader, in
1971, Snedden went on to say:

> I served Mr McMahon and I will continue to serve as best I can. As to
> whether Mr McMahon will continue to lead the party, [that] is for him
> to determine. If he should vacate the position I have a willingness to
> serve and I will offer myself.

Headlines the next day were blaring: 'Mr Snedden willing to stand
for leadership.'[20] McMahon was incensed when he heard of this. He
regarded it as a distraction to the campaign, to say nothing of abundant
disloyalty to him. Subsequent clarifying statements from Snedden did
nothing to repair the damage, not least because he continued to mention
that the Liberal Party was 'just chockfull of so much talent'.[21] Other
ministers appeared to have given up on McMahon and the prospect of
victory. When Don Chipp fronted a group of Young Liberals in Sydney
in the final days of the campaign, he spoke of the need for a new
generation of leaders, in tune with the times. 'He clearly meant *he* was
that leader,' Bruce MacCarthy recalled. Annoyed by Chipp's preening
and disloyalty, MacCarthy said that there were still four days left in the
campaign and a win, though unlikely, was still possible. 'Do you really
think that?' a disbelieving Chipp asked. 'Do you *really* think that?'[22]

Anthony also appeared to endorse the idea of deposing McMahon
after the election. Already of the opinion that McMahon's campaigning
was 'pretty poor', Anthony found himself having to deflect questioners
asking why he could not be prime minister.[23] He would usually grin and
say that it was the last job he could ever want. 'It's a most onerous task,'
he would say. Aware that the questions spoke to a deep dissatisfaction
with McMahon's leadership, Anthony subsequently began to speak as if
McMahon would not be leader for long, should the government retain
office. Speaking in Perth on 28 November, Anthony told radio listeners:

> It is wrong for people to interpret Australian elections as a presidential
> election. You cannot judge who is going to be the leader of any party, or
> who will be Prime Minister, until after the election. You elect a whole
> series of individuals and it is the right of those individuals to determine
> who is going to be the leader of their party.[24]

For McMahon, Sonia, and the staff working around him, the conclusion of all this was clear. The coalition was fracturing. The Liberal Party was giving up. McMahon's colleagues were running dead. They were all abandoning him. He was going to have to fight the election alone.[25]

CRISES continued to rile McMahon and to set the campaign off course. On 12 November, Whitlam announced that, should he win the election, Nugget Coombs would advise him on the economy. 'I shall personally be seeking the advice of Dr H.C. Coombs who, on high economic matters and more recently on Aboriginal affairs and the universities and the arts, has rendered such service to the nation.'[26] Whitlam took no small pleasure when reporters pointed out that Coombs was supposedly McMahon's 'guiding philosopher'. Playing on their disagreements over Aboriginal policy, Whitlam said that the difference between Coombs's advice to McMahon and his potential advice to Whitlam was that Whitlam would accept it. The press saw the development for what it was: a clear sign of confidence in Whitlam and of no confidence in McMahon. 'The news will be a severe blow to the government in this early stage of the campaign,' *Sydney Morning Herald* journalist Brian Johns wrote.[27]

The apparent switch of allegiance prompted criticism from McMahon, his ministers, and his staff. But Coombs subsequently argued that he had accepted Whitlam's offer largely out of what he believed was an even-handed approach to politics. In Coombs's view, McMahon's public discussion of his role had suggested a 'close political-style association' between them, one that implied partiality and bias. To refute that, to establish his political impartiality, Coombs decided he should agree to overtures from Whitlam to advise him—but only under the same conditions that he already advised McMahon.[28] The reasoning was sound, but it would never convince Coombs's critics. 'This now shows up Coombs in his true colours,' Howson wrote in his diary.[29]

Another story, on the same day that Whitlam announced Coombs would advise him, was small, but would grow in prominence and significance: that of a speech by the senior auxiliary bishop in the

Catholic archdiocese of Sydney, Archbishop James Carroll. Speaking at the opening of a library at St Augustine's College, Brookvale, the archbishop noted that now both the Liberal and Labor parties supported the dual system of education—private and public schools. What differences remained, Carroll said, were variously 'relatively unimportant', 'secondary', and 'of a passing phase'. Carroll's note of these small disagreements and the general consensus was not unimportant: indeed, it was one of the first times that this had been noted. Moreover, it led to the crucial section of his speech:

> The conscientious Christian in a free democratic society should cast his vote thoughtfully, unselfishly and patriotically. In earlier times, such a Christian has given his support to this or that Party, this or that candidate, not without some reluctance, because all Parties and all candidates seemed to be ignoring the question of the just claims of parents who wished education for their children in non-government schools. At this stage of our history, that reason for reluctance has been removed.[30]

Coming amid statements from other Catholic bishops that were critical of Labor, Carroll's remarks represented a significant break in the wall of opposition to the ALP's policies on state aid. In effect, Carroll was dismissing any suggestion that the ALP's policy should be a barrier preventing Catholics from voting for Whitlam and the Labor Party. As journalists Laurie Oakes and David Solomon would subsequently write, Carroll's remarks shattered the illusion that the Catholic hierarchy was united in wanting a Liberal victory.[31] Notwithstanding that right-wing bishops and Catholic-affiliated spokespeople continued to criticise the ALP policy, it was clear that Carroll's intervention was a blow to McMahon's campaign. A plank that had helped to support Menzies and Holt and Gorton was now gone, right when McMahon needed it.

Another blow landed on 23 November. A letter signed by sixteen prominent Australians was published in many of the country's daily newspapers: 'We, the undersigned, who are not members of any political party, believe that Australia's interests will be best served by a change of Government as a result of this election,' it began.[32] The identity of the sixteen who signed the letter—historians Manning

Clark and Keith Hancock, academics MacMahon Ball and Hedley Bull, scientists Frank Fenner and Macfarlane Burnet, writers Judith Wright and Patrick White—would not have surprised the government. Nor was its provenance much of a surprise: it had been drafted by *Age* columnist Bruce Grant, who was widely acknowledged to be sympathetic to the ALP.[33] The letter would not have been such a blow, had it not been for the presence of the name of Kenneth Myer, chairman of Myer Emporium Ltd. The only businessman of note to have signed, Myer's support for a change of government gave the letter an aura of bipartisanship; moreover, it lent Labor a respectability that was important in Victoria, where the antics of the left-wing ALP executive had long tarnished the party's name. McMahon attempted to negate the value of Myer's signature by circulating a telegram from Dame Merlyn Myer, Kenneth's mother, who wrote to assure him of her own support for McMahon's government. Other ministers circulated similarly dissenting letters from the Myer family, but the damage was done.[34] Just as with Coombs's apparent defection to the ALP, and just as with Archbishop Carroll's endorsement of the ALP's policy on state aid, the letter fed into a consensus that it was finally time for a change.

DIVISIONS within the Liberal Party and McMahon's own office hampered the effectiveness of the campaign. Sonia was scathing of the quality of speeches that were prepared for her husband, and would rewrite them herself. 'He had some terrible speechwriters,' she said later. 'The language was so convoluted and full of jargon.'[35] She was bitter about the conduct of the Victorian division of the Liberal Party, and thought darkly of John Howard's participation: she thought him a spy for the New South Wales division.[36] Senator John Carrick, the former general secretary of that division of the party, joined Howard to try to instill some stability in the campaign. But it was chaotic. As Carrick said later:

We travelled all over Australia with the Prime Minister in that last month of the campaign, mostly sleeping on the floors of aircraft, trying to write things on the floor of an aircraft, with the feeling that the Party was facing defeat.[37]

In mid-November, McMahon's press secretary, Jonathan Gaul, contracted chickenpox and was forced to return home. McMahon had to have a Varicella vaccine, in an enormous needle, to protect him against getting sick. 'He probably didn't thank me for that,' Gaul said later.[38] Edgar Holt did not aid morale. 'The feel I get is that it will be a landslide,' he said to journalists on the campaign plane. 'The tragedy is that everyone knows it except the little fellow.'[39]

In Gaul's absence, relations between the press and McMahon's office went steadily downhill. Journalists were frustrated by the lack of understanding and know-how from McMahon's office. Advance copies of speeches were non-existent. Statements were rarely issued. The campaign's itinerary was tightly held. McMahon would not do press conferences, would not talk on the record. It was partly a fault of personnel: Keith Sinclair did not think much of issuing statements, and Reg MacDonald, McMahon's erstwhile press secretary, had been forced into a job at which he was not adept. It made for a terrible time.

Back in Canberra, Phil Davis, a former police-rounds reporter who now worked as press secretary to Phillip Lynch, was horrified by what he heard from journalists with the campaign. Although a member of the ALP, Davis took little pleasure in what was going on. 'You bastards are mad,' he told Lynch. 'Look at what's happened out there.' Lynch passed on Davis's criticism, and within days Davis had been brought on board to work with McMahon, in what Gaul would later say was fortuitous timing.

'Billy was very difficult to work with,' Davis later wrote, 'although no more difficult than any PM would be under siege. At the stage I worked for him, he didn't trust anybody, rightly or wrongly, [and] he was a hard man to work for. He would switch allegiances at the drop of a hat.'[40] Davis thought the situation was dire. He persuaded McMahon that he should take responsibility for liaising with the press, and had McMahon agree the campaign should give out press releases for the morning and evening papers, so that reporters had material to work with. Most of all, he advised McMahon to stop viewing reporters as the enemy.

Davis nevertheless encountered resistance. Sinclair scorned the idea of issuing press statements. 'You can't manufacture news,' he said.[41] MacDonald told Davis people were suspicious of him: 'A lot of people are not very happy about you joining us, you know.'[42] Davis was unrepentant. It was his job to provide an expertise that seemed otherwise absent. He advised McMahon on what colour shirts to wear: 'No, Mr Mac, yellow's not good for TV—blue or pink is fine.'[43] In a campaign visit to Moonee Ponds, someone handed McMahon a Chiko roll. Aware of rumours about McMahon's sexuality and words that could flow from an inopportune photo, Davis snatched it away. 'Oh, what did you do that for?' McMahon asked. Davis did not enlighten him.

'It was commonsense really,' Davis said later. 'I looked good because no one else was doing it. Billy called the staff in then and said, "Do anything this man wants." Of course that had the effect of losing his staff's support from that moment on, but I coped. They came around.'[44]

But McMahon would not always be agreeable or amenable to advice. He resisted Davis's urging to do away with the teleprompter, and he would not always accept guidance on what to say. On 23 November, as he prepped for a television interview with Channel 7, McMahon told Davis that he was going to talk about how much he had done as the party's leader, how he had taken decisions himself. Davis told him immediately it would be a silly thing to do and not to do it. Had McMahon not been lauding his cabinet only recently? Had he not been comparing it, favourably, with Whitlam's shadow cabinet? Would this not sound like criticism of his cabinet? But McMahon would not be dissuaded.[45] When he was asked during the interview what he had learned over the past twenty months of his prime ministership, he answered without hesitation:

McMahon: I have learned a lot. I have learned, first of all, the fact that I now must make more decisions than I had intentions of making when I first became the Prime Minister. I wanted to be the head of a team. I wanted to delegate the authority to the relevant Ministers responsible for the Departments.

Interviewer: What went wrong with that principle?

McMahon: I couldn't get the work done quickly enough and I found frequently that the political approaches to it were not as good as I thought they should be. So from September last year I gradually started to change, and I have been changing a little more quickly as the days have gone by—and I believe with success.[46]

McMahon undoubtedly believed the comments. He had long spoken of his belief that he was the engine room of the government, that he was both its best political judge and actor. He had told newspapers and businessmen, associates, and people in the Liberal Party of his frustration with his colleagues in the ministry: that they were unable to make the right decisions, that he had to carry the government on his own back. 'You know, I had to fight for every one of those initiatives. All of them,' he told two journalists on a flight from Adelaide to Melbourne.[47] But however true McMahon felt these were, they were poor sentiments to voice during an election campaign. Bolstering his own image in this way undermined his colleagues. 'It was an inept answer,' John Howard thought.[48]

'I'm worried about that,' Davis said to MacDonald, when he heard McMahon. 'It looks like criticism of the ministry.' MacDonald told him not to worry, that McMahon had said it all before: 'There's nothing new in it.'[49] Unfortunately, two journalists—the ABC's Ken Begg and News Ltd's Robert Baudino—were in the studio listening to McMahon speak. They reported the comments immediately, before anyone could intervene to have them edited or cut from the programme. 'Well, he's fucked himself now,' Baudino said.

It took very little time for McMahon to realise that he had erred. Amid a wave of telephone calls and criticism, he soon realised the gravity of the mistake. Initially, he lashed out and attempted to blame Davis, who turned to Sonia. 'Mrs Mac, you've got to help,' Davis said. 'What did I tell him?'[50] But Sonia knew that McMahon required support, too. On a plane from Brisbane to Sydney, seeing him sitting silent and shattered, she knelt in the aisle, by his seat, to hold his hand. She refused entreaties from the flight attendant to return to her own seat. 'I will stay here,' she said.

When the plane landed, Davis had a statement issued denying that McMahon had intended any kind of reflection on his ministry and asserting that his remarks had been 'misconstrued'. The real issue, the statement went on, was Whitlam's twenty-seven-man cabinet and how impracticable it would be.[51] The statement did nothing to alter the consensus that McMahon had stumbled again; if anything, it simply drew more attention to the issue.

McMahon's ministers were aghast. Anthony was scathing of the blunder. 'My Party worked flat out to try to keep in harmony with McMahon until the last week when he made that statement that he couldn't trust our Party and some of his own members,' he recalled. 'It put us in a difficult position.'[52] Snedden buried his head in his hands when he saw the comments broadcast. 'It's the end,' he said. 'We're finished.'[53] Howson despaired of the headlines as much as of what followed: when he tried to find guidance for a suitable response, he could get nothing from McMahon's campaign.[54] McMahon's allies were blunt about the effect the comments had. 'If you hadn't lost it already, you did it tonight on TV,' Harry Bland told McMahon over the phone.[55]

The fallout caused the government to change its tactics. New South Wales DLP senator Jack Kane had warned McMahon that the election was likely to be lost without some eye-catching issue to campaign on, and thus pushed for an attack on the 'permissive society', on abortion, on censorship. New South Wales premier Bob Askin, who had already been speaking on these issues, agreed on grounds that it could put Labor on the run, particularly amid a planned all-out bombardment from religious groups and the DLP on Labor's policy regarding abortion. The hesitation in McMahon's office faded once the results of that weekend's Gallup poll became known. Labor's forecast 49 per cent share of the vote dwarfed the 41 per cent polled for the Liberal and Country parties. The voices in McMahon's office spoke as one: he should go on the attack.

Phil Davis urged McMahon to do it. He enlisted Sonia's help to convince McMahon. While travelling to a campaign stop, Davis told McMahon that abortion was an issue in the campaign. 'Before he could answer, I said, "What do you think, Mrs Mac?" And she and I had this conversation that we had pre-planned. And Billy ran with it.'[56] But whether McMahon believed it was another matter. 'I'm not sure that the PM really had his heart in that line of advocacy,' Howard would say later.[57]

Nonetheless, what appeared on the following Monday's *Sydney Morning Herald* was a full-throated attack on Labor's policies on 'moral issues'.[58] McMahon's campaign had issued a statement to the press that called attention to differences between the government and Labor, and papers like the *Herald* ran it almost in totum. Although admitting that morals should be private and a matter for individual conscience, McMahon argued that if moral actions impinged on others and were likely to corrupt them, the government should intervene. Therefore, his government did not believe in abortion on demand or request, but there was justification for 'therapeutic abortion'. Drug addicts should receive treatment, yes—but 'we would not, as some Labor Party members urge, remove the penalties for drug-taking, including marihuana'. And while the government should not be heavy-handed or paternalistic on censorship issues, it was his view that 'the Australian people expect us to act on hard-core pornography and we will continue to do so'.[59] Askin was similarly inflammatory: 'When people declare that their private lives are no concern of the government or of anyone else, they are talking like a cancerous cell that no longer obeys the laws of the body.'[60]

Was this line of attack effective? Only a day later, divisions among Catholic and Protestant clergy over the question of a conscience vote on abortion, as well as dissension over the effectiveness of both party's policies on poverty, suggested that moral issues were eye-catching but not necessarily likely to gain traction for the government.[61] Admissions from McMahon's ministers that they had different ideas about abortion, censorship, drugs, and pornography also made the attacks less effective. By 29 November, when McMahon attended a scheduled lunch at the National Press Club (where he would speak and turn the sod for the new site), it seemed that the issue had failed. Under questioning from journalists, McMahon admitted that, like Labor's policy had it, he would prefer a conscience vote on abortion, were it to come up in the Parliament.[62]

But McMahon would never stop searching for a way to regain the initiative and sharpen the lines of difference with Labor. Some of his criticisms and arguments were prescient. In his speech to the Press Club, McMahon went to great lengths to cite the economic effects of Labor's promises, should they be enacted. He argued that Whitlam's stated reliance on the continued growth of Commonwealth receipts to pay for his promises were 'too clever by half' and unrealistic. Arguing that Whitlam was attempting to buy his way into office, McMahon pointed out that estimates of the costs of Labor's promises were $1,330m—against $375m for his own election proposals. 'That is four times the cost,' McMahon said. 'Either taxes will have to be increased or many of Labor's promises would have to be quietly dropped as forgotten election gimmicks.' It was all 'Mandrake economics', McMahon said.[63] According to Gaul, the attack was not insincere: 'He was very apprehensive about the size of the promises Labor was making for the 1972 election.'[64]

McMahon also tried to revive questions about who would control Labor and the type of administration Australians could expect under an ALP government. 'It may well be that a Labor government in the 1970s would be more subject to outside, non-elected direction than in the 1940s,' he said. 'It is certainly true that the influence of the left-wing unions through Mr Hawke and the ACTU executive is stronger.' McMahon cited his 'good friend' Bob Askin's claim that Labor wished to 'murder' the state governments. McMahon criticised Labor's tendency for centralism and the growth of government power. 'The whole thrust of the socialist takeover scheme is the concentration of all political power here in Canberra,' he said.[65] Coming barely seven days after his comment that he wished the Commonwealth could secure powers to control prices and wages, the attack was ineffective.[66] Neither issue—union control nor Labor's centralism—would bite during those final days. They were too late, and too shopworn from use in elections of the past. 'We decided to kick the commie can at the end of the campaign, which went down like a lead balloon,' Davis recalled. 'We made an error there. I should have talked him [McMahon] out of that one.'[67]

McMahon had known that the speech at the Press Club was important. He had chosen the date knowing it was the final occasion on which political matters could be broadcast on television and radio before the mandated election blackout, and had thought the occasion significant enough to use the preceding day to prepare for it. But his aim of delivering an effective speech was almost immediately undermined by his manner. When he reached the stage and faced the room, he turned away, sheltering his face behind his arm. The lights were too bright. He gesticulated for the television crews to turn them down. 'It was something an ordinary person might do,' one journalist thought. 'That was the trouble.'[68]

There was also the unfavourable contrast with Whitlam. Only two days before, Whitlam had arrived and spoken without notes, confidently and proudly. McMahon, however, had insisted on using the autocue. Gripping its edges, microphones aimed at his sternum, he read his speech dutifully, carefully. Representatives of the Press Club were displeased. To their 'considerable annoyance', the lectern that bore the Press Club's name had been replaced by the autocue. Moreover, the need for an uninterrupted line of sight between McMahon and the autocue operator created an opportunity for confusion to occur. 'The autocue operator had a good view as long as everyone was sitting down,' Peter Sekuless, the club's treasurer, recalled, 'but as waiters flitted back and forth along the official table his view was blocked and the prime minister's flow of words became erratic.'[69]

McMahon's gratuitous complaints about the burden he carried as prime minister tinged coverage as the campaign went into the blackout period. 'What I would change most, if I could, would be to get quicker decisions in government itself,' he said. 'And I would also wish to change the quantity of work that has to be handled by the prime minister, so that he can tend to the important issues that have to be faced and make quick decisions on those issues. The critical [element] for me has been the amount of work that comes across my table. Much of it could be handled by somebody else.' It was silly. He sounded small, not up to the task of being prime minister. Then he lashed out at the press. On *This Day Tonight*, he said that the press had tried to destroy Harold Holt and John Gorton, and was now trying to do the same to him. He said that some sections of the press had 'tasted blood' and thought it good to destroy the Liberal Party.[70] 'I think now there has been more unfairness than I can remember for a long time,' he said elsewhere. '... Some sections of the media, particularly one section, have been malevolent, even malicious.'[71]

McMAHON'S complaints about the media were not incorrect—but he hardly told the full story. Some sections of the media were adamantly opposed to him; others were still in his favour. What became notable over the course of the campaign was the ways that the government reacted to these allies and enemies, and its hurt when its long-held advantages in the media were overturned.

That Sir Frank Packer might try to help McMahon, for example, was a given—but his initial interventions, in mid-November, were so clumsy and heavy-handed that they did not pass muster.[72] At seven o'clock on 15 November, just as stations in the Channel 9 network expected to see the weekly broadcast of *A Current Affair*, an editorial written by David McNicoll was played instead. 'It will not take the solid, middle-of-the-road voter long to work out which policy—Mr Whitlam's or Mr McMahon's—is the best for Australia and the best for him,' it began. The editorial pasted Labor as decadent, secretive, unrealistic, and McMahon's government as entirely the opposite. But the broadcast came unstuck almost immediately. Mike Willesee, compère of *A Current Affair*, complained that he had not known of it, and Colin Bednall, a former managing director for Packer at GTV-9 now standing for Labor in the seat of Flinders, angrily pointed out that the editorial had breached the Broadcasting and Television Act.[73] Bednall was quite right, but the ability of the Australian Broadcasting Control Board to enforce a penalty—such as demanding equal time for Labor—was non-existent. A week later, with brazen impunity, TCN-9 and GTV-9 would screen another editorial criticising Labor. Staffers in Packer's employ were never particularly embarrassed by what they did. Clyde Packer admitted that he had deliberately kept Labor people out of the news, and the company continued to allow Brian Morelli to help McMahon's television campaign. Moreover, strong evidence would later emerge that Packer had given almost $19,000 worth of free television advertising time to the DLP.[74]

Other press organisations were less friendly, more intractable, unrelentingly hostile. McMahon was not imagining it: there were journalists who took no small degree of pleasure in chronicling every fault and flaw in the campaign. Gaul was certain of it: 'I had to deal with them every day, and I can attest to that.'[75]

Richard Farmer, a self-described 'strange little git with long hair and everything' who had written for Maxwell Newton but now wrote for *The Daily Telegraph*, provoked anger with his coverage of McMahon's campaign. Assigned to write a column that took readers behind the scenes, Farmer took regular shots at McMahon. 'That was my job: to make fun of this man, wherever I could,' Farmer explained later. '[Rupert] Murdoch had decided he had to go.' McMahon had no idea that complaining about Farmer would be ineffectual. After antagonising McMahon with a particular line of questioning, Farmer received a telephone call from Murdoch. McMahon had telephoned him, Murdoch said, to demand that Farmer be reined in or transferred from the campaign. But Murdoch would do no such thing; in fact, he would alter long-held plans for Farmer to cover Whitlam's campaign. 'You'd better stick with McMahon the whole way,' Murdoch said.[76]

On Wednesday 22 November, while arguing that his government was keeping up with the times, McMahon told a radio audience about the review of Australia's policy on China that he had initiated while minister for foreign affairs. 'Everyone should get a copy of it and read it,' he intoned. But when reporters tried to do so, they found that the review was secret. It would not be released until it was declassified; its contents would not be known unless it was leaked. When quizzed, McMahon's team claimed that McMahon had referred to a speech, not a briefing. Writing about this for the next day's *Telegraph*, Farmer was sceptical. 'Could a copy be made available so the Australian people could see this memorable document? Well, unfortunately, no.'[77]

When McMahon read that report the next day, while on the plane to Hobart, he grew angry. After the plane had landed, he spied Farmer emerging from the steps near the tail. He broke off from talking with the delegation that had turned out to meet him, walked across to Farmer, and began to harangue him about the report, saying that he was wrong, that he *had* referred to a speech. Farmer was unmoved: all he had done was report what had happened. This calm response seemed to make McMahon angrier. 'He was furious,' Farmer said later. McMahon seemed out of control to Farmer, so much so that he thought McMahon might hit him. Recalling that McMahon had once boxed tempered Farmer's willingness to continue the conversation. Davis intervened when it became clear that the argument was becoming dangerously heated. How about they discussed this elsewhere, later, he suggested pointedly, and *not* in view of the cameras?

Thinking it was over, Farmer turned to go. 'Well, don't run away in fear,' McMahon said, scornfully, to his back. Farmer turned around to continue the talk, and Davis had to intervene again.[78] A drink between them that afternoon allowed McMahon's team to say that the matter had been smoothed over, but McMahon was still incensed. 'He rang Murdoch again to complain,' Farmer recalled. Murdoch's response was a shrug. As he relayed to Farmer, Murdoch told McMahon that he was a difficult reporter to control. 'He didn't say that he had instructed me [to be difficult],' Farmer said later. Then, unbelievably, at Murdoch's suggestion, McMahon invited Farmer to his home for breakfast, as though to get to know him. Said Farmer:

> It was extraordinary. We sat outside. It was a summer's day. He had no idea what was happening to him. His mind had gone. He didn't realise that Rupert was against him … I had this lovely breakfast, said, 'Thank you very much,' and continued to do the same thing. Everywhere he went, I went. The fact that he could allow himself to get so upset by one journalist was extraordinary.[79]

Extraordinary, yes—but also understandable. Farmer had worked with Newton, been an ally with Newton, when McMahon was fighting McEwen over tariff policy. McMahon could not have failed to be aggrieved at this seeming change of sides. Nor could he fail to have been aggrieved by the knowledge that the *Telegraph* was against him. He could not rely on its support, as all his predecessors had. At the moment when he needed it most, McMahon could not rely on his former constant ally.

Murdoch was forthright about the change. 'We did some dreadful things to the other side,' he said later. 'A lot more happened than even they managed to find out.' His long-held dislike and scorn for McMahon had caused him to urge Bob Askin to support a late challenge from Gorton. When Askin declined to support this, Murdoch told Snedden that if he challenged McMahon, he would throw his support behind the government.[80] A meeting with McMahon in Sydney—taken in spite of advice from McMahon's staff that the media baron should come to him, to the prime minister's office—did not change Murdoch's mind about the merits of the McMahon government.[81] 'It was an unsuccessful meeting,' Gaul said later.[82]

Murdoch's involvement with the Labor campaign, and his willingness to offer advice and free advertising in his newspapers, were the logical culmination of his disenchantment with McMahon and the Liberal-Country Party government. Murdoch would admit that he and his papers had been unfair to McMahon. 'I should have had more reserve, but I got emotionally involved. I allowed, with my eyes open, some of the journalists to go beyond being sort of partisans into almost being principals.'[83] *The Daily Telegraph* was the most strident, he acknowledged. It had gone 'overboard' in seeking a change. 'We all really threw ourselves into the fight, to get a change. It did break twenty years of conservative government.'[84] Certainly the *Telegraph's* editorial on 2 December, advocating a vote for Labor, was unequivocal: 'We have no hesitation in recommending a vote for Mr Whitlam and his party.'[85]

Other newspapers that withdrew or tempered their support rubbed salt in McMahon's wounds. Aside from his dalliance with Labor in 1961, the conservative chairman of the Fairfax stable, Sir Warwick Fairfax, had been a steady supporter of the government and had exercised his influence to ensure that his newspapers echoed that support. But this time would be different. *The Sydney Morning Herald* would offer some support—running a dubious story, wholly on Fairfax's urging, on Labor's immoral social policies.[86] But *The Australian Financial Review* leaned so obviously towards Labor that Fairfax made a complaint about its 'lack of enthusiasm' for the government. 'There was not one leader or one sentence that said positively that, summing matters up, the policy of the government was to be preferred to that of Labor,' he wrote.[87] Most egregious, however, was *The Age.*

Under editor Graham Perkin, *The Age* became far more active and incisive on political issues, pursuing an editorial independence that was much to the chagrin of its board. The Liberal Party's president, Robert Southey, had found the paper difficult all year. '*The Age* is having a very destructive effect in Victoria, and is much more bilious than most of the Australian newspapers which I see,' he had written to McMahon in March.[88] Certainly, Perkin was not enamoured of McMahon. After lunching with him in May, Perkin conceded that the prime minister was 'really dazzling company', but thought him disconnected from reality. 'The funny little man has convinced himself that he is a brilliant success and sees himself winning handsomely in November,' wrote Perkin to a colleague, 'and remaking the nation in the following three years; leading them to victory in 1975 and then retiring with honours thick upon him. God save us all!'

Whatever his regard for McMahon, however, Perkin was intent on giving his readers the knowledge to make an informed decision. He ensured there was considerable space devoted to analysing the politics of both parties, and invited McMahon and Whitlam to lunch with the editorial staff before the election. The successive lunches saw the contrast between prime minister and leader of the opposition exposed. Where Whitlam came looking a winner, confident and tall, McMahon arrived looking lost, hopeless. 'He looked like a retired jockey who was on his way to the bowls club,' Les Carlyon recalled. That McMahon later telephoned Perkin to request that a 'misjudged' comment be removed from an interview transcript only confirmed the poor impression. Perkin had been amazed at the request: 'Remove it? My dear Prime Minister, it's in 72-point headlines on page one.'[89] It was no surprise, then, that *The Age's* election-day editorial was simple and clear:

> Should we persist with a Government of modest accomplishment, considerable disunity and no clear vision for the future? Or should we decide for change, with the risks that change inevitably involves, and look forward to the stimulation of new ideas and new purposes? This paper believes change, and Labor, ought to be given the opportunity.[90]

MCMAHON spent polling day in Lowe, in Sydney's inner west. He had no fear of losing his seat. There were only nuisances about: an eccentric who had sued to have the election stopped over problems with his filing fee; a local who had changed his name by deed poll to 'M.D. Aussie-Stone' in the hope of attracting the donkey vote; and an Australia Party candidate who had suggested people vote for the poof who lived in the seat.[91] McMahon's electorate chairman drove him around. John Howard and Sonia accompanied McMahon for part of the day. McMahon visited polling booths, chatted with workers, and shook hands. He went to booths in the seat of Evans, held by Malcolm Mackay, which he knew the government might lose. In the mid-afternoon, he went home to Bellevue Hill. He went for a swim.

Inside, showered and dressed, with the curtains tightly closed, McMahon sat down with friends and family. John and Janette Howard went to the house after dinner. At McMahon's invitation, Bruce MacCarthy left the party faithful who had gathered at the back of the Strathfield L.J. Hooker, by the builder's shed that had once been McMahon's own headquarters, to come over. He arrived to see food and wine everywhere, laid out for a party. Davis, meanwhile, holed himself up in the kitchen to draft a concession speech. When someone asked what he was doing, Davis replied, 'Trying to bury everything.'[92]

At eight o'clock, the polls closed. McMahon's party watched the returns come in on television sets in the lounge room. Bede Hartcher, the Liberal Party director, called repeatedly on one of the two telephones with messages and news of numbers. Settled beside one of the phones, McMahon calmly used it to follow results himself. He scribbled on a notepad to keep track of the seats that were falling, calculating the swing, noting what was certain and what was not. There were bright spots in the evening. The government won the Victorian seat of Bendigo and the South Australian seat of Sturt, and it took the Western Australian seats of Forrest and Stirling, as per McMahon's prediction. But seats also fell the other way. Evans was gone; Cook slipped away; Lilley was lost by a handful of votes. The bright spots were blacked out, forgotten. It became a steady stream of losses. 'It was a tough night,' Gaul would say later.[93] The atmosphere, Howard thought, was one of 'calm acceptance'.[94] Denison, Diamond Valley, Holt, La Trobe: they all fell to the Labor Party. Seats that McMahon had thought he might win—St George, Eden-Monaro—did not come his way. More seats fell: Macarthur, McMillan, Mitchell, Phillip. Overnight, it would become clear that Casey, held by Howson, would also crumble.[95]

Just after nine o'clock, speaking on Channel 9's election coverage, Alan Reid confirmed it. 'If the trend continues,' he said, 'I'd say Labor is home and hosed.'[96] There was a swing, not as big as that which had swept Chifley away in 1949, not as big even as that which had so damaged Gorton three years before. This was some solace to McMahon: 'At least we didn't lose as many seats as in 1969,' he would say.[97] On a two-party-preferred measure, the swing was only 2.5 per cent. But it was enough. The government would take only 41.4 per cent of the nation-wide primary vote; with almost 500,000 more votes, Labor would take 49.6 per cent. By ten o'clock, two hours after the polls had closed, McMahon could tell that the government had lost office. In spite of the caution advised by Hartcher, telling him to wait just in case, McMahon knew that there was no coming back. There were too many seats being lost. 'Where did we go wrong?' McMahon wondered, at one point.[98] For that night, at least, he would not answer questions like that. 'That's something for deep consideration,' he would soon say.

Most in the room believed that McMahon knew what the election result would be. 'I think by then he had realised the most likely result was a loss,' said Gaul, later.[99] Howard agreed, though he did not think Sonia was quite prepared. But she was dignified, just as her husband was, he recalled.[100] Certainly, McMahon was composed throughout the evening. He did not tear up. When he spoke, his voice did not tremor. Sonia admired it. 'He was marvellous,' she said of her husband.[101]

Gorton appeared on television to confirm the defeat. Chipp followed. Snedden added his concession. Whitlam's Labor had won office with a nine-seat majority. The loss was not huge. It could have been worse. An additional 1,917 votes, spread over five seats, would have seen the government retain office. There was no landslide. 'It's not that bad,' McMahon told MacCarthy. 'We're only going to lose by eight or nine seats.'[102]

Knowing that he would need to say something, McMahon took the statement that Davis had drafted. He had a cup of tea and, with Gaul, retired to the family room to look it over. McMahon tweaked the draft, then had a stenographer type the new version so that he could read it without his glasses.

Whitlam came on the television at just after 11.30pm to announce that Labor had won. Speaking from the sunroom of his home in Cabramatta, sitting on a white piano stool in a crush of press, Whitlam claimed a 'very good mandate' for his party's policies and said he would await a call from the governor-general. McMahon watched the impromptu press conference in silence. He re-read his own statement, and made a final note on the back. 'Let's get it over with,' he said. He went outside, plunging through a tunnel of press, down the gravel driveway to the front lawn. Sonia accompanied him. 'Nothing would stop me going out with him,' she told Davis. A crowd of neighbours and friends watched from McMahon's right as the television crews and reporters clustered around him. Wearing a blue suit, a white shirt, and a crimson tie, McMahon became the first prime minister to concede on television. 'Mr Whitlam has obviously won, and he's won a handsome victory,' he said.

McMahon thanked those who had voted for the government.

Glancing at the paper in his hands, he promised that the Liberal Party would stick to 'our Liberal principles' and give Whitlam 'vigorous opposition whenever we feel that he is taking action which is contrary to the interests of the Australian people'.

Then he departed from the statement. The hand that held the paper fell to his side. 'Above all,' McMahon said, 'I want to thank my own staff who have been driven relentlessly over the last few months and have stuck with me, they've helped me, and they've never wilted under the most heavy and severe oppression.'

The remarks surprised his staff. They were generous and unprompted, and, coming from a man who had read from an autocue throughout the campaign, were surprisingly eloquent. His speech would provide a lingering memory of considerable dignity and grace. 'He showed real true grit,' Davis would say.[103] The sword had fallen, Ian Grigg would later recall, and despite the hurt, what was clear was McMahon's professionalism. 'I was stunned at his calmness and the way that he handled the whole thing,' Grigg said later. '… He stood and said that this is how it would happen; this is how the change of government would take place. I think that was really where all his ministerial background came to the fore. He knew that government had to go on … He was a real professional.'[104] Whitlam would echo the sentiment. McMahon's concession was 'a brief, brave television appearance of memorable charm and grace'.[105]

McMahon made his way through the well-wishers and press to return to the house. After sitting alone, sombre and quiet, McMahon brightened up. His staff had brought champagne in case of a miracle. 'Let's open it,' he said.[106]

It was finished. The election had been lost. McMahon's time in government was over.

CHAPTER FORTY-NINE

As Matters Stand

1984

On 19 June, McMahon called Bowman into his office. Sonia had received a letter from an editor at Macmillan, he said, suggesting that she should write her autobiography. The letter also, McMahon said, inquired how matters stood with her husband's book. Did he have anything? How was it all going?

The letter was but a way for McMahon to complain about his own publisher. He was annoyed at the work that was going into the book, annoyed that Bowman was leaving, and believed that Richard Smart and Collins were not doing enough to help. Bowman told him that he believed Smart was only interested in getting a manuscript: 'He didn't want to be otherwise involved.' Bowman told McMahon that he should commit himself to the material that had been given to him: no more changes, no more rethinking the structure and theme.

The advice fell on deaf ears. 'WM said for the umpteenth time that Smart had said it [the manuscript] needed to be more readable—"easier to read",' Bowman recorded. McMahon could not be dissuaded from his belief that Smart and Collins were at fault, that they were the problem. He told Bowman he would get the editor from Macmillan to come to Sydney for a discussion about his own book.[1]

But the reference to McMahon's book was an invention of McMahon's mind. When Bowman remarked about the letter from Macmillan the next day, Joyce Cawthorn scoffed: 'Oh, the old liar!' She ran from the room and retrieved the letter for Bowman to see. 'There was no final sentence about WM's work – no mention whatsoever!'[2]

It was hard to deny that the work was going poorly. No matter how hard he tried to stick to his plan, and the structure that had been agreed upon before, Bowman was always battling to keep McMahon on track. 'WM does indulge in some extraordinary monologues at times,' he wrote, on 20 June. 'Rambles from one topic to another, misunderstands one's comments—quite mad.'

He was complaining 'bitterly' about the early chapters of the book—again. George Campbell had supposedly done terrible things to the first chapter, but Bowman saw through it: 'Clearly WM is restoring my cuts, and new material ...' McMahon had not hidden his tracks well: only that morning he had given Bowman old material on Billy Hughes, and asked if it should be used. 'I explained that we had retained several Billy Hughes stories, and that readers didn't want to hear all about Hughes but wanted to hear about McMahon.' That convinced McMahon, but Bowman was sure that it would be only momentary: 'No doubt he'll consider it tomorrow as an entirely new problem, and make the opposite decision.'

Then McMahon told Bowman that he had decided he had had enough of his publisher, Richard Smart, and Collins:

> He said he thought it best to get rid of Collins. They had done nothing for him. I said that, like any publisher, they wanted a usable manuscript. However, they could, I felt, have been more helpful with their advice (if they had been frank, he would probably have discarded them anyway!). He proposed to sack them today. He did not see any legal problems.

Bowman did not bother to argue. There was no point. At McMahon's mention of potential legal problems, Bowman went along with him: 'I said that on my knowledge of the dealings with Collins, I didn't either.'[3]

CHAPTER FIFTY

In the Wilderness

1972–1975

Losing the election did not mean that the phone calls stopped. McMahon was up long into the night, telephoning colleagues and officials. When the sun rose on Sunday morning, McMahon was back on the phone. He called Sir John Bunting and Clarence Harders (of the attorney-general's department) to consult about procedures for the change of government.[1] He telephoned the governor-general, Paul Hasluck, to propose a meeting at 11.30am on Tuesday, at which he would tender his resignation and advise that Whitlam be commissioned as prime minister, ostensibly on the Thursday. He was following the precedent set by Chifley in 1949, he said. Hasluck thought the suggestion reasonable, and, with McMahon's agreement, said he would consult Bunting and Harders for further advice.[2] Then McMahon returned to his calls to colleagues within the party.

By the time Phil Davis arrived at the house that morning, McMahon had made enough of these calls to persuade himself of the belief that he still had a future. Told by Davis that he had to quit as leader of the Liberal Party, McMahon surprised him. 'Oh,' he said, 'I've been ringing around and I've still got the numbers.'

Davis was astonished. He and McMahon had discussed the leadership the night before. They had agreed that McMahon would not quit explicitly—he would just not stand when the position was inevitably declared open at the next party meeting. 'It's nicer,' Davis thought. Apparently, however, morning had brought a new idea. Pity prompted Davis to be honest and blunt. 'They're just being nice to you, Mr Mac. Don't do it.' He told McMahon that he had conceded defeat with dignity and grace. But if he stood for the leadership, the end was certain. He would be humiliated.

At this, the defeated prime minister broke into tears. As he left the room, Sonia told Davis to stop. 'That's enough, Phil.'

'I had to tell him,' he said.

'I know, but that's enough.'[3]

More realistic colleagues soon delivered the same message. McMahon resisted, but his vestigial hopes were scattered once Nigel Bowen announced he would stand for the leadership. Knowing that the vote of New South Wales would split between him and Bowen, McMahon gave in. When he called upon Hasluck two days later, he was bitter and the defeat was still sinking in. The loss was not bad, but it was clear enough to overcome any thought of staying on as Liberal Party leader.

'In the course of the conversation he expressed a mixture of disappointment and of relief at the results of the election,' Hasluck recorded. 'He was not sure what he would do about his own future but, later in the conversation, when we discussed the reconstruction of the Liberal Party, he said he "would not be there" at the 1975 election.'

McMahon might well have been disengaging, but anger and resentment were palpable. 'He thought [the defeat] was due to the faults of others and the wickedness of the Labor Party,' wrote Hasluck. McMahon let on that he believed Gorton was organising to retake the leadership. He dismissed the thought of Billy Snedden, Don Chipp, Malcolm Fraser, Phillip Lynch, Andrew Peacock, or Tony Street as successors, saying they were no good. Hasluck's attempts to draw McMahon on the future of the party, and its need for rejuvenation, went nowhere:

> He said that there had been too much disagreement and scheming inside the Liberal Party and mentioned the disappointment and 'disgust' of his wife Sonia at some of the things she had heard said by Liberals. Nigel Bowen was so disgusted with some of them that he talked of resigning from the party. The disloyalty was terrible.[4]

But there was no time for an extensive talk between the two men. Whitlam had not wished to wait until Thursday to meet Hasluck. The prime minister-elect was coming at 12.15pm.

Barely two hours later, Whitlam called McMahon and told him that he would be sworn in as prime minister that afternoon. McMahon was surprised. The counting of votes had not yet finished. Had Whitlam 'consulted the appropriate people'? Whitlam assured McMahon of the legality of his plans, and said he wished to begin enacting his party's agenda. Suddenly aware that his prime ministership would be ended within a few hours, McMahon was gracious. He wished Whitlam luck, and said that he hoped Whitlam would be given a fair go.[5]

At 3.30pm, it was done. Whitlam was prime minister.

THE Liberals moved on quickly. On 20 December, the party held its leadership contest. Staving off Malcolm Fraser, John Gorton, Jim Killen, and Nigel Bowen, Billy Snedden was elected leader; Phillip Lynch emerged as his deputy. The close-fought ballot, and the immediate wrangle over whether Lynch or Anthony should occupy the office space set aside for the deputy leader of the opposition, augured a turbulent time for the Coalition. 'We have no present memory of what it is like to be in opposition,' Snedden admitted.[6]

Blame for that new status was soon allocated. In an influential article published the following January, academic and future minister David Kemp blamed the election loss on a 'failure of leadership' that produced further problems. There were substantial criticisms of McMahon. His 'dismal failure' of a policy speech was 'dull, poorly presented' and so 'crammed full of promises' that it sounded 'like a cynical effort to buy votes'. His 'apparent criticism' of his own ministers was misjudged, and the instability of the party's leadership was an implicit dig at McMahon, who had played such a large part in the white-anting of colleagues.[7]

Over the next twelve months, there were suggestions from all and sundry about what could have been done to prevent the loss. Some offered policy suggestions: Billy Wentworth said that if the Coalition had actually abolished the means test, rather than just promising to, it would have won.[8] Others said that lowering the voting age to eighteen could have done it. For a few, it was a matter of timing: Doug Anthony continued to believe that if they had gone to the election right after the budget, they could have done better.[9] Most echoed Kemp's criticisms, and blamed a failure of leadership. Howard Beale, a veteran of the Menzies government, wrote that McMahon's administrative experience and skill 'were not matched by the magnetic quality necessary to draw men to him and pull the party together'. David Fairbairn was silent for the moment, but had criticisms of McMahon's television performances, public comments, and constant slip-ups. But he also blamed the press: 'Eighty per cent of journalists tend to be Labor—Labor in outlook, anyway.'[10]

Peter Howson agreed with this, but reserved real fire for colleagues he believed were more intent on preserving personal power than staying in government: McMahon, he wrote in his diary, 'fought the campaign without the teamwork that one would normally have expected from Ministers and this was particularly noticeable with the Victorian Ministers, particularly Snedden, Chipp, and Peacock.'[11] But a pseudonymous Liberal favourably compared those MPs to the 'doddering' sixty year-olds re-endorsed in New South Wales, who couldn't possibly appeal to a young electorate.[12] Some blamed infighting with the Country Party; others blamed communication woes.

Most within the party thought that defeat was inevitable. The success of the Labor Party's slogan pervaded this acknowledgement. The Coalition had been in office for twenty-three years, and it was simply time for a change. The government had run out of puff. It had little to offer, particularly in contrast to the energetic and wide-ranging programme of the Labor Party. Whitlam, too, thought it. 'They would have been beaten under anybody,' he had said, on election night. 'It's just too silly for them to blame—or us to thank—Mr McMahon.'[13]

However far-ranging or apt the criticisms, McMahon rarely admitted personal fault. The journalist Ray Aitchison once put it to McMahon that he was an example of the Peter Principle—that he was a successful person who had been promoted just one step further than his competence. McMahon flatly disagreed. 'I instituted a programme of reform legislation and often pushed it through despite great difficulties in the path of it. I did not have much time available to me, but I am proud of what was achieved in that time.'[14] When asked to explain why the government lost, he always returned to the same issues: the disloyalty of colleagues, the wickedness of the ALP, bias in the press. Of all the reasons that Labor had won, he said, 'I believe the first one was disloyalty within our own party.' He targeted the Country Party, too: 'We weren't completely at one.' There were continual invocations of how he had carried the government on his own shoulders. 'Time beat me,' he said. 'I couldn't fit any more into twenty-four hours a day.'[15] If there was a failing he would admit, it was of working too hard. He told Alan Reid that advice to 'think' through his problems, rather than work through them, was sound but unused. 'I couldn't take it because of the rush of events.'[16] His focus on the defeat and evident hurt was such that one journalist was to write that year:

> William McMahon is essentially a lost man, hoping that someone will help lead him out of the wilderness. He spends most of these days in a comfortable, and none too modest, office in the Commonwealth Bank Building in Martin Place, Sydney, and much of his conversation is morbidly concerned with the newspaper-Liberal Party-Labor Party conspiracy that dumped him from office.[17]

McMahon was happy to feed disinformation to journalists wherever it would make him look good, irrespective of what effect it would have on others. In February 1973, an account of the 1972 campaign by journalists Laurie Oakes and David Solomon, entitled *The Making of an Australian Prime Minister*, was published with the claim that a special political steering committee had been appointed by McMahon to look at election planning—but had never met.[18] Nigel Bowen collared Solomon in the opposition lobbies at Parliament House soon afterward, and told him that he and Oakes had held Bowen up to 'hatred, ridicule, and contempt'. Aware that this was the formula used to assert a claim of defamation, Solomon asked what was wrong. Bowen pointed out the claim. 'That is false,' he said. 'You have my permission to ask Sir John Bunting for details of when we met.' Then, Bowen added, 'You should have known better than to believe anything that silly little bugger told you.'[19] Later that year, McMahon told another journalist that the president of the Liberal Party had not agreed with his desire to have a unified, and co-ordinated advertising campaign for the election. Southey did not disagree that such a campaign would have been better, but he had no compunctions about writing to correct McMahon: Southey *had* attempted to have a unified campaign.[20]

Whatever his colleagues thought of the loss, whatever they thought of McMahon's responsibility, was to no effect. Most of them simply thought that his time was past. 'He didn't make much impact and wasn't liked,' Anthony recalled. 'I didn't blame him publicly [for the election loss] but I felt that way.'[21] And now, though he sat at the top table alongside Snedden, Anthony, and Lynch during joint party meetings, McMahon was not a senior figure. Like Gorton, McMahon was on Snedden's frontbench, but unlike Gorton he had no specific portfolio. He had asked for one and one alone; when Snedden refused that choice, McMahon preferred to take nothing. 'I'm not prepared to push it,' McMahon would say later. 'I'm not prepared to try to stake a claim. If I'm not asked, then I'm not interested.'[22] In the face of McMahon's unhappiness, Snedden had to be diplomatic: 'Mr McMahon feels that he would like to be able to be a fatherly figure.'[23]

This was hardly ever going to be the case. McMahon was jaded, unwilling to work for people he blamed and so distrusted. Snedden found him impossible to deal with. 'McMahon did not do his homework sufficiently,' he said later, 'was very impetuous and would state a point of view, be totally committed to it, and then literally within minutes he would change his mind.'[24] The past dominated the party. In meetings of the shadow cabinet, the dislike between McMahon, Snedden, Gorton, and Fraser would always be palpable. Gorton would wait for McMahon to say something and then pick him off.[25] 'There was a three-way artillery match going on, on any issue that cropped up,' said Bowen later. 'It was a waste of time. If McMahon put something forward, first Gorton would snipe at him and then Fraser would snipe at Gorton.'[26] They could all be petty. In October 1973, upon hearing a suggestion that he and McMahon be invested as Companions of Honour together, Gorton reacted sharply. He would not share a ceremony with 'that little lying bastard'.[27]

McMahon was also unwilling to allow any suggestion that his career was over. Throughout 1973, he denied widely circulating rumours that he had canvassed leaving politics after the election defeat. 'Whoever conveyed that information to you,' he said to one journalist, 'could have no knowledge of me at all, none, because I have never expressed that opinion to anyone and I haven't talked about it to anyone else in an in-depth fashion other than to my wife.'[28] Nor would he agree with suggestions that he was finished. He still had a contribution to make, he insisted. He still had skills and talent to use.

But he did have to admit that it was harder now. McMahon made no bones about how tough he found opposition. On his sixty-fifth birthday in February 1973, McMahon had to cancel lunch and dinner to work. For most of his career, he said, he had public servants to help him. 'Now I have to do the work myself, and the effort to do it has been both difficult and enormous.'[29] It stung that he could not simply reach for the telephone as he once had. 'If you get in touch with former friends in the department,' he said, 'they have to say: "Please don't get in touch with me. The repercussions will be too serious." I just keep away from them. You've got to do it all yourself.'[30]

Taking on the Whitlam government was going to be a significant challenge. Its pace of work was immense. Within days of taking office, the so-called 'duumvirate' of Whitlam and Barnard had announced the end of conscription, the release of draft-dodgers, and the dropping of all charges against those who had violated the *National Service Act*. Whitlam and Barnard had decided to give a passport to Wilfred Burchett, to close Australia's embassy in Taipei and establish diplomatic relations with the People's Republic of China, to reverse McMahon government instructions and support imposition of sanctions on the Rhodesian government, most notably in the UN, to re-open the equal-pay case that the McMahon government had opposed, to remove the excise on wine, to end British honours, and to ban racially selected sporting teams from touring Australia. There were additional measures to have the contraceptive pill placed on the National Health Scheme, to offer new grants in the arts and new spending for schools and education, to sign UN covenants on civil, political, economic, social, and cultural rights, and there were plans to institute a royal commission on land rights in the Northern Territory.

The Whitlam government also acted to withdraw the final 128 members of the Australian Army Training Team from Vietnam. This decision led to the popular belief that Australia's military involvement in Vietnam was wound down and completed by Whitlam alone. Whitlam *had* been the one to achieve the final cessation of Australia's involvement, but it had been the McMahon government that had significantly wound down Australia's military presence and terminated a combat role.

It was an example of the way that the legacies of McMahon's time in office would be overshadowed, and even built over. Memory of the establishment of the National Urban and Regional Development Authority would be all but wiped away when Whitlam rebadged it the Cities Commission, and created the Department of Urban and Regional Development; the huge increases in education spending would be overshadowed by even larger increases from the Whitlam government, especially in secondary education; the legislation for Commonwealth involvement in childcare would be superseded by the Whitlam government's expansion of that involvement; the controls against foreign takeovers that McMahon had legislated would allow Whitlam to halt a proposed takeover of manufacturing firm MB John & Hattersley, and to claim credit for protecting Australian companies. Even the poverty enquiry that McMahon had announced in August 1972 would be reshaped and expanded by Whitlam. As Donald Horne was to write, the years before Whitlam might seem to have been an 'interregnum period, rather shapeless, a little silly, not leading anywhere'. But this was false. These were the years of critical change. In terms of objective results, Horne claimed, McMahon had modernised the political agenda, and given voice to the changes underway in Australian society—even if those efforts had been borne of expediency and the need to win an election.

McMahon's efforts to defend his government and his time in office, rather than attacking Labor, could leave him exposed to ridicule and derision, to charges of hypocrisy or bitterness. After Whitlam ended conscription, McMahon publicly said that he regretted not having done the same. When Whitlam transformed the working of ministerial offices by introducing political staffers who could provide advice and challenge that of the public service, McMahon lauded the idea and criticised the efforts of those who had worked for him.[31] In May, while attacking the Whitlam government's Conciliation and Arbitration Bill, McMahon recalled a confrontation with Jim Healy, of the Waterside Workers Federation, when McMahon was minister for labour and national service. McMahon said he had threatened sanctions would be imposed should Healy not ensure industrial peace on the waterfront. 'He did in fact tremble in his shoes,' McMahon said. But Labor pulled up this grandstanding immediately. Healy had been dead for four years at the time McMahon nominated, Labor noted.[32] When the US withheld an invitation for Whitlam to visit the White House, following Whitlam's condemnation of its so-called Christmas bombings of Hanoi and Haiphong, McMahon mocked and provoked him in the House. Whitlam was scornful in response. 'We all remember the "McMann" visit,' he said.[33]

At other times, McMahon's efforts could simply produce incongruous headlines. When, by 1974, Labor's problems with the Treasury department began to make headlines, McMahon was only too happy to offer support—for Labor. Spurred by his experiences dealing with a department that, in his view, was doctrinaire and responsible for the economic downturn that had helped lose him the 1972 election, McMahon went on television to warn Whitlam against accepting Treasury's advice.[34] This was an especially notable *volte-face*. McMahon could also, at times, offer sympathy. 'When I looked at Gough Whitlam after he had become Prime Minister, I saw how fatigued he had become,' McMahon said. 'I knew exactly how he felt and I was sorry for the poor brute.'[35]

Labor could defend itself. It ran attacks on McMahon and his government. The effects of the 1972–73 budget and the government's refusal to revalue the dollar throughout 1972 were, in Whitlam's opinion, a 'baleful legacy'. In Whitlam's view, the decisions taken and not taken led to a gross undervaluation of the dollar, excessive liquidity in the economy, rising unemployment, and inflationary pressures that would come to affect his government profoundly.[36] His task would not be made easier by decisions of the Organisation of the Petroleum Exporting Countries to embargo oil sales to much of the West, cut production and then raise the price. The developments sent economies around the world into shock.

Whitlam's task of managing the government and economy was made no easier by the Liberal and Country parties. They were unfamiliar with opposition, unwilling to unify, and unwilling to respond to the fast-paced, progressive reforms of the Whitlam government with anything but outraged howls. 'We were very rowdy in the opposition,' Snedden later said.[37]

They were outraged by Labor senator and attorney-general Lionel Murphy's decision to 'raid' ASIO offices in Canberra and Melbourne in March 1973, an incident that brought back on to the agenda McMahon's handling of the Sydney Travel Agency bombings in September 1972.[38] They were aghast at plans to abolish fees for university and technical education, to repeal penal sanctions against workers, to introduce universal health insurance, and to reform Australia's electoral law by giving the vote to eighteen-year-olds and reducing the permissible variation in electorates to a maximum of 10 per cent. The government's mid-July decision to implement a 25 per cent cut in tariffs was a sharp shock that prompted outrage, and polls that followed suggested that the Liberal and Country parties had regained enough support to win an election, should one be held.[39] This point was most evidently borne out when the Liberal Party retained Nigel Bowen's marginal seat of Parramatta in a by-election after the former foreign affairs minister resigned to join the New South Wales Court of Appeal.[40]

Elements of the coalition parties regarded the Whitlam government as an aberration, the result of a temporary bout of insanity in the electorate, and advocated as a cure for that insanity the use of radical measures—most notably, the blocking of the government's supply Bills in order to force it to the polls. Snedden held out against this idea for some time, but he maintained the Coalition's obstruction in the Senate, which repeatedly rejected or deferred Whitlam government Bills.

By April 1974, the obstruction was undeniable. Aware that a half-Senate election was necessary within the next few months, Whitlam saw an opportunity to increase the ALP's strength by inducing former DLP leader Vince Gair to accept an appointment as ambassador to Ireland. But the controversial and underhanded attempt to create an extra vacancy at the half-Senate election, which Labor might win, went awry. The Country Party's Queensland premier, Joh Bjelke-Petersen, secured the writs for only five vacancies, not six. The controversy over Gair's appointment and outrage at Whitlam's scheming led Snedden to succumb to internal party pressure, including from McMahon, to block supply. Snedden announced that the Coalition parties would exploit their numerical strength in the Senate and refuse supply until Labor went to an election. 'I think some of them [his colleagues] were in favour of it rather recklessly,' Snedden said later, 'feeling "Let's give the bastards a go, we'll win." You know, let's kick them out. You know, they were gung ho.'[41]

The threat, along with the six Bills languishing in the Senate—Bills that would establish Medibank, Senate representation for the Northern Territory and the ACT, ensure greater equality between electorates, and establish the Petroleum and Minerals Authority—was all the reason Whitlam needed to bring on the election. He went to Hasluck to secure the dissolution of both houses of Parliament, with an election scheduled for 18 May.

McMahon was an enthusiastic proponent of getting rid of the Whitlam government via an early election. As he had said in March, 'It is time—time to think again; time to act; time—a little more than a year later—to give the Australian voter the opportunity to kick out this Labor Government; time to do so before irreparable damage is done to the fabric of the Australian economy and society.' To McMahon, the Labor government was most egregiously offensive in its mishandling of the economy. He accused it of fuelling inflation by failing to restrict the growth of government expenditure. To him, it was obvious that voters would see matters as he did.[42]

They did not. The election saw the Whitlam government returned with 49.3 per cent of the vote, the DLP wiped out in the Senate, and Labor supporters elated.[43] It was the first time that a Labor prime minister had won consecutive terms, and Whitlam claimed that the result was a renewal of the mandate of 1972. But it was an election from which all but the DLP could draw succour. The government had been re-elected, yes—but it did not have control of the Senate; it had lost a minister, in Al Grassby, and its majority in the House had fallen from nine seats to five. Largely the consequence of two new seats that had been added to the House, the Liberal and Country parties could count all these as victories. The ability to draw this kind of conclusion allowed Snedden, the next day, to deny that the government had a mandate.

The Coalition's loss at the 1974 election resulted in McMahon's dismissal from the frontbench. In the wake of the defeat, Snedden recognised that preference could no longer be given to eminences and elders, particularly those who were getting in the way. Therefore, he sacked Gorton, senator Kenneth Anderson, and McMahon. Snedden had had enough of the former prime minister. In addition to urging Snedden to bring on the election, and then disavowing it once it failed,[44] McMahon had made a nuisance of himself. Snedden was sick of having to deal with him. 'He wanted to talk on every issue and was, to put it frankly, a hindrance to the proper progression of consideration of issues,' Snedden recalled.[45]

But, as Snedden later found, sackings invariably result in enemies. McMahon was not impressed by his ignominious removal, and a year later had the satisfaction of watching Snedden also be dispatched. 'There are a lot of people who feel they would like this problem of leadership determined very quickly,' McMahon said.[46] Although Malcolm Fraser was still an object of considerable venom within the Liberal Party, disliked and distrusted for sparking Gorton's downfall, his formidable talent could not be denied. In late 1974, Tony Staley, the Liberal member for the Victorian seat of Chisholm, came to the view that Snedden simply 'should not be Prime Minister', and decided to begin working for Fraser's election in Snedden's place.[47] It took two attempts, but eventually it was successful.[48] McMahon voted for Fraser, and, on 21 March 1975 had the satisfaction of watching an enraged Gorton hurry from the party room to spit at the journalists waiting outside: 'That bastard's got it!'[49]

McMahon was quick to ingratiate himself with his new leader. When Snedden returned to his office following the meeting, McMahon followed soon after. 'Well, that little twirp [sic] McMahon is here asking for Mr Fraser,' Snedden's secretary told him. 'He thinks he is in the office already!'[50]

Fraser, however, had no trust in McMahon whatsoever. Prompted by his experiences working alongside him and suspicions about his honesty, Fraser would not countenance a glorious return for the former prime minister. A position in the shadow cabinet was not in the offing. McMahon stayed on the backbench. 'I don't think he had any future in a senior or leadership role,' said John Howard, who had entered the House as member for Bennelong at the 1974 election.[51] Why was McMahon staying in Parliament, then? Why was he not packing it in, retiring, as he had intimated to Hasluck in 1972?

A faith in the rewards of endurance may have influenced McMahon's refusal to retire. If there was one lesson that his experience gave him, it was surely the value of persistence. He had outlasted Menzies; survived McEwen; prevailed, in the end, over Gorton. Why would it now be any different? Even outside the question of a particular position or role, however, McMahon believed he still had things to give. 'I don't believe that he had in mind that there would be a return to power,' said Robert Ashley, who worked as McMahon's private secretary for two bouts between 1973 and 1975. 'I think his role gave him a platform and public position to achieve what he was looking to achieve ... Sonia would have said to him, "You having something to offer, Bill. Keep at it."'

Nor was McMahon wholly fixed on the past, in Ashley's opinion. McMahon had ideas. 'He didn't slow down. We were always writing something—a speech, an article. There was always something on the boil.' McMahon was still energetic, still hardworking, still demanding, still desirous of being involved. He was always building his knowledge bank, whether through books, articles, briefing papers, or by phone. The days were long, beginning before eight o'clock and usually running until after McMahon went home at seven o'clock. 'The pressure on staff was really quite demanding.'

Moreover, there was a clear public appetite for McMahon's presence. However much colleagues might grumble about him, the party had no hesitation about using him in campaigns. 'There was a serious bit of stardust about Bill and Sonia,' Ashley recalled. 'There was a lot of glamour. He was amazingly friendly with people. So was Sonia. He was an electioneering asset for them, but they were very careful about how they used him.' No doubt the attention—'They need me,' he would frame it—flattered McMahon. Politics, Sonia would say, was his passion: 'What else was he going to do with himself? He didn't have many other interests. He played squash and golf, but he never dwelt on his political defeat.'[52]

Staying ensured that McMahon could continue to assert and protect his legacy. 'He was also looking to put some perspective on his time in office, on saying what was behind his decisions,' recalled Ashley. 'He would challenge any articles. He was always available for television interviews. He was always on *AM*. He always enjoyed exposure.'[53] But there were also, always, clear signs that McMahon was looking forward to the time when he could say everything that he wanted. Once, when it was put to him that his legacy might be more easily defended if he could set out all that had happened—the crises and compromises, the personal animosities and secrets—McMahon simply grinned. 'I'll give my side of it eventually—when I write my memoirs.' *But when would that be?* 'When I feel that the time is right, but not now.'[54]

Ashley was in no doubt about it. Shortly before he returned to work for McMahon in 1974, McMahon moved from his longstanding office in the Commonwealth Bank Building to one at Westfield Towers. The amount of paper that came with him was enough to fill the boardroom 'wall-to-wall'. 'McMahon was determined to write his autobiography,' Ashley recalled. 'Quite anxious to do so, too.'[55]

NO longer being prime minister was, in some ways, a godsend for McMahon. As he was later to say, he was no longer as exhausted as he once was; nor was there so much pressure on him. He could enjoy life with Sonia and their three growing children, largely out of the media spotlight.

It also gave him time to join the Freemasons, the theistic fraternal organisation brought to Australia at the time of the First Fleet.[56] While McMahon did not speak publicly of the decision, it seems to have been prompted by an experience he had as prime minister. Attending a series of lectures organised by Lodge University of Sydney in the Great Hall on 27 August 1971, impressed by the regalia and tradition in evidence, McMahon presented a petition to the Lodge in November 1973 to be initiated as a Freemason. After a ballot in February 1974, he was initiated and passed in the following month. In doing so, McMahon joined a series of former prime ministers who had also been Freemasons: Edmund Barton, George Reid, Joseph Cook, Stanley Bruce, Earle Page. Even his own contemporaries Menzies, Fadden, McEwen, and Gorton were members. 'To have an ex-Prime Minister among our members was a great distinction,' wrote one of McMahon's new peers, 'just as it was to have a man of such mature age and sound judgement seeking to join our assemblies.'[57] Whether it prompted any reconsideration of his religious beliefs is unknown.

In the three years that followed McMahon's loss of office, long-palpable changes in Australia's society were given legislative effect. They exposed gaping fissures on all sides of politics, and foreshadowed how McMahon's beliefs could leave him isolated from his party. The Whitlam government's reform of family law was but one example.

McMahon was a keen participant in and supporter of its changes. 'It is path-breaking in the sense that it introduces liberal principles into family law,' he said.[58] Believing that the government should act to remove the anguish and fear associated with divorce proceedings, McMahon sought to redefine marriage, not as a 'voluntary union entered into for life', but rather a 'union intended to be permanent' that 'should not be dissolved by law unless the marriage ... has irretrievably broken down'.[59] He believed that there should be no demonstration that a marriage was irretrievably broken beyond a twelve-month separation. 'Irretrievable breakdown is a fiction,' he said. 'The real ground is twelve months separation.'[60] Votes on that Bill made for a curious display of the varying attitudes towards marriage: on the bellwether vote, McMahon, Gorton, and Whitlam sat on the same side of the House—opposite Fraser, Keating, and Howard.[61]

Another matter that would draw attention was McMahon's comments on the intelligence community. In August 1974, Whitlam acceded to long-running calls to establish a royal commission on intelligence and security, to be chaired by New South Wales Supreme Court justice Robert Hope. The decision followed a meeting with ASIO's acting director-general that had been prompted by the leaking of an ASIO file on Jim Cairns (who had just displaced Lance Barnard as Labor's deputy leader and thus deputy prime minister). Told, in that meeting, that ASIO had undertaken considerable surveillance of Australian political figures, Whitlam moved to establish a commission into the history, administrative structures, and functions of Australia's national security agencies.

McMahon had gone some way to stoke the issue. In an appearance on Channel 9's *Federal File*, on 23 June 1974, McMahon had let slip the existence of a secret intelligence agency known only to very few: the Australian Secret Intelligence Service (ASIS), also known by the codename M09, which obtained and distributed foreign intelligence about threats to Australian interests in Asia and the Pacific. Asked about the ASIO file on Cairns, McMahon denied having anything to do with it, and criticised ASIO for acting without authority. The law should be changed so that it was accountable, he said. What about the other intelligence arms, his interlocutor asked. 'The JIO and M09,' McMahon replied. 'Yes, I know a fair bit about them too. Particularly

JIO, when I was Minister for Foreign Affairs and Cambodia was on. I had a fair bit of information coming in to me daily about the operations there. But M09 too, again I took a deep interest in ...'[62]

There was, immediately, speculation about what McMahon was referring to, and whether his response had been deliberate.[63] Rob Ashley had no doubt that it was accidental: 'He was a bit concerned about it, how it had slipped out, and he tried very hard to make good.'[64] Whether or not it was accidental, it certainly ensured that the prospect of a royal commission could linger in the public consciousness.

McMahon gave evidence to the Hope commission just under a year later, on 29 May.[65] He pointedly admitted to, and discussed, the utility of intelligence that he received while minister for labour and national service. Believing that the relationship between Harry Bland and Sir Charles Spry (then director-general of ASIO) was central to the sharing of that intelligence, McMahon said it was used to 'pre-empt' moves by militant or communist-controlled unions. 'You would give a warning to the people involved and they would be, to a considerable extent, able to ensure that they could take anticipatory action,' McMahon explained. But in every one of his roles after that, McMahon said, ASIO intelligence was next to useless. 'During the time I was Prime Minister, I became extremely disturbed about the quantity and quality of the information that was coming to me from ASIO.' It was so bad and so little, McMahon said, that sometimes he wondered if the agency even existed.

Telling then director-general Peter Barbour of his regard for ASIO did nothing, McMahon claimed. He recounted how, in the aftermath of the travel-agency bombings in September 1972, he had decided to cut ASIO out of the handling of the investigation. According to McMahon, it was only the police investigation of the first bombing that enabled the truth to emerge that it was far from a deliberate terrorist attack: 'So it was pretty complicated and rather amusing, I felt,' he said.

But McMahon also felt clear anger that he had not been able to air this in the House, in order to dispel suggestions that the government had ignored extremism within the Croatian community. To McMahon, it was merely the latest example of how he had been ignored or unable to speak:

I wasn't given a brief to speak on Vietnam, and yet I was the only person in the government, in the Parliament, who knew of John Kennedy's famous operational order, 24 ot [sic] 34A, when he first committed … to go ahead with further commitment of American advisers and military technicians and experts into North Vietnam [sic]. I was the only one who knew about the operations, the decisive influence, that Governor Averell Harriman had in stopping the Americans from going over the border into North Vietnam … I was the only one who knew anything at all of the mission here of Clark Clifford and Maxwell Taylor and the offer of what they wanted us to do and our refusal to give a battalion so that the Americans could step up efforts and bomb Hanoi and Hai Phong and the industrial centres. I knew more about the Guam doctrine, which was the beginning of our failure, and the end, so far as I was concerned, of a need for participation there [in Vietnam] … And so we too when we accepted the doctrine of privilege sanctuary and gave up the rights of hot pursuit. So I was the only one who knew these things.

He was disappointed he had not been able to speak publicly on these matters, he said, but 'you suffer your disappointments in some anguish, particularly when you know that the others haven't a clue what it is all about'.

And yet McMahon did not appear to have all the clues to hand, either. Confessing that he had first heard of ASIS/M09 through journalist Max Suitch, McMahon said that he had been 'bewildered' by the setup and expense of operating the agency. He called a meeting with Sir John Bunting and Sir Keith Waller, he said, to tell them that it was a waste of money. 'And they laughed,' McMahon said. They 'giggled'. He was shocked. Then they told him that they would prefer he do nothing about it. McMahon accepted the advice, but maintained his annoyance at ASIS. Speaking of the intelligence sent by one ASIS station, McMahon described it as 'bedroom gossip … without any association with the realities of life'. Nor was it intelligence that would have any impact on the government's policy. 'It would have been valueless.'

Asked for his suggestions for reform, McMahon argued that there should not be tenure for ASIO directors-general on grounds that long-established heads of department become 'inbred', 'self-centred', and 'build their own empires'. He illustrated his point with the Treasury and Sir Frederick Wheeler:

> I only agreed to the 1971–72 budget on the basis that if their [Treasury's] estimates turned out to be correct, and I believed they would turn out to be correct, then they would have to give me another budget because I said they were confused with the various types of inflationary pressures, cost pressures, and demand pressures. They gave me an assurance on the third of September when America went off gold and out of Bretton Woods. I got the Reserve Bank and the Treasury together and told them they would have to give me a mini-budget. They both said I was silly but I called another meeting three weeks later and Treasury said I was still wrong. Reserve said I was right. I asked them to give me a mini-budget. It took me until the twenty-first of May [1972] to get it and if you see the correspondence on it and the records of conversation, you would be horrified. So you can't get this inbredness, this self-centredness, this determination to run their own race because nobody else knew what was good or what was right, so I do agree with you.

Towards the end of the session, McMahon said that he had two points to make. The first was on wasted resources. The second, in the event, escaped him. 'The other point I have forgotten, but when I do remember it in the car ...'

'Would you let us know?'

'Yes, I will give you a ring,' McMahon promised.

He would never ease up on his criticism of ASIS and ASIO. He recounted his attempts to abolish ASIS on television in 1977, and again in 1983, when a botched mock-raid by ASIS staff resulted in a second royal commission to be headed (again) by Justice Hope. 'ASIS should have been abolished as a non-feasible part of our intelligence service ten years ago,' McMahon would say. 'It is no use to any government. It is sheer madness to have the leader of the country and his top cabinet ministers kept in the dark by people who believe themselves to be under no obligation to consult or answer to their government.'[66]

CHAPTER FIFTY-ONE

Never

1984

When Bowman handed in a formal note of his resignation on 6 June, McMahon came to his office to discuss it. 'Yes, I accept what you say here,' he said, pointing to the note in his hand, 'but there is a point that isn't here—I spoke with Smart, and twice he said it was just to be made easier to read.'

It was back to the manuscript. For the third time, Bowman recapitulated what he had said about the changed nature of the work: how they had decided to rewrite the manuscript, how the autobiography had become a memoir, how an editing job had become a writing job. McMahon nodded, understood, agreed that this had been discussed already. But it was in one ear and out the other. He was already moving on, ignoring his ghostwriter's advice. He intended to hand over all of the post-Menzies material to his publishers, and leave it to them to sort out, he said. He needed a private secretary, he went on, and left the office, waving the now heavily underlined note and saying as he went, 'Don't you worry, I accept this.'

Soon enough, Campbell was telling Bowman that McMahon was talking about starting all over again, with the original manuscript, as though Bowman had never been there.[1]

McMahon's emphatic belief that everyone had it wrong but him affected all that he did. His book—the way to correct those views, to rebut them—was all-important. Any kind of slight on it was a slight on him, too. On 15 June, he came into the office complaining that Sonia had upset him. While out the night before, Sir Roden Cutler had asked how the work on the autobiography was going. Before he could answer,

Sonia had interrupted: 'Oh, don't ask him about that—he'll never be finished.'[2]

She was right, but he did not want to hear it. McMahon was ready to accept any sign of progress, anything that might seem like the book was getting done. He gave Campbell an old draft of the beginning of the manuscript—potentially the first ever done, in Bowman's opinion—and told him to type it up. Campbell's response was to put in front of him the most recent version by Bowman and ask if he really wanted it replaced. At this, McMahon gave his best about-face: 'He read it and said it was the best so far, and he had never seen it before. He was adamant,' Bowman recorded. 'Never.'[3]

His moods oscillated between indecision and reverie, between pettiness and silliness, between reality and seriousness. When Phillip Lynch died on 19 June, journalists called the office for a comment, and McMahon gave a rare performance. 'From his office,' wrote Bowman, 'float tributes to Lynch. *Man of commonsense ... Never sought the highest office but sought to serve in the national interest ... Very sad ... Deserves to be remembered with gratitude by the people of this country.* All delivered in the most unctuous tones. No hesitation. Constant stream of words.'[4] And then the next day there was the silliness: McMahon 'lolling about in a chair, speaking with a slur, waving two fingers to show Gorton's sexual proclivities' as he imitated Menzies ridiculing the suggestion that Gorton might have gone to Washington as Australia's ambassador in the 1960s.[5]

Inevitably, McMahon was backsliding, forgetting, falling into the belief that all around him were failing him. On 21 June, when George Campbell rang the office to say that he would be late that day, McMahon told Cawthorn to call him back and fire him. He would not be needed, he told her. Cawthorn decided that hiring and firing staff was not her business, and did not tell Campbell.[6] When Campbell returned, McMahon said nothing.

He was jittery, frantic, disconcerted, and obsessed. 'I've got to rush this book through,' he told Cawthorn. 'I've been eighteen months at it!'[7]

But time was slipping away from him. Bowman was leaving, with repeated reminders that it was soon. When his ghostwriter left a note saying that Canberra needed to be informed of his imminent departure, McMahon hurried down to his office. 'Yes, yes, I'll fix that,' he said.

'Unless you can stay for another week?'

Bowman would not countenance it. 'I'm sorry—I've made other arrangements. I'm afraid it's not possible. I'm sorry.'

'No no,' McMahon said, 'that's quite understandable.'[8]

He was in the golden day's decline, tiring and weakening. During one visit to Bowman's office, McMahon's announcement that he hated going out at night prompted the ghostwriter to see something ineffably sad in him. 'He was rather pitiful, [the] poor man,' wrote Bowman.[9]

On Bowman's final day at work, McMahon had him in for a cup of coffee. He told him about his family and an uncle who had married his housekeeper while lying on his deathbed. He told him about a journalist who was always inviting himself over for dinner, and who, when McMahon was prime minister, glowered at him while on a plane trip and told him not to speak with him. 'My job is to cut you down, and there are others in the plane on the same mission.' The long talk was of no use to the book. This was McMahon being nice. So, too, was his invitation, declined, that Bowman join him for a drink after work.[10]

One of the ghostwriter's last acts was to supply a list of publishers and a note to Campbell setting out where the manuscript stood. As of 29 June, there were eight fully drafted chapters completed, he said. They were to be re-drafted and revised as the rest of the book took shape, but, for the moment, they were readable and coherent, shorn of repetition and adhering to accepted fact. There were also a series of sections from the original manuscript that, while polished, did not fit into the structure of the book. A note of resignation permeated Bowman's advice. 'None of this matters much, at this stage anyway,' he wrote, 'because Sir William has taken all the material referred to above, and rewritten it and restored earlier material. I have not seen the outcome.'[11]

Despite his skills and work, his efforts and the trials, Bowman had failed at the basic task of the ghostwriter: to write the book that McMahon was himself unable to write. It was a failing of both his and McMahon's, and, understandably, not one that bothered Bowman. He was finished.

McMahon, however, was not.

CHAPTER FIFTY-TWO

Persistence

1975–1982

The Liberal and Country parties unified under Malcolm Fraser. Driven in no small part by the government's economic woes—including what was, by early 1975, the highest levels of inflation ever known in Australia—the Coalition parties were growing increasingly concerned by the way the country was being governed. Fraser had deferred the prospect of blocking supply unless 'reprehensible circumstances' presented themselves; and yet, inevitably in the months that followed, those circumstances appeared to have arisen.

The key issue was the so-called 'Loans Affair', in which the government sought to raise loans for large infrastructure projects by sourcing money from the Middle East, which was awash in petro-dollars following the surge in oil revenue. A Pakistani money-dealer called Tirath Khemlani promised that he could secure adequate funds, and a meeting of the Executive Council on 13 December authorised minerals and energy minister Rex Connor to seek a loan of up to US$4,000m. This authority was revoked on 7 January 1975, but three weeks later Connor would receive authority to seek US$2,000m. Leaks from the Treasury and press investigations would eventually see Connor's authority revoked once and for all on 20 May, but claims and allegations about the effects of such a loan and payments caused a furore that was further inflamed by revelations, in June, that treasurer and deputy prime minister Jim Cairns had signed a letter promising to pay a brokerage fee for funds raised by an Australian broker. Because it contradicted Cairns' statements in the House about such matters, Whitlam sacked the treasurer.

Whitlam sought to avert the rising press criticism and re-establish his control of matters by calling a special sitting of Parliament and tabling all documents related to the matter. But the ploy was undermined when *The Sydney Morning Herald* obtained copies of telexes between Khemlani and Connor that heavily implied Connor had continued to pursue loans after his authority to do so had been revoked. Whitlam was forced to sack Connor—not for continuing to communicate with Khemlani when his authority had been revoked, but for causing Whitlam to mislead Parliament when he tabled all the documents relating to the loan-raising attempts.

McMahon was scathing about the Whitlam government's conduct. Speaking in June, McMahon ticked off a litany of failures: the Murphy raid on ASIO, the Gair affair, and the way that Whitlam had forced the resignation of Speaker Jim Cope.[1] Not a month later, he was speaking caustically about the Loans Affair. During the special sitting that Whitlam called in July, McMahon compared his record in raising loans overseas with Labor's, and pointed out the importance of maintaining Australia's credit rating:

> What we are arguing about now is the means adopted by the Australian Labor Party to get these loans, that is about those it has treated as agents, the degree of secrecy and the motivation for that secrecy ... The Cairns and Khemlani affairs have made us a laughing stock.[2]

Fear that Australia's reputation was sinking into the mire, as well as an awareness that the government still had at least eighteen months to run until the next (scheduled) election, Fraser announced that the opposition had decided that the threshold of 'reprehensible circumstances' had been met: 'We must use the power vested in us by the Constitution and delay the passage of the government's money Bills through the Senate, until the Parliament goes to the people.'[3]

McMahon was wholly in favour of this decision. As he told students while appearing at the University of New South Wales on 21 October, the opposition had the 'legal power' to stop appropriation Bills, and on moral grounds the time was right for an election. 'We would be wise to reject the appropriation Bills,' he said. 'The present federal government crisis should be put to the vote.' Students at the university were not convinced: between the cheers, some heckled and threw fruit peels at him.[4]

Two days later, McMahon appeared alongside Neville Wran, leader of the opposition in New South Wales, at a meeting at Macquarie University. Understandably, given the intense coverage that the issue was getting, McMahon spoke about the Loans Affair and the opposition decision to block supply. It was a wide-ranging talk. McMahon said that he did not believe the House of Representatives should determine who governed the country, as Whitlam had recently stated. 'My own view is that the people of this country are sovereign,' he said. 'They should be given a vote to decide what government they want ... I want the people to be able to express their views freely and adequately. It's time they were given the chance to do so.' McMahon was dismissive of Khemlani, calling him 'Old rice and monkey nuts,' and he argued that because of the dubious caveat that the government's sought-after loans were only ever to be temporary, there had been a conspiracy to undermine the constitution. Under section 86 of the constitution, that was a criminal offence, he said. After discussing the economy, McMahon emphasised yet again that 'we have to get him [Whitlam] out and let the people judge'.

The first question that he was faced with, however, spurred a deeper explanation of what McMahon thought should *not* happen once supply had been blocked or rejected. Asked to describe the power the governor-general possessed under the constitution to dissolve Parliament, McMahon answered that, per Edmund Barton and Quick and Garran's *Annotated Constitution*, the prerogative rights of the Queen's representative and the demitted powers of the governor-general in council 'can never be executed without the advice of a responsible minister'.[5] There might be room for exceptions, McMahon admitted. Should a governor-general get involved? According to McMahon, the answer was no:

I would be fearful of the exercise of such a power by the governor-general in his own right. It could well involve an appointment to this office, which is part of the constitutional government, for purely political purposes. We don't want this happening ...[6]

McMahon's comments were significant, even if (as he was to say later) 'nobody seemed to care' about what he had said. His comments represented a very public consideration of whether the governor-general, Sir John Kerr, should intervene in the developing stand-off between Whitlam and Fraser. Fraser was apparently confident that Kerr would intervene, if unsure what that intervention would look like. For his part, Kerr, who had been appointed by Whitlam in 1974, was uncertain: he approached Nugget Coombs to ask what action he should take. Coombs told him to make the Senate vote on supply; if it would not, he should 'dismiss either the whole Senate or that part which was due for earliest re-election'.[7] Kerr approached Whitlam to ask if he could seek advice from the High Court, but, after reading advice prepared by the former solicitor-general and current Liberal MP Robert Ellicott, seemed ready to scotch the idea of intervention. 'It's bullshit, isn't it?' he said.[8] Legal and political advice of varying degrees of merit and self-interest was being sent to Kerr: Menzies issued a statement that was then rebutted by the former judge of the Commonwealth Industrial Court, Sir Richard Eggleston; Richard McGarvie, a future governor of Victoria, expressed alarm at the idea of intervening; and advice prepared for the Liberal Party boiled the issue down to one of legality alone, where questions of politics, constitution, and convention were rendered irrelevant.

Whether McMahon was aware that Kerr was looking for advice or alarmed at the prospect that Kerr might make some intervention is unknown; nonetheless, within a fortnight of making the remarks at Macquarie University, he had a copy made and sent to Government House. Rob Ashley, McMahon's private secretary, was asked to take the sealed envelope to the gatehouse at the governor-general's residence. 'They're expecting it,' McMahon said. It was an unusual request. Delivering papers was not one of Ashley's normal duties, nor was it normal to have him take a Commonwealth car. Delivering the envelope could well have been handled by a driver, too. The peculiarity of the request is what caused it to lodge in Ashley's mind. 'When I got there [to Government House],' Ashley said later, 'I jumped out and said, "You're expecting these from Sir William McMahon." And they said, "Yes, we are."'[9]

McMahon would also recall the delivery of that envelope for years.

The governor-general, he would say, had 'acknowledged receipt' of it. Kerr was aware of the counsel it contained. Though it must be noted that McMahon could have altered the effect of that counsel in a covering letter, his remarks were a clear reflection of his long-held beliefs against use of reserve or other powers to dismiss an elected representative. Contrary to what Malcolm Fraser might want, John Kerr might do, and Sir John Peden might once have taught, McMahon believed that the governor-general did not have the power or the constitutional right to dismiss an elected representative in this way.[10] In years to come, he would argue that Parliament should define by statute the ambiguity and potentiality of the use of reserve powers by a governor-general.[11]

But that was what happened. On 11 November, after weeks of escalating tension and back-and-forth between both sides in the Parliament, Kerr dismissed the Whitlam Labor government and appointed Fraser as caretaker prime minister, with an assurance that Fraser would secure the passage of supply and subsequently recommend the dissolution of both Houses of Parliament. Fraser did both, but not before a motion of no confidence was passed by the new Labor opposition that afternoon. Robert Ashley thought it staggering. 'No one can continue in office after that,' he said. McMahon's response was immediate: 'Malcolm Fraser is the only man in Australia who would.'[12] Kerr's subsequent refusal to see the Speaker of the House, and receive the motion of no confidence, was a withdrawal of the power of the House of Representatives. It was, as Jenny Hocking has termed it, the *second* dismissal of the day, even if overshadowed by the drama of the initial dismissal. It was a blow that ensured the Labor Party staggered into the immediate election campaign, due to culminate on 13 December. It was the act that brought Parliament into the greatest disrepute, McMahon would later agree.[13]

That day, as word spread that Kerr had terminated Whitlam's commission and protesters descended on Parliament House, McMahon went outside to watch. He stood on the steps, waving 'gaily' at the shouting crowd, at one point lifting a small child onto his shoulders so the child could see all the action.[14]

But while his colleagues were wholly elated by Whitlam's dismissal and their restoration to government, McMahon had significant reservations. In addition to disagreeing with Kerr's decision to dismiss

Whitlam, he disagreed with Fraser's undertaking to Kerr to refrain from investigating the legality of the loans affair and a criminal pursuit of those involved. McMahon believed that a criminal conspiracy had occurred—and he was determined to pursue it.

Thus, on 14 November, three days after Whitlam was dismissed, McMahon had his staff call the office of the secretary of the Executive Council. They sought information about the minutes, memoranda, and schedules for the Executive Council meeting where the authority to seek the loans had been granted. When those enquiries were deflected, McMahon himself picked up the phone. On 17 November, he spoke with David Reid, the secretary of the Executive Council, about the documents. At first, he was uncertain about the nature, use, and confidentiality of the documents. Reid 'refreshed' his memory. Then McMahon asked Reid to provide him with copies. Reid's refusal, on grounds of propriety, 'disturbed' McMahon:

> He [McMahon] explained that he understood Mr Fraser had given the Governor-General an understanding that the caretaker Government would not initiate a court case against the ministers who participated in the meeting on 13 December 1974 but that he (McMahon) had overcome this problem by arranging for a private person to initiate a civil action against them.[15]

He already had a copy of the minute, McMahon told Reid, but he needed the schedule and memorandum in order to complete the documentation necessary for that court case. If Reid would agree to provide it, McMahon would send a staff member to his home to collect it. Reid was disbelieving. If he, McMahon, were still prime minister, he asked, would he really expect a departmental officer to agree to a request like this?

But McMahon just laughed. If the court case proceeded, he went on to say, the documents would likely be subpoenaed anyway. He rang off. Fifteen minutes later, Reid's phone rang again. It was the QC tasked with preparing the case, ringing to express his disappointment that he was not releasing the documents to McMahon.[16]

That disappointment, however, halted nothing. Three days later, still in the throes of the campaign, solicitor Danny Sankey launched a court

case against Whitlam, Cairns, Murphy, and Connor, accusing them of
offences under the *Crimes Act*. It was a dubious case that would drag
on for years, and while it attracted considerable press attention, and
would come to place pressure on Fraser to go back on his undertaking
with Kerr, there was initially more concern within the government and
bureaucracy about McMahon.

Word of his approach to Reid reached Fraser's ears. He told
McMahon that he was 'not to be involved in any activities designed
to circumvent the guidelines' of caretaker government and Fraser's
undertaking.[17] McMahon reluctantly agreed to follow the order,
confirming it in a subsequent call to Reid on 22 November.[18]

Now the secretary of the attorney-general's department became
involved. Upon reading Reid's notes of the approach, Harders informed
his minister, senator Ivor Greenwood, that McMahon himself might
be guilty of contravening the *Crimes Act*. Inciting a Commonwealth
official to leak material contravened section 7a of the Act when it was
read alongside section 70, Harders wrote; inciting that offence in order
to have others charged with an offence made McMahon's actions even
'more worrying'.[19]

Greenwood met with Fraser on 3 December to let him know of
Harders' concern,[20] which the secretary summed up more formally two
days later:

> On the question of law that has been raised it might be said that the
> approach to Mr Reid [by McMahon] was only a suggestion and that it
> fell short of inciting, by Reid [sic]. However, the dividing line, if there is
> one, must be very faint and the circumstances, looked at as a whole, are
> worrying.[21]

But then there was the election. On 13 December, despite Whitlam's
energetic campaign and the fury directed towards Fraser and Kerr, the
caretaker Liberal-Country Party government was elected in stunning
fashion. Labor lost thirty seats, almost half of its previous total, and
Fraser's power was confirmed with the largest House majority of any
Australian government. The emphatic result underscored Fraser's
refusal to investigate the Loans Affair. 'The people had passed their
judgment,' he said later. 'That was it, so far as I was concerned.'[22]

McMahon's actions, and the potentially serious consequences that could follow from them, were an irritant that needed to be brushed away. So, despite Greenwood's letter advising that '*prima facie*, there has been conduct warranting serious concern,'[23] Fraser declined to pursue it. He delivered the message to McMahon to keep his hands off. The matter was over. McMahon got the message. 'I knew McMahon was running around up to his tricks,' Fraser said later. 'I couldn't control what he did, but I could make damn sure that the government, my government, did not get involved.'[24]

This message rankled with McMahon. Though he observed it, he never agreed with it. In the years that followed, he criticised Fraser about it in the party room. He argued in public for the pursuit of Whitlam, Cairns, Connor, and Murphy. And he cheered when Robert Ellicott, who succeeded Greenwood as attorney-general on 22 December 1975, tried to handle the case unbound by Fraser's undertaking. But throughout it all, Fraser refused to budge. Two years later, in 1977, Ellicott would resign as attorney-general, arguing that Fraser's view—expressed in a cabinet decision on 26 July 1976—prevented him from exercising his duty. In a subsequent newspaper column, McMahon cast Ellicott's resignation in a noble light, and grabbed some of it for himself. The rule of law 'is what Mr Ellicott is fighting for,' he wrote. 'So am I.'[25]

FRASER had no time for McMahon. His distrust of McMahon and dislike for him never went away. 'McMahon had an insatiable ambition,' he would say later. 'He had no sense of value. He wasn't immoral; he was totally amoral.'[26] The two men would repeatedly clash in the years that followed Fraser's assumption of office. In public, McMahon would pay Fraser his due; in private, he was far less effusive, more critical. 'He never lost a desire to be listened to and taken account of,' Howard later said. 'Looking back, I guess he probably was frustrated that his counsel was not sought more frequently.'[27] If there was one point that would cause McMahon to lose his enthusiasm and his energy for political work, it was this. He could not stand to be ignored.

He sought to display his expertise and experience publicly. From 1976 onward, McMahon wrote a fortnightly column for *The Sun* newspaper, dispensing advice and arguments about economics, housing, budgetary measures, uranium, taxation, and other areas of interest. He put forward his own proposals, and criticised his party when they were ignored. 'I presented these policies to the Government in October 1977,' he wrote in March 1978. 'As usual, it is only nibbling at the problem of guaranteeing repayment of [housing] deposits.'[28]

He was needling Fraser. He was restless without a portfolio, and unbound by cabinet solidarity. He had not been accorded the respect he felt he deserved as a former prime minister and party leader. In addition to his columns, he fed questions to Labor. 'On several occasions, in opposition,' Barry Jones recalled, 'the telephone would ring in my office and I would hear the familiar quavering voice: "Bill here. Have you looked at page 3 of the *Age*? What the government is doing is an outrage. At Question Time, why don't you ask Malcolm …"'[29]

Fraser was not unaware of McMahon's disgruntlement. Letters from McMahon expressing this were frequent. 'I refer to your letter of March 5, in which you say that you are disappointed to find that I was receptive to media mischief,' McMahon wrote to Fraser, in 1979. 'Your assumption is incorrect. I seldom rely on hearsay information and did not do so on this occasion.' Fraser knew when not to inflame a situation. 'Don't answer,' his office scrawled on the letter.[30] A few months later, after Tony Staley and Doug Anthony were nominated by Fraser to represent him at functions for migrant communities in Lowe, McMahon wrote to lambast Fraser for ignoring him and the make-up of the electorate:

> It is essential that we sustain the support of the various ethnic groups in Lowe if we are to keep on winning the seat … I can assure you that Mr Staley means nothing to the Italian community in my part of the world … These matters are politically important. The ethnics are emotional and volatile. It is better to let them know that we care for them rather than to send a representative who has little emotional commitment to their cause.[31]

To this, Fraser was diplomatic, not stooping to engage: 'I will keep the points you made very much in mind,' he said.[32] Fraser wanted McMahon gone. Peter Kelly, who returned to work for McMahon in

the wake of the 1975 election as his press secretary, recalled an approach
from treasurer Phillip Lynch, who asked what could be done to stop
McMahon's 'irritating criticism', which was getting on Fraser's nerves:

> I told him the best way was to take his [advice]. He asked me when
> did I think the former Prime Minister would retire and I said there was
> no sign of it and in any event certainly not until he had been awarded
> a knighthood. He [Lynch] said he would see what he could do ...
> Several weeks passed and as I had heard nothing I asked Phillip [Lynch]
> what had happened. With great embarrassment, he said that he had
> had no luck and that Malcolm was adamant [that there was to be] no
> knighthood.

McMahon was eventually knighted, in October 1977—but only
at the insistence of an influential Liberal Party officer, Kelly later
claimed.[33]

Attempts to press a claim for some revival would always go astray.
Fraser would have none of it. When, in 1977, Lynch was forced to
step down from his role amid health problems and allegations of
corruption, there were brief suggestions that McMahon be returned
to the Treasury. He disavowed them, but his heart was not in it. 'I
am not an anxious aspirant for Treasury honours,' he said. 'However,
if I was asked to be Treasurer, and the terms were right, of course I
would accept.'[34] That was never going to happen. Fraser opted to give
a vaulting promotion to a young John Howard, the minister for special
trade negotiations.

But McMahon's future in politics was coming under pressure. His
longtime seat was moving slowly but surely from a reliably Liberal-
voting electorate to one that was much more uncertain. It did not help
that McMahon—still living in Bellevue Hill, maintaining an office
out of the electorate—no longer enjoyed the prestige of a minister, or
the excuses that an absent minister could offer to constituents. As a
seventy-year-old and Father of the House, he could not claim to be a
young up-and-coming member, full of promise.

Thus, in the lead-up to the 1977 election, McMahon faced repeated
challenges to keep hold of his seat. Aware that a mooted redistribution
would have put Lowe into the Labor Party's hands, McMahon had

to beat that back and simultaneously fight a preselection challenge from John Abel, the Liberal member for Evans, whose seat was being abolished.[35] McMahon's Labor opponent at the election, Richard Hall—a former Whitlam staffer—was intent on giving McMahon a scare, and had a public following from his work as an author and journalist. On election night, the scare momentarily appeared to have worked when voting figures suggested that McMahon had lost. McMahon was written off, Alan Wright recalled, in those tense, vital hours. Television and news reporters were telephoning to ask McMahon about conceding. But McMahon dismissed the suggestions, pointing out that results from the vital Strathfield booth had not been counted yet. 'He called it right,' Alan Wright recalled. 'He knew he had won.' McMahon did win the seat—but there was a 3.4 per cent swing against him.[36]

Rumours that McMahon would retire swirled within the Liberal Party and in the seat, encouraged in no small part by McMahon himself. Bruce MacCarthy, who had worked on McMahon's behalf and represented him for years in the electorate, believed that he had an undertaking from McMahon: come the next election, McMahon would announce his intention to retire and endorse MacCarthy as his successor. When MacCarthy and his wife, Leanne, sought to get a home loan, McMahon telephoned the bank manager and made that understanding explicit. 'Why didn't you tell us that your husband was going to be the next member for Lowe?' the bank manager asked Leanne.[37]

But when the question of preselection came up, ahead of the 1980 election, McMahon announced he would re-contest. MacCarthy was shocked. It made little sense. Why did McMahon not retire? As one observer had recalled of Billy Hughes, was it just that McMahon, while bereft of much interest in causes or principles, still preserved an interest in 'the game'?[38]

McMahon later claimed that he had only done so because of fears within the party that Lowe would be lost if he were to retire. 'I wanted to go before the last election,' he would say later, 'but my seniors in the party didn't want that.'[39] For all the party's dislike of and frustration with McMahon, it does seem to have been the case that they acted to ensure McMahon got through without a challenge. 'If it hadn't been arranged,' Alan Wright recalled, 'McMahon would have lost his last preselection.'

McMahon was also considerate of his superannuation. Under changes mooted by Fraser and the minister for finance, Eric Robinson, McMahon's superannuation payouts would have been irreparably harmed should he continue to stay in politics. As he wrote to Fraser in 1980, drafted changes to his retirement benefit would have seen either a $15,802.99 reduction in his annual pension entitlement or a loss of $293,367.92, were he to take it as a lump sum. 'The figures highlight in a dramatic way the unfairness and injustice of the scheme,' he wrote.[40]

He wanted out, he told Robinson a fortnight later, and he wanted a guarantee that he would not be disadvantaged by any future scrutiny of the parliamentary superannuation scheme. 'Bill, I can not give you any details because the only decision taken is that the Act will be looked at,' Robinson told him. Were ministers sympathetic to his situation? McMahon asked. 'Yes, there is an understanding by ministers that the Act has worked against your interests, and a desire for amendments to occur.' Robinson told him that whatever McMahon thought, he should do what he felt was in his best interests.[41]

McMahon agreed to stand. As Alan Wright claimed, Fraser promised in exchange that he would make sure McMahon's pension was unaffected. At the election in October, the government lost twelve seats. The swing against McMahon was 4.1 per cent, just under the national average. Commentating on television that night, he appeared shaken by the result.

BY the end of 1981, McMahon decided that he had had enough. He had been palmed off and ignored for too long. His advice that increases in the sales tax should be offset by lower income-tax rates had gone unheeded in John Howard's spring budget. 'I drafted documents to this effect last February and to my horror, when I thought it had been accepted, it was disowned,' he said. Other measures in the budget horrified him. McMahon blamed the 'far too great' influence of the public service: 'I do not think the government gives enough consideration to the views of people other than bureaucrats'. He reached back to his own time to burnish his criticisms. 'In the time when I was Treasurer and again Prime Minister,' he said, 'I made the decisions together with my parliamentary colleagues. I did not allow the bureaucrats to dominate me or the government.'[42]

Crucially, he felt that Fraser had not lived up to their bargain. He met with the prime minister on 17 December. According to McMahon, the meeting was relatively conciliatory—at least at the beginning. McMahon said that he did not believe Labor would elect Bob Hawke as its leader and that he doubted the government would lose an election in 1983. He criticised Peacock and Snedden. He said he might write a book about Fraser's election to the leadership. He discussed the economy, how it was faltering. He believed Fraser was impressed by what he had to say. Then he told him that he was going to resign. The year had been a lost one, he said. Fraser's government had failed to act wisely on almost everything—financially, economically, taxation, housing. He complained that Fraser and Howard had shut him out of vital discussions. Therefore he would resign.[43]

McMahon announced the decision on 4 January. He repeated his criticism of the 'lost year' of 1981. 'I don't want to have to repeat it,' he told reporters. 'There is no point working your insides out for nothing,' he said. He made a point of noting that it was not *retirement*. It was resignation.[44]

He announced the decision at his home in Drumalbyn Road, Bellevue Hill. He did it in the downstairs sitting room. Sonia sat next to him on the green-and-white divan, her arm in his. Thirty-or-so reporters clustered on the orange, brown, and green armchairs in front of them, separated by a small glass coffee table. Though he had put on a suit for the occasion, the sultry afternoon heat saw McMahon remove his jacket and throw it over the arm of the divan. The end was to be informal and resentful.

He was done with Canberra's bureaucrats, done with Malcolm Fraser, done with the inhibitions of the parliamentary party, he told the press. 'I'd rather be freed from the necessity to continuously work without achieving the objectives I thought were essential ... I would not go on and waste my time there knowing that my opinions were so different to those of the government,' he said.

'I do not believe I could put up with another year like last year. It did not matter what contribution I made or what experience I had, no notice was taken.' Although there were no leadership contenders, he argued that Fraser had to listen more to his backbenchers. 'They are closer to the people and not dominated by bureaucratic opinion.'

McMahon told the reporters that he was looking forward to spending time with his family. 'Darling, I hope you're going to have a better world,' he told Sonia, midway through the press conference. 'I'll even do my best to help you with the kids.'[45]

After forty-five minutes, conscious of the media deadlines, Sonia tugged him outside. For the TV reporters, he repeated his criticisms; for the photographers, he and Sonia posed. He affected nonchalance and relaxation in the flicker and flashes; she smiled and gripped his shoulder tightly. His press secretary handed out bottles of KB for the sweating print journalists.

It was impossible to deny that his timing was painful. The New South Wales Liberals had no money to contest a by-election. The 1.2 per cent margin with which they held the seat would not be enough. Even with a very good candidate, McMahon admitted, they were unlikely to hold it. He would not bet on it himself.[46]

'A loss for the Government would put added strain on Mr Fraser's leadership which could be compounded by any setback the Liberal Party receives in the Victorian State election,' wrote one journalist.[47] Despite suggestions that Sonia stand for the seat, speculation that Neville Wran would make a move to Canberra, or even that a brash young lawyer by the name of Malcolm Turnbull would take it, the candidates remained colourless.[48]

McMahon would not hear of suggestions that he had timed his resignation deliberately to target Fraser. As he recounted, he had been implored to resign repeatedly, only for these to be suddenly contradicted. 'In 1976 I was invited by the wizards in Canberra to resign … After I had received preselection in 1980 I was again invited to retire … After considerable discussion I was asked to contest the election.' The timing would never be great, but he was quite willing to admit that the look on Fraser's face when told of his resignation was 'horrified'.[49]

As ever, he returned to his time as prime minister. 'At the end of 1972 we put up a record that I don't believe has ever been equalled.' Look at unemployment, he said. Unemployment was 88,000 people in October 1972, and the government 'had the five best months we ever had' just before Christmas. Inflation was low, he argued. But there were considerable regrets, he said. 'There were many forces against me and there were many unbelievable problems within my own party. I never had a chance as Prime Minister.'[50]

Everyone would understand soon. Everyone would know what he had done, what he had grappled with. They would be shocked. 'When I publish my autobiography and tell of the things I had to put up with,' he said, 'none of you will believe it.'[51]

CHAPTER FIFTY-THREE

A Liberal View

1984-1988

The work continued. McMahon pressed on. Bowman's departure was not going to dissuade him.[1] He approached other writers, sought assistance, hunted for feedback. But word had spread. The book had become notorious, and there were few who wanted to deal with its misshapen, unpublishable mass.

Those who had been involved believed that there was a remedy. The manuscript, Richard Smart said later, 'will remain unpublished until Sir William allows someone to take it away and knock it into shape.' Even after all the tribulations with Bowman, Smart still saw some commercial potential in the work, thinking that somewhere in the morass of material was a 'bloody good story'.[2] But McMahon's unwillingness to hand over control ensured it was unlikely to be heard any time soon. 'As it was,' Smart said elsewhere, 'it was unpublishable. Sir William would not accept that. To him it was like Moses's slabs, so we couldn't continue with it.'[3]

The contract with Collins was abandoned, with both parties claiming they had walked away. The supposed flare of interest from Macmillan faded quickly once they got wind of the nature of the work. A submission to Angus and Robertson finished with rejection. Another, to the Hutchison Publishing Group, ended the same way: there would be too much work involved to get the manuscript into shape, Hutchison informed McMahon, in July 1985.[4] The University of New South Wales Press was the next to consider the manuscript; they, too, passed.

Throughout it all, McMahon was undeterred. He continued to proclaim that his autobiography would set everything straight, that it was all coming together. 'I have completely finished the writing and only have to make a decision about the photographs,' he said. 'It's absolutely extraordinary what I have done.'

Few believed him. His attempts to write the book, the veritable industry of ghostwriters and assistants who had worked on it, the list of publishers who had read it and backed away—these all began to loom larger than the history he was trying to write. Commentary from previous staff members fuelled the notoriety. While Bowman was restrained, saying only that his six months with McMahon were 'an interesting experience', others were more forthright. Mark Hayne, who had worked for McMahon for three months before resigning with a plea of ill-health in 1983, was cutting:

> I wouldn't have minded if he [McMahon] had wanted to tell lies—that's his right, it's his biography … But I was employed to produce something that was coherent, grammatical, interesting to the reader and, of course, publishable. None of that made any impression on him and I realised I was just wasting my time.[5]

Others were more generous. The journalist Paul LePetit, who worked on the manuscript for more than a year, thought it viable commercially and historically. 'It's a good book and it's a good read,' he said.[6] Yet even he could not see the work brought up to a publishable standard. In 1986, following the surprising success of Jim Killen's memoir, *Killen: inside Australian politics*, the publisher Methuen agreed to consider McMahon's manuscript. No contract was signed, but the publisher managed to extract an agreement that McMahon hand over some editorial control. It was no use: soon enough, Methuen had backed away.

McMahon continued to seek advice and help. Richard Farmer was surprised to receive a phone call from a researcher at the National Library, who told him that she was calling on McMahon's behalf. The former prime minister wished to cite an article in *The Daily Telegraph* in which Farmer had stated that McMahon would have won the 1972 election had it been held two weeks later. 'But,' she went on, 'I've looked everywhere, at everything you wrote, and I can find no record of this. But when I went back and told Mr McMahon that I couldn't find it he said, "No, it's there, you go back ..."' Listening over the phone, Farmer could not help but laugh. He had written no such thing. Never. 'But he [McMahon] had decided that *even* Richard Farmer, the man who had caused him *all* this trouble, had said that he would have won if it had gone on two weeks longer,' Farmer said, later. 'He had totally rewritten history in his mind.'[7]

Phillip Adams also found himself on the receiving end of an approach. Woken in his hotel one evening, Adams endured three bumbling attempts by McMahon's staff to connect a telephone call. Finally, McMahon's shrill pipe came down the line to greet Adams and declare that he wanted help with the book. 'I want you to edit it for me,' McMahon told him.

To Adams' reply that he was not an editor, McMahon begged: 'Please, could you at least read it for me?'

A great pile of paper bound with thick rubber bands was delivered to Adams by courier the next day. Sitting at the end of his hotel bed with the manuscript in front of him, Adams read it through carefully and guiltily. By now, the book had no title. The long sections on Sonia had disappeared. But the writing was poor and the story flat. 'It was really, really bad,' Adams said later.

Not sure how to tell McMahon this, coming up short with advice and feedback that might be useful, Adams sent the manuscript on to Barry Jones. Could Jones advise him on how to respond? he asked.

Jones read the manuscript. As he said later, 'dreadful' was the charitable way to describe it. 'He [McMahon] seemed to suffer from total recall and to feel that every sentence he had uttered deserved to be preserved for all time,' Jones said. 'He had superior analytical skills and a waspish sense of humour, but was completely unable to apply either to himself.'[8]

Then Jones lost the book. Adams had to make a grovelling apology to McMahon for doing so—and that was the end of his relationship with McMahon.[9]

McMahon approached the publisher Corgi and Bantam. Their consideration of the manuscript progressed further than any previous submission: the book went through three readers' reports that variously focused on the story, the structure, and, finally, the political and legal aspects. 'Virtually, we are at the point of making a decision, but we haven't got a contract,' said its managing director. 'It could go either way.'[10] Three months later, Corgi and Bantam had also rejected it.[11]

These were blows, but McMahon persevered. He was not willing to give up. He was not willing to change direction. The book had to come out. It had to be finished.

But reminders of his late age were growing ever more frequent. McMahon's brother, Sam, died in December 1985. Alan Reid died two years later. Colleagues and supporters, too, began to pass away. And while McMahon scrupulously held to his regimen of squash and swimming, his health was suffering. In November 1984, he discovered a lump the size of a fingernail on the outer rim of his left ear. It was removed, and he underwent a dose of radiation therapy. But then doctors realised that the cancer had reappeared, this time behind the ear and inside it. McMahon was told that his ear would have to be removed. 'It was a bit of a shock at first but I quickly became resigned to the operation,' he said.[12] He grew his hair long to disguise its absence, laughed off the jokes and suggestions of self-consciousness, talked of returning to work on the memoirs. Whatever he said publicly, it was clear that such blows took their toll: LePetit, working with McMahon throughout this time, recalled the former prime minister's frustration as his memory continued to fade and his hearing difficulties increased. 'Yet, he continued, as far as possible, to keep to his daily routine: travelling to his office, reading the papers, underlining sections for his staff to file, and keeping in touch with his business affairs,' said LePetit.[13] For his family, this was bravery. 'He was wonderful then, when things were very grim,' said Sonia later.[14]

The quality that characterised much of McMahon's career—a dogged refusal to countenance defeat, a willingness to confront obstacles, an indomitable instinct for survival, of persistence—would not abate. Even at the fag end of 1987, he persisted in his work. He would continue, determined that his memoirs and his views be published.

It was not to be. McMahon would die, of complications due to pneumonia, in his sleep, in the early hours of 31 March 1988. All work on the book would cease. The twenty-seven filing cabinets of papers and files on the nineteenth floor of Westfield Towers would be emptied, packed into boxes, and sent to Canberra. Upon its donation, the McMahon papers would constitute one of the National Library of Australia's largest individual collections, rich and vast—but access to those papers and files would be closed.[15] Drafts of the autobiography would be scattered through the collection. Sonia's own copy would vanish: 'I've mislaid it,' she said, years later.[16] The book, it seemed, would never see the light of day.

It is hard to think that, even had McMahon finished the book, it would have prompted the recognition he so desperately sought. Even had he lived another decade, had he been in the best of health when he wrote, it would have been a fiendishly difficult task. To take his readers back through his life required a sense of history that, for all his first-hand experience, McMahon could not muster. He could not make the past live again. To make his readers understand the unrealised nightmares that had pervaded the 1950s—nightmares of nuclear war, communist revolutions, economic ruin—required an act of historical imagination for which McMahon's storytelling abilities were simply inadequate. To extend that imagination to the 1960s, and through to the 1970s, was too much for McMahon. 'At times *everything* seemed to be changing,' Donald Horne wrote of this period. 'Was it?'[17]

For a man so fixed in his views, seemingly so out of his time, apprehending that change and wrestling it into a convincing book would have been a mighty, mighty task. Most crucially, to show readers the options that were open to him, amid all the daily uncertainties, and have them understand the decisions he made and the actions he took, commendable and disreputable, right and wrong, would have been beyond him. McMahon could not admit fault. Would not admit fault. Rarely even *saw* fault. And that would be crippling. 'Autobiography is only to be trusted when it reveals something disgraceful,' wrote George Orwell. 'A man who gives a good account of himself is probably lying, since any life when viewed from the inside is simply a series of defeats.'[18]

The failure to produce a publishable manuscript, and to see it published, would have a profound effect on McMahon's precarious legacy. His side of the story—the history he witnessed while in the Menzies government, the actions he took under Holt and Gorton, the perspective he might offer as a former prime minister—would remain untold. His opportunity to explain and argue for what he had done, at length, was gone. The potential to salvage his time as prime minister from the dustbin of history was lost. Those who had known him had little doubt that this would be the case. 'Because he led the Liberal-Country Party Government to defeat,' Peter Kelly would write, shortly after McMahon's death, 'he was never given the full credit for the numerous policies that he implemented.'[19] David Fairbairn, speaking at McMahon's memorial service at St Andrew's Cathedral on 8 April, echoed the remarks: 'I believe he was never given full credit for some of the policies which he implemented as prime minister.'[20]

'Death is swallowed up in victory,' the governor-general, Sir Ninian Stephen, read that morning. 'O death, where is thy sting? O grave, where is thy victory?'[21]

The victory would be of the sort that is visited on all men and women. What Henry James described as 'the hand of death' would smooth the folds of McMahon's image, simplifying it, summarising it, making it more typical and general.[22] Within a few years, McMahon would be known in profile form only, as a silhouette cut from the confusion of life, a one-dimensional figure of little consequence or merit. He would become a punchline, a by-word for failure, silliness, ridicule. Historians would concur: he would be entrenched as the worst prime minister Australia had ever had.[23] And where every other prime minister attracted a Boswell, McMahon would be nearly ignored. Only the 'shilling life', as Auden called it, would be told.[24]

Throughout all this, his widow—and, upon her death in 2010, his children Melinda, Julian, and Deborah—would become the keepers of the McMahon flame. 'I'm so proud of him,' Sonia would say. 'In his twenty-one years as a minister, he served with distinction in just about every portfolio and, I believe, was a particularly fine treasurer and prime minister.'[25] The toll of continuing derision was palpable. 'It hurts when someone attacks and ridicules the man you love, questions his achievements and wonders if his life has been largely a lie,' Sonia would say. What his family wanted—for a man who was a husband and father far more than a politician or prime minister—was fairness. 'Bill deserves a fair go,' Sonia told a prospective biographer.[26]

Fairness, however, would mean making a judgement about McMahon—this man who in death became a byword for silliness and treachery, but who in life was a mass of contradictions and change; whose youth was buoyed by wealth and opportunity, but blighted by death and deprivation; whose gaiety and charm gilded a naked ambition and hidden determination; whose absorption of a conservative, upper-class milieu propelled him to the law and then to politics; whose hearing difficulties isolated him but never silenced him; whose desire for advancement compelled him to act nefariously and unconscionably; whose propensity for hard work was almost without equal, yet also aroused jealousy and dislike; whose flaunting of wealth, fashion, and pomp betrayed his almost total lack of self-awareness; whose exercise of power was alternately informed by principle, pragmatism, and pure political expediency; who, holding that power, vacillated between periods of administration, change, and complete inaction; whose desire to hold and extend that power was tenacious, despite the tolls and setbacks; who, through the highs and lows of a long career, survived, endured, persevered where others faltered and gave in; who never stopped believing that one day there would be vindication for all he had done; and who, to the end, persisted in a quest to find recognition for the years he had served, the things he had done, and the battles he had fought, lost, and won.

David Bowman had seen this side of McMahon quite clearly, quite early on. In February 1984, amid a torrid few days of bad moods and forgetfulness, McMahon had asked Bowman to record him practising a speech. Bowman organised it, but later in the day became curious. What was the speech like? How had it gone? He abandoned the manuscript he had been toiling over, retrieved the tape, and listened to an excerpt. What he heard evinced grudging respect.

'His voice was strong, unhesitating. The old warhorse,' Bowman wrote in his diary, 'sniffing the breeze of a battle.'[27]

Acknowledgements

This book was written without the co-operation of the McMahon family, and without access to McMahon's papers, which are held at the National Library of Australia. In light of these absences, this book would not have been possible without the considerable generosity of interviewees, the efforts of staff at archives and libraries across Australia and the United Kingdom, and the contemporaneous work of an array of journalists, biographers, scholars, and historians. The notes that append this work speaks to the debt that I owe to all these people, and the thanks that are their due.

I am grateful to staff of the National Library of Australia (in particular, those staff in the oral history and manuscript reading room sections, and those who maintain the wonderful Trove), the National Archives of Australia, the British National Archives in Kew, London, the Noel Butlin Archives at the Australian National University, the Library at the University of Canberra, and the National Film and Sound Archives in Canberra. Thanks are also due to Bridget Minatel, archivist at Sydney Grammar School, and Karin Brennan, archivist at Sydney University, for their helpful and informative responses to my queries; and to Adam Carr, whose *Psephos* archive is invaluable.

I thank those who helped facilitate this work through advice, interviews, answers to queries, correspondence, and permissions. These include the Hon. John Howard, David Joliffe, Tony Stephens, Dianne Davis, Robert Macklin, Richard Farmer, Bruce MacCarthy, Leanne MacCarthy, the Hon. Sir John Carrick, the Hon. Tom Hughes QC, the Hon. Doug Anthony, David Bowman, Margarita Bowman, Ian Hancock, Richard Smart, Michael Morton-Evans, Prof. Cameron Hazlehurst, Phillip Adams, Sir Eric McClintock, Sir Peter Lawler,

Tony Eggleton, the family of Frederick Osborne, the family of Alan Reid, John Stone, Prof. Jacques E.C. Hyman, Alan Wright, Lorna Wright, Peter Samuel, C.R. 'Kim' Jones, the Hon. Neil Brown QC, Dr David Solomon, Mungo MacCallum, Nicholas Hasluck, Rob Ashley, Bob Bowker, the Sydney Grammar School Archives, the Whiddon Group, Alan Ramsey, Richard Woolcott, Sir Lenox Hewitt, Eric Bogle, Ian Grigg, Jonathan Gaul, Stephen Holt, Reg MacDonald, and Fr Paul Smithers.

I gratefully acknowledge the support of the Centre for Creative and Cultural Research at the University of Canberra, and the Australian Prime Ministers Centre, at the Museum of Australian Democracy. The award of fellowships from both of these institutions was invaluable to the early stages of my research on McMahon. The museum also generously provided funds for the compilation of the index, for which I thank them. In turn, I thank Mei Yen Chua for compiling the index.

This biography was in no small way prompted and encouraged by the award of the 2015 Scribe Nonfiction Prize for Young Writers. I am therefore very grateful for the support and advice offered by Julia Carlomagno, then at Scribe, in response to the proposal for this book. I am also profoundly grateful to Henry Rosenbloom, Scribe's publisher and this book's editor. Henry has generously supported this book, even though it is unlikely to make him any money, and in doing so has given me the benefit of his experience and sharp eye: I thank him.

Professor Tom Sheridan read a draft of chapter eight and offered perceptive comments: I thank him. Professor Matthew Ricketson offered wisdom, encouragement, and guidance throughout this work, proving once again his abundant generosity. Ian Hancock read the manuscript in draft form and provided much encouragement and suggestions. John Nethercote, adjunct professor, Canberra campus, Australian Catholic University, made a significant contribution: he read the manuscript and offered encouragement, valuable comments, suggestions, and corrections.

My siblings and extended family, whose good humour has always sustained me, have been wonderful throughout. My wife, Kate, in putting up with this endeavour over years and several continents, has been my rock: without her, nothing is possible. My parents, for their love and support, have never wavered: thank you.

Appendix

McMahon government cabinet and ministry, 11 March 1971–5 December 1972

Cabinet

Prime Minister	William McMahon
Minister for Trade and Industry	Doug Anthony
Treasurer	Les Bury*
	Billy Snedden**
Minister for Primary Industry	Ian Sinclair
Minister for Health	Jim Forbes*
	Sen. Ivor Greenwood (22 March 1972–2 August 1971)
	Sen. Kenneth Anderson***
Minister for National Development	Reginald Swartz
Minister for Foreign Affairs	William McMahon*
	Les Bury (22 March 1971–2 August 1971)
	Nigel Bowen***
Minister for Defence	John Gorton†
	David Fairbairn††
Postmaster-General; Vice president of the Executive Council; Minister administering the Department of Vice president of the Executive Council (until 30 May 1971)	Alan Hulme
Minister for Shipping and Transport	Peter Nixon
Minister for Labour and National Service	Billy Snedden*
	Phillip Lynch**
Minister for Education and Science	Nigel Bowen*
	David Fairbairn (22 March 1971–20 August 1971)
	Malcolm Fraser†††

Outer Ministry

Minister for Air	Sen. Thomas Drake-Brockman
Minister for Immigration	Phillip Lynch[*] Jim Forbes[**]
Minister for Social Services	William Wentworth
Minister for Works	Sen. Reginald Wright
Minister for Civil Aviation	Sen. Robert Cotton
Minister for Customs and Excise	Don Chipp
Minister for Repatriation and Minister assisting the Minister for Trade and Industry	Rendle Holten
Minister for External Territories	C.E. Barnes[‡] Andrew Peacock[††]
Minister for the Interior	Ralph Hunt
Attorney-General	Tom Hughes[*] Nigel Bowen (22 March 1971–2 August 1971) Sen. Ivor Greenwood[***]
Minister for the Navy	Jim Killen[*] Malcolm Mackay[**]
Minister for Housing	Sen. Annabelle Rankin[*] Kevin Cairns[**]
Minister for the Environment, Aborigines and the Arts, Minister-in-charge of Tourist Activities (from 31 March 1972)	Peter Howson
Minister for Supply	Sen. Kenneth Anderson[†††] Victor Garland[***]
Minister for the Army	Andrew Peacock[§] Robert Katter[††]

Assistant Ministers and Ministers Assisting

Minister in charge of Aboriginal Affairs under the Prime Minister	William Wentworth[§§]
Minister assisting the Prime Minister	Andrew Peacock[§§§]
Assistant Minister assisting the Prime Minister	Don Dobie[†††]
Minister in charge of Tourist Activities under the Minister for Trade and Industry	Sen. Reginald Wright[§§]
Minister assisting the Minister for Trade and Industry	Rendle Holten[†††]
Assisting Minister assisting the Minister for Primary Industry	Robert King[¶]
Assistant Minister assisting the Postmaster-General	Ian Robinson[†††]
Minister assisting the Treasurer	Phillip Lynch[*] Andrew Peacock (27 May 1971–2 February 1972) Victor Garland[¶¶]
Minister assisting the Minister for National Development	Don Chipp[¶¶¶]
Assistant Minister assisting the Minister for Labour and National Service	Tony Street[†††]
Assistant Minister assisting the Minister for Health	Sen. John Marriott[¥]
Assistant Minister assisting the Minister for Civil Aviation	John McLeay[†††]

[*]	until 22 March 1971	[###]	until 2 August 1971
[**]	from 22 March 1971	[§]	until 2 February 1972
[***]	from 2 August 1971	[§§]	until 31 May 1972
[†]	until 13 August 1971	[§§§]	until 27 May 1972
[††]	from 13 August 1971	[¶]	from 5 October 1971
[†††]	from 20 August 1971	[¶¶]	from 21 March 1972
[‡]	until 25 January 1972	[¶¶¶]	from 27 May 1971
[‡‡]	from 2 February 1972	[¥]	from 14 September 1971

Abbreviations

AAEC	Australian Atomic Energy Commission
ABC	Australian Broadcasting Commission
ACP	Australian Consolidated Press
ACT	Australian Capital Territory
ACTU	Australian Council of Trade Unions
AFR	*Australian Financial Review*
AIDC	Australian Industry Development Corporation
AIF	Australian Imperial Force
ALP	Australian Labor Party
AMA	Australian Medical Association
ANU	Australian National University
ANZUS	Australia–New Zealand–United States (Security Treaty)
ARDB	Australian Resources Development Bank
ARU	Australian Rugby Union
ASIA	Australian Stevedoring Industry Authority
ASIO	Australian Security Intelligence Organisation
ATN	Amalgamated Television Networks
AG	Attorney-General
BIG	Basic Industries Group
CAA	Council for Aboriginal Affairs
CHOGM	Commonwealth Heads of Government Meeting
CP	Country Party of Australia
CPD	Commonwealth Parliamentary Debates
CSR	Colonial Sugar Refinery
DLP	Democratic Labor Party
DT	*Daily Telegraph*
GATT	General Agreement on Tariffs and Trade
GCMG	Knight Grand Cross of the Most Distinguished Order of Saint Michael and Saint George
GG	Governor-General
HMAS	Her Majesty's Australian Ship
HoR	House of Representatives
IAEA	International Atomic Energy Agency
ILO	International Labour Organization
IMF	International Monetary Fund

IPEC	Interstate Parcel Express Company
JETRO	Japanese External Trade Organisation
JIO	Joint Intelligence Organisation
LP	Liberal Party of Australia
MiG	Mikoyan-and-Gurevich designed Soviet fighter aircraft
MLA	Member of the Legislative Assembly
MLC	Member of the Legislative Council
MLC	Mutual Life and Citizens' Assurance Co.
MoAD	Museum of Australian Democracy
MP	Member of Parliament
MVD	Russia Ministry of State Security
NAA	National Archives of Australia
NFSA	National Film and Sound Archive
NLA	National Library of Australia
NSW	New South Wales
OECD	Organisation for Economic Co-operation and Development
OPEC	Organisation of Petroleum Exporting Countries
P&O	Peninsular and Oriental Steam Navigation Company
PIR	Pacific Islands Regiment
PM	Prime Minister
PMO	Prime Minister's Office
PNG	Papua New Guinea
PRC	Peoples' Republic of China
QC	Queen's Counsel
RAAF	Royal Australian Air Force
RAN	Royal Australian Navy
ROC	Republic of China (Taiwan)
RSL	Returned Services League
SEATO	Southeast Asia Treaty Organization
Sen.	Senate
SMH	*Sydney Morning Herald*
UAP	United Australia Party
UK	United Kingdom
UN	United Nations
USA	United States of America
USSR	Union of Soviet Socialist Republics
VIP	Very Important Person
WWF	Waterside Workers Federation of Australia

Notes

Chapter 1: End to End

1 With the exception of the 1961 election, Lowe had been a safe Liberal seat for much of McMahon's career. In the late 1970s and early 1980s, however, demographic changes and redistributions had made it far more marginal.

2 Peter Rees, 'McMahon quits in protest', *Sun*, 5 January 1982, p. 2.

3 Reynolds, 2005, pp. 16–17.

4 Reid, 1917; Menzies, 1967, p. 2; Hughes, 1947, p. v.

5 Mark Hayne, 'The autobiography that never was', *SMH*, 11 April 1988, p. 15.

6 Hughes, for example, had written: 'About what was said—and who said it—I shall say nothing, for in the nature of things all was (and as far as I am concerned will remain) highly confidential.' See Hughes, 1947, pp. 153–54.

7 Hugh Crawford, 'My one regret', *Herald*, 5 January 1982, p. 4.

8 ibid.

9 Edited by an uncredited Dale Dowse, Helen Shepherd, and Germanus Pause, the book was published in mid-1972 as a send-up of McMahon and a parody of Mao Tse-Tung's *Little Red Book*. See 'McMahon authors own up', *DT*, 5 October 1972, p. 7.

10 Author's interview with Michael Morton–Evans, 27 September 2016.

11 ibid.

12 Author's interview with Richard Smart, 24 August 2016. Morton-Evans wrote to McMahon on 20 August 1983 to tell him that William Collins was interested in the project.

Chapter 2: Building Character

1 Biographical information on James 'Butty' McMahon is drawn from: 'A Self-Made Man: the story of Mr "Jimmy" McMahon', *ACL*, 1 August 1906, pp. 21–23; 'Death of Mr James McMahon', *SMH*, 18 November 1914, p. 8; 'Carrier King: the life story of Mr James McMahon', *SW*, 10 May 1914, p. 1; *CP*, 19 November 1914, p. 23; 'The late Mr James McMahon', *The Newsletter*, 28 November 1914, p. 4; 'Died last week "Butty" McMahon', *Bulletin*, 26 November 1914, p. 16; and Anthony Norman, 2005, 'McMahon, James (Jimmy) (1838–1914)', *ADB*, supp. vol., Melbourne University Press. See also ADB file on James McMahon, Noel Butlin Archives, ANU, AU ANUA 312–6239. Unless otherwise noted, 'Butty' McMahon quotes are drawn from 'A Self-Made Man: the story of Mr "Jimmy" McMahon', *ACL*, 1 August 1906, pp. 21–23.

2 'Scene at McMahon's yard', *SMH*, 16 September 1890, p. 5.

3   Alan Stewart, 'Oh darlings, said the PM, you'll get me into trouble when your mother comes home', *Herald*, 3 April 1971, pp. 27–28.

4   See birth certificates, New South Wales State Archives: James McMahon (3284/1865), Agnes McMahon (3474/1868), John McMahon (4933/1873), William Daniel McMahon (5295/1875), James Thomas McMahon (5356/1877), Daniel Ernest McMahon (6647/1879), and Patrick Joseph McMahon (6646/1879); '"Smiths's" personalities—no. 102: wants a wharf laborers' tariff', *Smiths Weekly*, 17 May 1920, p. 4.

5   'The late Mr James McMahon', *Newsletter*, 28 November 1914, p. 4.

6   'Death of WD McMahon', *Referee*, 20 October 1926, p. 20.

7   Peter Coleman, 'Bill McMahon: from "Christus Veritas" to the Department of Labour', *Bulletin*, 10 August 1963, p. 17; Oakes and Solomon, 1973, p. 66; and WD McMahon and ME Walder marriage certificate, New South Wales State Archives, 5381/1903.

8   Peter Spearitt, 1990, 'Walder, Sir Samuel Robert (1879–1946)', *ADB*, vol. 12, Melbourne University Press; see also notes from T.D. Mutch, *An Account of the Family of William Walder*, contained in 'Walder, Sir Samuel Robert', *ADB* file, ANUA 312/697, Noel Butlin Archives, Canberra.

9   For information on James McMahon, see 'Death of Mr James McMahon', *SMH*, 18 November 1914, p. 8, and 'Wants a wharf laborers' tariffs', *SW*, 17 May 1920, p. 4; for information on William Daniel's career as a referee, see *Referee*, 11 September 1907, p. 10; *Referee*, 4 August 1909, p. 10; *SSM*, 28 July 1909, p. 2; *Arrow*, 21 August 1909, pp. 2–3; *Arrow*, 20 September 1920, pp. 8–9, and 'Death of WD McMahon', *Referee*, 20 October 1926, p. 20.

10   See the birth (19939/1905) and death (7749/1905) certificates of James McMahon, who lived only two days, in the New South Wales State Archives; and James McMahon's birth certificate, New South Wales State Archives, 38472/1906.

11   For WD McMahon's work as a clerk and admittance as a lawyer, see: WD McMahon and ME Walder marriage certificate, New South Wales State Archives, 5381/1903 and *MDM*, 21 November 1908, p. 4. For his work as a lawyer, see: 'In divorce', *SMH*, 27 May 1924, p. 6; 'Appeal court', *SMH*, 23 February 1924, p. 14; 'Quarter sessions', *SMH*, 23 August 1923, p. 6; '£500 damages', *DE*, 19 October 1921, p. 4; 'Whitehead v. Whitehead', *SMH*, 29 May 1919, p. 5; 'District court', *SMH*, 15 March 1918, p. 4; 'Drysdale v. Drysdale', *SMH*, 30 March 1916, p. 5. For his burgeoning name and reputation, see 'The late Mr James McMahon', *Newsletter*, 28 November 1914, p. 4.

12   William McMahon's birth certificate, New South Wales State Archives, 7911/1908; 'Births', *SMH*, 6 October 1908, p. 12.

13   Samuel McMahon's birth certificate, New South Wales State Archives, 19153/1910; Agnes McMahon's birth certificate, New South Wales State Archives, 32803/1911.

14 Alan Stewart, 'Oh darlings, said the PM, you'll get me into trouble when your mother comes home', *Herald*, 3 April 1971, pp. 27–28.

15 I draw here, in particular, on Horney, 1951.

16 John Edwards, 'Inside Billy McMahon', *AFR*, 31 May 1972, p. 3.

17 'Camperdown: address by Mr Fitzpatrick', *SMH*, 19 November 1913, p. 14; and 'Camperdown: a keen struggle', *SMH*, 22 November 1913, p. 22; 'New South Wales Elections Links: Camperdown—1913 (Roll: 11,469)', *Parliament of New South Wales*.

18 James McMahon's death certificate, New South Wales State Archives, 15004/1914.

19 'Died last week "Butty" McMahon', *Bulletin*, 26 November 1914, p. 16.

20 'New South Wales Elections Links: Darling Harbour—1917 (Roll: 9,685)', *Parliament of New South Wales*.

21 See Mary Ellen Amelia McMahon's death certificate, New South Wales State Archives, 5469/1917.

22 John Edwards, 'Inside Billy McMahon', *AFR*, 31 May 1972, p. 3.

23 Carroll, 1978, p. 151; Oakes and Solomon, 1973, p. 66. There has been much confusion about how old McMahon was when his mother died. For example, Williams draws on Sekuless (in Grattan (ed.), 2001, p. 315) and writes that McMahon was four (2013, p. 154). Fricke (1990) makes the same claim.

24 James McMahon's death certificate, New South Wales State Archives, 24369/1919.

25 Curson and McCracken, 2006, pp. 103–07.

26 'The pains of recovery', *DT*, 4 December 1919, p. 4.

27 'Solicitor Sued: law clerk's action against William McMahon', *Truth*, 8 February 1925, p. 5.

28 John Edwards, 'Inside Billy McMahon', *AFR*, 31 May 1972, p. 3.

29 Abbotsholme College Prospectus, c. 1925, Kur-ring-gai Local History Centre (KLHC); 'Abbotsholme College, Killara: the open-air school', *SM*, 15 December 1920, p. 22; Griffen-Foley, 2000, pp. 25–26; 'At Abbotsholme—boys' healthy life', *EN*, 30 January 1923, p. 4; 'Mr J. Fitzmaurice—death announced—teacher and benefactor', *SMH*, 29 January 1924, p. 8.

30 Griffen-Foley, 2000, pp. 25–26; Frame, 2005a, pp. 4–8.

31 'Abbotsholme College', *Sydney Stock and Station Journal*, 2 January 1920, p. 2.

32 Turney, 1989, pp. 169, 185–86.

33 *The Sydneian*, no. 252, August 1923.

34 Herbert Dettman, 1934, 'Headmaster's report, December 1934', *Trustee's Report*, p. 2.

35 Turney, 1989, p. 175.

36 *The Sydneian 1924–26*, August 1926, Sydney Grammar School, pp. 26–27.

37 ibid.

38 John Edwards, 'Inside Billy McMahon', *AFR*, 31 May 1972, p. 3.

39 'Rowing: head of the river regatta', *Referee*, 21 April 1926, p. 13.

40 *The Sydneian 1924–26*, August 1926, Sydney Grammar School, p. 22.

41 Courlay, in *Sir William McMahon: this is your life*, 12 March 1978, ep. 4/008, NFSA.

42 Baptismal registry, St Vincent de Paul Redfern Catholic Church. McMahon

was baptised by Fr J. McCormack. His godparents were his aunt and uncle, Agnes McMahon and Ernest McMahon.

43   Peter Coleman, 'Bill McMahon: from "Christus Veritas" to the Department of Labour', *Bulletin*, 10 August 1963, p. 17; Robbie Swan, 'McMahon never made the pages of Penthouse', *CT*, 10 April 1988, p. 4. A complete lack of familiarity with the Bible is difficult to credit: Sam McMahon told a story about McMahon accidentally setting off some fireworks while staying with the Blunts in Lucknow, with the upshot that they were sent to church as punishment.

44   Turney, 1989, pp. 10, 189–91.

45   John Edwards, 'Inside Billy McMahon', *AFR*, 31 May 1972, p. 3.

46   Whitington, 1972, pp. 146–47.

47   Peter Coleman, 'Bill McMahon: from "Christus Veritas" to the Department of Labour', *Bulletin*, 10 August 1963, p. 17.

48   Robbie Swan, 'McMahon never made the pages of Penthouse', *CT*, 10 April 1988, p. 4.

49   Peter Coleman, 'Bill McMahon: from "Christus Veritas" to the Department of Labour', *Bulletin*, 10 August 1963, p. 17.

50   Temple, 1925, p. 8.

51   'Civic By-election: reform candidate selected', *SMH*, 11 August 1924, p. 8.

52   This was evident throughout McMahon's life; speeches and clippings make regular reference to his having grown up around prominent politicians. See also Walder to Hughes, 18 November 1941, 'Papers of William Hughes', NLA MS1538, 1/3796.

53   Robbie Swan, 'McMahon never made the pages of Penthouse', *CT*, 10 April 1988, p. 4.

54   William Daniel McMahon's death certificate, New South Wales State Archives, 19201/1926.

Chapter 3: The Ghostwriter

1   Henry Bland, interviewed by Mel Pratt, 1975, NLA Oral History, TRC 121/60, 4:1/182B.

2   Hazlehurst to McMahon, 18 August 1983, copy in the author's possession.

3   Mark Hayne wrote to McMahon on 9 August 1983 confirming he would be a private secretary and 'consultative historian' for McMahon as he worked on the autobiography. On 14 October 1983, however, Hayne resigned, pleading ill-health but writing that he was confident that the book would be published. This was very different from the position Hayne expressed after McMahon's death in 1988.

4   Bowman diary, 16 January 1984.

5   Souter, 1981, pp. 458–59; Bowman, 1988, pp. 128–29.

6   This section draws on notes made by Bowman as he read through the manuscript, which are in the author's possession.

7   Bowman diary, 16 January 1984.

8   ibid., 19 January 1984.

9   ibid., 3 February 1984.

10   ibid., 18 January 1984.

11   ibid., 20 January 1984.

12   ibid., 18 January 1984.

Chapter 4: Shelter and the Law

1   Iremonger, 1970, p. 4.

2   ibid., p. 11.

3   Oakes and Solomon, 1973, pp. 67–68.

4   Whitington, 1972, pp. 146–47.

5   Tess Lawrence, 'I need a good laugh … I can get one out of cartoonists', *Herald*, 22 September 1976, p. 17.

6   *The Pauline*, no. 30, November 1932, p. 15.

7   Sir Richard Kirby, interviewed by Catherine Santamaria, NLA Oral History, TRC 228.

8   *The Pauline*, no. 24, November 1927, p. 16.

9   John Edwards, 'Inside Billy McMahon', *AFR*, 31 May 1972, p. 3.

10 *The Pauline*, no. 30, November 1932, p. 15.

11 ibid., no. 26, November 1928, pp. 4, 36; no. 27, November 1928, p. 4; no. 28, November 1930, pp. 4, 11; no. 29, November 1931, p. 4.

12 ibid., no. 27, November 1929, pp. 8, 44; no. 28, November 1930, p. 9.

13 ibid., no. 30, November 1932, pp. 15–16; no. 26, November 1928, p. 9.

14 ibid., no. 24, November 1927, p. 16.

15 F.C. Huntley in Bavin (ed.), 1940, pp. 142–47.

16 R.O. McGechan in Bavin (ed.), 1940, p. 94.

17 See *Calendar of the University of Sydney for the Year 1930*, 1930, Angus and Robertson, Sydney, pp. 575, 794–95.

18 John M. Ward, 1988, 'Peden, Sir John Beverley (1871–1946)', *ADB*, vol. 11, Melbourne University Press.

19 Cowper, 1946, pp. 64–68.

20 H.V. Evatt in Bavin (ed.), 1940, pp. 34–37; Marr, 1980, pp. 10–11; Hall, 1978, pp. 20–21.

21 Hugh Robson interviewed by John Farquharson, 21 November 2000, NLA Oral History, TRC 4642, p. 95.

22 See *Calendar of the University of Sydney for the Year 1930*, 1930, Angus and Robertson, Sydney, pp. 247–48.

23 Dicey, 1979, p. 433.

24 Marr, 1980, p. 11.

25 Barwick, 1983, p. 85.

26 Tennant, 1970, pp. 32, 35; Judy Mackinolty in Mackinolty and Mackinolty (eds), 1991, p. 73.

27 Evatt, 1936.

28 Kerr, 1978, p. 52. See also Kelly and Bramston, 2015.

29 Ward, in Radi and Spearitt (eds), 1977, pp. 160–78.

30 Bede Nairn, 1983, 'Lang, John Thomas (Jack)(1876–1975)', *ADB*, vol. 9, Melbourne University Press; Foott, 1968; Lang, 1970; Radi and Spearitt (eds), 1977; Nairn, 1986.

31 Foott, 1968, p. 179; Marr, 1980, p. 21.

32 Foott, 1968, p. 198.

33 Peden thought Lang's dismissal was justified on the ground that the governor was the supreme guardian of the constitution.

34 Peter Coleman, 'Bill McMahon: from "Christus Veritas" to the Department of Labour', *Bulletin*, 10 August 1963, p. 18.

35 Mackinolty, in Mackinolty and Mackinolty (eds), 1991, pp. 76–77.

36 Tess Lawrence, 'I need a good laugh … I can get one out of cartoonists', *Herald*, 22 September 1976, p. 17.

37 Martha Rutledge, 2007, 'Cowper, Sir Norman Lethbridge (1896–1987)', *ADB*, vol. 17, Melbourne University Press.

38 Excerpt of McMahon's unpublished autobiography, NLA MS8725, box 97, folder 130/20, pp. 13–21.

39   Lawson, 1995, pp. 36–72; Allen, 1964, pp. 7–32.

40   Peter Coleman, 'Bill McMahon: from "Christus Veritas" to the Department of Labour', *Bulletin*, 10 August 1963, p. 18; Robertson, Hohmann, and Stewart, 2005, pp. 241–75.

41   Norman Cowper in Bavin (ed.), 1940, pp. 148–54.

42   Lawson, 1995, p. 64.

43   John Edwards, 'Inside Billy McMahon', *AFR*, 31 May 1972, p. 3.

44   Arthur Wigram Allen diaries, 13 May 1932, New South Wales State Library, MLMSS 1317, CY2892.

45   See *Calendars of the University of Sydney*, 1929–1933, for the course structure that McMahon would have followed.

46   Griffen-Foley, 1999, pp. 20–24; Griffen-Foley, 2000, pp. 63–84.

47   'Sydney "World" changes to new control!', *NN*, 1 November 1932, p. 1.

48   McMahon, *CPD HoR*, vol. 73, 17 August 1971, pp. 21–26.

49   'Australian company news', *DCN&SL*, 21 December 1932, p. 3; 'Memorandum and articles of association of Sydney Newspapers Limited', John Williamson & Sons, 1933, George Warnecke Papers, New South Wales State Library, MLMSS 8031, Box 1, Folder 6.

50   A former secretary to Clyde Packer, Maisie McMahon was also rumoured to be a former girlfriend of Frank's. She would soon become a journalist, writing stories on beauty and fashion under the name Carolyn Earle. See, for example: Maisie McMahon, 'I was made up by Hollywood's ace cosmetician', *AWW*, 18 October 1941, p. 9, and Maisie McMahon/Carolyn Earle, 'Try for good looks rather than beauty', *AWW*, 30 March 1946, pp. 32–33.

51   'Associated Newspapers Ltd. and The Star', *NN*, 1 December 1932.

52   Arthur Wigram Allen, 14 March 1933, New South Wales State Library, MLMSS 1317, CY2893.

53   *SMH*, 15 April 1939, p. 18.

54   Arthur Wigram Allen, 21 July 1933, New South Wales State Library MLMSS 1317, CY2893.

55   ibid., 28 July 1933.

56   Lawson, 1995, pp. 59–62.

57   Arthur Wigram Allen, 3 April 1939, New South Wales State Library, MLMSS 1317, CY2899.

58   John Edwards, 'Inside Billy McMahon', *AFR*, 31 May 1972, p. 3.

59   *New South Wales Law Almanac for 1940*, 1940, Thomas Henry Tennant, Sydney, p. 98.

60   Arthur Wigram Allen, 3 April 1939, New South Wales State Library, MLMSS 1317, CY2899.

61   Allen, 1964, p. 32.

Chapter 5: The Central Figure

1   Bowman to McMahon, 12 March 1984, copy in the author's possession.

2   As Andrew Crofts writes, this is the core task of a ghostwriter. See Crofts, 2004, p. 109.

3   Bowman diary, 23 January 1984.

4   ibid., 3 February 1984.

5   ibid., 7 February 1984.

6   ibid., 14 February 1984.

7   ibid., 15 February 1984.

8   ibid., 2 February 1984.

9   ibid., 20 February 1984.

10 ibid.

11 ibid.

Chapter 6: A Time of Transformation

1 Lyons, 1965, pp. 265–77; P.R. Hart and C.J. Lloyd, 1986, 'Lyons, Joseph Aloysius (Joe)(1879–1939)', *ADB*, vol. 10, Melbourne University Press; Henderson, 2011.

2 Keith Murdoch to Clive Baillieu, 4 January 1939, Sir Keith Murdoch Papers, NLA MS2823, Box 2, Folder 11.

3 Edwards, 1965, pp. 261–63.

4 Greene, 1969, p. 116.

5 Arthur Wigram Allen, 8 April 1939, New South Wales State Library MLMSS 1317, CY2899.

6 See, for example, Curthoys to Darling, 24 April 1939, in Martin, 1993, pp. 277–78.

7 'Attack on Mr Menzies', *Argus*, 21 April 1939, p. 2. This account draws from the *Argus* because of the considerable evidence that Page, regretting the speech, later had *Hansard* altered to soften his statements.

8 'Attack on Mr Menzies', *Argus*, 21 April 1939, p. 2.

9 Rowland James, *CPD*, vol. 159, 20 April 1939, p. 16.

10 'Attack on Mr Menzies', *Argus*, 21 April 1939, p. 2.

11 Menzies, 1969, pp. 14–15.

12 Menzies to Page, in Martin, 1993, p. 287; and in Edwards, 1965, pp. 270–71.

13 A.B.K.I. Bridge in Bavin (ed.), 1940, p. 95.

14 Sir Richard Kirby interviewed by Catherine Santamaria, NLA Oral History, TRC 228.

15 John Edwards, 'Inside Billy McMahon', *AFR*, 31 May 1972, p. 3.

16 Hasluck, 1952, p. 104.

17 Casey to Page, 19 July 1957, Earle Page papers, NLA, MS 1633, Folder 1773.

18 Day, 2003, pp. 6–7.

19 Popple, 1982, pp. 44–48.

20 Menzies, in Neale (ed.), 1976, pp. 221–26.

21 Excerpt of McMahon's unpublished autobiography, NLA MS8725, box 97, folder 130/20, p. 14.

22 Menzies, in Neale (ed.), 1976, p. 226.

23 Spender, 1972, p. 53.

24 'Extract of record of service', 1 September 1972, 1940–1984, NAA: B883, NX100034.

25 Arthur Wigram Allen, 17 February 1941, New South Wales State Library, MLMSS 1317, CY 2901; and Lawson, 1995, pp. 56–58.

26 'Mobilization Attestation Form', NAA: B883, NX100034.

27 ibid. Oakes and Solomon write that McMahon was injured in the leg while at university, leaving him bed-ridden for six months and bearing a six-inch scar (1973, p. 68). There is no note of such a scar in McMahon's medical records; nonetheless, it is possible that this is the same injury that caused McMahon to be assessed as Class II.

28 Peter Coleman, 'Bill McMahon: from "Christus Veritas" to the Department of Labour', *Bulletin*, 10 August 1963, p. 18.

29 NAA: B883, NX100034.

30 Peter Coleman, 'Bill McMahon: from "Christus Veritas" to the Department of Labour', *Bulletin*, 10 August 1963, p. 18.

31 For an overview of the characteristics of Australian soldiers in World War II, see Johnston, 1996.

32   Martin, 1992, p. 383.

33   Souter, 1988, p. 340.

34   Spender, 1972, p. 165.

35   Hasluck, 1997, p. 31.

36   Fadden, 1969, pp. 65, 68.

37   Hasluck, 1997, p. 82.

38   Souter, 1988, p. 338.

39   Ronald Cross to Lord Cranbourne, 20 January 1942, in Day, 2003, p. 179.

40   Allan Fraser, in Thompson (ed.), 1962, p. 64.

41   Curtin, in Crowley (ed.), 1973, pp. 49–52.

42   *National Geographic*, March 1943, p. 36.

43   Martin, 1993, p. 393.

44   Menzies, 1969, p. 56.

45   'UAP cave formed: 17 send letter to leader', *SMH*, 2 April 1943, p. 4.

46   Holt, 1966, p. 19.

47   Martin, 1993, p. 409.

48   Souter, 1988, p. 356.

49   Peter Coleman, 'Bill McMahon: from "Christus Veritas" to the Department of Labour', *Bulletin*, 10 August 1963, p. 18.

50   Souter, 1988, p. 358.

51   ibid., p. 366.

52   Menzies, 1969, p. 287.

53   Fitzherbert, 2004, pp. 209–43; Henderson, 1994, pp. 61–90; Hancock, 2000, pp. 122–131; Starr (ed.), 1980, pp. 64–107.

54   Menzies, 1969, p. 284.

55   Menzies, in Starr (ed.), 1980, pp. 69–70.

56   Holt, 1969, pp. 45–49; Henderson, 1994, pp. 61–90; Crayton Burns, 'Liberal Party aims to encourage individual initiative', *Argus*, 18 December 1944, p. 3.

57   Menzies, *CPD*, vol. 181, 21 February 1945, p. 19.

58   Souter, 1988, p. 376.

59   Chifley in Crowley (ed.), 1973, p. 129.

60   'DA & QMG', 6 September 1945, and 'NX100034 MAJ W.McMAHON', 11 September 1945, NAA: B883, NX100034.

61   'Appendix to University Calendars for the years 1944–1945–1946–1947–1948; University Examination Results for the years 1943–1944–1945–1946–1947', *University of Sydney*, 1950, A.H. Pettifer, pp. 124, 126.

62   ibid., pp. 208–09.

63   Excerpt of McMahon's unpublished autobiography, NLA MS8725, box 97, folder 130/20, p. 15.

64   ibid. McMahon's 1978 appearance on *This Is Your Life* refers to his having been a patient of Lempert's.

65   Renouf, 1980, p. 28.

66   Alan Renouf, interviewed by Michael Wilson, NLA Oral History, TRC 2981/6.

67   Peter Coleman, 'Bill McMahon: from "Christus Veritas" to the Department of Labour', *Bulletin*, 10 August 1963, p. 18; John Edwards, 'Inside Billy McMahon', *AFR*, 31 May 1972, p. 3.

68   'Australian legislative election of 28 September 1946', *Psephos*, <http://psephos.adam-carr.net/countries/a/australia/1946/1946reps1.txt>, accessed 1 January 2017.

69   Walder's death certificate, New South Wales Registry of Births, Deaths and Marriages, 28656/1946; and Walder's *ADB* file, Noel Butlin Archives, ANU, Canberra, ANUA 312/697.

70   Connell, Sherington, Fletcher, Turney, and Bygott, 1995, pp. 204–06.

71   ibid.

72 'Australian economic history is the major part of all Australian history,' Butlin wrote. See Butlin, 1986.

73 Information provided to the author by University of Sydney Archives.

74 University of Sydney, 'Calendar supplement for the year 1947', Thomas Henry Tennant, p. 424.

75 Arndt, 1985, pp. 12–13.

76 ibid.

77 Souter, 1988, p. 383.

78 *Bank of New South Wales v Commonwealth*, [1948] HCA 7; (1948) 76 CLR 1 (11 August 1948).

79 Crisp, 1963, p. 328.

80 Menzies, *CPD*, vol. 194, 23 October 1947, pp. 1279–91.

81 Marr, 1980, pp. 56–63.

82 Coleman, Cornish, and Drake, 2007, pp. 80–86; Arndt, 1985, p. 18.

83 Arndt, 1985, p. 18; Heinz Arndt interviewed by Peter Coleman, 23 May 1992, NLA Oral History, TRC 2825, p. 88.

84 Francis Bland, 'Criticism of the decision', *SMH*, 18 August 1947, p. 1.

85 Ross Curnow, 1993, 'Bland, Francis Armand (1882–1967)', *ADB*, vol. 13, Melbourne University Press.

86 University of Sydney, 'Calendar supplement for the year 1947', Thomas Henry Tennant, p. 429.

87 Peter Coleman, 'Bill McMahon: from "Christus Veritas" to the Department of Labour', *Bulletin*, 10 August 1963, p. 18.

88 McMahon's student card. Information provided to the author by the University of Sydney Archives.

89 Arndt, 1985, p. 14.

90 McMahon's student card. Information provided to the author by the University of Sydney Archives.

91 Arndt, 1985, p. 14. Arndt also told the story to John Stone, who recalled that McMahon believed he should have received first-class honours and the University Medal. The faculty disagreed on both instances, and McMahon threatened to sue the University to 'have this wrong, righted'. Said Stone: 'He [McMahon] was, of course, personally very wealthy, and the legal costs would not have worried him.' Author's correspondence with John Stone, 6 January 2017.

92 Peter Coleman, 'Bill McMahon: from "Christus Veritas" to the Department of Labour', *Bulletin*, 10 August 1963, p. 18.

93 Hughes, Wilson (ed.), 1976, (audio).

94 Dennis Minogue, 'When the chief is underdog', *Aus.*, 21 October 1972, p. 15.

95 Peter Coleman, 'Bill McMahon: from "Christus Veritas" to the Department of Labour', *Bulletin*, 10 August 1963, p. 17.

Chapter 7: Rumours

1 Bowman diary, 22 February 1984.

2 ibid., 23 February 1984.

3 I. Benedek to McMahon, 27 February 1984, copy in the author's possession.

4 McMahon to Secretary of the Central Army Records Office, 27 February 1984, NAA: B883, NX100034.

5 Bowman diary, 27 February 1984.

6 ibid.

7 ibid., 7 March 1984.

8 ibid., 9 March 1984. Bowman would later write Dame Pattie's obituary

for the London *Daily Telegraph*, and mention this supposed wish. See 'Dame Pattie Menzies', *Daily Telegraph* (London), 31 August 1995, p. 19. For Heather Henderson's (née Menzies) response to this, see Henderson, 2013, p. 213.

Chapter 8: Lowe

1   McMahon, 'Naïve economics', *SMH*, 11 February 1949, p. 2.

2   Souter, 1988, p. 398.

3   'Mission from Moscow', 1948, recording copy held by the University of Melbourne Library.

4   Hancock, 2000, p. 97.

5   Carrick, in Hancock, 2000, p. 107. See also Starr, 2012, pp. 119–50.

6   Hancock, 2000, p. 107.

7   John Kennedy McLaughlin, 1993, 'Cassidy, Sir Jack Evelyn (1893–1975)', *ADB*, vol. 13, Melbourne University Press.

8   This paragraph and the remainder of the section draws on the excerpt of McMahon's unpublished autobiography, NLA MS8725, box 97, folder 130/20, pp. 16–21; Hughes, 1976; and John Edwards, 'Inside Billy McMahon', *AFR*, 31 May 1972, p. 3.

9   McMahon to Hughes, 2, 10, and 19 February 1949, NLA, W.M. Hughes papers, 28/4861, 28/4864, 1/10254.

10 Excerpt of McMahon's unpublished autobiography, NLA MS8725, box 97, folder 130/20, pp. 19–21.

11 These were long-running issues and the Australian Women's National League had a long-running involvement in lobbying on them. See Fitzherbert, in Nethercote (ed.), 2001, pp. 98–112.

12 Hancock, 2007, p. 69.

13 ibid., pp. 68–70, and H.T.E. Holt, 1975, pp. 227–29.

14 Shortland, 'Banking Bill: public's emphatic opposition', *SMH*, 13 August 1948, p. 2.

15 Shortland, 'Dictators on the Air: broadcasting powers', *SMH*, 30 October 1948, p. 2.

16 'Women want "world fit for men to live in"', *SMH*, 17 November 1949, p. 12.

17 'Lady as Liberal Senate candidate', *FA*, 13 May 1949, p. 3.

18 'Woman quits party because of "discrimination"', *SMH*, 18 June 1949, p. 4.

19 ibid.

20 See excerpt of McMahon's unpublished autobiography, NLA MS8725, box 97, folder 130/20, p. 19.

21 'Women want "world fit for men to live in"', *SMH*, 17 November 1949, p. 12.

22 'How women will vote', *Charleville Times*, 20 October 1949, p. 11.

23 Shortland, in 'Women want "world fit for men to live in"', *SMH*, 17 November 1949, p. 12.

24 'Commonwealth of Australia, the Commonwealth of Australia Electoral Act. State of New South Wales. Electoral Division of Lowe', *SMH*, 1 December 1949, p. 17.

25 See excerpt of McMahon's unpublished autobiography, NLA MS8725, box 97, folder 130/20, pp. 19–21.

26 'W.M. Hughes tipped for ballot', *SMH*, 17 March 1949, p. 1.

27 'Lowe: Liberals tip decisive win', *Sun*, 17 November 1949, p. 26.

28 Arndt, 1985, p. 14.

29 Author's interview with Alan Wright, 6 December 2016.

30 Author's interview with Lorna Wright, 6 December 2016.

31 Crisp, 1963, pp. 368–69.

32 Souter, 1988, p. 402.

33 Hancock, 2000, pp. 92–93.

34 Souter, 1988, p. 402.

35 'Boy of nine gives election addresses', *SMH*, 27 November 1949, p. 5; 'Nine-year-old aids Liberals', *Age*, 28 November 1949, p. 3; '9-year-old campaigner makes election speeches', *DM*, 28 November 1949, p. 1.

36 McMahon to Hughes, 27 July 1949, W.M. Hughes Papers, 28/4933, NLA.

37 Dennis Minogue, 'When the chief is underdog', *Aus.*, 21 October 1972, p. 15.

38 Wakeling, in *Sir William McMahon: this is your life*, 12 March 1978, ep. 4/008, NFSA. The same story was told to the author by multiple interviewees. Hancock (2000, p. 302) also puts this story to paper.

39 See 'Commonwealth of Australia Legislative Election of 10 December 1949', *Psephos*, <http://psephos. adam-carr.net/countries/a/ australia/1949/1949repsnsw.txt>, accessed 14 November 2016.

Chapter 9: Gaps

1 Bowman, notes on McMahon's autobiography, undated.

2 ibid., 2 April 1984.

3 ibid., undated.

Chapter 10: Red

1 Cameron, *CPD*, vol. 206, 22 February 1950, pp. 18–19.

2 Governor-General's Speech, *CPD*, vol. 206, 22 February 1950, pp. 6–12.

3 Clive Turnbull, 'Canberra comes to life again', *Argus*, 23 February 1950, p. 1.

4 Holt, 1969, p. 61.

5 McMahon, *CPD*, vol. 206, 2 March 1950, pp. 313–17.

6 Cramer, 1989, p. 124. This was a regular criticism of McMahon, particularly in his early years in politics. See, for example, Anderson, *CPD*, vol. 206, 28 March 1950, pp. 1250–53.

7 See 'M.P. Apologised: Blazer brought "rebuke"', *Sunday Herald*, 21 May 1950, p. 7.

8 McMahon, *CPD*, vol. 206, 28 March 1950, pp. 1245–50.

9 See, for example, Chifley, *CPD*, vol. 207, 20 April 1950, p. 1703.

10 Cowper, 1950, pp. 5–12.

11 Menzies, *CPD*, vol. 207, 27 April 1950, pp. 1994–2007.

12 ibid.

13 Menzies, *CPD*, vol. 207, 9 May 1950, p. 2242.

14 McMahon, *CPD*, vol. 207, 17 May 1950, pp. 2756–59.

15 This draws upon McMahon, *HoR CPD*, vol. 90, 1 October 1974, pp. 1953–54 and vol. 109, 23 May 1978, pp. 2232–34. The story is largely the same in both instances, though it is likely to have been exaggerated or misremembered. Harrison had been appointed to London by the time the Communist Party Dissolution Bill was introduced in 1950, which suggests that it could not have been *that* Bill where this took place. Whenever this incident occurred, the salient point is that McMahon's contributions in the Parliament improved markedly after his first speech.

16   Alan Reid, *DT*, 20 April 1955, p. 11.

17   Alan Reid, 'This politician shuns limelight', *Sun*, 18 July 1950, p. 14. Hal Myers shows McMahon's propensity to ingratiate. See Myers, 1999, p. 106.

18   McMahon, *CPD*, vol. 209, 3 October 1950, pp. 153–57.

19   McMahon, *CPD*, vol. 209, 11 October 1950, p. 591.

20   William McMahon interviewed by John Edwards, NLA Oral History, TRC 168/8.

21   See 'Appointment of Mr Arndt: view of Mr Menzies', *CT*, 27 October 1950, p. 4. After these statements, Sen. Neil O'Sullivan made a statement in the Senate about Menzies' inclinations on this matter; see *CPD*, vol. 210, 31 October 1950, p. 1562.

22   Tennant, 1970, p. 262; Crisp, 1963, pp. 391–97.

23   Souter, 1988, p. 414.

24   Menzies, *CPD*, vol. 212, 13 March 1951, pp. 364–68.

25   Kerr, 1978, pp. 134–35.

26   George Blaikie, 'Who is this Dr. Burton?', *CM*, 19 June 1952, p. 2.

27   'How Burton Quit Post: Spender's accusations', *SMH*, 31 March 1951, p. 1.

28   'Dr. Burton is "untrustworthy", says Harrison', *NN*, 10 April 1951, p. 1.

29   See 'Commonwealth of Australia Legislative Election of 28 April 1951', *Psephos*, <http://psephos. adam-carr.net/countries/a/ Australia/1951/1951repsnsw.text>, accessed 22 July 2016.

30   'Field narrows for final cabinet post', *NS*, 2 June 1951, p. 5.

31   Fred Osborne interviewed by Ron Hurst, NLA, Oral History, TRC

4900/108. The quotes attributed to Osborne in the remainder of this chapter are drawn from this interview. See also Myers, 1998, p. 112. According to Osborne, Menzies later told him that he agreed Osborne had had his throat cut by his colleagues.

32   ibid. See also Jeff Bate, in Evan Whitton, 'Mr Prime Minister: Jeff Bate, MHR, rates the 4 he served under', *DT*, 24 October 1972, p. 8. Bate's claim that McMahon was promoted because of his ingratiating and extensive quotation of Menzies in the Parliament is impossible to confirm. Certainly, in a speech on the Communist Party Dissolution Bill he gave on 3 July, McMahon *did* quote extensively from his prime minister. It is unlikely that such conspicuous flattery would have worked on Menzies.

33   McMahon, *CPD HoR*, vol. 109, 23 May 1978, pp. 2232–34. Following McMahon's promotion, Arndt wrote to congratulate his old student. He seemed to have been undaunted by the political attacks McMahon had made. 'First, I was gratified that one of my students had attained Cabinet rank,' Arndt explained later. 'Second, it was comforting to learn that Mr Menzies was giving preferment to members with qualifications in Economics; and third, while I knew that he [McMahon] had thought my appointment purely political, I was hopeful his would not be purely academic.' (1985, p. 21). McMahon replied with some humour, telling Arndt that his was one of the first congratulatory letters he had opened and that Arndt's 'contribution to

my intellectual development was not negligible'. McMahon said he was glad to be Arndt's first cabinet minister. 'I hope they are not all as difficult as me,' he finished, 'though time does temper one's judgment and makes you tolerant of other's views.' (in Coleman, Cornish, and Drake, 2007, p. 118).

Chapter 11: Disgust

1   Bowman diary, 19 March 1984.

Chapter 12: The Colours of Ambition

1   'New Federal minister', *HM*, 20 July 1951, p. 4, and 'New cabinet minister', *CQH*, 19 July 1951, p. 16.

2   Cabinet notebook, 17 July 1951, NAA: A11099, 1/13.

3   Menzies, *CPD*, vol. 213, 5 July 1951, pp. 1076–81.

4   Tennant, 1970, p. 282. See also Bongiorno, 2013, pp. 54–70.

5   'Dr. Evatt's accusation of "fascist tendencies"', *WA*, 6 September 1951, p. 2.

6   'Labour split on referendum', *CT*, 7 September 1951, p. 4.

7   'Fadden strongly criticises Evatt', *Newcastle Morning Herald and Miners' Advocate*, 11 September 1951, p. 3.

8   'Minister says—confident of "yes" vote', *QT*, 14 September 1951, p. 2.

9   See comments from Menzies, Harrison, and Hughes, in Webb, 1954, p. 157.

10   It is also noteworthy that until this point only four proposals to alter the constitution had succeeded at referendums.

11   O'Neill, 1985, pp. 346–70, 467–77. See also 'Proposal to purchase additional aircraft from the United Kingdom to replace wastage of Meteors of No. 77 Squadron in Korea—decision 105', NAA: A4905, 81.

12   McMahon was among twelve ministers for the navy who held the portfolio as their first ministerial role: Jens Jensen (1915–17), William Laird-Smith (1920–21), Frederick Stewart (1939–40), Archie Cameron (1940), Norman Makin (1941–46), Bill Riordan (1946–49), Charles Davidson (1956–58), John Gorton (1958–63), Fred Chaney, Sr. (1964–66), Don Chipp (1966–68), Jim Killen (1969–71), and Malcolm Mackay (1971–72). This is reflected in the questions asked of McMahon in the House, few of which were troublesome or went to his handling of the portfolio. Some of the questions he received, in fact, were outright ludicrous. See, for example, Alexander Downer's question about whether 'flying saucers' were a novel form of espionage or simply 'an aerial version of the Loch Ness monster'. See, too, his follow-up, where he asked whether McMahon regarded flying saucers as a 'problem for psychologists rather than defence authorities'. McMahon, thankfully, confirmed his belief that it was an issue for psychologists to deal with. See Downer and McMahon, *CPD*, vol. 218, 13 August 1952, p. 223; *CPD HoR*, vol. 2, 20 November 1953, p. 364.

13   Hyslop, 1990, p. ix.

14   Stephens, 1995.

15 'Was caddy a sailor?', *BT*, 4 August 1951, p. 20; Eddie Ward, *CPD*, vol. 214, 2 October 1951, pp. 190–93. McMahon would claim in drafts of his autobiography that there was no caddy, and that he was merely playing a round with three Navy personnel.

16 Reid, 1969, p. 31.

17 Frank Browne, *TIH*, no. 362, 14 January 1954, p. 4.

18 'Lawrie Anderson interviewed by Frank Heimans', Millers Point Oral History Project, <http://www.sydneyoralhistories.com.au/lawrie-anderson/>, accessed 15 September 2016.

19 Author's interview with Alan Wright, 9 December 2016.

20 Stephens, 1995, p. 74. See also James McCarthy, 2007, 'Hardman, Sir James Donald Innes (1899–1982)', *ADB*, vol. 17, Melbourne University Press.

21 McMahon, *CPD*, vol. 214, 11 October 1951, pp. 596–97. For the criticism that followed, see the speeches that followed McMahon's declaration.

22 Jones, 1988, p. 146.

23 'Re-organisation of the RAAF [Royal Australian Air Force]—information submission', NAA: A4905, 578.

24 See the draft minute prepared by the board on 27 November 1951, contained within 'Air Board Agenda 12201–12350', NAA: A4181, vol. 88.

25 Stephens, 1995, p. 75.

26 Air Board Agendum no. 12339, in 'Air Board Agenda 12201–12350', NAA: A4181, vol. 86; Air Board Agendum no. 11988 and 11989, in 'Air Board Agenda 11801–12000 (July–Sep. 1951)', NAA: A4181, vol. 86.

27 Cabinet submission, 'Acquisition of property 'Briarcliffe', Glenbrook, New South Wales, for RAAF', 10 December 1951, NAA: A4940, C2768.

28 Cabinet decision no. 274, 6 December 1951, submission no. 188, and McMahon's own submission: 'Ground control approach equipment for naval aviation—RAN [Royal Australian Air Force—decision 274', NAA: A4905, 112. See also Stephens, 1995, pp. 345–46.

29 Stephens, 1995, pp. 241–42; O'Neill, 1981, pp. 282–83.

30 'Glen Davis cement project', *SMH*, 10 July 1951, p. 4.

31 Ward, *CPD*, vol. 216, 20 February 1952, pp. 144–49. Labor MP Tony Luchetti made similar allegations; see *CPD*, vol. 215, 8 November 1951, pp. 1831–32.

32 Beale, *CPD*, vol. 218, 12 August 1952, pp. 158–59.

33 McMahon, *CPD*, vol. 218, 12 August 1952, pp. 157–58. The report that prompted McMahon to reply was also rebutted by *The Sun*, which inserted, midway through an article containing McMahon's denial, an editor's note that declared Eddie Ward was 'roaming in fantasy'. See 'No suppression, says minister', *Sun*, 12 August 1952, p. 2.

34 For further background, see Steinback, 2001, pp. 19–26; and Wilson, 2003, pp. 15–22.

35 *Australian Constitution*, ch. v, section 116.

36 *Codex Iuris Canonici* (Code of Canon Law), 1917, Canon 1258, cited in Wilson, 2003, p. 17.

37 'Duntroon question solved', *Catholic Weekly*, 18 February 1954, p. 1. Letters and memoranda between the involved parties suggest that McMahon was insisting on the observance of tradition. In his statement to the press, following the work of organising the presentation, McMahon emphasised the 'consecration and presentation' was being 'carried out at the express wish of Her Majesty the Queen, Elizabeth II'. See McMahon's statement, 23 August 1952, in 'Flags—Queen's colour for the RAAF', NAA: A462 828/2/15.

38 McMahon's copy of the programme for proceedings, 'Presentation of the Queen's colour to the Royal Australian Air Force', NAA: A11598/1; McMahon's speech, 17 September 1952, 'Presentation of the Queen's colour to the Royal Australian Air Force', NAA: A11598, 2; 'Queen's colour for RAAF', *SMH*, 18 September 1952, p. 3.

39 McMahon to Commonwealth Bank of Australia, 6 January 1953, NAA: A462, 114/32.

40 'Minister's message to Korea men's relatives', *Truth*, 7 December 1952, p. 4.

41 'McMahon urges big defence review', *SMH*, 16 December 1952, p. 4.

42 McMahon to McEwen, 16 April 1953, NAA: M58, 342.

43 McEwen to McMahon, 8 June 1953, ibid.

44 See, for example, McMahon, *CPD*, vol. 217, 7 May 1952, pp. 81–84.

45 One editor of the *SMH*, for example, thought McMahon 'young and ambitious', 'bright', but also a lightweight. See Pringle, 1973, pp. 86–87.

46 Ward and McMahon, *CPD*, vol. 219, 18 September 1952, p. 1769. *Truth*, a newspaper never particularly friendly towards the Coalition government, perhaps put it rightly when it suggested that 'some people' thought McMahon 'a fop, and an inconsequential political windbag'. See 'Statesmen are needed to lead Australia!', *Truth*, 28 March 1954, p. 9.

47 This paragraph, and the discussion of McMahon's paper, draws from the book produced from that forum. See McMahon, in Davis (ed.), 1954, pp. 29–51.

48 Mannix to Menzies, 12 February 1954, NAA: MS2576, 112.

49 Mannix to Menzies, 16 February 1954, ibid.

50 Cabinet minute, 12 February 1954, 'Without memorandum—ceremony at Duntroon', decision no. 930, NAA: A4909/1, vol. 8.

51 'Catholics fall out of naval rite', *BT*, 18 February 1954, p. 2; '400 "fell out" at rehearsal', *Argus*, 19 February 1954, p. 5; and 'RC's will attend colour ceremony', *CM*, 19 February 1954, p. 5.

52 '400 "fell out" at rehearsal", *Argus*, 19 February 1954, p. 5.

53 Cabinet minute, 18 February 1954, decision no. 946, 'Without memorandum—consecration of colours at Flinders', NAA: A4909/1, vol. 8.

54 Drawn from an undated aide-mémoire composed, it is likely, for McMahon's autobiography, a copy of which is in the author's possession.

55 'Procedure at Naval Base ceremony', *Age*, 20 February 1954, p. 4. McMahon's letter to Gilroy, containing both his press statement and noting Mannix's accession to the new plan, was sent 20 February 1954. Copies may be found in the Sydney Archdiocesan Archives.

56 'Catholics to "fall out" at parade', *SMH*, 20 February 1954, p. 3.

57 'Duke presents colour at naval parade', *Examiner*, 3 March 1954; and 'Duke joked with his old shipmates', *Argus*, 3 March 1954, p. 12.

58 Cabinet had decided the date of the election on 12 February. See cabinet minutes, 12 February 1954, decision no. 932, 'Without memorandum—election', NAA: A4909/1, vol. 8.

59 Menzies, *CPD HoR*, vol. 3, 13 April 1954, pp. 325–26. For the authoritative study of the Petrov affair, see Manne, 2004.

60 'Menzies given attentive hearing', *SMH*, 5 May 1954, p. 3.

61 'Fighting programme', *Advertiser*, 7 May 1954, p. 1.

62 'This "gimme" election', *Sun-Herald*, 16 May 1954, p. 20; 'Evatt policy "ridiculous"', *BT*, 17 May 1954, p. 13; 'Labour "divided" on means test', *Advocate*, 14 May 1954, p. 13.

63 '"Not using" Petrov inquiry evidence', *CM*, 15 May 1954, p. 3; 'Liberals' tour part of long range plan', *Advocate*, 1 May 1954, p. 3.

64 'Gerrymander plan alleged', *Cairns Post*, 6 May 1954, p. 1; 'Fadden speaks of red threat', *Morning Bulletin*, 6 May 1954, p. 1; 'Means test abolition "impracticable"', *CT*,

6 May 1954, p. 1; 'Changing tune on arbitration', *Sun*, 14 May 1954, p. 7; 'Secret ballot guards unions', *Advocate*, 12 May 1954, p. 17; 'Home building, contrast by minister', *Morning Bulletin*, 20 May 1954, p. 9.

65 'Communism must be "destroyed"', *Age*, 18 May 1954, p. 4.

66 There was no swing to or against McMahon in Lowe. See 'Commonwealth of Australia, legislative election of 29 May 1954', *Psephos*, <http://psephos. adam-carr.net/countries/a/ australia/1954/1954repsnsw.txt>, accessed 19 September 2016.

67 'Ultimate reshuffle considered certain', *Age*, 31 May 1954, p. 4, or 'Post-election prospects', *QT*, 12 June 1954, p. 9, for example.

68 Downer, 1982, pp. 19, 32.

69 In his biography of Menzies, Martin (1999, pp. 269–71) makes no mention of an elected ministry, but cites letters suggesting Menzies wished to make radical changes.

70 Harold Cox interviewed by Mel Pratt, NLA Oral History, TRC 121/43, 1:2/77–78.

71 'A reshuffle without reconstruction', *SMH*, 9 July 1954, p. 2.

72 Menzies, *Joint Policy Speech: federal election 1954*, p. 18.

73 McMahon, *CPD HoR*, vol. 5, 23 September 1954, pp. 1587–93; Kewley, 1973, pp. 283–91; Dixon, 1977, pp. 91–101. McMahon continued to obtain rises in pensions while minister for social services; for example see 'Fifth Menzies ministry cabinet decisions', vol. 3, 'Cabinet minute 543, 28 July 1955,' NAA: A4910.

74 McMahon, *CPD HoR*, vol. 5, 23 September 1954, pp. 1587–93.

75 Joske, *CPD HoR*, vol. 5, 29 September 1954, p. 1712.

76 Author's interview with Alan Wright, 6 December 2016.

77 Ward, *CPD HoR*, vol. 4, 26 August 1954, p. 713.

78 McMahon, *CPD HoR*, vol. 5, 21 October 1954, pp. 2200–04.

79 Haylen, *CPD HoR*, vol. 5, 28 October 1954, p. 2439.

80 Calwell and McMahon, *CPD HoR*, vol. 5, 28 October 1954, p. 2488.

81 McMahon, *CPD HoR*, vol. 5, 3 November 1954, pp. 2553–56.

82 Menzies, 1970, p. 124.

83 Haylen, *CPD HoR*, vol. 5, 11 November 1954, pp. 2876–81.

84 Kewley, 1973, pp. 312–25; M.A. Jones, 1983, pp. 262–63.

85 See, for example, Gough Whitlam's question to McMahon's successor as minister for social services, Hugh Roberton, asking if he intended to continue McMahon's practice of handing over cheques in person, with great ceremony and publicity. See *CPD HoR*, vol. 9, 20 March 1956, p. 906.

86 Browne, 1981, p. 63.

87 Daly, 1977, p. 128.

88 McMahon and Evatt, *CPD HoR*, vol. 8, 19 October 1955, pp. 1697–98.

89 Menzies to Henderson, 31 October 1955, NLA, MS4936/40/572/2.

90 'Commonwealth of Australia Legislative Election of 10 December 1955', *Psephos*, <http://psephos.adam-carr.net/countries/a/australia/1955/1955repsnsw.txt>, accessed 20 September 2016.

91 McMahon to Menzies, 11 August 1955, NAA: MS2576, 2.

Chapter 13: The Undoctored Incident

1 Bowman diary, 5 March 1984.

2 Bowman's annotation on excerpt of unpublished autobiography, NLA MS8725, box 97, folder 130/20, p. 14.

3 Bowman diary, 28 February 1984.

4 ibid., 20 February 1984.

5 Bowman to McMahon, 21 February 1984, copy in the author's possession.

6 Bowman diary, 21 February 1984.

7 Handwritten and undated notes authored by McMahon; untitled chapter from McMahon's autobiography, in the author's possession.

8 Menzies to McMahon, undated, NAA: M2576, 2, p. 4.

9 'A-bomb jet fleet may guard north', *Argus*, 15 March 1954, p. 7.

10 McMahon to Menzies, 15 March 1954, NAA: M2576, 2, p. 3.

11 Menzies to McMahon, undated, NAA: M2576, 2, p. 1.

12 Bowman diary, 5 April 1984.

13 Menzies claimed that it was his own measure, prompted at the urging of his wife. Dame Pattie, in the company of Keith and Elizabeth Wilson, had visited homes for the elderly in South Australia and wondered why the Commonwealth government was not helping to provide similar homes. See Joske, 1979, p. 28.

Chapter 14: Control

1 Schedvin, 2008, pp. 133–40; McEwen, 1983, p. 49. Golding questions the story of the creation of the new department, and McEwen's role in shaping it: see Golding, 1996,

pp. 178–79. McMahon later claimed to have had an instrumental role in both McEwen's decision to take on the Department of Trade and in the department's formation. See McMahon, *CPD HoR*, vol. 120, 25 November 1980, pp. 32–33.

2   McEwen, 1983, p. 49.

3   Harold Cox interviewed by Mel Pratt, NLA Oral History, TRC 121/43, 1:2/78.

4   Calwell, *CPD HoR*, vol. 9, 15 February 1956, p. 41. See also Reid, 1969, pp. 31–35.

5   Daly, *CPD HoR*, vol. 16, 19 September 1957, pp. 857–63. Menzies had a habit of appointing ministers to portfolios with which they were not necessarily best acquainted. For criticism, see Frank Browne, *TIH*, no. 462, 26 January 1956, p. 3.

6   Robinson, *CPD HoR*, vol. 160, 12 April 1988, p. 1410.

7   See McMahon to Menzies, 11 August 1955 and 29 September 1955, NAA: M2576, 2.

8   Cabinet notebook, NAA: A11099, 1/19.

9   McMahon, 'Aide-mémoire: short history of difficulties with Mr McEwen', 9 November 1967, NAA: MS3787, 32.

10   McMahon, *CPD HoR*, vol. 120, 25 November 1980, pp. 32–33.

11   Golding, 1996, p. 180.

12   This section draws on a series of unpublished and undated aide-mémoires authored by McMahon, copies of which are in the author's possession. The accuracy of information in these aide-mémoires is uncertain, and their reliability is subject to considerable caveats.

13   McMahon, 'Aide-mémoire: short history of difficulties with Mr McEwen', 9 November 1967, NAA: MS3787, 32. A copy of the above aide-mémoire is in the author's possession; however, this is a photocopy of another copy, and it bears annotations in McMahon's hand. In those annotations, McMahon attributes Menzies' decision to include Hasluck in cabinet to Harrison's influence. This is doubtful.

14   Frank Crean, *CPD HoR*, vol. 9, 15 February 1956, pp. 47–48.

15   Frank Browne, *TIH*, no. 460, 12 January 1956.

16   Martin, 1999, p. 318.

17   Reid, 1969, p. 33.

18   Myers, 1999, p. 158.

19   Hill, 2010, p. 160.

20   Fred Osbourne interviewed by Ron Hurst, NLA, Oral TRC 4900/108.

21   McMahon, *CPD HoR*, vol. 120, 25 November 1980, pp. 32–33.

22   McMahon, 9 November 1967, NAA: MS3787, 32.

23   ibid.

24   Drawn from an undated aide-mémoire composed by McMahon, a copy of which is in the author's possession. The Dorothy Dixer was from Alexander Downer. See *CPD HoR*, 10 April 1956, vol. 9, p. 1122.

25   Leslie and McMahon, *CPD HoR*, vol. 10, 2 May 1956, p. 1639.

26   McEwen, 1983, p. 45.

27   McMahon, 1956, 'Cabinet submission no. 215: dairy industry stabilisation plan—assessment of imputed costs', Sixth Menzies Ministry Cabinet Submissions, vol. 10, NAA: A4926.

28 McMahon, 'Cabinet submission no. 216: dairy industry stabilisation plan—bounty arrangements for 1956/57', Sixth Menzies Ministry Cabinet Submissions, vol. 10, NAA: A4926.

29 Cabinet minutes 281 and 282, 20 June 1956, in Sixth Menzies Ministry Submissions, vol. 10, NAA: A4926.

30 Martin, 1999, p. 330.

31 Hudson, 1989, p. 55.

32 Cabinet notebook, 'Notetaker EJ Bunting—notes of meetings 7 February 1956–7 August 1956', NAA: A11099 1/33.

33 ibid.

34 Stan Correy, 'The Suez Crisis 1956', ABC Background briefing, 24 September 2006.

35 Beale, 1977, pp. 91–92.

36 Menzies, 1967, p. 158.

37 ibid.

38 Stan Correy, 'The Suez Crisis 1956', ABC Background briefing, 24 September 2006.

39 George Kerr, 1956, 'Menzies, sadder and wiser, is due home today', Argus, 18 September, p. 4.

40 Martin, 1999, p. 340.

41 Crawford (ed.), 1968, p. 211.

42 Anderson, 1956, p. 6.

43 McEwen, 1983, p. 52.

44 ibid., p. 53.

45 Crawford (ed.), 1968, p. 343.

46 'New Agreement on UK trade', CT, 13 November 1956, p. 1.

47 McMahon, 9 November 1967, NAA: MS3787, 32.

48 Golding, 1996, p. 182.

49 Author's interview with Sir Eric McClintock, 28 October 2016.

50 McMahon, 9 November 1967, NAA: MS3787, 32.

51 ibid.

52 Cabinet notebook, 'Notetaker EJ Bunting—notes of meetings 9 August 1956–19 February 1957', NAA: 11099, 1/34, 16 January 1957.

53 'Submission no. 576: dairy industry stabilisation', Sixth Menzies Ministry Cabinet Submissions, vol. 23, NAA: A4926.

54 McMahon, CPD HoR, vol. 15, 15 May 1957, pp. 1412–15.

55 McMahon, CPD HoR, vol. 15, 22 May 1957, pp. 1752–54.

56 'Submission 491: funds for wool research and extension', Sixth Menzies Ministry Cabinet Submissions, vol. 20, NAA: A4926. See cabinet minute no. 597, 18 December 1956, for cabinet's approval.

57 McMahon, CPD HoR, vol. 15, 14 May 1957, pp. 1335–39.

58 McMahon, CPD HoR, vol. 21, 30 September 1958, pp. 1747–53; Muller, 1996, pp. 1–20.

59 Frank Browne, TIH, vol. 562, 30 January 1958.

60 Marr, 1980, p. 137.

61 Kelly and Bramston, 2015, pp. 60–61 (which draws from 'John Kerr Oral History Interview, 1974–76' NLA Oral History, TRC 440, pp. 157–60); McClelland, 1991, p. 206.

62 'Menzies asks for "vote of confidence" in record', SMH, 30 October 1958, p. 1.

63 Journalist Ray Aitchison would later note that McMahon was an early recogniser of the value of a careful approach to television. See Aitchison, 1978, p. 64.

64 'The Great Debate', broadcast 14 November 1958, NFSA, no. 16168.

65   Rawson provides a thorough overview of the 1958 election and its results. See Rawson, 1961.

66   McEwen, 1983, p. 57.

67   Author's interview with Sir Eric McClintock, 28 October 2016.

68   Frame, 2005a, pp. 99–101; Hasluck, 1997, p. 128.

69   ibid.

Chapter 15: Perception

1   McMahon, 9 November 1967, copy in the author's possession.

2   McMahon, draft autobiography, extract stapled to Bowman letter to McMahon, 22 May 1984, in possession of author. See also McMahon, 'Menzies the man', *Sun*, 16 May 1978; McMahon, *CPD HoR*, vol. 109, 23 May 1978, pp. 2332–34.

3   Menzies, 1967, p. 158.

4   Bowman to McMahon, 22 May 1984, in possession of author.

5   ibid.

6   See also Paul LePetit, 'Sir Billy: playboy at 18 with a string of racehorses', *Sunday Telegraph*, 3 April 1988, pp. 8–9; Cameron, 1990, pp. 542–43.

7   The story is difficult to credit, but it is possible that Menzies was inducing McMahon to stand in order to split the vote among members from New South Wales, thus weakening the candidacy of senator William Spooner, in favour of Harold Holt.

Chapter 16: War and Strife

1   Henry Bland interviewed by Mel Pratt, 1975, NLA Oral History, TRC 121/60.

2   ibid., amendment note, p. 11.

3   Henry Bland interviewed by Mel Pratt, 1975, NLA Oral History, TRC 121/60.

4   ibid.

5   Reginald Reed, in *Sir William McMahon: this is your life*, 12 March 1978, ep. 4/008, NFSA.

6   E.R. Wilkins to W.F. Foster, 6 February 1959, Noel Butlin Archives, E217/198, 60.

7   Henry Bland interviewed by Mel Pratt, 1975, NLA Oral History, TRC 121/60.

8   Wilson, *CPD HoR*, vol. 24, 22 September 1959, pp. 1227–29.

9   'Social services—budget proposals', July 1959, NAA: A5818, 259, and cabinet minute no. 304 (M), 13–16 July 1959, NAA: A5818, 259.

10   'Note of conversation between the Prime Minister and the Minister for Labour and National Service, 23 September, 1959', NAA: M2576, 2. There is evidence that the envelope was opened in 1960. Menzies' reaction may also have been prompted by concern about Wilson's proposal, which on 24 September received debate in the party room. See Bert Kelly diary, 24 September 1959, NLA MS7424.

11   See Fraser and Simons, 2009, pp. 162–63; Henderson, 1994, p. 207; Golding, 1996, pp. 218–19. Bland recalled that McMahon 'charged' down to Melbourne in the days following this meeting with Menzies and told Bland about it three times—each version 'bore very little resemblance' to one another. See Henry Bland interviewed by Mel Pratt, 1975, NLA Oral History, TRC 121/60.

12 See Sir Garfield Barwick interviewed by J.D.B. Miller, NLA Oral History, TRC 499/1, p. 37.

13 Hasluck, 1997, p. 133; Sir Garfield Barwick, interviewed by J.D.B. Miller, NLA Oral History, TRC 499/1, p. 37; Dudley Erwin interviewed by Robert Linford, NLA Oral History, TRC 4900/7, 5:10.

14 Fraser and Simons, 2009, pp. 162–63.

15 Dudley Erwin interviewed by Robert Linford, NLA Oral History, TRC 4900/7, 5:10.

16 Hasluck, 1997, p. 185.

17 In 1965, for example, Menzies asked McEwen to consult with colleagues for candidates for a new governor-general. McEwen consulted with Holt and Shane Paltridge, but went no further. The likely reason lies in a handwritten list of other ministers to consult. Beside McMahon's name is written: 'Not safe'. See NAA: A7394, 1.

18 McMahon, in Killen, 1985, p. 41.

19 Doug Anthony, correspondence with author, 15 August 2016.

20 Downer, 1982, p. 25.

21 Sir Garfield Barwick interviewed by Clyde Cameron, NLA Oral History, TRC 1045.

22 Hasluck, 1997, p. 95.

23 D'Alpuget, 1977, p. 17. See also Sir Richard Kirby interviewed by Catherine Santamaria, NLA Oral History, TRC 228.

24 Dennis Minogue, 'When the chief is underdog', *Aus.*, 21 October 1972, p. 15.

25 Henry Bland interviewed by Mel Pratt, 1975, NLA Oral History, TRC 121/60.

26 See, for example, McMahon, 27 April 1960, NAA: AA1968/119, 16; or 'An industrial charter', April 1960, NAA: M2576, 2.

27 Bland had been intent on using the prospect of long-service leave to enforce change for some time. In February 1959, E.R. Wilkins noted that some reckoning with it was likely to be imminent: 'The ASIA [Australian Stevedoring Industry Authority] have given McMahon an estimate of the labour position over the next few years and it is obvious that the WWF requirements will continue to shrink. In other words, the redundancy problem will become more acute and whilst Bland is now opposed to long service leave, he could well come to light with some proposition in relation to both long service leave and pensions which would pave the way for an amendment to the Stevedoring Act in connection with redundancy which would be acceptable to the WWF.' See E.R. Wilkins to W.F. Foster, 6 February 1959, Noel Butlin Archives, E217/98, 60.

28 Sheridan, 2006, p. 282.

29 Bland to McMahon, 7 March 1961, NAA: B142, SC61/32.

30 Bland to McMahon, 27 March 1961, ibid.

31 'Measures to improve discipline on the waterfront', NAA: A5818, 1041, and 'Notetaker E J Bunting—notes of meetings 6 February 1961–3 May 1961', NAA: A11099, 1/50.

32 McMahon, *CPD HoR*, vol. 31, 10 May 1961, pp. 1698–1700.

33 Calwell, *CPD HoR*, vol. 31, 10 May 1961, p. 1719.

34 Killen, *CPD HoR*, vol. 31, 11 May 1961, p. 1814.

35 Called 'The Waterfront Jungle', these articles discussed the tribulations of William Phillips, a seaman who had faced intimidation and harassment after speaking out against communist influences in the Australian Seamen's Union. See *Bulletin*, 15 July 1961, pp. 12–16; 22 July 1961, pp. 12–16; and 29 July 1961, pp. 15–16.

36 McMahon, 'Long service leave for waterside workers', 16 August 1961, NAA: AA1968/119, 16.

37 'Report of the committee of inquiry into public service recruitment', Chairman: Sir Richard Boyer, November 1959, Commonwealth Government of Australia.

38 Bland to McMahon, 4 September 1961, NAA: B142, SC61/23.

39 Bunting to Menzies, 10 October 1961, NAA: A4940, C3548.

40 McMahon to Menzies, 15 July 1961, NAA: M2576, 2.

41 Calwell's policy speech, 16 November 1961, <http://electionspeeches. moadoph.gov.au/speeches/1961-arthur-calwell>, accessed 11 November 2016.

42 See Maxwell Newton, 'Remember 1961!', *Incentive*, vol. 1, no. 12, 11 April 1972, p. 3.

43 Calwell, 1972, pp. 204–05.

44 McNicoll, 1978, pp. 272–91.

45 McMahon, *CPD HoR*, vol. 29, 19 October 1960, pp. 2196–98.

46 Alan Reid interviewed by Daniel Connell, NLA Oral History, TRC 2172, pp. 73–74.

47 'Menzies firm: "no rest" until all in jobs', *DT*, 30 November 1961, pp. 1, 3; 'Mr Menzies talks sense on jobs', *DT*, 1 December 1961, p. 1.

48 McMahon to Menzies, 9 November 1961, NAA: M2576, 2.

49 'Commonwealth of Australia: legislative election of 9 December 1961', *Psephos*, <http://psephos. adam-carr.net/countries/a/ australia/1961/1961repsnsw.txt>, accessed 11 November 2016.

50 Killen, 1985, p. 49.

51 Author's interview with Bruce and Leanne MacCarthy, 5 August 2016.

52 Whitington, 1971, p. 270.

53 Author's correspondence with John Stone, 6 January 2017.

54 See Reid, 1969, p. 40; Reid, 1976, pp. 31–32.

55 Author's correspondence with John Stone, 6 January 2017.

56 McEwen, 1983, p. 91.

57 Bland had noted this possibility in September 1961. See Bland to McMahon, 4 September 1961, NAA: B142, SC61/23.

58 McMahon's annotation on Bland to McMahon, 21 May 1962, ibid.

59 McMahon to Bland, cited in Sheridan and Stretton, 2004, p. 94.

60 Henry Bland interviewed by Mel Pratt, 1975, NLA Oral History, TRC 121/60.

61 Item (r), 'Submission no. 201—amendment of the Stevedoring Industry Legislation', cabinet minute, decision no. 256, 12 June 1962, NAA: A5819, 201.

62 McMahon to Bland, 31 July 1962, copy in the author's possession.

63 Beasley, 1996, pp. 200–07.

64 Sheridan, 2006, p. 282.

65 'Background notes', undated briefing material about the waterfront, copy in the author's possession.

66 McMahon to Cook, 22 May 1963, NAA: M1171/0/807.

67 Introducing his amendments to enact the agreed-upon terms, McMahon acknowledged that there would likely be problems in the future. See *CPD HoR*, vol. 40, 10 October 1963, pp. 1671–73.

68 Peter Coleman, 'Bill McMahon: from "Christus Veritas" to the Department of Labour', *Bulletin*, 10 August 1963, pp. 18–19.

69 McMahon to Menzies, 13 September 1963, NAA: M2576, 2.

70 Alan Reid, 'Waiting for instructions from their bosses', *DT*, 22 March 1963, p. 5.

71 Souter, 1988, p. 451.

72 McMahon to Menzies, 22 August 1963, NAA: M2576, 2.

73 McMahon to Menzies, 13 September 1963, ibid.

74 Menzies proposed the date at his cabinet meeting on 22 October, and, after agreement from his colleagues, announced it that day. See 'Notetaker E J Bunting—notes of meetings 22 October 1963–4 November 1963', NAA: A11099, 1/64.

75 Smart, 1978, pp. 29–30.

76 'Notetaker E J Bunting—notes of meetings 22 October 1963–4 November 1963', NAA: A11099, 1/64.

77 Santamaria had lobbied Holt for a 'breakthrough' in education allowances following the 1961 election, and, when given early news of such a breakthrough, took word to Archbishop Mannix, who commented: 'I have never stopped speaking about this question in all the years since I came from Ireland. But I thought I had wasted my time. I haven't wasted my time.' Overall, Santamaria thought, the move was 'as politically effective as it was ironic'. See Santamaria, 1987, pp. 261–70.

78 Mills, 2014, p. 59.

79 See 'Commonwealth of Australia Legislative Election of 30 November 1963', *Psephos*, <http://psephos. adam-carr.net/countries/a/ australia/1963/1963repsnsw.txt>, accessed 16 November 2016.

80 Edwards, 1992, pp. 259–60.

81 ibid., p. 304.

82 Pemberton, 1987, p. 197.

83 Cabinet submission no. 521, 'Services Manpower Review: summary of conclusions', November 1964, NAA: A4940/1.

84 Cabinet minute no. 596, 4–5 November 1964, NAA: 5827, vol. 16.

85 Labor MPs quoted many of Forbes' comments back to him after the National Service Bill was introduced.

86 See Menzies, *CPD HoR*, vol. 44, 10 November 1964, pp. 2715–24; and McMahon, *CPD HoR*, vol. 44, 11 November 1964, pp. 2836–38.

87 So much so, in fact, that McMahon's successor at Labour and National Service, Les Bury, noted that McMahon had informed the cabinet about the 'main elements of the scheme' orally only. See cabinet submission no. 117, 'National Service—extension to aliens', NAA: A5841, 117.

88 Ham, 2007, p. 168

89 Menzies, *CPD HoR*, vol. 44, 11 November 1964, p. 2785.

90 Calwell, *CPD HoR*, vol. 44, 12 November 1964, pp. 2920–28.

91 'Australian Senate election of 5 December 1964', *Psephos*, <http://

psephos.adam-carr.net/countries/a/
australia/1964/1964senate1.txt>,
accessed 16 November 2016.

Chapter 17: Exposure

1   'McMahon sees an easy Labor win,
    but tips Greiner for next time', *SMH*,
    8 March 1984, p. 5.
2   Bowman diary, 14 March 1984.
3   ibid., 3 May 1984.

Chapter 18: Preparing the Way

1   McMahon press release, 'Miss
    Wheatley', 21 January 1969;
    Mitchell, 2007, p. 40.
2   Henry Bland interviewed by Mel
    Pratt, 1975, NLA Oral History, TRC
    121/60.
3   D'Alpuget, 1978, p. 193.
4   ibid.
5   Henry Bland interviewed by Mel
    Pratt, 1975, NLA Oral History, TRC
    121/60.
6   ibid.
7   ibid.
8   Peter Kelly, 'A courageous and
    persistent man', *Age*, 2 April 1988,
    p. 6.
9   Author's interview with Peter Kelly,
    1 October 2016.
10 ibid.
11 ibid.
12 ibid.
13 This biographical information on
    Newton is drawn from: Murray Goot,
    2012, 'Newton, Maxwell (1929–
    1990)', *ADB*, vol. 18, Melbourne
    University Press, Carlton; Cryle,
    2008, pp. 1–32; Newton, 1993.
14 Author's interview with Peter Kelly,
    1 October 2016.

15 Henry Bland interviewed by Mel
    Pratt, 1975, NLA Oral History, TRC
    121/60.
16 John Edwards, 'Inside Billy
    McMahon', *AFR*, 31 May 1971, p. 3.
17 D'Alpuget, 1978, p. 225.
18 William McMahon interviewed by
    John Edwards, NLA Oral History,
    TRC 168/8.
19 Author's interview with Bruce and
    Leanne MacCarthy, 5 August 2016.
20 Henry Bland interviewed by Mel
    Pratt, 1975, NLA Oral History, TRC
    121/60.
21 Killen, 1985, p. 138.
22 Peter Kelly, 'A courageous and
    persistent man', *Age*, 2 April 1988,
    p. 6.
23 Author's interview with Peter Kelly,
    1 October 2016.
24 Mitchell, 2007, p. 8. As far back as
    1956, McMahon's colleagues had
    laughed about his bachelorhood: see
    'The egg ... and the MP', *Argus*,
    8 June 1956, p. 3.
25 Author's interview with Alan Ramsey,
    31 January 2018.
26 Paul LePetit, 'Sir Billy: playboy at 18
    with a string of racehorses', *Sunday
    Telegraph*, 3 April 1988, pp. 8–9;
    Mitchell, 2007, pp. 7–8.
27 Author's interview with Peter Kelly,
    1 October 2016.
28 Wheatley told Susan Mitchell that
    McMahon judged the woman to be
    not of a 'high enough social level' for
    him: Mitchell, 2007, pp. 7–8.
29 Julian Leeser, 'Gracious, stylish and
    steadfast', *Aus.*, 5 April 2010, p. 11.
30 Mitchell, 2007, p. 7.
31 ibid., p. 16.
32 Author's interview with Peter Kelly,
    1 October 2016.

33 Edwards, 1992, p. 254.

34 ibid., pp. 361–62.

35 Martin and Edwards make the same, caveated judgement. See Martin, 1999, p. 519; Edwards, 1997, p. 388. Don Chipp claimed later that Menzies told him he knew who had leaked the news; if true, it is again perplexing that Menzies did not dismiss McMahon, as he had previously threatened.

36 'Report of the Committee of Economic Enquiry', May 1965, vol. 1, para. 17.73.

37 Author's correspondence with John Stone, 7 January 2017.

38 McMahon to Menzies, unsent letter, 15 January 1962, copy in the author's possession.

39 Wilson to McMahon, 4 August 1965, copy in the author's possession.

40 ibid.

41 Author's interview with Peter Kelly, 1 October 2016; Golding, 1996, p. 221.

42 Author's correspondence with John Stone, 6 January 2017.

43 Howson, 1984, p. 167.

44 McEwen, 1983, p. 66.

45 Maxwell Newton, *Incentive*, no. 16, 22 September 1965, p. 2.

46 Menzies, *CPD HoR*, vol. 47, 21 September 1965, pp. 1078–86.

47 Supposedly, McMahon urged Barwick to accept the post while the two crossed the tarmac at Canberra airport: Barwick, 1995, p. 209.

48 'Federal minister urges "more jobs for wives"', *CM*, 9 September 1964, p. 3.

49 'Why should they work?', *CM*, 10 September 1964, p. 2.

50 McMahon and Bland, 1 September 1965, NAA: B142, SC61/23.

51 'Using our work force efficiently', *Aus.*, 1 September 1965, p. 8.

52 Beasley, 1996, p. 210.

53 Gourley, 1969, p. 185.

54 Sheridan, 2006, p. 282.

55 Woodward, 2005, pp. 107–08.

56 Bland had suggested the prospect of an inquiry to McMahon in March. See 'Papers maintained by Sir Henry Bland. Waterside 1965', NAA: M2438, 2, p. 4.

57 ibid.

58 Henry Bland interviewed by Mel Pratt, NLA Oral History, TRC 121/60.

59 ibid.

60 Henry Bland interviewed by Allan Martin, NLA Oral History, TRC 2549.

61 Author's interview with Peter Kelly, 1 October 2016. See also Short, 1992, p. 234.

62 McMahon, 'Chapter 5: The Waterfront Imbroglio', copy in the author's possession.

63 Author's interview with Peter Kelly, 2 May 2017.

64 Bland to McMahon, 1 August 1965, NAA: M2438, 1.

65 Bland to Norman J. Hood, 1 August 1965, ibid.

66 Bland to Sir Edwin Hicks, 1 August 1965, ibid.

67 Bland to Wally Talbot, 1 August 1965, ibid.

68 Bland to McMahon, 3 August 1965, ibid.

69 Cabinet submission no. 1016, 'The stevedoring industry', 25 August 1965, NAA: A5827, 1016.

70 Henry Bland interviewed by Mel Pratt, NLA Oral History, TRC 121/60.

71 'Notetaker EJ Bunting—notes of meetings 10 August 1965–7 September 1965', NAA: A11099, 1/75.

72 Cabinet minute no. 1203, 1 September 1965, 'Submission no. 1016—the stevedoring industry', NAA: A5827, 1016.

73 Henry Bland interviewed by Mel Pratt, NLA Oral History, TRC 121/60.

74 Howson, 1984, p. 174.

75 McMahon, *CPD HoR*, vol. 47, 23 September 1965, pp. 1249–56.

76 Menzies, *CPD HoR*, vol. 48, 1 October 1965, p. 1594.

77 Henry Bland interviewed by Mel Pratt, NLA Oral History, TRC 121/60.

78 Maxwell Newton, *Incentive*, no. 17, 29 September 1965, p. 2.

79 Howson, 1984, p. 174.

80 McMahon, *CPD HoR*, vol. 48, 29 September 1965, p. 1373.

81 ibid., 30 September 1965, p. 1478.

82 ibid., 12 October 1965, p. 1658.

83 ibid., 30 September 1965, p. 1481.

84 ibid., 12 October 1965, p. 1653.

85 Bland to McMahon, 14 October 1965, NAA: M2438, 2.

86 McMahon's annotations on letter, Bland to McMahon, 14 October 1965, NAA: M2438, 2. The underlining is McMahon's. In a letter to Norman Hood dated 4 November 1965, Bland asked the ASIA chairman to destroy the records that had been cited.

87 Gourley, 1969, p. 174.

88 Henry Bland interviewed by Mel Pratt, 1975, NLA Oral History, TRC 121/60.

89 Sawer (ed.), 1996.

90 Hayden and Menzies, *CPD HoR*, vol. 47, 14 September 1965, p. 808; Hayden, *CPD HoR*, vol. 48, 14 October 1965, pp. 1861–64.

91 Bunting to Menzies, 11 November 1965, NAA: A4940, C3548.

92 Helen Crisp interviewed by Ian Hamilton, 21 September 1982, NLA Oral History, TRC 1170.

93 Cabinet minute no. 1416, 30 November 1965, 'Submission no. 1124: employment of married women in the Commonwealth public service', NAA: A5827, 1124. Hayden brought up the marriage bar in the House two days after the cabinet decision, and was undercut by McMahon's announcement that it was being studied. See Hayden and McMahon, *CPD HoR*, vol. 49, 2 December 1965, pp. 3484–92.

94 Mitchell, 2007, pp. 16–17.

95 Charles 'Bert' Kelly interviewed by Bruce Edwards, NLA Oral History, TRC 4900/30; Kelly, 1978, p. 92.

96 See 'Minister to wed in October', *CT*, 25 October 1965, p. 3.

97 Larry Writer, 'Sonia McMahon—the truth about my marriage', *AWW*, 1 November 2007.

98 Author's interview with Peter Kelly, 1 October 2016.

99 Henry Bland interviewed by Mel Pratt, NLA Oral History, TRC 121/60.

100 'Mr McMahon married', *Mercury*, 13 December 1965, p. 8.

101 Bolton, 2015, p. 389. Frame notes that senator Reg Withers recalled Menzies telling him that the Privy Councillorship was a 'blessing' on Hasluck's aspirations. See Frame, 2005a, p. 137.

102 Author's interview with Tom Hughes, 16 August 2016.

103 Maxwell Newton, *Incentive*, no. 31, 19 January 1966.

104 Gordon Freeth interviewed by John Ferrell, NLA Oral History, TRC 4900/89.

105 Les Bury interviewed by Mel Pratt, NLA Oral History, TRC 121/70.

106 Peter Hastings, 1965, 'McMahon', *Bulletin*, 11 December 1965, p. 9; Henry Bland interviewed by Mel Pratt, NLA Oral History, TRC 121/60.

107 Official transcript: 'Press, radio and television conference given by Sir Robert Menzies at Parliament House, Canberra, on 20th January, 1966'.

108 Howson, 1984, p. 202.

109 Peter Bowers, 'Out of the shadow into the blaze', *SMH*, 27 January 1966, p. 1.

Chapter 19: Lauding the Headmaster

1 Bowman to McMahon, 12 March 1984, copy in the author's possession.

2 McMahon, *CPD HoR*, vol. 109, 23 May 1978, pp. 2332–34.

3 McMahon, in 'The leaders', *This Fabulous Century*, 14 November 1978, NFSA.

4 K.L. Menzies, 'Menzies on record', *SMH*, 22 December 1979, p. 10; Martin, 1999, p. 562. Menzies' regard for McMahon was subsequently confirmed in letters he had exchanged with his daughter: Henderson (ed.), 2011.

5 McNicoll, 1978, pp. 210–31.

6 'Menzies' stinging appraisal of colleagues', *SMH*, 22 November 1979, p. 3.

7 What follows draws on drafts and notes of McMahon's autobiography, some authored by Bowman, others of unknown authorship. Copies in the author's possession.

8 Barwick had a different recollection: see Barwick, 1995, pp. 208–11.

Chapter 20: Protection (I)

1 Rob Chalmers, *IC*, 27 January 1966, vol. 19, no. 3, p. 1.

2 Hancock, 1930, p. 97.

3 James Jupp, in Davidson (ed.), 1986, p. 81. See also Anderson and Garnaut, 1987, pp. 40–51.

4 McEwen, 1983, p. 67.

5 ibid., p. 68.

6 Veitch, 1996, pp. 237–44. See also Stewart, in Prasser, Nethercote, and Warhurst (eds) 1995, pp. 185–201.

7 Fadden's correspondence with Ulrich Ellis, NLA MS1006, Box 30. Fadden was also aggrieved by McEwen's decision to not appoint him chairman of the Commonwealth Banking Corporation board.

8 Reid, 1969, p. 44.

9 McEwen, 1983, p. 85.

10 Charles 'Bert' Kelly interviewed by Bruce Edwards, NLA Oral History, TRC 4900/30.

11 ibid.

12 Jonathan Gaul, 'McMahon, the man behind the federal budget', *CT*, 13 August 1966, p. 2.

13 Later, McMahon claimed to have rejected an early Treasury assessment of the economy and demanded that the economy be stimulated. See William McMahon interviewed by John Edwards, NLA Oral History, TRC 168/8.

14   Rob Chalmers predicted 'some serious and even violent clashes' between McMahon and Wilson, and suggested (correctly) that Wilson might not remain long at Treasury. See *IC*, vol. 19, no. 3, 27 January 1966, p. 1.

15   John Farquharson, 'Wilson, Sir Roland (1904–1996)', *SMH*, 29 October 1996, p. 33.

16   Cornish, in King (ed.), 2007, pp. 310–15; author's correspondence with John Stone, 8 January 2017. Wilson's retirement was forecast earlier than this: in August, when the budget was handed down, economics editor for *The Age* Rolf Lie intimated that Wilson was expected to retire soon. See Rolf Lie, 'The story behind the budget', *Age*, 16 August 1966, p. 2.

17   Treasury 1966, 'The Australian economy 1966', Commonwealth of Australia, p. 3.

18   'Queensland dairy industry—request by Queensland government for commonwealth financial assistance', 26 May 1966, NAA: A5841, 221.

19   'Cabinet minute, decision no. 306', 15 June 1966, NAA: A5841, 221.

20   'Superphosphate bounty', 31 May 1966, NAA: A5841, 223; 'Analysis of submission no. 369 superphosphate bounty', 31 May 1966, NAA: A5841, 302; 'Cabinet minute, decision no. 400 (M)', 21 July 1966, NAA: A5841, 302.

21   'Treasury analysis of submission no. 353—assistance to flying training', 31 May 1966, NAA: A5841, 303; 'Cabinet minute, decision 402 (M)', 21 July 1966, NAA: A5841, 303.

22   McEwen press release, 'Government policy toward the Australian motor vehicle industry', 18 February 1966; Maxwell Newton, *Incentive*, no. 36, 23 February 1966, p. 1.

23   Peter Howson, the minister for air who was assisting McMahon in Treasury, describes it as a deliberate attempt by Treasury to be 'ethical'. See Howson, 1984, p. 208.

24   Howson, 1984, pp. 211–12.

25   'Research and development in Australian secondary industry', 29 March 1966, NAA: A5842, 105.

26   'Notes on submission: no. 105—research and development in Australian secondary industry; no. 127—research and development in secondary industry; no. 198—research and development in secondary industry', 17 May 1966, NAA: A5842, 105, 127, 198.

27   'Cabinet minute, decision no. 268', 17 May 1966, NAA: A5841, 105, 127, 198. Peter Howson later claimed it as a win for Treasury. See Howson, 1984, p. 222. Cabinet notebooks suggest that the debate between McMahon and McEwen was harmonious. See 'Notetaker EJ Bunting—notes of meetings 4 April 1966–24 May 1966', NAA: A11099, 1/79.

28   Frame, 2005a, p. 159.

29   Martin Collins, 'The trials of being a week-day widow', *Aus.*, 25 March 1966, p. 20.

30   Noel Pratt, 'McMahons choose a local flat', *Aus.*, 5 May 1966, p. 15.

31   Mitchell, 2007, p. 20.

32   'Baby for MP's wife', *Sun-Herald*, 29 May 1966, p. 2. Peter Howson thought McMahon 'skittish' about the news. Howson, 1984, p. 224.

33 McNicoll, 1978, p. 273.

34 Jonathan Gaul, 'McMahon, the man behind the federal budget', *CT*, 13 August 1966, p. 2.

35 For the notes on those meetings, see 'Notetaker EJ Bunting—notes of budget meetings 19 July 1966–21 July 1966', NAA: A11099, 1/80.

36 Howson, 1984, pp. 230–31.

37 This would appear to be the instance cited in Mitchell, 2007, p. 25.

38 McMahon draft autobiography, copy in the author's possession.

39 John Stubbs, 'Laughter—and some blushes', *Aus.*, 17 August 1966, p. 1.

40 In July, the ministry had decided that a 'working ceiling' of $1,000m for the defence proposals should be adopted, in order to 'preserve flexibility within the Budget'. It noted as well that this still represented a 33 per cent increase in defence expenditure since 1965–66. See cabinet minute, decision no. 366 (M), 'Submissions nos. 361, 291, 272, 271, 355, 329, 327, 328, 326, 335, 363, 357, 362—Defence', 20 July 1966, NAA: A5841, 366.

41 McMahon and Calwell, *CPD HoR*, vol. 52, 16 August 1966, pp. 11–24.

42 Howson, 1984, p. 236.

43 John Stubbs, 'Laughter—and some blushes', *Aus.*, 17 August 1966, p. 1.

44 'Editorial: a good job done against difficulties' and 'Not enough', *DT*, 17 August 1966, p. 2.

45 Alan Ramsey, 'It's a half-speed-ahead budget', *Aus.*, 17 August 1966, p. 1; 'Editorial: defence at a price', *Age*, 17 August 1966, p. 2.

46 McMahon to Holt, 5 April 1966, NAA: M2684, 132.

47 'Employment of married women in a permanent capacity in the Commonwealth public service. Decision 481', NAA: A5841, 414.

48 'Notetaker EJ Bunting—notes of meetings 1 June 1966–13 October 1966', NAA: A11099, 1/81.

49 ibid. The tensions surrounding this are also detailed in Howson, 1984, pp. 237–39.

50 McEwen was often criticised for putting recommendations into the terms of reference.

51 'Notetaker EJ Bunting—notes of meetings 1 June 1966–13 October 1966', NAA: A11099, 1/81.

52 Maxwell Newton, 'A very dangerous precedent indeed in the Chemical Tariff Report', *Incentive*, no. 72, 2 November 1966. It was notable that Newton had run an article outlining the basic contents of the report in June, some four months before cabinet considered the report. See Maxwell Newton, 'Bounties recommended by Tariff Board on chemicals', *Incentive*, no. 51, 8 June 1966, p. 5.

53 Transcript of McMahon press conference, 4 January 1982, copy in the author's possession.

54 Holt, in Warhaft (ed.), 2004, pp. 123–24.

55 Author's interview with Peter Kelly, 1 October 2016.

56 McMahon, 'Liberals: we alone can ensure security at home', *DM*, 18 November 1966, p. 6.

57 McMahon, speech to the annual convention of the Liberal Party, 9 September 1966, NAA: M4250, 48.

58 'McMahon sees Calwell as Santa Claus', *Aus.*, 12 November 1966, p. 3.

59 Liberal Party research notes would subsequently indicate that the

Liberal Reform Group contained no Liberal Party members of any status. See 'The Australia Party', 1972, Sir Robert Southey papers, NLA MS9901/1/3.

60 Maxwell Newton, 'Suddenly political leaders are in doubt about public attitude on conscription', *Incentive*, no. 73, 9 November 1966, p. 1.

61 'Country Party Leader attacks Basic Industries Group', *CT*, 16 November 1966, p. 15.

62 See 'Commonwealth of Australia legislative election of 26 November 1966', *Psephos*, <http://psephos. adam-carr.net/countries/a/ australia/1966/1966repsnsw.txt>, accessed 3 December 2016. James later claimed that he had been friends within McMahon since the 1950s and described him as 'a hard-working, highly efficient administrator'. See James, in Aitchison (ed.), 1974, p. 90.

63 Sue Jordan, 'Come look at her, says a new father', *Aus.*, 30 November 1966, p. 1.

64 'Personages', *Pauline*, no. 64, 1966, p. 48.

65 Val Kentish, in *Sir William McMahon: this is your life*, 12 March 1978, ep. 4/008, NFSA.

66 Hocking, 2008.

67 See McMahon and Whitlam, *CPD HoR*, vol. 16, 12 September 1957, p. 560; 18 September 1957, p. 778; 19 September 1957, pp. 790, 792–94, and 868–71. Whitlam made sure to spell out the word for *Hansard* reporters.

68 Hocking, 2008, p. 172; Whitlam, *CPD HoR*, 1 October 1957, vol. 16, p. 883.

69 Freudenberg, 1987, p. 106.

Chapter 21: Protection (II)

1 Howson, 1984, p. 272.

2 McMahon, *CPD HoR*, vol. 93, 20 February 1975, pp. 560–63.

3 McMahon to Holt, 15 May 1967, NAA: M2684, 132.

4 McMahon, 27 March 1967, NAA: M4250, 67.

5 Holt's brother Cliff died 24 March 1967, following a fifteen-month battle with cancer. Holt described it as a 'terrible blow'. See Frame, 2005a, p. 205; Howson, 1984, pp. 279–80.

6 Charles 'Bert' Kelly interviewed by Bruce Edwards, NLA Oral History, TRC 4900/30, 4:12.

7 Beaton, McEwen, and the Speaker, *CPD HoR*, vol. 54, 11 April 1967, p. 1076; also see *IC*, vol. 20, no. 14, 13 April 1967, p. 1.

8 McEwen, 1983, p. 75.

9 ibid.

10 Hasluck, 1995, p. 149.

11 Paul Hasluck interviewed by Clyde Cameron, NLA Oral History, TRC 1966, p. 22.

12 Author's correspondence with David Solomon, 24 September 2017.

13 Don Chipp interviewed by Bernadette Schedvin, NLA Oral History, TRC 4900/73, 7:9.

14 Author's interview with Alan Ramsey, 31 January 2018.

15 Doug Anthony, in 'It's alright, Boss', *The Liberals*, TV programme, 1994.

16 Sir John Bunting interviewed by Ian Hamilton, 26 June 1983, NLA Oral History, TRC 1428.

17 Author's interview with Richard Farmer, 15 July 2016.

18 Peter Howson interviewed by Jonathan Gaul, NLA Oral History, TRC 229, 9/9.

19   Author's interview with Richard Farmer, 15 July 2016.

20   Author's interview with Peter Kelly, 1 October 2016.

21   Golding, 1996, p. 259.

22   McEwen, *CPD HoR*, vol. 54, 4 April 1967, pp. 834–35.

23   McMahon, *CPD HoR*, vol. 93, 20 February 1975, pp. 560–63.

24   McMahon to Holt, 15 May 1967, NAA: M2684, 132.

25   'First details of overseas capital plan', *CT*, 15 May 1967, p. 1.

26   'Notetaker EJ Bunting—notes of meetings 4 May 1967–28 July 1967', NAA: A11099, 1/85.

27   Maxwell Newton, 'Mr Sinclair is out campaigning for "The McEwen Bank"', *Incentive*, no. 98, 17 May 1967.

28   Randall to McMahon and Holt, 1 June 1967, 'Trade and Industry Proposals: Australian industry development corporation', NAA: M2684, 132.

29   Tom Frame, 2005b. McMahon had launched *Voyager* while minister for the navy and air.

30   Chipp and Larkin, 1978, pp. 74–75.

31   St John, *CPD HoR*, vol. 55, 16 May 1967, pp. 2167–72.

32   Holt, ibid., p. 2169.

33   Not since Whitlam, in fact, had been interrupted by McEwen in 1953. See Whitlam and McEwen, *CPD*, vol. 221, 19 March 1953, pp. 1423–28.

34   Freudenberg, 1987, p. 108.

35   See Holt, *CPD HoR*, vol. 55, 18 May 1967, p. 2309.

36   Howson, 1984, p. 299.

37   Maxwell Newton, 'Mr McEwen does badly in Geneva', *Incentive*, no. 99, 24 May 1967.

38   Howson, 1984, p. 301.

39   Reid, 1969, p. 64.

40   Jonathan Gaul, 'CP leader upraids BIG again', *CT*, 22 June 1967, p. 1; 'BIG will fight Country Party nationally', *CT*, 30 June 1967, p. 1.

41   McMahon to Holt, 20 June 1967, NAA: M2684, 132.

42   Howson, 1984, pp. 302–03.

43   This was confirmed in the days that followed. See Ian Fitchett, 'Holt still to discuss BIG issue', *SMH*, 26 June 1967, p. 1; Jonathan Gaul, 'PM defends McEwen, denies BIG links', *CT*, 28 June 1967, p. 1.

44   Ian Fitchett, 'Holt still to discuss BIG issue', *SMH*, 26 June 1967, p. 1.

45   'Note of a meeting at the Ministry of Defence', 14 June 1967, UK National Archives, Kew, PREM 13/1323, p. 8.

46   Casey to Michael Adeane, 21 January 1969, in Hudson, 1986, p. 306.

47   In his 1972 Queale Memorial Lecture, Paul Hasluck wrote that while a governor-general 'may ask a Minister to call to discuss matters of current interest', he or she should exercise discretion in doing so: 'He would stray beyond his functions if he took sides in any argument between his advisers or preferred one Minister to another, or tried to intervene in the domestic arguments of any political party.' Hasluck was careful to disavow any comment on his predecessors or successors, but it is difficult to read this without thinking of Casey's offer to intervene in the McMahon–McEwen dispute. The governor-general 'could cause mischief and have little hope of doing good if he tried to be a ruler or if he tried to manipulate politicians'. This was

most certainly the result of Casey's
intervention. See Hasluck, 1979.

48   Author's interview with Alan Ramsey,
     31 January 2018.

49   Maximilian Walsh, 'The myths and
     the facts of Billy McMahon', *National
     Times*, 20 September 1971, pp. 3–4.

50   Author's interview with Peter Kelly,
     1 October 2016.

51   Robert Haupt, 'What we didn't know
     of McMahon', *SMH*, 4 April 1988,
     p. 2.

52   Author's interview with Peter Kelly,
     1 October 2016. *Hansard* officer John
     Campbell recalled that McMahon
     used to make many changes. See
     'John Campbell interviewed by
     Edward Helgeby', 27 March 2008,
     MoAD Oral History.

53   McMahon, *CPD HoR*, vol. 56,
     15 August 1967, pp. 6–21. Howson
     notes that changes to the family
     allowances were originally knocked
     back by cabinet but that they were
     reinstated a week before the budget.
     News that this had occurred found
     its way into the press with favourable
     mention of McMahon. See Maxwell
     Newton, 'Mr McMahon's last minute
     budget intervention', *Incentive*,
     no. 114, 6 September 1967, p. 4;
     Howson, 1984, p. 316.

54   See '"No worry" budget to aid family
     man', *Age*, 16 August 1967, p. 1;
     'No-shock budget aids family man',
     DT, 16 August 1967, p. 1; 'No answer
     to the old questions', *Aus.*, 18 August
     1967, p. 2.

55   Maxwell Newton, 'Government
     restraint', *Age*, 16 August 1967, p. 2.

56   Howson, 1984, pp. 325–340.

57   ibid., p. 313. On 23 August,
     McMahon wrote a letter to Holt

detailing a conversation with Bob
Askin, the premier of New South
Wales. Askin had told McMahon
that there was a 'swing' against
the Liberal Party in the state, with
'hostility everywhere'. To McMahon's
question for an explanation, Askin
named Vietnam as one of the premier
reasons. See McMahon to Holt,
23 August 1967, NAA: M2684, 132.

58   Graham Freudenberg suggested
     that McMahon had done this
     while under the influence of bad
     champagne. McMahon denied
     it. See Freudenberg, 1987, p. 111;
     McMahon, *CPD HoR*, vol. 107,
     25 October 1977, pp. 2314–16.

59   Freudenberg, 1987, p. 111.

60   Mitchell, 2007, p. 25; 'The Treasury',
     extract of draft of McMahon's
     autobiography, in possession
     of author. There has long been
     ambiguity about the circumstances
     of McNamara's appointment.
     McNamara himself was later to
     remark, in the 2003 documentary *Fog
     of War*, that he was not sure whether
     he had 'quit or was fired' from the
     Defence department.

61   McMahon to Holt, 2 October 1967,
     in Edwards, 1997, pp. 154–55.

62   ibid.

63   Undated memo, no author listed,
     NAA: M4298, 2.

64   Crean, *CPD HoR*, vol. 56,
     26 September 1967, p. 1273.

65   Tony Eggleton to Holt, 14 October
     1967, NAA: M4298, 2.

66   Anonymously authored memo, 'A',
     6 October 1967, NAA: M4298, 2.

67   'Record of discussion with
     P. Goldsworthy, proprietor of
     Union Offset Company, Pirie

Street, Fishwyick [sic] on Thursday, 29 February 1968', NLA, Papers of W.L. Carew, MS 7524.

68 Author's correspondence with Tony Eggleton, 26 November 2016.

69 Packer, 1984, pp. 118–19.

70 Author's correspondence with John Stone, 8 January 2017.

71 Newton, 1993, p. 165.

72 Clarke, 2006, pp. 2–9.

73 Reid, 1969, p. 75.

74 Author's interview with Robert Macklin, 11 July 2016.

75 Author's interview with Jonathan Gaul, 24 February 2018.

76 Reid, 1969, p. 69.

77 'Replacement of VIP aircraft. Decision 1407', NAA: A5827, 1152.

78 Howson, 1984, p. 211.

79 David Fairbairn interviewed by Mel Pratt, 1976, NLA Oral History, TRC 121/74. Gordon Freeth recalls McMahon similarly ignoring the availability of commercial flights: see Gordon Freeth interviewed by John Ferrell, NLA Oral History, TRC 4900/87.

80 Daly and Holt, CPD HoR, vol. 51, 13 May 1966, p. 1913.

81 Turnbull, CPD Senate, vol. 33, 2 March 1967, pp. 259–66; 8 March 1967, p. 320; vol. 34, 16 May 1967, pp. 1594–600; 17 May 1967, pp. 1624–5; vol. 35, 31 August 1967, p. 407; 7 September 1967, p. 593; Hancock, 2004, p. 24.

82 CPD Senate, vol. 35, 26 September 1967, pp. 875–80, 897.

83 ibid., pp. 880–97.

84 Murphy, ibid., 27 September 1967, pp. 965–66.

85 CPD Senate, vol. 36, 5 October 1967, pp. 1191–266.

86 'Cabinet minute—VIP [Very Important Person] aircraft—WITHOUT MEMORANDUM', decision 630, 12 October 1967, NAA: A5840, 630.

87 Whitington, 1972, p. 135.

88 Holt, CPD HoR, vol. 57, 24 October 1967, pp. 2149–52.

89 Cameron, ibid., pp. 2156–58.

90 Gorton, CPD Senate, vol. 36, 25 October 1967, pp. 1633–34.

91 ibid., pp. 1665–66.

92 Howson, 1984, p. 347.

93 Ian Fitchett, 'Gorton: a man to watch', SMH, 31 October 1967, p. 2.

94 McMahon to Holt, 9 November 1967, NAA: M4298, 2.

95 Hasluck, 1995, pp. 147–51.

96 ibid., pp. 150–1; 'Copy of Newton's contract with JETRO', NAA: M4298, 2.

97 John Gorton interviewed by Clyde Cameron, NLA Oral History, TRC 1702, vol. 1, pp. 63–64.

98 John Gorton interviewed by Clarrie Hermes, NLA Oral History, TRC 4900/47, 6:7.

99 Hasluck, 1995, p. 152.

100 ibid.; John Gorton interviewed by Clyde Cameron, NLA Oral History, TRC 1702, vol. 1, pp. 63–64.

101 Author's correspondence with Tony Eggleton, 26 November 2016.

102 Author's interview with Peter Kelly, 1 October 2016.

103 ibid.

104 See Reid, 1969, pp. 69–74.

105 'McEwen's shock departure', IC, vol. 20, no. 42, 26 October 1967.

106 McMahon, 'Devaluation of sterling', Press Release, 19 November 1967.

107 Aitchison, 1978, p. 81.

108 Howson, 1984, p. 352.

109   Howson writes that Treasury's draft submission had suggested devaluing the currency by 7.5 per cent, but that it had been removed at McMahon's urging: ibid., p. 359.

110   'Notetaker EJ Bunting—notes of meetings 22 August 1967–20 November 1967', NAA: A11099, 1/87.

111   'Devaluation of pound sterling', Press release, 20 November 1967, PM no. 122/1967.

112   Author's correspondence with John Stone, 8 January 2017.

113   Alan Reid interviewed by Daniel Connell, NLA Oral History, TRC 2172, pp. 75–76.

114   Hancock, 2002, pp. 134–35.

115   Gorton, in 'It's alright, Boss', *The Liberals*, TV programme, 1994.

116   Author's correspondence with David Solomon, 24 September 2017.

117   Sir William Aston interviewed by Ron Hurst, 12 June to 7 November 1986, NLA Oral History, TRC 4900/95.

118   Gordon Freeth interviewed by John Ferrell, NLA Oral History, TRC 4900/89.

119   Sir James Plimsoll interviewed by Clyde Cameron, NLA Oral History, TRC 1967, p. 184.

120   According to Paul LePetit, this was the second meeting between the pair; an initial meeting, three weeks before, went over the same matters without resolution. See Paul LePetit, 'The day Holt tried to sack the governor-general', *Sunday Telegraph*, 3 April 1988, p. 9.

121   McMahon to Holt, 11 December 1967, NAA: M1945, 1.

122   Casey to Holt, 9 December 1967, in Hudson, 1986, pp. 307–08.

123   Hasluck, 1995, p. 155.

124   Harold Cox interviewed by Mel Pratt, NLA Oral History, TRC 121/43, 1:2/75–76.

125   Author's interview with Peter Kelly, 1 October 2016.

126   McEwen, statement, 11 December 1967. The statement was widely carried in newspapers the next day.

127   Frame, 2005a, pp. 240–41.

128   Hasluck, 1995, p. 154.

129   Peter Bailey interviewed by Garry Sturgess, NLA Oral History, TRC 6552, p. 222.

130   'Devaluation: reaffirmation of government's decision', 13 December 1967, PM no. 135/1967, NAA: M4295, 22.

131   Wallace Brown, *CM*, 'Holt critics think again after the McEwen "crisis"', 13 December 1967, p. 2.

132   Tom Fitzgerald, 'Getting a bit back of Jack', *SMH*, 13 December 1967, p. 21.

133   Hasluck, 1995, pp. 153–54; 'Government measures to assist industry', 15 December 1967, PM no. 136/1967, NAA: M4295, 22.

134   R.G. Casey diaries, 13 December 1967, NLA MS6150.

135   Fitzgerald and Holt, 2010, pp. 179–80.

136   Frame, 2005a, pp. 245–46.

137   Howson, 1984, pp. 362–63.

Chapter 22: The Story and the Fact

1   Hasluck, 1995, pp. 147–49.

2   ibid.

3   Ashley, 1968, p. 16.

4   Peter Kelly, 'Politics the day Holt died', *Aus.*, 13–14 December 1986, p. 2.

5 Author's interview with Peter Kelly, 1 October 2016.

6 For discussion of Casey's activism as governor-general, see Rodan, 2013, pp. 547–58.

7 After McMahon's death in 1988, Paul LePetit wrote that McMahon had repeated this story to him. In LePetit's account, the 8 December meeting was the second meeting between McMahon and Casey. According to this account, McMahon attempted to storm out only to be restrained by Casey, who begged McMahon to stay in order to preserve social niceties and prevent Casey's staff from observing that there was something wrong. See 'The day Holt tried to sack the governor–general', *Sunday Telegraph*, 3 April 1988, p. 9.

8 Author's correspondence with Tony Eggleton, 26 November 2016.

9 Author's interview with Peter Kelly, 1 October 2016.

10 *The Harold Holt Mystery*, 18 February 1985, NFSA.

11 McMahon said much the same thing in 1985: 'He [Holt] was very suspicious about whether or not it was me [plotting to replace him]. And it was one of the only occasions in which I had difficulty with him by saying I can't believe that he could possibly do it.' See *The Harold Holt Mystery*, 18 February 1985, NFSA.

12 In May 1968, Peter Howson described a dinner with McMahon where this incident was recounted. See Howson, 1984, p. 427.

13 Frame, 2005a, p. 274.

14 John Cloke, in *The Harold Holt Mystery*, 18 February 1985, NFSA.

15 Author's correspondence with Tony Eggleton, 26 November 2016.

16 ibid.

17 McMahon, in *The Harold Holt Mystery*, 18 February 1985, NFSA.

18 Lawless, in *The Harold Holt Mystery*, 18 February 1985, NFSA. McMahon continued to deny it, even claiming at one point that it could not have been him as people called him Bill, not Billy.

19 Hasluck, 1995, p. 143.

Chapter 23: Cold Water

1 Killen, 1985, p. 119.

2 Howson, 1984, p. 363.

3 McMahon, in *The Harold Holt Mystery*, 18 February 1985, NFSA.

4 Golding, 1996, p. 267.

5 Hancock, 2002, p. 137.

6 Hasluck, 1997, pp. 146–47.

7 Peter Kelly, 'Politics the day Holt died', *Aus.*, 13–14 December 1986, p. 2.

8 Hancock, 2002, p. 137.

9 Author's correspondence with Tony Eggleton, 26 November 2016.

10 According to Simon Warrender and Peter Blazey, McMahon also called the Victorian Premier, Henry Bolte. See Warrender, 1973, p. 169; Blazey, 1990, p. 204.

11 Trengrove, 1969, p. 176.

12 Author's interview with Sir Peter Lawler, 22 November 2016.

13 ibid.

14 Author's correspondence with Doug Anthony, 25 July 2016.

15 Hasluck, 1997, pp. 148–49.

16 Nigel Bowen interviewed by Ron Hurst, NLA Oral History, TRC 4900/61.

17 R.G. Casey diaries, 17 December 1967, NLA MS6150; Barwick, 1995, p. 290.

18   John Bunting to Murray Tyrrell, 16 February 1968, NAA: M1945, 1.

19   Tiny Lawless, in *The Harold Holt Mystery*, 18 February 1985, NFSA.

20   R.G. Casey diaries, 17 December 1967, NLA MS6150.

21   McEwen, 1983, p. 74.

22   R.G. Casey diaries, 17 December 1967, NLA MS6150.

23   Sir James Plimsoll interviewed by Clyde Cameron, NLA Oral History, TRC 1967, pp. 185–86.

24   John Gorton interviewed by Clyde Cameron, NLA Oral History, TRC 1702, vol. 1, pp. 58–60.

25   Hasluck, 1997, pp. 149–50.

26   These times are based on the movements of Gorton, McEwen, and Hasluck, as detailed in Golding, 1993, pp. 268–69; Hancock, 2002, p. 139; and Hasluck, 1995, p. 148.

27   Hasluck, 1997, p. 149.

28   Golding, 1996, pp. 269–70.

29   John Gorton interviewed by Clyde Cameron, NLA Oral History, TRC 1702, vol. 1, p. 59.

30   Hancock, 2002, p. 139.

31   Bolton, 2015, p. 406.

32   Hudson, 1986, p. 310.

33   ibid.

34   R.G. Casey diary, 18 December 1967, NLA MS6150.

35   Dudley Erwin interviewed by Robert Linford, NLA Oral History, TRC 4900/7, 3:6–7.

36   John McEwen interviewed by Ray Aitchison, NLA Oral History, TRC 311, 2:1/3.

37   Alan Reid interviewed by Daniel Connell, NLA Oral History, TRC 2172, p. 36.

38   McEwen, 1983, p. 76.

39   Peter Kelly, 'Politics the day Holt died',

40   *Aus.*, 13–14 December 1986, p. 2.

40   ibid.

41   See, for example, 'Country Party warns: anybody but McMahon', *AFR*, 19 December 1967, p. 1.

42   Reid, 1969, p. 135.

43   Alan Ramsey, 'The power game', *Aus.*, 27 December 1968, p. 7.

44   Hasluck, 1997, p. 151.

45   Howson, 1984, pp. 367, 373, 376.

46   Peter Howson, in 'It's alright, Boss', *The Liberals*, TV programme, 1994.

47   McEwen, 1983, p. 76.

48   'Prime Minister, Mr J. McEwen, meets with press', Canberra, 20 December 1967, no. 1742, APMC Transcripts.

49   Casey to Michael Adeane, 8 January 1968, in Hudson, 1986, p. 309.

50   Killen, 1985, p. 124.

51   Holt's stepson, Sam, had suggested that he might put himself forward for the seat. By Boxing Day, he had retreated from this. See Hancock, 2002, p. 143.

52   Alan Ramsey, 'Power game', *Aus.*, 27 December 1968, p. 7.

53   Author's correspondence with Tony Eggleton, 26 November 2016.

54   Howson, 1984, pp. 365–66.

55   Fitzgerald and Holt, 2010, pp. 192–93; Reid, 1969, pp. 132–42.

56   McNicoll, 1978, p. 233.

57   Dennis Minogue, 'Packer's $15 million deal', *New Times*, September 1977, pp. 4–5. Frank Jennings, a private secretary to Holt at the time, recalled that when arrangements for the memorial service were being made, the putative contenders—Gorton, Hasluck, McEwen, Fairhall, Bury, and McMahon—were not allowed

to ride in the same plane together. McMahon was given use of a DC3, a point that he was unhappy about. See Frank Jennings interviewed by Barry York, 10 October 2007, MoAD Oral History Project.

58 Norman Abjorensen, 'Black Jack McEwen almost a Lib PM', *CT*, 13 September 1992, pp. 1, 2.

59 'Kent Hughes wants McEwen to stay as PM', *Aus.*, 30 December 1967, p. 1.

60 David Eric Fairbairn interviewed by Robert Linford, NLA Oral History, TRC 4900/72.

61 Alan Reid interviewed by Daniel Connell, NLA Oral History, TRC 2172, p. 78; McNicoll, 1978, pp. 233–34.

62 ibid.

63 One was apparently Alan Reid. See John Gorton, 'I did it my way', *Aus.*, 15 August 1971, p. 10.

64 McMahon aide-mémoire, 7 December 1969. Copy in the author's possession. According to it, Hasluck gave a similar guarantee face to face.

65 Menzies to Henderson, 4 January 1968, in Henderson (ed.), 2011, pp. 171–76.

66 McNicoll, 1978, pp. 234–35.

67 Peter Kelly, 'Politics the day Holt died', *Aus.*, 13–14 December 1986, p. 2.

68 Author's interview with Peter Kelly, 1 October 2016.

69 ibid.

70 ibid.

71 See, for example, 'McEwen did his duty: Hasluck; BIG denies link with McMahon', *CT*, 29 December 1967, p. 1; or 'BIG not main issue in govt. rift—McEwen', *SMH*, 29 December 1967, p. 1.

72 Ian Fitchett interviewed by Heather Rusden and Mungo Wentworth MacCallum, NLA Oral History, TRC 2249, 9:2/5.

73 Brian Toohey, 'The Austeo papers', *National Times*, 6 May 1983, pp. 3–7.

74 The story is conspicuously flattering: 'Economic observers complain that his administration has been so nearly right that they are almost out of business as critics,' it says at one point. See 'The success story of William McMahon', *DT*, 4 January 1968, pp. 8–9; and Alan Reid, 'McMahon seen as able treasurer', *DT*, 6 January 1968, p. 3. The *Telegraph* followed this up, on 7 January, with a forthright editorial: 'We believe, and have, for a long time, that Mr William McMahon would, if he stood, be worthy of the leadership.' See 'Wanted—a tough but wise leader', *Sunday Telegraph*, 7 January 1968, p. 2.

75 'McEwen—strength through growth', *Aus.*, 4 January 1968, p. 7.

76 Author's interview with Alan Ramsey, 31 January 2018.

77 Golding, 1996, p. 276.

78 'Why McEwen vetoed McMahon', *Aus.*, 6 January 1968, p. 1.

79 Rokuro Sase, 'Japan Trade Centre replies to McEwen's statement', *CT*, 9 January 1968, p. 10.

80 'Newton's contract with Japanese', *SMH*, 9 January 1968, p. 1.

81 See Alan Barnes, 'Bid to depose McMahon', *Age*, 9 January 1968, pp. 1, 2; Eggleton to Gorton, 8 March 1968, NAA: M3787, 32. Alan Reid writes that it was Robert Macklin, McEwen's press secretary,

who confirmed the reports; Reid also claims to have checked with Macklin that it was he, and that his comments had been reported accurately. See Reid, 1969, p. 185. In an interview with the author (11 July 2016), Macklin denied leaking these stories or confirming them, and stated that it was a colleague who had done so.

82   Hasluck, 1997, p. 155.
83   Reid, 1969, pp. 179–94.
84   Hancock, 2002, p. 144.
85   Tom Hughes said that he thought Gorton a 'fresh face with a reasonably radical, open-minded approach to the leadership'. While Hasluck enjoyed 'considerable respect', Hughes did not see him as 'the leader to take the Liberal Party forward'. Author's interview with Tom Hughes, 16 August 2016.
86   Peter Kelly later claimed that McMahon's support for Gorton was 'the deciding factor'. See Peter Kelly, 'Politics the day Holt died', *Aus.*, 13–14 December 1986, p. 2. Other writers, less definitively, have made similar statements. See, for example, Hancock, 2002, p. 147; Hasluck, 1997, p. 154; Howson, 1984, p. 379.
87   Aitchison, 1978, pp. 96–103.
88   Howard, 1972, p. 225.
89   Reid, 1969, p. 198.
90   McMahon, 'Speech delivered by the chairman and deputy leader at the Liberal Party meeting on Tuesday, 9 January 1968', copy in possession of author.
91   Gordon Freeth interviewed by John Ferrell, NLA Oral History, TRC 4900/87.
92   Menzies to Henderson, 4 January 1968, in Henderson (ed.), 2011, p. 173.
93   Don Chipp interviewed by Bernadette Schedvin, NLA Oral History, TRC 4900/73, 7:11.
94   Author's interview with Tom Hughes, 16 August 2016.
95   Hancock, 2002, p. 147; Reid, 1969, p. 200.
96   Howard, 1972, pp. 225–26; Reid, 1969, p. 201.
97   Hasluck, 1997, p. 155. McMahon had played his cards well. Certainly it is the case that McEwen's veto, and McMahon's decision to refrain from contesting the leadership, allowed the weakness of his support to go unexposed.

Chapter 24: Privilege

1   Bowman diary, 14 March 1984.
2   ibid.
3   ibid., 22 March 1984.
4   ibid., 6 April 1984.
5   ibid., 2 May 1984.
6   ibid., 11 April 1984.
7   ibid., 16 April 1984.
8   ibid., 1 May 1984.
9   ibid., 20 June 1984.
10   ibid., 18 May 1984.
11   ibid., 24 February 1984.
12   Hasluck, 1997, p. 187.
13   ibid., p. 128.
14   ibid., p. 187.
15   Buckley, 1991, pp. 211–12.
16   Malcolm Fraser interviewed by Clyde Cameron, NLA Oral History, TRC 2162, pp. 100–02.
17   Author's interview with Alan Ramsey, 31 January 2018.
18   Bowman diary, 25 June 1984.

Chapter 25: The New Man

1   McMahon to Gorton, 12 January 1968, NAA: M3787, 32.

2   Author's correspondence with Tony Eggleton, 26 November 2016.

3   'McMahon should step down', *Aus.*, 9 January 1968, p. 6.

4   'Clean slate', *Aus.*, 10 January 1968, p. 6.

5   Hancock, 2002, pp. 161–62.

6   Spry to Gorton, 5 February 1968, NAA: M3787, 12.

7   McMahon was well aware of the difficulties that would be involved in Gorton attempting to remove him. As he told Peter Howson later that year, 'Gorton knows he can't afford to drop me from the Cabinet.' See Howson, 1984, p. 434.

8   'Notetaker EJ Bunting—notes of meetings 28 February–3 April 1968', NAA: A11099, 1/91.

9   McEwen acknowledged this in the House. See Whitlam and McEwen, *CPD HoR*, vol. 58, 13 March 1968, p. 29.

10 Cabinet meetings on 28 February 1968 and 12 March 1968, 'Notetaker EJ Bunting—notes of meetings 28 February–3 April 1968', NAA: A11099, 1/91.

11 Holt to Johnson, 6 October 1967, NAA: A5882/2, CO77.

12 Murray Groot and Rodney Tiffen in King (ed.), 1983, p. 131.

13 Foreign Affairs and Defence Committee meeting, 12 March 1968, 'Notetaker EJ Bunting—notes of meetings 28 February–3 April 1968', NAA: A11099, 1/91.

14 Robert Collins, 1996, 'The economic crisis of 1968 and the waning of the "American Century"', *American Historical Review*, vol. 101, no. 2, April, pp. 396–422.

15 Cabinet meeting 18 March 1968, 'Notetaker EJ Bunting—notes of meetings 28 February–3 April 1968', NAA: A11099, 1/91.

16 See Ham, 2007, p. 362; Cabinet meeting 2 April 1968, 'Notetaker EJ Bunting—notes of meetings 28 February–3 April 1968', NAA: A11099, 1/91.

17 Gorton believed both Bunting and Howson had misled the Parliament. See John Gorton interviewed by Clyde Cameron, NLA Oral History, TRC 1702, vol. 1, p. 50; Hancock, 2004, p. 90.

18 Bunting to Trumble, 11 March 1968, NAA: M321, 1.

19 Author's interview with Sir Peter Lawler, 22 November 2016.

20 Gorton, 22 January 1968, in Hancock, 2002, p. 154.

21 See Howson, 1984, p. 430.

22 Trengrove, 1969, p. 214.

23 Howson, 1984, p. 411.

24 Alan Ramsey, 'The power game', *Aus.*, 27 December 1968, p. 7.

25 Aitchison, 1974, p. 15.

26 Howson, 1984, p. 427.

27 Author's interview with Alan Ramsey, 31 January 2018.

28 Mitchell, 2007, p. 38.

29 Aitchison, 1974, p. 15.

30 Howson, 1984, p. 431.

31 Killen, 1985, p. 131.

32 Author's interview with Peter Kelly, 1 October 2016.

33 Author's interview with Sir Peter Lawler, 22 November 2016.

34 'William McMahon talks about everything except the budget', *Aus.*, 8 August 1969, p. 22.

35   Author's interview with Peter Kelly, 1 October 2016.

36   Author's correspondence with John Stone, 8 January 2017.

37   'William McMahon talks about everything except the budget', *Aus.*, 8 August 1969, p. 22.

38   Whitlam, 19 April 1968, in Hocking, 2008, pp. 314–15.

39   Cairns, 24 April 1968, in Hocking, 2008, p. 318.

40   Cabinet discussed Bolte's decision to introduce a receipts tax in Victoria on 25 January 1968. Though McMahon took the lead in the discussion, it is clear from the records that he and Gorton were in agreement about the Commonwealth position on this—and the likely response. See 'Notetaker EJ Bunting—notes of meetings 11 January 1968–23 February 1968', NAA: A11099, 1/90.

41   'Commonwealth/State financial relations—DECISION 299', NAA: A5868, 130.

42   'Bolte attacks PM on finances', *CT*, 13 December 1968, p. 3.

43   'Premiers out-pointed', *CT*, 28 June 1968, p. 1.

44   Reid, 1969, p. 74.

45   Author's interview with Peter Kelly, 1 October 2016.

46   *Incentive*, no. 154, 1 July 1968.

47   McMahon press release, 'Miss Wheatley', 21 January 1969.

48   McEwen's press secretary, Robert Macklin, approached Tony Eggleton about having Newton's representatives excluded from prime ministerial briefings. See Eggleton to Gorton, 8 March 1969, NAA: M2093, 14.

49   Laurie Oakes, 'Govt upset by resignation of secretary', *Sun*, 22 January 1969, p. 3. In April 1969, there were moves to have Wheatley appointed as Head of Service for *The Independent*, a new Perth newspaper. Peter Kelly, who telephoned Tony Eggleton to inform him of this news, 'hoped that Miss Wheatley might be kept in mind on those occasions when Mrs. Gorton was seeing the ladies of the Press'. Whether Wheatley took up the position is not known. See Tony Eggleton to Gorton, 29 April 1969, NAA: M2093, 14.

50   'William McMahon talks about everything except the budget', *Aus.*, 8 August 1968, p. 22.

51   Mitchell, 2007, pp. 20–21.

52   *The Australian Economy 1968*, Treasury, Commonwealth of Australia, Canberra, p. 7.

53   McMahon, *CPD HoR*, vol. 60, 13 August 1968, pp. 35–48.

54   Author's correspondence with John Stone, 8 January 2017.

55   Howson, 1984, p. 441.

56   'A give and take budget', *Aus.*, 15 August 1968, p. 10.

57   'Budget has a place for humanity', *DT*, 14 August 1968, p. 2.

58   'Warning by Askin on financial policy', *DT*, 14 August 1968, p. 10.

59   Maximilian Walsh, 'Has cabinet miscounted the votes?', *AFR*, 14 August 1968, p. 1.

60   Howson, 1984, pp. 450, 453.

61   Aitchison, 1978, p. 158.

62   Gorton press statement, 22 September 1968, 'Amendment to ACT Companies Ordinance', PM no. 83/1968.

63 Gorton, *Sunday Aus.*, 15 August 1971, p. 11; 22 August 1971, p. 10; 12 September 1971, p. 6.

64 John Gorton interviewed by Clyde Cameron, NLA Oral History, TRC 1702, vol. 1, p. 58.

65 Gorton, in Reid, 1971, p. 129.

66 See also 'Sir John Bunting', NAA: A11099, 1/96; Hancock, 2002, pp. 127–28.

67 See Reid, 1971, pp. 127–28.

68 Howson, 1984, p. 474.

69 Alan Ramsey, 'The power game', *Aus.*, 27 December 1968, p. 7.

70 Gorton, 'Flinders electorate Liberal Party luncheon, Mornington, Vic', 14 October 1968, no. 1938.

71 Fadden to Bunting, 20 October 1968, NAA: M321, 1.

72 Kiernan, 1986, p. 70.

73 ibid., p. 95.

74 Golding, 1996, pp. 29–30.

75 John Gorton interviewed by Clyde Cameron, NLA Oral History, TRC 1702, vol. 1, p. 291.

76 Cabinet notebook, 'Sir John Bunting', NAA: A11099, 1/97; 'Cabinet minute—exchange control—News Limited—WITHOUT SUBMISSION [1 page]', NAA: A5872, decision 731.

77 Hancock, 2002, p. 338; Griffen-Foley, 2003, pp. 153–54.

78 Whitwell, 1986, pp. 156–59.

79 Gorton and McMahon press statement, 5 December 1968, 'Overseas takeovers of Australian companies', PM no. 96/1968. See too McMahon's press statement, 2 April 1969, on overseas investment, which simultaneously deplored foreign takeovers and asserted the benefits they could bring: NAA: M58, 220.

80 Alan Ramsey, 'The power game', *Aus.*, 27 December 1968, p. 7.

81 Maxwell Newton, 'Mr McMahon's economic principles go out the window', *Incentive*, no. 177, 9 December 1968, p. 3.

82 'The new economics? ... none', *AFR*, 9 December 1968, pp. 1, 28.

83 'I think that he reflected the views of Treasury almost completely,' Gorton later said. See John Gorton interviewed by Clyde Cameron, NLA Oral History, TRC 1702, vol. 1, p. 63.

84 Maxwell Newton published the full text of Gorton's 11 December press conference for his subscribers. See 'The Prime Minister, the Rt Hon. John G. Gorton, full text of his press conference, 11 December 1968'.

85 Cabinet meeting 18 December 1968, 'Sir John Bunting', NAA: A11099, 1/98.

86 Maxwell Newton, 'Hot water bags—and damn the cost', *Incentive*, no. 178, 13 January 1969, p. 3.

87 Alan Ramsey, 'It's in the book—or is it?', *Aus.*, 7 October 1968, p. 7.

88 Howson, 1984, pp. 479, 484, 491; Fitzgerald and Holt, 2010, p. 207.

89 Howson, 1984, pp. 491–92.

90 Mungo MacCallum interviewed by Mel Pratt, NLA Oral History, TRC 121/44, p. 24.

91 Dudley Erwin interviewed by Robert Linford, NLA Oral History, TRC 4900/7.

92 Alan Reid states these rumours forthrightly. See Reid, 1971, p. 81.

93 Hasluck, 1995, p. 158.

94 See, for example, Menzies to Henderson, 21 February 1969, in Henderson (ed.), 2011, pp. 206–07.

95 Maxwell Newton, *Insight*,

10 February 1969.

96   Frank Browne, *TIH*, no. 1079, 6 December 1968; no. 1080, 13 December 1968; no. 1084, 31 January 1969.

97   James, *CPD HoR*, vol. 62, 19 March 1969, pp. 694–95.

98   Killen and Hughes, ibid., pp. 695–98.

99   Aston, ibid., pp. 698–99.

100 McMahon, ibid., pp. 701–02. Jim Killen was scathing about McMahon's intervention. It 'put the incident on the front page of newspapers', he wrote. See Killen, 1985, p. 140.

101 Barnard, *CPD HoR*, vol. 62, 19 March 1969, pp. 702–03.

102 Gorton, Whitlam, and McEwen, *CPD HoR*, vol. 62, 20 March 1969, pp. 709–14.

103 Fitzgerald and Holt, 2010, pp. 206–10.

104 St John, *CPD HoR*, vol. 62, 20 March 1969, pp. 790–92.

105 Gorton, ibid., pp. 792–93.

106 Sam McMahon told newspapers that he would oppose St John for pre-selection should Liberal Party branches in St John's electorate of Warringah not withdraw his nomination. His decision was made without the knowledge or influence of his brother, he said. See 'Mr S. McMahon offers to stand', *CT*, 27 March 1969, p. 1.

107 Hancock, 2002, pp. 222–23.

108 Tony Eggleton, Gorton's press secretary, kept a file on Newton and the activities of his reporters: NAA: M2093, 14.

109 'The Prime Minister, the Rt. Hon. John G. Gorton, Full text of his press conference, 11 December 1968'

may be found as an addendum in compilations of *Incentive*.

110 *Incentive*, 7 April 1969; and cabinet minute no. 922, 'Cabinet document—"Incentive"', 15 April 1969, NAA: A5872, 922; Interview notes between F. Mills and Newton, 15 April 1969, NAA: M3787, 12.

111 Maxwell Newton, 'Australian ambassador talks with French foreign minister', *Management Newsletter*, 13 May 1969, pp. 3–4.

112 The prime minister's office was following matters closely, as a dossier on the matter shows: NAA: M3787, 12. According to Gorton, the whole of cabinet agreed on the raid. See John Gorton interviewed by Clyde Cameron, NLA Oral History, TRC 1702, vol. 1, p. 322.

113 Cabinet decision no. 922, 15 April 1969, NAA: A5872, 922.

114 Newton, 1993, p. 178.

115 Author's interview with Peter Kelly, 1 October 2016, 1 May 2017.

116 ibid. John Stone, who had known Newton for many years, was told about this telephone call by Newton, who stated definitively that it was McMahon on the other end: Author's correspondence with John Stone, 8 January 2017.

117 Supreme Court of Australian Capital Territory, 1969, 14, Federal Law Reports, *The Queen v. Tillett and others; ex parte Newton and others*, pp. 101–28. After the charges were dismissed, Newton supposedly sent Gorton a pithy, gloating telegram: 'Ho-de-hum.' See Aitchison, 1978, p. 200. Peter Kelly recalls that the telegram read only 'Ho-hum.' When he queried whether Newton should

say more in the reply, Newton grinned and said that it was enough. Clyde Cameron mentioned to Gorton the possibility that McMahon had tipped off Newton about the raid. Gorton's response was non-committal, though he agreed Newton 'probably' would have known it was coming. See John Gorton interviewed by Clyde Cameron, NLA Oral History, TRC 1702, vol. 1, p. 320.

118 In April, McMahon told Howson of his doubts and fears about Gorton but said he would do nothing. Howson also records a conversation with the president of the Senate, Senator Alister McMullin, who said that Frank Packer had warned Gorton about his treatment of McMahon: if Gorton continued to denigrate the treasurer, Packer supposedly said, Packer would turn his press against him. This may have been in response to a conversation Gorton had in March with New South Wales premier Bob Askin, when Gorton said he was going to move McMahon from the Treasury. See Howson, 1984, pp. 499–500, 502–05, 509–16 and Reid, 1971, p. 78.

119 *The Australian Economy 1969*, Department of the Treasury, Canberra.

120 McMahon, *CPD HoR*, vol. 64, 12 August 1969, p. 31.

121 Howson, 1984, p. 539.

122 McMahon, *CPD HoR*, vol. 64, 12 August 1969, pp. 31–43.

123 'A budget for progress and humanity', *DT*, 13 August 1969, p. 2.

124 David Lowe, 'Time bombs with a welfare veneer', *AFR*, 13 August 1969, pp. 1, 26.

125 Maxwell Newton, 'An act of vandalism', *Incentive*, no. 209, 18 August 1969, p. 5; Maximilian Walsh, 'To the polls while the illusion lasts', *AFR*, 13 August 1969, pp. 1, 5.

126 'Policies', *Aus.*, 13 August 1969, p. 12.

127 For an account of Freeth's fitness, compared with McMahon's, see Hasluck, 1997, pp. 188–89.

128 Reid, 1971, pp. 196–98.

129 Freeth, *CPD HoR*, vol. 64, 14 August 1969, pp. 310–17.

130 Whitlam, ibid., pp. 317–23.

131 It was often overlooked that the sections on the USSR had been drafted, at least in part, by Freeth's permanent head, Sir James Plimsoll. See Hearder, 2015, pp. 204–08. Killen suggests that the speech caused the budget to fade 'into relative insignificance'. See Killen, 1985, p. 144.

132 Howson, 1984, p. 541.

133 Reid, 1971, p. 304.

134 Ian Hancock writes that the Liberal Party's staff planning committee had concluded in June 1969 that a campaign fought on domestic matters should be avoided. Whether Gorton received this advice is unclear; nonetheless, his shift towards defence late in August was notable. See Hancock, 2002, pp. 228, 235.

135 Gorton, 'Kingston electorate Liberal Party dinner', 12 September 1969, PMC Transcripts.

136 Gorton, 'Federal elections 1969 policy speech', 8 October 1969, PMC transcripts.

137 Reid, 1971, p. 308.

138 See Howson, 1984, pp. 549–54.

139 Menzies to Henderson, 24 October 1969, in Henderson (ed.), 2011, pp. 222–25.

140 Jonathan Gaul, 'Ten more worrying days for Mr Gorton', *CT*, 14 October 1969, p. 2.

141 'No direct answer on McMahon', *CT*, 20 October 1969, p. 11.

142 Arthur Fadden to Ulrich Ellis, 21 October 1969, NLA MS1006, Box 30.

143 'Whitlam says McMahon being humiliated', *CT*, 21 October 1969, p. 10.

144 Author's correspondence with Mungo MacCallum, 4 October 2017; MacCallum, 2002, p. 188.

145 Jonathan Gaul, 'Up to PM, McMahon says', *CT*, 22 October 1969, p. 7.

Chapter 26: Fragments and Credit

1 Salter, 1995, p. 35.

2 Mark Hayne, 'The autobiography that never was', *SMH*, 11 April 1988, p. 15.

3 Gorton later claimed that McMahon's good reputation as treasurer stemmed from his doing exactly as his department urged. See John Gorton interviewed by Clyde Cameron, NLA Oral History, TRC 1702, vol. 1, p. 63. Don Chipp also thought that McMahon was lucky to have inherited the good economic conditions from Harold Holt. See Chipp and Larkin, 1978, p. 125.

4 Dudley Erwin interviewed by Robert Linford, NLA Oral History, TRC 4900/7.

5 Billy Snedden interviewed by Catherine Santamaria, NLA Oral History, TRC 455.

6 Author's correspondence with John Stone, 6 January 2017.

7 Mark Hayne, 'The autobiography that never was', *SMH*, 11 April 1988.

8 Bowman diary, 4 June 1984.

9 Author's correspondence with John Stone, 8 January 2017.

10 Peter Sekuless, in Grattan (ed.), 2001, pp. 313–23.

Chapter 27: Subsequent Plots

1 Adam Carr, 'Australian Legislative election of 25 October 1969', *Psephos*, <http://psephos.adam-carr.net/countries/a/australia/1969/1969reps1.txt>, accessed 29 December 2016.

2 Jonathan Gaul, 'The PM meets the press', *CT*, 27 October 1969, p. 8.

3 Irwin wrote to all Liberal and government MPs in this vein. See Hancock, 2002, p. 243.

4 John Carrick to Fred Osborne, cited in Hancock, 2002, p. 244.

5 Alan Reid, 'Qld Liberals to review elections', *DT*, 28 October 1969, p. 3.

6 David Fairbairn interviewed by Mel Pratt, NLA Oral History, TRC 121/74.

7 Fairbairn to Gorton, 30 October 1969, NAA: M3787, 48.

8 Jonathan Gaul, 'Power struggle', *CT*, 31 October 1969, p. 1.

9 Author's interview with Tom Hughes, 16 August 2016.

10 Howson, 1984, p. 563.

11 ibid., p. 564.

12 ibid., p. 566.

13 ibid., p. 568.

14 ibid.

15 'Editorial', *Sunday Telegraph*, 2 November 1969, p. 2.

16 Paul Hasluck, 'Events following the election of October 25, 1969', NAA:

M1767, 3. McEwen and Hasluck met at the Melbourne Cup on 4 November. In the course of that conversation, McEwen informed Hasluck that he did not believe Gorton had learned 'a thing' from the election, had found him 'immovable', and stated that he would keep out of the leadership fight, believing a veto of McMahon would do no good. 'If the Liberal Party elected McMahon, however,' wrote Hasluck, 'he (McEwen) would want to do some "pretty hard talking" and he would want any arrangement for a coalition put down in writing in a form that would enable him to keep McMahon pinned down to his promises.'

17   McEwen, 1983, p. 76. Others have attributed McEwen's recission of his veto to McMahon's attempts to flatter him. Peter Howson suggests that both men were clearly concerned by Gorton's policies on defence and foreign relations: Howson, 1984, pp. 546–47, 570.

18   McEwen, press statement, 3 November 1969.

19   McEwen, 1983, p. 79.

20   Laurie Oakes, 'Laurie Oakes' remarks at launching of *John McEwen: his story*', 21 October 2014, <http://www. mattcanavan.com.au/laurie_oakes_ remarks>, accessed 29 December 2016.

21   'Fairbairn would serve', *CT*, 4 November 1969, p. 1.

22   'Fairbairn's statement: questioning the policies of Mr Gorton', *CT*, 4 November 1969, p. 8.

23   Author's correspondence with Doug Anthony, 25 July 2016.

24   Alan Reid, 'McMahon to stand as leader', *DT*, 4 November 1969, p. 1.

25   Gorton, 'Declaration of Higgins poll', 5 November 1969, APMC Transcripts.

26   Howson, 1984, pp. 564–65.

27   Alan Reid, *Bulletin*, 8 November 1969, p. 18.

28   Reid, 1971, pp. 362–65.

29   Author's interview with Bruce MacCarthy, 5 August 2016. The rescission motion ensured that the motion was held over until November, by which time Gorton had been re-elected. According to MacCarthy, a vote to withdraw the motion was held in his absence and the count was deliberately left unreported in issues of *The Australian Liberal*. Alan Reid records this, too. See Reid, 1971, p. 362.

30   'McMahon "a federalist"', *CT*, 5 November 1969, p. 3.

31   McNicoll, 1978, p. 273.

32   John Gorton interviewed by Clarrie Hermes, NLA Oral History, TRC 4900/47, 6:6.

33   Author's interview with Tom Hughes, 16 August 2016.

34   Charles 'Bert' Kelly diary, 11 November 1969, NLA MS7424. See also Kelly, 1978, pp. 112–13. Freeth's poor opinion of McMahon did not prevent him from accepting a subsequent offer from McMahon to become Ambassador to Japan. See Gordon Freeth interviewed by John Ferrell, NLA Oral History, TRC 4900/87.

35   Menzies to Henderson, 29 October 1969, in Henderson (ed.), 2011, pp. 222–25.

36   Howson, 1984, p. 571.

37   Aitchison, 1978, p. 234.

38   Howson, 1984, p. 575. See also Reid,

1971, p. 375. If true, this would
have been an egregious example of
interference; however, it should be
noted that Howson's interpretation
and record of the conversation may
not be wholly accurate.

39   Unsigned note, NAA: M3787, 48.
40   Reid, 1971, p. 377.
41   ibid.
42   'Mr Gorton sees "unity, strength"',
      CT, 8 November 1969, p. 13.
43   Aitchison, 1978, p. 235.
44   'Two shook hands', CT, 8 November
      1969, p. 1.
45   Killen, 1985, p. 150.
46   Hasluck, 'Events following the
      election of October 25, 1969', NAA:
      M1767, 3.
47   Howson, 1984, p. 576.
48   Max Newton, 'A great body of men',
      Incentive, no. 221, 10 November
      1969, pp. 6–7.
49   Howson, 1984, pp. 576–77.
50   Hasluck, 'Events following the
      election of October 25, 1969', NAA:
      M1767, 3.
51   ibid.
52   ibid.

Chapter 28: Loyalty

1   McMahon, aide-mémoires from
     conversations with Fairbairn, 30 and
     31 October 1969, copies in the
     author's possession.
2   McMahon aide-mémoire from
     conversation with Gorton,
     30 October 1969, copy in the author's
     possession. Any assessment of this
     aide-mémoire should take into
     account that the note of the need
     for a practised political hand in
     External Affairs may be reflective of

     McMahon's need to attach prestige to
     the portfolio he would soon take over.
3   McMahon aide-mémoire from
     conversation with McEwen,
     3 November 1969, copy in the
     author's possession.
4   McMahon aide-mémoire from
     conversation with senator Robert
     Cotton, 28 October 1969, copy in the
     author's possession.
5   McMahon aide-mémoire from
     conversation with Les Bury,
     12 November 1969, copy in the
     author's possession.
6   McMahon aide-mémoire from
     conversation with Dudley Erwin,
     11 November 1969, copy in the
     author's possession.
7   Confidential memo, 28 October
     1969, no author listed, copy in the
     author's possession.
8   Author's interview with Peter Kelly,
     2 May 2017.

Chapter 29: A New Stage

1   See Hancock, 2016, pp. 129–30;
     Killen, 1985, p. 142; Robert 'Duke'
     Bonnett interviewed by Peter
     Sekuless, 21 April–21 July 1983,
     NLA Oral History, TRC 1454.
2   The so-called cocktail Cabinets were
     a point of criticism: see Reid, 1971.
3   Howson, 1984, p. 577.
4   'Federal election campaign', report
     to Federal Executive from the Staff
     Planning Committee, 19 November
     1969, Robert Southey papers, NLA
     MS9901/1/30–31.
5   Howson, 1984, p. 577.
6   Author's interview with C.R. 'Kim'
     Jones, 2 June 2017.
7   Author's interview and

correspondence with C.R. 'Kim' Jones, 2 June, 3 June, and 10 June 2017.

8   Keith Waller interviewed by J.D.B. Miller, NLA Oral History, TRC 314, pp. 29–31.

9   Chipp and Larkin, 1978, p. 125.

10   Hunt, *CPD HoR*, vol. 160, 12 April 1988, p. 1407.

11   Author's correspondence with Mungo MacCallum, 4 October 2017.

12   On 30 November, McMahon was telling Howson of his concerns about lack of forward planning in areas such as disengagement from Vietnam, the future of Thailand amid Chinese encroachment, the USSR and the Indian Ocean, and Australia's policy towards Japan. See Howson, 1984, p. 584.

13   See Hearder, 2015.

14   Waller, 1990, p. 42; Philip Flood interviewed by Gregory Wood, NLA Oral History, TRC 6350/5.

15   Tange, 2008, p. 20.

16   Bruce Juddery, 'Tange, Sir Arthur Harold (1914–2001)', *CT*, 11 May 2001, p. 13.

17   Tange to McMahon, 5 December 1969, in Edwards, 2006, p. 173.

18   McMahon to Tange, 12 December 1969, ibid.; Tange, 2008, p. 20.

19   ibid.

20   'Record of conversation: Prime Minister and Mr McMahon at 2.10PM, Thursday 27 November 1969', NAA: M3789, 39.

21   Sir James Plimsoll interviewed by Clyde Cameron, NLA Oral History, TRC 1967, p. 350.

22   Hearder, 2015, pp. 209–10.

23   ibid.

24   Freeth had requested Gorton appoint

him to an overseas post after losing the election. Gorton's first choice was London, then Washington. McMahon suggested Japan. See 'Record of conversation: Prime Minister and Mr McMahon at 2.10PM, Thursday 27 November 1969', NAA: M3789, 39.

25   Waller, 1990, p. 42. See also Waller to Casey, 3 February 1970, NAA: M1129, WALLER/K Part 1.

26   Hearder, 2015, p. 210.

27   Writing to Richard Casey, McMahon stated that his first weeks in External Affairs had left him 'inundated with the cables' and that his first effort had been South Vietnam. See McMahon to Casey, 18 December 1969, NAA: M1129, MCMAHON/W.

28   Howson, 1984, p. 594.

29   McMahon to Gorton, n.d., 'Withdrawal of Australian forces from Vietnam', NAA: A1838, TS696/8/4/11 Part 3.

30   Mark Uhlmann, 'Gorton as forthright as ever', *CT*, 13 February 1988, p. 15.

31   Reynolds and Lee (eds.), 2013, pp. xvii–liv.

32   Walsh, 1997, pp. 1–20.

33   'Nuclear Tests Conference: control posts in Australia', 13 June 1961, NAA: 5818, 1156.

34   Seaborg and Loeb, 1987, p. 252; Fairbairn, *CPD HoR*, vol. 54, 11 April 1967, pp. 1070–71; *CPD HoR*, vol. 54, 13 April 1967, p. 1214.

35   Gorton, *CPD Sen*, vol. 10, 8 May 1957, pp. 604–09; Trengrove, 1969, pp. 204–05, 250.

36   Carr, 1979, p. 169.

37   Sir James Plimsoll interviewed by Clyde Cameron, NLA Oral History, TRC 1967, p. 121.

38 Hubbard, 2004, pp. 526–43; Clohesy and Deery, 2015, pp. 217–32.

39 Hewitt to Gorton, 'The nuclear treaty', 28 April 1968, NAA: A5619, C48 Part 1.

40 Mozley Moyal, 1975, pp. 365–84.

41 Hubbard, 2004, pp. 526–43; Sir James Plimsoll interviewed by Clyde Cameron, NLA Oral History, TRC 1967, p. 121.

42 Walsh, 1997, pp. 1–20.

43 Gorton, 'Federal elections 1969 policy speech', 8 October 1969, PMC Transcripts.

44 Walsh, 1997, pp. 12.

45 See McMahon's cabinet submission no. 772, 'Construction of a Commonwealth sponsored nuclear power station in Australia', 8 September 1969, NAA: A5882/2, CO11 Part 1.

46 Mozley Moyal, 1975, p. 373.

47 'American embassy Canberra (Rice) to Secretary of State [Secret]', 30 January 1970, RG 59, Box 1688, Folder 'Def 7 Ausl–US–1/1/70', US National Archives, Maryland. My thanks to Professor Jacques E.C. Hymans, who provided me with the text of this cable.

48 McMahon to Gorton, 6 February 1970, NAA: M4251, 19 Part I.

49 Cabinet submission no. 120, 'Treaty on the non-proliferation of nuclear weapons', 13 February 1970, NAA: A5869, 120.

50 Gorton's marginalia on cabinet submission no. 120, 'Treaty on the non-proliferation of nuclear weapons', 13 February 1970, NAA: A5619, C48 Part 2.

51 Cabinet meeting, 17 February 1970, 'Sir John Bunting', NAA: A11099,

1/108. For another of the records of the meeting, see cabinet meeting, 17 February 1970, 'PJ Lawler', NAA: A11099, 1/284.

52 Cabinet decision no. 141, 'Treaty on the non-proliferation of nuclear weapons', 18 February 1970, NAA: A5869/1, vol. 6, 141.

53 Martin Reith, 27 February 1970, FCO 24/677, British National Archives, Kew, London.

54 Robert Howard's uncertain explanation for why cabinet had seen fit to reverse course on a commitment made only months before is indication of how the matter was overshadowed. See Howard, 1970, pp. 109–16. See also Stan Hutchinson, 'Australia to sign atom pact', *SMH*, 19 February 1970, pp. 1, 6.

55 McEwen to Gorton, 7 January 1970, quoted in Hancock, 2002, p. 266.

56 Hewitt to Gorton, quoted in Hancock, 2002, p. 266.

57 Cabinet submission no. 97, 'Proposal to establish an Industry Development Corporation of Australia', 23 January 1970, NAA: A5869, 97.

58 Cabinet notebook, 'PJ Lawler', NAA: A11099, 1/282.

59 Cabinet minute no. 87, 'Proposal to establish an Industry Development Corporation of Australia', 28 January 1970, NAA: A5869, 97.

60 Cabinet decision no. 115, 'Proposal to establish an Industry Development Corporation of Australia', 5 February 1970, NAA: A5882, CO817 Part 1.

61 Cabinet notebook, 'PJ Lawler', NAA: A11099, 1/283.

62 Les Bury interviewed by Mel Pratt, NLA Oral History, TRC 121/70.

63 Malcolm Fraser interviewed by Clyde Cameron, NLA Oral History, TRC 2162, p. 447.

64 John Gorton interviewed by Clyde Cameron, NLA Oral History, TRC 1702, vol. 1, pp. 322–24.

65 See inset, p. 4, 'Sir John Bunting', NAA: A11099, 1/107.

66 Howson, 1984, p. 597.

67 ibid., p. 602. When, late in February, the charter for the AIDC was presented to the parliamentary draughtsman for comment (the night before cabinet was to consider it), the draughtsman was moved to write to the attorney-general that the charter was 'full of commercial jargon and gobbledegook, and uses words that I suspect do not even exist in the English language'. Moreover, the charter did 'not have a constitutional feather to fly with'. See inset, 'Sir John Bunting', NAA: A11099, 1/109.

68 Fraser's talent had early been recognised by US observers. In 1964, he was one of two parliamentarians to be awarded a US-funded grant to study overseas. Whitlam was the other.

69 McMahon wrote to Gorton on 6 February suggesting he speak on 10 or 12 March and that 'logically' his statement should precede Fraser's defence statement. By the time Gorton replied to that letter, on 21 February, he noted that events had overtaken them, and that Fraser's statement needed to occur as soon as possible, with McMahon's to follow thereafter. See Gorton to McMahon, 1 December 1969; McMahon to Gorton, 4 December 1969; McMahon to Gorton, 6 February 1970; and Gorton to McMahon, 21 February 1970, NAA: M3787, 39.

70 Howson, 1984, p. 601. Fraser had also given a speech on 12 February to a Perth audience of Young Liberals that encroached on McMahon's territory. See John Bennetts, 'Defence sets the foreign policy pace', CT, 31 March 1970, p. 2.

71 Plimsoll to McMahon, 5 March 1970, NAA: M3789, 39.

72 Fraser and Simons, 2009, pp. 189–90.

73 Kellow and Carroll, 2011, pp. 93–111; Carroll and Kellow, 2012, pp. 512–25; Carroll, 2015, pp. 229–40.

74 Flood, 2011, p. 55.

75 McMahon to Gorton, 2 April 1970, NAA: M4251, 19 Part 1.

76 Cabinet minute no. 305, 30 April 1970, NAA: A5873, 305.

Chapter 30: Le Noir

1 J.G. Crawford's note, loose insertion in copies of *John McEwen: his story*, ed. R.V. Jackson. A copy of this note, annotated by McMahon, is in the author's possession.

2 McEwen, 1983, pp. 75–76, 79–80.

3 McMahon, *CPD HoR*, vol. 120, 25 November 1980, pp. 32–33.

4 McEwen, 1983, p. 85.

5 Bowman to McMahon, 12 March 1984, copy in the author's possession.

Chapter 31: Battles

1 When McMahon corresponded with Gorton about the prospect of a ministerial statement, in December 1969, he specifically cited Freeth's statement and emphasised that 'it was a prudent practice to make

a submission to cabinet prior to important statements being made involving changes of policy'. See McMahon to Gorton, 4 December 1969, NAA: M3787, 39.

2   As Malcolm Booker, a diplomat with the department at this time, was later to note, attempts to persuade McMahon to give 'a firm public lead on the Russian issue were met with the response that he was not going to let what happened to Freeth happen to him'. See Booker, 1978, p. 200.

3   Howson, 1984, pp. 611–12.

4   McMahon, *CPD HoR*, vol. 65, 19 March 1970, pp. 675–85.

5   ibid.

6   John Bennetts, 'Defence sets the foreign policy pace', *CT*, 31 March 1970, p. 2; 'Our foreign policy', *CT*, 21 March 1970, p. 2; Howson, 1984, p. 612.

7   For background to Malik's proposal, and Indonesia's positions during the conference, see Teik Soon, 1972.

8   Cabinet decision no. 299, 'Conference of Asian Foreign Ministers on Cambodia', 30 April 1970, NAA: A5873, 299.

9   'Australia backs meeting on Cambodia', *CT*, 28 April 1970, p. 1.

10   Cabinet notebook, 'PJ Lawler', NAA: A11099, 1/287.

11   Gorton, *CPD HoR*, vol. 66, 5 May 1970, pp. 1603–05.

12   Howson, 1984, pp. 623–24.

13   Gorton, *CPD HoR*, vol. 66, 22 April 1970, pp. 1456–59.

14   Whitlam, ibid., pp. 1459–62.

15   'Talks still relevant, McMahon says', *CT*, 15 May 1970, p. 11.

16   Author's interview with C.R. 'Kim'

Jones, 2 June 2017.

17   Teik Soon, 1972.

18   'Joint Communiqué—issued by the Conference of Foreign Ministers on Cambodia held in Jakarta', *Foreign Affairs Malaysia*, vol. 3, no. 1, June 1970, pp. 50–53.

19   McMahon acknowledged this in the House. See McMahon, *CPD HoR*, vol. 66, 19 May 1970, pp. 2346–47.

20   I concur with Geoffrey Bolton, who called it McMahon's 'finest hour'. See Geoffrey Bolton, in Tyler, Robbins, and March (eds), 2014, pp. 23–69.

21   Later, McMahon claimed that the most significant achievement of the conference was recognition that responsibility for regional problems—whether military, political or economic in nature—rested with the countries in the regions. See 'Hope of Soviet help', *CT*, 8 June 1970, p. 1.

22   McEwen, *CPD HoR*, vol. 66, 5 May 1970, pp. 1597–603; Howson, 1984, p. 628.

23   Howson, *CPD HoR*, vol. 66, 20 May 1970, pp. 2456–57.

24   Daly, ibid., pp. 2472–73.

25   Cabinet minute no. 74, 21 January 1970, NAA: A5873, 74.

26   Howson, 1984, p. 627.

27   Snedden and Schedvin, 1990, p. 89.

28   Howson, 1984, pp. 629–31.

29   Fairbairn, *CPD HoR*, vol. 66, 8 May 1970, pp. 1897–1901.

30   Howson, 1984, p. 631.

31   ibid.

32   ibid., pp. 632–33.

33   Gorton, *CPD HoR*, vol. 66, 15 May 1970, pp. 2242–46.

34   Patterson, ibid., p. 2246.

35   Gorton, ibid., p. 2246.

36 Fairbairn, ibid., pp. 2256–60.
37 Martin Reith, n.d., 'Visit to Sydney and Queensland, 21–22 May 1970', FCO 24/677, British National Archives, Kew, London.
38 John Bennetts, 'A battle won, but the war goes on', *CT*, 19 May 1970, p. 2.
39 Hasluck, 1997, p. 175.
40 Hasluck, 'Events following Gorton's crisis in May, 1970', NAA: M1767, 3.
41 Howson, 1984, pp. 639–40.
42 ibid., pp. 641–42.
43 Author's interview with Tom Hughes, 16 August 2016.
44 Author's correspondence with Tony Eggleton, 26 November 2016.
45 Hearder, 2015, p. 229.
46 Alan Reid to Sir Frank Packer, 20 May 1970, David McNicoll Papers, ML MSS 7419/3/1.
47 Author's interview with C.R. 'Kim' Jones, 2 June 2017.
48 Martin Reith, 27 February 1970, FCO 24/677, British National Archives, Kew, London.
49 Chipp and Larkin, 1978, pp. 94–95.
50 Author's interview with Tom Hughes, 16 August 2016.
51 John Bennetts, 'Liberals want federalism retained', *CT*, 9 June 1970, p. 1.
52 John Bennetts, 'PM favours evolving federal system', *CT*, 9 June 1970, p. 11.
53 Killen, 1985, p. 159.
54 Don Chipp would later suggest that understanding Gorton's downfall required study of the Liberal Party machine. See Chipp and Larkin, 1978, p. 93.
55 Author's interview with Bruce MacCarthy, 5 August 2016.
56 Maxwell Newton, 'Economic Report',
Incentive, no. 247, 1 June 1970, p. 5; 'Economic Report', *Incentive*, no. 253, 13 July 1970, p. 5.
57 Jim Killen later argued that McMahon's leaking of the budget was 'reprehensible' and 'one of the most serious indictments ever to be presented against a senior Minister of the Crown'; had it been known, Killen commented, McMahon's ascent to the prime ministership would have been 'made much more difficult' and 'somewhat miserable'. See Killen, 1985, p. 162.
58 Howson, 1984, pp. 647–50.
59 McMahon, *CPD HoR*, vol. 66, 22 April 1970, p. 1510; *CPD* HoR, vol. 69, 20 August 1970, p. 264; *CPD HoR*, vol. 70, 20 October 1970, p. 2454.
60 Phillip Darby, 'What British force for the region?', *CT*, 16 July 1970, p. 2.
61 C.H. Johnston to FCO, 4 August 1970, 10/78 and Carrington to FCO, 1 August 1970, telegram 862, FCO 24/645, British Archives, Kew, London.
62 McMahon, Fraser, Carrington, 31 July 1970, NAA: A5882/2, CO98.
63 See Howson, 1984, pp. 651–53.
64 'Settlement basis', *CT*, 4 July 1970, p. 1.
65 McMahon, *CPD HoR*, vol. 69, 3 September 1970, pp. 981–84; 'Cambodian aid lifted to $2m', *CT*, 4 September 1970, p. 1; Cabinet minute no. 659, 3 September 1970, NAA: A5873, 659.
66 McMahon to Gorton, 10 March 1970, NAA: M4251, 19 Part 1.
67 Bruce Juddery, 'Department had external-aid victory', *CT*, 2 September 1970, p. 25.

68 Whitlam, *CPD HoR*, vol. 69, 3 September 1970, pp. 984–87; Cabinet decision no. 657, 3 September 1970, NAA: A5873, 657. The so-called 'Pearson Report', named for former prime minister of Canada, Lester B. Pearson, who chaired the commission that authored the report, presented proposals for international co-operation and spelt out the responsibilities of donor and recipient countries. For information, discussion and a summary of the report, see the February 1970 edition of the *UNESCO Courier*.

69 Whitlam, *CPD HoR*, vol. 69, 15 September 1970, pp. 1144–46.

70 'Record of conversation with His Excellency Mr Shizuo Saito, Japanese Ambassador on Wednesday 1st, April 1970', NAA: M4252, 10.

71 Flood, 2011, pp. 63–64.

72 Griffen-Foley, 2014, p. 241.

73 Handwriting on the bottom of the note indicates that McMahon spoke with Packer that day. 'Olwen' [OMB] to McMahon, 17 August 1970, NAA: M4252, 8.

74 Plimsoll diary, 18 September 1970, Papers of James Plimsoll, NLA MS8048, Series 3, Box 9.

75 'Visit by Minister for External Affairs to Japan and United States: itinerary', NAA: M4252, 18.

76 Howson, 1984, pp. 657, 659; 'Vietnam debate needed, says McMahon', *CT*, 25 September 1970, p. 6.

77 Plimsoll diary, 24 September 1970, 'Papers of James Plimsoll', NLA MS8048, Series 3, Box 9.

78 Hearder, 2015, p. 229.

79 Cabinet minute no. 707, 'Senate election date', 30 September 1970, NAA: A5873, 707.

80 Hocking, 2008, pp. 355–62.

81 Hancock, 2016, pp. 156–60.

82 Snedden, *CPD HoR*, vol. 66, 7 May 1970, pp. 1783.

83 Cabinet minute no. 738, 'Demonstrations Bill', 20 October 1970, NAA: A5873, 738.

84 Howson, 1984, p. 663.

85 By November, Jess Bate was suggesting much the same thing. Howson, 1984, pp. 656, 675.

86 Cabinet minute no. 727, 'Tri-Service Officer Cadet Academy', 14 October 1970, NAA: A5873, 727.

87 See John Bennetts, 1970, 'Mr Fraser to resubmit caded college plan', *CT*, 16 October, p. 3.

88 Howson, 1984, p. 667.

89 ibid., p. 672.

90 Adam Carr, 'Australian Senate election of 21 November 1970', *Psephos*, <http://psephos. adam-carr.net/countries/a/ australia/1970/1970senate1.txt>, accessed 13 April 2017.

91 Howson, 1984, p. 674.

92 ibid.

93 ibid., p. 676.

94 Tony Eggleton, 2014, 'Reflections', *Commonwealth Oral History*, <http:// www.commonwealthoralhistories. org/2014/tony-eggleton-reflections/>, accessed 11 April 2017, p. 1.

95 'Commonwealth Heads of Government Meeting, Singapore January 1971, minutes', 16 January 1971, CAB 164/813, British National Archives, Kew, London.

96 McEwen, *CPD HoR*, vol. 70, 30 October 1970, pp. 3151–53.

97   Rattigan, 1986, pp. 80–89.

98   'Tariff policy', NAA: 5869, 631, 669.

99   ibid.

100 Kenneth Davidson, 'McEwen hits tariff role', and 'McEwen's Tariff Board move destined to fail', *Aus.*, 18 December 1970, pp. 1, 12. See too Kelly, 2016.

101 Bert Kelly diary, 15 January 1971, NLA MS7424.

102 Rattigan, 1986, p. 87.

103 'McEwen's last stand', *Age*, 26 January 1971, p. 9.

104 Cabinet minute no. 843, 27 January 1971, NAA: 5869, 669.

105 McCarthy, 2000, p. 96.

106 Kenneth Randall, 'Farewell to Black Jack', *Aus.*,1 February 1971, p. 7.

107 Bert Kelly diary, 28 January 1971, NLA MS7424.

108 Bruce Juddery, 'A McMahon view of External Affairs', *CT*, 28 January 1970, p. 2; 'Tinkering only at External Affairs', *CT*, 29 January 1970, p. 2; 'Planning policy in a think tank', *CT*, 2 February 1970, p. 2.

109 McMahon to Waller, 6 April 1970, NAA: M4252, 8A.

110 This was almost certainly a slight on Hasluck, who largely discounted and eschewed policy guidance sourced from within the department. See Porter, 1993, pp. 275–76.

111 Bruce Juddery, 'External Affairs deputy chosen', *CT*, 29 April 1970, p. 1.

112 Peter Sekuless, 'Promotion for 63 Australian diplomats', *CT*, 1 May 1970, p. 3; G.M. Reith, n.d., 'The Federal council meeting of the Liberal Party Canberra 8–9 June 1970', FCO 24/677, British National Archives, Kew, London.

113 Author's interview with C.R. 'Kim' Jones, 2 June 2017.

114 Author's interview with Richard Woolcott, 2 February 2018.

115 Gorton to McMahon, 4 September 1970, NAA: M3787, 39; Cabinet decision no. 660, 'Department of Foreign Affairs', 3 September 1970, NAA: A5873, 660. See also 'Dept's new name', *CT*, 7 November 1970, p. 1.

116 For some background on the reorganisation, see Fewster, 2018, pp. 182–86.

117 '"Radical" overhaul at Foreign Affairs', *CT*, 21 December 1970, p. 1; Bruce Juddery, 'Foreign Affairs changes in a changing world', *CT*, 21 December 1970, p. 2.

118 Woolcott, 2003, pp. 106–07. See also Waller, 1990, pp. 46–47.

119 'Mr McMahon's first year', *Aus.*, 16 December 1970, p. 12.

120 Waller, 1990, p. 44.

121 Cooper to McIntyre, 11 March 1969, in Doran and Lee (eds), 2002, pp. 297–99.

122 McIntyre to Cooper, 12 June 1969, ibid., pp. 300–01.

123 Anderson to Waller, 2 October 1970, Plimsoll to Waller, 15 October 1970, and Dunn to Waller, 23 October 1970, ibid., pp. 316–18, 321–25, 327–30.

124 Renouf to Waller, 15 October 1970, ibid., p. 326.

125 Waller to Renouf, 23 October 1970, ibid., pp. 330–31.

126 Waller, 1990, p. 43.

127 A.J. Forbes to McMahon, 14 October 1970, NAA: M4252/1, 4.

128 McMahon, *CPD HoR*, vol. 70, 14 October 1970, p. 2087. See also Whitlam and McEwen, and

Whitlam and Swartz, *CPD HoR*,
vol. 70, 30 September 1970, pp. 1856,
1861.

129 Eastman to McMahon, 28 October
1970, and McMahon's annotations, in
Doran and Lee (eds), 2002,
pp. 331–36.

130 Savingram to Canberra, 1 December
1970, ibid., pp. 338–41; David
Solomon, 'China and UN: Australia's
policy, re-appraised', *CT*, 8 December
1970, p. 2.

131 Holdich to Anderson and Policy
Planning Paper LP No. 2,
10 December 1970, in Doran and
Lee (eds), 2002, pp. 346–56.

132 McMahon to Shann, 17 December
1970, ibid., pp. 356–57.

133 Author's interview with C.R. 'Kim'
Jones, 2 June 2017.

134 Keith Waller interviewed by J.D.B.
Miller, NLA Oral History, TRC 314,
p. 29.

135 Gorton to McMahon, with
McMahon's annotations, 5 January
1971, NAA: M4251, 44.

136 Reid, 1971, p. 401. Kim Jones
believed that far from feeling
humiliated, McMahon was probably
relieved not to have to share a plane
with Gorton.

137 Howson, 1984, pp. 687–91.

138 ibid., p. 691.

139 Ian Wood interviewed by Ron
Hurst, 1984, NLA Oral History,
TRC 4900/84; see also Reid, 1971,
pp. 405–11; Hancock, 2002, p. 308.

Chapter 32: A Transient Phantom?

1 Bolton, in Tyley, Robbins and March
(eds), 2014, p. 44. The line is drawn

from Disraeli's *Endymion*.

2 Sir James Plimsoll interviewed by
Clyde Cameron, NLA Oral History,
TRC 1967, pp. 5, 41. Plimsoll stated
on two occasions that McMahon
was *the* weakest, but added later that,
on consideration, Les Bury was the
weakest, mostly owing to his health
problems.

3 Laurence 'Jim' McIntyre interviewed
by Mel Pratt, NLA Oral History,
TRC 121/67.

4 Flood, 2011, pp. 68–69.

5 Submission no. 250, 'Development of
Japanese Foreign Policies', 27 April
1970, NAA: A5869, 250; Cabinet
minute no. 300, 30 April 1970,
NAA: A5873, 300; Cotton, in Tyler,
Robbins, and March (eds), 2014,
pp. 109–50.

6 These comments are drawn from
Hearder, 2015, p. 209.

7 Keith Waller interviewed by J.D.B.
Miller, NLA Oral History, TRC 314,
pp. 26–28.

8 That McMahon went, too, was a
point in his favour, as *The Age* argued
at the time. See 'Partner in Asia', *Age*,
29 April 1970, p. 2.

9 Credit for the reorganisation
remained a touchy point for Waller.
When Nigel Bowen noted that
McMahon had reorganised the
department, Waller leaped out of his
chair: 'Nothing of the sort! What
utter rubbish!' See Keith Waller
interviewed by J.D.B. Miller, NLA
Oral History, TRC 314, p. 27.

10 Author's interview and
correspondence with C.R. 'Kim'
Jones, 2 and 3 June 2017.

11 Juddery, 1974, pp. 104–05.

12 'It was McMahon's voice rather

than that of either of his two foreign ministers who seemed to speak for Australia in 1971 and 1972,' wrote Geoffrey Bolton later. See Bolton, in Tyler, Robbins, and March (eds), 2014, p. 47.

13 Renouf, 1979, p. 24.

14 The official historian of Australia's involvement in Vietnam made this point. See Edwards, 1997, pp. 346–47.

15 Bowman notes, undated, in the author's possession.

Chapter 33: A Natural Development

1 McEwen noted this point himself: 'With my retirement,' he wrote, 'a particular political age was just about over.' See McEwen, 1983, p. 81.

2 Author's correspondence with Doug Anthony, 25 July 2016.

3 'Premiers empty-handed', *CT*, 5 February 1971, pp. 1, 13.

4 'Election climax', *SMH*, 8 February 1971, p. 6.

5 Howson, 1984, p. 693.

6 ibid., p. 694.

7 McMahon to Gorton, 4 February 1971, in Doran and Lee (eds), 2002, pp. 369–75.

8 Submission to cabinet, 9 February 1971, ibid., pp. 375–91.

9 Waller commented later that, in driving this reconsideration of Australian policy, he was suggesting 'a different strategy in the [UN] General Assembly and not immediate recognition of Communist China'. Though—as he says—it was 'strange' that McMahon took a long time to grasp this, his comment makes

clear that the department was only recommending incremental change in Australia's policy. See Waller, 1990, p. 44.

10 'Attitude on China reaffirmed', *CT*, 18 February 1971, p. 10.

11 Only as recently as November, McEwen had declared that he did not believe recognising the PRC would have 'any impact' on its trade relationship with Australia. Moreover, McEwen said, 'I will not contribute to anything that will set us apart from the United States, and the United States won't recognise China.' See McEwen, interviewed on *This Week*, HSV-7, 11 November 1970.

12 Cabinet minute no. 902, 23 February 1971, NAA: A5869, 678.

13 *Incentive*, no. 282, 23 February 1971, p. 1.

14 Whitlam, *CPD HoR*, vol. 71, 18 February 1971, pp. 274–82.

15 McMahon, ibid., pp. 282–88.

16 Maxwell Newton, 'Economic report: McMahon treads softly', *Incentive*, no. 282, 23 February 1971, p. 5.

17 Paul Hasluck, 'Gorton's reconstruction of Cabinet in February, 1971', NAA: M1767, 3.

18 Howard, 2014, p. 541.

19 Howson, 1984, p. 693.

20 ibid., p. 696.

21 Author's interview with C.R. 'Kim' Jones, 2 June 2017.

22 Author's interview with Tom Hughes, 16 August 2016.

23 Brown, 1993, p. 58.

24 Fraser, in 'It's alright, Boss', *The Liberals*, 1994, TV programme.

25 Submission no. 259, 'Aid to South Vietnam', 1 May 1970, NAA: A5869, 259; Cabinet minute no. 391, 27 May

1970, NAA: A5873, 391.

26 See McMahon to Gorton,
3 September 1970, NAA: M62, 28.

27 'Military civic action plan 1971/72',
3 February 1971, in Fraser and
Simons, 2009, p. 751.

28 Ayres, 1987, p. 177.

29 ibid.

30 David Solomon, 'Army "sabotage" on
Vietnam', CT, 22 February 1971, p. 1.

31 See Barnard, Fraser, Morrison,
Lucock, Bryant, Killen, CPD HoR,
vol. 71, 24 February 1971, pp. 564–78.

32 Reid, 1971, p. 417.

33 ibid., p. 419.

34 Daly, 'It's alright, Boss', The Liberals,
1994, TV programme.

35 Fraser and Simons, 2009, p. 215.

36 Reid, 1971, p. 420.

37 Tony Eggleton, 'It's alright, Boss',
The Liberals, 1994, TV programme.

38 Killen, 1985, pp. 165–66.

39 Peter Samuel, 'The Australian army's
"revolt" in Vietnam', Bulletin,
6 March 1971, pp. 11–12.

40 Author's interview with Alan Ramsey,
31 January 2018.

41 Alan Ramsey, 'General says Fraser
is disloyal to service', Aus., 4 March
1971, p. 1.

42 Ramsey, 'It's alright, Boss',
The Liberals, 1994, TV programme.

43 Howson, 1984, p. 697.

44 Daly, in 'It's alright, Boss',
The Liberals, 1994, TV programme.

45 Hancock, 2002, p. 318.

46 In his memoirs, Fraser claimed that
Menzies did not give him advice
about his resignation. This is highly
suspect, at best. Contemporaneous
notes made by Hasluck tell of
Fraser's emphasis that he 'had
been given advice that there was

no other proper thing to do. This
was a very experienced person who
had gone over the matter carefully
with him—one whose judgement
and advice I [Hasluck], too, would
respect.' Fraser then told Hasluck
he had spoken at least twice with
Menzies about it. See Hasluck,
'Gorton's crisis in March, 1971',
NAA: M1767, 3.

47 McNicoll, 1978, p. 241.

48 Howson, 1984, p. 698.

49 Hasluck, 'Gorton's crisis in March,
1971', NAA: M1767, 3.

50 David McNicoll, 'Time for a change
of leader', DT, 7 March 1971, p. 2.

51 Alan Reid, 'Resign call to Fraser', DT,
7 March 1971, p. 1.

52 Howson, 1984, p. 699.

53 Griffen-Foley, 2003, p. 165.

54 Reid, 1971, p. 426.

55 Ayres, 1987, p. 182.

56 Hancock, 2002, p. 320.

57 Fraser, in 'It's alright, Boss',
The Liberals, 1994, TV programme.

58 Author's correspondence with Tony
Eggleton, 26 November 2016.

59 After the Meet the Press broadcast,
Ian Fitchett rang Peter Howson
to 'confirm' Howson's view that
'something big is brewing for later
this week.' See Howson, 1984, p. 699.

60 'Gorton's crisis in March, 1971',
NAA: M1767, 3.

61 Chipp and Larkin 1978, p. 97–98.

62 Hasluck makes a point of noting
that these were Fraser's exact
words: Hasluck took them down
in shorthand as they spoke on the
phone. There is no statement about an
announcement of Fraser's resignation
in the letter. See 'Gorton's crisis in
March, 1971', NAA: M1767, 3.

63 ibid.

64 Howson, 1984, p. 700.

65 Bert Kelly diary, 9 March 1971, NLA MS7424.

66 ibid.

67 Howson, 1984, p. 701.

68 Fraser, *CPD HoR*, vol. 71, 9 March 1971, pp. 679–84.

69 Gorton, ibid., pp. 684–89. Ramsey's interjection is on p. 687.

70 See Whitlam, Hayden, Mackay, Calwell, Turner, Cairns, Gorton, and Whitlam, ibid., pp. 689–92.

71 Chipp, 'It's alright, Boss', *The Liberals*, 1994, TV programme.

72 Hearder, 2015, p. 230.

73 Robert 'Duke' Bonnett interviewed by Peter Sekuless, 21 April–21 July 1983, NLA Oral History, TRC 1454.

74 Author's interview with C.R. 'Kim' Jones, 2 June 2017.

75 David Fairbairn interviewed by Robert Linford, 4 June 1985–27 June 1985, NLA Oral History, TRC 4900/72.

76 Howson, 1984, p. 701.

77 ibid.

78 Bert Kelly diary, 9 March 1971, NLA MS7424.

79 Howson, 1984, pp. 701–02.

80 Brown, 1993, p. 59.

81 John Gorton interviewed by Clyde Cameron, NLA Oral History, TRC 1702.

82 Howson, 1984, pp. 701–02.

83 Ian Wood interviewed by Ron Hurst, NLA Oral History, TRC 4900/84.

84 Killen, 1985, p. 173.

85 Bert Kelly diary, 10 March 1971, NLA MS7424.

86 Chipp and Larkin, 1978, pp. 98–99.

87 Author's interview with Tom Hughes, 16 August 2016.

88 ibid.

89 Chipp and Larkin, 1978, p. 99.

90 Howson, 1984, p. 703.

91 Bert Kelly diary, 10 March 1971, NLA MS7424.

92 Brown, 1993, p. 60.

93 Snedden and Schedvin, 1990, p. 92.

94 John Gorton interviewed by Clyde Cameron, NLA Oral History, TRC 1702, vol. 2, p. 50; John Gorton interviewed by Mel Pratt, NLA Oral History, TRC 121/78.

95 Author's interview with Tom Hughes, 16 August 2016.

96 Howson, 1984, p. 703.

97 Author's interview with Tom Hughes, 16 August 2016.

98 Bert Kelly diary, 10 March 1971, NLA MS7424.

99 Author's correspondence with Tony Eggleton, 26 November 2016.

100 Reid, 1971, p. 443.

101 'New Prime Minister: press, radio and TV conference given by the leader of the Liberal party, Mr William McMahon', 10 March 1971, APMC Transcripts.

102 Clem Lloyd interviewed by Mel Pratt, 8 September 1975–14 July 1976, NLA Oral History, TRC 121/64.

103 Freudenberg, 1987, p. 188.

104 Paul Hasluck interviewed by Clyde Cameron, NLA Oral History, TRC 1966, p. 216.

105 Author's interview with C.R. 'Kim' Jones, 10 June 2017.

Chapter 34: Activity and Responsibility

1 See Griffen-Foley, 2001, pp. 499–513.

2 Beazley, *CPD HoR*, vol. 71, 15 March 1971, pp. 839–43.

3   Whitlam, *CPD HoR*, vol. 73, 17 August 1971, pp. 16–21.

4   Beazley, *CPD HoR*, vol. 71, 15 March 1971, pp. 839–43.

5   Mr Y, 1971, pp. 2–7. Historian Stephen Holt revealed Peter Samuel was Mr Y in 2010. Samuel had confessed to it in an interview with the National Library of Australia: 'That article of mine is 90 per cent correct but there was another 10 per cent that was somewhat mischievous,' Samuel said, 'done out of a sense of fun as much as anything.' See Peter Samuel interviewed by Mel Pratt, NLA Oral History, TRC 121/47, p. 73. Today, Samuel is uncertain whether he wrote it. 'I do recall it appearing. I'm not definitely denying I wrote it. I just don't remember.' Author's correspondence with Peter Samuel, 25 April 2017.

6   Mr Y, 1971, pp. 2–7.

7   Reid, 1971, p. 417.

8   St John, 1971, pp. 115–25.

9   Edwards, 1977, p. 66.

10   Hancock, 2002, p. 332.

11   Martin Reith, n.d., 'Visit to Sydney and Queensland, 21/22 May 1970', FCO 24/677, British National Archives, Kew, London.

12   McMahon, 'It's alright, Boss', *The Liberals*, 1994, TV programme.

13   Oakes, 2008, p. 259.

14   Ramsey, 2009, p. 38.

15   Lenox Hewitt, 'It's alright, Boss', *The Liberals*, 1994, TV program; author's interview with Sir Lenox Hewitt, 2 February 2018.

16   Reid, 1971, p. 444.

17   Southey, 'It's alright, Boss', *The Liberals*, 1994, TV programme.

18   Howson, 1984, p. 712.

19   Killen, 1985, p. 166.

20   ibid., p. 173.

21   For hints of Fraser's suspicion, see Ayres, 1987, pp. 179–80 and Fraser and Simons, 2009, p. 212. His interview with Clyde Cameron was the most detailed articulation of his suspicions.

22   Malcolm Fraser interviewed by Clyde Cameron, NLA Oral History, TRC 2162, p. 350.

Chapter 35: The Crumbling Pillars (I)

1   Author's interview with Tony Eggleton, 26 November 2016.

2   Author's interview with Sir Lenox Hewitt, 2 February 2018.

3   Howard, 2014, p. 516.

4   Author's correspondence with Tony Eggleton, 26 November 2016.

5   Bunting to Garner, 26 June 1971, NAA: M321, 11.

6   Author's interview with Sir Lenox Hewitt, 2 February 2018.

7   See McMahon's comments in Hughes, 1976, ed. Wilson (audio).

8   Author's interview with Sir Peter Lawler, 22 November 2016.

9   Author's interview with C.R. 'Kim' Jones, 10 June 2017.

10   Author's correspondence with Tony Eggleton, 26 November 2016.

11   McMahon hired MacDonald on 16 March for a three-month trial appointment. See Bunting, note for file, 30 March 1971, NAA: M319, 26.

12   'Fairbairn offer: Foreign Affairs', *SMH*, 12 March 1971, p. 1; Howson, 1984, p. 704.

13   ibid.

14   Jim Oram, 'I couldn't sleep a wink',

DM, 11 March 1971, p. 4.

15 'A time to look forward', *DT*, 11 March 1971, p. 2.

16 'A tough role for a tough pro', *DM*, 11 March 1971, p. 2.

17 Edgar Holt interviewed by Mel Pratt, NLA Oral History, TRC 121/93.

18 'Leadership crisis did great harm—Anthony', *SMH*, 11 March 1971, p. 3.

19 Stan Hutchinson, 'Rebuke for Qld party head', *SMH*, 10 March 1971, p. 8.

20 John O'Hara, 'Askin's "wait and see" on McMahon', *SMH*, 12 March 1971, p. 12.

21 Edwards, 1977, p. 68.

22 'Gorton gives reason for casting vote', *SMH*, 12 March 1971, p. 12.

23 Edwards, 1977, p. 68; Howson, 1984, pp. 704–05.

24 ibid., p. 705.

25 Hasluck, 'The resignation of Mr Gorton', NAA: M1767, 3.

26 In the press release announcing the department's creation, McMahon stated that the new department was completely separate and independent of the Executive Council itself: 'New administrative arrangements', 12 March 1971, PM no. 29/1971, APMC Transcripts.

27 McMahon remained of the view that Hasluck was unduly worried. See Bunting, note for file, 13 March 1971, NAA: M319, 26.

28 ibid. Kim Jones recalled later being asked by McMahon to retrieve the announcement going out: Author's interview with C.R. 'Kim' Jones, 10 June 2017.

29 ibid.

30 Howson, 1984, p. 706.

31 Whitlam, *CPD HoR*, vol. 71, 15 March 1971, pp. 827–33.

32 McMahon, ibid., pp. 833–39.

33 Cabinet meeting, 15 March 1971, 'Sir John Bunting', NAA: A11099, 1/117.

34 Howson, 1984, p. 706.

35 Clem Lloyd interviewed by Mel Pratt, 8 September 1975–14 July 1976, NLA Oral History, TRC 121/64.

36 Bert Kelly diary, 16 March 1971, NLA MS7424.

37 Ramsey, 2009, p. 265. Rankin subsequently claimed that McMahon had approached her about a foreign posting while serving as Minister for Foreign Affairs, and that she was 'thrilled, absolutely thrilled' by the renewed offer in 1971. See Annabelle Rankin interviewed by Pat Shaw, NLA Oral History, TRC 4900/15.

38 Killen, 1985, pp. 174–76.

39 Author's interview with Tom Hughes, 16 August 2016.

40 McMahon's creation of assistant ministers was criticised on grounds that it represented an accrual of power to the executive. See, for example, Magnus Cormack, *CPD Sen*, vol. 48, 12 May 1971, pp. 1751–55; David Solomon and Peter Sekuless, 'The Week', *CT*, 15 May 1971, p. 2; 'PM forced to allow debate on appointments', *CT*, 21 August 1971, p. 11.

41 Author's interview with Tom Hughes, 16 August 2016. See also Hancock, 2016, pp. 188–89.

42 Snedden and Schedvin, 1990, p. 113.

43 'The resignation of Mr Gorton', NAA: M1767, 3.

44 Killen, 1985, pp. 176.

45 David Fairbairn interviewed by Mel

Pratt, NLA Oral History, TRC
121/74, pp. 113–14.

46   Howson, 1984, p. 709.

47   Peter Howson records that
McMahon 'indicated' that Howson
should continue to pressure Gorton
in his electorate, which was making
noises about Gorton's preselection:
ibid., p. 712.

48   'The prospects of the McMahon
government', 5 April 1971, NAA:
M1767, 3. Peter Howson records that
Hasluck told him the Liberals would
have trouble in the electorate. See
Howson, 1984, p. 711.

49   Bunting to Garner, 26 June 1971,
NAA: M321, 11.

50   Peter Samuel interviewed by Mel
Pratt, NLA Oral History, TRC
121/47, p. 73.

51   Horne, 2000, pp. 152–53.

52   Fadden to Ulrich Ellis, 17 March
1971, NLA MS1006, Box 30.

53   Fadden to Bunting, 16 March 1971,
NAA: M321, 11.

54   Morrice James, 'Mr McMahon in
Britain', 8 December 1971, British
National Archives, Kew, London,
PREM 15/744.

55   Menzies to McMahon, 11 March
1971, NLA MS4936, 1/132.

56   Author's correspondence with Doug
Anthony, 15 August 2016.

57   Alan Reid diary, 31 March 1971,
NLA MS7796.

58   Snedden and Schedvin, 1990, p. 130.

59   Howson, 1984, p. 714.

60   'New-look deal', CT, 11 March 1971,
p. 10.

61   'Premiers take hopeful view', CT,
5 April 1971, p. 1.

62   'Premiers' conference: agreement
reached', CT, 6 April 1971, p. 8.

63   'Leaders go home happier', CT,
6 April 1971, p. 8.

64   David Solomon, 'Oh, what a change
for the States', CT, 6 April 1971, p. 2.

65   Turner, CPD HoR, vol. 72, 4 May
1971, pp. 2484–86.

66   Killen, ibid., pp. 2480–81.

67   'Keeping the House at work', Aus.,
6 May 1971, p. 13.

68   Alan Reid diary, 6 May 1971, NLA
MS7796.

69   In July, McMahon told Peter Howson
that the chaos of the session's end was
one of his failures as prime minister.
See Howson, 1984, p. 751.

70   Hasluck, 'Appointment of new
minister, May 1971', NAA: M1767, 3.

71   Cabinet decision no. 145, 'Australian
Membership of OECD', 4 May 1971,
NAA: A5908, 80; Cabinet decision
no. 168, 'The National Gallery and
High Court, Australian National
Gallery', 11 May 1971, NAA:
A5908, 79; Cabinet decision no. 115,
'Rural reconstruction programme',
27 April 1971, NAA: A5908, 21;
Cabinet decision no. 89, 'Papua
and New Guinea—constitutional
development', 20 April 1971, NAA:
A5908, 45.

72   Following this meeting on 25 May,
Hasluck discovered that McMahon
had not followed the proper
procedures to have the Department
created. See Hasluck, 'Appointment
of new minister, May 1971', NAA:
M1767, 3.

73   ibid.

74   Howson, 1984, pp. 723–24.

75   ibid., p. 726.

76   ibid., p. 728.

77   ibid., p. 729.

78   *Milirrpum v Nabalco Pty Ltd* (1971),

17 FLR 141, pp. 266–67.

79 Bunting, note for file, 7 May 1971, NAA: M319, 27.

80 Coombs, 1981, p. 278.

81 Dexter, 2015, p. 179.

82 Barrie Dexter noted this in a letter. See Dexter to Bunting, 15 March 1971, NAA: M321, 11.

83 Coombs, 1981, p. 280.

84 'Aboriginal affairs policy: statement by the prime minister', 23 April 1971, Cairns, APMC transcripts.

85 Coombs, 1981, p. 282. See also Cabinet decision no. 150, 4 May 1971, NAA: A5908, 76.

86 Cabinet committee, 3 August 1971, 'PH Bailey', NAA: A11099, 336.

87 This section draws on: Heenan and Dunstan, 2015, pp. 1110–31; Murray, 2003, pp. 162–71; Nick Scott, 2015, pp. 145–63.

88 *Australian Cricket Yearbook*, 1970, *Modern Magazines*, Rushcutter's Bay, New South Wales, pp. 6–7. See also Menzies, 1970, pp. 276–85.

89 McMahon, *CPD HoR*, vol. 71, 6 April 1971, pp. 1455–56.

90 Bunting, 5 April 1971, NAA: M319, 26.

91 Cabinet minute no. 70, 6 April 1971, NAA: A5909, 90.

92 See Waller to Australian high commissioner in Lagos, 23 April 1971, 'South Africa—relations with Australian sporting teams', NAA: A1838, 201/10/10/3 Part 1.

93 Australian mission to the UN, New York, 14 April 1971, ibid.

94 Cabinet minute no. 524, 9 November 1971, NAA: A5909, 524.

95 Fred Wells, 'More unions in ban on Sth Africans', *SMH*, 28 April 1971, p. 2.

96 'ACTU certain to boycott South African tours', *CT*, 14 May 1971, p. 3.

97 'ACTU executive minutes, 13 May 1971', in Hagan (ed.), 1986, pp. 208–10.

98 Bunting, note for file, 10 June 1971, NAA: M319, 28.

99 Bunting, notes for file, 12.10pm and 1.40pm, 23 June 1971, ibid.

100 McMahon had been canvassing the idea for several days. See Bunting, note for file, 19 June 1971, NAA: M321, 15.

101 Alan Reid diary, 23 June 1971, NLA MS7796.

102 'PM offers RAAF', *CT*, 26 June 1971, p. 1.

103 Harris, 1972, p. 81.

104 ibid., p. 63.

105 'Mr Hawke postpones his departure', *CT*, 26 June 1971, p. 1.

106 Harris, 1972, p. 62.

107 'Violence racks the city', *Age*, 2 July 1971, p. 1.

108 David Solomon, 'Snap election: PM weighs chances', *CT*, 6 July 1971, p. 2; Howson, 1984, p. 746; 'Interview given by the Prime Minister, Mr William McMahon, on TVW Channel 7—Perth', 3 July 1971, APMC Transcripts.

109 Harris, 1972, p. 54.

110 Bunting, notes for file, August 1971, NAA: M319, 29 Part 2.

111 Cabinet meeting 24 August 1971, 'Sir John Bunting', NAA: A11099, 1/120.

112 Cabinet meeting 24 August 1971, 'PJ Lawler', NAA: A11099, 1/301.

113 Cabinet meeting 24 August 1971, 'Sir John Bunting', NAA: A11099, 1/120.

114 'Cricket tour of Australia by South African Team', 24 August 1971, NAA: A5882, CO1274.

115 Perry, 2000, p. 575.

116 Murray, 2003, pp. 162–71.

117 'PM blames minority', *SMH*, 9 September 1971, p. 1.

Chapter 36: The Crumbling Pillars (II)

1 McMahon, *CPD HoR*, vol. 71, 30 March 1971, pp. 1147–49.

2 McMahon press statement, 'Further Vietnam withdrawals', 8 April 1971, PM no. 43/1971, APMC Transcripts.

3 Howson, 1984, p. 719; Bunting to Tange, 10 May 1971, NAA: A5882, CO60 Part 2; Bunting to McMahon, 2 June 1971, NAA: M319, 28.

4 McMahon press statement, 'Vietnam correspondence', 19 June 1971, PM no. 82/1971, APMC transcripts; 'Menzies: entered war at request', *CT*, 18 June 1971, p. 8.

5 McMahon, '*New York Times* articles on Vietnam', 22 June 1971, PM no. 64/1971, APMC transcripts.

6 For criticisms in addition to those of Swartz, see Alan Reid diary 19 April, 26 May, 31 May 1971, NLA MS7796.

7 Bunting, note for file, 12 June 1971, NAA: M321, 15.

8 Author's correspondence with Tony Eggleton, 26 November 2016.

9 Howson, 1984, pp. 714–15.

10 ibid., pp. 722–23.

11 'Australia: she'll be right, Mate—maybe', *Time*, 24 May 1971, pp. 24–36.

12 Alan Reid diary, 10 May 1971, NLA MS7796.

13 Bunting, note for file, 6 June 1971, NAA: M321, 15.

14 John Bunting interviewed by Ian Hamilton, 26 June 1983, NLA Oral History, TRC 1428.

15 Howson, 1984, p. 735.

16 Bert Kelly diary, 19 July 1971, NLA MS7424.

17 Aitchison, 1974, p. 8.

18 Benvenuti, 2008, pp. 153–62.

19 Cabinet (ad hoc), 7 April 1971, 'PH Bailey', NAA: A11099, 1/335.

20 Decision no. 85 (ad hoc), 7 April 1971, NAA: A5882, CO133 Part 3.

21 McMahon to Yew, 7 April 1971, ibid.

22 Yew to McMahon, 12 April 1971, ibid.

23 Bunting, 'Note for file', 15 April 1971, ibid.

24 Gorton to McMahon, 15 April 1971, ibid.

25 Gorton to McMahon, 16 April 1971, ibid.

26 McMahon to Gorton, undated, ibid.

27 Bunting, note for file, 7 July 1971, NAA: M319, 29 Part 1.

28 In the cabinet meeting where this was discussed, Gorton made his feelings clear: 'I believe this a mistaken decision and we will lose in defence and technical expertise more than what we make up in econ[omic gain].' See cabinet, 8 June 1971, 'PH Bailey', NAA: A11099, 1/335.

29 Mozley Moyal, 1975, pp. 365–84.

30 'More money is "needed for defence"', *CT*, 21 June 1971, p. 7

31 See Cabinet decision no. 197, 8 June 1971, NAA: A5908, 107.

32 Cabinet, 8 June 1971, 'PH Bailey', NAA: A11099, 1/335; Edwards, 1997, p. 302; Howson, 1984, p. 735.

33 Alan Reid diary, 22 June 1971, NLA MS7796.

34 Howson, 1984, p. 737.

35 ibid., pp. 738–39.

36   Alan Reid diary, 23 June 1971, NLA
      MS7796.

37   ibid., 26 June 1971.

38   Submission to cabinet, March 1971,
      in Doran and Lee (eds), 2002,
      pp. 410–12.

39   McMahon, 5 May 1971, 'Sir John
      Bunting', NAA: A11099, 1/118.

40   Cabinet decision no. 158, 5 May
      1971, NAA: A1838, 158.

41   Cablegram to Canberra, 2 April
      1971, in Doran and Lee (eds), 2002,
      pp. 417–18.

42   Cablegram to Washington, 7 April
      1971, ibid., pp. 421–22.

43   Pitty, 2005, p. 445.

44   Author's interview with Richard
      Woolcott, 2 February 2018.

45   Keith Waller interviewed by J.D.B.
      Miller, NLA Oral History, TRC 314,
      p. 35.

46   Howard, 1971, pp. 97–108.

47   Whitlam, *CPD HoR*, vol. 5, 12
      August 1954, pp. 272–76.

48   For background on the ALP
      delegation, see Griffths, 2012, and
      FitzGerald, 1972.

49   Gough Whitlam to Zhou Enlai,
      14 April 1971, NLA MS8725,
      51/15/2.

50   Alan Reid diary, 13 April 1971, NLA
      MS7796.

51   'National Press Club luncheon',
      15 April 1971, APMC Transcripts.

52   McMahon, *CPD HoR*, vol. 71, 20
      April 1971, p. 1667.

53   Cabinet decision no. 165, 11 May
      1971, NAA: A1838, 165.

54   Alan Reid diary, 12 May 1971, NLA
      MS7796.

55   Cablegram to Washington, 13 May
      1971, in Doran and Lee (eds), 2002,
      pp. 445–46.

56   Appling to McMahon, 14 July 1971,
      ibid., pp. 500–01.

57   Cablegram to Paris, 22 May 1971,
      ibid., pp. 452–54.

58   Cablegram to Canberra, 27 May
      1971, ibid., pp. 455–58.

59   Cablegram to Canberra, 1 June 1971,
      ibid., p. 462.

60   Cablegram to Canberra, 2 July 1971,
      ibid., p. 485.

61   Griffiths, 2012, p. 25.

62   'No common sense by Peking, says
      PM', *SMH*, 5 July 1971, p. 1.

63   Whitlam, 1985, p. 56.

64   Quotes from this meeting are drawn
      from the transcript recorded by AAP
      journalist David Barnett. See 'China
      talk with Chou', NAA: A1838,
      3107/38/12/7 Part 2.

65   Whitlam, 2002, p. 329.

66   McMahon was also trying to find
      out when China had been considered
      during his time as minister for
      external/foreign affairs. See Bunting
      to McMahon, 27 July 1971, NAA:
      M319, 29 Part 1.

67   Alan Reid diary, 7–8 July 1971, NLA
      MS7796.

68   John O'Farrell, 'Chou had Whitlam
      on a hook, says PM', *SMH*, 13 July
      1971, p. 1.

69   Howson, 1984, p. 748.

70   Whitlam, 2002, p. 330.

71   Cablegram to Canberra, 15 July 1971,
      ibid., pp. 502–03.

72   'President Nixon's statement 15 July
      1971', *Survival*, vol. 13, iss. 9, p. 292.

73   Freudenberg, 1987, p. 211.

74   Author's interview with Richard
      Woolcott, 2 February 2018.

75   Griffiths, 2012, p. 54.

76   Whitlam, 1985, p. 57.

77   Oakes, 1973, p. 225.

78 Curran, 2015, pp. 124–26.

79 Cablegram to Washington, 18 July 1971, ibid., pp. 509–11.

80 Cablegram to Canberra, 19 July 1971, ibid., pp. 513–14.

81 Bunting, note for file, 18 July 1971, NAA: M321, 15.

82 Howson, 1984, p. 751.

83 'PM says: it's also our policy', SMH, 17 July 1971, p. 1.

84 Griffiths, 2012, p. 59.

85 Curran, 2015, p. 126.

86 Bunting, note for file, 17 July 1971, NAA: M321, 15.

87 Hasluck, 'Mr Bury's resignation', NAA: M1767, 3.

88 ibid.

89 Les Bury interviewed by Mel Pratt, NLA Oral History, TRC 121/70.

90 See, notably, Bunting's note for file, 28 July 1971, NAA: M319, 29 Part 1.

91 Current Notes, Department of Foreign Affairs, vol. XLII, no. 7, July 1971, pp. 385–88.

92 'Gair attacks PM over China policy', Age, 30 July 1971, p. 3.

93 Cablegram to Canberra, 7 September 1971, Waller to Bowen, 9 September 1971, and submission to Bowen, 14 September 1971, in Doran and Lee (eds), 2002, pp. 596–98, 601–02.

94 See Bunting, notes for file, October– December 1971, NAA: M319, 30 Part 2 and 30 Part 3.

95 Anderson to Waller, 30 September 1971; Cablegram to Hong Kong, 4 October 1971; Cablegram to Hong Kong, 4 October 1971; Note for file by Bailey, 8 October 1971; Record of conversation between Waller and Kibel, 13 October 1971; Cablegram to Canberra, 14 October 1971, in Doran and Lee (eds), 2002,

pp. 610–11, 615–19, 621–25, 626–28. See also 'Red faces over China trade move', NT, 18–23 October 1971, p. 6; Eric Walsh, 'McMahon's 'no' to Peking', NT, 13–18 December 1971, p. 1; Hugh Armfield, 'Peacock visit to China vetoed', Age, 13 December 1971, p. 1; and Richard Zachariah, 'The man between', Aus., 19 December 1971, p. 11. Edmund Fung provides a narrative overview of the to-and-fro of the proposal: see Fung, 1983, pp. 39–59.

96 Cablegram to Canberra, 8 November 1971, in Doran and Lee (eds), 2002, pp. 651–52.

97 Hugh Armfield, 'Peacock visit to China vetoed', Age, 13 December 1971, p. 1.

Chapter 37: The Crumbling Pillars (III)

1 Alan Reid diary, 28 July 1971, NLA MS7796.

2 Ross Fitzgerald and Stephen Holt provide the authoritative account of the background to Reid's work. See Fitzgerald and Holt, 2010, pp. 242–47.

3 Reid, 1971, p. 9.

4 Gorton, 'I did it my way', Sunday Aus., 8 August 1971, p. 10.

5 Howson, 1984, p. 753.

6 Richard Farmer, 'This was the chance the Prime Minister was waiting for', Aus., 15 August 1971, p. 4.

7 See Alan Reid diary, 1–10 August 1971, NLA MS7796; Hancock, 2002, pp. 349–50; Fitzgerald and Holt, 2010, pp. 246–47.

8 Bunting to McMahon, 'Points to mention to Prime Minister', 9 August

1971, copy in possession of author. In a separate note for file, Bunting noted that Peter Howson had already asked McMahon to be absolved from obligations to secrecy in order to respond to Gorton's statements on the VIP affair. See Bunting, note for file, 9 August 1971, NAA: M319, 29 Part 2.

9   Bailey to Bunting, 8 August 1971, copy in possession of author.

10 McMahon aide-mémoires, 8–15 August 1971, copies in possession of author.

11 Griffen-Foley, 2003, pp. 1972–73; Whitlam, *CPD HoR*, vol. 73, 17 August 1971, p. 19.

12 Bert Kelly diary, 10 August 1971, NLA MS7424.

13 Alan Reid diary, 12 August 1971, NLA MS7796.

14 McMahon, record of conversation with Gorton, 12 August 1971, copy in author's possession.

15 Mark Uhlmann, 'Gorton as forthright as ever', *CT*, 13 February 1988, B1, B14.

16 McMahon to Gorton, 12 August 1971; Gorton to McMahon, 12 August 1971, copies in author's possession.

17 Maxwell Newton, 'Billy's got guts', *Incentive*, no. 306, 18 August 1971, pp. 4–6.

18 John Gorton, 'I did it my way', *Sunday Aus.*, 15 August 1971, pp. 4–5.

19 Howson, 1984, p. 761.

20 Hancock, 2002, pp. 352–53.

21 Killen, 1985, p. 180.

22 Whitlam, *CPD HoR*, vol. 73, 17 August 1971, pp. 16–21.

23 McMahon, ibid., pp. 21–26.

24 Bert Kelly diary, 17 August 1971, NLA MS7424.

25 Howson, 1984, p. 760.

26 Bert Kelly diary, 16 March 1971, NLA MS7424.

27 See, for example, Bunting, notes for file, 5.55pm and 5.45pm, 9 June 1971, NAA: M321, 15.

28 Snedden and Schedvin, 1990, pp. 117–19.

29 ibid.

30 Snedden, *CPD HoR*, vol. 73, 17 August 1971, pp. 38–133.

31 Bunting to Randall, 4 August 1971, NAA: M319, 29 Part 2.

32 Bert Kelly diary, 17 August 1971, NLA MS7424.

33 Author's correspondence with John Stone, 9 January 2017.

34 Snedden and Schedvin, 1990, pp. 126–28.

35 ibid.

36 According to Bowen, he had advised McMahon to make Malcolm Fraser minister for foreign affairs. The idea was blocked when McMahon sought Snedden's thoughts and his treasurer threatened to resign. See Nigel Bowen interviewed by Ron Hurst, NLA Oral History, TRC 4900/61.

37 Jess, Turner, Kelly and Hughes, *CPD HoR*, vol. 73, 20 August 1971, pp. 420–7, 435–50.

38 Cormack, *CPD Sen.*, vol. 48, 12 May 1971, pp. 1751–55.

39 'Task for a leader', *CT*, 17 August 1971, p. 2.

40 'Withdrawal of Australian forces from Vietnam', Cabinet decision no. 319, 26 July 1971, NAA: A5909, 319.

41 McMahon and Whitlam, *CPD HoR*, vol. 73, 17 August 1971, pp. 226–32.

42 Alan Reid diary, 27 August 1971, NLA MS7796.

43 Whitlam and McMahon, *CPD HoR*, vol. 73, 7 September 1971, pp. 803–04. McMahon had privately confirmed the previous year that he had not been to PNG for a decade. See Jones to McMahon, with McMahon's annotations, 1 April 1970, NAA: M3787, 39.

44 Peter Bailey interviewed by Garry Sturgess, NLA Oral History, TRC 6552.

45 Author's interview with Sir Peter Lawler, 22 November 2016.

46 John Bunting interviewed by Ian Hamilton, 21 September 1983, NLA Oral History, TRC 1428/7.

47 ibid.

48 Alan Reid diary, 23 March 1971, NLA MS7796.

49 McEwen, Barber, O'Neill, 8 July 1970, British National Archives, Kew, London, FCO: 30/802.

50 Ward, in Bridge, Bongiorno, and Lee (eds), 2010, pp. 145–163.

51 Davey, 2008, p. 152.

52 Ward, in Bridge, Bongiorno, and Lee (eds), 2010, p. 158.

53 Coombs, 1981, pp. 283–84; 'Report of Inter-departmental Committee on Aboriginal Affairs', Cabinet decision no. 486 (AA), 14 October 1971, NAA: A5909, 486/AA.

54 Coombs, 'Note on conversation with Prime Minister on 30th August 1971 by telephone', 30 August 1971, NAA: M321, 15.

55 Bunting, note for file, 3 October 1971, NAA: M319, 30 Part 2.

56 'Press conference given by the Prime Minister before leaving for overseas—27 October 1971', 71/940, APMC Transcripts.

57 Howard, 2014, pp. 557–58.

58 Gorton and Howson, *CPD HoR*, vol. 73, 16 September 1971, pp. 1402–03.

59 Author's interview with Phillip Adams, 12 October 2016.

60 ibid.

61 Howson, 1984, p. 773.

62 McMahon, *CPD HoR*, vol. 74, 7 October 1971, pp. 2020–21.

63 Howson, 1984, p. 783.

Chapter 38: The Crumbling Pillars (IV)

1 Downer to Heath, 14 October 1971, British National Archives, Kew, London, PREM 15/744.

2 Author's interview with Richard Woolcott, 2 February 2018.

3 Morrice James, 8 December 1971, 'Summary: Mr McMahon in Britain', British National Archives, Kew, London, PREM 15/744.

4 ibid.

5 Menzies to Henderson, 27 October 1971, in Henderson (ed.), 2011, p. 238.

6 See, in particular, Daly, *CPD HoR*, vol. 74, 28 and 29 October 1971, pp. 2787–89.

7 Coombs, 1981, pp. 287–88.

8 Author's interview with Richard Woolcott, 2 February 2018.

9 Woolcott, 2003, pp. 108–09; Ramsey, 2009, p. 38.

10 Woolcott, 2003, p. 110; author's interview with Richard Woolcott, 2 February 2018.

11 'Press conference at Blair House', 2 November 1971, APMC transcripts.

12 Curran, 2015, p. 130.

13 When, during the turmoil of the Dismissal, Henry Kissinger confessed

he could not remember the last 'conservative prime minister' of Australia, one of his advisers supplied the answer: 'The guy with the wife—McMahon': ibid., p. 290.

14 Author's interview with Alan Ramsey, 31 January 2018.

15 Heath, 21 November 1971, 'Record of a conversation with Mr McMahon, the Prime Minister of Australia on Tuesday 9 November 1971', British National Archives, Kew, London, PREM 15/744.

16 ibid.

17 McMahon to Heath, 20 December 1971, British National Archives, Kew, London, PREM 15/744.

18 Heath to McMahon, 14 December 1971, quoted in Bunting to Tange, 18 January 1972, NAA: M319, 31 Part 1.

19 'Visit of the Australian Prime Minister to the United Kingdom 7–13 November 1971, United Kingdom record of a meeting held at 10 Downing Street on Tuesday 9 November 1971 at 12.20pm', British National Archives, Kew, London, PREM 15/744.

20 Waller to Bunting, 20 August 1971, NAA: A1209, 1971/9949 Part 1.

21 Ward, in Bridge, Bongiorno, and Lee (eds), 2010, pp. 159–61. See also Ashton, Bridge, and Ward (eds), 2010, pp. 853–92.

22 Alan Reid diary, 14 November 1971, NLA MS7796.

23 Alan Reid, 'Prime Ministers I have known', *Bulletin*, 19 February 1980, pp. 59–60.

24 McMahon, 19 November 1971, 'Sir John Bunting', NAA: A11099, 1/120.

25 Bunting, note for file, 20 November 1971, NAA: M319, 30 Part 3.

26 Morrice James, 'Mr McMahon in Britain', 8 December 1971, British National Archives, Kew, London, PREM 15/744.

27 Foster, *CPD HoR*, vol. 70, 7 October 1971, pp. 2121–22.

28 Alan Reid diary, 8 October 1971, NLA MS7796.

29 ibid. McMahon's conduct may also have been influenced by discussions he was having with Arthur Calwell, who informed him of ALP positions on the matter. See Bramston, 2015, p. 10.

30 Malcolm Fraser interviewed by Clyde Cameron, NLA Oral History, TRC 2162, p. 35.

31 Cabinet, 20 December 1971, 'PJ Lawler', NAA: A11099, 1/306.

32 Alan Reid diary, 20 December 1971, NLA MS7796.

33 Loose-leaf draft statement, 'PJ Lawler', NAA: A11099, 1/306.

34 McMahon, aide-mémoires, 20, 21, and 22 December 1971, copies in the author's possession.

35 Alan Reid diary, 21 December 1971, NLA MS7796.

36 Cabinet, 22 December 1971, 'PJ Lawler', NAA: A11099, 1/306.

37 Nigel Bowen interviewed by Ron Hurst, NLA Oral History, TRC 4900/61.

38 Author's correspondence with John Stone, 25 May 2017.

39 'Backdown', *SMH*, 24 December 1971, p. 6.

40 Alan Reid diary, 23 December 1971, NLA MS7796.

41 Bunting to Garner, 26 June 1971, NAA: M321, 11.

42 Freudenberg, 2005, p. 129.

Chapter 39: The Stories Told

1 Bowman diary, 4 June 1984.
2 Tiffen, 1988, pp. 25–29.
3 'Diary of a Liberal: even friends take a knock', *SMH*, 28 May 1984, p. 2.
4 Bowman diary, 28 May 1984.
5 ibid., 4 June 1984.
6 ibid., 6 June 1984.
7 Maximilian Walsh, 'Public McMahon and Private Billy: the facts and the myths', *National Times*, 20–25 September 1971, pp. 3–4.
8 See Gerard Henderson, in Bramston (ed.), 2010, p. 84; or Henderson, 2015, p. 291.
9 Author's interview with Alan Ramsey, 31 January 2018.
10 Mitchell, 2007, pp. 38–39.
11 Mungo MacCallum interviewed by Mel Pratt, NLA Oral History, TRC 121/44, p. 33.
12 Author's correspondence with Mungo MacCallum, 4 October 2017.
13 Author's interview with C.R. 'Kim' Jones, 10 June 2017.
14 Author's interview with Ian Grigg, 16 April 2018; author's interview with Jonathan Gaul, 24 February 2018.
15 This section draws on: Bruner, 2004, pp. 691–710; Mandler, 1984; Schacter, 2001, pp. 138–60; and Sartre, 1964.
16 Bowman diary, 6 June 1984.

Chapter 40: Survival Mode

1 Hughes, 1972a, pp. 92–101.
2 Bunting, note for file, 4.25pm, 23 January 1972, NAA: M321, 16.
3 Author's interview with Ian Grigg, 20 February 2018.
4 Oakes and Solomon, 1973, pp. 80–81.
5 See APMC Transcripts: 'Army re-organisation', 26 January 1972, 11/1972; 'Payment of pensions overseas', January 1972, 8/1972; 'Retirement of the Honourable C.E. Barnes, MP', 25 January 1972, 7/1972; 'Release of Sheikh Mujimur Rahman', 10 January 1972, 3/1972; 'President Nixon's peace proposals', 26 January 1972, 10/1972.
6 Bert Kelly diary, 24 January 1972, NLA MS7424; Hughes, 1972b, pp. 261–70.
7 Snedden and Schedvin, 1990, p. 115.
8 Bunting, notes for file, 15 January 1972, NAA: M321, 16; Bunting, note for file, 13 January 1972, NAA: M319, M31 Part 1; Snedden and Schedvin, 1990, pp. 116–18.
9 Bunting note for file, 23 January 1972, NAA: M321, 16.
10 Hasluck, 'Mr McMahon's plans in February, 1972', NAA: M1767, 3.
11 Alan Reid diary, 4 and 14 February 1972, NLA MS7796.
12 Hasluck, 'Mr McMahon's plans for February, 1972', NAA: M1767, 3.
13 'Premiers' Conference opening statement by the Prime Minister', 14 February 1972, APMC Transcripts.
14 'Interview given by the Prime Minister, the Rt Hon. William McMahon, CH, MP on ABC national television', 14 February 1972, APMC Transcripts, 72/23B.
15 Alan Reid diary, 15 February 1972, NLA MS7796.
16 See, for example, *CPD HoR*, vol. 76, pp. 107–18.
17 Alan Reid diary, 16 February 1972, NLA MS7796.
18 Bunting, 16 February 1972, NAA: M319, 31 Part 2.

19 Bunting, 17 February 1972, NAA: M319, 31 Part 3.

20 Snedden and Schedvin, 1990, p. 138.

21 Bert Kelly diary, 22 February 1972, NLA MS7424.

22 Alan Reid diary, 22 February 1972, NLA MS7796.

23 McMahon and Hurford, *CPD HoR*, vol. 76, 22 February 1972, p. 7.

24 Bunting, note for file, 20 January 1972, NAA: M321, 17.

25 Alan Reid diary, 20 January 1972, NLA MS7796.

26 ibid., 23 February and 7 March 1972.

27 Howson, 1984, p. 813.

28 Coombs, 1981, p. 289. Late in September 1971, McMahon wrote to Howson of his 'deep' concern at the delay—which he argued was 'damaging to the credibility and standing of the government'—and his 'general agreement' with the submissions made by the CAA to Howson's inter-departmental committee. See McMahon to Howson, 28 September 1971, NAA: M1368, 51 Part 1.

29 When McMahon attended a meeting of the Aboriginal affairs committee of cabinet on 14 October, he said: 'I do not believe we could sensibly contemplate granting leases on basis of traditional association.' See 'PH Bailey', NAA: A11099, 1/336.

30 Aboriginal affairs committee of cabinet, 13 October 1971, 'PH Bailey', NAA: A11099, 1/336.

31 Howson, 1984, p. 792.

32 ibid., p. 799; 'Committee on Aboriginal Affairs—cabinet minute—leases on Aboriginal reserves—submission 457', 6 December 1971, NAA: A5909, 613.

33 Lawler, 'Land for Aborigines', 3 January 1972, NAA: M319, 31 Part 1.

34 Dexter, 2015, p. 216.

35 McMahon, 'The PM's statement on policy', *CT*, 26 January 1972, pp. 12–13.

36 'A chance lost', *CT*, 27 January 1972, p. 2.

37 'A price on our guilt', *Aus.*, 26 January 1972, p. 3.

38 This paragraph draws on Foley, 2014, pp. 22–41; and Robinson, 1994, pp. 49–63.

39 Michael Anderson interview with Brenda Gifford, in Foley, Schaap, and Howell (eds), 2014, pp. 119.

40 Howson, 1984, p. 818. Barrie Dexter recalled later that McMahon considered his statement 'a major turning point in Aboriginal Affairs in Australia'. See Dexter, 2015, p. 217.

41 'Aboriginal women record dissent', *CT*, 31 January 1972, p. 1.

42 *CN*, 31 January 1972, quoted in Foley, 2014, p. 32.

43 Coombs, 1981, p. 290.

44 Harris, 1972, p. 19.

45 McNally, 1973, p. 44.

46 Perkins, 1975, p. 167.

47 'Black Power salute to Mr Suharto', *CT*, 8 February 1972, p. 3.

48 'Labor promises Aborigines land', *CT*, 9 February 1972, p. 3.

49 'This Week', McMahon interviewed by John Boland and Max Grant, 5 March 1972, APMC Transcripts.

50 Whitlam and McMahon, *CPD HoR*, vol. 76, 29 February 1972, pp. 331–37.

51 Souter, 1988, p. 501.

52 Alan Reid diary, 29 February 1972,

NLA MS7796.

53 Bert Kelly diary, 8 March 1972, NLA MS7424.

54 Paul Hasluck, 'Dissension in the cabinet, May 1972', NAA: M1767, 3.

55 Alan Reid diary, 1 March 1972, NLA MS7796.

56 'Who is it?', *Age*, 17 March 1972, p. 9.

57 Neither of the Kibels were from Manchester; neither Kibel was Jewish.

58 Berinson, Bowen, Hughes, McMahon, *CPD HoR*, vol. 76, 23 March 1972, pp. 1090, 1096.

59 ibid., pp. 1096–103.

60 Alan Reid diary, 23 March 1972, NLA MS7796.

61 Howson, 1984, p. 838.

62 ibid., pp. 836–37.

63 Alan Reid diary, 22 March 1972, NLA MS7796.

64 Howson, 1984, p. 840.

65 'Killen's "crisis a teacup storm"', *CM*, 28 March 1972, p. 3.

66 Alan Reid diary, 26 March 1972, NLA MS7796.

67 Bert Kelly diary, 24 March 1972, NLA MS7424.

68 Alan Reid diary, 26 March 1972, NLA MS7796.

69 Snedden and Schedvin, 1990, pp. 134–35.

70 Alan Reid diary, 29 March 1972, NLA MS7796.

71 Howson, 1984, p. 841.

72 Snedden, *CPD HoR*, vol. 77, 12 April 1972, pp. 1428–32.

73 Bunting, note for file, 20 March 1972, NAA: M321, 17.

74 Author's interview with Jonathan Gaul, 24 February 2018.

75 The quotes from Crean, Anthony and *The Aus.* are drawn from Hughes, 1972b, pp. 261–70.

76 Hasluck, 'Mr McMahon's views on Honours', NAA: M1767, 3.

77 Bunting, 3 March 1972, NAA: M321, 17.

78 Bunting, 11 March 1972, ibid.

79 Bunting, 7 June 1972, NAA: M319, 35 Part 1.

80 Author's interview with Sir Lenox Hewitt, 2 February 2018.

81 Bunting, 1 June 1971, Bunting to Wheeler, 7 June 1971, NAA: M319, 28.

82 Bunting to Collings, 17 June 1971, ibid.

83 Bunting, 'Trade with Japan', n.d., June 1971, ibid.

84 Bunting, 'Discussions with Sir Frederick Wheeler', 20 January 1972, NAA: M319, 31 Part 1.

85 Bunting, note for file, 15 March 1972, NAA: M321, 16.

86 Author's interview with Jonathan Gaul, 24 February 2018.

87 Bunting, note for file, 12 June 1971, NAA: M319, 28.

88 Lawler, note for file, 27 December 1971, NAA: M321, 15.

89 Lawler, note for file, 29 December 1971, ibid.

90 Bunting, note for file, 15 May 1972, NAA: M321, 16.

91 Bunting, note for file, 7 September 1972, NAA: M319, 37.

92 Bunting, note for file, 8 September 1972, ibid.

93 Bunting, note for file, 9.45am, 8 September 1972, ibid.

94 Bunting to McMahon, 8 September 1972, ibid.

95 Bunting, note for file, 7.45am, 6 October 1972, NAA: M319, 38.

96 Author's interview with Ian Grigg, 20 February 2018.

97 See, for example, Howson, 1984, pp. 735, 751–54, 828, 831, 836–37.

98 Peter Howson interviewed by Jonathan Gaul, NLA Oral History, TRC 229, 10/16.

99 Bruce Juddery, 'Making something of the environment', *CT*, 10 December 1971, p. 2.

100 Author's interview with Sir Lenox Hewitt, 2 February 2018.

101 Howson, 1984, pp. 796–97; Cabinet decision no. 583, 'Proposal for a committee of enquiry into the quality of the environment', 30 November 1971, NAA: A5909, 583.

102 McMahon, 30 November 1971, 'Sir John Bunting', NAA: A11099, 1/121.

103 Howson, 1984, p. 807.

104 ibid., p. 816. In that cabinet meeting, McMahon said, 'We need something but we won't get it out of this paper.' See McMahon, 25 January 1972, 'Sir John Bunting', NAA: A11099, 1/121; 'PH Bailey', NAA: A11099, 1/336.

105 Cabinet decision no. 500, 'Commonwealth Advisory Committee on the Environment', 25 January 1972, NAA: A5909, 500.

106 Howson, 1984, pp. 833–34, 842–43; McMahon, 'Australian Environment Council Meeting', 6 April 1972, PM no. 33/1972, APMC Transcripts.

107 ibid., pp. 848–55.

108 ibid., p. 858; Bunting, note for file, 29 April 1972, NAA: M319, 33 Part 2.

109 Joseph Glascott, 'Now that the environment is here …' *SMH*, 2 May 1972, p. 6.

110 Howson, 1984, pp. 860–61.

111 Cabinet decision no. 978, 'Appointment of Chairman of Commonwealth Advisory Committee on the Environment', 16 May 1972, NAA: A5909, 978; Howson, 1984, pp. 867–69.

112 Howson, *CPD HoR*, vol. 78, 24 May 1972, pp. 2970–79.

113 Howson, 1984, p. 873.

Chapter 41: On Edge

1 Bowman diary, 10 March 1984. For more on this treatment, and follow-up treatment a year later, see Jerry Featherston, 1985, 'Cancer scares for Sir William and Lady McMahon', *Women's Day*, 13 May, pp. 4–5.

2 Bowman diary, 14 March 1984.

3 ibid., 15 March 1984.

4 ibid., 19 March 1984.

5 ibid., 20 March 1984.

Chapter 42: Constant Threats

1 Chipp and Larkin, 1978, p. 102.

2 John Edwards, 'Inside Billy McMahon', *AFR*, 31 May 1972, p. 3.

3 David Solomon, 'MPs seek ban on "Schoolbook"', *CT*, 17 April 1972, p. 1.

4 David Solomon, 'Mr Chipp to win on "Schoolbook"', *CT*, 18 April 1972, p. 3.

5 Chipp and Larkin, 1978, p. 127.

6 'Archbishop's call for "Schoolbook" banning', *CT*, 24 April 1972, p. 3.

7 'Mackay says nation faces moral siege', *CM*, 1 May 1972, p. 10.

8 'Anthony flays "Schoolbook"', *CT*, 15 May 1972, p. 3; Kane, *CPD Sen.*, vol. 52, 26 April 1972, p. 1333.

9 Bunting drafts, in McMahon's name, for Katter, Cotton, Wentworth,

Holten, and Howson, NAA: M319, 34 Part 2.

10 Alan Reid diary, 18 April 1972, NLA MS7796.

11 Hancock, 2016, p. 198.

12 Killen, 1985, pp. 191–92. According to Alan Reid, Killen told McMahon to 'Go dive in a lake'. See Alan Reid diary, 9 May 1972, NLA MS7796.

13 According to Howson, at least. See Howson, 1984, pp. 869–70.

14 The Bill received debate again on 18 October, but out of a need to have it deferred once more. See Gorton, Patterson, Killen, Connor, Bowen, and Whitlam, *CPD HoR*, vol. 81, 18 October 1972, pp. 2770–89.

15 'Challenge to Labor over wanted candidate', *Aus.*, 11 February 1972, p. 2.

16 Paul, 1972, pp. 99–100.

17 Brown, Hughes, Whitlam and Killen, *CPD HoR*, vol. 76, 2 March 1972, pp. 479–89.

18 Hughes, 1972b, p. 269.

19 'Dangerous to future', *CT*, 4 May 1972, p. 3.

20 Howson, 1984, pp. 831, 857.

21 Bruce Grant, 'The question is: Who is entitled to govern?', *Age*, 8 March 1972, p. 8.

22 Laurie Oakes, 'PM's very difficult year', *Advertiser*, 11 March 1972, p. 4.

23 ibid.

24 ibid.

25 'Reports of cabinet proceedings', cabinet decision no. 698, 26 January 1972, NAA: A5909, 698.

26 'Press briefing given by the Prime Minister Mr William McMahon to Heads of Bureaux in the parliamentary Press Gallery, Canberra', 26 January 1972, APMC Transcripts, 72/10B.

27 Max Walsh had written of this perceptively the year before. See Maximilian Walsh, 'Public McMahon and Private Billy: the facts and the myths', *National Times*, 20–25 September 1971, pp. 3, 4.

28 Wallace Brown, 'McMahon's first year as Prime Minister', *CM*, 9 March 1972, p. 2.

29 Bunting, note for file, 23 February 1972, NAA: M319, 31 Part 3; Howson, 1984, pp. 825–26.

30 Bunting, note for file, 24 February 1972, ibid.

31 Alan Reid diary, 9, 10, 11 August 1972, NLA MS7796; Bunting, note for file, 30 August 1972, NAA: M319, 36 Part 2.

32 Mungo MacCallum interviewed by Mel Pratt, NLA Oral History, TRC 121/44, p. 27.

33 Howson, 1984, p. 826.

34 Alan Reid diary, 23 February 1972, NLA MS7796.

35 Coombs, 1981, pp. 292–93.

36 Bunting, 31 January 1972, NAA: M319, 31 Part 1.

37 Bunting, 26 May 1972, NAA: M319, 34 Part 2.

38 Author's interview with Jonathan Gaul, 24 February 2018.

39 ibid.

40 Barnard, Whitlam, Foster and Gorton, *CPD HoR*, vol. 77, 12 April 1972, pp. 1491–94, 1556–62. See also Howson, 1984, p. 847.

41 Casey to McMahon, 14 August 1972, NAA: M1129, MCMAHON/W.

42 Allan Barnes, 'Whitlam to have same radio time as PM', *Age*, 22 April 1972, p. 3.

43 Author's interview with Jonathan Gaul, 24 February 2018.

44 Fairfax to Carroll, in Souter, 1981, p. 478.

45 Killen, 1985, pp. 189–90.

46 Alan Reid diary, 1 May 1972, NLA MS7796. See also Bunting, notes for file, 1 May 1972 and 2.30pm 1 May 1972, NAA: M319, 34 Part 1.

47 Hughes, 1972b, pp. 261–70; 'Treasurer bent on suicide?', DT, 8 March 1972, p. 6.

48 Fitzgerald and Holt, 2010, pp. 241.

49 McMahon, CPD HoR, vol. 107, 25 October 1977, pp. 2314–16. Accounts of this meeting differ. According to Graham Freudenberg, Murdoch telephoned McMahon, who was in London, to tell him of the deal: 'I can promise you, Prime Minister, that we will be as fair to you as you deserve.' In the background, Packer could be heard to say, 'If you do that, you will murder him.' McMahon, however, was not in London in June 1971. See Freudenberg, 1987, p. 221.

50 Sonia McMahon, 'It's alright, Boss', The Liberals, TV programme, 1994.

51 Freudenberg, 1987, p. 221.

52 Tange, 2008, p. 40.

53 Edwards, 2006, p. 195.

54 Tange subsequently wrote of approaching Fairbairn that year with a suggestion that the government establish a review of the organisation of the Defence group of ministers and departments. Fairbairn's answer was unsurprising: McMahon would not want to open up such a controversial matter. See Tange, 2008, p. 46.

55 David Solomon, 'Two-tier defence for Australia', CT, 29 March 1972, p. 1; Fairbairn, CPD HoR, vol. 77, 28 March 1972, pp. 1247–56.

56 Edwards, 2006, p. 197.

57 Allan Barnes, 'PM off to Asia, minus two trumps', Age, 2 June 1972, p. 9.

58 In a February conversation with Paul Hasluck, McMahon said he believed Lee had behaved 'in the most extraordinary manner' when he informed McMahon of this decision to stay away. 'He must have taken leave of his senses', McMahon said, of Lee's explanation that he would delay any visit in to see 'who was really going to be the Prime Minister of Australia'. The letter he sent was 'most offensive'. See Hasluck, 'McMahon's plans for February, 1972', NAA: M1767, 3.

59 Allan Barnes, 'Jakarta to get $75m in new aid', Age, 7 June 1972, p. 1.

60 Hugh Armfield, 'Liberal gloom, Labour joy on that speech', Age, 10 June 1972, p. 1.

61 John Lombard, 'Fairbairn is upset, too', Sun, 10 June 1972, p. 2.

62 Author's interview with Bob Bowker, 24 January 2018.

63 Neil O'Reilly, 'Govt "interference"', Sun, 13 June 1972, p. 6; Allan Barnes, 'PM in new Asia defence row', Age, 13 June 1972, p. 1, 7.

64 Author's interview with Richard Woolcott, 2 February 2018.

65 Author's interview with Jonathan Gaul, 24 February 2018.

66 Neil O'Reilly, 'Govt "interference", Sun, 13 June 1972, p. 6.

67 Author's interview with Bob Bowker, 24 January 2018.

68 'Political leaders in trouble', CN, 13 June 1972, p. 2.

69 Jim Quirk, 'Aussies blush at PM's blues', DM, 13 June 1972.

70 'Defence myths exploded: MP', Age,

14 June 1972, p. 5.

71 'South-East Asian Visit', McMahon television statement, 18 June 1972, APMC Transcripts.

Chapter 43: The Unequal Struggle

1 Bowman diary, 21 March 1984.
2 ibid., 22 March 1984.
3 ibid., 23 March 1984.
4 ibid., 3 April 1984.

Chapter 44: Dither and Irresolution

1 Maximilian Walsh, 'Byelection could be key to backing for Govt', *SMH*, 25 June 1972, p. 11.
2 'Still no noise on nuclear test', *DM*, 13 June 1972, p. 4.
3 Bunting to McMahon, 'Mr Anthony', 27 June 1972, Bunting, note for file, 'Conversation with Waller', 26 June 1972, and Bunting, note for file, 8.40am, 17 June 1972, all in NAA: M319, 35 Part 1; 'French envoy, PM differ on N-tests', *CT*, 20 June 1972, pp. 1, 3.
4 Bunting, note for file, 8.40am, 17 June 1972, NAA: M321, 16.
5 McMahon, 'Nuclear tests', 21 June 1972, APMC Transcripts.
6 McMahon, interviewed by John Boland and Max Grant, 'This Week', 25 June 1972, APMC Transcripts.
7 See McMahon, 'Commonwealth/State Relations: Macquarie Network Weekly Broadcast', 28 June 1972, APMC Transcripts.
8 Alan Reid diary, 22 June 1972, NLA MS7796.
9 Rohan Rivett, '17-year reign may end in August', *CT*, 22 June 1972, p. 13.

10 Henry Bolte interviewed by Mel Pratt, NLA Oral History, TRC 121/73, 1:1/16.
11 Hasluck, 'Mr McMahon's views on honours', 2 May 1972, NAA: M1767, 3.
12 McMahon, 'Sir Henry Bolte's retirement', 11 July 1972, PM no. 66/1972, APMC Transcripts.
13 Coombs to McMahon, quoted by Brennan, in Bramston (ed.), 2013, p. 256.
14 Cabinet decision no. 1303 (AA), 'Acquisition of Wave Hill Lease from Vesteys; surrender of land from Wave Hill Station', 24 August 1972, NAA: A5909, 1303/AA.
15 'Campers on Parliament House Lawns', aide-mémoire, 27 June 1972, NAA: A5882, CO1396.
16 ibid. McMahon signed and dated the list on 27 June 1972.
17 Bailey to McMahon, 27 June 1972, 'Aboriginal campers on lawns in front of Parliament House', ibid.
18 Harris, 1972, p. 28.
19 McNally, 1973, pp. 85–86.
20 ibid.
21 ibid.
22 Waugh to McMahon, July 1972, NAA: A463, 1972/3200 Part 1.
23 Bobbi Sykes, in Foley, Schaap, and Howell (eds), 2014, pp. 165–68.
24 See Coombs, 1981, pp. 290–91.
25 Howson, 1984, p. 892.
26 Hunt, *CPD HoR*, vol. 79, 15 August 1972, pp. 22–26.
27 Bunting, note for file, 13 September 1972, NAA: M319, 37.
28 Killen, *CPD HoR*, vol. 80, 13 September 1972, pp. 1306–09.
29 Whitlam, ibid., pp. 1282.
30 Bunting note for file, 23 January

1972, NAA: M321, 16.

31 Alan Reid diary, 1 February 1972, NLA MS7796.

32 Lynch, *CPD HoR*, vol. 75, 7 December 1971, pp. 4176–89.

33 Cameron, ibid., pp. 4189–204.

34 'DLP threat on arbitration', *CT*, 10 January 1972, p. 1. For the legal background of the amalgamation of the AMWU, see: Michael Kirby, 2014, pp. 123–45.

35 See Alan Reid diary, 22 February 1972, NLA MS7796; David Solomon, 'Backbench anger at union merger', *CT*, 25 February 1972, p. 1; 'Government defies DLP', *CT*, 1 March 1972, p. 3.

36 Howson, 1984, p. 829.

37 Snedden and Schedvin, 1990, pp. 131–2; Chipp and Larkin, 1978, p. 127.

38 'Aid for unionists fighting move for merger', *CT*, 6 April 1972, p. 1.

39 'At least 51pc vote sought in merger plans', *CT*, 26 April 1972, p. 13.

40 Howson, 1984, p. 853. Don Chipp would later claim that McMahon had held up the discussion of the measures until he had learned the DLP's views. When the DLP's opposition came through—on grounds that abolition of compulsory unionism would loosen its grip on the Federated Clerks' Union—McMahon abandoned it, in spite of the apparent support of a majority of cabinet. See Chipp and Larkin, 1978, p. 127.

41 Howson, 1984, p. 856.

42 'Minor changes in arbitration', *CT*, 28 April 1972, p. 2.

43 'Oil talks within the week demanded', *CT*, 15 June 1972, p. 9.

44 'Oil workers defy strikes ban', *CT*,

22 June 1972, p. 8.

45 'Refinery men walk off job', *CT*, 23 June 1972, p. 3.

46 'Oil strikers to meet', *CT*, 14 July 1972, p. 1.

47 'Oil unions seek return on Tuesday', *CT*, 15 July 1972, p. 1.

48 Bunting, 'Oil industry dispute', 22 July 1972, NAA: M319, 35 Part 2.

49 Bunting, 'Oil industry dispute', 26 July 1972, ibid.

50 'Ad Hoc Committee—cabinet minute—oil industry—industrial dispute—without submission', NAA: A5909, 1226/AD HOC.

51 D'Alpuget, 1982, p. 204.

52 David Solomon, 'Oil companies demand full end to strike', *CT*, 28 July 1972, pp. 1, 8.

53 'Without submission—oil industry dispute', 30 July 1972, NAA: A5909, 1243/AD HOC.

54 Bunting, 'Oil industry dispute', 29 July 1972, NAA: M319, 35 Part 2.

55 Bunting, 'Oil industry dispute', 30 July 1972, ibid.

56 'PM's statement', *CT*, 31 July 1972, p. 6.

57 Bunting, notes for file, 7.45am and 31 July 1972, NAA: M319, 35 Part 2.

58 Bunting, 'Oil', 31 July 1972, ibid.

59 Howson, 1984, p. 893.

60 'Unnecessary: Hawke', *CT*, 31 July 1972, p. 1.

61 'Pledge by PM', *CT*, 1 August 1972, p. 1.

62 Bunting, 'Oil', 8.05am 1 August 1972, NAA: M321, 16.

63 Bunting, note for file, 7.05pm 1 August 1972, NAA: M319, 36 Part 1.

64 After a conversation with Malcolm Fraser, Peter Howson had noted the existence of a 'militant' faction within

the cabinet, who were supposedly
egging McMahon on. See Howson,
1984, p. 893.

65 'Without submission—oil strike
legislation', 1 August 1972, NAA:
A5909, 1259/LEG.

66 McMahon, 'Oil industry dispute:
Meeting of Parliament', 1 August
1972, PM no. 76/1972, APMC
Transcripts.

67 David Solomon, 'Judge's action opens
way to settlement', *CT*, 2 August
1972, pp. 1, 12.

68 Alan Reid diary, 1 August 1972,
NLA MS7796.

69 ibid., 2 August 1972.

70 Tony Stephens, 'PM had "no focus,
no trust, not up to job"', *SMH*,
1 January 2003, p. 3.

71 Snedden and Schedvin, 1990, p. 134.

72 Bunting, note for file, 2 August 1972,
NAA: M319, 36 Part 1.

73 Alan Reid diary, 3 August 1972,
NLA MS7796.

74 Tony Stephens, 'PM had "no focus,
no trust, not up to job"', *SMH*,
1 January 2003, p. 3.

75 Snedden, *CPD HoR*, vol. 79,
15 August 1972, pp. 40–53.

76 Whitlam, *CPD HoR*, vol. 79,
22 August 1972, pp. 509–19.

77 'Liberal minister fears means test is
killer', *Aus.*, 11 February 1972, p. 1.

78 Cabinet decision no. 1209 (BRE),
'Means test', 23 July 1972, NAA:
A5909, 1209 (BRE); cabinet decision
no. 1211, 'Means test', 27 July 1972,
NAA: A5909, 1211; Snedden and
Schedvin, 1990, pp. 122–24.

79 Lawler, 'Note for file, 'Handling of
social and welfare submissions for
budget', 16 July 1972, NAA: M319, 16.

80 Bunting, n.d., August [?] 1972, NAA:

M319, 36 Part 1.

81 Bunting, n.d., July 1972, NAA:
M319, 35 Part 2.

82 Bunting, 22 July 1972, ibid.

83 Bunting, 'Budget meetings', n.d., July
1972, ibid.

84 David Solomon, 'Budget leaks and
car prices', *CT*, 15 August 1972, p. 2.

85 McMahon, 'The 1972/3
budget—Snedden and Reid',
aide-mémoire, undated, copy in the
author's possession.

86 Alan Reid diary, 8 July and 4 August
1972, NLA MS7796.

87 ibid., 15 August 1972.

88 Whitlam, *CPD HoR*, vol. 79,
15 August 1972, p. 139 and
22 August 1972, pp. 509–19.

89 Snedden and Schedvin, 1990,
pp. 135–37.

90 Author's correspondence with Doug
Anthony, 25 July 2016.

91 Bert Kelly diary, 23 August 1972,
NLA MS7424.

92 Alan Reid diary, 23 August 1972,
NLA MS7796.

93 Oakes and Solomon, 1973, pp. 81–82.

94 Hughes, 1973, pp. 63–81.

Chapter 45: Tributes

1 David Bowman diary, 11 April 1984.

2 ibid., 13 April 1984.

3 ibid., 17–27 April 1984.

4 ibid., 30 April 1984.

5 ibid., 1 May 1984.

Chapter 46: 'Where We Are Heading'

1 McMahon to Hartcher, August 1971,
in Starr, 1980, p. 246.

2 McMahon to Fraser, 31 August 1972,

NAA: M442, 41.

3   Minutes of Joint Standing
     Committee on federal policy,
     3 September 1971, quoted in Starr,
     1980, pp. 246–47.

4   Robert Southey, 'Changes and
     challenges', 29 May 1972, quoted
     in Starr, 1980, p. 247; Oakes and
     Solomon, 1973, pp. 114–15. For
     substantial documentation of the
     results, see 'Policy sub-committees
     1969–1972', Papers of Robert
     Southey, NLA MS9901/1/143.

5   Oakes and Solomon, 1973, p. 120.

6   Martin Reith, 'The Federal Council
     Meeting of the Liberal Party,
     Canberra, 8/9 June 1970', FCO
     24/677, British National Archives,
     Kew, London; Oakes and Solomon,
     1973, p. 129.

7   Bunting, note for file, 23 September
     1972, NAA: M319, 37.

8   Cabinet decision no. 1462, 'Secrecy
     in Government', 25 October 1972,
     NAA: A5908, 907.

9   Drake-Brockman, *CPD Sen.*, vol. 53,
     12 September 1972, pp. 689–92.

10   Kenneth Anderson interviewed by
     Mel Pratt, NLA Oral History, TRC
     121/90.

11   Anderson, *CPD Sen.*, vol. 47,
     8 March 1972, pp. 551–53.

12   Kenneth Anderson interviewed by
     Mel Pratt, NLA Oral History, TRC
     121/90.

13   Cabinet decision no. 270 (M),
     'Assistance to students —
     Commonwealth Advanced Education
     Scholarship Scheme', 21 July 1971,
     NAA: A5908, 170.

14   Cabinet decision no. 1179, (BRE),
     'Assistance to tertiary level students',
     21 July 1972, NAA: A5908, 756.

15   Cabinet decision no. 141 (GA),
     'Constitution of the Commonwealth
     Advisory Committee on Advanced
     Education as a Statutory Advisory
     Body', NAA: A5909, 141/GA;
     Cabinet decision no. 1155 (BRE),
     'Financial assistance to universities
     and colleges of advanced education
     1973–1975', 21 July 1972, NAA:
     A5909, 1155/BRE; Cabinet decision
     no. 1233 (BRE), 'Financial assistance
     to universities and colleges of
     advanced education', 27 July 1972,
     NAA: A5909, 1233/BRE.

16   McMahon, *CPD HoR*, vol. 78,
     11 May 1972, pp. 2455–58.

17   Cabinet decision no. 1156 (BRE),
     'The teaching of Asian languages and
     culture', 21 and 23 July 1972, NAA:
     A5908, 746.

18   Cabinet decision no. 1232 (BRE),
     'Assistance to secondary level
     students', 27 July 1972, NAA: A5908,
     757.

19   McMahon, 'The budget', 16 August
     1972, APMC Transcripts.

20   McMahon to Fraser, 1 September
     1972, NAA: M442, 41.

21   Gorton, 'Federal Elections 1969
     Policy Speech', 8 October 1969,
     APMC Transcripts.

22   Lynch, *CPD HoR*, vol. 81,
     10 October 1972, pp. 2288–95.
     Tony Street, the minister assisting
     the minister for labour and national
     service, said during the debate that
     'everybody would agree that the best
     place for a very young child is with its
     mother'. See *CPD HoR*, vol. 81,
     24 October 1972, pp. 3061–62.

23   Brennan, 1998, pp. 67–69.

24   Logan, Sumsion, and Press, 2013,
     pp. 84–91.

25   'Education and child care: Macquarie Network weekly broadcast', 14 September 1972, APMC Transcripts.

26   Denoon, 2005, p. 101.

27   Troy Bramston, 'Andrew Peacock: Colt from Kooyong on what might have been', *Aus.*, 17 December 2016, p. 18.

28   Cabinet decision no. 1347 (AD HOC), 'Papua New Guinea programme of movement towards internal self-government report on initial discussions', 12 September 1972, NAA: A5909, 1347/AD HOC; cabinet decision no. 980 (PNG), 'Papua New Guinea: programme of movement towards internal self-government', 18 May 1972, NAA: A5909, 980/PNG.

29   Troy Bramston, 'Andrew Peacock: Colt from Kooyong on what might have been', *Aus.*, 17 December 2016, p. 18.

30   Loane, in Paul, 1972, pp. 106–09.

31   Kelly and McMahon, *CPD HoR*, vol. 77, 26 April 1972, pp. 1976–77.

32   Cabinet decisions 972 and 1004, 'Poverty Enquiry', 16 May and 24 May 1972, NAA: A5909, 972; A5909, 1004.

33   McMahon, interviewed by John Boland and Max Grant, 'This Week', 25 June 1972, APMC Transcripts.

34   Cabinet decision no. 1228, 'Poverty enquiry', 20 July 1972, NAA: A5909, 1228.

35   'Gorton calls for means-test end', *CT*, 28 July 1972, p. 3.

36   Cabinet decision no. 1255, 'Poverty enquiry', 15 August 1972, NAA: A5909, 1255; Brown, McMahon, *CPD HoR*, vol. 79, 15 August 1972, p. 10.

37   Cabinet decision no. 1271, 'Poverty enquiry', 17 August 1972, NAA: A5909, 1271.

38   Cabinet decision no. 1273, 'Poverty enquiry', 22 August 1972, NAA: A5909, 1273; McMahon, 'Enquiry into poverty', 29 August 1972, APMC Transcripts.

39   McMahon, interviewed by Paul Lynch, 'The budget', 16 August 1972, APMC Transcripts.

40   McMahon, 'Terrorist attack at Munich', 6 September 1972, PM no. 83/1972, APMC Transcripts.

41   Waller, 'Terrorist attack on Israeli athletes competing at Olympic Games, Munich 1972', 11 September 1972, NAA: A1209, 1972/6887.

42   McMahon, Whitlam, Cohen, *CPD HoR*, vol. 80, 12 September 1972, pp. 1119–20.

43   Aarons, 2001, p. 428.

44   ibid., p. 431.

45   Cameron, in Hocking, 1997, p. 146.

46   Murphy, *CPD Sen.*, vol. 53, 19 September 1972, pp. 918–22.

47   Bunting, note for file, 9.40am 18 September 1972, NAA: M319, 37.

48   Bunting, 'Violence and terrorism', 18 September 1972, NAA: A5882, CO1528.

49   McMahon's annotations on Greenwood submission, 'Terrorism and violence in Australia', 29 September 1972, ibid.

50   Cabinet decision no. 1406, 'Terrorism and violence in Australia', 10 October 1972, NAA: A5909, 1406.

51   For an overview of how the September attacks and the government's response figures in the development of counter-terrorism in

Australia, see Finnane, 2015, pp. 817–36.

52   'The role of the Commonwealth in urban affairs', 3 March 1972, NAA: A5908, 572.

53   Bunting, 5.15pm and 10.30pm 12 April 1972, NAA: M319, 33 Part 1.

54   Quoted in Bunting, 'Decentralisation and urbanisation situation report', 24 June 1972, NAA: M319, 35 Part 1.

55   Bunting, 13 April 1972, NAA: M319, 33 Part 1.

56   Bunting, 23 May 1972, NAA: M319, 34 Part 2.

57   Cabinet decision no. 1351 (AD HOC), 'Urban and regional development', 14 September 1972, NAA: A5909, 1351/AD HOC.

58   McMahon, *CPD HoR*, vol. 80, 19 September 1972, pp. 1577–79.

59   Whitlam, ibid., pp. 1579–82.

60   Alan Reid diary, 19 September 1972, NLA MS7796.

61   McMahon, *CPD HoR*, vol. 81, 11 October 1972, pp. 2382–84.

62   'The cities', *SMH*, 13 October 1972, p. 6.

63   Author's interview with Jonathan Gaul, 24 February 2018.

64   *Strickland v Rocla Concrete Pipes Ltd* ("Concrete Pipes case") [1971] HCA 40; (1971) 124 CLR 468 (3 September 1971).

65   Bannerman, *Commissioner of Trade Practices Fifth Annual Report for Year 1971–72*, October 1972, Parliamentary Papers, vol. 7, no. 112, p. 1.

66   Greenwood, *CPD Sen.*, vol. 52, 24 May 1972, pp. 1955–68. According to Alan Reid, McMahon had said that he should introduce the trade practices legislation. 'With me doing it,' Reid quoted McMahon saying, 'it would add another one per cent to the polls. Greenwood isn't real value.' See Alan Reid diary, 11 May 1972, NLA MS7796.

67   Kane, *CPD Sen.*, vol. 52, 9 May 1972, pp. 1422–44.

68   Snedden and Schedvin, 1990, pp. 136–37.

69   Bunting, note for file, 10.10am, 17 August 1972, NAA: M321, 16.

70   Cabinet decision no. 1361 (AD HOC), 'Foreign takeovers of Australian businesses, a new approach to overseas investment', 14 September 1972, NAA: A5909, 1361 (AD HOC).

71   McMahon, *CPD HoR*, vol. 80, 26 September 1972, pp. 1916–20.

72   McMahon interviewed by Paul Lynch, 'Overseas investment in Australia', 27 September 1972, APMC Transcripts.

73   McMahon, interviewed by Paul Lynch, 'Foreign takeovers, unemployment', 5 October 1972, APMC Transcripts.

74   Bunting, note for file, 6 October 1972, NAA: M319, 38 Part 1. Bunting believed that McMahon had become mixed up with legislation relating to the National Urban and Regional Development Authority.

75   Bunting, 1.30pm 6 October 1972, NAA: M319, 38 Part 1.

76   McMahon, *CPD HoR*, vol. 81, 24 October 1972, pp. 3080–83.

77   *CPD HoR*, vol. 81, 25 October 1972, pp. 3182–207.

78   Oakes and Solomon, 1973, p. 121.

79   Georges, *CPD Sen.*, vol. 53, 12 September 1972, pp. 721–32.

80   See Wright, *CPD Sen.*, vol. 54, 27
     September 1972, pp. 1205–09.
81   Whitlam, *CPD HoR*, vol. 81, 12
     October 1972, pp. 2544–50.
82   McMahon, ibid., 17 October 1972,
     pp. 2625–27.
83   Whitlam, ibid., 19 October 1972, pp.
     2869–74.
84   Waller to Casey, 2 November 1972,
     NAA: M1129, WALLER/K Part 2.
85   David Solomon, 'A principle often
     breached', *CT,* 24 October 1972, p. 2.
86   David Fairbairn interviewed by Mel
     Pratt, NLA Oral History, TRC
     121/74, p. 123.
87   Barnard, Hayden, Fairbairn, Foster,
     Jess and Cameron, *CPD HoR*, vol. 81,
     25 October 1972, pp. 3127–31.
88   McMahon, Barnard and Jess, *CPD
     HoR*, vol. 81, 26 October 1972,
     pp. 3279–90.
89   David Fairbairn interviewed by Mel
     Pratt, NLA Oral History, TRC
     121/74, p.124.
90   Author's correspondence with David
     Solomon, 24 September 2017.
91   Author's interview with Alan Ramsey,
     31 January 2018.
92   Eric Bogle, 'Poor Wee Billy
     McMahon', *Down Under, Volume 2*
     [bootleg], lyrics by permission of Eric
     Bogle.
93   Mitchell, 2007, p. 43.
94   Mungo MacCallum interviewed by
     Mel Pratt, NLA Oral History, TRC
     121/44, pp. 30–31.
95   Howson, 1984, p. 797; Alan Ramsey,
     'A remake of Mr McMahon', *Aus.*,
     7 December 1971, p. 9.
96   Bunting, 29 June 1972, NAA: 319,
     35 Part 1.
97   Bunting, 21 August 1972, NAA:
     M319, 36 Part 2.

98   Oakes and Solomon, 1973, p. 127.
99   'I pray for poll victory: PM', *CT*, 31
     August 1972, p. 1.
100 Alan Reid diary, 30 August 1972,
     NLA MS7796.
101 Frost and Whitlam, 1974, p. 40.
102 Whitlam, 1985, pp. 10–11.
103 Edgar Holt interviewed by Mel Pratt,
     NLA Oral History, TRC 121/93,
     2:2/9.
104 Author's correspondence with Doug
     Anthony, 25 July 2016.
105 Whitlam, *CPD HoR*, vol. 81,
     10 October 1972, p. 2295.
106 Howson, 1984, p. 916.
107 Bert Kelly diary, 26 October 1972,
     NLA MS7424.
108 Hasluck, 'Dissolution of Parliament,
     November 1972', NAA: M1767, 3.

Chapter 47: Finishing
1   Bowman diary, 7 May 1984.
2   ibid., 17 May 1984.
3   ibid., 18 May 1984.
4   ibid., 28 May 1984.
5   ibid.
6   James, 1986, p. 611.
7   Ashley, 1968, pp. 22–37.
8   Bowman diary, 4 June 1984.

Chapter 48: In Calm and in Crisis
1   Edgar Holt interviewed by Mel Pratt,
    NLA Oral History, TRC 121/93.
2   Howard, 2014, p. 566; author's
    interview with John Howard,
    22 April 2016.
3   Howson, 1984, p. 920.
4   Author's interview with Jonathan
    Gaul, 24 February 2018.
5   Howson, 1984, pp. 917–18.
6   Oakes and Solomon, 1973, p. 129.

7   Edgar Holt interviewed by Mel Pratt, NLA Oral History, TRC 121/93.

8   Oakes and Solomon, 1973, pp. 175–76.

9   McMahon, 'Election Policy Speech', 14 November 1972, MoAD.

10 Howson, 1984, p. 920.

11 Freudenberg, 1977, p. 229.

12 'Steady as you go', SMH, 15 November 1972, p. 6.

13 Oakes and Solomon, 1973, p. 205.

14 ibid., p. 200.

15 Edgar Holt interviewed by Mel Pratt, NLA Oral History, TRC 121/93.

16 Oakes and Solomon, p. 211.

17 Author's interview with John Howard, 22 April 2016.

18 Oakes and Solomon, 1973, p. 260.

19 Howson, 1984, p. 920.

20 'Mr Snedden willing to stand for leadership', CT, 23 November 1972, p. 15.

21 'Mr McMahon as PM "indefinitely"', CT, 28 November 1972, p. 13.

22 Author's interview with Bruce MacCarthy, 5 August 2016.

23 Author's correspondence with Doug Anthony, 25 July 2016. .

24 Oakes and Solomon, 1973, pp. 221–22.

25 Author's interview with Jonathan Gaul, 24 February 2018.

26 David Solomon, 'Dr Coombs adviser if ALP elected', CT, 13 November 1972, p. 1.

27 Brian Johns, 'Labor calls in Dr Coombs', SMH, 13 November 1972, p. 1.

28 Coombs, 1981, p. 294.

29 Howson, 1984, p. 920.

30 I quote from Croke, 2001, pp. 41–42. There are other, though largely similar versions, of this speech. See, for example, 'Archbishop clears ALP policy on schools aid', SMH, 13 November 1972, p. 2; Croke, 2001, pp. 41–42.

31 Oakes and Solomon, 1973, p. 156.

32 'A change of government', CT, 23 November 1972, p. 2.

33 Grant, 2017, pp. 190–97.

34 Oakes and Solomon, 1973, pp. 266–7; 'Treasurer on letter', CT, 24 November 1972, p. 10.

35 Mitchell, 2007, p. 45.

36 Julian Leeser, 'Gracious, stylish and steadfast', Aus., 5 April 2010, p. 11.

37 Carrick, in Starr, 2012, p. 216.

38 Author's interview with Jonathan Gaul, 24 February 2018.

39 Oakes and Solomon, 1973, p. 268.

40 Phil Davis, unpublished memoirs, p. 7, copy in the author's possession.

41 Oakes and Solomon, 1973, p. 260.

42 ibid., p. 257.

43 Mitchell, 2007, p. 44.

44 Davis, unpublished memoirs, p. 8.

45 ibid.

46 Oakes and Solomon, 1973, p. 269.

47 David Solomon, 'All the load on one pair of shoulders', CT, 28 November 1972, p. 2.

48 Howard, 2014, p. 572.

49 Oakes and Solomon, 1973, p. 269.

50 Davis, unpublished memoirs. p. 8.

51 'PM's view of his team: stir on report', SMH, 25 November 1972, p. 1; McMahon, 'The Channel 7 (Brisbane) Interview', PM no. 105/1972, APMC Transcripts.

52 Author's correspondence with Doug Anthony, 25 July 2016.

53 Brown, 1993, p. 67.

54 Howson, 1984, p. 924.

55 Henry Bland interviewed by Mel Pratt, NLA Oral History, TRC 121/60.

56   Davis, unpublished memoirs, p. 8.
57   Howard, 2014, p. 570.
58   'Lab under attack on moral attitudes',
     SMH, 27 November 1972, p. 1.
59   McMahon, 'Moral issues in the
     election', 26 November 1972, PM
     no. 106/1972, APMC Transcripts.
60   'Lab under attack on moral attitudes',
     SMH, 27 November 1972, pp. 1, 3.
61   'Morality issue divides churchmen',
     SMH, 28 November 1972, p. 1.
62   'Abortion: PM, too, favours free vote',
     SMH, 30 November 1972, p. 1.
63   McMahon, 'National Press Club',
     29 November 1972, APMC
     Transcripts.
64   Author's interview with Jonathan
     Gaul, 24 February 2018.
65   McMahon, 'National Press Club',
     29 November 1972, APMC
     Transcripts.
66   'Prices power wanted', SMH,
     23 November 1972, p. 2.
67   Davis, unpublished memoirs, p. 9.
68   Tony Thomas, 'PM with the gift of
     the gaffe', Age, 5 January 1982, p. 9.
69   Lewis, 2014, p. 147.
70   Oakes and Solomon, 1973, p. 282.
71   'Final TV, radio appeal to voters',
     SMH, 30 November 1972, p. 2.
72   Griffen-Foley, 2003, pp. 177–203.
73   Mayer (ed.), 1973, p. 198.
74   Mayer (ed.), 1973, pp. 198–200.
75   Author's interview with Jonathan
     Gaul, 24 February 2018.
76   Author's interview with Richard
     Farmer, 16 July 2016.
77   Richard Farmer, 'Must "reading" held
     in secrecy', DT, 23 November 1972,
     p. 2.
78   This account of the confrontation is
     drawn from 'PM-Writer clash over
     report', DT, 24 November 1972,

     p. 13; author's interview with Richard
     Farmer, 16 July 2016; and Oakes and
     Solomon, 1973, p. 268.
79   Author's interview with Richard
     Farmer, 16 July 2016.
80   Sir Robert Askin interviewed by
     Mel Pratt, NLA Oral History, TRC
     121/83, p. 2:2/8–10; Snedden and
     Schedvin, 1990, pp. 134–35.
81   Author's interview with Ian Grigg,
     20 February 2018.
82   Author's interview with Jonathan
     Gaul, 24 February 2018.
83   Henderson, 1990, p. 255.
84   Shawcross, 1993, pp. 162–63.
85   'Let's give Whitlam a chance', DT,
     1 December 1972, p. 1.
86   Bowman, 1986, p. 117.
87   Fairfax, 7 December 1972, in Souter,
     1981, pp. 478–80.
88   Southey to McMahon, 7 March
     1972, in Reid, 1976, pp. 34–38. The
     original carbon may be found among
     Southey's papers at the NLA.
89   This section on Perkin and The Age is
     drawn from Hill, 2010, pp. 426–28.
90   Age, 2 December 1972, p. 1.
91   Thompson, in Mayer (ed.), 1973,
     p. 250.
92   Carol Summerhayes interviewed
     by Edward Helgeby, MoAD Oral
     History Project, OPH-OHI 153.
93   Author's interview with Jonathan
     Gaul, 24 February 2018.
94   Howard, 2014, p. 624.
95   Howson, 1984, p. 927.
96   FitzGerald and Holt, 2010, p. 258.
97   Oakes and Solomon, 1973, p. 7.
98   ibid.
99   Author's interview with Jonathan
     Gaul, 24 February 2018.
100 Author's interview with John
     Howard, 22 April 2016.

101 Mitchell, 2007, p. 46.
102 Author's interview with Bruce MacCarthy, 5 August 2016.
103 Davis, unpublished memoirs, p. 9.
104 Author's interview with Ian Grigg, 13 March 2018.
105 Whitlam, 1985, p. 13.
106 Oakes and Solomon, 1973, p. 7.

Chapter 49: As Matters Stand

1 Bowman diary, 19 June 1984.
2 ibid., 20 June 1984. McMahon may have been mixed up. A draft memorandum of understanding with MacMillan, dated October 1983, was among McMahon's papers. The contract stated that the entirety of the mooted $10,000 advance was to be paid to a professional writer—not McMahon —and that McMahon was to accept that writer's final manuscript and not withhold consent to publish the manuscript unreasonably. It appears, however, that the contract was not signed.
3 ibid.

Chapter 50: In the Wilderness

1 Bunting, note for file, 3 December 1972, NAA: M319, 40.
2 Hasluck, 'The defeat of McMahon', NAA: M1767, 4.
3 Davis, unpublished memoirs, p. 9; Oakes and Solomon, 1974, p. 60; Allen, in Aitchison (ed.), 1974, p. 19.
4 Hasluck, 'Mr Whitlam takes office', NAA: M1767, 4.
5 McMahon, in Bramston (ed.), 2013, pp. xxiv–xxv.
6 David Solomon, 'Snedden faces his first problem', CT, 21 December 1972, p. 3.
7 Kemp, in Mayer (ed.), 1973, pp. 48–59.
8 William Charles Wentworth interviewed by Ron Hurst, NLA Oral History, TRC 4900/104, 11:8.
9 Howard, 2014, p. 564.
10 David Fairbairn interviewed by Robert Linford, NLA Oral History, TRC 4900/72, 7:4–7:5, and David Fairbairn interviewed by Mel Pratt, NLA Oral History, TRC 121/74, session 5.
11 Howson, 1984, p. 928.
12 Laurence in Mayer (ed.), 1973, pp. 60–61.
13 Hocking, 2012, p. 3.
14 Aitchison, 1974, p. 4.
15 'McMahon blames 'disloyal' party', CT, 11 June 1973, pp. 1, 3.
16 Alan Reid, 'Prime Ministers I have known', Bulletin, 19 February 1980, pp. 59–60.
17 Dennis Minogue, 'Leading role or is it the final act?', Age, 20 August 1973, p. 9.
18 Oakes and Solomon, 1973, p. 121.
19 Author's correspondence with David Solomon, 24 September 2017.
20 Southey to McMahon, 29 August 1973, NLA MS9901/1/127.
21 Author's correspondence with Doug Anthony, 25 July 2016.
22 Dennis Minogue, 'Leading role or is it the final act?', Age, 20 August 1973, p. 9.
23 Reid and Lloyd, 1974, p. 315.
24 Snedden and Schedvin, 1990, p. 168.
25 ibid.
26 Nigel Bowen interviewed by Ron Hurst, NLA Oral History, TRC 4900/61.

27 Hasluck, 'Adjustment of ministry, October 1973', NAA: M1767, 4.

28 McMahon and Minogue, transcript of conversation, copy in the author's possession.

29 'McMahon faces new task', SMH, 24 February 1973, p. 3.

30 Dennis Minogue, 'Leading role or is it the final act?', Age, 20 August 1973, p. 9.

31 Aitchison, 1974, p. 8.

32 McMahon and Riordan, CPD HoR, vol. 83, 9 May 1973, pp. 1865–68.

33 McMahon and Whitlam, CPD HoR, vol. 84, pp. 2834–35.

34 John Edwards, 'Treasury barons under siege', NT, 9–14 September 1974, pp. 32–35.

35 Aitchison, 1974, p. 8.

36 Whitlam, 1985, p. 12.

37 Billy Snedden interviewed by Bernadette Schedvin, NLA Oral History, TRC 4900/57.

38 McMahon and Whitlam, CPD HoR, vol. 83, 4 April 1973, pp. 1045–46.

39 Gruen, 1975, pp. 7–20.

40 'Top Liberal resigns to become judge', CT, 12 July 1973, p. 1.

41 Billy Snedden interviewed by Bernadette Schedvin, NLA Oral History, TRC 4900/57.

42 McMahon, CPD HoR, vol. 88, 12 March 1974, pp. 284–85.

43 'Australian legislative election of 18 May 1974', Psephos, <http://psephos.adam-carr.net/countries/a/australia/1974/1974reps1.txt>, accessed 5 January 2017.

44 McMahon had predicted a large victory for the Coalition. When that failed to eventuate, he criticised the strategy for bringing the election on. See 'Gorton denies CP charges', CT, 30 May 1974, p. 12.

45 Snedden and Schedvin, 1990, p. 168.

46 'Snedden says no rejection of Supply', CT, 17 March 1975, p. 1.

47 Fraser and Simons, 2009, p. 261.

48 According to Reid, McMahon moved, in the first challenge, that the first ballot be secret. In the second, McMahon objected to Gorton's amendment of a motion by Billy Wentworth to declare the leadership vacant. The effect of Gorton's amendment—in effect, that all leadership positions, in addition to the leadership, be declared vacant—might have been to push wavering MPs to vote with greater regard to their own positions in the party, rather than on a sole, leadership basis. See Reid, 1976, pp. 154, 333.

49 Ayres, 1987, p. 233; Schneider, 1980, p. 22. When Gorton announced his resignation from the Liberal Party and his intention to stand at the next election as an independent candidate for one of the two Senate seats available in the ACT, McMahon was happy to gloat. 'From 1969 we did become disorganised,' he told a Brisbane audience. 'However, now we have come back, gaining unity, and the departure of John Gorton will help to consolidate that process.' See 'Gorton's secretary resigns in protest', CT, 26 May 1975, p. 1.

50 Snedden and Schedvin, 1990, p. 185.

51 Author's interview with John Howard, 22 April 2016.

52 Mitchell, 2007, p. 46.

53 Author's interview with Rob Ashley, 28 December 2017.

54 Aitchison, 1974, p. 14.

55 Author's interview with Rob Ashley, 28 December 2017.

56 Cramp, McLoskey, and Stewart, 1974, p. 208.
57 ibid., p. 198.
58 McMahon, *CPD HoR* vol. 95, 21 May 1975, pp. 2601–02.
59 McMahon, ibid., 20 May 1975, pp. 2499–500.
60 McMahon, *CPD HoR*, vol. 95, 19 May 1975, pp. 2418–19.
61 ibid., p. 2441.
62 'McMahon reveals spy group', *SMH*, 24 June 1974, p. 1.
63 'Mr McMahon sets off a minor furore', *CT*, 25 June 1974, p. 2.
64 Author's interview with Rob Ashley, 28 December 2017.
65 The following passages, which describe McMahon's evidence to the Hope Royal Commission, are drawn from: 'Private hearings (secret hearings of non-official evidence)—transcript pages 171 to 201—hearing at Canberra 29 May 1975—evidence by Rt Hon William McMahon (pages 171–183); Peter Hastings (pages 184–201)', NAA: A8913, 3/1/5.
66 Peter Gibson, 'Get rid of ASIS—MPs', *Daily Mirror*, 2 December 1983, p. 2. See also: Toohey and Pinwill, 1989, p. 146; 'ASIS: Who needs it?', *Daily Mirror*, 2 December 1983, p. 8; 'Marvellous house protection: McMahon', *CT*, 7 May 1983, p. 1.

Chapter 51: Never
1 Bowman diary, 6 June 1984.
2 ibid., 15 June 1984.
3 ibid., 19 June 1984.
4 ibid., 19 June 1984.
5 ibid., 20 June 1984. Gorton later stated that McMahon had urged him to take the ambassadorship. See John Gorton interviewed by Clyde Cameron, NLA Oral History, TRC 1702, vol. 1, p. 471. Barwick, who made the offer, recorded that Menzies believed Gorton would not take the position because of his ambition to become prime minister. See Barwick, 1995, pp. 206–07.
6 Bowman diary, 21 June 1984.
7 ibid., 25 June 1984.
8 ibid., 26 June 1984.
9 ibid., 28 June 1984.
10 ibid., 29 June 1984.
11 Bowman to Campell, 29 June 1984, copy in the author's possession.

Chapter 52: Persistence
1 McMahon, *CPD HoR*, vol. 95, 5 June 1975, pp. 3419–22.
2 McMahon, ibid., 9 July 1975, pp. 3651–54.
3 Ian Frykberg, 'No choice—Fraser', *SMH*, 16 October 1975, p. 1.
4 'Rowdy reception for a former PM', *SMH*, 21 October 1975, p. 11.
5 See Quick and Garran, 1976 [1901], pp. 404–06. McMahon specifically quotes this in his remarks.
6 'Questions and answers on address by the Rt. Hon. William McMahon, CH MP to students at Macquarie University on Thursday, 23 October, 1975', copy in the author's possession.
7 Coombs, 1981, p. 320.
8 Hocking, 2012, pp. 258, 264.
9 Author's interview with Rob Ashley, 28 December 2017.
10 Jan Goldie, 'Whitlam dismissal hurt Parlt: McMahon', *SMH*, 5 February 1979, p. 3.

11   McMahon, 'Use and abuse of "reserve powers"', *SMH*, 5 June 1979, p. 7.

12   Hocking, 2016, p. 74.

13   ibid.

14   Reid, 1976, p. 421.

15   David Reid, 'Note for file', 21 November 1975, NAA: M4081, 3/13 Part 1.

16   ibid.

17   John Menadue, 'Note for file', 24 November 1975, ibid.

18   David Reid, 'Note for file', 24 November 1975, ibid.

19   C.W. Harders to Ivor Greenwood, 21 November 1975, ibid.

20   Greenwood to Fraser, 16 December 1975, ibid.

21   C.W. Harders to Ivor Greenwood, 5 December 1975, ibid.

22   Fraser and Simons, 2009, p. 339.

23   Greenwood to Fraser, 16 December 1975, NAA: M4081, 3/13, Part 1.

24   Fraser and Simons, 2009, p. 338.

25   McMahon, 'Bob Ellicott … and the "rule of law"', *Sun*, 16 September 1977; McMahon, 'Sankey's Cost: a moral obligation', *Sun*, 2 March 1979, p. 18.

26   Fraser and Simons, 2009, p. 163.

27   Author's interview with John Howard, 22 April 2016.

28   McMahon, 'Housing: get the money moving', *Sun*, 10 March 1978.

29   Jones, *CPD HoR*, vol. 126, 12 April 1988, p. 1408.

30   McMahon to Fraser, 8 March 1979, NAA: M1266, 28 Part 2.

31   McMahon to Fraser, 3 May 1979, ibid.

32   Fraser to McMahon, 7 May 1979, ibid.

33   Peter Kelly, 'Petulant Fraser', *Age*, 3 July 1986, p. 12.

34   'Bashful ex-treasurer would take post again', *CM*, 30 November 1977, p. 8.

35   Errol Simper, 'Sir William's battle won', *CT*, 30 November 1977, p. 18.

36   Author's interview with Alan Wright, 9 December 2016.

37   Author's interview with Bruce and Leanne MacCarthy, 5 August 2016.

38   Pringle, 1973, p. 89.

39   'McMahon calls it a day', *Sun*, 4 January 1982, p. 2.

40   McMahon to Fraser, 12 August 1980, NAA: M1266, 28 Part 2.

41   Eric L. Robinson, 'Record of conversation with Sir William McMahon at 4pm, 27 August 1980', ibid.

42   Norm Lipson, 'Sir Billy: why I quit', *DT*, 5 January 1982, pp. 1, 2.

43   McMahon, aide-mémoire, 20 December 1981, copy in the author's possession.

44   Norm Lipson, 'Sir Billy: why I quit', *DT,* 5 January 1982, pp. 1, 2; Michael Wilkinson, '"The last year has been a lost year"', *Sun*, 5 January 1982, p. 8.

45   Peter Rees, 'McMahon quits in protest', *Sun*, 5 January 1982, pp. 1–2.

46   Tony Parkinson and Hugh Crawford, 'Labor Shapes up for the battle of Lowe', *SMH*, 5 January 1982, p. 3.

47   Greg Hartung, 'Sir Billy has the last laugh', *DT*, 5 January 1982, p. 10.

48   Murray Trembath and Tony O'Leary, 'McMahon quits Parlt', *Sun*, 4 January 1982, p. 1; Tony Parkinson and Hugh Crawford, 'Labor shapes up for the battle of Lowe', *SMH*, 5 January 1982, p. 3.; Teresa Mannix, 'McMahon's "suggestion for Lowe candidate"', *CT*, 6 January 1982, p. 1.

49   Peter Rees, 'McMahon quits in protest', *Sun*, 5 January 1982, pp. 1–2.

50 Michele Ferguson, 'McMahon retires with one regret', *Aus.*, 5 January 1982, p. 1.

51 Peter Rees, '33 years on …' *Sun*, 5 January 1982, p. 2.

Chapter 53: A Liberal View

1 Word of Bowman's experience with McMahon did leak, and was perhaps even leaked by McMahon. By October 1985, Clyde Cameron was relating that McMahon had sacked Bowman for refusing to write what he wanted. 'I know my facts,' McMahon supposedly said—indicative of McMahon's relationship with the truth. See Paul Hasluck interviewed by Clyde Cameron, NLA Oral History, TRC 1966, p. 184.

2 Andrew McCathie, 'The saga of Sir William's memoirs', *AFR*, 30 August 1985, pp. 1, 3.

3 Ben Hills, 'The strange tablets of Moses McMahon', *SMH*, 5 July 1986, pp. 1, 7.

4 Andrew McCathie, 'The saga of Sir William's memoirs', *AFR*, 30 August 1985, pp. 1, 3.

5 Ben Hills, 'The strange tablets of Moses McMahon', *SMH*, 5 July 1986, pp. 1, 7.

6 John Messer, 'The McMahon saga may yet hit print', *Times*, 26 July 1987, p. 2.

7 Author's interview with Richard Farmer, 15 July 2016.

8 Barry Jones, *CPD HoR*, vol. 160, 12 April 1988, pp. 1407–08.

9 Author's interview with Phillip Adams, 12 October 2016.

10 John Messer, 'The McMahon saga may yet hit print', *Times*, 26 July 1987, p. 2.

11 Robin Hill, 'The story behind Sir Billy's own story', *SMH*, 3 October 1986, p. 11.

12 Jerry Fetherston, 'Cancer scares for Sir William and Lady McMahon', *Women's Day*, 13 May 1985, pp. 4–5.

13 Paul LePetit, 'Sir Billy: playboy at 18 with a string of racehorses', *Sunday Telegraph*, 3 April 1988, pp. 8–9.

14 Larry Writer, 'Sonia McMahon: the truth about my marriage', *AWW*, 1 November 2007, accessed via Factiva.

15 For the terms under which McMahon donated his papers and their content, see Graeme Powell, 2005, 'The first in the field: Prime Ministers' papers in the National Library of Australia', *Australian Academic and Research Libraries*, vol. 36, no. 1, pp. 54–64.

16 Mitchell, 2007, p. 42.

17 Horne, 1980, p. 6.

18 Orwell, in Orwell and Angus (eds), 1968, p. 185.

19 Peter Kelly, 'A courageous and persistent man', *Age*, 2 April 1988, p. 6.

20 Fran Hernon, 'Friends and foes farewell Sir Billy', *DT*, 9 April 1988, p. 9.

21 Tony Stephens, 'Lady Sonia, a lady in mourning', *SMH*, 9 April 1988, accessed via Factiva.

22 James, 1956, pp. 77–106.

23 Paul Strangio discusses the various surveys and rankings of Australia's prime ministers. See Paul Strangio in Strangio, 't Hart and Walter (eds), 2013.

24 Auden, 1950, p. 78.

25 Larry Writer, 'Sonia McMahon: the truth about my marriage', *AWW*, 1 November 2007, accessed via Factiva.

26 Julian Leeser, 'Gracious, stylish and steadfast', *Aus.*, 5 April 2010, p. 11.

27 Bowman diary, 15 February 1984.

Bibliography

Personal Papers

National Library of Australia
Papers of W.L. Carew, MS 7524
Papers of R.G. Casey, MS 6150
Papers of Richard Hall, MS 8725
Papers of William Hughes, MS 28/4861, 28/4865, 1/10254, 28/4933, 28/4949
Papers of Bert Kelly, MS 7424
Papers of David Marr, MS 9356
Papers of Robert Menzies, MS 4936.
Papers of Sir Keith Murdoch, MS 2823
Papers of Earle Page, MS 1633
Papers of James Plimsoll, MS 8048
Papers of Alan Reid, MS 7796

New South Wales State Library
Arthur Wigram Allen Diaries, MLMSS 1317
George Warnecke Papers, MLMSS 8031

Government Reports
Report of the committee of inquiry into public service recruitment (Chair: Sir Richard Boyer), November 1959, Commonwealth Government of Australia.
Report of the committee of economic enquiry (Chair: Sir James Vernon), May 1965, Commonwealth Government of Australia.
Australian Defence Review, 1972, Commonwealth Government of Australia.

Books
Mark Aarons, 2001, *War Criminals Welcome: Australia, a sanctuary for fugitive war criminals since 1945*, Black Inc., Melbourne.
Ray Aitchison, 1978, *From Bob to Bungles and Now to Billy*, Sun Books, Melbourne.
— (ed.), 1974, *Looking at the Liberals*, Cheshire Publishing, Melbourne.
Blanche d'Alpuget, 1977, *Mediator: a biography of Sir Richard Kirby*, Melbourne University Press, Carlton.
— 1982, *Robert J. Hawke: a biography*, Schwartz Press, Melbourne.
Dundas Allen, 1964, *The Elizabeth Street Cottage*, Halstead Press, Sydney.
Kym Anderson and Ross Garnaut, 1987, *Australian Protectionism: extent, causes and effects*,

Allen & Unwin, Sydney.

R.W.C. Anderson, 1956, *Basic Reasons Why the Ottawa Agreement Must be Reviewed*, Associated Chambers of Manufactures of Australia.

Heinz Wolfgang Arndt, 1985, *A Course Through Life: memoirs of an Australian economist*, National Centre for Development Studies, ANU, Canberra.

Maurice Ashley, 1968, *Churchill as Historian*, Secker and Warburg, London.

S.R. Ashton, Carl Bridge and Stuart Ward (eds), 2010, *Documents on Australian Foreign Policy: Australia and the United Kingdom, 1960–1975*, Australian Department of Foreign Affairs and Trade, Canberra.

W.H. Auden, 1950, *Collected Shorter Poems, 1927–1957*, Faber & Faber, New York.

Philip Ayres, 1989, *Malcolm Fraser: a biography*, Mandarin, Melbourne.

David Barnett and Prue Goward, 1997, *John Howard: prime minister*, Viking, Ringwood.

Garfield Barwick, 1983, *Sir John Did His Duty*, Serendip Publications, Wahroonga.

— 1995, *A Radical Tory*, Federation Press, Sydney.

Diane E. Barwick, Jeremy Beckett and Marie Reay, 1985, *Metaphors of Interpretation: essays in honour of W.E.H. Stanner*, ANU Press, Canberra.

Basic Industries Group, 1967, *The Great Hoax: a public affairs discussion forum on the dairy industry*, Sydney.

Thomas Bavin (ed.), 1940, *The Jubilee Book of the Law School*, Halstead Press, Sydney.

Howard Beale, 1977, *This Inch of Time: memoirs of politics and diplomacy*, Melbourne University Press, Carlton.

Margo Beasley, 1996, *Wharfies: a history of the Waterside Workers' Federation of Australia*, Halstead Press, Rushcutters Bay.

Brian D. Beddie and Sue Moss, 1982, 'Some aspects of aid to the civil power in Australia', *Occcasional Monograph no. 2*, Department of Government, Faculty of Military Studies, University of New South Wales, Canberra.

Andrea Benvenuti, 2008, *Anglo-Australian Relations and the 'Turn to Europe', 1961–1972*, Boydell Press, Woodbridge.

Peter Blazey, 1990, *Bolte: a political biography*, Mandarin, Melbourne.

Geoffrey Bolton, 2015, *Paul Hasluck: a life*, UWA Press, Crawley.

Malcolm Booker, 1978, *The Last Domino: aspects of Australia's foreign policy*, Sun Books, Melbourne.

— 1993, *Nuclear War: present and future dangers*, Left Book Club Co-Operative, Sydney.

David Bowman, 1988, *The Captive Press*, Penguin, Ringwood.

Troy Bramston (ed.), 2015, *The Whitlam Legacy*, Federation Press, Annandale.

Deborah Brennan, 1998, *The Politics of Australian Child Care: philanthropy to feminism and beyond*, Cambridge University Press, Melbourne.

Carl Bridge, Frank Bongiorno and David Lee (eds), 2010, *The High Commissioners: Australia's representatives in the United Kingdom, 1910–2010*, Department of Foreign Affairs and Trade, Canberra.

Neil Brown, 1993, *On the Other Hand … Sketches and Reflections from Political Life*, Poplar Press, Canberra.

Wallace Brown, 2002, *Ten Prime Ministers*, Longueville Books, Sydney.

Waveney Browne, 1981, *A Woman of Distinction: the Honourable Dame Annabelle Rankin D.B.E.*, Boolarong Publications, Ascot.

Jerome Bruner, 1990, *Acts of Meaning*, Harvard University Press, Cambridge.

Brian Buckley, 1991, *Lynched: the life of Sir Phillip Lynch, mastermind of the ambush that ended Gough's run*, Salzburg Publishing, Melbourne.

John Bunting, 1988, *R.G. Menzies: a portrait*, Allen & Unwin, Sydney.

S.J. Butlin, 1986, *The Australian Monetary System*, (ed.) J.F. Butlin, privately published, Sydney.

Nancy Buttfield, 1992, *Dame Nancy: the autobiography of Dame Nancy Buttfield*, Adelaide.

Arthur Calwell, 1972, *Be Just and Fear Not*, Lloyd O'Neil, Victoria.

Clyde Cameron, 1990, *The Cameron Diaries*, Allen & Unwin, Crows Nest.

Brian Carroll, 1978, *From Barton to Fraser: every Australian prime minister*, Cassell, Stanmore.

— 2004, *Australia's Prime Ministers: from Barton to Howard*, Rosenburg, Kenthurst.

Richard Casey, 1972, *Australian Foreign Minister: the diaries of R.G. Casey, 1951–60*, (ed.) T.B. Millar, Collins, London.

Rob Chalmers, 2011, *Inside the Canberra Press Gallery*, (eds) Sam Vincent and John Wanna, ANU E-Press, Canberra.

Don Chipp and John Larkin, 1978, *Don Chipp: the third man*, Rigby, Adelaide.

Peter Coleman, Selwyn Cornish and Peter Drake, 2007, *Arndt's Story: the life of an Australian economist*, ANU E-Press, Canberra.

W.F. Connell, G.E. Sherington, B.H. Fletcher, C. Turney and U. Bygott, 1995, *Australia's First: a history of the University of Sydney, 1940–1990*, vol. 2, Hale & Iremonger, Sydney.

Selwyn Cornish, 2010, *The Evolution of Central Banking in Australia*, Reserve Bank of Australia, Sydney.

H.C. Coombs, 1981, *Trial Balance: issues of my public life*, MacMillan, South Melbourne.

John Cramer, 1989, *Pioneers, Politics and People*, Allen & Unwin, Sydney.

Karl R. Cramp, H.L. McLoskey and E.K. Stewart, 1974, *The History of the Lodge University of Sydney, No. 544 U.G.L. of New South Wales, 1924–1974*, Hogbin, Poole, Sydney.

J.G. Crawford, 1968, *Australian Trade Policy: 1942–1966: a documentary history*, Australian National University Press, Canberra.

L.F. Crisp, 1963, *Ben Chifley: a biography*, Longmans, London.

Andrew Crofts, 2004, *Ghostwriting*, A&C Black, London.

F.K. Crowley (ed.), 1973, *Modern Australia in Documents*, vol. 2, Wren Publishing, Melbourne.

Denis Cryle, 2008, *Murdoch's Flagship: twenty–five years of the Australian newspaper*, Melbourne University Publishing, Carlton.

James Curran, 2015, *Unholy Fury: Whitlam and Nixon at war*, Melbourne University Press, Carlton.

Blanche D'Alpuget, 1982, *Robert J. Hawke: a biography*, Schwartz/Lansdowne Press, Melbourne.

Fred Daly, 1977, *From Curtin to Kerr*, Sun Books, Melbourne.

Paul Davey, 2008, *Politics in the Blood: the Anthonys of Richmond*, UNSW Press, Sydney.

— 2010, *90 Not Out: the National Party of Australia, 1920–1910*, UNSW Press, Sydney.

— 2011, *The Country Party Prime Ministers: their trials and tribulations*, Chatswood.

A.F. Davies, 1972, *Essays in Political Sociology*, Cheshire Press, Melbourne.

J. Davidson (ed.), 1986, *The Sydney–Melbourne Book*, Allen & Unwin, North Sydney.

Phil Davis, unpublished memoirs, copy in the author's possession.

S.R. Davis (ed.), 1954, *The Australian Political Party System*, Angus and Robertson, Sydney.

David Day, 2003, *The Politics of War*, HarperCollins, Pymble.

Warren Denning, 1937, *Caucus Crisis: the rise and fall of the Scullin government*, Cumberland Argus, Parramatta.

Donald Denoon, 2005, *Trial Separation: Australia and the decolonization of Papua New Guinea*, ANU E-Press, Canberra.

Barrie Dexter, 2015, *Pandora's Box: the Council for Aboriginal Affairs 1967–1976*, (ed.) Gary Foley and Edwina Howell, Keeira Press, Australia.

A.V. Dicey, 1979 [1885], *Introduction to the Study of the Law of the Constitution*, tenth edition, Macmillan, London.

Stuart Doran and David Lee (eds), 2002, *Australia and Recognition of the People's Republic of China 1949–1972*, Department of Foreign Affairs and Trade, Canberra.

Alexander Downer, 1982, *Six Prime Ministers*, Hill of Content Publishing, Melbourne.

Dale Dowse, Helen Shepherd and Germanus Pause (eds), 1972, *The Wit and Wisdom of William McMahon*, Thomas Nelson, Australia.

Cecil Edwards, 1965, *Bruce of Melbourne: man of two worlds*, William Heinemann, London.

John Edwards, 1977, *Life Wasn't Meant To Be Easy: a political profile of Malcolm Fraser*, Mayhem, Sydney.

Peter Edwards, 1992, *Crises and Commitments: the politics and diplomacy of Australia's involvement in southeast Asian conflicts 1948–1965*, Allen & Unwin/Australian War Memorial, Sydney.

— 1997, *A Nation at War: Australian politics, society and diplomacy during the Vietnam War 1965–1975*, Allen & Unwin/Australian War Memorial, St Leonards.

— 2006, *Arthur Tange: last of the mandarins*, Allen & Unwin, Crows Nest.

P.G. Edwards, R.G. Neale, H. Kenway (eds), 1975, *Documents on Australian Foreign Policy 1937–49*, vol. 2, Australian Government Publishing, Canberra.

Sol Encel, 1974, *Cabinet Government in Australia*, Melbourne University Press, Carlton.

Herbert Vere Evatt, 1936, *The King and His Dominion Governors*, Oxford University Press, London.

Arthur Fadden, 1969, *They Called Me Artie: the memoirs of Sir Arthur Fadden*, Jacaranda Press, Melbourne.

Alan Fewster, 2018, *Three Duties and Talleyrand's Dictum: Keith Waller, portrait of a working diplomat*, Australian Scholarly Publishing, North Melborne.

Ross Fitzgerald and Stephen Holt, 2010, *Alan 'The Red Fox' Reid: pressman par excellence*, NewSouth, Sydney.

Stephen FitzGerald, 1972, *Talking with China: the Australian Labor Party visit and Peking's foreign policy*, ANU Press, Canberra.

Margaret Fitzherbert, 2004, *Liberal Women: Federation to 1949*, Federation Press, Annandale.

— 2009, *So Many Firsts: Liberal women from Enid Lyons to the Turnbull era*, Federation Press, Annandale.

Philip Flood, 2011, *Dancing With Warriors: a diplomatic memoir*, Arcadia, North Melbourne.

Gary Foley, Andrew Schaap and Edwina Howell (eds), 2014, *The Aboriginal Tent Embassy: sovereignty, black power, land rights and the state*, Routledge, Oxon.

Bethia Foott, 1968, *Dismissal of a Premier: the Philip Game papers*, Morgan Publications, Sydney.

Tom Frame, 2005a, *The Life and Death of Harold Holt*, Allen & Unwin, Crows Nest.

— 2005b, *The Cruel Legacy: the HMAS Voyager tragedy*, Allen & Unwin, Crows Nest.

Malcolm Fraser and Margaret Simons, 2010, *Malcolm Fraser: the political memoirs*, Miegunyah Press, Carlton.

Robert Freestone, 2010, *Urban Nation: Australia's planning heritage*, CSIRO Publishing, Canberra.

Graham Freudenberg, 1977, *A Certain Grandeur: Gough Whitlam in politics*, MacMillan, South Melbourne.

— 2006, *A Figure of Speech*, John Wiley & Sons, Milton.

Graham Fricke, 1990, *Profiles of Power: prime ministers of Australia*, Houghton Mifflin, Ferntree Gully.

Brian Galligan and Winsome Roberts (eds), 2007, *The Oxford Companion to Australian Politics*, Oxford University Press, Melbourne.

Leon Glezer, 1982, *Tariff Politics: Australian policy-making 1960–1980*, Melbourne University Press, Carlton.

Peter Golding, 1996, *Black Jack McEwen: political gladiator*, Melbourne University Press, Carlton.

Michelle Grattan (ed.), 2001, *Australian Prime Ministers*, New Holland, Australia.

Frank Green, 1969, *Servant of the House*, William Heinemann, Melbourne.

Bridget Griffen-Foley, 1999, *The House of Packer: the making of a media empire*, Allen & Unwin, Sydney,

— 2000, *Sir Frank Packer: the young master*, HarperCollins, Pymble.

— 2003, *Party Games: Australian politicians and the media from the War to Dismissal*, Text, Melbourne.

Billy Griffiths, 2012, *The China Breakthrough: Whitlam in the Middle Kingdom, 1971*, Monash University Press, Clayton.

Richard Hall, 1978, *The Real John Kerr: his brilliant career*, Angus and Robertson, Sydney.

Paul Ham, 2007, *Vietnam: the Australian War*, HarperCollins, Pymble.

Ian Hancock, 2000, *National and Permanent? The federal organisation of the Liberal Party of Australia 1944–1965*, Melbourne University Press, Carlton.

— 2002, *John Gorton: he did it his way*, Hodder, Sydney.

— 2004, *The VIP Affair, 1966–67: the causes, course and consequences of a ministerial and public service cover-up*, Australasian Study of Parliament Group, Canberra.

— 2007, *The Liberals: a history of the New South Wales division of the Liberal Party of Australia 1945–2000*, Federation Press, Annandale.

— 2016, *Tom Hughes QC: a cab on the rank*, Federation Press, Annandale.

W.K. Hancock, 1930, *Australia*, Ernest Benn, London.

Søren Hansen and Jesper Jensen, 1971, *The Little Red Schoolbook*, (trans) Berit Thornberry, Stage 1, UK.

Stewart Harris, 1972, *Political Football: the Springbok tour of Australia, 1971*, Gold Star Publications, Melbourne.

— 1972, *This Our Land*, Australian National University Press, Canberra.

Paul Hasluck, 1952, *The Government and the People, 1939–1941*, Australian War Memorial, Canberra.

— 1979, *The Office of Governor-General*, Melbourne University Press, Carlton.

— 1991, *Crude Impieties*, Rainy Creek Press, Victoria.

— 1995, *The Light That Time Has Made*, NLA, Canberra.

— 1997, *The Chance of Politics*, (ed.) Nicholas Hasluck, Text, Melbourne.

Bill Hayden, 1996, *Hayden: an autobiography*, Angus & Robertson, Sydney.

Cameron Hazlehurst (ed.), 1979, *Australian Conservatism: essays in twentieth century political history*, ANU Press, Canberra.

— 1979, *Menzies Observed*, George Allen & Unwin, Hornsby.

Jeremy Hearder, 2015, *Jim Plim: ambassador extraordinary: a biography of Sir James Plimsoll*, Connor Court, Ballarat.

Anne Henderson, 2011, *Joseph Lyons: the people's prime minister*, NewSouth, Sydney.

Gerard Henderson, 1983, *Mr Santamaria and the Bishops*, Hale & Iremonger, Sydney.

— 1990, *Australian Answers*, Random House, Milsons Point.

— 1994, *Menzies' Child: the Liberal Party of Australia, 1944–1994*, Allen & Unwin, Sydney.

— 2015, *Santamaria: a most unusual man*, Miegunyah Press, Carlton.

Heather Henderson (ed.), 2011, *Letters To My Daughter: Robert Menzies, letters, 1955–1975*, Murdoch Books, Millers Point.

— 2013, *A Smile for My Parents*, Allen & Unwin, Sydney.

Ben Hill, 2010, *Breaking News: the golden age of Graham Perkin*, Scribe, Melbourne.

Jenny Hocking, 1997, *Lionel Murphy: a political biography*, Cambridge University Press, Oakleigh.

— 2008, *Gough Whitlam: a moment in history*, Miegunyah Press, Melbourne.

— 2012, *Gough Whitlam: his time*, Miegunyah Press, Melbourne.

Edgar Holt, 1966, *Politics is People: the men of the Menzies era*, Angus and Robertson, Sydney.

H.T.E. Holt, 1975, *A Court Rises: the lives and times of the judges of the district court of New South Wales*, Law Foundation of New South Wales, Sydney.

Donald Horne, 1980, *Time of Hope: Australia 1966–72*, Angus and Robertson, Sydney.

— 2000, *Into the Open: memoirs, 1958–1999*, HarperCollins, Pymble.

Karen Horney, 1951, *Neurosis and Human Growth: the struggle toward self-realization*, Routledge & Kegan Paul Ltd, London.

J.C. Horsfall, 1974, *The Liberal Era: a political and economic analysis*, Sun Books, Melbourne.

Frederick Howard, 1972, *Kent Hughes: a biography*, Macmillan, South Melbourne.

John Howard, 2010, *Lazarus Rising*, HarperCollins, Sydney.

— 2014, *The Menzies Era: the years that shaped modern Australia*, HarperCollins, Sydney.

Peter Howson, 1984, *The Life of Politics*, (ed.) Don Aitkin, Viking Press, Ringwood.

W.J. Hudson, 1986, *Casey*, Oxford University Press, Melbourne.

—1989, *Blind Loyalty: Australia and the Suez crisis, 1956*, Melbourne University Press, Carlton.

William Hughes, 1947, *Crusts and Crusades: tales of bygone days*, Angus and Robertson, Sydney.

Jacques E.C. Hymans, 2006, *The Psychology of Nuclear Proliferation: identity, emotions, and foreign policy*, Cambridge University Press, Cambridge.

Robert Hyslop, 1990, *Aye, Aye, Minister: Australian naval administration 1939–59*, AGPS Press, Canberra.

Martin Indyk, 1979, 'Influence without power: the role of the backbench in Australian Foreign Policy 1976–1977', *Australian Parliamentary Fellow Monograph*, Australasian

Political Studies Association and the Parliament of Australia, Canberra.

Lucille Iremonger, 1970, *The Fiery Chariot: British prime ministers and the search for love*, Chatto and Windus, London.

Henry James, 1956, *The American Essays of Henry James*, (ed.) Leon Edel, Princeton University Press, Princeton.

Robert Rhodes James, 1986, *Anthony Eden*, Weidenfeld and Nicolson, London.

Dean Jaensch, 1994, *The Liberals*, Allen & Unwin, St Leonards.

L.W. Johnson, 1983, *Colonial Sunset: Australia and Papua New Guinea 1970–74*, University of Queensland Press, St Lucia.

George Jones, 1988, *From Private to Air Marshal: the autobiography of Sir George Jones KB CB DFC*, Greenhouse Publications, Richmond.

M.A. Jones, 1983, *The Australian Welfare State: growth, crisis and change*, George Allen & Unwin, Sydney.

Percy Joske, 1979, *Sir Robert Menzies: 1891–1978, a new, informal memoir*, Angus and Robertson, Sydney.

Bruce Juddery, 1974, *At the Centre: the Australian bureaucracy in the 1970s*, Cheshire, Melbourne.

James Jupp, 1982, *Party Politics: Australia 1966–1981*, Allen & Unwin, North Sydney.

C.R. Kelly, 1978, *One More Nail*, Brolga Books, Adelaide.

Paul Kelly and Troy Bramston, 2015, *The Dismissal: in the Queen's name*, Penguin, Melbourne.

John Kerr, 1978, *Matters for Judgment: an autobiography*, Aprolon Limited, South Melbourne.

T.H. Kewley, 1973, *Social Security in Australia 1900–72*, Sydney University Press, Sydney.

Thomas Kiernan, 1986, *Citizen Murdoch*, Dodd Mead, New York.

James Killen, 1985, *Killen: inside Australian politics*, Methuen, North Ryde.

J.E. King (ed.), 2007, *A Biographical Dictionary of Australian and New Zealand Economists*, Edward Elgar, UK.

Peter King (ed.), 1983, *Australia's Vietnam: Australia in the second Indo–China War*, George Allen & Unwin, Sydney.

Jack Lang, 1970, *The Turbulent Years*, Alpha Books, Sydney.

Valerie Lawson, 1995, *The Allens Affair: how one man shook the foundations of a leading Australian law firm*, MacMillan, Sydney.

Steve Lewis, 2014, *Stand and Deliver: celebrating 50 years of the National Press Club*, Black Inc., Melbourne.

Clem Lloyd, 1988, *Parliament and the Press: the federal parliamentary press gallery, 1901–88*, Melbourne University Press, Carlton.

David Lowe, 2010, *Australian Between Empires: the life of Percy Spender*, Pickering & Chatto, London.

David Lowe, David Lee and Carl Bridge (eds), 2016, *Australia Goes to Washington: 75 years of Australian representation in the United States, 1940–2015*, ANU Press, Canberra.

Enid Lyons, 1965, *So We Take Comfort*, Halstead Press, Sydney.

— [1972] 1997, *Among the Carrion Crows*, Lansdowne Publishing, Sydney.

Mungo MacCallum, 1994, *Australian Political Anecdotes*, Oxford University Press, Melbourne.

— 2002, *Mungo: The Man Who Laughs*, Duffy & Snellgrove, Potts Point.

— 2012, *The Good, the Bad and the Unlikely: Australia's prime ministers*, Black Inc., Melbourne.

Stuart Macintyre, 2015, *Australia's Boldest Experiment: war and reconstruction in the 1940s*, NewSouth, Sydney.

John and Judy Mackinolty (eds), 1991, *A Century Down Town: Sydney University law school's first hundred years*, Sydney University Law School, Sydney.

Jean Mandler, 1984, *Stories, Scripts, and Scenes: aspects of schema theory*, Hillsdale, New Jersey.

Robert Manne, 2004, *The Petrov Affair*, rev. edn., Text, Melbourne.

David Marr, 1980, *Barwick*, George Allen & Unwin, Sydney.

A.W. Martin, 1993, *Robert Menzies: a life, vol. 1, 1894–1943*, Melbourne University Press, Carlton.

— 1999, *Robert Menzies: a life, vol. 2, 1944–1978*, Melbourne University Press, Carlton.

— 2007, *The Whig View of History: and other essays*, (ed.) J.R. Nethercote, Melbourne University Press, Carlton.

Henry Mayer, 1973, *Labor to Power: Australia's 1972 election*, Angus and Robertson, Sydney.

John McEwen, 1983, *John McEwen: his story*, (ed.) R.V. Jackson, privately published.

Ian McLean, 2013, *Why Australia Prospered: the shifting sources of economic growth*, Princeton University Press, Princeton.

Jim McClelland, 1991, *Stirring the Possum*, Australian Large Print, Melbourne.

David McNicoll, 1979, *Luck's A Fortune*, Wildcat Press, Sydney.

Robert Menzies, 1967, *Afternoon Light*, Penguin, Australia.

— 1970, *The Measure of the Years*, Cassell, Melbourne.

Stephen Mills, 2014, *The Professionals: strategy, money and the rise of the political campaigner in Australia*, Black Inc., Collingwood.

Susan Mitchell, 2006, *Margaret Whitlam: a biography*, Random House, Milsons Point.

— 2007, *Stand By Your Man*, Random House, Milsons Point.

Frank Moorhouse, 1988, *The Everlasting Secret Family*, Sirius, North Ryde.

Lawrie Muller, 1996, *Australian Dairy: the comprehensive reference to the Australian dairy industry*, Morescope Publishing, Camberwell.

John Murphy, 2016, *Evatt: a life*, NewSouth, Sydney.

Bruce Murray and Christopher Merrett, 2004, *Caught Behind: race and politics in Springbok cricket*, WITS University Press and University of KwaZulu-Natal Press, Johannesburg.

Robert Murray, 1970, *The Split: Australian Labor in the fifties*, Cheshire, Melbourne.

Hal Myers, 1999, *The Whispering Gallery*, Kangaroo Press, Sydney.

Bede Nairn, 1986, *The 'Big Fella'*, Melbourne University Press, Melbourne.

R.G. Neale (ed.), 1976, *Documents on Australian Foreign Policy 1937–49*, vol. 2, Australian Government Publishing Service, Canberra.

J.R. Nethercote (ed.), 2001, *Liberalism and the Australian Federation*, Federation Press, Annandale.

Sarah Newton, 1993, *Maxwell Newton*, Fremantle Arts Centre Press, Fremantle.

Peter Nixon, 2012, *An Active Journey: the Peter Nixon story*, Connor Court, Ballan.

Laurie Oakes, 1973, *Whitlam PM: a biography*, Angus and Robertson, Sydney.

— 2008, *Power Plays: the real stories of Australian politics*, Hachette, Sydney.

Laurie Oakes and David Solomon, 1973, *The Making of an Australian Prime Minister*, Cheshire, Melbourne.

— 1974, *Grab For Power: Election '74*, Cheshire, Melbourne.

Robert O'Neill, 1981, *Australia in the Korean War 1950–53, vol. I: strategy and diplomacy*, AGPS, Canberra.

— 1985, *Australia in the Korean War 1950–53, vol. II: combat operations*, AGPS, Canberra.

George Orwell, 1968, *The Collected Essays, Journalism and Letters of George Orwell, vol. 3: As I Please, 1943–1945*, (eds) Sonia Orwell and Ian Angus, Secker and Warburg, London.

Clyde Packer, 1984, *No Return Ticket*, Angus and Robertson, North Ryde.

Gregory Pemberton, 1987, *All the Way: Australia's road to Vietnam*, Allen & Unwin, Sydney.

Charles Perkins, 1975, *A Bastard Like Me*, Ure Smith, Sydney.

Kevin Perkins, 1968, *Menzies: last of the Queen's men*, Rigby, Adelaide.

Roland Perry, 2000, *The Don: the definitive biography of Sir Donald Bradman*, Ironbark, Sydney.

Robert Porter, 1993, *Paul Hasluck: a political biography*, UWA Press, Nedlands.

Scott Prasser, J.R. Nethercote and John Warhurst (eds) 1995, *The Menzies Era: a reappraisal of government, politics and policy*, Hale & Iremonger, Sydney.

John Douglas Pringle, 1973, *Have Pen, Will Travel*, Chatto and Windus, London.

John Quick and Robert Garran, 1976 [1901], *The Annotated Constitution of the Australian Commonwealth*, Legal Books, Sydney.

Heather Radi and Peter Spearitt (eds), 1977, *Jack Lang*, Hale & Iremonger, Sydney.

Alan Ramsey, 2009, *A Matter of Opinion*, Allen and Unwin, Crows Nest.

D.W.Rawson, 1961, *Australia Votes: the 1958 election*, Melbourne University Press, Melbourne.

Alan Reid, 1969, *The Power Struggle*, Shakespeare Head Press, Sydney.

— 1971, *The Gorton Experiment*, Shakespeare Head Press, Sydney.

— 1976, *The Whitlam Venture*, Hill of Content, Melbourne.

George Reid, 1917, *My Reminiscences*, Cassell and Co., Sydney.

G.S. Reid and C.J. Lloyd, 1974, *Out of the Wilderness: the return of Labor*, Cassell, Sydney.

Alan Renouf, 1979, *Frightened Country*, MacMillan, Melbourne.

— 1980, *The Champagne Trail: experiences of a diplomat*, Sun Books, Melbourne.

P.L. Reynolds, 1974, *The Democratic Labour Party*, Jacaranda Press, Milton.

Wayne Reynolds and David Lee (eds), *Documents on Australian Foreign Policy: Australia and the nuclear non-proliferation treaty 1945–1974*, Australian Department of Foreign Affairs and Trade, Canberra.

Tim Rowse, 2000, *Obliged to be Difficult: Nugget Coombs's legacy in Indigenous affairs*, Cambridge University Press, Sydney.

— 2002, *Nugget Coombs: a reforming life*, Cambridge University Press, Sydney.

James Salter, 1995, *Light Years*, Vintage, New York.

B.A. Santamaria, 1981, *Against the Tide*, Oxford University Press, Melbourne.

Jean-Paul Sartre, 1964, *The Words*, Braziller, New York.

Marian Sawer (ed.), 1996, *Removal of the Commonwealth Marriage Bar: a documentary history*, Centre for Research in Public Sector Management, University of Canberra.

Daniel Schacter, 2001, *The Seven Sins of Memory: how the mind forgets and remembers*, Houghton Mifflin, Boston.

C.B. Schedvin, 1992, *In Reserve: central banking in Australia, 1945–72*, Allen & Unwin, Sydney.

— 2008, *Emissaries of Trade: a history of the Australian trade commissioner*, Department of Foreign Affairs and Trade, Canberra.

Russell Schneider, 1980, *War Without Blood*, Angus and Robertson, Sydney.

Glenn Seaborg and Benjamin Loeb, 1987, *Stemming the Tide: arms control in the Johnson years*, Lexington Books, Massachesetts.

R. Seth, 1960, *Robert Gordon Menzies*, Cassell, London.

William Shawcross, 1993, *Murdoch*, Pan Books, London.

Tom Sheridan, 2006, *Australia's Own Cold War: the waterfront under Menzies*, Melbourne University Press, Carlton.

Susanna Short, 1992, *Laurie Short: a political life*, Allen & Unwin, Sydney.

Marian Simms, 1982, *A Liberal Nation: the Liberal Party and Australian politics*, Hale & Iremonger, Sydney.

Don Smart, 1978, *Federal Aid to Australian Schools*, University of Queensland Press, St Lucia.

Billy Mackie Snedden and M. Bernie Schedvin, 1990, *Billy Snedden: an unlikely Liberal*, Macmillan, South Melbourne.

Gavin Souter, 1981, *Company of Heralds: a century and a half of Australian publishing by John Fairfax Limited and its predecessors 1831–1981*, Melbourne University Press, Melbourne.

— 1988, *Acts of Parliament: a narrative history of the Senate and House of Representatives Commonwealth of Australia*, Melbourne University Press, Melbourne.

Percy Spender, 1972, *Politics and a Man*, William Collins, Sydney.

Jim Spigelman, 1972, *Secrecy: political censorship in Australia*, Angus and Robertson, Sydney.

Graeme Starr (ed.), 1980, *The Liberal Party of Australia: a documentary history*, Heinemann/Drummond, Victoria.

— 2012, *Carrick: principles, politics and policy*, Connor Court, Ballarat.

Alan Stephens, 1995, *Going Solo: the Royal Australian Air Force 1946–1971*, AGPS Press, Canberra.

Paul Strangio, Paul 't Hart, James Walter (eds), 2013, *Understanding Prime-Ministerial Performance: comparative perspectives*, Oxford University Press, Oxford.

— 2015, *Settling the Office: from Federation to Reconstruction*, Melbourne University Press, Carlton.

— 2017, *The Pivot of Power: Australian prime ministers and political leadership, 1949–2016*, Melbourne University Press, Carlton.

Arthur Tange, 2008, *Defence Policy-Making: a close-up view, 1950–1980*, (ed.) Peter Edwards, ANU E-Press, Canberra.

William Temple, 1925, *Christ's Revelation of God*, Student Christian Movement, London.

Kylie Tennant, 1970, *Evatt: politics and justice*, Angus and Robertson, Sydney.

John Thompson (ed.), 1962, *On Lips of Living Men*, Cheshire, Melbourne.

Rodney Tiffen, 2017, *Disposable Leaders: media and leadership coups from Menzies to Abbott*, NewSouth, Sydney.

Andrew Tink, 2013, *Air Disaster Canberra: the plane crash that destroyed a government*, NewSouth Publishing, Sydney.

Brian Toohey and William Pinwill, 1989, *Oyster: the story of the Australian Secret Intelligence Service*, William Heinemann Australia, Port Melbourne.

Alan Trengrove, 1969, *John Grey Gorton: an informal biography*, Cassell, Melbourne.

Clifford Turney, 1989, *Grammar: a history of Sydney Grammar School 1819–1988*, Allen & Unwin, Sydney.

Melissa Tyler, John Robbins and Adrian March (eds), 2014, *Ministers for Foreign Affairs 1960–1972*, Australian Institute of International Affairs, Canberra.

Peter van Onselen and Wayne Errington, 2007, *John Winston Howard*, Melbourne University Press, Carlton.

David Veitch, 1996, *McEwen's Way*, David Syme College of Economics, Melbourne.

Keith Waller, 1990, *A Diplomatic Life: some memories*, Centre for the Study of Australia-Asia Relations, Griffith University.

Maximilian Walsh, 1979, *Poor Little Rich Country: the path to the eighties*, Penguin, Ringwood.

James Walter, 1980, *The Leader: a political biography of Gough Whitlam*, University of Queensland Press, St Lucia.

Sally Warhaft (ed.), 2004, *Well May We Say: the speeches that made Australia*, Black Inc., Melbourne.

Simon Warrender, 1973, *Score of Years*, Wren, Melbourne.

Leicester Webb, 1954, *Communism and Democracy in Australia: a survey of the 1951 referendum*, Cheshire, Melbourne.

Patrick Weller, 1989, *Malcolm Fraser PM: a study in prime ministerial power*, Penguin, Ringwood.

— 2007, *Cabinet Government in Australia, 1901–2006*, University of New South Wales Press, Sydney.

Patrick Weller, Joanne Scott and Bronwyn Stevens, 2011, *From Postbox to Powerhouse: a centenary history of the Department of Prime Minister and Cabinet*, Allen & Unwin, Sydney.

Katharine West, 1965, *Power in the Liberal Party: a study in Australian politics*, Cheshire, Melbourne.

Don Whitington, 1964, *The House will Divide: a review of Australian federal politics*, Lansdowne Press, Melbourne.

— 1972, *Twelfth Man?*, Jacaranda Press, Milton.

— 1975, *The Witless Men*, Sun Books, Melbourne.

Don Whitington and Rob Chalmers, 1971, *Inside Canberra: a guide to Australian federal politics*, Rigby, Australia.

R.S. Whitington, 1971, *Sir Frank: the Frank Packer story*, Cassell, Sydney.

Gough Whitlam, 1985, *The Whitlam Government 1972–1975*, Viking, Ringwood.

Greg Whitwell, 1986, *The Treasury Line*, Allen & Unwin, North Sydney.

Craig Wilcox, 1998, *For Hearths and Homes: citizen soldiering in Australia, 1854–1945*, Allen & Unwin, Sydney.

Roy Williams, 2013, *In God They Trust?: the religious beliefs of Australia's prime ministers 1901–2013*, Bible Society, Australia.

Edward Woodward, 2005, *One Brief Interval: a memoir*, Miegunyah Press, Carlton.

Academic Articles

n.a., 'Joint Communiqué — issued by the Conference of Foreign Ministers on Cambodia held in Jakarta', *Foreign Affairs Malaysia*, vol. 3, no. 1, June 1970, pp. 50–53.

Joel Atkinson, 2011, 'Australian support for an independent Taiwan prior to the recognition of the People's Republic of China', *Australian Journal of Politics and History*, vol. 57, no. 1, pp. 68–85.

Luke Auton, 2013, 'Opaque Proliferation: The Historiography of Australia's Cold War Nuclear Weapons Option', *History Compass*, vol. 11, no. 8, pp. 561–72.

Andrea Benvenuti and Moreen Dee, 2010, 'The Five Power Defence Arrangements and the reappraisal of the British and Australian policy interests in Southeast Asia, 1970–75', *Journal of Southeast Asian Studies*, vol. 41, no. 1, pp. 101–23.

Frank Bongiorno, 2013, 'Herbert Vere Evatt and British Justice: The Communist Party Referendum of 1951', *Australian Historical Studies*, vol. 44, no. 1, pp. 54–70.

Troy Bramston, 2004, 'Wherefore art thou Billy?: Revisiting the government of Billy McMahon', *Eureka Street*, April, pp. 33–35.

Jerome Bruner, 2004 [1987], 'Life as narrative', *Social Research*, vol. 71, no. 3, pp. 691–710.

Aynsley Kellow and Peter Carroll, 2011, 'Australia and the OECD', *Revista de Economía Mundial*, no. 28, pp. 93–111.

— 2012, 'Fifty Years of the OECD and Forty Years of Australian Membership', *Australian Journal of Politics and History*, vol. 58, iss. 4, pp. 512–25.

Peter Carroll, 2015, 'Gaining greater access to Western European Decision-Makers: A Motive for Australian Membership of the OECD', *Australian Journal of Politics and History*, vol. 60, no. 2, pp. 229–40.

Patricia Clarke, 2006, 'On a roller coaster with Maxwell Newton Publications', *Canberra Historical Journal*, iss. 57, July, pp. 2–9.

Lachlan Clohesy and Phillip Deery, 2015, 'The Prime Minister and the Bomb: John Gorton, W.C. Wentworth and the quest for an atomic Australia', *Australian Journal of Politics and History*, vol. 61, no. 2, pp. 217–32.

Robert Collins, 1996, 'The Economic Crisis of 1968 and the Waning of the "American Century"', *American Historical Review*, vol. 101, no. 2, April, pp. 396–422.

Brian Croke, 2001, 'Prelates and Politics: The Carroll Style', *Journal of the Australian Catholic Historical Society*, vol. 22, pp. 31–45.

Peter Curson and Kevin McCracken, 2006, 'An Australian perspective of the 1918–1919 influenza pandemic', *New South Wales Public Health Bulletin*, vol. 17, no. 7–8, pp. 103–7.

Norman Cowper, 1946, 'A Roman Character', *Australian Quarterly*, vol. 18, no. 3, September, pp. 64–68.

— 1950, 'Action against communism', *Australian Quarterly*, vol. 22, no. 1, March, pp. 5–12.

Dickenson, J 2010, 'Journalists Writing Political History', *Australian Journal of Politics and History*, vol. 56, no. 1, pp. 105-119.

John Dixon, 1977, 'Australia's policy towards the aged: 1890–1972', *Canberra Series in Administrative Studies*, no. 3, Canberra College of Advanced Education, pp. 91–101.

Sol Encel and Allan McKnight, 'Bombs, Power Stations and Proliferation', *Australian Quarterly*, vol. 42, no. 1, March 1970, pp. 15–26.

Erik Erikson, 1956, 'The Problem of Ego Identity', *Journal of the American Psychoanalytic Society*, vol. 4, no. 1, pp. 56–121.

Mark Finnane, 2015, 'The Munich Olympics Massacre and the Development of Counter-Terrorism in Australia', *Intelligence and National Security*, vol. 30, no. 6, pp. 817–36.

Lorna Froude, 2002, 'Petrol rationing in Australia during the Second World War', *Journal of the Australian War Memorial*, iss. 36, May.

Edward Fung, 1983, 'Australia's China Policy in Tatters 1971–72', *Australian Journal of Chinese Affairs*, no. 10, July, pp. 39–59.

Bridget Griffen-Foley, 2003, 'A "Civilised Amateur": Edgar Holt and His Life in letters and Politics', *Australian Journal of Politics and History*, vol. 49, no. 1, pp. 31–47.

— 2010, 'Sir Frank Packer and the leadership of the Liberal Party, 1967–71', *Australian Journal of Political Society*, vol. 36, no. 3, pp. 499–513.

F.H. Gruen, 1975, 'The 25% Tariff Cut: Was it a mistake?', *Australian Quarterly*, vol. 47, no. 2, June, pp. 7–20.

Ian Hancock, 2000, 'The Liberal Party — and the neglect of history', *Sydney Papers*, Winter, p. 122–131.

Tom Heenan and David Dunstan, 2015, 'The dark side of the Don: Bradman, the board and Apartheid', *Sport in Society*, vol. 18, no. 9, pp. 1110–31.

Robert Howard, 1970, 'Foreign Policy Review January–June 1970', *Australian Quarterly*, vol. 42, no. 3, September, pp. 109–116.

— 1971, 'Foreign Policy review', *Australian Quarterly*, vol. 43, no. 3, September, pp. 97–108.

Christopher Hubbard, 2004, 'From ambivalence to influence: Australia and the negotiation of the 1968 Nuclear Non-Proliferation Treaty', *Australian Journal of Politics and History*, vol. 50, no. 4, pp. 526–43.

Colin A. Hughes, 1972a, 'Australian Political Chronicle: September — December 1971', *Australian Journal of Politics and History*, vol. 18, no. 1, pp. 92–101.

— 1972b, 'Australian Political Chronicle: January — April 1972', *Australian Journal of Politics and History*, vol. 18, no. 2, pp. 261–70.

— 1972c, 'Australian Political Chronicle: May — August 1972', *Australian Journal of Politics and History*, vol. 18, no. 3, pp. 402–14.

— 1973, 'Australian Political Chronicle: September — December 1972', *Australian Journal of Politics and History*, vol. 19, no. 1, pp. 63–81.

Colin A. Hughes and J.S. Western, 1972, 'Hunting the PM: The Sequel', *Australian Quarterly*, March, vol. 4, no. 1, pp. 30–41.

Jacques E.C. Hymans, 2000, 'Isotopes and Identity: Australia and the Nuclear Weapons Option, 1949–1999', *Nonproliferation Review*, Spring, pp. 1–23.

Mark Johnston, 1996, 'The civilians who joined up, 1939–45', *Journal of the Australian War Memorial*, iss. 29, November.

Paul Kelly, 2016, 'Economic reform: A lost cause or merely in eclipse?', Alf Rattigan Lecture, 7 December, ANZSOG.

Michael Kirby, 2014, 'Present at the creation: The strange eventful birth of the Amalgamated Metal Workers' Union', *Journal of Industrial Relations*, vol. 56, no. 1, pp. 123–45.

Helen Logan, Jennifer Sumsion, and Frances Press, 2013, 'The *Child Care Act 1972:* a critical juncture in Australian ECEC and the emergence of "quality"', *Australasian Journal of Early Childhood*, vol. 38, no. 4, December, pp. 84–91.

Nigel McCarthy, 2000, 'Alf Rattigan and the journalists: advocacy journalism and agenda setting in the Australian tariff debate 1963–1971', *Australian Journalism Review*, vol. 22, no. 2, pp. 88–102.

David McKnight, 2008, 'Partisan improprieties: Ministerial Control and Australia's security agencies, 1962–72', *Intelligence and National Security*, vol. 23, no. 5, pp. 707–25.

Anne Mozley Moyal, 1975, 'The Australian Atomic Energy Commision: A case study in Australian Science and Government, *Search*, vol. 6, no. 9, pp. 365–84.

Patrick Mullins, 2015, 'Chasing the future — journalists writing political history', *Australian Journalism Review*, vol. 37, no. 2, pp. 95–107.

Bruce K. Murray, 2003, 'The sports boycott and cricket: the cancellation of the 1971/72 South African Tour of Australia', *South African Historical Journal*, vol. 49, no. 1, pp. 162–71.

J.B. Paul, 1972, 'Political Review', *Australian Quarterly*, vol. 44, no. 2, June, pp. 99–111.

Roderic Pitty, 2005, 'Way Behind in Following the USA over China: The lack of any Liberal tradition in Australian Foreign Policy, 1970–72', *Australian Journal of Politics and History*, vol. 51, no. 3, pp. 440–50.

Jeff Popple, 1982, 'The Australian Militia 1930–39', *Australian Defence Journal*, no. 33, March/April, pp. 44–48.

Graeme Powell, 2005, 'The first in the field: Prime Ministers' papers in the National Library of Australia', *Australian Academic and Research Libraries*, vol. 36, no. 1, pp. 54–64.

David Reynolds, 'Churchill the Historian', *History Today*, February 2005, vol. 55, no. 2, pp. 16–17.

Wayne Reynolds, 2015, '"To the brink of Manufacture": Nuclear weapons, the Anglo-American alliance and Australia's approach to the Nuclear Non-Proliferation Treaty', *Australian Historical Studies*, vol. 46, iss. 2, pp. 269–84.

Kel Robertson, Jessie Hohmann, and Iain Stewart, 2005, 'Dictating to one of "us": the migration of Mrs Freer', *Macquarie Law Journal*, vol. 5, pp. 241–75.

Geoffrey Robinson, 2008, 'The All for Australia League in New South Wales: a study in political entrepreneurship and hegemony', *Australian Historical Studies*, vol. 39, iss. 1, pp. 36–52.

Paul Rodan, 2013, 'Crossing the line: Richard Casey Re-Visited', *Australian Journal of Politics and History*, vol. 59, iss. 4, pp. 547–58.

— 2014, 'Not so bland after all: Paul Hasluck as Governor-General', *Journal of Australian Studies*, vol. 38, no. 2, pp. 190–204.

Sean Scalmer and Jackie Dickenson, 2010, 'The march of the insider', *Overland*, iss. 199.

Nick Scott, 2015, 'Black-bans and black eyes: Implications of the 1971 Springbok Rugby Tour', *Labour History*, no. 108, May, pp. 145–63.

Tom Sheridan, 1999, 'Regulator Par Excellence: Sir Henry Bland and industrial relations 1950–1967', *Journal of Industrial Relations*, vol. 41, no. 2, June, pp. 228–55.

Tom Sheridan and Pat Stretton, 2004, 'Mandarins, Ministers and the bar on married women', *Journal of Industrial Relations*, vol. 46, no. 1, March, pp. 84–101.

Lau Teik Soon, 'Indonesia and regional security: The Djakarta Conference on Cambodia', *Occasional Paper* no. 14, Institute of Southeast Asian Studies, May 1972.

John Steinback, 2001, 'Sectarianism's last stand? Mannix, Menzies and the 1954 Duntroon colours controversy', *Australian Defence Force Journal*, no. 146, January/February, pp. 19–26.

Edward St John, 1971, 'The Gorton fiasco', *Australian Quarterly*, vol. 43, no. 4, December, pp. 115–20.

Rodney Tiffen, 1988, 'A Politician's Experiences with the News: Insights from the
    Howson diaries', *Media Information Australia*, no. 49, pp. 25-29.
Jim Walsh, 1997, 'Surprise down under: the secret history of Australia's nuclear ambitions',
    Nonproliferation Review, Fall, pp. 1–20.
Elizabeth Ward, 1997–98, 'Call Out the Troops: An examination of the legal basis
    for Australian Defence Force involvement in 'non-defence' matters', *Australian
    Parliamentary Research Paper 8*, Commonwealth Parliamentary Library, Canberra.
Gough Whitlam, 2002, 'Sino-Australian diplomatic relations 1972–2002', *Australian
    Journal of International Affairs*, vol. 56, no. 3, pp. 323–36.
Greg Whitwell, 2001, 'Commodity Price Stabilisation schemes: A case study of the
    Australian wheat industry's Stabilisation scheme, 1948 to 1989', *Australian Economic
    Review*, vol. 24, iss. 3, pp. 52–60.
Graham Wilson, 2003, 'Error of judgment or outright bigotry? The colours controversy of
    the 1950s', *Sabretache*, vol. 44, September, pp. 15–22.
Mr Y, 1971, 'A Packer Plot?', *Australian Quarterly*, vol. 43, no. 2, June, pp. 2–7.

Newspapers and Periodicals

The Advertiser
The Advocate
The Age
The Argus
The Arrow
The Australian (Aus.)
Australian Country Life (ACL)
The Australian Dictionary of Biography (ADB)
The Australian Financial Review (AFR)
The Australian Journal of Politics and History (AJPH)
The Australian Quarterly (AQ)
The Australian Women's Weekly (AWW)
The Brisbane Telegraph (BT)
The Bulletin
The Cairns Post
Canberra News (CN)
The Canberra Times (CT)
The Catholic Press (CP)
The Central Queensland Herald (CQH)
The Charleville Times
The Courier-Mail (CM)
The Daily Commercial News and Shipping List (DCN&SL)
The Daily Examiner (DE)
The Daily Mirror (DM)
The Daily News (DN)
The Daily Telegraph (DT)
The Evening News (EN)
The Examiner
The Forbes Advocate (FA)

The Herald

The Hobart Mercury (HM)

Incentive

Inside Canberra (IC)

Insight

The Maitland Daily Mercury (MDM)

The Morning Bulletin

The National Geographic

The Newcastle Morning Herald and Miners' Advocate (NMHMA)

The National Times (NT)

The New Times

The Newsletter

The Newspaper News (NN)

The Northern Star (NS)

The Queensland Times (QT)

The Referee

Smith's Weekly (SW)

The Sun

The Sunday Times (ST)

The Sydney Mail (SM)

The Sydney Morning Herald (SMH)

The Sydney Sportsman (SA)

The Sydney Stock and Station Journal (SSSJ)

Things I Hear (TIH)

Truth

The West Australian (WA)

Oral Histories

Lawrie Anderson, interviewed by Frank Heimans, Millers Point Oral History Project, <http://www.sydneyoralhistories.com.au/lawrie-anderson/>, accessed 15 September 2016.

Heinz Arnd, interviewed by Peter Coleman, 23 May 1992, NLA Oral History, TRC 2825.

Sir William Aston interviewed by Ron Hurst, 12 June to 7 November 1986, NLA Oral History, TRC 4900/95.

Peter Hamilton Bailey interviewed by Garry Sturgess, NLA Oral History, TRC 6552.

Garfield Barwick interviewed by J.D.B. Miller, NLA Oral History, TRC 499/1.

Garfield Barwick interviewed by Clyde Cameron, NLA Oral History, TRC 1045.

Henry Bland interviewed by Mel Pratt, 1975, NLA Oral History, TRC 121/60.

Henry Bland interviewed by Allan Martin, NLA Oral History, TRC 2549.

Robert 'Duke' Bonnett interviewed by Peter Sekuless, 21 April — 21 July 1983, NLA Oral History, TRC 1454.

Nigel Bowen interviewed by Ron Hurst, NLA Oral History, TRC 4900/61.

Wallace Brown interviewed by Tom Duffy and Noel Goddard, MoAD Oral History, OPH-OHI 52.

John Bunting interviewed by Ian Hamilton, 26 June 1983, NLA Oral History, TRC 1428.

Les Bury interviewed by Mel Pratt, NLA Oral History, TRC 121/70.

Nancy Buttfield interviewed by Clyde Cameron, NLA Oral History, TRC 1688/1 and 2.

John Campbell interviewed by Edward Helgeby, 27 March 2008, MoAD Oral History Project.

Don Cameron interviewed by Barry York, 5 April 2011 and 5 June 2013, NLA Oral History, TRC 6100/74.

Don Leslie Chipp interviewed by Bernadette Schedvin, NLA Oral History, TRC 4900/73.

Harold Cox interviewed by Mel Pratt, NLA Oral History, TRC 121/43.

Helen Crisp interviewed by Ian Hamilton, 21 September 1982, NLA Oral History, TRC 1170.

Paul Davey interviewed by Barry York, 12 April 2011, MoAD Oral History.

Dudley Erwin interviewed by Robert Linford, NLA Oral History, TRC 4900/7.

David Fairbairn interviewed by Robert Linford, NLA Oral History, TRC 4900/72.

David Fairbairn interviewed by Mel Pratt, NLA Oral History, TRC 121/74.

Ian Fitchett interviewed by Heather Rusden and Mungo Wentworth MacCallum, NLA Oral History, TRC 2249.

Philip Flood interviewed by Gregory Wood, NLA Oral History, TRC 6350/5.

Malcolm Fraser interviewed by Clyde Cameron, NLA Oral History, TRC 2162.

Gordon Freeth interviewed by John Ferrell, NLA Oral History, TRC 4900/89.

John Gorton interviewed by Clyde Cameron, NLA Oral History, TRC 1702.

John Gorton interviewed by Mel Pratt, NLA Oral History, TRC 121/78.

John Gorton interviewed by Clarrie Hermes, NLA Oral History, TRC 4900/47.

Paul Hasluck interviewed by Clyde Cameron, NLA Oral History TRC 1966.

Edgar Holt interviewed by Mel Pratt, NLA Oral History, TRC 121/93.

Peter Howson interviewed by Jonathan Gaul, NLA Oral History, TRC 229.

Frank Jennings interviewed by Barry York, 10 October 2007, MoAD Oral History Project.

Charles Robert Kelly interviewed by Bruce Edwards, NLA Oral History, TRC 4900/30.

Richard Kirby interviewed by Catherine Santamaria, NLA Oral History, TRC 228.

Mungo MacCallum interviewed by Mel Pratt, NLA Oral History, TRC 121/44.

John McEwen interviewed by Ray Aitchison, NLA Oral History, TRC 311.

William McMahon interviewed by John Edwards, NLA Oral History, TRC 168/8.

Laurence 'Jim' McIntyre interviewed by Mel Pratt, NLA Oral History, TRC 121/67.

Frederick Osborne interviewed by Ron Hurst, NLA, Oral History, TRC 4900/108.

James Plimsoll interviewed by Clyde Cameron, NLA Oral History, TRC 1967.

Annabelle Rankin interviewed by Pat Shaw, NLA Oral History, TRC 4900/15.

Alan Reid interviewed by Daniel Connell, NLA Oral History, TRC 2172.

Alan Renouf interviewed by Michael Wilson, NLA Oral History, TRC 2981/6.

Hugh Robson interviewed by John Farquharson, NLA Oral History, TRC 4642.

Billy Snedden interviewed by Catherine Santamaria, NLA Oral History, TRC 455.

Billy Snedden interviewed by Bernadette Schedvin, NLA Oral History TRC4900/57.

Carol Summerhayes interviewed by Edward Helgeby, MoAD Oral History Project, OPH-OHI 153.

Keith Waller interviewed by J.D.B. Miller, NLA Oral History, TRC 314.

William Charles Wentworth interviewed by Ron Hurst, NLA Oral History, TRC 4900/104.

Ian Alexander Christie Wood interviewed by Ron Hurst, NLA Oral History, TRC
   4900/84.
Richard Woolcott interviewed by John Farquharson, NLA Oral History, TRC 3484.

Interviews and Correspondence

Author's interview with Phillip Adams, 12 October 2016.
Author's correspondence with Doug Anthony, 15 August 2016, 11 May 2017.
Author's interview with Rob Ashley, 28 December 2017.
Author's interview with Bob Bowker, 24 January 2018.
Author's interview with David Bowman, 23 August 2016.
Author's interview with Neil Brown, 20 September 2017.
Author's interview with Sir John Carrick, 5 August 2016.
Author's correspondence with Tony Eggleton, 26 November 2016.
Author's interview with Richard Farmer, 15 July 2016.
Author's interview with Jonathan Gaul, 24 February 2018.
Author's interview with Ian Grigg, 20 February and 13 March 2018.
Author's interview with Sir Lenox Hewitt, 2 February 2018.
Author's interview with John Howard, 22 April 2016.
Author's interview with Tom Hughes, 16 August 2016.
Author's interview with C.R. 'Kim' Jones, 2 June and 6 June 2017.
Author's interview with Peter Kelly, 1 October 2016, 1 and 2 May 2017, 8 April 2018.
Author's interview with Sir Peter Lawler, 22 November 2016.
Author's correspondence with Mungo MacCallum, 4 October 2017.
Author's interview with Bruce and Leanne MacCarthy, 5 August 2016.
Author's interview with Reg MacDonald, 21 May and 8 June 2018.
Author's interview with Robert Macklin, 11 July 2016.
Author's interview with Sir Eric McClintock, 28 October 2016 and 17 September 2017.
Author's interview with Michael Morton–Evans, 27 September 2016.
Author's interview with Alan Ramsey, 31 January 2018.
Author's correspondence with Peter Samuel, 25 April 2017.
Author's interview with Richard Smart, 24 August 2016.
Author's correspondence with David Solomon, 24 September 2017.
Author's correspondence with John Stone, 6, 8, 9 January, 24 and 25 May 2017.
Author's interview with Richard Woolcott, 2 February 2018.
Author's interview with Alan and Lorna Wright, 6 December 2016.

Theses

Luke Auton, 2008, *A sort of Middle of the Road Policy': forward defence, alliance politics and
   the Australian nuclear weapons option, 1953–1973*, PhD thesis, University of New
   South Wales.
Anna-Eugenia Binnie, 2003, *From Atomic Energy to Nuclear Science: a history of the
   Australian Atomic Energy Commission*, PhD thesis, Macquarie University.
Michael Carr, 1979, *Australia and the Nuclear Question: a survey of government attitudes
   1945–1975*, MA thesis, University of New South Wales.
P.D. Gourley, 1969, *An Industrial Relations Analysis of the Stevedoring Industry in the Port of
   Hobart*, Masters thesis, University of Tasmania.

TV, Radio, Audio Broadcasts

Sir William McMahon: This Is Your Life, 12 March 1978, (television) ep. 4/008, National Film and Sound Archive.

Colin Hughes, 1976, *William McMahon: The Politics of Power*, ed Paul R Wilson, University of Queensland, St. Lucia (audio).

'Mission from Moscow', 1948, (radio) spoken by Richard Matthews, written by Sim Rubensohn and Pip Cogger, recording copy held by the University of Melbourne Library.

'The Great Debate', 14 November 1958, (television), no. 16168, National Film and Sound Archive.

'The Leaders', *This Fabulous Century*, 14 November 1978, (television) National Film and Sound Archive.

The Harold Holt Mystery, 18 February 1985, (television), National Film & Sound Archive.

'Tribute to a leader', *British Movietone–AP*, <https://www.youtube.com/watch?v=_sOLqsKgSpM>, accessed 13 December 2016.

The Liberals, 'It's alright, Boss', 1994 (television program), YouTube, accessed 1 April 2017.

Index